Adapting Early Childhood Curricula for Children with Special Needs

Seventh Edition

Ruth E. Cook
Santa Clara University

M. Diane Klein
California State University—Los Angeles

Annette Tessier
California State University—Los Angeles (Emerita)

PEARSON

Merrill
Prentice Hall

Upper Saddle River, New Jersey
Columbus, Ohio

Library of Congress Cataloging-in-Publication Data

Cook, Ruth E.
  Adapting early childhood curricula for children with special needs / Ruth E. Cook,
M. Diane Klein, Annette Tessier. — 7th ed.
      p. cm.
  Includes bibliographical references and index.
  ISBN-13: 978-0-13-172381-8
  ISBN-10:   0-13-172381-2
  1. Children with disabilities—Education (Preschool)   2. Children with disabilities—Education
(Preschool)—Curricula.   3. Mainstreaming in education.   I. Klein, M. Diane.   II. Tessier, Annette.   III. Title.
  LC4019.2.C66 2007
  371.9′0472—dc22

                                                                                          2007024337

Vice President and Executive Publisher: Jeffery W. Johnston
Executive Editor: Ann Castel Davis
Editorial Assistant: Penny Burleson
Production Editor: Sheryl Glicker Langner
Production Coordination: Rebecca K. Giusti, GGS Book Services
Photo Coordinator: Lori Whitley
Design Coordinator: Diane C. Lorenzo
Cover Design: Bryan Huber
Cover Image: Fotosearch
Production Manager: Laura Messerly
Director of Marketing: David Gesell
Marketing Manager: Autumn Purdy
Marketing Coordinator: Brian Mounts

This book was set in Garamond and Optima by GGS Book Services. The text and cover were printed and bound by
R. R. Donnelley/Harrisonburg.

Additional photo credits: Photos on pp. 7, 24, 46, 105, 138, 147, 152, 160, 179, 190, 201, 204, 227, 233, 237, 245, 248, 265, 276,
301, 315, 342, and 371 were supplied by the authors.

Pearson Education Ltd.   Pearson Education Australia Pty. Limited
Pearson Education Singapore Pte. Ltd.   Pearson Education North Asia Ltd.
Pearson Education Canada, Ltd.   Pearson Educación de Mexico, S.A. de C.V.
Pearson Education—Japan   Pearson Education Malaysia Pte. Ltd.

10 9 8 7 6 5 4 3 2 1
ISBN-13: 978-0-13-172381-8
ISBN-10:   0-13-172381-2

We dedicate this edition to children with special needs around the world
and the practitioners who serve them.

Foreword

For over two decades this text, *Adapting Early Childhood Curricula for Children with Special Needs*, has served as a major resource for early educators and related services personnel and for the faculty members who teach them. Its tremendous success lies in its blend of developmental and learning theories with practical suggestions for delivery of services to young children with special needs and their families.

While today's children with special needs are enrolled in the full range of early childhood education programs, many of these programs have limited exposure to strategies for modifying or expanding the curricula for these children. In most cases, only minor adaptations may be needed to ensure that all children can become full members of the group and benefit from the activities. Nevertheless, these adaptations can pose challenges to service providers who are engaged in meeting the diverse needs of a wide range of children in their programs.

This text is aimed at supporting those personnel. Its focus is on enhancing collaboration, consultation, and problem solving among educators and other service personnel in community-based inclusive early education settings, whether they are in child care homes, centers, or classrooms. Emphasis is placed on assisting practitioners to identify the strengths that children and families bring to the programs and on involving families through family-centered, relationship-based approaches. These strategies can only be optimally implemented by planned coordination and collaboration among the many personnel who work in these settings and who come from a variety of disciplines, such as special education, early childhood education, physical and occupational therapy, speech and language pathology, psychology and counseling, health services, and so on.

The training and clinical experience of the authors, Ruth Cook, Diane Klein, and Annette Tessier, mirror the varied disciplines that provide services to young children with special needs and their families. These authors together bring years of experience and active engagement in the field of early intervention and early education. Their collective knowledge is reflected in their effective translation of theoretical information into practical techniques that can be implemented in a range of early education settings.

This text covers topics such as recommended practices in the field, family concerns and experiences, child assessment, individualized program planning for children, implementation of instructional strategies, managing and understanding child behavior, and the integral involvement of families in their children's programs. Specific curricular strategies in developmental domains, such as language, motor, social, concept development, and emergent literacy, also are described. Other useful features of the text include charts and descriptions of typical child development, information on specific types of disability, and resources available through web sites and periodicals.

Adapting Early Childhood Curricula for Children with Special Needs is a highly readable and comprehensive resource for early educators. This text appeals to the needs of a wide range of readers who seek to support the development of young children with special needs and their families through inclusive early education programs.

Marci J. Hanson, Ph.D.
Professor
Early Childhood Special Education
San Francisco State University

Preface

This book is written with you, the student of either early childhood or special education, in mind. Whether you are studying to become a teacher of young children with special needs or are an early interventionist with a related background who wishes to develop greater versatility in your chosen field, we have designed this to be an easy-to-read, interesting, and comprehensive resource for you. It provides extensive use of examples, dialogues, practical illustrations, vignettes, and a focus on the best practices in the field.

When this text was originally published, intervention with young children with special needs was in its formative years. Since that time the field has expanded, and this book has successfully grown with it. Young children with special needs are now enrolled in a variety of settings and are served by professionals and paraprofessionals with diverse backgrounds. Our objective now, as it was in the first six editions, is to present a text that will play a major role in the development of all who serve young children. The focus is on the skills necessary to assist infants, young children, and their families to meet their special challenges and develop to their fullest potential.

Distinguishing Features

This book has four main strengths that make it a compelling self-teaching resource:

1. It emphasizes the importance of understanding the natures of all young children and how they learn. Adapting curricula and intervention approaches for children with special needs works effectively only when professionals build on a strong foundation of understanding what is common to all young children. On the basis of this necessary foundation, students can consider strategies for meeting the developmental and educational needs of infants and young children who have disabilities or who experience circumstances and conditions that potentially interfere with optimal growth and adjustment.

2. The approach taken in this text stresses the absolute necessity of understanding young children within the context of the family. Every family is unique and complex, reflecting the many influences of history, culture or ethnicity, economics, and family dynamics. Early interventionists must focus not on the detailed analysis of these many factors but on ways of supporting families that will maximize their day-to-day fulfillment as caregivers of their young. As explained in the text, your job, in part, is to help parents develop a sense of competence in their own abilities to nurture their children regardless of family circumstances. Appreciation of families' roles in the development of children and respect for families' concerns and priorities are critical to effective curriculum design and program development.

3. A significant portion of the text is organized according to traditional developmental domains: social-emotional, motor, communication, and cognitive skills. As an early childhood special education professional, you will seek to develop these growth areas in the children entrusted to you. Thus, you must develop a thorough understanding of each of these complex domains.

4. Finally, you must ultimately understand that all the growth areas and individual and family background factors must be synthesized into a view of

the whole child. As in any other form of synergy, the whole child is much greater than the sum of his or her parts. This holistic view relates directly to the book's emphasis on activity-based and play-based approaches to intervention. You will learn how to integrate goals and objectives for all domains into developmentally appropriate and motivating activities in inclusive, community-based settings. You will also learn how to work collaboratively with others in inclusive community-based settings in an itinerant consultation role. Throughout, best practices are explained for home, center, or classroom application.

What is new about this seventh edition? The four points just mentioned suggest the framework and approach that have consistently made this book appealing to readers of six earlier editions. They have been time tested and consistently found to be helpful. This edition includes legal updates related to the Individuals with Disabilities Education Improvement Act and increased attention to school readiness skills, particularly the area of emergent literacy.

Organization

The text opens with a presentation of our philosophy for working with children who have special needs. It explores human likenesses and value differences and discusses our belief in the importance of providing services in the most normalized settings possible. Chapter 1 highlights the historical contributions of the fields of early childhood education and special education. Important features and implications of Public Laws 94-142, 99-457, 101-336, 101-476, 102-119, 105-17, and 108-446 are summarized. Evolving trends in the field and alternative approaches to service delivery including the unique challenges involved in supporting inclusion are discussed.

Chapter 2 presents techniques to involve families in a collaborative partnership with the variety of professionals with whom they must interface. In developing a family-focused approach, students are encouraged to view families from a systems perspective. Special attention is given to the various methods of parent involvement that can accommodate cultural diversity, language differences, and unique family situations.

Issues and methods of infant and child assessment, including both formal and informal methods, are presented in chapter 3. The importance of becoming a skilled observer of children is stressed. Students are introduced to team approaches and the importance of ecologically valid assessments. Linking assessment to curriculum and monitoring the progress of children is shown to be critical. Chapter 4 defines the components of individualized education programs and individualized family service plans. Techniques for writing goals and objectives are illustrated. Strategies for collaborative program and transition planning are outlined. Chapter 5 focuses on curriculum development within a framework of generic instructional strategies. Facilitation of play, the development of appropriate schedules, and optimal environmental arrangement contribute to the success of early intervention. Disability-specific adaptations for young children with special needs, including those with autism or who have been prenatally exposed to alcohol, provide a point of departure for facilitating inclusion.

Chapter 6 begins by describing the stages of psychosocial development as a precursor to understanding how to facilitate social skills through the medium of play. Considerable attention is given to helping children who experience particular emotional and behavioral challenges and working with those who have been maltreated. The use of positive behavioral supports is discussed in detail.

After describing typical development of motor skills, chapter 7 examines atypical motor development. Practical intervention strategies are offered, including handling and positioning guidelines as well as techniques for facilitating self-help skills. The role of movement education and music in the development of motor skills is considered.

Chapters 8 and 9 focus on the development of communication and cognition. The importance of caregiver–child interactions and the role of play in optimal development is recognized throughout. Special attention is devoted to specific strategies for enhancing communication skills in children with severe disabilities, autism, visual impairments, and hearing

impairments. Attention is given to children from non–English-speaking families. Unique is the section devoted to understanding the social and linguistic factors related to children's emergent literacy skills and strategies for encouraging these skills. Facilitation of phonological and phonemic awareness along with a brief synthesis of premath skills is included in this section.

The final chapter provides an overview of models, strategies, and challenges for providing inclusion support to young children with disabilities who are included in community-based early childhood settings. The chapter also contains helpful considerations for working with paraprofessionals.

As in previous editions, the appendices include a wealth of practical information, such as developmental guidelines, curricular adaptations for children with specific needs, modifications, and checklists to assist facilitation of inclusion. Specific communication strategies to enhance collaboration and the sequence of training steps for milieu approaches have been added. Finally, it includes a list of competencies that we hope will be developed by each and every reader.

Acknowledgments

We present this book with gratitude to the hundreds of children and parents who have been our teachers. From them we have learned to value and nurture the uniqueness of each child regardless of background, skills, or abilities. We believe we have found a way to meet children's unique needs in whatever setting they appear. It has been our purpose to convey the essence of this process to anyone interested in working with young children.

We wish to thank sincerely the many colleagues and friends who assisted and supported us throughout the many years since the original edition of this book. We are especially grateful for the conscientious efforts of those who so kindly read and commented on the prospectus and rough drafts of the present edition. These include former students Carole Osselaer, who readily offered helpful comments from an instructors point of view, and Lisa Wadors, who provided photos of the adorable students in her class. Special gratitude goes to the following reviewers for

their time, attention, and feedback: Geralyn A. Arango, Holy Family University; Lynne S. Arnault, Mississippi State University; Lorraine Martin, Grossmont College; and Lynda A. Nelson, Central Missouri State University.

There are many people who enrich and enhance one's personal as well as professional life along the way. We are grateful to Dr. Marci Hanson for graciously providing the foreword to this edition. We have always admired the impact Dr. Hanson has made on our field and feel honored that she has helped to enhance our contribution to the future of early childhood special education.

Gratitude is also expressed to Anne Marie Richardson-Gibbs, Sharon Kilpatrick, Carol Dale, Shirley Sparks, and the Santa Clara University graduate students and the California State University at Los Angeles for helping us learn what good teachers need to know. Deep appreciation is extended to the parents, children, and outstanding staff of Centro de Niños y Padres, at California State University at Los Angeles, the Southern Illinois University Early Childhood Center, and the Mount Saint Mary's College at Los Angeles Child Development Center, whose inspiration is a source of strength.

Throughout this project, the personal support of those with whom we live and work has been invaluable. Very special thanks go to Erin Klein and Christopher and Kimberly Cook Bodemar, without whom our understandings of child growth and development would have been superficial, at best. Sincere gratitude goes to Curtis Cook, whose patience, tolerance, and editorial skills over the years made this project possible. Ruth wishes to publicly express her appreciation to her parents, Peggy and (the late) Ray Ellis, for always being there with the love all children deserve.

The editors and staff at Merrill/Prentice Hall have worked hard to keep us on target. Particular praise and gratitude go to our editors, Penny Burleson and Ann Davis; their attention and prompt responses have been invaluable throughout the acquisition and development of this manuscript. Finally, we offer our thanks to Lori Whitley, our photo coordinator, and Rebecca Giusti, production editor from GGS Book Services, for their conscientious efforts and expertise throughout production.

Discover the Merrill Resources for Special Education Website

Technology is a constantly growing and changing aspect of our field that is creating a need for new content and resources. To address this emerging need, Merrill Education has developed an online learning environment for students, teachers, and professors alike to complement our products—the *Merrill Resources for Special Education* Website. This content-rich website provides additional resources specific to this book's topic and will help you—professors, classroom teachers, and students—augment your teaching, learning, and professional development.

Our goal is to build on and enhance what our products already offer. For this reason, the content for our user-friendly website is organized by topic and provides teachers, professors, and students with a variety of meaningful resources all in one location. With this website, we bring together the best of what Merrill has to offer: text resources, video clips, web links, tutorials, and a wide variety of information on topics of interest to general and special educators alike. Rich content, applications, and competencies further enhances the learning process.

The *Merrill Resources for Special Education* Website includes:

- Video clips specific to each topic, with questions to help you evaluate the content and make crucial theory-to-practice connections.

- Thought-provoking critical analysis questions that students can answer and turn in for evaluation or that can serve as the basis for class discussions and lectures.

- Access to a wide variety of resources related to classroom strategies and methods, including lesson planning and classroom management.

- Information on all the most current relevant topics related to special and general education, including CEC and Praxis™ standards, IEPs, portfolios, and professional development.

- Extensive web resources and overviews on each topic addressed on the website.

- A search feature to help access specific information quickly.

To take advantage of these and other resources, please visit the *Merrill Resources for Special Education* Website at

http://www.prenhall.com/cook

Brief Contents

Contents

2   In Partnership with Families   32

3 Recognizing Special Needs and Monitoring Progress 80

4   Developing Individualized Intervention Plans and Programs   110

5   Implementing Intervention and Instructional Strategies   138

6   Promoting Emotional and Social Development   172

7   Helping Young Children Develop Motor and Self-Help Skills   216

9 — **Encouraging the Development of Cognitive Skills and Literacy**   **292**

Providing for Special Needs in Early Education: The Challenge

Photo by Lisa Wadors

KEY TERMS

(Note: Terms are discussed within the text and/or defined in the glossary.)

Americans with Disabilities Act
best practices
developmentally appropriate
   practices
early intervention
family-centered approach
free appropriate public
   education

Individuals with Disabilities
   Education Act
Individuals with Disabilities
   Education Improvement Act
inclusion
inclusion support
inclusive settings
interdisciplinary collaboration

least restrictive environment
mainstreaming
natural environments
relationship-focused intervention
   model
standards-based practices
transactional
transdisciplinary approach

- The goal of early intervention is to optimize each child's learning potential and daily well-being and to increase opportunities for the child to function effectively in the community.

- The current focus in early childhood special education is not *whether* young children with special needs can be served in inclusive (typical) environments but *how* inclusive programs can be designed most effectively.

- Programs for infants and toddlers with special needs must be based on the same developmentally appropriate strategies that are considered best practices for *all* young children.

- A child with special needs must be viewed as a child first; the special need or disability is secondary.

- All children are best understood within the context of their families rather than within the context of their disabilities. To successfully include young children with special needs, educators must make careful curricular adaptations.

- Success is dependent on systematic planning of responsive environments, consideration of individual needs, parent–professional partnerships, respect for cultural diversity, and collaboration among families, professionals, and community agencies.

- Early childhood special education reflects influences and recommended practices derived from the fields of both early childhood education and special education.

- Increasingly, attention is being focused on the impact of caregiver–child relationships.

- Public pressure resulted in federal legislation that provided an important impetus to the development of programs for infants and young children with special needs through a variety of service delivery models and within various settings.

- The role of early childhood special educators is changing to meet the unique challenges of providing effective inclusion support for children. This new role requires additional training in collaboration and teaming.

From the mother of a 5-year-old with special needs:

I have come to accept that my daughter will not be quite like everybody else when she grows up, but then who of us is? We are all unique individuals, and we should appreciate our differences rather than scorn them. We all have our strengths and weaknesses, and how many of us, even without disabilities, ever realize our full human potential?

Lora Jerugim

Helping children with special needs to realize their full human potential—this is our challenge. By recognizing the human similarities in each of us and by positively valuing differences, parents and educators together can provide each child the opportunity to develop his or her unique strengths. For children who appear to have developmental disabilities or characteristics that interfere with normal growth and learning, the stage must be prepared more thoughtfully. It is expected that parents, educators, and other community resource members will work together to create a nurturing environment sensitive to, but not solicitous of, children's special needs.

Many aspects of mental and physical development seem to "just happen" to most children. They are, however, the result of interaction between innate capacities and appropriate environmental experiences. With most children, comparatively little

3

deliberate effort has to be made to synchronize capacities and experiences. Most have a repertoire of skills and interests that motivate them to explore, experiment, and therefore learn. However, children with special needs may not be able to learn easily and spontaneously from the play experiences and daily routines that they naturally encounter. Educators can learn to build on naturally occurring encounters by adapting materials, equipment, space, instructions, and expectations to provide opportunities for experiences conducive to learning within the child's natural environments.

VIEWING THE CHILD WITH SPECIAL NEEDS AS A CHILD FIRST

We cannot overstate the point that children with special needs are children first—children who have the same characteristics and needs as so-called typical children. The beauty of being young and "new" is the potential for growth and change. All infants and young children, no matter how significantly challenged or disabled, will benefit from those best practices that create supportive and nurturing environments for all young children. This belief must be the foundation of early childhood special education.

For some children, additional strategies, techniques, and adaptations will be required to maximize their opportunities to experience, enjoy, and learn from the world around them. Thus, early childhood special education students must master two sets of skills: one related to facilitating learning and healthy growth and development in all children and another related to the specific and special needs of children with disabilities. Appendix E provides a sample list of important competencies for professionals in early childhood special education to master.

INCLUSION OF YOUNG CHILDREN WITH SPECIAL NEEDS IN COMMUNITY-BASED SETTINGS

A fundamental shift in the most beneficial way to provide services to young children with special needs and their families is taking place. Intervention services have been changing "from a services-based,

professional-driven approach that has focused on deficits and needs to a supportive approach emphasizing child and family strengths and natural routines and parents as the agents of change in their child's development" (Childress, 2004, p. 163). Yes, to a greater extent, young children with disabilities are included in typical early childhood settings, including their home, child care, Head Start, and public and private preschools. Encouraged by legal mandate and professional "best practices," infants, toddlers, and preschool children increasingly are receiving part or all of their early intervention and early education services in these natural settings. The intent of this text is to provide information and strategies that early childhood and special educators can use to support children's growth and development and full participation in natural settings and to establish collaborative, supportive partnerships with families and colleagues in this effort.

The commitment to inclusive intervention and education for infants and young children is well established in federal law. Part C of the Individuals with Disabilities Education Act of 1997 states that (1) "To the maximum extent appropriate, early intervention services are provided in natural environments; and (2) the provision of early intervention services occurs in a setting other than a natural environment only when early intervention cannot be achieved satisfactorily for the infant or toddler in a natural environment" (Sec. 635 [a][16]). Part B addresses the needs of preschoolers by stating that "To the maximum extent appropriate, children with disabilities are educated with children who are not disabled." This part also goes on to state in Section 612 that preschoolers are not to be removed from the regular educational environment unless "education in regular classes with the use of supplementary aids and services cannot be achieved satisfactorily." The most recent law, **Individuals with Disabilities Education Improvement Act** (IDEIA 2004), continues to support the mandate that encourages services for infants and toddlers in **natural environments** and it requires school districts to educate children in the **least restrictive environment.** Some specifics of these educational shifts are noted in Exhibit 1–1.

Trends in Early Childhood Special Education

Evolving trends in the field include:

- Community-based inclusive settings
- Emphasis on child and family strengths
- Relationship-focused interventions
- Family-centered approaches
- Interdisciplinary collaboration
- Increased cultural competence
- Coordinated, comprehensive services
- Standards- and evidence-based practices
- Involvement of inclusion support specialists

PHILOSOPHY OF THIS TEXT

This text emphasizes that the goal of early intervention is to optimize each child's learning potential and daily well-being as well as to increase opportunities for the child to function effectively in the community. We believe this is best accomplished by facilitating the child's underlying developmental processes by encouraging the child's active and dynamic interactions with the world around him or her, particularly the social world. Perhaps the term that best reflects this orientation is **transactional.** It is through the child's active and successful transactions with the social environment that optimal growth and development can best be achieved.

To achieve this end, early interventionists must first have a thorough understanding of how children learn. Programs for infants and young children with special needs must be based on developmentally appropriate practices that are effective for *all* children. In addition, systematic planning to meet the individualized needs of each child is critical to the success of early childhood programs that include children with special challenges and disabilities. This cannot be accomplished without establishing mutually respectful partnerships between early childhood professionals and families. Successful assessment and intervention require a thorough understanding of the child within the context of the family system and a respect for the diverse cultural backgrounds represented by families in early childhood centers.

The importance of collaboration among families, professionals, and community agencies is acknowledged throughout the text. Understanding the roles of various disciplines and specialists and the importance of assisting families in accessing community agencies and resources are also critical elements in the success of early intervention.

Many tools and strategies are available to assist the early childhood special educator. This text describes the basic developmental domains of human learning and the principles of how children learn as well as specific teaching strategies. It also demonstrates applications of these principles and strategies to meet the needs of a wide range of children within inclusive environments.

As we continue to strive toward successful inclusion of young children with special needs, it is interesting to note that we are still struggling with the primary issue put forth by Guralnick (1990) nearly two decades ago:

Perhaps the single most significant achievement in the field of early childhood education in the decade of the 1980s was the repeated demonstration that mainstreamed programs can be implemented effectively. The contemporary issue is clearly not whether early childhood **mainstreaming** is feasible and should be encouraged, but rather how one can design programs to maximize its effectiveness. *(p. 3)*

Though much progress has been made toward the goal described by Guralnick in 1990, it has not been fully realized. More recently, he pointed out that clear guidelines and policies for decision making around placements in **inclusive settings** still need to be established (Guralnick, 2000). This text provides early childhood special educators with the knowledge and skills to enhance progress toward understanding how to design programs that will maximize the effectiveness of **inclusion.**

EARLY CHILDHOOD SPECIAL EDUCATION: AN EVOLVING FIELD

Whereas the 1980s opened with concern for the rights of individuals with disabilities, the 1990s recognized the rights and needs of the *families* of children with special needs. The 2000s recognize the value of serving young children with disabilities in what has become known as their natural environments. Children are no longer viewed in isolation; attention is focused on understanding the needs of the child within the context of his or her family. It is recognized that *all* children should have the opportunity to be served in environments where they would naturally function if they did not have a disability.

Early intervention services gained new momentum as the nation recognized its responsibility to provide services from the moment of birth. However, the field of early childhood special education is relatively new. Its historical roots are derived not only from typical early childhood education, compensatory education, and school-aged special education but also from allied fields such as medicine, psychology, human development, nursing, and sociology. A few of the major historical forces shaping the expanding field of early childhood special education are outlined in this section.

Photo by Lisa Wadors

Pioneering Influences

Jean-Marc Itard undertook one of the first documented efforts to provide intervention services to a child with special needs. In 1800, a child approximately 12 years old was found living in the forest near Aveyron, France. The boy, named Victor, was thought to have been raised by animals and was described as "an incurable idiot." Itard refused to accept the idea that Victor's condition was incurable and irreversible. Itard believed in what later became known as an "interactionist viewpoint" (Bijou, 1977). That is, Victor's learning potential could be enhanced through intervention that changed the stimulation in his environment. Therefore, Itard undertook to humanize Victor through a series of carefully planned lessons stimulating the senses.

Itard's feelings of optimism, frustration, anger, hope, and despair were published in a 1962 edition of *The Wild Boy of Aveyron*. Teachers today who work with children who have extreme disabilities may easily recognize these feelings. Although Itard did not achieve the success he visualized, his efforts had a significant impact on the future of special education. Itard was one of the first to demonstrate and record an attempt to understand empathically the needs of a child with disabilities. It was Itard's student, Edouard Sequin, who could be considered a pioneer in the area of early intervention. This is evident in his statement, "If the idiot cannot be reached by the first lessons of infancy, by what mysterious process will years open for him the golden doors of intelligence?" (quoted Talbot, 1964, p. 62).

Casa dei Bambini

About a century later, another physician, Maria Montessori, was busy in Italy creating a nursery school, *Casa dei Bambini*, that revolutionized the notion of early education. Because of her training, early interests, and the nature of the school she was asked to develop, Montessori stressed cleanliness, order, and housekeeping skills as well as reading, writing, and arithmetic. Aspects of both the discovery approach to learning and programmed instruction

can be found in the techniques developed by Montessori. She suggested that teachers observe the natural, spontaneous behavior of children and then arrange learning experiences to encourage their development.

Like Itard, Montessori believed in developing the child's natural curiosity through systematic training of the senses. Both proceeded with optimism and determination to train those whom some might believe to be beyond hope. Today, Montessori's "sensorial" materials are advocated for use with children with disabilities because they are manipulable, three-dimensional, and concrete. Advocates cite the emphasis on task analysis, sequencing, and individualization evident in the Montessori approach as worthy for use with children who have limited abilities as well as those who are gifted.

Piaget's Theory of Cognitive Development

Until his death in 1980 at the age of 84, Jean Piaget continued to influence our understanding of cognitive development. Piaget proposed an inborn tendency toward adaptation that, in its encounter with the environment, results in categories of knowledge that are remarkably similar among all human beings. Piaget's concept of child development and his stages of cognitive development will be considered again in Chapter 9. His prolific writings and those of followers continue to remind us of the need to be aware of the unfolding internal mental capacities of children.

According to Piaget, the purpose of education is to provide opportunities that allow a child to combine experiences into coherent systems (schemes) that constitute the child's knowledge. "Knowledge" then is constructed from within rather than acquired from without (Furth, 1970). Therefore, each child's capacity to learn is thought to be uniquely experientially based. Piaget's concept of the child as an active learner stimulated by inborn curiosity has prompted the development of preschool programs designed to allow the child to become an active initiator of learning experiences. From a developmental point of view, a child's strengths, rather than deficits, receive emphasis. Most notable of the Piagetian-based programs is the Perry Preschool Project developed in the late 1950s in Ypsilanti, Michigan. An extension known as the High/Scope First Chance Preschool serves as a model program for those desiring to integrate preschoolers with disabilities into programs with their typical peers (Banet, 1979).

Recognition of the Role of Early Experiences

Even though Sequin recognized the critical importance of early intervention, it was the work of Skeels and Dye that drew pupil attention to the impact of early relationships. One of the earliest attempts to demonstrate the close relationship among nurturing, environmental stimulation, and mental growth processes grew out of the Iowa growth studies in the late 1930s. Skeels and Dye (1939) transferred 12 children under 3 years of age from an orphanage to an institution for individuals with mental retardation. In the institution the children were cared for with great affection by adolescent girls who were considered to have retardation. A comparison group of children remained in the orphanage, where they received no specialized attention. Follow-up testing demonstrated that those placed in the stimulating environment increased their intelligence test scores, whereas those who remained in the orphanage decreased their intelligence test scores (Skeels, 1942). Twenty-one years later, Skeels (1966) found dramatic differences between those who had been placed in the enriching environment and those who had not. The 12 children in the experimental group were found to be self-supporting. Of the comparison group, 4 had been institutionalized and 1 had died. Educationally speaking, 4 of those who had been in the enriching environment completed college, and the others had a median high school education. On the other hand, the median education for the comparison group was only at the third-grade level.

Kirk (1958) also conducted experiments on the influence of early experiences on the development of young children with mental disabilities. In his textbook, Kirk's suggestion that an inadequate cultural environment might be a cause of mental retardation helped to convince politicians of the need for compensatory educational programs for young children. Perhaps more convincing was the conclusion reached by Bloom (1964), who claimed that about "50% of the [intellectual] development takes place between conception and age 4, and about 30% between ages 4 and 8, and 20% between ages 8 and 17" (p. 88).

Bloom's argument was built on J. McVicker Hunt's popular book *Intelligence and Experience* (1961), which argued eloquently against the notion of fixed intelligence. Attempting to lay to rest the heredity versus environment controversy, Hunt supported well his contention that heredity sets the limits, whereas environment determines the extent to which the limits will be achieved. And so, under the belief that children's intelligence develops early and rapidly and that enrichment early in life can have profound influences on the child's development, federal funding for Project Head Start was provided in 1965.

Project Head Start: A Breakthrough

The primary purpose in passing the Economic Opportunity Act of 1964 was to break the cycle of poverty by providing educational and social opportunities for children from low-income families. The result was the implementation of Head Start during the summer of 1965 with approximately 550,000 children in 2,500 child development centers. Parent involvement both within the Head Start classroom and on policy committees set a precedent. This has, no doubt, influenced legislators to require parent involvement in current decisions involving children with disabilities.

The Head Start program had a significant impact on the development of early childhood special education. It was the first major public exposure to the importance of early educational experiences. As Caldwell (1973) pointed out, "The implicit strategy of early Head Start was to devise a program that fits the children as they are found and that institutes remedial procedures to correct whatever deficiencies they have, whether they are nutritional, experiential, or medical" (p. 5).

Legislation enacted in 1972 required Head Start programs to include children with disabilities to the extent of at least 10% of their enrollment. Including children with disabilities in classrooms with typical children has become a major activity of Head Start. In fact, even as early as 1985, Head Start enrollment of preschoolers with disabilities exceeded 60,000.

Today, service to very young children has increased considerably with the addition of Early Head Start.

Doubts

After the extreme optimism that accompanied the establishment of Head Start, it came as a shock to those who worked daily with the children and their parents that the program failed to produce documented gains. The Westinghouse report of 1969 cited data suggesting that measured gains made by Head Starters faded rapidly. By the end of the first grade, there often were no significant differences between the overall academic performance of children who had attended Head Start programs and those from the same kinds of homes who had not. Doubting the validity of this investigation, influential people fought for a stay of execution (Gotts, 1973). Among them was Edward Zigler, a member of the original planning committee that conceptualized Head Start and later director of the Office of Child Development. Zigler (1978) retorted, "I ask my colleagues in the research community to forego the temptation of delivering definitive pronouncements concerning the fade-out issue and await instead the collection and analyses of more data" (p. 73).

Impact of Early Intervention

Indeed, Zigler was to be rewarded for his faith. It wasn't long until great attention was given to the work of Lazar and Darlington (1979, 1982) and the Consortium on Developmental Continuity. These researchers conducted longitudinal investigations into the persistence of the effects of early intervention programs throughout the United States. The evidence from the projects clearly indicated that there were long-lasting positive effects from early intervention programs. Tracing children who had been involved in preschool programs into their teens or early 20s, Lazar found that children with some form of early education were far less likely to require special education or to be held back a grade.

A powerful case for federal support of early intervention programs appeared in the report of a

Exhibit 1–2

Effects of Early Education/Intervention

Children who have participated in early education programs:

1. Are less likely to be assigned to special education classes or to be held back a grade.
2. Have more positive attitudes toward high school and are more likely to graduate.
3. Are less likely to be arrested as youth and young adults.
4. Are less likely to experience teen pregnancy.
5. Are more likely to secure gainful employment after leaving school.

well-designed 19-year longitudinal study of the effects of the Perry Preschool Project (Schweinhart & Weikart, 1988). Exhibit 1–2 lists some of the gains attributed to early intervention with children who are primarily at risk and disadvantaged. Although children in these programs did not have disabilities, they were considered to be at risk. The progress of these children definitely helped to promote financial and social support of programs providing early intervention. Recently, Reynolds, Temple, Robertson, and Mann (2001) reported on a 15-year follow-up of low-income children who received early intervention services in their public schools. They found that by the age of 20, those who had received services were significantly more likely to complete high school and have less involvement in delinquency and crime.

Early Intervention for Children with Disabilities

In interpreting the findings of early intervention research, it is important to keep in mind the diversity with which this field deals. When policy makers ask, "What are the benefits of early intervention?" the

response will inevitably be, "It depends." This is not because researchers lack agreement or because of the limitations of research methods but because of the great diversity among children and families and the circumstances in which they live. There is no one best intervention for everyone all of the time. There is not even one best intervention for a very narrowly defined group such as infants with Down syndrome and their families. Even infants with Down syndrome differ so much from one another that any specific intervention for a group of these infants probably would not be very successful. Research does provide some pieces of this complex, highly individualized puzzle, indicating that early intervention can yield important benefits. Because of the complexities involved in documenting positive effects of early intervention, professionals in the field do not yet know enough to put the complete picture together (Guralnick, 1997; Shonkoff & Meisels, 2000).

Nevertheless, a recent two-and-a-half-year project resulting in the now-famous volume *From Neurons to Neighborhoods,* edited by Shonkoff and Phillips (2000), sheds a spotlight on the very early years and the critical influence of quality early intervention. The following conclusion is worthy of considerable reflection:

Model early childhood programs that deliver carefully designed interventions with well-defined objectives and that include well-designed evaluations have been shown to influence the developmental trajectories of children whose life course is threatened by socioeconomic disadvantage, family disruption, and diagnosed disabilities. Programs that combine child-focused educational activities with explicit attention to parent-child interaction patterns and relationship building appear to have the greatest impacts. In contrast, services that are based on generic family support, often without a clear delineation of intervention strategies matched directly to measurable objectives, and that are funded by more modest budgets, appear to be less effective. (p. 11)

Relationship-Focused Models of Early Intervention

As noted above, considerable attention has been given to the role of caregiver–child interaction in early intervention (Greenspan & Weider, 2003). Mahoney, Boyce, Fewell, Spiker, and Wheeden (1998)

examined the developmental outcomes achieved in four independent intervention research studies. Findings provide support for assumptions underlying the **relationship-focused intervention model.** That is, intervention effectiveness is dependent on parent–child interaction. In fact, intervention effects on child development did not appear to occur unless mothers changed their style of interaction with their child. The absence of close, supportive relationships with adult caregivers appears to put children at risk for varied and multiple problems, especially in the area of social and cognitive development (Kelly & Barnard, 2000).

The mechanism that maintains child change over time has become obvious. The parent or caregiver is the factor that assists the child in maintaining the advantage stimulated by early intervention. Research shows that when family-centered intervention provides emotional and informational support, positive outcomes for children and families are increased (Bruder, 2000; McWilliam & Scott, 2001). Even though a great deal of additional research is needed to explore how specific interventions can influence caregiver–child relationships, research results suggest a cumulative-transactional model of development (Foley & Hochman, 1997–1998).

If the mechanism that facilitates and maintains the impact of early intervention services is the caregiver, intervention programs need to focus on the caregiving environment as much as on the infant or child. Changes in the child may enhance parental attitudes as well as improve the interactional nature of the parent–child relationship. Conversely, changes in parent responses can reinforce and build desired responses in the child. Thus, a mutually reinforcing cycle of parent–child interactions will help to maintain the impact of early intervention services. As Meisels stated as early as 1985, "The primary intervention target should not be the child, but the child within the context of the family" (p. 8).

This recommendation was underscored by Kelly and Barnard (2000) in a review of research:

With a better understanding of how to examine areas of individual strengths and concerns in the parent–child

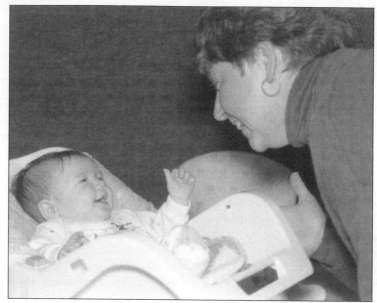

Photo by Anne Vega/Merrill

relationship, parents and professionals will be able to work together to ensure caregiving environments that help children reach their full developmental potential. (p. 282)

Therefore, throughout this text, the importance of caregiver–professional collaboration is emphasized, especially in Chapter 3.

CHANGING POLICIES: THE ENABLING IMPACT OF PUBLIC PRESSURE AND LEGISLATION

Concerned citizens and active parent and professional associations have played a vital role in changing public policy toward children with special needs.

Development of Professional Groups

It has been said that Alexander Graham Bell, inventor of the telephone and a strong advocate of oral education of the deaf, should be given credit for organizing professional advocates of special education. He petitioned the National Education Association (NEA) to establish a division to be concerned about the needs of people with disabilities. In 1897, the NEA established such a division and named it the Department of Education of the Deaf, Blind, and the Feeble-Minded. As attitudes toward and knowledge of this population changed, this name was later changed to the Department of Special Education.

The formation of the International Council for Exceptional Children in 1922 provided the impetus for what some believe to be the most influential advocacy group continuing to provide national leadership on behalf of children with special needs. The 1930 White House Conference on Child Health and Protection was a milestone in marking the first time that special education had received national recognition. Today, over 7,000 educators turn to the Division for Early Childhood of the Council for Exceptional Children as a continuing source of advocacy for young children with disabilities.

The Power of Private Citizens

Several factors came together after World War II to give rise to the development of strong parent organizations in the late 1940s. Professional knowledge was expanding, the country felt responsible for aiding its

wounded, and prominent people such as Pearl Buck, Roy Rogers and Dale Evans, and the Kennedy family were visibly calling for better education of individuals with special needs. Parents no longer felt the need to hide their children with disabilities. Pressure groups such as the United Cerebral Palsy Association, the National Association for Retarded Citizens, and the American Foundation for the Blind began to demand alternatives other than institutionalization for the education of their children with disabilities.

Professional groups joined parent groups in capitalizing on the historic Supreme Court decision in *Brown v. Board of Education* (1954). Although primarily a racial integration initiative, the Court ruled that state laws that permitted segregated public schools were in violation of the Fourteenth Amendment's "equal protection under the law" clause. Realizing that decisions applicable to one minority group must be applicable to another, pressure groups sought to secure legislation that would create significant educational changes on behalf of children with special needs. However, little actually occurred until after the publication of an article by Dunn (1968) that provided a blueprint for changes recognizing the rights of students with disabilities.

The First Chance Program

In 1968, Congress recognized the need for seed money to develop model programs to spur the development of services for children with disabilities from birth through age 8. Legislation in the form of P.L. 90–538 was enacted to establish the Handicapped Children's Early Education Program (HCEEP), better known as the First Chance program. These projects were required to include parents in their activities, run inservice training, evaluate the progress of both the children and the program, coordinate activities with public schools, and disseminate information on the project to professionals and the public. In 1980, the total number of funded projects was 177, with 111 including infants in their population (Swan, 1981). These projects served two basic purposes: (a) to provide models of exemplary services that can be

replicated for young children with disabilities and (b) to disseminate information that will encourage this replication.

Model Delivery Systems

The concept of delivery systems applies to how, when, and where services are delivered to children and their families. Karnes and Zehrbach (1977) summarized the unique approaches of 120 HCEEP programs. The majority of these fell under the following delivery system headings: (a) home, (b) home followed by center, (c) home and center, (d) center, and (e) technical assistance and consultative services.

Most projects that delivered only home-based services viewed the parents as the primary teachers of their children. Beller (1979) described these as "parent-oriented" programs. Such programs were especially useful in rural areas or where parents are reluctant to have their children leave home. For example, the Portage Project (Shearer & Shearer, 1976) developed a home-based program to meet the needs of children where geography prevented transportation. Such home-based programs had the advantage of allowing intervention within the natural setting of the home. However, these programs put added stress on the parents, who had little respite from their children and had to take on teaching responsibilities.

Many of the children originally served only at home often entered a center program around the age of 18 months. Some received services both in a center and at home. Staff members modeled appropriate teaching techniques in the child's home. A number of the center-based programs not only were cross-categorical but also included children who had no disabilities. According to Beller (1979), center-based programs tended to be child oriented, emphasizing direct intervention with the child. Finally, those centers that used technical assistance did so for help with diagnosis and inservice training.

The HCEEP seed money was well spent. Hebbeler, Smith, and Black (1991) reported that of the demonstration projects funded, 80% were able to locate

funding to continue to operate beyond the funding period. After 10 years, the 140 outreach projects resulted in 1,991 known replications of the models. These replications served nearly 108,000 children.

Public Law 94–142: The Education for All Handicapped Children Act of 1975

In 1975, with the passage of P.L. 94-142 (EHA), the right to a **free appropriate public education** was mandated for all children of school age. This law was limited in that it did not require states to offer services to young children with disabilities, but it did provide financial incentives for states to provide services to children with special needs as young as 3 years of age.

Purpose. The purpose of P.L. 94-142 is "to insure that all handicapped children have available to them . . . a free, appropriate public education which includes special education and related services designed to meet their unique needs, to insure that the rights of handicapped children and their parents or guardians are protected, to assist States and localities to provide for the education of all handicapped children and to assess and insure the effectiveness of efforts to educate handicapped children" (Sec. 601 [c]). In addition, the National Center for Clinical Infant Programs was founded in 1977 to recognize and support the needs of very young children and their families.

Free Appropriate Public Education. The law requires that a qualified school representative, teacher, the parents or guardian, and whenever possible the child join together in the development of an individualized education program (IEP). This written statement must include (a) a statement of the child's present level of academic functioning, (b) a declaration of annual goals complete with appropriate short-term instructional objectives, (c) a description of specific educational services to be provided to the child and the degree to which the child will participate in regular educational programs, (d) the

proposed date for initiation and estimation of the required length of services, and (e) annual evaluation procedures specifying objective criteria designed to determine whether the short-term instructional objectives have been met (Sec. 602, 19).

Procedural Safeguards. The law requires that children with disabilities be served in the **least restrictive environment** appropriate to their educational needs. Children can be placed in separate classes or schools only when their disabilities are so severe that regular school placement is considered inappropriate. The act also requires nondiscriminatory testing and the use of multiple criteria in the determination of placement (Sec. 612, 5, C). This requirement implies the need for all teachers to become skilled in the education of children who exhibit a variety of educational needs. P.L. 94-142 provided for the right of parents or guardians to examine all records, obtain independent evaluation, and require written notification in their native language when there are plans to change a child's educational program. The intent is to ensure that the child's rights are legally protected. Parents or guardians are entitled to a hearing before termination, exclusion, or classification of a student into a special program.

Public Law 99–457: The Education of the Handicapped Act Amendments of 1986

P.L. 99-457 is thought by some to be the law that legitimized the field of early childhood special education (Bricker, 1988). At the very least, it created a national agenda that has federal, state, and local planners collaborating with parents in unprecedented efforts to develop new and expanded services for infants and young children who have disabilities or are at risk and their families. Part B of the law required all states to extend all of the provisions of P.L. 94-142 to children 3 to 5 years old by the 1990-1991 school year. States that did not comply were to lose federal monies they had been receiving for other preschool services.

Part H.   Part H of P.L. 99–457 established a discretionary program for states to facilitate the design and implementation of comprehensive systems of early intervention services for infants and toddlers with developmental delays or disabilities. As defined by the law, early intervention services "are designed to meet a handicapped infant's or toddler's developmental needs in any one or more of the following areas: physical development; cognitive development; language and speech development; psychosocial development; or self-help skills" (Sec. 672).

Part H defined the eligible population as all children from birth through age 2 (up to the third birthday) who have developmental delays, have conditions that typically result in delay, or are at risk for significant developmental delay. States have had to make independent decisions about the definition of developmental delay and "at risk" as well as the criteria used to make these determinations. Therefore, the populations of children eligible for services varies from state to state. In order to design "a statewide, comprehensive, coordinated, multidisciplinary, interagency program of early intervention services for all handicapped infants and their families" (Sec. 671), each governor appointed a lead agency and established an interagency coordinating council. States continue to struggle through the conceptual morass and face the political challenges that determined the nature of early intervention services in 2000 and beyond. Major features of Part H of P.L. 99–457 are listed in Exhibit 1–3.

Public Law 101–476: The Education of the Handicapped Act Amendments of 1990

P.L. 101–476, an amendment to P.L. 99–457, changed the title of EHA to the **Individuals with Disabilities Education Act** (IDEA). By dropping the phrase "handicapped children" and replacing it with "individuals with disabilities," Congress intended that children with special needs be recognized as children first and, if necessary, as children with disabilities second. Throughout the law, all phrases putting the term *handicapped* before children

---

Exhibit 1–3

Major Features of P.L. 99–457

- Establishes state-level interagency councils on early intervention.
- Institutes individualized family service plans.
- Provides case management services to families.
- Maintains a public awareness program that includes a comprehensive child find system and a central early intervention resource directory.
- Establishes a single line of responsibility for general supervision and monitoring of services.
- Requires the development of a multidisciplinary, coordinated interagency model of service delivery.
- Establishes procedural safeguards.
- Acknowledges the family to be the central focus of service.
- Provides for smooth transitions as a family moves from one service or system to another.
- Facilitates development of a comprehensive system of personnel development.

---

or youth were deleted. This law became known for its "person-first" language. It also reauthorized and expanded the discretionary programs and mandated transition services and the inclusion of assistive technology services.

Public Law 102–119: The Individuals with Disabilities Education Act Amendments of 1991

IDEA was amended again in 1991 in the form of P.L. 102-119. There were two sections of the amended IDEA that contributed to the expansion and improvement of the mandate for services to infants, toddlers, and preschoolers with disabilities and their families. The first is Part H, initially included

in the 1986 amendments as discussed earlier. Recall that it created a new, discretionary program designed to provide the incentive to states to develop and implement a statewide system of comprehensive, coordinated, multidisciplinary, interagency services for all children from birth to age 3 with disabilities and their families. The second section of direct interest is Part B, Section 619, also included in the 1986 amendments, which extended the mandate to full provision of a free appropriate public education to 3- to 5-year-olds and increased funding through the Preschool Grant Program. IDEA places special emphasis on the provision of services designed to facilitate a smooth transition from services required through Part H to services provided through Part B.

Public Law 105–17: The Individuals with Disabilities Education Act Amendments of 1997

Amendments were made to IDEA again in 1997 that became effective in 1998. These amendments repealed the old Part H and reauthorized the early intervention program under a revised Part C. The new Part C allows states greater flexibility to serve at-risk infants and toddlers. It also requires individualized family service plans (IFSPs) to contain statements about the natural environments in which early intervention services will be provided. The IFSP must include a statement of justification when services are not provided in the natural environment.

States were also encouraged to employ appropriately trained paraprofessionals to help provide early intervention services. Part B now requires that school districts must participate in transition planning when children move from early intervention into preschool special education services. It also allows states to use the term *developmental delay* for children aged 3 to 9 instead of more detrimental labels such as *mental retardation*. In addition, Part B funds can be used for special education and related services as required on IEPs even if children without disabilities benefit from these services.

Public Law 108–446: The Individuals with Disabilities Education Improvement Act of 2004

Improvements were again made to IDEA in 2004. Of particular importance to early education is the requirement that services to young children be developed from "scientifically based research." To that end, the authors of this text continue to include and emphasize strategies and techniques substantiated by empirical research as best practices. This reauthorization of IDEA also allows states to continue early intervention services from age 3 until a child enters kindergarten. Parents and providers are, therefore, given the flexibility to determine when a child is ready, developmentally, to move from Part C to Part B services. The arbitrary age of 3 no longer dictates that move. Other improvements will be discussed at appropriate points in this text.

Public Law 101–336: The Americans with Disabilities Act of 1990

The **Americans with Disabilities Act** (ADA) is the most significant federal law ensuring the full civil rights of individuals with disabilities. Although the laws described previously focused primarily on education and related services, this law is broad-reaching in guaranteeing equal opportunity in employment, public accommodation, transportation, state and local government services, and telecommunications. Of particular significance is the fact that child-care centers and family day-care homes are included in the law's definition of public accommodations. According to the ADA, child-care centers must make reasonable modifications in their policies and procedures to accommodate children and adults with disabilities. This may mean that centers that do not normally accept children who are not yet toilet trained may have to make accommodations to do so if a disability is an obstacle to the toilet training. A center must also provide auxiliary aids and services when they are necessary to ensure communication with children or parents with hearing, vision, or

speech disabilities. Physical access to the center is also required. Although this law creates many questions to clarify its full impact, the intent is, nevertheless, clear. Society is expected to move toward full inclusion of individuals with disabilities in all aspects of daily living. The most significant legislation is summarized in Exhibit 1-4.

EVOLVING TRENDS IN EARLY CHILDHOOD SPECIAL EDUCATION

After reviewing the major public policy changes influencing the field of early childhood special education, it is important to note the trends that continue to evolve as policy is being implemented. Major philosophical changes are discussed below.

Family-Centered Services

The original framers of P.L. 99-457 recognized the family as the constant in the life of the child as evidenced in their mandate for a family-centered approach to implementation of the law. Rather than the traditional focus on the child, a **family-centered approach** views the child's development within the context of the family system. Increasingly, it is recognized that effective service delivery is guided by a thorough understanding of family systems—including family stresses, factors influencing family functioning, and the family's ability to cope with the challenges of raising a child with special needs. Professionals are being urged to reexamine traditional agency roles and practices as they promote the collaborative family-directed partnerships essential to success in planning processes such as assessment, prioritizing goals, and designing and implementing intervention plans.

Community-Based Inclusive Settings

One of the basic premises of IDEA is the inclusion of young children with special needs in the least restrictive environment. Indeed, Part C states that early intervention services for children from birth to age 3 are to be provided in "natural environments, including the home, and community settings in which children without disabilities participate" (P.L. 105-17, 1997). Each child's individual plan must state the degree to which the child will receive services in "natural environments." **Natural environments** include not only the child's home but also neighborhood play groups, child development centers, Head Start programs, and any other setting designed for children without disabilities.

The practice of fully including children with special needs in programs and settings designed primarily for children without disabilities received a boost through the 1990 passage of the ADA. The challenge of providing services sufficient to enable all young children to function as optimally as possible within normal environments appears to be the challenge of the new millennium. At the very least, early childhood special educators are being asked to move outside the walls of a self-contained classroom and to become integrated into early education programs within the community.

Interdisciplinary Collaboration

In addition to the mandate of delivering coordinated multiagency services, the field of early childhood special education is confronted with the need to avoid the difficulties inherent in a strict categorical response to the needs of young children and their families. Part C mandates service coordination designed to provide the critical mechanism for coordinating among complex and diverse human service personnel. Deliberate service coordination reduces duplication of intake procedures, assessment of child and family needs, and direct service delivery.

This focus on interagency and **interdisciplinary collaboration** facilitates the learning of skills necessary to work in teams comprising various disciplines, sometimes from several agencies. As discussed further in Chapter 3, the **transdisciplinary approach** allows the child and family to benefit from the expertise of several disciplines without necessarily having to be handled by, or meet face-to-face with, a myriad of professionals. Professionals from various disciplines

Exhibit 1–4

Significant Legislation

1968	Public Law 90–538 Handicapped Children's Early Education Assistance Act	Significant to the education of preschool children with disabilities; established experimental early education programs through the Handicapped Children's Early Education Program (HCEEP).
1972	Public Law 92–424 Economic Opportunity Act Amendments	Established a preschool mandate that required that not less than 10% of the total number of Head Start placements be reserved for children with disabilities.
1974	Public Law 93–380 Education Amendments Buckley Amendment, Title V	Preceded P.L. 94–142 and established a total federal commitment to the education of children with disabilities; concerns included education within the least restrictive environment, nondiscriminatory testing, and privacy rights.
1975	Public Law 94–142 Education for All Handicapped Children Act	Revised and expanded P.L. 93–380; provided a free appropriate public education with related services to all children with disabilities between ages 3 and 21.
1983	Public Law 98–199 Education of the Handicapped Act Amendments of 1983	Provided financial incentives for states to extend service levels down to birth.
1986	Public Law 99–457 Education of the Handicapped Act Amendments of 1986	Extended P.L. 94–142 to include 3- to 5-year-olds; added a grant program to assist states in establishing a comprehensive system of early intervention services for infants and toddlers with disabilities and their families.
1990	Public Law 101–336 Americans with Disabilities Act (ADA)	Ensures full civil rights for all individuals with disabilities including reasonable accommodations in preschools and day-care centers.
1990	Public Law 101–476 Individuals with Disabilities Education Act (IDEA)	Reauthorization of P.L. 94–142 to reflect a change in philosophy away from labeling children as "handicapped children" to referring to them as individuals first, with "disabilities" following as a secondary description.
1991	Public Law 102–119 Individuals with Disabilities Education Act of 1991	Reauthorization of P.L. 101–476 ensuring comprehensive early intervention services to young children and their families.
1997	Public Law 105–17 Individuals with Disabilities Education Act of 1997	Reauthorization of P.L. 102–119 authorizing comprehensive services for infants and toddlers under Part C and for preschoolers under Part B.
2004	Public Law 108–446 Individuals with Disabilities Education Improvement Act of 2004	Reauthorization of P.L. 105–17 continuing authorization of preschool services under Part B and early intervention services for infants and toddlers under Part C with allowance to continue early intervention services until kindergarten.

work together cooperatively to educate one another so that any one professional can provide a broader range of essential services. For example, a teacher or caregiver may, on the advice of a speech-language pathologist, redirect an informal playground activity to facilitate language development. (See Chapter 3 and the glossary for definitions of *interdisciplinary* and *transdisciplinary*.)

Cultural Competence

Naturally, the families of young children with disabilities reflect the diversity of families in the general population. The past two decades have brought dramatic changes in the concept and reality of the family. Increasingly, definitions of the family conceptualize it as any unit that defines itself as a family. A family includes any persons who are related by blood or marriage as well as those who have made a commitment to share their lives (Hanson & Lynch, 2004). Family characteristics will continue to become more diverse and complex. Early intervention service delivery models will continue to undergo reconceptualization in order to serve effectively the families of the 2000s and beyond.

Given the great diversity found among families, moving from a child-oriented view to a child and family service orientation creates a continuing challenge for change. Viewing the family as the primary mediator of child development necessitates a reconsideration of service goals. Part C recognizes this need by requiring parents to be the primary decision makers when outcomes or goals are targeted in the service plan. A culturally pluralistic, sensitive orientation is essential to service delivery mechanisms that can respond to constantly changing family characteristics.

Coordinated, Comprehensive Services

Collaboration between parents and professionals and among agency professionals is essential to the provision of coordinated, comprehensive services as required by the law. There are definite challenges created by significant shifts in role emphasis as professionals develop partnerships not only with families but also with an increasing array of community service providers. The literature increasingly discusses the shift away from stimulation and/or remediation programs to a new paradigm reflecting the ecological view of the child and family embedded within the larger community (Noonan & McCormick, 2006).

To meet the demands of this paradigm shift, training programs have moved away from curricula that follow traditional disciplinary boundaries toward curricula that foster multiagency and multidisciplinary collaboration. Such programs enable professionals from several disciplines to work together with families through a variety of approaches, integrating the best of the consultant, transdisciplinary, and multidisciplinary models with the best practices from special and "regular" early childhood education.

Standards-Based Curriculum

By 2005, 45 states had developed curriculum standards for 3- to 5-year-olds, and some had or were working on standards for children from birth to 3 years old (Gronlund, 2006). The number of items included in the list of standards differ from state to state, and the standards are given various titles. In Colorado, they are called *Early Learning Guidelines*, whereas in Washington they are known as *Early Learning and Development Benchmarks*. Although it is not important to remember the title given to the list of standards, it is important to remember that they are considered to be the expectations for the learning and development of young children. That is, they articulate the specific knowledge or skills that children should acquire and demonstrate through performance. Professionals see both risks and benefits in the movement toward early learning standards (National Association for the Education of Young Children [NAEYC], 2002). Together, the NAEYC and the National Association of Early Childhood Specialists in Departments of Education issued four essential features for success in leading to high-quality early education programs. These are found in Exhibit 1-5.

Creating the Conditions for Success

1. Effective early learning standards emphasize significant, developmentally appropriate content and outcomes.

2. Effective early learning standards are developed and reviewed through informed, inclusive processes.

3. Early learning standards gain their effectiveness through implementation and assessment practices that support all children's development in ethical, appropriate ways.

4. Effective early learning standards require a foundation of support for early childhood programs, professionals, and families.

Source: NAEYC (2002).

BUILDING ON BEST PRACTICES

Fortunately for all young children, the two major professional groups that relate to early intervention services have issued definite statements of **best practices** for developmentally appropriate procedures to guide program development and evaluation. In 1986, the NAEYC issued position statements on developmentally appropriate practices in early childhood programs. These have been revised and issued in the form of books (Bredekamp & Copple, 1997; Copple & Bredekamp, 2005).

While the NAEYC's **developmentally appropriate practices** serve as the primary context in which to develop curriculum, age appropriateness and individualization are essential to the understanding of effective practices within early childhood special education. As Noonan and McCormick (2006) state,

Infants and young children with severe disabilities, however, will not always be ready to learn the same activities as their age peers with mild or no disabilities. To support the integration of infants and young children with and without disabilities, however, curricular activities should be age appropriate, even when the activities do not correspond to readiness levels. The activities should serve as a context for instruction. Specific objectives, or the way in which children with disabilities participate in activities are individualized to address unique needs. (p. 85)

It is useful to consider some key recommendations that emerged from the NAEYC framework related to curriculum (see Exhibit 1–6). NAEYC also offered essential noncurricular recommendations that focus on adult–child interactions, family involvement, and evaluation (see Exhibit 1–7).

Collaboration Between Early Childhood Education and Early Childhood Special Education Professionals

A second major professional group, the Division for Early Childhood (DEC) of the Council for Exceptional Children, issued *DEC Recommended Practices in Early Intervention/Early Childhood Special Education* (Sandall, Hemmeter, Smith, & McLean, 2004; Sandall, McLean, & Smith, 2000). Although there is substantial overlap between the developmentally appropriate practices from NAEYC and the recommended practices from DEC, there are certain differences.

The NAEYC guidelines for developmentally appropriate practices were generated by early childhood education (ECE) professionals who were dismayed at the growing emphasis on academic performance and structure in preschool and kindergarten classrooms. Thus, the major focus of the original NAEYC (1987) guidelines was on expectations and learning environments that were appropriate for the developmental levels of typical young children. There was also a negative reaction to strongly teacher-directed approaches and to the teaching and tracking of specific skills. NAEYC practices valued the *process* rather than the *products* of learning.

Early childhood special education (ECSE) professionals, on the other hand, have been strongly influenced by the values and tenets of special education and P.L. 94–142. The DEC-recommended

Exhibit 1–6

NAEYC Curriculum Recommendations

- Curriculum development is responsive to families' goals and priorities as well as the individual needs of children.
- Educational goals are incorporated into all daily activities. Objectives are not taught in isolation but are integrated into meaningful activities and events.
- To the maximum extent possible, educational experiences are derived from research-based practices.
- Curriculum planning and intervention are based on specific observations of each child made by parents and the intervention team in natural contexts.
- Learning is an *interactive* process. Children's interactions with adults, peers, and the physical environment are all important.
- Learning activities and materials must be concrete and *relevant* to children's lives. Teachers should make use of real-life objects and activities (e.g., make a trip to the fire station, not just read a story about fire engines).
- Programs must be able to meet a wide range of interests and abilities. Teachers are expected to *individualize* instructional programs.
- Teachers must increase the difficulty and challenge of activities gradually and skillfully.
- Teachers must be able to facilitate *engagement* of each child by offering choices, making suggestions, asking questions, and describing events in ways that are meaningful and interesting to the child.
- Children should be given opportunities for *self-initiation, self-direction,* and *repeated practice.*
- Teachers must accept and appreciate cultural differences in children and families and avoid ethnic and gender stereotypes.
- Programs must provide a balance between rest and activity and should include outdoor activities each day.
- Outdoor activities should be *planned,* not simply opportunities to release pent-up energy.
- Programs must create careful *transitions* from one activity to the next. Children should not be rushed, and schedules should be flexible enough to take advantage of impromptu experiences.

practices emphasize the identification of specific expected outcomes, accountability of professionals for ensuring steady progress toward these outcomes, the importance of direct instruction, and a strong commitment to individualized instruction. The field of ECSE also places strong emphasis on parent–professional collaboration and family empowerment, transition planning and training for the next environment, and interdisciplinary and interagency collaboration.

While there continue to be some differences between NAEYC's developmentally appropriate and DEC's recommended practices, there has long been a trend toward mutual incorporation of the best practices and philosophies from both fields. Over a decade ago, Bredekamp (1993) suggested that ECE had recognized the importance of the ECSE practices. Similarly, the field of ECSE also recognized the importance of several key developmentally appropriate practices from ECE (Carta, Atwater, Schwartz, & McConnell, 1993; Wolery & Wilbers, 1994). Collectively, these practices are summarized in Exhibit 1–8.

The goal of many professionals in the fields of ECE and ECSE is that there be no division between the two. Especially in light of the growing diversity

Exhibit 1–7

NAEYC Noncurricular Recommendations

Adult–Child Interaction

- Adults should respond quickly and directly to children's needs and attempts to communicate. Whenever possible, adults should be at eye level with children.

- Children must be provided with a variety of opportunities to communicate. Interaction is best facilitated on a one-to-one basis or in groups of two to three children. Large-group instruction is less effective in facilitating communication.

- Professionals must be alert to signs of stress and provide sensitive, appropriate assistance to children.

- Adults must facilitate the development of self-esteem by being respectful and accepting of children, regardless of the child's behavior.

- Adults must use disciplinary techniques that enhance the development of self-control. These include setting clear, consistent limits; redirecting inappropriate behavior; valuing mistakes; listening to children's concerns and frustrations; helping children solve conflicts; and patiently reminding children of rules as needed.

- Adults must be responsible for all children at all times. Health and safety issues must be addressed constantly.

- Adults must plan for gradually increasing children's independence.

Family Involvement

- Families have the right and the responsibility to share in decision making regarding their children's care and education. Families are considered to be equals in a partnership and their vision guides program planning. Professionals must maintain frequent contact, and families should be encouraged to participate.

- Professionals must regularly share information and resources with parents, including information regarding stages of child development. They must also obtain and respect caregivers' views of individual children's behavior and development.

Evaluation

- Child evaluations should not rely on a single instrument.

- Evaluations should identify children with special needs and provide information that will lead to meaningful early interventions.

- Evaluations must be culturally appropriate.

and special needs of children from multirisk families and communities, all early childhood professionals need the range of skills that currently characterize professional development within each field. This goal was recognized by Bredekamp and Copple in their 1997 revision of developmentally appropriate practices. They suggested continuing convergence of philosophies as noted in greater emphasis on forming partnerships with parents and the importance of social and cultural contexts when considering appropriateness of practices.

A Cautionary Note

Students of ECSE must realize that, as is the case with any progressive field, early childhood special education is constantly evolving. The ideas and notions that make up today's best or recommended practices may

Some Recommended Best Practices from NAEYC and DEC

Early Childhood Special Education Recommended Practices

1. A stronger emphasis on collaboration with families and other professionals
2. Greater emphasis on supporting the specific needs of individual children
3. Greater emphasis on the birth-to-3 age range
4. Viewing teacher centered versus child centered not as a dichotomy but as a continuum; understanding that child-centered approaches do not exclude the use of teacher-directed strategies in certain situations
5. Greater emphasis on transition planning

Early Childhood Developmentally Appropriate Practices

1. Training in natural environments, particularly within the context of play
2. Importance of child-initiated activities
3. Deemphasis of standardized assessment and integration of assessment and curriculum
4. Importance of active child engagement throughout the day in naturally occurring routines and activities
5. Emphasis on social interaction
6. The importance of cultural sensitivity and competence

be very different from those that evolve a decade from now. Early intervention professionals must have a thirst for knowledge and a genuine desire to better understand how to meet the needs of young children with disabilities. They must also have considerable tolerance for ambiguity as the field continues to

define itself and its methodologies. Finally, early interventionists must have an understanding of the potential contribution of research.

Practitioners must be responsible for maintaining an important two-way dialogue with the field's researchers. They must help identify important research questions, insist on the use of research methods that are appropriate to answer those questions, and then apply the findings of that research by incorporating evidence-based techniques into their daily instructional routines whenever possible. Perhaps one of the best current examples of the importance of looking to research for guidance is in the active research on causes and intervention effectiveness in the area of autism spectrum disorders (Lord & McGee, 2001; Ozonoff, Rogers, & Hendren, 2003; Simpson, 2005).

SERVICE DELIVERY

A parameter of service delivery of particular interest today is the target of intervention, that is, whether intervention is directed primarily toward the child or the caregiver. P.L. 99–457 and subsequent reauthorizations and amendments clearly intend for the family to be the primary focal point and context within which the infant or toddler is viewed. However, even within this family-centered framework, intervention is still too often focused solely on intervention for the child with relatively little concern for the role of the family in the child's development.

Child-Focused Approaches

Bricker and Veltman (1990) defined child-focused programs as those that have as their primary focus the enhancement of the child's development. They stated that such programs are based on two theoretical assumptions: (a) that biological problems can be overcome or ameliorated and (b) that early experience is important. Related to the latter assumption is another assumption: that the potential to have a positive impact on children's development is greater when intervention occurs at younger ages.

Traditionally, under the influence of behavioral theories and the field of special education, child-focused programs have been more teacher directed than child directed. Such approaches have been characterized by carefully planned and highly structured programs that were controlled primarily by a teacher using behavioral analysis techniques. (Note: While the field has begun to move away from the teacher-directed approach, this continues to be the philosophy of many programs designed for children with autism [Scheuermann & Webber, 2002].)

Currently, child-focused programs are more child directed than teacher directed. Child-directed programs assume that the child's development can best be facilitated through opportunities for self-initiation and exploration that are carefully mediated by responsive adults. Child-focused programs do not ignore family needs. Family involvement is primarily in the context of enabling family members to meet the child's needs while at the same time having some of their own needs met. Parents are included as partners with professionals and as members of the child's intervention team.

Caregiver-Focused Approaches

As professionals have become more attuned to practices supported by research, they have turned to a functional approach that works across disciplines (Rapport, McWilliam, & Smith, 2004). They realize that for children to learn skills and make developmental gains, they must have repeated interactions with their environment that are dispersed over time. As services from different disciplines are provided intermittently, it becomes clear that these sessions must support daily caregivers in order for the interventions to be effective.

Caregiver-focused approaches, mentioned earlier, are most commonly used in early intervention programs with infants and toddlers. These approaches concentrate primarily on the delivery of services to parents. Within this category there are two fairly distinct kinds of programs. The first seeks to

establish a clinical therapeutic relationship with the parents, usually the mother, in an effort to promote mental health relationship-building principles (Barnard, Morisset, & Spieker, 1993; Knitzer, 2000). For example, this may include changes in the caregiver's view of herself and how she perceives and experiences her infant. In this approach, it is assumed that once these psychoemotional changes are brought about, the mother's interactions and relationship with her child will automatically be positive and facilitative. Other, related approaches may be less focused on a therapeutic relationship, but they continue to assume that providing emotional support and guidance for the caregiver will have positive effects on the infant (Klass, 2003; Wasik & Bryant, 2000). Even services that provide only respite for parents have been found to have an incredible impact on parents' well-being, thus making them more available to their child (Mullins, Aniol, Boyd, Page, & Chaney, 2002).

A second major category of caregiver-focused intervention programs involves those that concentrate specifically on the facilitation of caregiver–infant interaction strategies, often focusing particularly on communicative interaction (Kelly & Barnard, 2000; Mahoney & Perales, 2003). These approaches attempt to change or enhance caregivers' behaviors as they care for their infants or young children within the context of daily routines (Klein, Chen, & Haney, 2000). This approach asks parents not to be trainers but rather to be responsive in particular ways to their infant's naturally occurring cues. (See Chapter 8 for a fuller discussion of the bases of these programs.)

It is readily apparent that the choice of how services will be delivered must result from careful collaboration between parents and professionals. The more in tune professionals are with child and family needs, the more likely it is that appropriate recommendations will be made. Rapport and colleagues (2004) reflected on the following challenges for professionals: (a) intervention suggestions need to be tailored to the individual caregiver within the context of the child's family and home, (b) professionals

need to readily give credit for child progress to the caregivers involved, and (c) hands-on work with the child should be for the purposes of demonstration, assessment, and showing the caregiver that the professional really cares for the child rather than as direct service to the child.

Further considerations for developing a productive partnership with the family will be discussed in the next chapter. It also discusses how families affect and are affected by children with special needs, and it offers a variety of involvement options for families.

Services for Infants and Toddlers

Providing services for infants and toddlers with special needs and their families is referred to throughout this text as **early intervention**. As noted earlier, Part C of IDEA states that early intervention services are to be provided in natural environments, including the child's home and a variety of community settings. To provide the most appropriate option for each child and family, communities are increasingly developing what is sometimes referred to as a "menu of services." For infants and children with severe disabilities, home-based services often are considered to be the least restrictive because they are in the most normal environment. Sometimes home-based services are offered in the home of a relative or child-care provider.

Home-based programs are determined by the individual needs of each child and family. Providers are able to assess the family's priorities and resources. Such assessment can be sensitive to the functional demands of the child's environment. Home visitors include a wide variety of professionals from various community agencies. For young infants, early intervention services may be provided by a public health nurse who focuses on health care issues. A nutritionist may work with a family when their child has unique nutritional needs. Or the visits may center around sensory stimulation activities modeled by an

infant educator or provided by an occupational or physical therapist. Increasingly, attention is being paid to the facilitation of quality caregiver–child interactions and the influence of parental mental health on these interactions (Fenichel, 2002).

Some toddlers attend center-based programs. These center-based programs are group settings to which families bring their children. Such programs provide important access to parent-to-parent support. They may also provide important "one-stop-shopping" access to a variety of service providers within the same setting. Center-based programs usually provide more frequent interdisciplinary contact than in-home programs. Some service delivery models combine home- and center-based services. For example, children may be enrolled in a center 3 days per week and receive a monthly home visit.

Center or group settings may include public and private child-care settings in natural environments. Some children may experience dual enrollment by attending an agency-sponsored segregated center-based program for children with disabilities for part of the day and participate in a typical child-care

setting for the remainder of the day. As P.L. 101–336, the ADA, increases in influence, a greater number of infants and toddlers will be served in normalized child-care settings.

Special Considerations for Infant and Toddler Group Care.   Any group care programs for children from birth to 3 years of age must be designed to create

and sustain *intimacy.* Five key components of group care for infants and toddlers offered some time ago by Lally, Torres, and Phelps (1994) are summarized in Exhibit 1–9.

It is imperative that individuals working with young children from cultures different than their own carefully examine the roots of their own biases and values. They must also be knowledgeable of the

---

Exhibit 1–9

Key Components of Group Care for Young Children

1. *Group size.* The adult-to-child ratio in programs serving young children under age 3 should be no greater than 1:3. However, the issue of group size is not simply the need to maintain a low adult-to-child ratio. Total group size is at least as important as ratio. As group size increases, so does the level of stimulation. This creates a stressful environment for both infants and staff. A noisy, chaotic environment makes it difficult for staff to be sensitive and responsive to child cues and decreases the opportunity for quiet, intimate interactions.

2. *Physical environment.* Arrangement of the physical environment can either facilitate or interfere with flexible, individualized, responsive care. For example, easy and frequent access to food and to outdoor space allows greater individualization. Furniture that is comfortable for adults, such as rocking chairs and couches, encourages holding and reading to infants. Reduction of off-limits items and areas minimizes discipline problems and negative adult–child interactions. Small, well-defined areas for certain types of play help control overstimulation and help young children focus.

3. *Assignment of primary caregiver.* An extremely important factor in center-based care for young children is the assignment of a primary caregiver to each child. This facilitates the development of trust and intimacy. This does not mean that the child interacts *exclusively* with one adult; rather, on most days there will be a familiar and "special" person on whom the child can rely. The assignment of a primary caregiver also increases the likelihood that at least one staff person knows each child well. A knowledge of temperament, communication cues, likes, dislikes, and fears can be shared with other staff members. This, in turn, increases the opportunity for responsive and appropriate interactions with the infant.

4. *Continuity of care.* Related to the issue of primary caregiver, Lally and associates (1994) also stressed the importance of continuity of care: "When a very young child loses a caregiver, he really loses part of his sense of himself and the way the world operates. The things that the child knows how to do, and the ways that he knows to be simply don't work anymore. Too many changes in caregivers can lead to a child's reluctance to form new relationships" (p. 6). Changing caregivers every 6 to 9 months can have a negative effect on infants and young children. Changing the caregiver (or teacher in an early intervention program) is also difficult for the child's parents. This requires the reestablishment of trust and communication patterns.

5. *Cultural and familial continuity.* Ideally, programs should employ staff whose cultural backgrounds match the families they serve. Children and parents are sensitive to significant mismatches in the childrearing values and practices of family and staff.

values and attitudes of the cultural groups in their community and work to avoid being judgmental when significant differences do exist.

Services for Preschoolers

Part B of IDEA also requires that children be placed in the least restrictive environment. Despite the trend toward placement in inclusive settings, the least restrictive environment for 3- to 5-year-olds with more complex needs may be a segregated preschool special education class usually provided by the public school system. Special education preschool classrooms are staffed by teachers with special education credentials. Some states have specific early childhood special education certification. The staff-to-child ratios are smaller than in standard child-care settings or Head Start classrooms. At least one teacher's aide must be available to assist. Although parents are usually encouraged to be present, they may be less involved than the parents of infants and toddlers, where attendance is usually required. In all specialized programs designed to serve young children with complex needs, a transdisciplinary team of service providers is essential to the progress of children. Throughout the text, the roles of related service personnel will be illustrated.

MEETING YOUNG CHILDREN'S NEEDS IN INCLUSIVE SETTINGS

There are many reasons why the early years should be optimal ones for including children with disabilities. First, most early education programs expect children to mature at varying rates during these years of enhanced growth and development. Differences in skills are expected and accommodated within the curriculum. The range of so-called normalcy in early education is much broader than that usually found in elementary school classrooms.

Unlike teachers of older children, early childhood educators tend to focus on the *process* more than the *product* of learning. They are busy setting up centers to allow for sensory exploration rather than grading spelling papers or preparing the next day's language test. In addition, the methods and materials usually found in early education centers are conducive to the development of all young children. Exploration, manipulation, expression, sharing, and active involvement provide easy opportunities for educators to structure and reinforce meaningful interaction between children with disabilities and those without. However, with the current emphasis on school readiness and standards-based education, this tradition may be changing as noted in the previous discussion on standards-based practices.

Anyone who has worked with young children is readily aware of their natural abilities to accept and even appreciate individual differences. Children respond to one another without making judgments and comparisons. Spontaneous friendships abound, with little in the way of ongoing expectations. When differences are observed, questions reflect a natural curiosity. If answered in genuine, thoughtful ways, children tend to accommodate and accept those who are different (Odom, 2002).

Unique Challenges Involved in Supporting Early Childhood Inclusion

Despite these favorable conditions for successful inclusion, there are also several challenges to successful inclusion in early childhood settings. Common examples of these challenges include lack of availability of quality child care, low pay for child care staff, and differences in administrative structure and educational philosophies (Hanline & Daley, 2002; Harris & Klein, 2002; Wesley & Buysse, 2004).

It is also important to acknowledge that simply placing children with disabilities in the same educational settings with nondisabled children does not accomplish the goals of inclusion (Bricker, 2000). Although much has been written about **inclusion support** strategies in K–12 education, less attention has been given to inclusion support in early childhood settings. As Harris and Klein (2002) illustrate, there are

Photo by Lisa Wadors

several challenges that are unique to early childhood inclusion. Some of these are discussed below:

1. In the K–12 inclusive classroom, the general education teacher is credentialed at the same level as the special educator who provides support to the children with special needs. There is generally "parity" in terms of training background, level of academic degree, credential/license status, and pay. This is very often not the case in early childhood settings. The lack of support as a society for quality child care results in inadequate resources and low staff salaries, particularly in urban communities. This can result in little motivation for advanced training in early childhood education, thus creating a "parity gap" between the training and salary level of ECE and ECSE teachers. This difference can lead to significant challenges for the inclusion support specialist. It requires understanding and perspective-taking skills to bring about successful collaboration and effective team building.

2. The level of experience and understanding of disabilities among ECE teachers (i.e., non-special

education teachers) and staff is highly varied. The inclusion support specialist must be able to explain the nature of a child's disability and learning style and to demonstrate specific strategies. Klein and colleagues (2000) described a project evaluation focus group in which families reported that one of the greatest values of the inclusion support specialist was her ability to help ECE staff understand the child's disability. Thus, early childhood support specialists must have a certain level of disability-specific expertise.

3. Often the ECSE support specialist must take on the unfamiliar role of providing services on someone else's turf. The support specialist must manage her own role and avoid being intrusive while at the same time establishing a collaborative relationship. On the other hand, the ECE teacher may be uncomfortable in her own relative lack of knowledge and experience with disabilities. She may also be unaccustomed to having someone observing in her classroom. Thus, the ECE teacher may be understandably defensive or wary and experience additional stress in an already stressful job. The challenges

posed to the development of a truly collaborative relationship in such situations can be significant.

4. Finally, even when the ECE staff are highly trained, there are sometimes significant philosophical differences between ECSE and ECE staff. Klein et al. (2000) found that this was perceived to be one of the major barriers to successful inclusion. These differences in philosophy and beliefs might include such issues as the following:

- The *purpose* of early childhood education— for example, opportunities for socialization versus training of specific developmental skills or school readiness.
- Beliefs about inclusion—for example, all children should be included regardless of severity or complexity of disability versus only certain children can be successfully included.
- Strict adherence to a particular early childhood curriculum versus more flexible, adapted implementation of the curriculum.
- The kinds of teaching and interaction strategies used—for example, very child-directed and unstructured versus a combination of more structured, teacher-directed teaching interventions.
- Organization of daily activities—for example, fairly unstructured, flexible daily schedules versus predictable daily routines.

Note: Given that there has been an important trend toward the development of "blended" ECE and ECSE personnel preparation programs, many of the challenges expressed above will eventually be resolved through the provision of common training experiences at the university level (Miller & Stayton, 1998).

Redefining the Role of the Early Childhood Special Educator

In order for children with special needs to meet their developmental and educational goals, someone must be available to structure the environment, adapt the materials, determine the child's most profitable mode of learning, and select appropriate teaching strategies to encourage specific behaviors. Inclusion does

not supplant the mandate for individualized planning and services as needed by each child. Research to date suggests that systematic intervention efforts guided by the teacher are necessary in order to promote successful inclusion (Bricker, 2000; Horn, Lieber, Sandall, Schwartz, & Li, 2000).

To fulfill such a multifaceted role, teachers must develop competencies characteristic of both the early childhood educator and the special educator. Fortunately, the skills needed include the same skills that are necessary to work with *all* young children. However, successful inclusion of children with disabilities requires additional skills and expertise.

The Case for Specific Training Related to Inclusion Support

A fairly recent study reported by Dinnebeil, McInerney, Roth, and Ramaswamy (2001) offered support for the need for specific training in inclusion support. They surveyed ECSE professionals serving in itinerant support roles for children in community-based settings. Dinnebeil et al. found that the primary strategy being used by these consultants was a direct instruction approach in which they simply carried out the teaching strategies they were accustomed to using in their segregated settings. They concluded that there is a significant need for training in collaborative consultation skills (see also Klein & Harris, 2004).

Exhibit 1-10 presents some examples of the kinds of support an inclusion specialist might need to be prepared to provide for a child placed in a community-based early childhood setting.

For our discussion we will use the term *inclusion support specialist* to refer to an early childhood special educator who provides support for one or more children with disabilities within an inclusive early childhood setting. The inclusion support specialist role may differ from that of the discipline-specific therapist (e.g., occupational therapist, physical therapist, or speech-language pathologist) or the disability-specific specialist (e.g., visual impairment specialist or deaf and hard-of-hearing specialist) who provides specific direct services or consultative services related to a particular special need. *In this text the role of the*

Exhibit 1–10

Examples of Inclusion Support Activities

- Inservice and information to staff members regarding the characteristics of the child's specific disability (e.g., autism, Down syndrome, or multiple sensory impairment).
- Demonstration or modeling of specific intervention and teaching strategies.
- Ongoing observation and assessment of the child within the setting.
- Ongoing discussion and written feedback to teachers regarding all areas of a child's development and performance (e.g., level of engagement and participation or development across the developmental domains, such as language, self-help, social-emotional, and so on).
- Ongoing discussion and feedback with parents about child's adjustment and progress.
- Occasional individual work with the child as necessary to encourage achievement of specific goals (e.g., participation in group activities, appropriate communication with peers, or behavior management).
- Modeling of peer training techniques.
- Creating or obtaining adapted equipment for child's use in the classroom (e.g., photographs for communication or various types of adaptive equipment and technology to assist self-help and communication).
- Participation in team meetings, including regular staff meetings and IEP or IFSP meetings to provide problem-solving and conflict resolution guidance as needed and team leadership and coordination.

inclusion support specialist is to support the optimal participation of the child in the inclusive setting through collaboration and coordination with other service providers and team members.

It is clear from examining the list in Exhibit 1–10 that the effective delivery of these services will depend not only on a wide range of knowledge and skills related to best practices in early intervention and ECSE but also on skills in the area of collaboration, consultation, teaming, adult learning styles, and strategies specifically targeted to the child's participation in the early childhood environment. To provide optimal support, an individual should have knowledge and skills across the following broad competency areas:

- Typical child development and developmentally appropriate practice in ECE.
- Disability-specific characteristics and best practices in early intervention and ECSE.
- Specific strategies and methods that support inclusion of children with disabilities and interactions with typical peers.
- Collaborative consultation and team building.

The goal of this text is to provide not only information related to the characteristics and learning needs of children with disabilities but also the specific guidance necessary to address these needs in inclusive settings. The knowledge and recommendations included within this text reflect a long history of research, policy, and practice that are derived from the two fields of early childhood education and special education. Chapter 10 discusses in detail approaches, skills, and specific strategies for providing effective support to young children with special needs and their families in inclusive settings.

Summary

This chapter offers perspectives on the evolving field of early childhood special education historically, theoretically, and with an introduction to best practices. Over the past 100 years, the lot of children with special needs has shifted from "hide and forget" to "identify and help." Jean-Marc Itard, Maria Montessori, and Jean Piaget were a few of the most notable pioneers in this field. Their contributions paved the way

for the development of curricular adaptations to accommodate young children with special needs in a variety of settings.

Results of several research studies led to greater acceptance by the mid-1960s of the belief that intelligence develops rapidly in the primary years of life and that early stimulation can influence this development. Head Start began as a federally funded project in 1965 to provide enrichment opportunities for young children in impoverished families and was subsequently extended to include at least 10% of children with disabilities. Initial research indicated that the immediate educational gains for Head Start children quickly faded, but longitudinal studies have substantiated long-term persistence of this early intervention. Children between birth and 8 years of age who have disabilities were given a boost in 1968 through legislation that created the Handicapped Children's Early Education Program. The resulting model programs emphasized inclusion of parents in their child's educational activities.

P.L. 94–142 mandated that appropriate public education be made available to all children with disabilities as early as possible. One significant provision of this law is that each child should have a written individualized education program. Children with disabilities also are to be served in the least restrictive environment that meets their needs. The law mandates inclusion in a regular classroom unless the child's disabilities are too severe. In effect, the thrust is to fit the schooling to the child rather than fit the child to the school. This goal is pursued through informed selection of intervention strategies, with preparation of the interventionist as the critical foundation.

P.L. 99–457 initiated legitimization of the field of early childhood special education. Federal, state, and local planners are collaborating with parents in unprecedented efforts to develop new and expanded services for infants and young children who have disabilities or are at risk and their families. Part H provides incentives for states to provide comprehensive, coordinated family-focused interagency programs for children from birth through age 2. Unique to this law and following amendments are the requirements for collaborative service coordination designed to implement individualized family service plans.

Strategies for inclusion of children with special needs in the early education curriculum have had several theoretical origins. Current approaches to early childhood special education continue to combine influences from both early education and special education fields, especially in advocating best practices. The child development and early education literature emphasizes the importance of child-directed methods that are developmentally appropriate and use play and social interaction as primary vehicles for teaching and learning. Special education legislation has mandated a focus on family involvement and education within integrated, community-based settings. The evolving delivery systems offer a variety of opportunities to meet the unique needs of each child and his or her family.

Discussion Topics and Activities

1. If an interventionist believes that a child's development is determined primarily by heredity or primarily by the environment, how will his or her behavior be influenced? What is your belief? As a teacher, how would your behavior be influenced?

2. Choose at least six articles about childrearing or education that have appeared in leading popular magazines during the past year. Discuss these in light of the beliefs espoused. How can these beliefs influence behavior of parents and early interventionists? Do you see any relationship between these beliefs and historical developments? In what way might these be setting precedents?

3. Contact the state department of education or local school district where you live and obtain a copy of their early learning standards, assuming they have been developed and adopted.

4. Discuss specific criteria an evaluator might use to determine whether a program encompasses the best practices of effective intervention programs listed in this chapter.

5. Obtain and study copies of guidelines explaining state and local legislation related to early intervention and special education preschool services for children from birth to five years of age.

6. Compare and contrast the National Association for the Education of Young Children's best practices with the recommended practices of the Division for Early Childhood Education.

7. Become informed about the service delivery options available in your area. Role-play a transdisciplinary team meeting to determine which would be the most appropriate options for children and families with differing needs.

chapter 2

In Partnership with Families

Photo by Laura Dwight/PhotoEdit Inc.

KEY TERMS

(Note: Terms are discussed within the text and/or defined in the glossary.)

active listening	family-centered intervention	family's quality of life
coaching	family functions	marital subsystem
confidentiality	family interactions	parental subsystem
cultural models	family life cycle	sibling subsystem
empathy	family resources	relationship-based intervention
empowered (empowerment)	family structure	(support-based intervention)
extended family subsystem	family systems perspective	routines

- Early intervention specialists must learn effective ways of supporting families who exhibit individual styles of coping with disability.

- A child with special needs can be understood only within the context of his or her family.

- Families are best understood as dynamic social systems. Each comprises its own values, roles and functions, and life cycle.

- Successful intervention for children with special needs is dependent on the formation of true partnerships with those who serve as the child's caregivers.

- Early intervention professionals must be able to use a variety of communication strategies to foster the involvement and meet the needs of individual families.

- Understanding the range of possible cultural differences among families and respecting those differences is essential to successful early intervention. Cultural stereotyping must be avoided.

- Early childhood special education professionals must acquire strategies for working with special populations of parents, such as those who have developmental disabilities or who are teen or foster parents.

Helping parents understand that parent–child interaction may be the single best predictor of child outcome is clearly a responsibility of early intervention specialists. Collaboration with parents or other caregivers is essential to the development of families' awareness of the importance of their role in facilitating, guiding, and supporting their child's development. With time and understanding, parents do become their child's best ally in interpreting his or her needs. The following parent perspective illustrates how time and professional concern helped enable one parent to develop the coping skills needed to face the day-to-day realities of parenting a young child with special needs. Although written over 20 years ago, involved professionals unfortunately will attest to its continuing relevance.

A Personal Perspective on Raising a Child with Developmental Problems

by Lora Jerugim

My daughter Elisa is 5 years old. She is a developmentally delayed child whose delays range from mild to borderline and are of unknown etiology. I do not have any research findings to present. I have no statistics for you. But what I can share with you is something that I know a lot about—what it *feels* like to raise a child with developmental problems.

When Elisa was born, I was ecstatic. I had two sons, and I had dreamed about having a daughter. I had fantasies about who she would be and what we would share. Of course she would be completely articulate by the age of 2, and someday I would teach her to play the piano. And when she grew older we would recommend books to each other to read, and I had images of our whole family sitting at a table assembling a thousand-piece puzzle together. So much for the fantasy.

Elisa's birth was 5 to 6 weeks premature, but it was normal and no one suspected that there was anything wrong with her. So I took home what I thought was a perfectly normal baby. Elisa always seemed alert and responsive, but by the time she was 6 months old and was not able to roll over, I sensed that something was wrong. Like so many parents, I was encouraged to believe that Elisa would catch up, and I only wish that pediatricians

could be as attuned to the signs of delay as parents are so that we would not lose so much precious time in getting help for our children. By the time Elisa was a year old, she couldn't sit up and was severely hypotonic. It was clear at that point that she was not developing normally, and we were finally referred to a developmental specialist. What was once like a dream come true had turned into a living nightmare. My first reaction was one of complete shock and disbelief. I would wake up in the morning and wonder if it was all just a bad dream. Certainly disabled children are born every day, but it couldn't be happening to me . . . not my child. I felt a sense of panic and helplessness as I waited for almost 2 months for the test results to come back. And when I learned that the results were negative, I felt relieved and yet confused. Elisa had no diagnosis and consequently no clear prognosis. I was told that she might have a brain dysfunction, but having a label to hold onto didn't seem to help much. We don't know what caused this dysfunction, and although I feel somehow responsible, I have nowhere to place my diffused sense of guilt. In a way I feel lucky that I do not know precisely what happened, because if I did I would probably run that moment over in my mind for the rest of my life wishing that I'd done something differently.

There are times when I feel such rage that this has happened to my child and to our whole family. I am angry with a world that is intolerant of people who are different—a society that is so focused on achievement that we often forget to look into a person's soul. I feel jealous and lonely as I listen to friends discuss whether their children are highly gifted or just gifted, while I'm praying that someday my daughter will be capable of leading an independent life. I feel so much pain as I watch Elisa at nursery school struggling to do things that younger children do with ease. I am exhausted because a special child requires twice the work to get half the distance. But most of all I live in fear of the unknown, because I don't know what limitations my daughter's handicap will impose on her, and I do not know how the world will respond to her being different.

Having a young child whose development is delayed but whose disability is not visible poses a number of special problems. These children seem to be caught somewhere between the normal world and the world of disabilities. Normal toddler programs are not quite appropriate, and yet early intervention programs in the area are populated with children whose disabilities are more severe and/or visible. When Elisa entered her first intervention program at 20 months, I was traumatized. I wept on and off for weeks. I had never had any exposure to handicapped children and being in their presence was a painful reminder of life's incomprehensible injustices. I also realized that I wasn't just visiting the class. I was there because my daughter was handicapped and this was her school! But it was this same environment that fostered my denial of Elisa's problems. After all, Elisa looked so "normal" compared to most of the other children.

Attending parent groups often made me feel more depressed. I felt so guilty that I experienced such despair over Elisa's condition, when other parents envied me and thought my daughter seemed like a genius compared to their children. Furthermore, most of the children had been diagnosed at birth, and not only did a diagnosis help the parents face the reality of their situations, but they'd had so much more time to come to terms with their children's disabilities, while I felt as though I was just beginning. They also had special support groups and an abundance of literature to refer to when dealing with their children's specific disabilities.

I also decided to place my daughter in a normal nursery school part time where she was the only child with disabilities, and although my daughter, who is very competent socially, adjusted fairly well, I felt lonely, isolated, depressed, and at times embarrassed. During my daughter's first few weeks there, when I stayed with her to ease her separation, I had to leave the room on a few occasions when I began to cry. Being around all those normal 3-year-olds was a constant reminder of how verbal and adept little children are and how far behind Elisa was in her development.

Furthermore, when my sons were in nursery school, I became acquainted with the other parents primarily through my children playing after school with other children or being invited to birthday parties. Elisa is rarely invited to birthday parties, and she has been invited to play at another child's house twice in 2 years. I have made some attempts to invite children over, but I not only have to find an appropriate playmate, I also must determine if the parent is the type who would be receptive to having their child play with a child who is "slow."

There were times in the past when my feeling of isolation became so pervasive that I found myself wishing that somebody I knew, whether family or friend, would give birth to a disabled child just so that someone close to me would truly understand what I was experiencing and that I would no longer feel so alone. Then, of course, just the idea that I could entertain such a terrible thought made me feel the most unbearable guilt. For several years I felt as though I was riding a roller coaster in the dark. I could never see when the dips were coming, and when they did, I would be dropped into a depression that could last for weeks. Sometimes a stranger's question would be enough to do it, like the woman who asked me how old my daughter was and proceeded to ask me why she couldn't talk. If Elisa had been in a wheelchair, that woman would never have dared to ask me that question.

Parents of children with delays must endure many types of stress. We live with financial stress, and we worry about governmental budget cuts and changes in the laws protecting handicapped children. We are responsible for selecting schools and therapies, but when our children are receiving such a variety of services, how are we supposed to determine what's working and what's not? Often we do not know from one year to the next where our children will go to school, because we can't predict what their needs will be in a year, and we don't know what programs will be available. Even a class that is appropriate now may not be appropriate 6 months from now just because the population of children in the class may change so radically. We

find ourselves battling with school districts and forever fighting against society's prejudicial attitudes towards the disabled. I've often wished that I could hire a full time advocate to deal with all these external stresses so that I could just focus my energies on raising my daughter.

There are constant family stresses as well, since one child requires more help and attention than the others. Resentments build up, and I find myself doing a perennial balancing act with my husband and children trying to make sure that everyone gets their fair share of me. All this is aggravated by the fact that when you have a delayed preschooler, what you really have on your hands is a child who seems to be stuck in the terrible twos. I'm sure any of you who have raised children will remember the nightmare of the terrible twos and how grateful you were that it only lasted a year. Try to imagine the shape our nerves are in after we've endured the terrible twos for 2 or 3 years and with no end in sight. Elisa is destructive without malintent and is forever testing us. She frequently spills her drinks, and the other day she tried to pour herself a bowl of cereal and poured cereal all over the floor. I sometimes wonder if she'll ever be fully toilet trained or if she will ever sleep through the night.

Testing is another source of stress for parents of delayed youngsters. Elisa's behavior and skills vary from day to day and often from one part of the day to another, so she is difficult to assess. Her most organized time of the day is usually the evening, and evaluations are generally done in the morning. Furthermore, her fine motor and language problems make assessment even more difficult. In one testing situation, she was asked to stack 1-inch cubes and was then scored in two areas: fine motor and cognitive. Her poor fine motor development prevented her from stacking more than a few blocks, so I asked the woman who was administering the test if she would try it again while steadying the tower for Elisa. Elisa then stacked all 10 blocks, and her cognitive score on that item jumped by 18 months! Sometimes Elisa can show where a puzzle piece should go but can't maneuver it into place. I often feel that the

standard tests used are designed for normal children and, consequently, are inadequate for handicapped children. They certainly fail to pick up the qualitative changes that our children's abilities undergo over time. Professionals also need to be aware that the whole concept of testing triggers a special response in well-educated parents, because for us, perhaps on a subconscious level, poor performance is equated with failure.

Perhaps one of my areas of greatest frustration, anger, and despair has been the area of diagnosis. How much more difficult it is to accept your child's handicap when you don't know what it is. I have received so many conflicting opinions about who Elisa is that I've stopped listening. I just don't care anymore about having a label for her, because the only appropriate label for my daughter is the one I gave her at birth: ELISA. One physician told me that I'd thoroughly confused Elisa's diagnosis by all the work I'd done with her. I remember thinking at the time that you can't teach a child anything they're not capable of learning. A psychologist labeled her mentally retarded, and 2 weeks later, I was told that according to test results from a research project, Elisa did *not* appear to be mentally retarded. I had another doctor tell me that Elisa would grow up and be able to feed herself and dress herself, while yet another doctor told me that we should have expectations of normalcy for Elisa and that she in turn would have those expectations for herself. He said that by working with disabled children for 30 years he knew by observing Elisa that she was not mentally retarded. Looking at the child seemed more important to him in his assessment than simply looking at test scores. He also told me that she would grow up and be able to lead a normal life, that she would not be a Phi Beta Kappa, but that where she would fall in between no expert could ascertain. The level she would attain would depend on many variables that could not be measured, and that the most important of them would be her own motivation to succeed.

This particular doctor deserves special mention, because he is not only a skilled physician, he is a humanist as well. He still sees Elisa regularly, and I feel that the way he has related to us over the years could well serve as an example to everyone in the helping professions. He has treated us with sensitivity and respect and has valued our input, recognizing that we, as Elisa's parents, probably know her better than anyone else in the world. He has been honest with us and has freely admitted that he doesn't have all the answers. He has always looked at Elisa as a human being and not simply as a composite of her problems. He has made us aware of her strengths, and he has acknowledged our efforts in providing Elisa with the help that she needs. He always questions us about our whole family and reminds us of the importance of keeping our lives in balance. But the most important lesson to be learned from this man is that you must not take parents' hope away. Hope is what keeps us going, even if it's only the hope that things will be a little better than they are today. Without hope, we would stop fighting for our children and working so hard to provide the services they need. I believe that parents and professionals share the same goals for our disabled children. We want them to grow up to be independent, productive, and self-actualized human beings, so we must be sure that we are working together towards these goals, rather than in opposition.

A friend of mine shared a quote with me that says, "Thank you, God, for reminding me that thorns have roses," and with that thought in mind, I want to share with you the joy and growth I've experienced in raising Elisa, and not just the pain and frustration.

Elisa has taught me more about love and patience than anyone I have ever known, and she has drastically altered my perception of what matters in life. And as I have watched her development and lived with the uncertainty of not knowing when or even *if* she will acquire certain skills, I have come to appreciate my sons' normal growth in a way that I never could before. She has shown me that a "spoken word" and a simple "step" are among life's greatest gifts and that the miracle of normal development must never be taken for granted.

I have come to accept that my daughter will not be quite like everybody else when she grows up, but

then who of us is? We are all unique individuals, and we should appreciate our differences rather than scorn them. We all have our strengths and weaknesses, and how many of us, even without disabilities, ever realize our full human potential?

I have struggled to redefine the meaning of joy in my life, and I have learned to live with sorrow and to move beyond it. I have discovered that life is very precious and that none of us has any guarantee of what the future will hold. Parenting Elisa has been a challenge for me, and I have found a strength within myself that I didn't know existed.

I've also become aware of the importance of seeing myself as a human being separate from mother and wife and of nurturing my own growth. And as I nourish myself, I find that I have just that much more to give. Elisa's education is in good hands, and I no longer want to be her teacher. I just want to be her mother and to teach her the things that I know about: appreciating life and being a caring human being. At the same time, she is teaching me, because Elisa has no prejudices and doesn't let her head get in the way of establishing human relationships. Instead, she seems to have a direct line to people's hearts.

I can honestly say that I love and accept my imperfectly perfect daughter for exactly who she is rather than for who she might have been. I hope that sharing my experiences will in some way help the professional community to be more sensitive to the needs of parents of delayed children and that we will be better able to work together to serve these children.

Courtesy, Lora Jerugim.

As this parent so clearly illustrates, all children do affect and are affected by their families. Historically, conceptual contributions such as the transactional model of child development elaborated by Sameroff and Fiese (2000) have played a significant role in helping early interventionists understand the continuous dynamic interactions of the child within the context of the family and community. Originally, when children with special needs began to receive early intervention services, parents were usually passive bystanders watching their children "receive" therapy or infant stimulation. In 1975, P.L. 94–142 formalized parents' participation in the educational planning process of school-aged children. Parents were encouraged to become involved, but the nature of the involvement was not clearly delineated. Parents of young children with special needs often were trained to carry out therapeutic or instructional activities with their children. Although many found their role as "teachers" to be fulfilling, others became frustrated with these teaching expectations. Their lives were too demanding to cope with even one more expectation.

P.L. 105–17 of 1997 strengthened the recognition of families as integral partners in the early intervention process. The recognition of the family as a legitimate client in early intervention was spelled out in the formal requirements of family assessment, family outcomes, and family services within the regulations of P.L. 105–17. Currently, P.L. 108–446, the Individuals with Disabilities Education Improvement Act of 2004, further supports the critical role that families play in their child's development by requiring that families receive written notification of their rights and responsibilities annually rather than just on initiation of services.

Experiences provided for the child are not to be viewed as independent of the family. The family is recognized as the essential component of the caregiving environment that influences and is influenced by the child over time, resulting in different outcomes for both the child and the family (Zeanah, 2000). To understand the reciprocal nature of the relationship between young children with special needs and their families, the family is viewed as a system with interacting subsystems. No family member is thought to function in isolation from other family members. Therefore, after reviewing some of the needs and emotions that appear to be characteristic of families with special needs, we will explore family dynamics from a **family systems perspective** (Turnbull & Turnbull, 2001).

EMOTIONAL NEEDS OF FAMILIES WITH CHILDREN WHO HAVE SPECIAL NEEDS

The majority of new parents start out with little or no preparation to meet the unique, ongoing challenges of caring for a newborn. Even experienced parents must readjust their style of living whenever another child is added to the family. The birth of any child brings adjustments within family systems. According to the annual report of the March of Dimes in 2000, every 3.5 minutes a parent is told that his or her child has a serious illness or disability. Parents of very young children with special needs must deal not only with the usual adjustments of parenthood but also with additional stresses and concerns for which they are not likely to be prepared. Each change in their child's condition brings about new questions, concerns, and challenges.

Today there are many ways parents can obtain help and emotional support. For example, they can join support and therapy groups composed of other parents of children with special needs. Participants offer support and encouragement to one another and exchange information about useful resources. Part C of P.L. 108–446 mandates that psychological and service coordination services be provided to families of children from birth to age 3 who may have developmental delays or be at risk for such delays. When emotionally supportive services are provided while children are very young, adjustments within family systems may be made more readily. However, it must be remembered that the emotional needs of families may be constantly changing, and the emotional and physical demands that accompany the advent of a child with special needs should never be underestimated. The following description of basic family needs and perceived emotional responses is offered to facilitate understanding of individual family reactions.

Indeed, the law requires professionals to specifically address the concerns and priorities of families through individualized family service plans (discussed in chapter 4). This requirement recognizes that it is difficult for families to have the time and energy necessary to address children's needs if the family's basic survival needs have not been met.

Basic Needs

Certain needs are basic to all parents who seek professional help. First, they want to be recognized as caring, intelligent people. They need to be viewed as individuals capable of effective parenting, and they want to know that they are seen in that way. Second, they want to be assured that they are receiving the best and most up-to-date information possible. They want to have confidence in those who profess to know how to help their child. Third, they want and urgently need guidance in what to do in the immediate *now*. Although they want positive opinions about what the future holds, they need to have useful suggestions immediately.

Failure to Consider Basic Needs

Many of the emotional reactions attributed to families may be heightened by the failure of those to whom the families have turned for help to consider their basic needs. There is no doubt that early intervention professionals, for the most part, have jumped wholehcartedly into practices designed to meet the needs of not only the child with special needs but also other family members. However, even if early interventionists do not mishandle the needs of parents, they should realize that some parents may have experienced inadequate and insensitive treatment by some professionals. We cannot deny that there are professionals who may fail to recognize a disabling condition, convey negative attitudes, withhold important information, or ignore parents' concerns. This understanding will help interventionists sustain the patience and develop the empathy necessary to work effectively with parents who are anxious, angry, or troubled.

The Need for Emotional Support

Parents need emotional support. In fact, it has been found that parents of children with disabilities typically experience a higher level of stress than those of typical children (Smith, Oliver, & Innocenti, 2001). Assuming that parents are seen as partners by all the professionals with whom they come into contact, parents' ability to cope effectively with their stress

will influence how responsive they can be to their child and his or her needs (Lessenberry & Rehfeldt, 2004). Parental responsiveness has, indeed, been shown to have a positive influence on child development and general well-being (Collins, Maccoby, Steinberg, Hetherington, & Bornstein, 2000).

PARENTAL REACTIONS

A number of writers, both parents and professionals, have described various phases of adjustment in parents' acceptance of their child and his or her disabling condition. Early on, Boyd (1950) discussed three levels of adaptation: the need to pull back and focus solely on one's own needs, a gradual turning toward the needs of one's immediate family, and a desire to aid others with similar problems. Writers later turned to the grieving process described by Kübler-Ross (1969) for an understanding of the possible emotional reactions of some parents to the perceived "death" of a normal child. Table 2–1 illustrates a summary of the phases of emotional reactions that may be experienced by families with children who have special needs.

Table 2–1 Possible parental reactions

Family Reactions	Stages	Possible Caregiver Reactions	What You Can Do
• Shame, guilt, unworthiness, overcompensation. • Disbelief. • "He's just like his father." • "Don't worry he'll grow out of it." • Shopping for a diagnosis. • Research mode (seeks all information/shuts down from communicating with others).	Shock, Disbelief, and Denial	• Frustration and concern that parent isn't moving fast enough or doing enough for the child. • Anger or resentment. • If you were the one to initially approach the parent, fear or uncertainty that maybe you made a mistake. • Discomfort.	• Listen with acceptance. • Employ active listening. • Work together on behalf of child. • Patience. • Provide resources, if appropriate (i.e., referral for parent to parent support or for assessment).
• Anger can be transferred to provider or other caregivers. • Verbal abuse common. • Blaming others. • Resenting others who have healthy or typical children or may not want to be around typically developing children.	Anger and Resentment	• Feeling hurt that parent is taking it out on you. • Concern that family may display anger around child, could be damaging to child. • "Get over it" attitude. • Easy to be provoked by parent, as they are looking for a "fight."	• Encourage patience, small steps. • Get parent busy—give resources. • Support and model positive parent–child interactions, suggestions for what works. • Understanding, compassion, caring.
• Delays acceptance of the inevitable. • Working with determination (or vengeance/vehemence). • Let's make a deal: "If I do this . . ." then this will happen. • Can lead to depression when things don't go well.	Bargaining	• In an effort to help the parent, it is easy to get hooked into their state or stage. • You can't "fix" the child, make him better or progress faster—can lead to your frustration.	• Show family "empathic understanding"—accept their feelings. • Help parents understand that their feelings are normal and that it's OK. • Communicate with honesty: "it must be very frustrating for you . . ."

Continued

Table 2–1 Possible parental reactions (*Continued*)

Family Reactions	Stages	Possible Caregiver Reactions	What You Can Do
• Feeling of "What's the use?" or "Why bother?" • Helplessness and hopelessness. • Mourning the loss of the "perfect" or healthy child.	Depression and Discouragement	• Potential to do too much for the child and family. • "When I hold her like this, she sits up better" can lead to the parent feeling like a failure ("She doesn't do that at home . . ."). • Setting up unrealistic expectations: "he'll be walking any time now." • Guilt that you can't "fix it."	• Focus on the positive, help parent identify the child's strengths—not focus on his or her needs. • Assure success of activities or interventions. • Help parents feel confident in their parenting skills. • Provide referrals for professional counseling or other support services.
• Realization that something can be done. • Adjustment in lifestyle. • Adaptation to the child's needs. • Willingness to do practical things.	Acceptance	• Relief. • Fear of the unknown, that you may not be able to meet the child's needs.	• Encourage comfort from other parents, link families to support systems. • Encourage patience. • Model positive interaction techniques. • Praise parents when child shows progress. • Maintain open, regular communication with family. • Partner with other service providers, invite them to visit your program. • Encourage family to request your presence at IFSP or IEP meetings, get copies of information.

Source: Adapted from Cook, Tessier, and Klein (1996).

It is important to remember, however, that parental reactions are unique. Some parents may take issue with the whole concept of stages or phases of emotional adjustment (Vacca & Feinberg, 2000). It must also be noted that much of the literature about grieving comes from the work of Euro-American professionals who are describing their cultural peers. *Understanding the impact of disabilities on the great diversity of families within our country is a continuing challenge to professionals, as the process of adaptation is not yet fully understood.* Early interventionists must therefore apply the concept of stages cautiously, realizing that the sequence and completeness of each phase of adjustment may differ with each individual. Family members may differ from each other in developing an accepting attitude. Some may never fully accept their child and his or her condition. It is the professional's responsibility to be prepared to listen with acceptance while providing accurate information and promoting access to available resources.

Shock, Disbelief, and Denial

Parents and professionals alike describe the primary stage of parental reaction as one of shock and disbelief on learning of a child's disability or disfigurement. This shock and possible disbelief may be accompanied by feelings of shame, guilt, and unworthiness.

As the reality of the child's condition is slowly assimilated, parents may try to deny the existing problems. Often, first attempts to find out what is wrong are really attempts to find someone who will say that nothing is wrong. For this reason, some parents go from doctor to doctor and from clinic to clinic seeking opinions. Some parents do this, however, because each professional recommends that they seek additional opinions. Diagnosis of problems in young children is far from an exact science. Rather, it is a piecing together of diverse observations, bits of information, and confusing evidence. Cause and effect interact to the point that it is difficult to decide which is which.

Some parents refuse to seek any guidance. They can be heard telling relatives and friends, "Oh, he's just like Uncle Joe. He didn't talk until he was 7," or "Aunt Susie never did learn how to do puzzles, and our Sally is just like her."

The Positive Role of Denial.
Ken Moses (1987), the father of a child with a disability and a pioneer clinician, summarized the role of denial in the parental grieving process as follows:

Denial buys the time needed to blunt the initial impact of the shattered dream, to discover the inner strengths needed to confront what has really happened, and to find the people and resources needed to deal with a crisis for which one could not be prepared. (p. 8)

It is important for professionals to allow parents the time they need to come to grips with their situation. They need professionals to listen with acceptance and exhibit genuine empathy.

Some parents may deprive the rest of their family while working diligently to prove diagnosticians wrong. They hope that intensive instruction will eliminate whatever developmental lag exists. But their nagging suspicions continue to grow. Unless parents can and will accept available guidance, precious time is lost. Fear that is allowed to grow undermines effective solutions to the simplest of problems.

Early Interventionists Can Help.
The interventionist can help if he or she suspects that a parent is feeling fearful, guilty, or anxious while experiencing shock, disbelief, or denial. The parent needs help to understand that these feelings and experiences are appropriate. It is normal and acceptable for parents temporarily to blame, reject, or even hate the child or themselves. Professionals should listen with patience. Pushing parents to "face the child's limitations" will only create defensiveness. Professionals must learn to allow family members to grieve and feel their feelings. They must be allowed to remain in denial until they have the psychological resources to deal with reality. This is a time when families turn to professionals for support. Professionals must be nonjudgmental, active listeners while providing information and appropriate referral sources.

Interventionists must remember that anxiety creates problems and that lack of knowing what to do creates anxiety. This is why parent–infant programs are needed. Initial fear and grief can be minimized if parents can be taught to do constructive things from the beginning. However, energy is wasted by grief and anger. Energy used to play with children in positive ways can minimize grieving time. Professionals should take to heart the words of this parent: "Encourage me not to make every moment with my child a therapy session. She just needs loving and fun parenting sometimes" (Poyadue, 1998, p. 9). Professionals must be sensitive enough to allow families the grieving time they need while being prepared with the resources that families need to move on.

Anger and Resentment

When parents can no longer deny the existence of their child or his or her condition, they move into a secondary phase and may feel anger, resentment, rage, or envy. Even though they may have accepted the child's problems intellectually, they may be so caught up in their emotions that they cannot focus on positive approaches to their concerns. They may even direct their anger at the very professionals who are trying to help the most. Suspicions about a professional's motives may explode in angry accusations. Other parents try to prove that the interventionist is "wrong." Verbal abuse is common. At this stage, interventionists need to demonstrate true

professionalism. They need to be understanding, compassionate, and gently caring.

Getting Parents Busy.   The anger will pass. It will pass more quickly if the parents are given appropriate activities to do with their children at which they absolutely cannot fail. This is not the time to try to make rapid progress with either children or their parents. Rather, the parents need to have constant reminders that they do indeed make a difference to their children. They must discover and rediscover that they have resources within themselves that they did not know were there. They must be provided with supports that match their individual needs. All of this must be done with a kindness that refuses to blame or to react to the excessive demands that accompany parental grief.

Bargaining

Some parents may try to resolve their anger and resentment by going through what Kübler-Ross (1969), in her classic resource, described as a process of bargaining. It resembles an attempt to postpone complete intellectual and emotional acceptance of the inevitable. During this time, parents and other family members may work with great diligence and determination. It is as if they are saying, "If I do everything you tell me to do, then surely this problem will go away." If progress is not as rapid or as great as they expect, bargaining is sometimes followed by the gray-black world of depression.

Empathy Is Essential.   To be helpful, interventionists must display empathic understanding by accurately perceiving, accepting, and actively trying to understand the natural feelings of the parents. Empathy is thought to be "the root of all caring about others: intimacy, ethics, altruism and morality itself" (Carter & McGoldrick, 1999, p. 34). Helping parents realize that their feelings and states of mind are normal can convey an attitude of interest and caring. A simple statement reflecting active listening such as "It must be very frustrating and tiring to have to take your child to so many medical appointments" shows an attempt to go beyond mere perception toward real understanding of some of the stress being experienced by the family. Although only the family members in the situation can have true understanding, genuine empathic responses by caregivers can go a long way in providing the support so critical to helping parents cope with the crises they face.

Depression and Discouragement

"What's the use?" and "Why bother?" can become the reaction of some parents to all suggestions. An oppressive weight of hopelessness can add new dimensions to the problems. It is common for parents to feel totally powerless. For some, this feeling of helplessness may make them more amenable to being helped. Because of feeling helpless, they may be more likely to ask for assistance. Santelli et al. (2001) point out that because these feelings are terrifying, "it is hard to believe that depression is a normal and necessary part of the grieving and adjustment process. Acknowledging and working through the sadness that accompanies personal loss is an important part of the adjustment process" (p. 7).

Focus on the Positive.   Professionals must focus on the positive and avoid adding to parents' depression by their own eagerness to get on with the task of teaching the child. During this time, activities must be planned for the parents in a way that ensures success. Interventionists must halt the growth of seeds of self-doubt about being a good parent. They should avoid all indirect and direct criticism. They must also avoid giving excessive, unwarranted praise because parents interpret it as insincere. Instead, they must believe in the resilience of families and in their ability to solve problems. By doing so, families can be empowered to handle the inevitable stresses they will face.

Parents who continue to suffer deep depression may need professional counseling. Interventionists should not hesitate to find some tactful way to suggest this. Often the simplest way is to listen carefully to the cry of "What's the use?" and then suggest that they may find help in many ways. Some parents will want

and need the counsel of psychologists and psychiatrists. Others may find great comfort from other parents who have passed through depression and have moved on to practical solutions to their problems. An informal parent support group may help some parents find comfort from one another. Many might benefit from an opportunity to look through a carefully developed file of local resources, including churches, synagogues, mental health agencies, and parenting groups. All parents need to know someone cares.

Adaptation and Acceptance

Adaptation and, it is hoped, acceptance is usually thought of as the final stage in parents' emotional recognition of the need to reorganize their lives or their interactions with the child with disabilities. Parents typically have an increasing willingness to do practical, useful things. Acceptance means that today's needs are recognized, not denied. It means they have a willingness to learn and to apply new knowledge to meet day-to-day demands. It means they have a deep conviction that each human being is unique, special, and worthy of love and affection.

Acceptance should not mean that the disabling condition is accepted as unalterable. Rather, parents accept the need to learn skillful ways to alter the negative effects of the condition. True acceptance includes the conviction that much needs to be done and that what is done will make a difference. Consider this father's reaction to his child's disability: "Your self-image as a father is influenced by roles and traditions. You may see yourself, consciously or unconsciously, as a 'provider,' 'hunter-gatherer' and the 'strong one,' more than as 'child rearer.' To the extent that these roles are valid, they were developed to help rear typical children. You need different traditions and roles to successfully father a child with a disability in today's world" (Bill, 2000, p. 1).

Encourage Patience.   Interventionists must encourage patience when parents have begun to accept their children as they are because most can achieve realistic expectations and give appropriate help. They will quickly and often eagerly learn new interaction techniques. There will be occasions, however,

Photo by Annette Tessier

when they will feel stupid and confused. They must be helped to understand that the disability they are dealing with is a new experience and they will need time to grow accustomed to it. Parents can be helped to learn to read their child's unique cues. Professionals must give the parents much praise for their child's progress and for the parents' participation. All parents feel better when they are able to see themselves as vital contributors to their child's progress. Parents who focus on positive interaction techniques will provide constructive options for mutually satisfying interactions.

A Father's Perspective

In responding to the request to share his feelings about raising a child with a disability, John stated,

You look at the world differently when you have a child with a disability. It takes a long time to orient your thinking to having a child with a disability and how it will affect your life. The reality comes as the child grows older. You try to lead a normal life, and you do what you have to do. It's often hard for fathers to talk about their child. Most interact with their typical children through sports, school, or other activities. If I want to find a father with my experience, it's very difficult. (Bill, 2000, p. 1)

In an effort to consider the unique needs of fathers, the Pacer Center (2000) offers the following

tips to fathers of children with disabilities: (a) learn about the disability, (b) build and continue good communication with the child's mother and other family members, (c) spend time with your child, (d) make necessary adjustments in your child's physical environment, (e) find or create support, and (f) enjoy your child.

Crisis Periods

Crisis periods can occur at any point from conception on through life. Parents often report that they "recycle" through the stages described earlier in this chapter. This is especially likely to occur at times of crisis. Some parents conceal these crises from professionals; others do not. Nevertheless, a supportive atmosphere that offers help and encourages adaptations can make a significant difference. Parents are comforted when they know someone understands their need to cry, yell, or scream.

Even though parents may have basically accepted their child and the disabling condition, adaptation may never be complete for some. Parents report that tears come even as the child grows into adulthood. Sometimes a crisis brings out the incompleteness of a parent's adaptation. Interventionists can avoid judging or comparing parents' coping skills. The reassurance that someone who understands is available to listen may make the difference between a productive reaction to a crisis and a debilitating one. Professionals will remember that the emotional needs of families are as unique as the needs of the child. Reactions to the shattering of parental expectations and to the real concerns of daily care and worry about the future must be coped with adequately before parents can fully participate in whatever parent involvement opportunities are available.

THE FAMILY AS A SYSTEM

From a **family systems perspective,** the reciprocal nature of the relationship between young children with special needs and their families becomes clearer. No family member is seen to function in isolation from other family members. Any intervention with one family member is found to affect other members and interactions in the family (Hanson & Lynch, 2004). The needs of the child and of the parents or siblings are viewed within the context of the entire family as it functions within the larger societal/ecological system. Every family system is composed of relational or interactive subsystems. Turnbull and Turnbull (2001) described four such subsystems: the **marital subsystem** (parent–parent), the **parental subsystem** (parent–child), the **sibling subsystem** (child–child), and the **extended family subsystem** (family–extended family). Of course, the actual makeup of families differs greatly. For example, single-parent families may have no marital subsystem. However, a single-parent family may have more than one person exercising a parental role if extended family members are actively involved.

How a family member functions in one role in a subsystem is not predictive of how he or she will behave in another subsystem. Parents behave differently when interacting with one another than they do when interacting with their children. Whole families behave differently toward one another at home than they do when visiting with their neighbors. The advent of a child with disabilities has implications for all four subsystems. The special needs of the child may impose additional stress on the marital relationships, whereas the extended family subsystem may be hardly affected. There may be no sibling subsystem if fear of giving birth to another child with special needs curtails future pregnancies. Alternatively, older siblings may be brought into the parental role to help alleviate the stress placed on either the marital or the parental subsystem. Anything that happens in one subsystem has effects on all the others.

The manner in which a child with special needs affects family members cannot be predicted or assumed because families differ along many dimensions. **Family structure** has changed dramatically in the past two decades. More and more children are living in single-parent or blended families. A growing number of grandparents have been thrust, once again, into the role of primary parents. Family membership

or structure is also changing in terms of gender makeup. Increasingly, same-sex couples are creating families that include children. Professionals can better understand and appreciate family dynamics by fostering an awareness of the changing dynamics within family systems today. Professionals who look at each family in relation to its own interactional system and the manner in which these interactions are used as tools to fulfill the tasks of daily life will find it easier to provide services to meet the total needs of the family.

It is clear that the unique needs of families cannot be met by providing the same prescribed set of services for each family. When designing early intervention services, Turnbull, Summers, and Brotherson (1983), over two decades ago, recommended adoption of the following four assumptions that remain critical today:

1. Each family is unique due to the infinite variations in membership characteristics, cultural and ideological styles.

2. The family is an interactional system whose component parts have constantly shifting boundaries and varying degrees of resistance to change.

3. Families have a variety of functions to fulfill for each member collectively and individually to aid their continued growth and development.

4. Families pass through developmental and nondevelopmental changes which produce varying amounts of stress affecting all members (pp. 4–5).

Interventions planned from a family systems perspective will also carefully consider four major family components described by Turnbull and Turnbull (2001). These include family resources, family interactions, family functions, and the family life cycle. **Family resources** include the characteristics and strengths each family member brings to the family as they interact to meet the needs of the family. *The nature of each individual's personality, values and beliefs, health status, motivation, and desires as well as cultural background will determine the nature of the interaction or relationships developed. The effectiveness of early intervention may depend on the existence of productive interactions between the resources of professionals and the resources of families.*

Family interactions are the processes families use to accomplish the duties or functions of the family system. Families meet their needs through such processes as sharing affection, planning together, resolving conflicts, teaching new skills, and accomplishing daily tasks. **Family functions** are the outputs of the interactional system. Hanson and Lynch (2004) have combined the basic family functions into seven components that are essential to the development of young children with disabilities: (a) love and affection, (b) daily care and health maintenance, (c) economic support, (d) identity development, (e) socialization and guidance, (f) educational and vocational development, and (g) recreation, rest, and recuperation. **Family life cycle** refers to the developmental and nondevelopmental changes that alter the family's structure and needs over time. Issues evolving at each stage in the family life cycle impact every member of the family. Turnbull and Turnbull (2001) list an array of possible issues encountered when the child with special needs is in the early childhood life cycle stage. These are noted in Table 2-2. Of course, it is not enough to support families during the early years. They must be helped to develop coping strategies that will help them avoid the burnout that can come from lifelong challenges.

As stated by Johnson and Kastner (2005), "A family's requirement for community supports depends not only on the characteristics of the child, but also on the structural, functional and external characteristics of the family" (p. 507).

SIBLING AND EXTENDED FAMILY NEEDS AND REACTIONS

As predicted from family systems theory, siblings and the extended family of the child also have needs and reactions. Grandparents grieve deeply, too. Theirs is often a double hurt because they not only experience pain for their grandchild but they also grieve for their own children. Seeing a loved son or daughter try to cope with long-term problems is disheartening. One grandfather arrived at a diagnostic clinic

Table 2–2   Possible issues encountered during the early childhood years

Life Cycle Stage	Parents	Siblings

Early childhood
Ages 0–5
	Obtaining an accurate diagnosis
	Informing siblings and relatives
	Locating services
	Seeking to find meaning in the
	   exceptionality
	Clarifying a personal ideology to
	   guide decision making
	Addressing issues of stigma
	Identifying positive contributions
	   of exceptionality
		Less parental time and energy for
		   sibling needs
		Feelings of jealousy over less
		   attention
		Fears associated with
		   misunderstandings of
		   exceptionality

Source: Barber, Turnbull, Behr, and Kerns (1988, p. 194).

with a blank check. "Just tell me what it costs," he said, "I'll find the money somehow."

Denial, blame, and anger may run rampant among grandparents. They may say, "It's because she smoked while she was pregnant," or "His family never was any good," or "If only they hadn't . . ." There is no doubt to whom the angry grandparents are referring.

Most grandparents and other close relatives, however, can be helped to provide needed moral, mental, and emotional support. Often relatives are the major source of babysitting relief for parents. All those who spend much time caring for a child with disabilities will find it helpful to be included in conferences and planning and teaching demonstrations. Often involved grandparents feel left out and deeply confused about what they should do. Professionals must be sensitive to this and, with the parents' approval, include these extended family members.

When viewing families from a systems perspective, it is readily apparent that attention must be paid to the changing needs of siblings without disabilities. For example, young children may need to be reassured that they cannot catch their sibling's disability. School-aged children need information to answer their own questions and those posed by peers about their sibling's disability. Teenagers and young adults need additional information about their sibling's future and the role they will play in that future. Bringing siblings "into the loop" through inclusion in meetings as valued members of the team benefits all members of the family.

Parents and professionals can help siblings cope with their feelings. An effective way is often to provide siblings with opportunities to participate in working with their brother or sister with disabilities. Even very young children can learn to be effective teachers. In fact, young children who have just learned how to do something themselves may be superior teachers. Given the immense variability in family members' responses to disability, it is imperative that parents and professionals be sensitive in their expectations and requests of siblings.

In reviewing the literature examining the relationship between siblings with and without disabilities, Moore, Howard, and McLaughlin (2002) noted the following possible characteristic reactions:

1. Young children frequently believe that they have caused their sibling's problem and may try to compensate by being particularly well behaved. However, feelings of jealousy and envy may arise when their needs are neglected by parents who are striving to cope. Then others may act out in response to feelings of isolation should their parents be preoccupied with the needs of their disabled sibling.

2. School-aged children may be expected to look after their disabled sibling if they attend the same school. They might also experience social stigmatization when their disabled sibling starts public school. The resulting frustration can be in conflict with their desire to defend their sibling. Nondisabled siblings who are younger may even worry about surpassing their older sibling with disabilities.

3. While adolescents may have a better understanding of their sibling's disability, they nevertheless often continue to encounter the stigma and embarrassment of having a sibling with disabilities. There may also be uncertainty regarding the potential for genetic inheritance of the disability. Although these are a few of the more characteristic reactions, it must be remembered that variations within family systems and the uniqueness of individual development create a multitude of potential responses. Even so, the most powerful predictor affecting sibling acceptance has been found to be parental attitude (Moore et al., 2002). Given this

predictor, it is imperative that early childhood professionals be prepared to provide both emotional and logistical support to parents.

On the other hand, Lavin (2001) acknowledged the positive characteristics exhibited by siblings that might be attributed to their unique experiences of being raised along with disabilities. They are often more mature, have a deeper understanding of life, are more accepting, are able to advocate for individuals with disabilities, and often choose to become a helping professional.

One should never assume that parents are unaware of the impact of a sibling with a disability on brothers and sisters. Professionals need to listen carefully and take the time to learn about the needs of the whole family—not just the child with special needs and his or her parents. Think about the words of a parent: "Let me talk about my child's siblings. They need time and attention and praise too. Especially when they are present, I like to and need to say nice things about them. Believe it or not, this helps them accept my delayed child. They get more involved with him that way, and that helps him" (Poyadu, 1998, p. 9).

In order to positively foster the relationships between children with disabilities and their siblings, the Pacer Center (2001) interviewed siblings and then offered these tips to parents: (a) provide honest communication about the disability and issues related to it, (b) include the child in activities at home and in the community, (c) teach your children to accept their sibling with a disability but encourage them to help the child to reach his or her potential, and (d) remember that as parents you are the model for how others will treat your child with disabilities.

Regardless of the age or the relationship of the extended family members, the interventionist must be tactful, open, and honest. The parents' feelings and attitudes must always be given careful consideration and top priority. Everyone in the family interacts in some way with everyone else. Insofar as the interventionist can influence these interactions in positive ways, the children will gain. Having faith that one can be a positive help to a child with special needs buoys young siblings and mature grandparents.

Specific tasks at which success is guaranteed are the place to begin. Then everyone benefits.

CAREGIVERS AS TEAM MEMBERS

Professionals have become more aware that caregivers play an important role not only in providing an emotional support system for the developing child but also as contributing team members in educating and instructing their child in classes and at home. However, some parents of young children with special needs feel that often too much emphasis is placed on the parent as teacher. To avoid creating additional stress, professionals should try not to overwhelm the parents as they become involved in their child's education.

In helping caregivers understand the intervention needs of their children, those who evaluate children's skills and developmental levels are expected to communicate the results of their testing to caregivers meaningfully. If caregivers are to become contributing team members who are **empowered,** they first need to understand what the professionals are talking about. This means that information must not be given in professional jargon. Professionals can translate test results and implications into layperson's language. For example, telling parents that their child may have a "visual perceptual problem" is meaningless to many of them. But parents can grasp their child's problem readily when the interventionist describes tasks using the eyes and the hands at the same time, such as buttoning, eating, doing puzzles, or stacking blocks. The caregiver's role in child assessment will be discussed further in chapter 4.

OPTIONS FOR FAMILY INVOLVEMENT

Just as children with special needs and children without disabilities are more alike than different, so are the parents of both groups more alike than different. They have needs, frustrations, hopes, fears, and dreams similar to those of any other parent, although they also have feelings that may be unique to parents of children with special needs. Even so, interventionists cannot expect to use the same method of working with all families, just as they cannot expect to use the same method of working with all children.

However, as professionals have increased their awareness of how families function and the impact of the family on the outcome of intervention efforts, a philosophy of intervention has emerged known as **family-centered intervention.** This philosophy moves intervention efforts from that of an agency-oriented approach to a family-oriented approach. The following tenets characteristic of family-centered practice were offered by Hanson and Lynch (2004): It (a) recognizes parents or primary caregivers as experts on their child; (b) acknowledges the family as the ultimate decision maker for their child and themselves; (c) views the family as the constant in the child's life and the service providers and systems as transitory; (d) respects and works to support family priorities, their goals for service, and the extent to which they choose to be involved; (e) values trusting, collaborative relationships between parents and professionals; and (f) works to ensure culturally competent services.

In an effort to become more family centered, professionals are urging early educators to recognize the impact of a **family's quality of life** on the success of early intervention and inclusion (Purcell, Turnbull, & Jackson, 2006). To that end, the Beach Center on Disability (2001) has developed a Family Quality of Life Survey. They have identified five quality-of-life domains: physical-material well-being, disability-related support, family interaction, parenting, and emotional well-being. This chapter emphasizes a family-centered approach and discusses a number of activities that will, it is hoped, enhance the quality of life of participating families.

As the tenets above suggest, the development and implementation of family-centered services requires a change in roles and relationships. Intervention is guided by family–professional collaboration with families who function as the primary decision makers. Professionals are no longer considered to be "the experts." Instead, parents and professionals are expected to create relationships built on respect and appreciation for what each can contribute to the development and implementation of effective intervention.

The individualized family service plan outcomes and individualized educational program goals and objectives are derived from each family's concerns and priorities. Family members are encouraged to choose how and when they wish to be involved. To the greatest possible extent, professionals are encouraged to provide opportunities for family involvement that will fit into the family's daily living routines.

It is extremely important to remember that families should clearly feel that participation is, indeed, an *option.* Professionals must help families understand the continuum of services and opportunities from which they may make choices. Procedures for helping families identify their resources and needs, as well as appropriate participation, will be discussed in chapter 4.

A Continuum

Even though P.L. 108–446 sets the stage for family-focused or family-centered early intervention, in reality family involvement will fall along a continuum. Some families may elect not to be involved in early intervention services, whereas others will seek the fullest possible involvement (Dabkowski, 2004.) It is hoped that families will be open to active participation in decision making, program implementation, and advocacy activities. Family needs, values, and lifestyles, as well as program characteristics, are likely to determine the level of family involvement. Early interventionists may be directly involved as therapists or teachers, or they may only provide referral information. It is the intent of the individualized family service plan to clearly delineate the level of both family and professional involvement. *It is important for professionals to avoid implying that the degree of parent involvement is synonymous with parent concern. Parent involvement is certainly not a measure of parent concern.*

Individual needs and capabilities must be balanced with the goals of parent involvement. Some parents will have a greater need and capacity for cognitive information delivered through lectures, panel discussions, and films. Other parents may most desire and need one-to-one conversations with the professional when privacy is ensured and they can feel comfortably accepted. Still other parents will thrive

on being shown how to teach their child. Whatever strategies early interventions use to encourage family involvement, success will most likely depend on the ability of the professionals to develop a sense of trust (Smith, Gartin, Murdick, & Hilton, 2006).

Much of this chapter focuses on the primary considerations to be thought through carefully in making each type of involvement effective. Unique needs are also discussed, along with helpful hints for the professionals who must work with these needs.

What Fathers Say About Their Involvement

Turbiville and Marquis (2001) surveyed 318 fathers of young children from six states. Of the respondents, 28% of the fathers had children with disabilities. They found that fathers of children with and without disabilities preferred activities in which both husband and wife could be involved. In fact, activities that were offered only to men resulted in the least father participation. Consistent with earlier literature, fathers preferred activities that involved both men and women learning about how to take action in order to help their child progress and how to solve problems. Degree of father involvement seemed to depend on being specifically invited at convenient times to activities that are perceived to have learning value. They did not care if the activities were all planned by women and if extras such as refreshments or child care were offered. Fathers appreciated being asked personally to participate (Guthrie, 2000).

Home-Based Intervention Programs

Home-based intervention programs as a model of service delivery was strengthened in the reauthorization of the Individuals with Disabilities Education Act, as it mandated that early intervention services should be provided in the "natural environment" to the maximum extent possible. Home visiting offers many advantages (Wasik & Bryant, 2000). Young children and parents are most natural at home. At home they do not have to develop the feeling of comfortable belonging; they do not have to be transported by either the parents or

a school bus. Interventionists can take the home life into consideration when planning for the child.

Within the past decade, best practices have reflected a shift from a focus on direct service to the child to what is referred to as **relationship-based intervention** or **support-based intervention** (McWilliam & Scott, 2001). Generally, a teacher, nurse, therapist, or trained paraprofessional makes regularly scheduled visits (weekly or monthly) to offer support that may involve educational services and sometimes social and health services. The focus is on the provision of support that helps parents develop healthy parent–child relationships that will meet the needs of the child. Parents are encouraged and taught how to interact positively with their own children using

household objects or materials. Embedding intervention activities into daily caregiving **routines** obviates the necessity for planning special times for "lessons." For instance, the parent of a young child with cerebral palsy might embed stretching exercises into diapering time or language activities during feeding. A conceptual framework for early intervention home visiting is presented in Exhibit 2-1.

In the past few years, early intervention personnel are also being encouraged to embrace the concept of **coaching** in regard to collaboration with families in natural settings (Hanft, Rush, & Shelden, 2004). Coaching is an interactive process of observation and reflection in which the "coach" promotes a caregiver's ability to support a child's participation in everyday

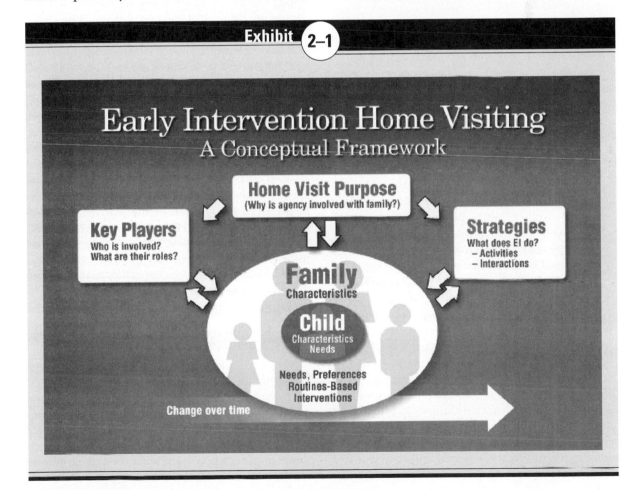

Exhibit 2-1

Early Intervention Home Visiting
A Conceptual Framework

Home Visit Purpose
(Why is agency involved with family?)

Key Players
Who is involved?
What are their roles?

Strategies
What does EI do?
– Activities
– Interactions

Family
Characteristics

Child
Characteristics
Needs

Needs, Preferences
Routines-Based
Interventions

Change over time

experiences and interactions with family members and others. It provides a supportive structure for promoting conversations among family members, child-care providers, and early interventions to select and implement meaningful strategies that achieve functional outcomes through the child's participation in natural settings.

At first, some parents may feel uncomfortable having a professional in their homes. Tact, courtesy, and sensitivity can overcome this initial discomfort very quickly. The professional or trained paraprofessional becomes an anticipated visitor. Toys to share, ideas that work, and a sympathetic ear usually endear the home visitor to both parents and children. Bernstein (2002) points out that the key to success may be related to focusing on the family's agenda rather than on that of the home visitor. However, the agenda of families is often driven by whatever is perceived as the immediate crisis. In order to avoid becoming burned out or bogged down in ensuing crises, Bernstein (2002) offers the following four recommendations to create effective home visiting programs:

1. Build positive relationships with families, while not becoming consumed by their problems.

2. Support parent-child relationships to support the children's development.

3. Identify and build on strengths.

4. Provide reflective supervision for home visitors to strengthen their skills and protect them from burnout (p. 4).

It is clear that the success of home visitations is highly dependent on the visitor's training and preparation. Exhibit 2-2 offers practical suggestions for effective home intervention and discusses important considerations when making home visits.

Additional Important Considerations When Making Home Visits

Exhibit 2-3 outlines some critical safety tips for home visitors.

In addition to the points noted above, home interventionists should remember the following:

1. Always keep in mind the importance of directly *modeling* and explaining responsive interaction techniques while observing parent-child interactions across daily routines and activities.

2. Plan to *demonstrate* activities and strategies. Showing is more effective than merely telling or describing. Honor the concerns and priorities of families by asking them what they would like to work on. When choices are offered, parents' interests and time demands can be accommodated.

3. Sometimes an older child can be helpful. Teach brothers and sisters appropriate activities. Often they can participate with the parent and the child for whom the activity was planned. Including other children serves two purposes: they are usually excellent teachers, and including them can prevent jealousy and feelings of being left out.

4. Call attention to the importance of interacting with the child at his or her level. It will come as a surprise to many parents that children learn little by failing. It is crucial to show parents how to develop activities at which their children can succeed. At first, home interventionists must be very explicit about the need to avoid activities that result in failure for children. Showing parents how to prompt their children and then gradually reducing and fading the prompting is important. This strategy is basic to successful home intervention. Give the parents specific guidelines such as those in Exhibit 2-4.

5. Be nonjudgmental. Some parents will be embarrassed about their homes or will be afraid of criticism. It is important to be blind to the things that are not relevant to working with the children and to notice things parents are proud of, especially things that they have done for their children.

6. Refer to the child's individualized education program (IEP) or individualized family service plan (IFSP) regularly. Help parents see how the home program relates to the IFSP outcomes or the IEP goals and objectives of the former and the outcomes of the latter.

Exhibit 2–2

Practical Suggestions for the Home Visitation

1. *Greet all family members* who are present including siblings and extended family.

2. *Clearly communicate the purpose of your visit.* Families need to know what is legitimate for the home visitor to address. If the home visitor tries to change the expectations of family members, he or she may encounter resistance or anger.

3. *Be aware of family rituals and customs, for example, removing your shoes at the door.*

4. *Take time to gain information on family life and daily schedules.* This knowledge gives insight into optimal times for home visits and how and when to encourage families to embed functional activities into the routines of their daily lives. Be especially careful to take the time to get to know the family's beliefs and practices about childrearing. Understanding the family's characteristics as well as those of the child allows you to accommodate their concerns and preferences.

5. *Ask the family how they would like to be involved.* It is important to know who in the family would like to be involved in the home visits and how much they wish to be involved. Their involvement may be critical to the success of the visits. However, some family members may take a while to "warm up." As they see that you are not there to judge them or be critical in any way, they will relax and look forward to your visits.

6. *Be informal but not too casual.* You are a professional.

7. *Deal with crises/heightened affect as necessary.* Listen reflectively. Try to refocus on the child by saying something like "How is _____ handling this?"

8. *Be prepared.* Have resources, materials, activity plans, and backup ideas ready. To interact more freely, try to avoid filling out forms. If writing is necessary, explain what you are doing and why.

9. *Be flexible.* If what was planned is inappropriate for any reason, change it at once. Also encourage parents to vary the activities to meet their needs as well as the child's needs. Do not plan too much for the parents to do. They have other responsibilities.

10. *Utilize items found in the child's home.* To the maximum extent possible, demonstrate intervention strategies using household items rather than commercially developed materials. Parents are more likely to follow up with a similar or the same activity if materials are readily available and familiar.

11. *Be ready to admire pet frogs, favorite toys, and other family treasures.* Take the time to know what the children and their parents are proud of and what they value most. Compliment the home in some way.

12. *Encourage parents to show or demonstrate how they interact with their child.* Remember that parents are the experts on their children. Focus comments and questions on the child's behavior rather than on the caregiver's. Show that their ideas are worthwhile. Express approval and admiration. Comments like "He really seemed to smile when you . . . " or "Did you notice how he quieted down when . . . ?" Avoid direct criticism. Rather, suggest changes by saying something such as "Some of the time you will want to try _____" or "Can you think of anything you did in the past that seemed to work better?" Such comments helps parents come up with their own solutions and take ownership of their own interactions.

13. *Avoid confrontations.* Even if parents insist that what has been suggested will not work or is not something they can or will do, the visitor must not argue or insist that parents should conform. Home visitors are obligated to accept what families choose to do. That does not mean they have to be in agreement or should not plan to share their own opinions and expertise at the appropriate time.

14. *Begin and end your visit on time.*

15. *Before you leave, schedule and discuss the next visit.* Review with the parents what you did today and collaboratively decide what you will do during the next visit and what the family will do during the coming week or two. Write out any suggestions for activities for parents to follow. Schedule the next visit and write the date and time on the activity plan form left with the parents. Assure them that they can reach you by telephone if they should have any questions or comments.

16. *Maintain confidentiality.* At all times, remember that you are a professional. Whatever you observe in the parents' home and any judgments you make are not to be discussed in public. Families have a right to their privacy and their choice of living style. The effectiveness of visits may depend on your ability to be mature, objective, and professional.

Exhibit (2–3)

Don't Let It Happen to You: Safety Tips for Home Visitors

Be Alert to High-Risk Situations:

- Different people in the home each week
- Isolated areas, no telephone, dirt roads
- People loitering outside
- Dangerous dogs
- Families who often will not let you into the house or ask you to wait outside for a while before letting you in
- Individuals in the home appear to be under the influence of drugs
- Drug paraphernalia in the home
- Indications of drug traffic in the home
- Your instincts tell you that "this is a high-risk situation"

Precautions to Prevent Problems

- Before going on a high-risk visit, let someone else know where you are going, when you are leaving, and when you expect to return (put this information in writing)
- Visit in pairs
- Make early morning appointments
- Avoid visits on days when welfare checks arrive
- Plan your route in advance
- Do not circle the block looking for the home (someone may think you are looking for drugs)
- Meet in a well-peopled place such as a popular restaurant
- Keep a cell phone within easy reach
- Do not carry a purse, wear jewelry, or take valuables with you

- Ask to be introduced to all people in the house
- Introduce yourself to apartment complex managers
- Research the area ahead of time—learn the gang colors of any existing gangs and do not wear them
- Do use cars marked as county or state vehicles
- Carry identification on your person
- Ask families about the safety of their neighborhoods
- Park in front of the home if at all possible
- Keep car doors locked and windows rolled up
- Do not hide an extra key anywhere in or on your car
- Be aware of avenues of escape
- Always stand to the side of the door when knocking
- *Assess* the situation before entering—give preliminary information outside—ask permission to enter—*Ask who is home* (watch body language)
- Do not walk in when someone yells "come in"
- Make other plans to visit if anyone in the household appears to be under the influence of alcohol or drugs
- Position yourself where no one can come in behind you
- Avoid isolating yourself in a room without a second exit
- Project an air of authority—keep your eyes direct and scan the environment with your head up; wear pants and flat shoes
- If there is an altercation outside, leave when you assess it is safe and ask someone from the house to accompany you

7. Help parents develop behavior management skills. Many parents are concerned about their child's inappropriate behavior and attribute it to the disability. Usually the basis of the problem is not the disability itself but rather not knowing how to communicate effectively with the child. If inappropriate behavior is reported at the supermarket, plan some intervention there. The interventionist's demonstration of effective controls can be immensely helpful to parents who are frightened and worried.

Role-playing, with the parent taking the part of the child, will help parents master the needed management skills. Most important, the interventionist must explain that behavior is learned. Changing habits and behavior patterns may not be easy, and improvement may not be made overnight. Parents may be helped by talking about their problems with other parents who have successfully learned improved child management skills.

8. Again, it is important to remember that parents know their children better than the professional does in some ways. Most parents are accurate observers of what their children do and do not do, but their interpretation of the observed behavior is often inappropriate. For example, a child who screams and has a tantrum when denied something that he or she wants may be described by the parents as "bad" or "just like Uncle Will." Usually children who behave in this way have been rewarded by receiving the things they want when they cry. This cause-and-effect relationship is not well understood by many parents.

Chapter 6 enumerates some of the ways early interventionists can help parents in this essential task. The goal is to assist parents in reinterpreting

Exhibit 2–4

Activity Guidelines for Parents

1. *Be ready to praise.* Praise your child's efforts and successes. Use hugs, pats, smiles, and positive words readily.

2. *Correct with care.* When your child makes mistakes, do not tell him or her or that he or she is wrong. Instead, gently show or tell him or her the preferred response. For example, if your child hands you a spoon instead of the requested fork, say. "You've handed me a spoon. Now hand me the fork," instead of "That's not a fork. I asked for the fork."

3. *Find an appropriate time and place.* Do not remove a child from an activity in which he or she is involved. Keep the activity short, from 5 to 15 minutes. Be certain your child is wide awake, not hungry or "keyed up." Prepare a place to work where the child is comfortable and not distracted by sound or sight.

4. *Do not use force.* Do not force your child to continue an activity. Attention spans vary with the child and with the activity. Treat your child with the same consideration you would give your friends. If your child senses that you are tense, angry, or critical, he or she will learn to dislike the activities.

5. *Be flexible.* Vary the activity and methods to fit the child's needs. If one approach does not work, try another. Some learn more quickly while being active; others prefer being more passive. Use as many senses as possible, especially if one or more of the senses is impaired.

6. *Speak clearly.* Don't talk too fast.

7. *Be prepared.* Assemble materials and prepare the working space in advance. Do not waste the child's attention on preparation activities. Consider taking the phone off the hook during the short activity period.

8. *Be enthusiastic.* Do not under any circumstances let your child feel that you are working with him or her because "you have to." If you do not feel like working with your child, he or she will feel your tension. Reschedule your activity. By selecting a rather consistent time each day, you will find it easier to manage your time. If you find you are not enjoying your involvement, talk this over with your child's teacher or other professional. An adjustment in the activities or the approach may bring greater enjoyment.

---

the behaviors they have called bad as something the children have learned and not something "in" them. By the interventionist's example and explanations, parents can learn to think about their children more constructively.

9. Playfulness and the expression of enjoyment are essential if children are to achieve their potential. Let the parents observe activities during which the interventionist is expressing these feelings. Be willing to play with children, enjoying the games they like. This is very effective interaction. Avoid being too serious.

10. Introduce parents to other parents who have similar interests and needs. Even if most of the intervention is done in the home, plan occasional get-togethers for parents who have similar needs and interests.

11. Be aware of cultural influences on parents' communication styles and locus of decision making.

12. Communication with all caregivers is essential. In some cases, the early interventionist may plan activities in the home to supplement the child's *regular* preschool or day-care center program. When this is the case, a system of reporting what is done can be very useful. Common goals and objectives are essential. Methods of communication include the following:

   a. Phone calls to the child's regular early childhood teacher, usually brief, to report on what was accomplished and to suggest carryover activities.

   b. Written goals and objectives, with copies given to parents and to the preschool or day-care teachers.

c. A passport notebook with comments and observations made by all concerned. This passport notebook may travel with the child and be used by all who are responsible for care and teaching. An example of a page from such a passport notebook is illustrated in Figure 2-1. The following guidelines for writing notes in a passport are derived from the work of Shea and Bauer (2002):

1. Be brief. (Parents and teachers are busy.)
2. Be positive. (Parents know their child has problems and need not receive constant negative reminders.)
3. Be honest. (Don't say a child is doing fine if he or she is not. However, write noncommittal comments or request a face-to-face or telephone conference in place of negative notes.)
4. Be responsive. (If a parent or teacher asks for help, respond immediately.)
5. Be informal. (All participants are equals.)
6. Be consistent. (If the passport is the communication system of choice, use it consistently and expect the same from other participants.)
7. Avoid jargon. (Parents may not understand educational jargon, and even professionals may use jargon at cross-purposes.)
8. Be careful. (No one should project personal feelings or the frustrations of a bad day onto the child, parent, or teacher.)

Supporting and Partnering with Parents in Early Intervention Programs

A major premise of this text revolves around the fact that families are considered to be the primary context of children's learning. This premise is not only supported by the advocates of early childhood education, but it is incorporated into recent legislation such as the 2001 reauthorization of both the Elementary and Secondary Education Act titled No Child Left Behind (P.L. 107–110) and the Individuals with Disabilities Education Improvement Act of 2004 (P.L. 108–446). Each of these laws contributes toward making parent's involvement in their children's education a national priority.

Experienced early childhood educators already realize that involving parents in daily classroom or center activities can be useful in a variety of ways. Teachers are able to model preferred techniques of teaching specific skills and effective approaches to behavior management. Many parents will then be able to translate some of what they have observed into more useful interactions in the home environment. Increasingly, studies are describing the benefits of parent involvement (Eldridge, 2001; Smith et al., 2006).

Parents with specific skills or talents such as in music or art can feel good about the contributions they can make to the center. Parents who accompany classes on field trips to familiar places such as the grocery store can observe and, ideally, generalize ways of using everyday activities to teach their child. Finally, many parents will feel that their child is more like other children than different from them. As they observe progress over time, they will feel encouraged and more hopeful.

Eldridge (2001) highlights three of the common barriers to the development of a strong parent–professional partnership: (a) parent availability, (b) parent and teacher awkwardness, and (c) parent and teacher scheduling conflicts. Regarding parent availability, they mention the feelings of alienation of those parents whose own negative experiences with schools lead them to consider schools unresponsive. Both parents and teachers have been found to experience some awkwardness in initiating conversations. Parents may have feelings of inadequacy and feel generally reluctant or are contacted only when a problem has developed. Teachers are often concerned with bothering overworked parents who are already coping with the stress resulting from responsibilities related to their child's disability. Of course, scheduling conflicts have long been recognized as a barrier to collaboration.

The key to effective parental involvement may be the development of a trusting relationship between the staff and the parents. Critical to the establishment

Dec. 10, Mrs. J. (Susan's mother):

Susan wouldn't eat her breakfast this morning. She didn't seem sick, just not hungry. Could you give her an early snack, please?

Dec 10, Ms. S. (Susan's teacher at daycare):

Susan _was_ hungry when she got here. Two glasses of juice and a piece of toast disappeared right away. And then she _asked_ to go "potty." We are making progress. No accidents today! Hooray.

Dec. 11, Mrs. J.:

Ms. R., Susan's home teacher, came yesterday afternoon. She suggested that we continue to work on teaching Susan the names of her clothes. I'm going to put her clothes on the bed, and then tell her to bring me each thing, one at a time. Could you help with this at school, please?

Dec. 11, Ms. S.:

We surely can. Susan brought me her boots and her tote bag when I asked her today. Progress is good.

Figure 2–1 A passport page used by the day-care teacher, parents, and the home interventionist
This page was chosen from notes written during the fourth month of center attendance. Susan is 3 years old and has been described as "developmentally delayed." She uses two-word "sentences" that are partially intelligible. She has frequent "accidents," wetting and soiling herself at home and at school.

Source: Adapted by P. Shaw (1999) from Cook, Tessier, and Klein (1996). *Adapting early childhood curricula for children in inclusive settings*, 4th Edition. Upper Saddle River, NJ: Merrill/Prentice Hall.

of a trusting relationship is the assurance that **confid-entiality** will be maintained. Parents need the security of knowing that information about their child or their family will not be discussed with other individuals without their written permission. This means that they or their child will not be identified by name any time or anywhere, including the lunch room or on the play-ground, without their knowledge and permission.

A strong parent–professional partnership can be built only through the creation of a classroom cli-mate that is open and accepting. The first few times parents come to the center or classroom will be diffi-cult for them and for their children. Some parents will feel compelled to direct and correct their own children constantly. They may be deeply distressed by every small infraction of the rules. Tears and tantrums are the outward signs of the distress of the children. Nervousness and apologizing for the child's "misbehavior" may be the parents' reaction. With careful planning, the center or classroom staff can prevent or at least minimize most of these problems.

First Step: Parents Meet Other Parents.
Before parents begin to observe or participate, they can benefit by meeting with "veteran" parents. Parents from previous years, whether or not their children are currently enrolled, can be called on to help. If these experienced parents assist with planning and presenting the program, it will be much more believ-able and useful to the new parents. The opportunity to talk with other parents who have been through the program is the best preparation for beginners.

Centers should plan the orientation program *with* parents, not *for* them. Parents themselves can plan the agenda, choosing items to be discussed and points to be emphasized. Both the nature of the com-munity and the characteristics of the children will influence what needs to be done.

A letter of invitation from the parents who are planning the meeting or from their children is more effective than a letter from the center. One parent group sent handwritten notes to each new parent 1 week in advance. A follow-up phone call, including an offer to pick up the new parents, resulted in nearly 100% attendance.

Although traditionally mothers have come to school, fathers can be especially helpful. Having one father call another helps make it seem less strange. Other family members should be included whenever practical.

Evening meetings are usually more convenient for parents. Parents who work at night, however, can be encouraged to come to the center during the day. Properly welcomed, parents have even been known to take a vacation day to attend.

Parents as Observers.
All parents will feel unsure at first, even if they hide their feelings well. They will wonder what their children will do and will expect the worst. Often their children will oblige. Program staff must strive to make parents feel comfortable and welcome, giving their children specific things to do to keep them from seeking attention in undesir-able ways.

Interacting With Their Own Child. Teachers should encourage parents to greet their own child and allow their own child to show them around. These social skills must be taught to many children. Initial awk-wardness can yield quickly to confidence and secu-rity if the program staff sets the stage and does a bit of managing. Cues such as "Show Dad where we keep our big blocks. I'll bet he can build a tall tower" or "Show Mother where we keep the easel and the markers. I wonder if she knows how well you can draw" may be effective. Naturalness, friendliness, and a comfortable feeling for all should be the goal.

If the parents indicate that they would enjoy it, encourage them to play a game with their own child and one or two others. A demonstration by a staff member starts the game, but then the professional should be busy with others to allow the parent the opportunity to develop his or her own style. The intent is to set the stage for parents and children to have a good time and feel at ease.

Keeping the Visit Short. The time schedule should be understood by everyone before the visit begins. Parents should be encouraged to vary the time of day they visit to create a more complete understanding of their child's involvement in the program.

Providing Observation Guidelines. Staff can help parents become astute observers by telling them what to look for. A short list of focus points might be helpful. For example, an interventionist may wish a parent of Danny, a child with a hearing disability, to observe his reaction to sound in the classroom. She could prepare the following short list:

1. What does Danny do when someone calls his name?

2. Does Danny act differently when I stand directly in front of him and speak to him than when he cannot see my face?

3. Does Danny respond to noises made behind him or anywhere out of sight?

Such a list of focus points makes it easier to discuss the observations with everyone focusing on the child's behavior rather than on more subjective aspects of the child, such as personality. An interventionist could prepare the following list to help the parent of Asha, a child who is hyperactive, understand his or her concerns:

1. What was the first thing Asha did? What was the second?

2. Approximately how long did Asha stay with each activity?

3. Which activity held Asha's attention the longest?

A sample of a parent observation form that helps focus the parent's attention is presented in Exhibit 2–5.

Exhibit 2–5

Parent Observation Report

Date: _____

Who was involved in this experience? _____

What happened first?

Then what did the child do?

What did you do, or what did another adult caregiver do?

What were the results?

Do you think you or the other adult caregiver might have done something better? Why or why not?

Follow-Up.   Whenever possible, every parent observation or participation experience should be followed by a brief discussion with the lead teacher either in person or over the telephone. This provides an opportunity for parents to have their questions answered, and teachers can explain any unique behavior and point out positive attributes of the child.

Parents as Participants.   In some centers, parents are encouraged to participate as aides. Some parents may be willing to assist the professional in individual center or classroom activities. Such experiences provide excellent opportunities for the professional to model desired strategies for working with young children. Exhibit 2–6 presents some parent participation guidelines developed by a participating parent.

It is often helpful to ask parents to play a game or direct a small-group activity. Children love repetition. If they have experienced the activity before, it will be easier for the parent to facilitate their involvement. The activity should be one that is useful for the

---

Exhibit 2–6

Sample Center Participation Guidelines

Dear Parents,

As you know, it is very important for you to come to our center regularly to help us in the classroom and to learn more about working with your children at home. But some of you have told me that you felt a little uncomfortable—that you really were not sure what to do sometimes. So I asked one of our "experienced mothers," Laura, to jot down some guidelines that will help you feel more at ease. Laura and I talked about these guidelines, and she helped me to understand how you feel. Both Laura and I hope you will suggest other things that will make your time at our center more useful and enjoyable. These suggestions are just a beginning. Here they are:

Guidelines for mothers (fathers, grandparents, and aunts, too)

1. *Relax.* The children are allowed to do *some* things at the center that they cannot do at home or that they do not normally do at home (using scissors, putting things into the refrigerator, or helping another child).
2. *Be patient.* If you want to talk about your child, wait until children are not present. Even if you do not think they will understand, never talk about them when they can overhear.
3. *Take time.* Try what the teacher suggests. It might seem the teacher's way makes matters worse, and sometimes it will, at first. But time (lots of it) will make a difference. Ms. McLynn says that with our children we are not just working for this minute. We want them to learn how to use self-control and good judgment. And this takes experience with "logical consequences" of things they do.
4. *Learn the class rules.* Find out what is a "no-no" and what's all right. For example, Hot Wheels—no riding inside, but the balance toys are okay. Moving the kitchen stuff around is okay, just like we change the room arrangement at home sometimes. Yelling is a "no-no." (That is an "outside voice.") Putting stuff away after you use it is also a rule. But some of them have not learned that yet.
5. *Ask.* If you are not sure what to do, ask. If you do not know why the teacher does things her way, ask. And do not be afraid to say how you feel. She will listen. Sometimes she misses something that happens, and it helps if you clue her in. (Remember, do not let the children overhear.) If you have a problem with your child, ask to talk about it with the teacher. She will find a way to talk to you so your child will not overhear. It is also important to tell the teacher if you do not agree with what is happening. Find out why it is happening. The reason will probably make it feel better.

6. *Talk.* Talk to the teacher and the children in the regular way. Ms. McLynn wants you to have "conversations" with the children except during "circle time." These conversations help the children learn. Those words on the bulletin board behind her desk are the cues for words they are working on. Try to use them often while you are talking to the children. Don't try to make them say things "the right way." Conversations should be fun. They help to teach language. Speech lessons are at a separate time, unless Ms. McLynn says otherwise, because trying to make a child correct a speech sound can make things worse. The child may just stop talking to you.

7. *Play with your child and other children at playtime.* You will learn, just as they will. Remember, someone else will be playing with your child. It averages out.

8. *Remember, every little bit helps.* It is really important to be there. Cutting stuff, helping clean up, or just listening are all important. Lots of things are important for the children to learn before kindergarten.

9. *Have an open mind when the teachers correct your child.*

Courtesy Laura Bridgeman

parent's own child. Suggestions such as the following can be put in a parent handout and can be posted or distributed when parents choose to participate:

1. Plan for success for both the parents and the children.

2. Choose an activity that can be demonstrated easily. Provide a brief written description of the objective and procedures of the activity.

3. Keep the group small (two or three children).

4. Explain the purpose of the activity. Be specific.

5. Emphasize that learning should be fun even if it is also hard work.

6. Do not emphasize "winning." Children just like to play. Winning and losing are artificial concepts that interfere with learning.

7. Select a game or activity parents can use at home. Most commercial games or lessons can be duplicated with things found in most homes. Whenever possible, choose an activity that will benefit the child and interest his or her parent.

8. Specifically explain how to manage children's errors and misbehaviors. Demonstrate and talk about various techniques. A mistake or "failure" is merely a clue to try another way.

Conferences with Parents

Individual conferences with parents can and should be one of the most effective methods of parent involvement. Inherent in this approach is flexibility. Either the parent or the professional can request the conference. It can be held at the center or at home at any convenient time as long as parents feel the comfort of privacy and confidentiality. The content varies with the needs of the parents, the child, and the professional. The professional can individualize the specific suggestions made and the level of language used. With conferences, parents who cannot read or understand written comments do not miss important information about their child's progress.

Effective conferences with families involve the development of the following important skills:

1. The ability to be culturally sensitive and develop rapport with all the family members

2. The ability to obtain information without appearing to be intrusive

3. The ability to understand what information the family needs and desires

4. The ability to provide the desired information in everyday language

Photo by Lisa Wadors

5. The ability to collaboratively problem solve

6. The ability to summarize, help identify new objectives, and make appropriate recommendations

By being aware of the need to develop competence in these important behaviors, professionals who are new to the field can focus on developing habits conducive to successful conferencing.

Preparing for the Conference. The objectives for conferences should be planned with situational needs in mind. For some the objectives will be general, such as merely becoming acquainted and helping to assure the parents that their child is well cared for and progressing. Another conference may be requested by the parent or the professional because of a specific concern. For example, an interventionist may need to know whether Asha is as inattentive and active at home as she is in the classroom. If the interventionist understands Asha's parents' attitudes and reactions, he may be able to work with her family in developing consistency between school and home. Of course, objectives will have to be flexible enough to accommodate the families' concerns and priorities as well.

The professional should be prepared to provide parents with adequate information. Consider the information gathered through the various observation techniques discussed in chapter 3. Samples of the child's work, anecdotal records, tape recordings, logs, and assessment data should be readily available on request. Special care must be taken to discuss this information in lay terms. At all times, professionals must ensure that all information exchanged will be held in confidence.

When conferences are initiated by professionals, personal invitations should be extended by telephone, through letters, or via e-mail. A duplicated note is not very personal. Whenever possible, parents should be given a choice of date and time. A quiet, uninterrupted setting must be prepared with comfortable, adult-sized chairs. The professional should not be seated behind a desk because this puts a distance between him or her and the parent, who may already be tense. Offering a beverage can make the parent feel more relaxed. Babysitting may need to be arranged because the presence of children distracts the conversation and destroys the confidentiality necessary. Scouts and aides can help out by taking the child and siblings to the playground or to another room.

Beginning the Conference. Often the initial few minutes of a conference are the most uncomfortable

and are perhaps the most critical in building the necessary rapport. Initial impressions can create defensiveness that gets in the way of objective thinking and the creation of a productive relationship. Greetings, a handshake, and thanking the parent for coming help the parent see that the professional appreciates his or her effort to become involved. To help the parent feel at ease, it is helpful to begin with nonemotional topics, although these must be brief because the parent is usually eager to get to the purpose of the meeting.

A time limit for the conference should be made clear so that the parent will not feel rejected when it is necessary to close the conversation. A statement such as the following can establish the time limit of a conference and clarify the purpose of the meeting: "I am so happy, Ms. Jones, that you are able to share the next 15 minutes with me today. I have so much to tell you about Jamie's progress, and I want to hear how you feel about it."

If the parent has initiated the conference, the professional might say, "I am so glad, Ms. Dickson, that you felt free to request this conference. I will be free until 4:00 and am eager to know where you would like to begin." If the parent hesitates, the professional should try not to become tense. If the silence or apparent reluctance of the parent to speak seems to go on too long, the professional should then make a facilitating comment such as "It is sometimes hard to express what we are thinking or feeling." All the while, the professional should try to show by body language that he or she cares, is ready to listen, and is not pushy.

Conducting the Conference.   Once the purpose of the conference is clarified, the parent should be encouraged to talk if he or she has said very little. The professional can make a facilitating comment such as "I thought you might share some of your observations and concerns about Jessica so that we might plan a way to work together to help her progress." The professional should then listen very carefully to whatever the parent says. Parents usually express their primary concerns at this time. The professional is also given a glimpse of the sophistication level of the parent and can gear his or her language to that level.

Listening Carefully.   Listening carefully is critical in the development of productive relationships with parents. Hanson and Lynch (2004) state, "Active listening is foundational to the ability to understand others. Good communication cannot occur without the ability to understand the other person's point of view or perspective" (p. 222). Listening is a difficult skill that takes effort to master. However, it is well known that the most effective means of establishing rapport is to show interest in others through attentive listening. Attentive listening not only encourages parents to express themselves but also demonstrates the professional's acceptance and concern. Simpson discussed the following six attending skills that continue to be basic to effective listening: (a) door-opening statements, (b) clarifying responses, (c) restatements or paraphrasing, (d) reflection, (e) silence, and (f) summarization.

Minimal encouragers to talk are expressions and nonverbal cues that let the speaker know you want to hear more of what he or she has to say. These are often referred to as *door-openers.* Typical of these are such comments as "un-huh," "yes," "that's interesting," and "hmmm." These can be useful in getting parents to continue talking, but they should not become overused or be used stereotypically. The professional should be certain not to interrupt the parent with these or other comments. Leaning somewhat forward is usually a sign of listening and trying to focus on what is being said.

Clarifying responses help the listener to understand the parent or family member when, for some reason, one is unable to follow what has been said. Responses such as "I'm not sure I understand exactly what you mean. Could you say that again?" elicits clarification. Such responses encourage the speaker to elaborate and demonstrate the professional's interest and concern. They can also be used when the professional isn't sure the information he or she has given has been clearly understood. For example, one might ask, "What is your understanding of what you have been told?"

Paraphrasing occurs when the professional attempts to restate to the parent in revised form what he or she has said. This demonstrates that what

the speaker said has been heard and gives the speaker the chance to clarify any misunderstanding the professional may have. Often parents are more able to absorb and understand their own thoughts and motivations when heard from another person. This process can also help secure agreement between what is being said and what is perceived. A professional might say, "If I understand correctly, you are afraid other children will not play with Sarah because she cannot talk clearly."

Reflection involves comments that let the parent know the professional has heard and understood what the parent is saying. It helps to focus the parent's comments by recognizing a specific comment. It is a cue to parents to elaborate on that specific idea, concept, or question. If the reflection also includes the *feeling* that is perceived, then the professional will be demonstrating *active listening*. Consider the following example of a partial reflection and a reflection involving feeling necessary to active listening:

Parent: I had thought that when he began physical therapy, his walking would improve.

Teacher: Would improve? Or, you're feeling pretty discouraged.

Exhibit 2–7, which depicts a home conference, illustrates the skills involved in effective communication.

Active listening allows the listener to show sensitivity to the feelings and emotions being expressed as well as the content. It legitimizes the speaker's feelings and communicates that the emotions being expressed are acceptable. Active listening enables the listener to (a) respond to the speaker's affect by accurately and sensitively perceiving the speaker's apparent and underlying feelings and (b) express understanding of those feelings in words that are attuned to the other person's experience at the moment (Turnbull & Turnbull, 2001). The listener can be effective only if she or he is willing and able to devote the time necessary to allow the speaker to fully express himself or herself. Considering the emotional needs of parents of children with disabilities, it is well worth the effort to invest the energy necessary to become a good active listener.

Silence can serve to facilitate listening. It allows the listener to concentrate on listening and observing nonverbal signals rather than talking. It may communicate a willingness to listen. Skillful use of silent periods can stimulate conversation and contribute to an effective listening environment.

Questioning.   Skillful use of questions serves two primary purposes: (a) to obtain specifically needed information or clarification and (b) to direct the parent's conversation when it runs astray. Questions such as "Can you tell me exactly what Lakeisha did that bothered you so much?" help focus the conversation and provide additional information. Such an open-ended question, which cannot be answered with a "yes" or a "no," encourages a reluctant parent. On the other hand, a closed question, which can be answered with a "yes" or a "no," helps narrow the focus of a disorganized parent. Because professionals need to avoid interrogation, they should practice becoming skilled in using productive questions.

Recognizing and Accepting Parents' Concerns.   This chapter has been emphasizing the importance of a warm, caring attitude that conveys understanding. Of course, this attitude and the skills to convey it are essential for an effective parent conference. Professionals must expect parents to be reluctant at first. They must be given time to learn that the professional cares. Reflective listening is one way to let parents know that their concerns have been heard and understood. Another is by being prepared and honest. If parents ask a question and the professional does not know the answer, he or she should say so. The early childhood interventionist is not a medical doctor or a psychotherapist and must not pretend otherwise by giving misleading information. He or she can and should be prepared to make appropriate referrals. A file or notebook listing names and telephone numbers of local agencies can be helpful. It is important not to be biased in referrals or to endorse anyone in particular. It is a good idea to obtain a list from the local special education regional office, school psychologist, social worker, nurse, or principal.

Exhibit 2–7

Dialogue: A Home Conference Between Parent and Teacher

Scene: Matt is a 4-year-old who has been described by his mother as "never still" and by his father as "all boy." In the past week, the mother reports that several of her favorite plants have crashed to the floor as Matt walked by. "He never does anything mean or on purpose," she said. He bumps into things and is surprised when adults complain or he breaks things. It is time for Ms. McLynn's first home visit. Matt's mother, Ms. G., greets her at the door.

Ms. G.: Hello. Matt has been so excited about your coming, and when he heard you knock, he hid under the bed!

Ms. McL.: Good to be here, Ms. G. At school Matt is so helpful. I can always count on Matt to see what needs doing and to do it. He seems to sense the other children's needs, as well as mine.

Ms. G.: But he is so rough. And always breaking something. My neighbors say he is hyperactive.

Ms. McL.: What does that mean to them?

Ms. G.: Oh, you know, never still. He just can't seem to be quiet for a minute.

Ms. McL.: But he has been very quiet since I've been here.

Ms. G.: He's still hiding under the bed. Oh, he can be quiet when *he* wants to be.

Ms. McL.: So you feel he really does have control of how active he is?

Ms. G.: Yes, I guess so. But just tell him to sit still and he bounces all over the place.

Ms. McL.: You feel he is too active.

Ms. G.: Yes. And he won't listen when I tell him to sit still. That burns me up.

Ms. McL.: His constant moving annoys you.

Ms. G.: You bet it does. What can I do to make him behave? I've tried spanking, but he forgets right away.

Ms. McL.: From watching at school and with what you told me, I'd like to suggest that we both try something. Let's catch him being quiet and gentle.

Ms. G.: When? How?

Ms. McL.: At school I'll keep a special paper on my desk. Every time he is quiet or gentle, I'll say something like, "Matt, I like the way you helped Missy with her coat. You were so gentle," or "Matt, you are doing a good job with that puzzle. You are so quiet that I can hear the birds singing outside." Then, I'll make a quick note—for example 9:03—Quiet and gentle. Helped Missy with coat. 9:10—Worked puzzle. Quiet 3 minutes.

Ms. G.: Well, it can't hurt.

Ms. McL.: I'll call you in 2 days to see how it's working.

And 2 days later when Ms. McLynn called, she was not surprised that Ms. G. could report more quiet and gentle times than noisy ones. So could Ms. McLynn.

Describing Children's Progress. The professional should be organized and positive in describing children's progress, giving specific examples of a child's skills or behavior whenever possible. The professional should encourage parents to discuss individual points of progress and to ask questions and should not overwhelm them with information or use jargon. Evasiveness or "fortune-telling" are to be avoided. The professional can discuss only what the child will be doing in the center, what the child

has accomplished, and what might be expected in the immediate next step. He or she cannot predict how the child will be functioning next year or the year after.

Summarizing. At periodic intervals, the professional should offer summarizing statements that respond to both perceived content and affect. This allows family members to, once again, verify the accuracy of the professional's perceptions. A summarizing comment might be as follows: "Can we say, then, that you are feeling very uncomfortable with Shane's placement in the early intervention program as you don't understand just what he will get out of being here every day?" In addition to summarizing content and affect, the family should be asked if they have additional concerns. Reticent families may be more able to share emotionally laden concerns because of the rapport built in the earlier stages of the conference. Of course, the professional must have the time to listen if, indeed, additional concerns are solicited.

Closing the Conference. The professional has the primary responsibility for ending the conference in conformity with the time limit. Comments such as "Given the few minutes we have left, could you explain . . . ?" or "It is about time to call it a day; do you have any additional questions?" are gentle reminders that the conference must come to an end. Arranging for future contacts ("Let's see, our next regularly scheduled meeting is . . . ") and thanking parents for their time helps to bring a conversation to a close. By standing, it is easy to demonstrate that time is up. Finally, switching back to social conversation, the professional can lead the way to the door.

After the Conference. Professionals need to allow enough time between conferences to record what has occurred during the conference. This record retains vital information, documents the visit, and helps create continuity between meetings. Although occasional notes may be taken during the conference, extensive note taking is unwise because it interferes with listening and often makes parents uncomfortable. Parents should be apprised of any notes that are taken and the purpose they will serve. Only information that can directly be used to assist the child is worth recording.

Involving Parents in Group Meetings

In many communities, parent involvement is synonymous with group meetings. If parents are invited to attend scheduled group meetings, then the center has fulfilled its commitment to parent involvement. Little attention is given to whether the planned meetings meet the needs of those invited to participate. Such meetings are usually designed to provide educational information to relatively large groups of people. Professionals are invited to speak, videos are shown, books are displayed, and refreshments are served. The level of vocabulary used may or may not be understood by the audience. Eager parents may be able to resolve their confusion only by taking advantage of the question-and-answer period. As a result, parents who manage to attend one meeting may not return for the next.

To maximize the value of group meetings, professionals will need to keep these factors in mind. They should realize that group meetings will meet the needs of some, but not all, parents. Group meetings are often welcomed by parents who wish to meet and talk with other parents who have children with similar disabilities. Other parents attend primarily to seek the knowledge of the experts in the field. Some rather shy parents may enjoy not being the focus of attention, whereas other parents may be too inhibited to come in the first place. Even though those parents who linger on are obviously enjoying the experience, some parents may feel awkward socializing or feel pressure to hurry home. Because of the great diversity of individual needs, meetings should provide a balance between educational concerns and social involvement. Not all parents can be expected to be equally involved in all activities. Professionals must observe carefully and try to plan activities that will meet the needs of all the parents at least some of the time.

Rationale for Parent Education Groups. If parents of children with similar problems are brought together, a supportive climate can be developed for families to learn about and share feelings concerning their children with disabilities. Parent education groups also enhance the opportunity to provide parents with knowledge in specific skill areas such as home-based teaching and child management. Alternative approaches to childrearing can be presented. Parents more readily become acquainted with local community resources. Finally, professionals have an opportunity to get to know parents in a setting that can be more relaxed than the parents' home or the child's classroom. Figure 2–2 provides a sample of topics typical of programs designed for parents of young children.

Guidelines for Developing Successful Group Meetings. A review of the literature indicates that parents are increasingly requesting a true partnership in all aspects of the education of their children and themselves (Turnbull & Turnbull, 2001). Parents who feel they have a voice in selecting topics, speakers, times, dates, and hours of meetings are usually more actively involved. This is why the suggestion was made earlier to involve parents in developing the orientation meeting. Parents who help plan have a tendency to recruit other parents to attend to realize the fruits of their labors. Note that Figure 2–2 not only presents possible program topics but also illustrates one way to assess the interests of parents.

Frequency of Meetings. Because large-group meetings should be only a part of the total parent involvement program, they should not be called too frequently. Parents cannot handle more than one such meeting a month. If small-group meetings involving parents with very similar needs have been developed to offer social and emotional support, more frequent meetings may be desirable. If these meetings are being organized by the parents with the professional acting as a consultant, the parents will probably create the needed flexibility for these more informal meetings.

Notification of Meetings. Large-group meetings must be advertised at least 1 month in advance. Multiple media should be used. Written flyers or notes sent home with the children, telephone calls through a calling chain, newspaper articles, and cable television and local radio announcements will be necessary for maximum participation. Follow-up notices approximately 1 week before the meetings will be helpful. Of course, small-group meetings with the responsibility for planning rotated among the interested participants will not take such elaborate notification. Usually one telephone call to each participant is sufficient.

Content of Meetings. The content of meetings is where the active participation of an advisory group of parents is critical. Parents know what they need and should be encouraged to express their needs. Besides a written needs assessment as illustrated in Figure 2–2, professionals can be alert to needs expressed during home visitations, parent conferences, or informal conversation. Speakers need to be dynamic and able to speak on a comprehensible and understandable level. The best recommendations usually come from the parents. Whenever possible, a speaker should be heard before he or she presents to a parent group. Videotapes should also be previewed ahead of time.

Child Involvement. Involving children's work or the children themselves can lure the parents into attending. Parents will come to see their child in a presentation, their child's work displayed, or their child on a film or a videotape. One early childhood center that had difficulty getting parents to form an advisory group planned an Easter egg hunt for the children. While the children were hunting eggs with the supervision of aides, the director offered the parents refreshments and conducted a brief but successful orientation and organizational meeting.

Interpreters. Interpreters can facilitate communication between professionals and parents who have limited English proficiency skills. An interpreter who understands the needs of family members and has

Dear Parents:

Listed below are a number of topics that can become the focus of one or more parent meetings. Because we would like to arrange meetings that will be helpful to you, we would appreciate your cooperation in filling out this questionnaire. Please indicate by checking the appropriate spaces below which meetings would interest you enough for you to take the time to join us. Your comments and opinions are really needed. Please complete this form today and return it with your child by Friday.

Sincerely,

Your Parent Planning Committee

	Yes	No	Maybe
1. How children grow and develop			
a. Learning to talk	[ ]	[ ]	[ ]
b. Learning to think	[ ]	[ ]	[ ]
c. Getting along with others	[ ]	[ ]	[ ]
2. Understanding my child's special needs			
a. A pediatrician's views	[ ]	[ ]	[ ]
b. A physical therapist helps	[ ]	[ ]	[ ]
c. Other: _____	[ ]	[ ]	[ ]
3. The importance of play			
a. Helping your child learn to play	[ ]	[ ]	[ ]
b. Choosing appropriate toys	[ ]	[ ]	[ ]
4. Living with your child			
a. Eating hassles	[ ]	[ ]	[ ]
b. Bedtime nuisances	[ ]	[ ]	[ ]
c. Toileting troubles	[ ]	[ ]	[ ]
d. The babysitter search	[ ]	[ ]	[ ]
e. Brothers and sisters	[ ]	[ ]	[ ]
f. Other: _____	[ ]	[ ]	[ ]
5. Nutrition	[ ]	[ ]	[ ]
6. Safety/first aid	[ ]	[ ]	[ ]
7. Community resources	[ ]	[ ]	[ ]
8. Helping my child behave	[ ]	[ ]	[ ]
9. Parent effectiveness training	[ ]	[ ]	[ ]

10. What we need the most is:

_____

_____

11. The best day(s) for meetings are:

_____ ___A.M. ___P.M.   _____ ___A.M. ___P.M.

Figure 2–2   Sample parent program topics (interest checklist)

Photo by Scott Cunningham/Merrill

sufficient training should be selected and, subsequently, treated as a respected member of the team. He or she should then be given time to translate presented information as well as time for clarification if the information is not understood.

Variety.   The need for variety is an important factor. Not every meeting should focus on a serious topic that calls for the complete attention of the parents. Humor and fun are a necessary part of the learning of many parents who must face serious problems every day. Each meeting should involve some socializing, and some meetings should be purely social. Some groups of parents will plan and enjoy an occasional potluck dinner involving just the parents or even whole families. Workdays can be a productive means of fostering informal communication. Some parents will feel much more comfortable in informal clothes, painting classroom furniture or making educational toys. Still other parents would gladly organize and conduct a garage sale with proceeds to benefit their children.

Child Care and Carpools.   The need for child care and carpools is another important factor. Parents of children with disabilities suffer from a lack of relief from physical demands and time constraints. It is irresponsible to expect such parents to use their limited babysitting resources to attend a parent meeting. The planning committee must arrange child care through local service clubs, high school students, or other volunteers. Carpools or other transportation arrangements may also increase the attendance at meetings. Such practical matters can be all important to parents who may already have more than they need in the way of problems.

Evaluation.   Evaluation is of crucial importance. The atmosphere during group meetings of any size must reflect friendliness, caring, and relaxation. If staff members are tense, then parents will find themselves responding to this tension. Professional staff must be alert to activities that lessen tension, bring smiles to faces, generate questions, prompt people to lean toward action, and are talked about positively during the socializing period. Attendance itself is only one form of evaluation. Evaluation can be informal anecdotal records or logs focusing on the items just mentioned, or it can be formal written reactions by the parents. Formal evaluations should be kept to a minimum.

Parent Support Through Family Resource Centers.   Professionals and parents involved in the planning phases of early intervention services are finding that parents' needs assessment survey results show a strong desire for increased emotional support and counseling. One of the most economical and

effective ways to provide needed support is through the development of parent support groups. One example of an effective group is Parents Helping Parents, Inc., which is described in Exhibit 2–8. This program provides parent-run support groups for families with a variety of needs; it also has become a well-established model parent resource center. Not only should early interventionists become familiar with whatever groups may be available in their areas, but they should also be prepared to assist in the development of such groups if none are available. Appendix I lists helpful Web sites, including

---

Exhibit 2–8

Parents Helping Parents, Inc.

In 1976, two mothers of children with Down syndrome cofounded Parents Helping Parents (PHP). With help from local agencies, PHP became incorporated and a United Way agency. Financial support is realized through individual donations, grant receipts from local foundations and corporations, memberships, and various fund-raising projects. Until 1985, it was an all-volunteer agency.

PHP philosophy: The most important thing a child with disabilities needs is well-informed, emotionally balanced, caring, accepting, and assertive parents. Parents Helping Parents gives to kids with special needs what they need most—special parents.

PHP purpose: To help children with disabilities receive the care, services, education, love, hope, and acceptance they need to enable them to become all they can be, through direct services to their parents.

PHP desire: To collaborate with professionals committed enough to the benefits of peer support that they themselves call and make the referrals. Their devastated clients should not be left to follow through on a suggestion and/or brochure laid in their unsure hands.

Like many parent support groups, PHP started because:

1. Other parents had much vital information about available resources as well as about the disability being confronted.

2. Peer counseling, with its immediate credibility and empathy, was paramount to working through the grief/loss process and on to recovery.

3. Many professionals lacked adequate knowledge about community resources and also lacked sensitivity to the financial, social, and emotional problems faced by entire families.

4. There was no easy way for new parents to meet experienced parents. Such meetings were too important to be left to chance.

Services include visiting parents, family guidance sessions, newsletters, telephone counseling, information packets, gifts to newborns with special needs, workshops for parents on the individualized education program process, peer counseling, a speakers bureau, symposiums, sibling fun days, and workshops for medical professionals in better ways of helping families cope with the advent of a child with special needs.

Parents Helping Parents distributes manuals to assist other groups in the development of similar programs throughout the world. Family groups include any kind of physical, mental, emotional, or learning disability due to birth defects, illnesses, accidents, and developmental delays. Divisions include parents of near drownings, preemies and intensive care nursery support parents, an information and support network for individuals with learning disabilities, and help for those who have experienced neonatal death.

Interested individuals may contact Mary Ellen Petersen, Executive Director, Parents Helping Parents, Suite #3041 Olcott Street, Santa Clara, California 95054. Telephone (408) 727-5775, (800) 397-9827.

that of the National Information Center for Children and Youth with Disabilities, which provides a listing by state of local parent support groups and family resource centers.

WORKING WITH CULTURALLY DIVERSE FAMILIES

Maria Diaz, the early interventionist from Centro de Niños, is knocking on the door of the Ramirez family to do her weekly home visit with Elena, a 30-month-old girl with severe cerebral palsy. The family of seven (including a grandmother) came to the United States from Mexico to obtain help for Elena. They are all currently living in a converted garage in a neighborhood known for gang activity, drugs, and high unemployment. As Maria waits for the door to open, she thinks of the risks in this area as well as the extensive number of concerns this family has. At this home visit Maria will help set up a corner chair for Elena to use so that she can sit on the floor and play with the other children. She will also listen to Mrs. Ramirez as she expresses disappointment at Elena's progress and the desire to seek services of a *curandera* (folk healer) rather than return to the hospital clinic. Mr. Ramirez is in agreement, but he is even more concerned about finding work.

Besides working with Elena at home and school, what is Maria's responsibility to this family? How do culture, values, language, and resources of the Ramirez family enter into the interactions between the family and Maria, other early intervention team members at Centro de Niños, and community agencies?

The rich diversity of today's population challenges traditional patterns of communications between professionals and families. This diversity demands communication patterns sensitive to all parents. Professionals are challenged to become personally aware and use culturally responsive interaction practices. Thus, the challenge for professionals working with young children, whether in early intervention for high-risk infants or in a migrant worker's day-care center, is to be responsive to individual family cultural and language difference. All families assume the role of socializing children to become

part of the larger community. An examination and understanding of the differences between "mainstream" values of communities and specific families within these communities are a critical part of the ecological approach to intervention (Hanson & Lynch, 2004). The role of early interventionists must include acknowledging different cultural perspectives and learning how to work effectively within the boundaries that are comfortable for the family while increasing the family's understanding of and improving their ability to work within the larger mainstream culture.

Cultural Models and Childrearing Practices

Insights into how parents view children and their upbringing are critical in developing working relationships with families. Beliefs about issues such as adult–child interactions, feeding, toileting, sleeping, and discipline will emerge as the early interventionist gathers information about the child and family. If "preschool goals, and values for children's learning, social and behavioral expectations, and demands for interactional and communication abilities differ from those that the children and their families possess, then potential differences (and possible conflict) may arise" (Hanson & Zercher, 2001, p. 418). In fact, having inappropriate cultural expectations for a child and/or his or her family could create more problems than the child's actual disability. **Cultural models** offer a useful way to think about childrearing behavior. A cultural model is a shared understanding that people have of their universe and of their behavior in that universe. Cultural models help people turn their beliefs into practice. As Finn (2003) states, "Practitioners who work with families with infants and toddlers need to acknowledge the experience and power of family and community beliefs about what is needed for healthy child development and who should provide it" (p. 41). This understanding will make it possible for support and intervention to be family centered and aligned with parental goals. As attitudes toward childrearing vary in many ways and

can create conflict between professionals and parents, a generalized respect for the diversity of childrearing beliefs and practices is critical. Below are examples of some of these variations.

Values of Independence and Autonomy Versus Interdependence and Obedience.

Certain Western industrialized societies, especially the United States, value the characteristics of independence and assertiveness. Most other cultures emphasize the family values of interdependence, obedience, harmony, and respect. These differences result in very different childrearing attitudes and practices. For example, in the United States, the young child's abilities to initiate verbally, to use language to make requests, and to carry on a conversation with adults are seen as important and positive skills. They are often included in the goals and objectives identified for young children with special needs. In many other cultures, however, such behavior in children is viewed as inappropriate. American middle-class children are often viewed by other cultures as disrespectful, aggressive, and overindulged. Children should be "seen and not heard." They should not initiate interactions with adults and should not assert their preferences and desires. Consider the conflict that may result for a family with such values when the early childhood teacher indicates they should be helping their child initiate requests. In this situation, it is important for the professional to explore the family's degree of comfort with such a goal and to communicate why this goal might be important for success in the mainstream culture.

Another related area of difference is often referred to as "individualistic" versus "collectivist" views of personal development and behavior. Being an individual is highly esteemed in mainstream U.S. culture. Phrases like "rugged individualist" and "pursuit of individual freedom" are considered positive and basic to the "American way." Many cultures, particularly Asian cultures, that are influenced by Confucian values (Gonzalez-Mena, 2001) revere harmony, proper behavior, and maintenance of social order (e.g., conformity and hierarchical lines of authority). Family and community members must learn their proper roles. The extent to which a child or adult carries out his or her expected role is a measure of success and family pride.

Discipline Approaches.

Discipline is another area that varies widely across cultures and is often an area of cultural mismatch between families and early childhood professionals. The greatest variance between mainstream U.S. culture and many other cultures can be found in authoritarian versus egalitarian (democratic) parenting styles. In authoritarian families, the parent is the absolute and final authority. In such families the use of corporal punishment tends to be more common. The more democratic views of childrearing and discipline are less likely to use corporal punishment, and the rules are less fixed. Children are given the opportunity to give their side of the story and sometimes may even participate in the selection of a specific punishment. Parents with an extreme egalitarian approach would be unlikely to say, "Do it because I say so." Authoritarian families place great emphasis on obedience and respect. For them the mark of a good parent is one who punishes children for disrespectful behavior or for not conforming to their expected role. Physical punishment or "shaming" are common disciplinary strategies (Banks, 2002).

Variation can also be seen in the age at which discipline becomes appropriate. For example, in some Asian cultures there is an abrupt shift in discipline practices that may occur around the age of 5 to 6 years (Chao & Tseng, 2002). Although parents may be very indulgent and not use discipline at all in the early years, the 4-year-old is expected to begin to conform to adult expectations. Harsh consequences may be used to facilitate this learning.

Also, there may be significant gender differences in how young children are disciplined. Boys may be indulged, whereas girls are punished more severely or vice versa. In many cultures boys are given very special status relative to girls.

Attitudes Toward Disability.

"Each culture has its own explanations for why some babies are born with disabilities, how these children are to be treated, and what responsibilities and roles are expected of

family members, helpers, and other members of society" (Lamorey, 2002, p. 67). Only when early interventionists understand and build on each family's cultural interpretations of disability is it possible to create nurturing partnerships with parents. The degree and nature of parent involvement in early intervention is related to their beliefs about the nature of disability and its causation. Religion frequently plays a part in how families view a child's disability. A child's disability may be seen as God's punishment for some earlier wrongdoing of the parent. Thus, in some cases the family will be shamed by the child, as the child's condition serves as a visible pronouncement of the parent's guilt. In other cultures, because the disability is seen as God's will, there may be a reluctance to intervene. Parents may be torn between the early intervention program's pressure for them to take an active role in facilitating the child's development versus their feeling that trying to change or "fix" the child is questioning God's authority.

The Influence of Racism.   Racism is a very real phenomenon in American society. Whereas racism and prejudice are experienced to some extent by all minority groups in the United States, no racism is as profound as that which is experienced by African American families. Racism can have a major impact on childrearing practices. African American parents must prepare their children to cope and survive against great odds. Holzman (2004) reported that although black males make up only 8.6% of public school enrollments, they represent 22% of expulsions and 23% of suspensions. Varias (2005) reminds us of the problems that result when such a large percentage of these children are left to wander the streets. And then there is the contention that a major agent in the disproportionately high representation of black boys in special education and in disciplinary interventions is the lack of accommodation for differences in learning styles (Kunjufu, 2005). African American children may inadvertently learn that life will not be fair. White middle-class professionals often view such attitudes as paranoid and may believe that parents are setting their children up to feel oppressed. Parents must struggle to

help their children reconcile three different influences in their lives: the racism experienced by being a minority culture, the heritage and traditions passed down from their African forebearers, and the values and behaviors dictated by U.S. mainstream culture.

Family Structure.   Another area of cultural difference often encountered by early childhood professionals is in family structure. The middle-class ideal (although certainly no longer the norm) is the "nuclear family." The nuclear family consists of two parents and their children, living in relative isolation from other family members. Actually, other kinds of family structure are becoming much more common in the United States. Single-parent households, especially those headed by divorced or never-married women, are increasingly common. Also, many families from minorities include numerous extended family members: grandparents, great-grandparents, sometimes aunts and uncles and cousins, and spouses of grown children and their children. Such large family units, often living in relatively small quarters, seem chaotic and confusing to professionals who have grown up in nuclear families. They may be concerned about overstimulation of the young child or inconsistent, unpredictable childrearing practices. In many cases, however, extended family households provide important support for parents and young children. Parents from a minority culture are often uncomfortable leaving their children with strangers or may not be able to afford day care. Extended family members provide trusted, culturally compatible care for their children while parents work. Extended family members also provide important opportunities for child interaction and nurturance.

Parents' Roles.   There are interesting cultural differences in how parents see their roles in terms of their children's development. Middle-class parents clearly view themselves as teachers of their children. They teach their children concepts and vocabulary and help them learn to solve problems. Some parents also see themselves as teachers of their children, but what they teach are morality and proper behavior, including self-help skills. For some families there is a strong focus on not spoiling children. This often

Photo by Lisa Wadors

entails not being overly responsive or indulgent. For some, the goal is to teach children— especially boys— to "be tough" and be able to defend themselves. Still other families may believe that all skills simply evolve as a normal developmental course and view their roles as teachers or interveners as minimal.

Caregiver–Child Communication.   Another area of great cultural variation that has major implications for early intervention is parent–child communication. In middle-class U.S. society, *talking* is highly valued. By the standards of other cultures, Americans are excessive talkers. This talking carries over into their interactions with young children. Parents typically respond *verbally* even to very young infants long before they have any intentional communication. It is not unusual for a parent to respond to an infant's burp or sigh as though he has just said something profound! Parents also value early development of language skills and verbal assertiveness in young children. Very young children are expected to be able to label, explain, and initiate and maintain a conversation. Parents also believe that they can play an important role in helping children learn these skills.

This kind of verbal interaction is unusual in many cultures. In some cultures, very young children are not consistently responded to until they can talk intelligibly. As mentioned earlier, in cultures where respect and obedience are emphasized, it may not be considered appropriate for young children to initiate; thus, being responsive to young children's communications would not be a high priority.

Common strategies suggested by early intervention professionals to facilitate children's development of communication skills include asking parents to consistently label objects, follow the child's lead, and expand on the child's utterance. For some parents, such interactions will be unnatural. It will require learning a skill not only that is new but that also may be contrary to the practices of their culture. In such cases it will be important for the professional to explain to the parents that although these may be unfamiliar interactions, they can prove beneficial to the language development of their child with special needs.

Medical Practices.   Differing views on medical practices may be a significant source of family and professional conflict. Families from a wide range of subcultures may hold on to traditional health

practices. Faith healers, herbs, massage, animal rites, and other rituals are often part of treatments that lead to misunderstandings. For example, some Vietnamese parents have been reported for child abuse when using the technique of "coining" to treat conditions such as colds, sore throats, and headaches. The process involves applying a medicated salve and then stroking the affected area with a hot coin. The superficial red marks raise suspicions of abuse. Such judgments often grow out of the assumption that these families are not concerned about or caring for their children. We must remember not to judge parents to be uncaring when they actually care differently for their children.

Language Differences

Perhaps the most obvious difference among subcultures is communication, both verbal and nonverbal. The inability to communicate directly with families in their primary language creates a great deal of frustration for both parents and professionals. It is often the source of misunderstanding and an inadequate transmission of information. The need for translation in both spoken and written communication is critical in any early intervention program serving other than English-speaking families. Some suggestions for working through a translator are found in Exhibit 2–9. It is equally imperative that

---

Exhibit 2–9

Communicating Through a Translator

For the Professional:

1. Spend a few minutes with the translator, prior to the meeting, discussing topics to be covered. Make sure the translator understands the concepts.
2. Your translator should be someone you trust, especially with confidential or sensitive information.
3. In a group situation, sit next to the translator.
4. Use simple words. Talk slowly and in a few sentences at a time.
5. Look at and talk to the parent, not the translator.
6. Use nonverbal communication when talking. Observe the nonverbal communication used by the parent.
7. Allow sufficient time for the meeting.
8. After the meeting, ask the translator for his or her overall impression of the meeting.
9. In families with both English- and non–English-speaking members, be aware of the tendency to ignore members who do not speak English.
10. When young family members speak English and adults do not, avoid using children as translators if possible.

For the Translator:

1. Develop reference materials for medical, educational, and psychological terminology.
2. Make it a point to understand the culture and beliefs of the families.
3. Ask clarifying questions if the meaning of statements is unclear.
4. If line-by-line translation is not clear, use your own words, verifying changes with the professional and the parent.
5. Be aware of both verbal and nonverbal communication.

materials such as reports, newsletters, and home programs be prepared in parents' languages.

One way to break through the language barrier and enhance the family's involvement in a child's program is to provide support and encouragement from other parents. One such program is Fiesta Educativa, founded in 1978 to educate and assist Latino families in the Los Angeles area to obtain services for their children. It provides parent support groups and training programs and holds annual conferences in much the same manner as Parents Helping Parents illustrated in Exhibit 2-8. This form of peer counseling and peer support assists other parents in understanding "the system" and community resources while offering much-needed emotional support.

As Maria Diaz discovered in her home visits with the Ramirez family, the effectiveness of her work is clearly tied not only to understanding the unique values of the family but also to her own cultural biases and values. Although Maria speaks Spanish fluently, her upbringing in an upper-middle-class family in Spain has little relation to the experiences of the Ramirez family. Conversations have raised a number of differences in the way they view issues such as health, childrearing, and education. Maria feels that in recognizing their differences, she has begun to work within the boundaries that are comfortable to the family while sharing with them information about the ways of the larger culture.

In her ongoing experiences with the Ramirez family and other parents in the intervention program, Maria and the rest of the early intervention team must continually use caution in making prejudgments based on attitudes toward and stereotypes of certain subcultures. The effectiveness of programs will depend on the development of ethnic competence and behavioral changes by the service providers. Professionals must recognize and clarify their own values and assumptions. Second, they must gather and analyze ethnographic information regarding the cultural community that they serve. Third, they must determine the degree to which the family has adopted society's values. Finally, they must examine each family's orientation to specific childrearing issues. Exhibit 2-10 offers some suggestions for working with culturally diverse families.

WORKING WITH SPECIAL FAMILY POPULATIONS

In addition to the challenges encountered in working with all parents, many professionals who work with young children will discover that they are working with parents who have unique needs themselves. The nature of the circumstances or disabilities of these parents will vary widely. Although overt behaviors may appear to be similar, concerns can be very different. It is unwise and dangerous to generalize; each parent is an individual with unique needs. In some way, each one can be assisted.

Parents with Developmental Disabilities

Children of parents with developmental disabilities are often enrolled in early intervention programs because they are considered at risk rather than because they have a diagnosed disability. Although all the suggestions already made for developing partnerships with parents are appropriate for working with parents with developmental disabilities, there are two specific goals to keep in mind. These include helping the parents become the most effective parents possible while also carefully monitoring the children's progress. In order to achieve these goals, the following guidelines may be useful:

1. *Establish priorities.* To help parents with developmental disabilities develop effective parenting skills, professionals must work with these parents in choosing their priorities carefully. The first priority may be to determine whether parents would benefit from assistance in managing the basic needs of daily living. Many parents with developmental disabilities are in the lowest socioeconomic bracket. Both resources and skill in budgeting may be limited. The early interventionist may be called on to help parents plan budgets and to connect

Exhibit 2–10

Suggestions for Working with Culturally Diverse Families

1. Make sure that program staffing reflects the cultures and languages of the children and families in the program.

2. Provide ongoing staff training related to family differences.

3. Encourage families to share their beliefs and traditions. Invite speakers to discuss all aspects of the culture and its relationship to disabilities, childrearing, medical practices, and so forth.

4. Network with other community resources that are meaningful to families, such as churches, community advisers from subcultural groups, and the media (local television, radio, newspapers, and so on).

5. In addition to using trained interpreters for all parent interactions, provide written materials in the language of the participating families. Be sensitive to the comprehension and reading levels required. Be creative in addressing the needs of parents with limited reading ability. Bilingual curriculum materials and activities should also be an integral part of the child's program.

6. Learn at least a few words of the languages represented in the program, especially common greetings and phrases used in speaking to children.

7. Avoid stereotyping. Within cultural groups, recognize individual differences in background experiences, coping styles, interests, economic levels, and so forth. Parents from the same cultural group do not always have the same needs. Meet individual families at their own level of need and life experience.

with available community resources. Assistance may also be needed in such daily living skills as selection and storage of food, in developing daily routines for both themselves and their children, and in securing transportation and attending to medical needs.

2. *Coordinate help.* As soon as possible, discover which other agencies are extending help to these families. If there are several, the development of a collaborative intervention plan with frequent communication among all those involved is essential.

3. *Make frequent, brief contacts.* Telephone calls are better than notes, and 10 minutes with the parent in the home can pay quick dividends.

4. *Avoid lengthy explanations.* Be brief. Be explicit. Show parents what to do and how to do it. They are usually willing to try if they understand what is wanted.

5. *Require little or no reading.* Send only one request or direction in notes if they can read. A list of things to do will probably be ignored.

6. *Model appropriate parent-child interaction.* As parent-child interaction may be limited, the early interventionist may need to model responsiveness to children's cues. Teaching parents simple "baby play" games such as peekaboo will help these parents become more involved with their children.

7. *Help parents interpret the child's behavior.* Parents with developmental disabilities may misinterpret their children's behavior and see them as "bad children" who need to be punished.

8. *Involve parents with developmental disabilities.* Whenever possible, include these parents in center observations, volunteer activities, parent conferences, and meetings. Answer their questions in short sentences and with simple

language. Supervise their activities closely. It is helpful to remember that they are with their child far more than the professional. If their interaction skills and behavior management can be improved, both parent and child will benefit.

Teen Parents

Although much attention has been given to the increasing numbers of teen pregnancies, little is found in the literature about the needs of young teen parents of children with disabilities. The developmental level of the teenager who, in many ways, is still a child herself must be considered. All teen parents appear to need emotional support and specific instruction in "parenting" while they are being helped to set and reach toward some realistic goals for themselves. Providing this emotional support in a way that enhances the teen parent's self-esteem is often a significant challenge, as early interventionists may represent authority figures at a time when teens tend to turn toward peers as their primary source of self-esteem and goal setting.

Teen parents who have, themselves, suffered from poor parenting will benefit from the same careful approaches to providing information and modeling "parenting best practices" discussed above. In addition, teen parents need to be linked to education, child-care services, social groups, and agencies that provide a wide range of support so they can develop the life and vocational skills necessary to be able to provide a stable environment for themselves and their children. There is a tendency for teen mothers to vocalize, touch, and smile at their infants less; to be less sensitive to and accepting of their

infants' behavior; and to hold less realistic developmental standards than do older mothers. To be effective, early interventionists must be accepting and able to provide consistent emotional support to a group of parents whose history is generally lacking in this essential element of healthy development.

Foster Caregivers

The foster child, in addition to possibly having developmental disabilities, often has overwhelming social-emotional needs. Caregivers and early interventionists must be concerned about such issues as attachment, diminished use of adults for comfort, passivity, inappropriate emotional responses, impulsivity, and fearfulness in their efforts to provide developmentally appropriate support to the young child. Because of the complexities associated with a child's removal from his or her natural parents, a team approach to placement, care, and reunification (when possible) is critical.

The implications for early interventionists are in working with foster families and encouraging participation in home and center activities. Intervention needs of the child with a developmental disability are developed with foster parent input as well as with the biological parent (as appropriate). In addition, the foster parents are encouraged to be a part of parent groups to take advantage of ongoing emotional support, training, and educational opportunities.

The next chapter will provide an overview of the current issues, trends, and controversies related to assessment. It will also elaborate on the role of interventionists in light of changing philosophies and practices.

Summary

Properly trained professionals will recognize and actively work toward involving families in a partnership of responsibility for their child's development. One of the first steps in bridging a link between parents and professionals is for the professional to recognize the emotional needs of families with children

with disabilities. Parents often react to the realization that their child has a disabling condition in stages similar to the emotional adjustment encountered with the loss of a loved one. The alert and informed professional can help parents work through each stage, from initial feelings of shock, disbelief, and denial through anger

and resentment, bargaining to make it go away, depression and discouragement, and on to acceptance. Understanding the family as a system is essential to true parent–professional collaboration.

Children and members of the extended family can be included in the process of emotional and educational adjustments. Siblings are especially valuable allies, as children typically accept a child who has disabilities without jealousy or anxiety. Especially in early sessions with family members, it is important to avoid jargon and technical concepts. Test results should be explained in terms of common behaviors.

A variety of methods of parent involvement are surveyed, such as home-based instruction, observations, passports, and meetings. For effectiveness in home visits and instruction, teachers learn to use two-way communication, taking time to listen and observe as well as to inform and demonstrate.

Guidelines are provided for working with parents within the center under a variety of purposes.

With planning, it is possible to create a developmental approach for bringing parents into contact with other parents of children with disabilities, orienting them to observation and eventual participation within the center. Parent education groups and parent–teacher conferences can be viewed as requiring special teacher skills rather than simply as opportunities for parents to meet.

Special consideration is given to working with culturally diverse families. Understanding cultural practices and language differences is essential to successful early intervention.

Finally, professionals are reminded that some parents of children with disabilities may have special needs themselves. These include parents who themselves have disabilities, teen parents, and foster parents. Throughout the chapter, sufficient details have been provided to encourage professionals to pick and choose the type and extent of involvement most appropriate for their parents, their children, and themselves.

Discussion Topics and Activities

1. Do additional reading and research into the emotional needs and feelings of parents of children with disabilities. Discuss these feelings with class members. If possible, try to empathize with these feelings.

2. Make a list of the public and private institutions in your area whose purpose is to help families of children with disabilities cope with their problems. Organize the list as a referral file including contact person, telephone number, and cost and type of services.

3. Visit and, if possible, volunteer in your local family resource center.

4. Review and discuss why parents may feel fearful about their meetings with center personnel. What can professionals do to help relieve these feelings?

5. Prepare and role-play an orientation meeting. Try to be as convincing as possible when giving the reasons why you would like to get your children's parents involved.

6. Develop a questionnaire that you can use to determine the interests and needs of parents for parent involvement. Try it out on a few parents. Compare it with that of classmates and revise when necessary.

7. Collect magazine, newspaper, and journal articles about working with parents. Make a file of useful ideas.

8. Role-play a home visit with classmates. Share constructive criticism.

9. Consider and discuss the possibility of a values collision between a home visitor and a family. How can such a collision be avoided? Have you ever been involved in such a situation?

10. As a class, discuss issues of confidentiality, privileged communication, and conversation in the teacher's lounge in relation to parent involvement.

11. Gather and discuss newsletters from local early childhood centers. Develop one that may be appropriate for an early intervention program.

12. Develop a "happygram" to be sent home to parents.

Recognizing Special Needs and Monitoring Progress

Photo by Anne Vega/Merrill

KEY TERMS

(Note: Terms are discussed in the text and/or defined in the glossary.)

assessment	curriculum-based assessment	ecological validity
authentic assessment strategies	(curriculum-referenced	eligibility
child-find	assessment)	etiology
construct validity	diagnosis	family-directed child assessment
content validity	dynamic assessment models	formative evaluation
criterion-referenced assessment	ecological approach	functional assessment

identification
interdisciplinary team approach
multidisciplinary team approach
naturalistic observation (direct
    observation)
norm-referenced tests

performance assessment
portfolio assessment
predictive validity (criterion-related
    validity)
program monitoring and evaluation
reliability

screening
standardized tests
summative evaluation
trained examiner
transdisciplinary team approach
validity

Key Concepts

- Developmental assessment is a process designed to deepen understanding of children's competencies and the environments most likely to help them reach their full potential.

- Philosophy and practices in identification, assessment, and evaluation are changing rapidly.

- A move toward an ecobehavioral approach to assessment facilitates understanding of environmental influences as well as the complex interactions of young children with their caregivers.

- Professionals must understand the usefulness and limitations of both criterion-referenced and standardized assessment measures as well as the critical role of informal measures such as observation of the child in natural settings and the use of parent interviews.

- Assessment should be an ongoing process that builds on multiple sources of information gathered, whenever possible, during authentic daily activities such as playtime.

- Observers of children's progress should be trained. They should choose to observe within relevant and typical environmental contexts and should focus on describing functional needs (i.e., those behaviors needed by the child in order to participate in meaningful and purposeful daily activities).

- When children with special needs are included, developmental information must be recorded, kept up to date, and made available to parents and the child's program planning team. Progress must be monitored on an ongoing basis.

There continues to be much debate and discussion regarding assessment in early childhood. That is because the very nature of young children creates many challenges for professionals attempting assessment of their skills and abilities. Children are leery of strangers and unfamiliar places and have short attention spans, limited communication skills, and difficulty following directions. Several texts are available that provide comprehensive information related to approaches and procedures for assessment of infants and young children across developmental domains. These include *Meaningful Assessments of Young Children* (Puckett & Black, 2007), *Assessing Infants and Preschoolers with Special Needs* (McLean, Wolery, & Bailey, 2004), *The Practical Guide to Assessing Infants and Preschoolers with Special Needs* (Bondurant-Utz, 2002), and *Interdisciplinary Clinical Assessment of Young Children with Developmental Disabilities* (Guralnick, 2000). The purpose of this chapter is to present not a thorough consideration of the topic of assessment but rather an overview of the issues, trends, and controversies in the field. It will begin with a currently accepted definition of developmental assessment and a discussion of the purposes of assessment.

The following key issues will be considered: changing philosophies and practices; issues related to the use of standardized tests with infants and young children; and current approaches to assessment, such as "authentic" assessment, including play-based assessment, portfolio assessment, and techniques for becoming skilled observers of children.

WHAT IS DEVELOPMENTAL ASSESSMENT?

According to Meisels (2001), **assessment** is defined "as the process of obtaining information for the purpose of making evaluative judgments. Assessment is a tool for answering questions about specific aspects of children's knowledge, behavior, skill or personality and contributes to the acquisition of knowledge and information about children" (p. 5). He continues on to state that "in order to work effectively with young children, we need a great deal of information, and we need to acquire this information on a continuing basis" (p. 5).

Assessment is conducted to help parents and professionals make a series of informed, evaluative decisions. The choice of the tool or process of observation and analysis must depend on the type of decision that is required. The type of decision to be made will determine the nature of the information to be obtained and, therefore, the purpose of the assessment process. The purpose will then guide the process. The following section will discuss typical purposes for the use of assessment activities with young children.

IDENTIFICATION

In order for eligible children to receive the free appropriate early intervention services to which they are entitled, they must be found and identified. Therefore, **identification** involves both the child-find and screening activities that locate and identify disabling conditions in children who either are not receiving early intervention or are receiving inadequate intervention services.

Child-Find

The process of **child-find** includes finding and identifying children with disabling conditions. Educational regions within states often hire child-find teams that are usually interdisciplinary in nature. These teams are responsible for planning and conducting a public awareness campaign to inform and educate community members concerning the right to a free appropriate education for all children. A primary goal of the public awareness campaign is to generate referrals for screening. In most communities there are numerous possible sources of referral. If public awareness activities are sensitive to community characteristics, a significant number of first contacts may be made by families themselves. Other referral sources may include staff from the hospital neonatal intensive care unit, local physicians, child-care workers, social service agencies, and family resource centers. Of interest is the fact that the Individuals with Disabilities Education Act (IDEA) of 2004 requires communities to be certain that their child-find efforts apply to highly mobile children including those who are migrants, homeless, or in foster homes.

Screening

Screening is the initial step in the assessment and intervention process intended to assist children in receiving an appropriate education. "Screening is a brief, first-level assessment that is conducted prior to referral for more in-depth diagnostic assessments to determine a need for specialized services" (Twombly, 2001, p. 37). Screening is a limited procedure. The intent is to identify those children who *might* have a problem that should be investigated thoroughly. Children with obvious or severe disabling conditions who have been located through child-find procedures should not be involved in the screening process. These children should be referred directly to the local department or agency responsible for thorough diagnosis of the disabling conditions.

Early Childhood Educator's Role.   Currently, the role of the interventionist in the processes of

Photo by Scott Cunningham/Merrill

child-find and screening varies with local areas and professional expertise. In some areas teachers and therapists have been asked to assist in public awareness activities and in conducting screening programs. At the very least, all educators of young children are expected to be able to recognize high-risk or danger signals of disabling conditions in the children within their classes (see Appendix D).

Professionals who consent to participate in screening young children should do so realizing the responsibilities involved in the process. Even though great efforts are usually taken to ensure that the screening process is fun for children, it is, nevertheless, a time of anxiety. Parents, especially, need support and encouragement to realize that screening is only a preliminary step and does not determine the definite existence of a disabling condition. Caution must be taken to avoid labeling children.

Although there is a tendency to replace standardized screening tests with information provided by parents and medical personnel as well as informed clinical observation, screening tests are still used. Extreme care must be taken in the selection of any screening tests. To begin with, they must be used in relation to the definition for eligibility adopted in any local area. For example, if a state uses a very broad

definition of developmental delay that would include children with even mild delays, then the screening criteria for referral for diagnosis to determine eligibility must be more liberal than in a state where the definition includes only children with severe developmental delays.

The selection committee must consider the following factors when selecting a screening instrument:

1. Qualifications of individuals who will use the test

2. Reliability (consistency or stability) of the test

3. Validity of the test (extent to which the test screens what it is supposed to screen)

4. Provision of items that cover the major functional areas, including language skills, cognitive skills, fine and gross motor skills, and social-emotional development

5. Similarity of the children used to establish the norms to those being screened

6. Degree to which the screening instrument discriminates against minority groups or specific disabling conditions

7. Cost and time factors

DETERMINATION OF ELIGIBILITY FOR SERVICES

Assessment processes may be performed in order to confirm or disconfirm the existence of a problem severe enough to make a child eligible to receive early intervention services. By clarifying the nature and extent of the problem through a multidisciplinary evaluation, a definitive **diagnosis** as to the **etiology,** or cause, of the condition may be made. In many cases, however, a specific cause of the delay cannot be identified. In such cases, the purpose of the diagnostic assessment is to determine whether the child is, in fact, sufficiently delayed to be eligible for services. Of course, this decision will depend on the local area's set of criteria specifying precisely how **eligibility** will be determined. Legally, states are discouraged from reporting or serving young children according to a disability category label. Therefore, many states have adopted criteria based on number of months of delay. This allows children to be made eligible according to their degree of *developmental delay* rather than by being placed in a disability category. It should be noted that IDEA uses the term *evaluation* to refer to the assessment procedures used in determining a child's eligibility for services.

Determination of Services

The interagency team, in collaboration with the parents, will use the information derived from the multidisciplinary assessment of the child's current level of performance to decide what service options are most appropriate for the child and family. In making this decision, consideration must be given to a match between the needs, abilities, and priorities of the child and family and the services available. Such decisions must be dynamic in that they may be changed quickly if deemed necessary by continuing, ongoing assessment of child and family needs.

It must be realized that during a child's early years, there are several critical points when decisions must be made. Of course, the number of decision-making points will depend on the characteristics of the child's disability and when this disability becomes apparent. For example, service decisions

may have to be made when the child is being discharged from the hospital, a few months later when delay is clearly recognized and an infant program is deemed appropriate, when the child transfers into preschool services, and when he or she becomes eligible for kindergarten.

Early Childhood Educator's Role.   Although historically teachers were not seen as active participants in decision making about children with problems, increasingly they are expected to be astute observers and communicators of their observations. Teachers are included as part of the multidisciplinary diagnostic team. This is especially true of teachers or therapists who have been asked to serve as service coordinators. Their careful observations are helpful in corroborating or refuting formal test results. Current practice requires that teachers understand what each specialist is saying and recommending. Teachers today must be alert to recognize conflicting advice, the failure of a specialist to use tests that take into account multiple problems, or the need to coordinate conflicting opinions and directions. It is critical that *all* information, whether derived from formal testing, parental interviews, or informal observations, be integrated and synthesized. It is often the teacher who must assume this responsibility in an effort to see that a comprehensive picture of the child's level of functioning is obtained.

Take the case of a child with a mild hearing problem who was judged to be severely cognitively delayed by a psychologist using norm-referenced IQ tests that required understanding and use of language. Because of the hearing loss, language was limited, scores were low, and an inappropriate diagnosis was made. This same child, tested by another psychologist who based decisions on performance testing (nonverbal IQ tests), was again described as being severely delayed. Even though the test scores were in the range of retardation, both the parents and the teacher were unconvinced that the child was indeed severely delayed. Fortunately, the second psychologist noted that "vision should be checked."

A thorough visual examination revealed severe myopia (nearsightedness). Provided with glasses and

Exhibit 3–1

Special Considerations in Assessment of Infants and Toddlers

1. Although standardized instruments are available for assessment of various aspects of infant and toddler development, they *must* be accompanied by extensive use of informal measures as well.

2. Infants and toddlers must be assessed within the context of their families, ideally within their natural home environment.

3. Special considerations must be given to infant behavioral and physiological states, which may change quickly and dramatically because of factors such as hunger, fatigue, and ability. Assessment sessions may need to be rescheduled several times. Also, infant state considerations will require that infants be observed on more than one occasion, at different times of the day.

4. Parents must play a key role in the assessment of infants and toddlers in terms of both the information they can provide to the professionals and the need to observe the infant's behavior in the most optimal environment—that is, with the caregiver.

teaching adapted to both vision and hearing problems, this 3-year-old began to learn. In this case, if the teacher had not observed that specialists were not communicating and if the teacher had not persisted in encouraging the parents to see that all the team members had all the information, the diagnosis of severe cognitive delay might have been accepted. The child's precious early learning years might have been lost.

Interventionists are expected to be completely familiar with the environmental aspects of their own classrooms. If asked whether a child would benefit from services in their particular classrooms, teachers should be able to answer with confidence.

Teachers can also develop understanding of their own personal teaching styles and the atmospheres they develop only through willingness to be honest and to seek feedback from others who observe them. They should initiate dialogues with directors, school psychologists, speech therapists, and nurses to help gain as objective a picture as possible of the characteristics of the classroom in which they teach. Use of audiotapes and videotapes may help teachers (a) determine whether they seem to have greater patience with one type of disability than with another, (b) see whether they seem to reinforce children differentially by age or

gender, (c) assess the degree of structure they impose in a classroom, and (d) discover their most effective techniques of child management. Just as children differ, so do teachers and parents. Honesty and objective observation will help create the learner–environment match that is increasingly being encouraged in the literature. Exhibit 3–1 summarizes considerations to be kept in mind when assessing young children as the early childhood special educator is contemplating his or her responsibilities as a professional.

ASSESSMENT FOR PROGRAM PLANNING

Historically, there has tended to be a mismatch between the information obtained from a thorough diagnosis and the information needed by early interventionists to plan and provide direct services. Originally, it was thought that information gathered during diagnosis would be useful in the development of instructional programs. However, such information is usually provided on only a very general level and may be very limited. Therefore, most early intervention programs require additional assessment on program entry and on a continuing basis. Currently, assessment is further defined "as the ongoing process

of gathering evidence of learning in order to make informed judgments about instructional practice" (Jones, 2004, p. 15).

The National Association for the Education of Young Children (NAEYC) and the National Association of Early Childhood Specialist in State Departments of Education (2004) issued a joint statement giving early childhood professionals the following challenge:

Make ethical, appropriate, valid and reliable assessment a central part of all early childhood programs. To assess young children's strengths, progress, and needs, use assessment methods that are developmentally appropriate, culturally and linguistically responsive, tied to children's daily activities, supported by professional development, inclusive of families, and connected to specific, beneficial purposes: (1) making sound decisions about teaching and learning, (2) identifying significant concerns that may require focused intervention for individual children, and (3) helping programs improve their educational and developmental interventions. (p. 51)

While the continuous process of assessment may use and build on information gathered in the diagnostic sequence, initially, it is necessary to use various informal and formal techniques to carry out in-depth observation in an effort to pinpoint each child's skills and deficits. What the child can or cannot do, and under what circumstances, must be determined to select appropriate behavioral objectives and effective instructional strategies. As the child's program progresses, ongoing assessment data should be collected to update individual objectives and intervention procedures.

Early Childhood Educator's Role

In the past, teachers followed an adopted curriculum and activity plans. Although good teachers have always individualized activities to some extent, current practice requires much more thorough initial assessment, increased ongoing assessment, and continuous adaptation of activities.

Assessment is essentially the first task in developing the individualized instruction program required for each child with disabilities. Useful assessment draws information from a variety of sources. It begins by carefully listening to parents and encouraging them to share the wealth of information they have about their child. Assessment requires frequent observation of children in a variety of situations. Observation may be done with the help of standardized (formal) or informal teacher-made observational tools. This observation helps to confirm or refute diagnostic testing results; at the same time, concerns are pinpointed and a basis for individualized planning is developed.

Program assessment procedures must be directly related to program objectives, which emanate from the program curriculum adopted. (The process of developing objectives is discussed in chapter 4.) This means that educators must be extremely familiar with the curriculum's goals and objectives, and these must be kept in mind whenever observing children or planning activities. A well-balanced program should use assessment procedures that reflect that balance. Some programs are designed to focus primarily on one area of curriculum, such as development of language and communication skills. Obviously, these skills do not develop in isolation. Nevertheless, assessment procedures should have a heavy dose of items related to the development of language and communication.

Early childhood educators who are expected to understand the meaning of norm-referenced or standardized test reports should consult the *Buros Mental Measurements Yearbook* (Spies & Plake, 2005), as assessment instruments are thoroughly critiqued in this reference.

PROGRAM MONITORING AND EVALUATION

As noted earlier, federal law does use the term *evaluation* to refer to the process used to determine eligibility for services (see chapter 4). Although *evaluation* is sometimes used interchangeably with the terms *assessment* and *diagnosis*, evaluation is considered here as separate and vital to the development of quality programs for young children with special needs. There are generally two purposes for

program monitoring and evaluation: (a) to collect evaluative information that is used as the basis for ongoing program decision making and (b) to provide evaluative information for external support agencies, such as the Office of Special Education and the Danforth Foundation.

Evaluative information is used in making value judgments as to whether an instructional program produced the desired results. Evaluators discuss two types of evaluation: formative and summative. With **formative evaluation,** data on the progress of children are collected periodically and used to make ongoing program changes. **Summative evaluation** is concerned with the overall effectiveness of a program. It is a final accounting of program success. Testing typically is done at the beginning of an instructional program and at the end to determine whether desirable learning changes have occurred.

Early Childhood Educator's Role

Often teachers in early intervention programs have had little input into curriculum planning and program evaluation. Present practice, demanding teacher accountability, makes their participation in these areas a necessity. Teachers may or may not be directly involved in the process of gathering information to determine the effectiveness of a program. Some programs choose to acquire assistance from an outside agency to conduct the evaluation. These evaluations are usually summative in nature.

However, evaluation procedures must be planned at the beginning of a program to ensure ease of information gathering and to avoid the hazard of gathering data that are not relevant to the instructional program. Information gathered during the formative or ongoing assessment of a child's progress is usually appropriate in making summative program evaluations. Whenever ongoing assessment information is used to make value judgments about a program's effectiveness, teachers are most certainly involved. Therefore, the more organized, objective, and thorough a teacher is when observing and recording, the easier program evaluation will be.

CHANGING PHILOSOPHIES AND PRACTICES

Practices in identification, assessment, and evaluation are changing rapidly. New systems for describing special education services and the children who need them are evolving. It should be recognized that practices in some communities may vary somewhat from those described here.

Over time, the trend has shifted away from categorical descriptions such as *retarded* and *learning disabled* and toward descriptions that convey an understanding of the intervention needs of children. The emphasis is not on diagnosis of a problem to be found in the child but rather on (a) analysis of the specific instructional needs of the child, (b) determination of services required to meet these needs, and (c) avoidance of the stigma that can accompany traditional labeling. Both the kinds of tests used and the interpretations made of resulting information are changing. Greater care is given to recognizing cultural influences, previous experiences, daily environment, and the stress placed on children during testing.

The recognition of the child's interaction with the environment has added a vital dimension to the assessment picture. The **ecological approach** includes community and cultural influences as well as the complex interactions young children with disabilities have with family and others in their life space. Gargiulo and Kilgo (2005) state that "assessment information is not very useful when little or no emphasis is placed on the context in which children develop and the influence the environment has on skill acquisition" (p. 126).

In the past, many developmental assessments focused on singular areas of functioning and used rigidly administered standardized tests. Because these tests lack breadth and depth, they led to fragmented views of a child's functioning and neglected to consider the larger environmental context in which the child functions. It was, then, difficult to construct a comprehensive intervention plan based on incomplete information. Currently, assessments are being designed to address a wider range of child

and parent caregiver behaviors and to be viewed within a broader context of a child's experiential world.

Ecological Validity

This move toward an ecobehavioral approach to assessment allows for understanding of the community and cultural influences as well as the complex interactions young children have with family and others in their life space. Greater effort is being made to observe children in settings with which they are familiar. Children are being followed as they behave in the context of normally occurring routines such as eating and playing. Parents are included as interacting partners to help ensure the **ecological validity** of the observations. Ecologically valid assessments not only help the interventionist understand what skills are demonstrated by the child at home but also give clues to those behaviors that are functionally relevant to the family. This practice allows parents and professionals to agree on intervention goals that have meaning and relevance within the child's real-life environment of home and community. Ecologically valid assessments would not allow a stranger to conduct assessment activities in unfamiliar settings, a traditional practice. Instead, parents would be included as significant partners in the assessment process. Focus should be on naturalistic observation of children's behavior in the context of normally occurring routines. By observing normal daily activities such as eating, interacting during circle time, or participating in an art activity, professionals are aware of the extent to which children actually use skills.

Meisels (2001) elaborated on the tendency for reliance on structured tasks or questions to produce error in interpretation of young children's capacities:

- Young children have a restricted ability to comprehend assessment cues.

- Young children's verbal and perceptual-motor response capabilities are limited.

- Some types of questions require complex information-processing skills that young children do not possess.

- Young children may have difficulty understanding what is being asked of them in an assessment situation, and they may not be able to control their behavior to meet these demands.

Unfortunately, professionals who are under pressure to make quick decisions too often revert to their experiences with procedures and instruments developed to assess competencies in older children. This tendency to assess functioning of infants and young children with tests or scales already in existence tends to underestimate the abilities of children in those areas that are hard to measure, such as social skill development and functioning of a child within the context of his or her family.

THE EARLY INTERVENTION TEAM

Today, the team approach is considered to be an essential component of good early intervention programs. The number and type of professional team members vary with the perception of the needs of the child and family, the approach taken, and the financial resources of the program. A brief description of the roles various specialists play on early intervention teams is found in chapter 10. It must be remembered that parents or other caregivers are an essential part of the team throughout all aspects of the early intervention process. To be effective, the team approach requires participants to collaborate fully with one another. To do so, they must possess good communication skills, the ability to solve problems, and knowledge of available resources. Most of all, team members must demonstrate respect for one another.

A review of the literature reveals three primary approaches to team development. The most traditional model is the **multidisciplinary team approach,** in which each professional conducts his or her own assessment and intervention in isolation. Although professionals may confer with one another, consultation is not necessarily systematic and planned. Team members who work through an **interdisciplinary team approach** often work together in the same environment. Even though each member carries out his or her

Photo by Anthony Magnacca/Merrill

own assessment and intervention, there is frequent communication and planning within the team.

A model that has recently received considerable emphasis is the **transdisciplinary team approach** (Grisham-Brown, 2000). Transdisciplinary team members share their expertise and may cross the boundaries of their professional disciplines. All team members become sensitive to understanding the professional perspectives of other team members. Transdisciplinary team members must be open to sharing their expertise with others and open to learning new skills. By doing so, they are in a position to maximize what they can offer to a child and his or her family. This approach is more thoroughly explained in chapter 10.

Family-Directed Child Assessment

When family members participate actively on early intervention teams, family-based assessment is more likely to occur. **Family-directed child assessment** involves selecting assessment questions that are important to the family. It also means choosing assessment procedures that can answer these high-priority questions and incorporating family input throughout the assessment process. Practitioners in

the field of early intervention must be certain to develop procedures that will enable assessment of a family's concerns, priorities, and resources along with the child's strengths and needs without being too intrusive into the family system. This topic will be covered in greater depth later in this chapter.

USE OF STANDARDIZED TESTS WITH YOUNG CHILDREN

Early intervention specialists are increasingly looking to observation of the child in interaction with trusted caregivers and appreciation of the child's core functional capacities as the cornerstone of assessment (Wieder & Greenspan, 2001). The use of **standardized tests** is increasingly being criticized, as these structured test approaches look at what a young child can and cannot do only in relationship to a defined set of stimuli. This "snapshot" of the child's capabilities taken with a particular instrument is not representative of the child's usual functioning in the context of everyday living.

Contributing to this move away from routine standardized testing are (a) the lack of reliability and validity of standardized tests for use with young children, (b) the need to obtain information that can easily be transformed into individualized instruction

plans, (c) the cultural biases built into many standardized instruments, and (d) the influence of situational factors on test performance. Therefore, we agree with those experts who believe that structured tests should be used only if absolutely needed and only as one part of a comprehensive approach to assessment. Even then, structured tests should be appropriate and used only if they provide additional meaningful information.

These concerns can be demonstrated in the following scenario. Imagine you are 4 years old. Your mother, who seems nervous, takes you to a place that sort of reminds you of the doctor's office.

A strange man introduces himself to me and says he would like to play with some toys and show me some pictures. He asks my mother to sit off to the side. Though I can't really see her, I know she is still worried about something.

The man talks funny. Though he says some words like my mother does, many words are unclear. The man shows me some toys which look kind of interesting, but I have trouble figuring out what he wants me to do with them. I have the feeling I need to be very careful and not do the wrong thing. He seems in a hurry because he only shows me each toy for about a minute or so. I turn around to check on my mother. She gives me a funny look. Is she upset?

Next the man shows me some pictures. Though I enjoy my picture books at home, these pictures are new to me, and I'm not sure what to call them. He asks me different questions like "What is that?" or "What do you do with this?" I'm surprised that he doesn't know the answers to these questions. If he doesn't know, I'm pretty sure I don't! I'm only 4.

The room seems hot; my new shirt is scratchy, I would like to leave now. It seems like hours since I got on the bus with my mother to come here.

This scenario is not exaggerated. Although we can see gradual changes in our approaches to assessment, standardized instruments are still in common use. Most young children do not perform optimally in situations that are not familiar to them: unfamiliar adults, perhaps speaking an unfamiliar dialect or language; unfamiliar materials; unfamiliar rooms and furniture; and unfamiliar emotions and behavior exhibited by their parents. Many young children will not perform on demand in such situations. Standardized tests constrain children's natural curiosity and initiative, placing them in a responsive mode. Also, such tests focus only on specific skills or products rather than on the processes of learning. Process characteristics such as cognitive style, locus of control, interaction style, mastery motivation, and tempo are rarely the focus of traditional assessment.

Cautious Use of Norm-Referenced Tests

Standardized tests are instruments designed to be administered by a **trained examiner** following specified, standardized procedures. Depending on the purpose, standardized tests or assessments could be completed by psychologists or psychometrists; speech, language, and hearing clinicians; pediatricians; or social workers. Typically, these examiners report test scores and norm-referenced information. Even though standardized instruments are often required when establishing eligibility for services, their misuse continues to be widespread. Therefore, considerable information about the use of norm-referenced or standardized tests is included in this chapter.

Norm-referenced test scores reflect comparison of the performance of the child being tested with performance of other children of the same chronological age who took the test when norms were being established. Thus, a child with a mental age of 3 years and 6 months (3–6) is said to have performed on the norm-referenced tests, such as the Stanford-Binet intelligence test, in a way that *most* children do who are three and a half years old.

If the child being tested were actually younger and still performs as a child of 3 years and 6 months, he would then be considered to be above average. If, on the other hand, the child being tested were much older and still performed as a child who is 3 years and 6 months of age, this much older child would be considered to be cognitively delayed according to the Stanford-Binet.

Instruments such as those that assess mental age are of little value when assessing the performance of children with disabilities or those from a minority culture if the normative standards do not take into

Photo by Anthony Magnacca/Merrill

account the influence of the children's unique conditions or the nature of their development. *Children who have developed in a different manner by virtue of having disabilities or being bilingual or deprived cannot be compared logically to children who have been raised in what society considers to be normal circumstances.* Only when used with caution by a skilled examiner can standardized, norm-referenced tests provide information worthy of consideration for planning individualized instruction programs.

For example, norm-referenced tables typically are used by speech, language, and hearing clinicians as a comparison for a child's receptive and expressive language skills. Usually children have internalized most of the rules of grammar and syntax by age 4. Those who do not speak distinctly and in grammatically correct ways by that age are described as having delayed speech and language development. Useful information can be gained about the specific nature of a child's delay by analyzing performance on individual items of standardized, norm-referenced tests. Practitioners who are skilled in analyzing performances on individual test items will note patterns in development and behavior that may contribute to instructional goals and objectives.

Awareness of specific task performance can also be helpful to the teacher who has an understanding of the thinking and acting processes involved in test items missed. Knowledge of weaknesses will allow the teacher to use informal observational techniques to observe the child doing similar tasks. This observation will create increased understanding of how or why the child missed the items. The opportunity to refute or corroborate the original test results is thus provided by observation.

When observing her student, Ms. McLynn, another teacher, had the uneasy feeling that Danny could not hear well, even though he had passed the auditory screening test (see Exhibit 3–2). She decided to play games with Danny, such as asking him to point to the source of sound when blindfolded and to repeat simple sentences. Danny had much more difficulty with these tasks than the other 4-year-olds in the room. Ms. McLynn became even more convinced that Danny must have a complete audiological examination. She spoke to Danny's parents, who agreed to take Danny to the speech and hearing clinic at the nearby university.

This illustration emphasizes that it is the responsibility of the teacher to determine whether a child's test scores are an accurate reflection of abilities. Only observation on a day-to-day basis can confirm or refute examiner conclusions based on test performance. After all, standardized tests provide only a sample of the child's behavior at a specific point in time.

Considerations for Interpreting Standardized Test Results

Educators need to be alert to hidden penalties that may understate test results of children who have disabilities and those who are culturally different. What amounts to impossible response requirements for some children distorts even further the inappropriateness of single-test normative samples. A recent example comes to mind. Consider the validity of a norm-referenced IQ on a child with severe visual disabilities who was given a Stanford-Binet test with no accommodations for the visual impairments. What is even more disturbing is the fact that the child's

Exhibit 3–2

Ms. McLynn's Observation

Ms. McLynn teaches a preschool class of 4-year-olds. For several weeks she has been puzzled about Danny. He just won't pay attention. Sometimes when she calls him he comes right away. Other times he pays no attention until she raises her voice and speaks firmly. Often he acts as if he hears her call, but then he looks for her in the wrong direction. Or when she tells him to do something he does something else. Then he just gives her a blank look when she explains all over again what she wants him to do. (At first Ms. McLynn had wondered whether he had a hearing problem, but the nurse said he had passed the hearing screening.) Today she has decided to observe him carefully and take notes. Her aide, Ms. Cain, is playing a game with 4 children, while 10 others, including Danny, are playing with various toys and games. Here is what she wrote.

April 1, 2007

Danny is playing in the corner with some toy animals. Another child called him but he didn't turn, so Susan poked him. He turned, surprised. Tim said, "Danny, I want that little duck." When Danny gave him the dog, Tim said, "Not dog, you silly. I want the duck." Danny obligingly gave him the toy truck! So Tim went over and picked up the duck.

Danny walked over to the clay table and began to pound the clay. He hit it with all his 4-year-old's vigor.

Remember to ask Danny's mother about allergies. His nose always seems to be dripping. Even though he passed our screening, he just doesn't seem to be hearing.

mental capacity was classified and reported according to the score received.

It is the teacher who may need to confirm or refute the face validity of test results. Do scores seem reasonable when reality tested against the teacher's observational experiences with the child? To provide assistance to teachers who will be expected to interpret the results of tests or reports filed by diagnostic specialists, selected measurement terms can be found in the glossary at the end of this text. An understanding of these helps teachers explain the results of assessment procedures to parents and/or instructional aides, just as they help in the use of test information for the development of instructional strategies.

But even before becoming involved in the assessment process, teachers should talk with the specialists involved in their children's multidisciplinary assessment. They should discuss the assessment procedures used by these specialists and techniques for interpretation and translation of diagnosis into instructional outcomes and goals. Such a discussion helps the teacher understand the situational factors that may influence the performance of children observed by these specialists.

Importance of Reliable and Valid Tests

Tests developed for young children usually lack rigor in terms of reliability and validity; therefore, it is difficult to use norm-referenced tests in developing educational plans with any confidence. The term **reliability** refers to the consistency or dependability of a testing procedure. It is the degree to which a child's score is a true score. That is, little or no error in measurement is present. The reliability of a test is often determined by comparing results from repeated administrations of the test (test–retest), by giving equivalent forms of the test, by comparing the results from each half (split-half), and by noting the consistency in rating between two or more scorers (interscorer). Even though it is essential to be certain that results do not reflect considerable error, many test manuals do not report results from efforts to determine the reliability. Consistency in

any performance is not characteristic of young children, but attempts must continue to be made to ensure as much reliability as possible when assessments are made.

When a test is reliable, it may not necessarily be valid. **Validity** refers to what a test measures and how well it does so. Does it measure what it is supposed to measure? For example, if a teacher wishes to determine a child's level of problem solving, then he or she must require the child to solve problems. Asking a child to identify pictures by pointing to those named and recording a resulting mental age score does not tell a child's potential for solving problems. A valid problem-solving test has not been given. Instead, a valid test for assessing a child's level of receptive language and ability to associate a verbal symbol with a visual symbol has been given.

Three types of validity are usually discussed: construct validity, content validity, and predictive validity. Of the three, **construct validity,** or the ability to determine how well a test measures the conceptual idea behind its construction, is the most difficult to determine. Today, many question whether intelligence tests actually measure the abstract quality called intelligence. **Content validity** assumes that the test has a representative sample of the behaviors it is supposed to measure. Tests of eye-motor coordination that omit eye-foot tasks do not include a truly representative sample of test items. **Predictive validity,** or **criterion-related validity,** is concerned with whether performance on the test items can predict actual achievement on another test that is supposed to measure related skills or future performance in related life skills.

Predictive validity is an issue of considerable concern to developers of screening or readiness tests. The very attempt to predict difficulties that have not occurred has long been known to be risky. Furthermore, ethical considerations interfere with attempts to do the research to determine if it is possible to accurately predict future behavior from assessment. That is, children are not expendable! When concerned adults learn of a child's potential learning problems through the diagnostic interpretation of testing, they feel compelled ethically to

implement remedial or preventive actions as soon as possible. If we know how to help children, it is unthinkable to withhold the help. Therefore, the researchers are prevented from conducting long-term studies to find out whether the predicted problems would occur if intervention were not available.

Rather than prevent children from obtaining the services they need, educators are choosing to rely less on test results and more on professional and parent observation and judgment. Increasing recognition of the serious lack of substantial reliability and validity characteristic of available instruments has left professionals little choice. The importance of what is sometimes called "clinical opinion" cannot be underestimated given the instability of intellectual abilities in young children and the variability from child to child. Well-trained professionals and observant parents, together, can contribute to well-informed clinical opinions.

Criterion-Referenced Techniques

Comparing a child's performance to that of other children the same age is the traditional norm-referenced assessment approach. By contrast, **criterion-referenced assessment** compares the child's performance to a standard or expected mastery of a skill. It also makes it possible to compare a child's performance to his or her previous performance as it is relative to some standard or criterion.

A few criterion-referenced instruments that provide information directly transferable to program objectives are the *Assessment, Evaluation and Programming Systems*, *Carolina Developmental Profile*, *Boehm Test of Basic Concepts*, and the *Brigance Diagnostic Inventory of Early Development*.

However, directors and teachers of preschools often choose to develop their own criterion-referenced measurement instruments. They have the advantage of being able to tie the assessment devices to the program objectives. In this era of standards-based curriculum, early educators can more readily determine if children are developing according to

appropriate standards (criterion) and can adjust their intervention techniques accordingly.

It should be readily apparent that criterion-referenced devices facilitate daily planning for children. Appropriate tasks are sequenced after doing a careful task analysis, and the child is requested to perform each item, beginning with the most difficult. Instruction begins with the first item a child cannot complete in a sequence. It is said that we assess from the top down, from the hardest to the easiest, and teach from the bottom up, from the easiest to the hardest. When assessing, concern is not with how well a child did in comparison to other children but with determining the next appropriate skill for a child to master. However, if the first item in a sequence is targeted, prerequisite skills must be considered and a task analysis completed in order to facilitate individualized instruction.

Although criterion-referenced tools, often in the form of checklists, do allow for the measurement of intraindividual progress, are readily translated into program objectives, usually cover a range of developmental areas, and allow for adaptations to accommodate disabilities, there are some process weaknesses to consider. First, items may not have been intended to be used as instructional goals, and the sequences of the items may not reflect the best teaching sequence. There may also be large gaps between items.

Some areas of the curriculum are more difficult to operationally define and task analyze than others (Alper & Mills, 2000). Of course, even though you may know what skill a child needs to develop, it takes creativity, knowledge, and patience to figure out how best to teach that skill. Alper and Mills (2000) list the steps in Exhibit 3-3 as typical of the development of criterion-referenced assessment. Task analysis is further discussed and illustrated in chapters 4, 5, and 7.

When planning a program for an individual child, a teacher obviously should be more concerned with identifying the specific skills that the child does or does not have than with knowing how the child compares to others. However, relying on data based on developmental milestones as the

---

Exhibit (3–3)

Developing Criterion-Referenced Assessment

1. Clearly define the specific set of instructional objectives to be assessed.
2. Task analyze each objective into a sequence of teachable steps or skills.
3. Operationally define each step in the task analysis.
4. Specify performance criteria for each skill assessed.
5. Select items to be assessed based on their match with skills taught in the curriculum.
6. Develop a reporting system that efficiently and accurately describes child performance.

---

primary source of instructional objectives can have a negative impact if a child's disabilities make attainment of typical milestones unrealistic. Also, the tendency to test very specific skills may not give a picture of any child's overall capability or potential. Finally, measuring skills that are being acquired does not consider whether a skill can be generalized. For example, there is a big developmental difference between a child who happens to place items correctly on a form board through trial and error and one who places the items correctly with obvious ease.

Curriculum-Based Techniques

Curriculum-based assessment, or **curriculum-referenced assessment,** is considered a form of criterion-referenced assessment. Therefore, the same cautions must be considered. Curricular objectives are used as the standard against which performance is judged. The child's performance is observed on tasks requiring skills that are targets of the curriculum. As Neisworth and Bagnato (2005) state, curriculum-based assessment is "a form of criterion-based assessment in which the standards to be achieved are the objectives that comprise the program of instruction or therapy" (p. 62).

An example of such a tool is the *Hawaii Early Learning Profile*, which includes a manual that includes activities for intervention. Curriculum-based

assessments are popular because they provide direct linkage between assessment and the development of curriculum-related intervention goals and objectives. Task analysis is also the procedure often used to break the curriculum-related skills into "testable" and "teachable" behavioral steps. Although criterion-referenced assessment allows direct measurement of a child's progress toward fulfillment of curricula objectives, it is valuable only if the curriculum is relevant and useful for that particular child.

Therefore, in order for the use of either criterion- or curriculum-referenced assessment techniques to be effective, the assessment team must be certain that the measures have high intervention or treatment validity (Neisworth and Bagnato, 2000). That is, there must be a definite link between the assessment items, individual program planning, and individual progress. To this end, citing the work of Wolery, Strain, and Bailey (1992), Gargiulo and Kilgo (2005) consider the elements in Exhibit 3–4 to be critical to solid program planning and delivery.

CURRENT APPROACHES TO THE ASSESSMENT OF YOUNG CHILDREN

The previous discussion points out only some of the serious issues that exist with regard to the validity and appropriateness of use of standardized assessment instruments with infants and young children with special needs. Many years ago, the NAEYC (1988)

Exhibit **3–4**

Critical Elements of Assessment

1. Assessment should include a variety of measures in a variety of settings.
2. Assessment results should provide a detailed description of the child's functioning.
3. Assessment activities should involve the child's family.
4. Assessment activities should be conducted by professionals from different disciplines.
5. Assessment activities should result in a list of high-priority objectives.

---

produced a position statement that decried the use of formal standardized instruments with young children who have no disabilities. Such arguments continue to be even more valid for young children with disabilities.

A more appropriate assessment model being described in the literature is dynamic assessment. **Dynamic assessment models** are concerned not with a child's current performance output but rather with understanding learning styles and potential through careful observation of how children learn in a dynamic, interactive setting.

Also more appropriate are **authentic assessment strategies,** which strive to obtain information from multiple sources (e.g., direct observation, parent report, child interviews, samples of the child's work, and so on). Authentic assessment occurs when the observations are embedded in the curriculum rather than used on demand (Meisels, 2001). The argument is presented that young children cannot possibly be understood and appropriately described on the basis of a single, highly structured, performance-based test at an isolated point in time.

Attention is being drawn to what Meisels (2001) and others describe as **functional assessment:** "This approach focuses on everyday, naturally occurring, practical behaviors and accomplishments that are easily recognized by parents and service providers and that are central to the emergence of children's competence" (p. 7). Daily achievements are learned in context and should be assessed in context. Linder's

(1993) classic *Play-Based Assessment* and the *Infant-Toddler Developmental Assessment* developed by Provence, Erikson, Vater, and Palmeri (1995) are examples of this approach. More recently published is the *Ounce Scale*, which provides yet another strategy for collecting functional information (Meisels, Dombro, Marsden, Weston, & Jewkes, 2002).

Building Assessment on Multiple Sources of Information

Early intervention specialists readily agree that the assessment process must build collaboratively on information derived directly from families. Part C reinforces this approach by requiring that the process begin with a thorough understanding of the family's concerns, priorities, and resources. Professionals are expected to seek from the parents a detailed description of their child's developmental history and current capacities in all primary areas of development. After listening carefully to parents' views of their child's strengths and challenges, it is recommended that there be direct observations of the child. These observations should include interaction with caregivers and unstructured play in a familiar setting. With very young children, it is further suggested that interaction between the child and clinician be arranged, if appropriate. Then specific assessments of individual functions can be scheduled if enough information to fulfill the purpose of assessment has not already been obtained.

By following this additive approach, a picture of the "whole" child can be developed by integrating the data obtained from multiple sources. Using a developmental framework, professionals and families can, through open dialogue, create an understanding of the child's competencies within the caregiving and learning environments that will lead to optimal program planning.

Using Naturalistic Observations

Naturalistic observation, or **direct observation,** is a method of gathering information about children that is currently being favored over gathering information through formal tests. Naturalistic observation occurs when assessment information is gathered about a child through careful, systematic observations of that child in his or her natural environment. Recordings about various aspects of a child's behavior can be gathered during one observation period. For example, by stepping back and watching children as they naturally play with one another or with a familiar adult, information can easily be gathered about aspects of behavior such as expressive communication, social skills, motor skills, and task persistence. Exhibit 3–3 illustrates one such naturalistic observation.

A major advantage of direct observation is that skills observed are not artificially divided as they are with traditional testing procedures. Direct observation allows the assessor to learn directly just how a child is capable of functioning when faced with the everyday demands of his or her environment. The guidelines in this chapter are included to help interventionists develop critical observation skills.

The term **performance assessment** represents procedures that require multiple observations within natural settings. Performance assessments refer to any methods "that allow children to demonstrate their knowledge, skills, dispositions, and other aspects of development and expression through solving problems, acting on their environments, interacting with individuals in their settings, experimenting, talking and moving" (Meisels, 1996, p. 37). Such

procedures allow for multiple observations on which to judge a child's performance from a more holistic, functional point of view. It allows us to make hypotheses built on observations during the process or within the context of intervention. We can then learn how to intervene more effectively.

Play-Based Assessment

One type of assessment considered to be more "authentic" than standardized tests is play-based assessment. Play-based assessment addresses some of the concerns raised about the appropriateness of standardized tests for young children with disabilities.

According to Linder (1993, 2000), play-based assessment offers a more authentic alternative to traditional formal assessment using standardized tests. An inviting play environment is created in a preschool classroom or child-care center or even in the child's own home. Various interesting toys and materials are used, and children are encouraged to explore and initiate their own play actions and interactions. In the transdisciplinary model of play-based assessment, only one professional and the parent interact with the child during the assessment. Other professionals may observe the interactions, but they do not directly conduct their own assessment. (This is an example of "arena assessment.") As mentioned earlier, the examiner in the play-based approach is a "facilitator"—someone who is highly skilled in encouraging and observing children's play.

The Linder model is not simply an open-ended free-play session. Rather, it is an organized sequence of play situations in which very specific observations are made across all developmental domains (e.g., cognition, communication, social-emotional, and sensorimotor). Linder recommends that the assessment be videotaped. The child is carefully observed by the transdisciplinary team in the following situations:

1. *Unstructured facilitation.* In this situation the child is free to play in any area. The facilitator follows the child's lead, occasionally attempting to encourage the next higher level of play.

2. *Structured facilitation.* Those skills that were not demonstrated in the first phase can be encouraged in this phase of the assessment. The facilitator becomes somewhat more directive; however, the flavor of the activity is still responsive and interactive.

3. *Child-child interaction.* In this phase of the assessment, another child who is familiar to the target child (if possible) is brought into the play area. The facilitator again assumes a responsive rather than a directive mode. If the two children do not interact with one another, the facilitator may attempt to encourage interaction—for example, through the introduction of an interesting toy or cooperative game.

4. *Parent-child interaction.* In this situation the parent is asked to engage the child in ways that would be typical of what they would do at home. Although the primary purpose of this phase is to obtain more typical responses from the child as he or she interacts with a familiar adult, it can also be used to observe the quality of parent–child interaction.

5. *Motor play.* In this phase the child is directed to the available large motor play equipment and encouraged to climb, ride a bike, crawl, and so on. The occupational or physical therapist may wish to be directly involved with the child at this point in order to better assess muscle tone, balance, and other physical factors.

6. *Snack.* The final phase of the assessment is a snack. The child included in the child–child phase should also be included in the snack activity, as is the parent. This activity provides the opportunity to observe various self-help skills as well as oral motor skills and social interactions.

Limitations of Play-Based Assessment.   Clearly, play-based assessment as described above offers a richness of qualitative information that cannot typically be obtained through standardized testing. In addition, such information can be used directly in program planning for the child. However, as with any single approach, there are limitations to consider. Play-based assessment is often time consuming and requires the coordination and cooperation of several

professionals. Also, some areas of development, such as receptive language or auditory processing, may be difficult to assess in a play situation and may still require more formal standardized measure. Children with severe physical disabilities may require more detailed assessment by a physical therapist. Finally, some of the very criticisms of standardized assessment may also be issues for play-based assessment. Some children from culturally different backgrounds may not be familiar or comfortable with many of the toys. Some children are not object oriented and do not typically play with "things." Also, some children will not play comfortably with a stranger or with several people watching. Children with severe cognitive disabilities, with multiple sensory disabilities, or with severe behavioral difficulties may not respond well to unstructured, unfamiliar play settings.

Despite these cautions, the shift toward more functional assessment models in the field of early childhood special education is an important one. It will no doubt significantly improve the quality and usefulness of assessment information and make the interface between assessment and intervention a much more seamless link.

BECOMING A SKILLED OBSERVER

As previously stated, the target, setting, time, and conditions should be determined by the purpose of the observation. Informal observations help provide a more comprehensive view of the child than the observations obtained solely with the aid of structured inventories, checklists, rating scales, and tests. The focus of the observation is limited only by the imagination and time of the observer. It is important to observe a variety of situations during different times of the day. The focus should be more general when teachers are assessing the overall development of a child.

On the other hand, if teachers are trying to determine whether a child has accomplished a particular objective, they will narrow their observation to a very specific behavior under specified conditions. Most teachers will refer to a written objective to guide

their observation. For example, if the individualized education program (IEP) requires the child to learn to button a coat, the observer will watch specifically to see whether the child can button a coat, under what conditions, and with what degree of skill.

Observing How Children Perform a Task

The primary purpose of most teacher observation is to determine the strengths and weaknesses in children's learning repertoires in order to develop instructional goals and strategies. The teacher should not be overly concerned with etiology (investigation of causative factors) or assignment of diagnostic labels. The teacher must instead be concerned with exactly what children can (and cannot) do and how they do it. In closely analyzing task performances, the teacher observes children's processes or styles of performance in addition to determining whether children can perform specific tasks.

For example, when asked to describe what is happening in a picture, does a child respond impulsively? Or does he or she give a more deliberate or reflective response, taking time to note details while carefully scanning the picture? When copying a figure, does the child seem to study the picture and plan? Or does he or she start drawing with only a brief reference to the drawing presented?

Considering the Special Challenges When English Is the Child's Second Language

Too many children are considered to be developmentally delayed because observers do not have sufficient experience with culturally and linguistically diverse children. Professionals have long been challenged with the dilemma of how to facilitate nonbiased assessment that does not penalize children from diverse backgrounds for the uniqueness of their background or experience. The tendency is to measure only skills and abilities valued by the dominant culture. Careful observation must include information about the child's development, the sociocultural context and values of

his or her family, and comparison of the child's development to the developmental patterns of other children from a similar background. For example, observation of self-help skills must take into account the fact that some Asian families do not promote self-feeding as early in life as does the dominant culture.

A variety of observation procedures should be used, including observation in natural environments; observation of play in comfortable, familiar settings; and interviews with family members and care providers. As Conroy and Paolini (2000) stated, "A culturally sensitive assessment begins with a nonbiased philosophy by professionals who are flexible and respectful of individual difference. Active family involvement in the assessment process should be encouraged and may help to minimize cultural bias" (p. 216). Given the importance of culturally fair assessment, techniques are given in Exhibit 3–5.

Realizing Environmental Influences on Assessment Results

Various researchers continue to discuss the importance of focusing on the interaction of the child with the environment rather than focusing on either the child or the environment independently. Finding very young children difficult to test, Salvia and Ysseldyke (2007) state,

Infants between 6 and 18 months are distressed by unfamiliar adults. Although they may have better responses to strangers when held by their caregivers, they may still refuse to respond to an unfamiliar adult. Infants and preschoolers may be very active, inattentive, and distractible; they frequently perform inconsistently in strange situations. Because the language of these children is, by definition, undeveloped, they may not completely understand even simple questions and oral requests. Thus traditional assessment formats in which students respond to examiner questions can be problematic. Not surprisingly, many toddlers and preschoolers are described as untestable. (p. 500)

The influence of situational factors again suggests that the teacher must thoroughly understand and be ready to vary the conditions of observation to get the most comprehensive view of a child's learning strengths and weaknesses.

Techniques to Accomplish Culturally Fair Assessment

1. Use multiple assessment techniques within naturalistic settings, involving the parents or other caregivers as significant partners in the process.
2. Examine test items to be certain they are not biased against children or families of a certain cultural background.
3. Examine test manuals to determine whether the group to which the child is being compared is culturally compatible.
4. Give directions in the child's native language.
5. Use a multidisciplinary or transdisciplinary process so that more than one professional, along with the parents, can contribute to hypotheses developed from the observations.

Recognizing the Interrelationship of Skills

Finally, observers must be aware of and attuned to the interrelationship of skills. Children who are concentrating on the development of a motor skill may or may not exhibit what might be considered to be normal verbal or social interaction with other children during that period. On the other hand, children who are skilled in the motor activity may exhibit greater verbal fluency because of their confidence in their motor skills and lack of verbal inhibition.

Young children do not develop skills in isolation. The most obvious example of the interdependence of skill development is noted by psycholinguists in their study of language development. Chapter 9 elaborates on the importance of realizing that the potential for language development is present during every waking moment, assuming the child does not

Photo by Lisa Wadors

have severe impairments and is in a relatively stimulating environment. The teacher then must be aware of the child's total performance even when focusing on a single aspect of behavior.

In summary, observation is a complex, critical skill that can be developed only through systematic practice. The importance of becoming skilled in objective, systematic observation is obvious. Therefore, it is imperative that teachers strive to incorporate the following six abilities into their observational repertoire:

1. In-depth understanding of what is considered to be normal behavior.

2. Skill in recognizing risk factors or danger signals.

3. Ability to follow the guidelines for responsible observation.

4. Ability to choose types of observational techniques appropriate to the purpose of the observation.

5. Awareness of the influence of performance styles, motivational factors, environmental variables, and extraneous behaviors on the judgments to be made about children's strengths and weaknesses.

6. Continuous practice of professionalism through respect for confidentiality, restraint from labeling, and attempts to counteract any tendencies toward placing stereotyped expectations on children.

Guidelines for Successful Observation

Observation is the skill of deliberately listening to and watching children's behaviors. They can be observed alone or in a group, at any time of the day, and under a variety of circumstances. While observing, the teacher notes aspects of appearance or behavior. Specific behaviors to be observed are determined by the purpose of the observation. Observers differ considerably in the process of recording information. Teachers often just make mental notes of what they see or hear, but use of an organized record-keeping form results in more systematic recording procedures. If the purpose of the observation is to assess the child's progress in an

individualized program, systematic recording is essential to ensure objective, comprehensive data collection. The following guidelines help prepare teachers to become systematic, objective observers.

1. *Focus on observing exactly what the child does.* Record special, detailed observations of precisely what the child *does* and *says*. Use action verbs. Note the date, time, setting, what preceded the child's action or reaction, and what followed the behavior. *Do not* record inferences or opinions. Write down what is actually seen or heard.

2. *Record the observational details as soon after the observation as possible.* With practice, teachers develop the ability to participate and observe simultaneously by making mental notes. However, it is important to plan schedules so that recording of details can be done as quickly as possible. Details are important and are easily forgotten.

3. *Observe in a variety of settings and at different times during the child's day.* Changes in time and setting will often provide clues about children's interests. For example, children who are not comfortable on the playground may seek the solitude they never seek when in the classroom. Or they may become bullies on the playground, whereas they are self-controlled within the classroom. Children may be overly active when playing with other children but not so when playing alone. There may be a certain time of day, perhaps just before lunch, when some children are especially irritable. Identifying these times and circumstances makes it possible to plan needed changes that create a smoothly run day. Watching for patterns often leads to an explanation of behavior.

4. *Be realistic in scheduling observations.* When the purpose of the observation is to determine the developmental level at which a child is functioning, it is critical to be able to observe and make notes as often and in as many situations as necessary to get a complete record of the developmental areas under concern. Observations that are haphazard or incomplete jeopardize the correctness of any resulting hypotheses. Be realistic when planning observation time. Be certain that there is a chance the observation

will actually occur. On some days the only available observation time might be free-choice time.

5. *Begin by focusing on one child at a time.* Focusing on one child at a time and using checklists or rating scales will help develop observational skills without running the risk of missing or forgetting information.

6. *Avoid being obvious.* Avoid calling attention to the child being observed or the fact that the observation is taking place. Interact as naturally as possible. Be seated in a place normal for the teacher to be during the activity that is being observed. For example, when observing playground activities, teachers usually post themselves in a spot providing optimal visibility. Stand or sit in the usual position when observing any activity.

7. *At all times, ensure confidentiality.* Notes must *never* be left around; a system of coding names should be developed to ensure privacy. *Never* discuss observations in front of other children or parents of other children. Read and become familiar with the Family Educational Rights and Privacy Act of 1974 (P.L. 93–380) because it is important to be aware of the parents' rights to read the records created. Never send or give data collected from observation or test scores to outside agencies or individuals without written parental permission.

8. *Choose a workable recording system.* Teachers often need to experiment with file cards, notebooks, and three-ring binders to determine exactly what process is most convenient for them. Of course, the system used depends on the purpose and method of the observation. Well-organized, easy-to-review notes will facilitate the detection of patterns of behavior that may be vital to real understanding of the child.

9. *Share your observational reports with parents as appropriate.* Objective evidence of child progress is always welcome.

The Portfolio and Its Use with Young Children

Teachers have always gathered together samples of students' work and assembled them into folders to display to parents at evening "open-house" gatherings.

This process has become known as **portfolio assessment** and is receiving attention as a form of authentic assessment. Mindes (2003) characterizes a portfolio as one type of performance-based assessment.

Jarrett, Browne, and Wallin (2006) describe the assessment portfolio as "a purposeful collection of productions that demonstrates the child's baseline development (i.e., developmental status at the beginning of the intervention plan), growth, progress, effort and achievement over time" (p. 23). A portfolio portrays his or her efforts in one or more areas. It is the place to keep all the information known about a child.

For a young child, a portfolio might include records of various forms of systematic observation, video or tape recordings, photographs, and samples of a child's productive efforts, such as drawings. In short, a portfolio (contained in a folder, box, expanding file, and so on) includes the visual evidence of the types of observations described below.

Decisions about what items to place in a portfolio will depend on the purpose of the portfolio. Noonan and McCormick (2006) suggested that "each entry should have a descriptive label that tells the date, the person who provided the entry, and a notation as to why it is important" (p. 114). Whenever possible, children should be involved in choosing the items to be included. All items should be dated and can be arranged according to curriculum area or category of development.

As an assessment technique, portfolios can be used to document an individual child's progress over time and can be compared with a standard of performance that is consistent with the curriculum and appropriate developmental expectations. Portfolios are, obviously, a terrific tool for facilitating communication with parents. The types of observation techniques that follow provide valuable information to be included in portfolios.

Types of Observation Samples

Teachers should observe children in a variety of situations with as many purposes as they have objectives for the children. The particular technique chosen should relate directly to the purpose established. The

following list describes some of the more common types of observation. As the list progresses, the techniques become more standardized (formal), requiring greater systematic planning and structure from the observer.

1. *Photographs.* Photographs provide a quick, easy method of obtaining children's reactions to various lessons. They provide an automatic record of involvement. These pictures can be taken at planned intervals to demonstrate sequential development. A dual purpose is served when the snapshots are used to stimulate language development, as discussed in chapter 8. Using photographs in bulletin board displays offers repeated chances to encourage the development of self-esteem. With the advent of digital cameras, children can receive instant feedback and parents can view the images from home.

2. *Electronic recordings.* With the advancement of instructional technology, more and more classrooms commonly utilize electronic recording techniques. Teachers have the advantage of participating directly in the activities and can later review the children's responses to their unique teaching styles. However, care must be taken to prevent the presence of recording equipment from distorting the observation. Children thoroughly enjoy observing and listening to themselves. Again, such techniques provide ideal opportunities for language stimulation and allow the teacher to collect language samples. Moving pictures have long been used to provide evidence of development in areas such as motor coordination and social interaction. Local service clubs are often willing to make donations to help with film and processing costs.

3. *Collection of children's work.* Although early childhood education is usually process oriented rather than product oriented, there are opportunities to collect children's work. Collecting samples of such things as a child's paintings, tracings, cuttings, and attempts to print his or her name allows the teacher to analyze progress and to make this obvious to parents.

4. *Activity lists.* Programs that provide activity centers with some degree of free-choice time may post lists of children's names to be dated or checked off at each center area. By listing each child's name and the length of participation, the child's interests and level of involvement can be determined. The teacher will need to decide whether choices should be limited or children should be encouraged to broaden their participation.

5. *Anecdotal records, diaries, and logs.* Teachers record specific details of their observation, including exact behavior; precisely what precedes the behavior; and any reactions to the behavior, time, setting, and individuals involved. Care is taken to avoid making judgments, choosing isolated events, or overgeneralizing from atypical incidents. Systematic and regular recording allows the teacher to study patterns of behavior.

6. *Passports.* The passport (Shea & Bauer, 2002) is an ordinary spiral notebook that the child carries daily to and from home and the intervention program. An example of a passport is found in chapter 2. All adults who work with the child are encouraged to make observational notations in the passport. Records are required to be brief, positive, honest, and consistent. The objective of the passport is to promote positive parent–teacher communication and cooperation.

7. *Time sampling and event recording.* In time sampling the observer selects specific behaviors that are readily observable and occur often. A few behaviors are chosen, and their occurrence is recorded on a prepared recording sheet during regularly scheduled, short observation periods. Unlike time sampling, event recording is not restricted to specific preplanned time intervals. A targeted behavior, such as temper tantrums, is recorded on occurrence. This method is often used with infrequently occurring behaviors.

8. *Checklists and rating scales.* Checklists and rating scales help specify exactly what the observer is to be observing. Use of such instruments makes it possible to vary the observer and still maintain consistency in the behavior that is observed. Illustrations of checklists and developmental scales are included throughout this text and in most texts in the field of early childhood special education. However, teachers are encouraged to design their own to ensure that

the behavior observed is related to the goals and objectives of their program.

9. *Criterion-referenced tests.* Criterion-referenced devices or tests are designed to compare a child with a set of standards rather than with other children. Commercial tools usually establish the set of standards by selecting and sequencing items from several standardized developmental scales.

10. *Norm-referenced tests.* Norm-referenced tests provide the most standardized information-gathering opportunities for observation. As stated earlier, the intent of norm-referenced measurement is to compare a child's performance to the performance of other children who are the same chronological age. Few norm-referenced instruments are useful in planning individualized programs for children. These tests tend to be less reliable with young children. Norm-referenced tests are most useful for establishing eligibility, whereas criterion-referenced measures can be linked directly to the curriculum. However, funding agencies sometimes do require norm-referenced tests to complete program evaluations. Cautions when using such tests were discussed earlier in this chapter.

LINKING ASSESSMENT TO CURRICULUM

During the past decade, early childhood special educators have become aware of the need to link assessment processes to the curriculum that is implemented. The *AEPS Curriculum for Birth to Three Years and AEPS Curriculum for Three to Six Years* (Bricker, 2002) is a frequently used system that builds on the opportunity of making direct use of information obtained during assessment in developing individualized outcomes, goals, and objectives. Individual needs can be better met when all aspects of the intervention process, including assessment, goals and objectives, intervention, and evaluation, are interrelated. Pretti-Frontczak and Bricker (2000) state, "Thus, higher quality IEP goals and objectives that are developed from a comprehensive assessment process, and directly linked to intervention and evaluation, are likely to contribute to the individualization of services and improved outcomes for young children" (p. 92).

The next chapter discusses how to develop individualized outcomes, goals, and objectives. Keep in mind, however, that the comments made within the next chapter are based on the belief that *there must be a direct link between what is learned during assessment and the activities planned for children.*

MONITORING CHILDREN'S PROGRESS

Record keeping in early childhood programs is not typically detailed with regard to specific learning objectives or training procedures. Nor is it individualized for each child. However, when children with special needs are included in the class, certain information must be recorded, kept up to date, and made available to parents and other members of the child's educational team. In other words, progress must be monitored on an ongoing basis. Record keeping must be designed to facilitate constant fine-tuning and adjustment of programs and procedures. Doing this in the simplest manner possible is very important. Unwieldy systems are either time consuming or simply not used. The goal of designing a record-keeping system is that it be simple, efficient, and functional.

Data collection and record-keeping systems must be designed to fit specific training needs. Particularly challenging training objectives often require very specific and careful data collection. This is especially true if the child's progress is slow or inconsistent. In such cases it may simply be impossible to determine whether progress is being made without painstaking data collection efforts. For example, a plan for toilet training a child with multiple disabilities or reducing the destructive tantruming of a child with a severe behavior disorder would require very careful and frequent data collection of the type shown in Figure 3–1. The form in Figure 3–1 is being used to try to determine Jon's urination pattern and help him learn to urinate in the toilet. During the first part of the week he is checked every half hour to see if he is wet or dry. In addition, he is placed on the potty when he vocalizes because his mother reports that recently at home he has begun

to signal when he is wet by vocalizing. Gradually Jon's urination pattern emerges. He is often wet around 8:30 a.m. and again around 11:00 a.m. If he is dry at these times, he is placed on the potty and praised if he urinates there. His vocalizations continue to be recorded to determine whether he is actually using vocalization as a signal that he is wet or that he needs to go to the bathroom.

Use of carefully planned motor prompts and hand-over-hand procedures to help a child who is blind learn to eat with a spoon might require keeping records of how much assistance was required on each bite during a meal, as shown in Figure 3–2. At the beginning of each meal, seven trials are recorded to determine the level of assistance required. Examining the data sheet, we see that early in the week Sharon required total motor prompts (total assistance) on all seven trials. Although her performance is somewhat inconsistent, we see that by Thursday Sharon appears to be needing less total assistance and increasing the number of independent bites.

For keeping track of progress made across all IEP goals (or outcomes for individualized family service plans [IFSPs]), weekly or biweekly anecdotal record keeping may be more useful. One simple strategy is to make a single page for each child, listing the IEP objectives in each domain along one side of the form and leaving ample space to write comments next to each objective (see Figure 3–3). Several copies of this sheet are made for each child and placed in the child's folder. Each week, one of the sheets is used to summarize progress and problems for each objective. This provides a running narrative of progress across all objectives. It also ensures that each objective is reviewed by the teacher and assistants weekly. Data sheets for specific problem behaviors as described above can be attached to these anecdotal overview sheets.

The important point about record keeping is that *it must be done*. No matter how competent the early childhood professional is, it will not be possible to carefully monitor the child's progress and the effectiveness of intervention procedures without such records.

This chapter has presented the primary sources of information used in recognizing children's special needs and in monitoring their progress. It has also discussed changing philosophies and practices and raised cautions to be considered when using standardized instruments. The next chapter will consider how assessment information can be used in determining eligibility and in developing individualized service plans and programs.

PROGRESS DATA

NAME: Jon

OBJECTIVE: Jon will urinate when placed on potty

KEY: D = dry   W = wet   V = vocalized
P = placed on potty
+ = urinated in potty   − = did not urinate in potty

Time	MONDAY	TUESDAY	WEDNESDAY	THURSDAY	FRIDAY
8:00 A.M.	D	D	D	D	D
8:30 A.M.	W	W	P−	VP+	P+
9:00 A.M.	D	D	W	D	D
9:30 A.M.	D	D	D	D	D
10:00 A.M.	D	VP−	D	D	D
10:30 A.M.	VP−	D	D	VW	VP+
11:00 A.M.	W	W	VP+	D	D
11:30 A.M.	D	W	D	D	D

Figure 3–1   Progress chart: Toilet training

PROGRESS SUMMARY

NAME: _Sharon_   WEEK: _Nov. 9–13_

OBJECTIVE: _Eat with spoon independently at lunch_

KEY: + = bring spoon to mouth independently
      ⊕ = support at elbow
      A = total assistance required

Trials	MONDAY	TUESDAY	WEDNESDAY	THURSDAY	FRIDAY
1.	A	A	⊕	A	
2.	A	A	A	A	
3.	A	⊕	A	⊕	
4.	A	⊕	⊕	+	
5.	A	A	+	+	
6.	A	A	A	⊕	
7.	A	A	A	⊕	

Figure 3–2 Progress chart: Self-feeding

STUDENT PROGRESS

NAME:_____   DATE:_____

OBJECTIVES	COMMENTS
Social Skills 1. 2. 3.	
Communication 1. 2. 3.	
Motor Skills 1. 2. 3.	
Self-Help 1. 2. 3.	

Figure 3–3   Progress chart: Monitoring IFSP/IEP objectives

Summary

There has been a movement away from categorical descriptions of children with disabilities toward an analysis of specific instructional needs of the child. Typically a multistage process is involved that consists of (a) initial identification of children with problems, perhaps involving observational comparisons against a developmental checklist and screening for medically related problems; (b) diagnosis resulting in multidisciplinary staff development of an individualized family service plan or an individualized education program; (c) teacher observation and determination of daily activities; and (d) monitoring of the child's progress on a continuous basis for the purpose of updating the child's program and periodically to review success of the overall program.

Several phases in the process of recognizing and accommodating a child's special needs require assistance of numerous specialists, but the early interventionist plays an instrumental role in the continuous success of the child's efforts. To be successful at this, part of the educator's role is to know what constitutes so-called normal behaviors. Armed with such knowledge, the teacher can then systematically observe for high-risk signals that might indicate the need for referral to specialized personnel or agencies. Guidelines and suggestions are given for how to strengthen this observational process.

Early childhood educators should be particularly cautious when using standardized tests as part of the assessment process. Norm-referenced tests that compare a child's scores with norms established by groups of children of the same age may distort a child's capabilities if disabilities or unique needs are not considered. Criterion-referenced assessment compares a child's performance to a developmental standard or sequence of skills to be mastered. But increasingly, play-based, teacher-developed techniques serve as the basis for assessment and evaluation.

This chapter emphasized that the ultimate responsibility for assessment, choice of daily activities, and effective teaching remains with the teacher. This is a responsibility for which few teachers feel prepared. To become skilled in the techniques of observation, formal and informal testing, and programming, practice and patience are essential.

Finally, this chapter has attempted to clarify some of the ambiguities in the whole arena of evaluation, bring to light some of the critical concerns surrounding evaluative procedures, and encourage study and practice.

Discussion Topics and Activities

1. Differentiate identification, diagnosis, assessment, and evaluation. Give the purposes of each process.
2. Select or construct your own developmental rating scale. Observe at least two children. If possible, observe a child suspected of having a disability and a child with no known deficits. Check and compare their performances according to your rating scale. Write a summary of the educational strengths and weaknesses you observed. Be certain you have parental permission and observe all aspects of confidentiality.
3. Design a few informal assessment procedures that you can use to determine the educational strengths and needs of a young child with disabilities. Note the behaviors you would look for in order for the procedure to be useful to you in writing plans for the child being assessed.
4. Differentiate norm-referenced and criterion-referenced tests and give the advantages and disadvantages of each type of test.
5. Use the *Buros Mental Measurements Yearbook* (Spies & Plake, 2005) to thoroughly research a commonly used assessment instrument such as the Peabody Picture Vocabulary Test. Present a critique to your classmates. Be certain to research important factors such as reliability, validity, and the characteristics of the normative sample.
6. Select a specific child with a severe disability. Plan what you would include in a portfolio to demonstrate the child's progress over a 6-month period.

Developing Individualized Intervention Plans and Programs

Photo by Anthony Magnacca/Merrill

KEY TERMS

(Note: Terms are discussed in the text and/or defined in the glossary.)

behavioral objectives
blended model
collaborative interchanges
community networking
concerns, priorities, and
  resources
criterion
dedicated and independent
  model

dedicated but not independent
  model
en route behavior
equivalent practices
family-centered approach to
  assessment
IEP annual goals and
  objectives
IFSP outcome statements

individualized education program
  (IEP) process
individualized family service plan
  (IFSP) process
program plan
service coordinator
task analysis
terminal objective
transition

- The Individuals with Disabilities Education Act requires that an individualized family service plan (IFSP) be generated for infants, toddlers, and their families and that individualized education programs (IEPs) be developed for preschoolers.

- Families should be seen as the primary decision makers in the individualized planning processes.

- The IFSP and IEP documents are of secondary importance to the **process** the team uses in developing them.

- Essential to the planning processes is a belief in collaboration among families and service providers.

- Identification of family concerns, priorities, and resources should be guided by a family-directed approach.

- Family concerns should be directly reflected in functional IFSP outcomes and IEP goals and objectives.

- Service coordination is a newly mandated service for infants and toddlers that can potentially enable parents to become their own advocates as their child enters into public school services.

- A multidisciplinary assessment team is expected to collaborate with the parents in determining appropriate goals and objectives for the IEP.

- Annual and periodic reviews of the IFSP and IEP should be a vehicle for continuous improvement of services.

- In order to minimize family stress, careful consideration should be given to planning steps in transition to the next educational environment.

The previous chapter introduced some of the major issues surrounding the processes of identification, diagnosis, assessment, and evaluation. Attention was given to preparing professionals for their primary role as astute observers of children's behavior. The options available for assessment within the classroom were discussed. This chapter will focus on the process of developing individualized programs and plans.

THE INDIVIDUALIZED FAMILY SERVICE PLAN PROCESS FOR INFANTS, TODDLERS, AND THEIR FAMILIES

The individualized family service plan (IFSP) is the written document specified in the Individuals with Disabilities Education Act (IDEA) to guide the implementation of early intervention services for children from birth to age 3 and their families. It is to be developed through **collaborative interchanges** between families and the professionals involved in assessment and service delivery.

The purpose of the IFSP is to identify and organize formal and informal resources to facilitate families' goals for their children and themselves. "It is not a product so much as a process and context for establishing and maintaining a productive and supportive professional-family relationship. There is continuous gathering, sharing, exchanging, and expanding of information as the family makes decisions about which early intervention services they want and need for their child and themselves" (Noonan & McCormick, 2006, pp. 56–57).

As noted, the written document, in and of itself, is not considered to be as significant as the *process* involved in the development of the written product. Service providers are expected to form partnerships

with families built on trust and respect that are designed to be a viable part of each child's program throughout the critical first few years of the child's life. The IFSP process is intended to support the natural caregiving role of families. In keeping with the family systems dynamics outlined in chapter 2, young children with special needs can be understood only within the context of their families. In this way, the IFSP is viewed differently from the individualized education program (IEP), to be discussed later in this chapter. The IFSP process is *family centered*, whereas the IEP tends to be child centered. The IFSP approach takes into account the fact that infants and toddlers are uniquely dependent on their families for physical and emotional sustenance.

The IFSP Process

The process for developing the IFSP consists of the gathering, sharing, and exchange of information between families and staff to enable families to make informed choices about the early intervention services they want for their children and themselves.

Families may move through the dynamic process differently according to their concerns, desires, and choices. However, several key activities are expected to occur. These include the following:

1. *First contacts and screening for eligibility.* As discussed in the previous chapter, when a child is referred for early intervention services, an evaluation is conducted to determine a child's eligibility for services. Criteria for eligibility must be consistent with each state's definition of developmental disability. Assessment plans are developed with the family to determine the child's status in each of five developmental areas: physical development, including vision, hearing, and health; cognitive development; communication development; social or emotional development; and adaptive development.

2. *Assessment of the family's resources, concerns, and priorities and the child's strengths and needs.* Child and family assessment involves interviews with caregivers designed to elicit family-directed expression of family resources, priorities, and concerns.

Families are also encouraged to identify the supports and services necessary to enhance the family's capacity to meet the developmental needs of their child.

3. *Development of a service plan document.* A meeting must be held within 45 days of referral to develop the initial IFSP document. The meeting must be held in settings and at a time convenient for families. It is required to be conducted in the native language of the family. An ongoing service coordinator is also designated at this meeting.

4. *Implementation and monitoring.* Services for an eligible child and family are expected to be implemented as soon as possible after the IFSP meeting. The service coordinator is responsible for coordinating, facilitating, and monitoring the timely delivery of early intervention services. A review of the IFSP must be completed every 6 months or more frequently if deemed appropriate. In addition, a full evaluation of the IFSP is to be conducted on an annual basis.

Participants in Initial and Annual IFSP Meetings

Participants in the initial and annual IFSP meetings usually include the following:

1. The parent or parents of the child.

2. Other family members as desired by the family.

3. An advocate or person outside the family, if the parent requests that the person participate.

4. The service coordinator who has been working with the family since the initial referral or who has been designated by the public agency to be responsible for the implementation of the IFSP.

5. A person or persons directly involved in the assessment process.

6. As appropriate, persons who will be providing services to the child or the family.

If any of these persons are unable to participate, arrangements are to be made to include their involvement through other means, such as arranging

Photo by Anthony Magnacca/Merrill

a telephone conference call; employing the services of a knowledgeable, authorized substitute representative; or making available pertinent records.

Identifying Family Concerns, Priorities, and Resources

Although P.L. 99–457 originally required identification of family strengths and needs as related to enhancement and development of the child, professionals are increasingly wary of the use of the term *needs*, which implies that families may need to be fixed. The term *concerns* is now used in an effort to encourage the view that families are competent and able to make choices based on their concerns and priorities. It is not that families are just "needy." It is *not* appropriate for early childhood special education professionals to decide what areas of family life should be assessed to determine family strengths and concerns. Therefore, the law specifically states that there must be "a *family-directed* assessment of the resources, priorities, and concerns of the family" (P.L. 105–17, Sec. 636).

When general problems in family functioning are suspected, it is appropriate to explore with the family the possibility of referring them to appropriate professionals for counseling or other forms of assistance. Only families can decide for themselves which aspects of their functioning are relevant to their ability to help

their child develop optimally. Professionals need to understand the concerns and priorities of the family from the family's point of view and then identify the concerns and priorities from the provider's point of view. Through collaboration, concerns are then prioritized before resources can be identified.

Florene Poyadue, former executive director of Parents Helping Parents (see chapter 2), has referred to **concerns, priorities, and resources** as the lifeline of families who have children with special needs. Once concerns are prioritized, the responsibility of both the professional community and families is the identification of viable resources. It is important that professionals assist families in identifying and building on their own resources and strengths while at the same time helping them link up with appropriate community resources. It must be remembered that only resources that are easily accessible to families are useful.

Considerable discussion has been generated among professionals and families as to the least intrusive way to help families identify their concerns, priorities, and resources. It is clearly acknowledged that professionals need training and experience in a more **family-centered approach to assessment** in order to balance their needs for specific information to determine eligibility and programming against families' priorities and concerns. As communities

work through implementation of Part C, they must be creative in designing data collection methods that maintain the integrity of each family as **primary decision makers.** This means that whenever there is doubt about a family's concerns or a child's need, the opinions of the family should be sought first. Whether families complete interview forms or provide information through descriptive stories about their children, they must be given a choice in the assessment procedures used. Essential to success of the whole collaborative process is a relationship between families and professionals built on trust and respect.

Hanson and Lynch (2004) listed four basic qualities professionals must develop in order to realize effective collaboration with families: (a) possessing knowledge and skills related to children with disabilites, (b) working within the context of the family and community, (c) being positve and open-minded, and (d) following through on promises. They further state, "Professionals who are perceived to be dishonest with families, do not share information fully, do not respect family roles and responsibilities, display negative attitudes toward families or their job, and are not well trained for their jobs are not able to form collaborative partnerships" (p 201)

The IFSP Document

In written form, the IFSP must contain the elements that are listed here. One important difference from the IEP includes a statement of "outcomes expected to be achieved for the infant or toddler and the family" (Sec 677) rather than goals. These **IFSP outcome statements** are to reflect changes family members want to see for their child or themselves. Each outcome is to be stated functionally in terms of what is to occur (process) and what is expected as a result of these actions (product). Even though an example format is shown in Figure 4-1, readers are cautioned that formats differ from state to state and within states. A telephone call to health, education, and social service agencies should be able to direct interested individuals to the right sources to obtain copies of the format used locally. Whatever formats are chosen, the following contents are required (Secs. 633 to 636).

1. A statement of the child's present levels of physical development (including vision, hearing, and health status), cognitive development, communication development, social or emotional development, and adaptive development based on objective criteria.

2. A statement of the family's resources, priorities, and concerns related to enhancing the development of the child.

3. A statement of measurable results or outcomes expected to be achieved for the child and family and the criteria, procedures, and time lines used to determine the degree to which progress toward achieving the outcomes occurs. Outcomes must include preliteracy language skills, as developmentally appropriate.

4. A statement of the specific early intervention services based on peer-reviewed research to the extent practical. Services listed should be necessary to meet the unique needs of the child and the family, including the frequency, intensity, and method of delivering services.

5. A statement of the natural environments in which early intervention services shall appropriately be provided, including a justification of the extent, if any, to which the services will not be provided in a natural environment.

6. Projected dates for initiation of the services and the anticipated duration of those services.

7. The name of the service coordinator who will be responsible for the implementation of the IFSP and coordination with other agencies and persons.

8. Steps or services to be taken to support the transition of the child, on reaching age 3, to the next program of services recognized to be appropriate.

9. The contents of the IFSP shall be fully explained, and informed written consent from the parents or guardian shall be obtained prior to provision of early intervention services described in the plan. The case of Cathy, which is given in Figure 4-1, illustrates one format that encompasses the requirements.

INDIVIDUALIZED FAMILY SERVICE PLAN (IFSP) for Children Birth to Three Years   SANTA CLARA COUNTY

Child's name: _Cathy Rae Wright_   Birth Date: _11-15-07_   Age: _26_ months   Sex: _F_

Parent(s)/Guardian(s): _Martha and Gary Wright_   Address: _1414 Coolidge Drive Cupertino_   Zip: _95014_

Home phone: _398-2461_ Work phone: _408 554-2490_   Primary language of the home: _English_   Other languages _____

Date of this IFSP _1/15/09_ Projected periodic review _7/15/09_ Projected annual review _1/15/11_ Tentative IFSP exit _11/15/10_
                              (at 6 months or before)

Service Coordinator Name	Agency	Phone	Date Appointed	Date Ended
Sandy Drohman	_Regional Center_	_408-461-2192_	_12/10/08_	_/ /_
			_/ /_	_/ /_
			_/ /_	_/ /_

Family's strengths and preferred resources (With the family, identify the family strengths and the resources they might find helpful in addressing family concerns and priorities.) Mr. and Mrs. Wright are well educated and constantly seek additional information about Cathy's condition. They are eager to help Cathy in any way possible. Mrs. Wright's family is very supportive. They provide child care for Cathy's older brother.

Because of Cathy's tendency to be medically fragile, Mr. and Mrs. Wright prefer a home-based early intervention program. They appreciate receiving written materials to help them understand how to work with Cathy. Mrs. Wright wants to be home when the home visitor comes so she can learn from her.

Family's concerns and priorities (With the family, identify major areas of concerns for the child with special needs and the family as a whole.) Mr. and Mrs. Wright are very concerned about Cathy's delays in walking, using her fingers to pick up things, and in talking with other children. They also worry about her small size. Cathy is their second child and was born at 24 weeks' gestation. Mr. and Mrs. Wright would like to have more information on the issues of prematurity and they would like to find an appropriate support group for themselves.

Page _1_ of _6_ total IFSP

Figure 4–1 Example of an IFSP

INDIVIDUALIZED FAMILY SERVICE PLAN (IFSP) for Children Birth to Three Years   SANTA CLARA COUNTY

Child's name: _____ Cathy Rae Wright _____   Chronological Age: __26__ months

CHILD'S STRENGTHS AND PRESENT LEVELS OF DEVELOPMENT

With the family, identify what the child can do and what the child is learning to do. Include family and professional observations in each of the following areas:

PHYSICAL *Based on parent report and HELP Strands

Health _Cathy is said by her parents to be healthy but is very petite. Her parents are working with a nutritionist to_
help Cathy gain weight.

Vision _Cathy has had corrective surgery for strabismus._

Hearing _She has had numerous ear infections and currently has tubes in her ears._

Gross Motor (large movement) _Cathy stands on tiptoes, runs on toes, makes sharp turns around corners when running,_
walks upstairs with one hand held.

Fine Motor (small movement) _Cathy grasps crayon adaptively and points with index finger; imitates horizontal_
strokes; builds 6-block tower; turns pages one at a time; has trouble picking up small objects.

COGNITIVE (responsiveness to environments, problem-solving) _Cathy finds hidden object; attempts and succeeds in activating_
mechanical toy; demonstrates use of objects appropriate for age.

COMMUNICATION (language and speech)

RECEPTIVE (understanding) _Cathy points to body parts when asked; obeys two-part commands._

EXPRESSIVE (making sounds, talking) _Cathy names 8 pictures, interacts with peers using only gestures;_
attempts to sing songs with words.

SOCIAL/EMOTIONAL (how relates to others) _Cathy expresses affection; is beginning to obey and respect simple rules;_
tends to be physically aggressive.

ADAPTIVE/SELF-HELP (sleeping, eating, dressing, toileting, etc.) _Cathy can put on socks and shoes; verbalizes need to use_
the toilet, but is not potty trained; feeds self.

DIAGNOSIS (if known) _____

Page __2__ of __6__ total IFSP

Figure 4–1   (continued)

116

INDIVIDUALIZED FAMILY SERVICE PLAN (IFSP) for Children Birth to Three Years   SANTA CLARA COUNTY

Child's name: _____ Cathy Rae Wright _____

IFSP OUTCOMES

With the family, identify the goals they would like to work on in the next six months.
These should be directly related to the family's priorities and concerns as stated on page one.

OUTCOME: Cathy will increase her attempts to vocally communicate in order to make her needs known and to positively interact with others.

	Service Type (Individual = I Group = G) / Location	Frequency of sessions / Length of each session	Start Date	End Date (anticipated)	Responsible Agency/ Group Including payment arrangements (if any)
Strategy or activity to achieve the outcome (Who do what and when will they do it?) AIM Infant Educator will model for Mr. and Mrs. Wright techniques to solicit Cathy's vocalization efforts. **Criteria** (How will we know if we are making progress?) Increased vocalization will be observed by parents and infant educator.	I – Home-based infant program	1 hour each week	1-23-09	11-10-09	AIM (funded by SARC) Family
Strategy or activity to achieve the outcome (Who do what and when will they do it?) Mrs. Wright will take Cathy to play with neighborhood children and will invite children to her home. She will encourage play and vocalization. **Criteria** (How will we know if we are making progress?) Mrs. Wright will observe and note extent of interaction.	G – Home and in the neighborhood	once each week for at least 30 minutes	2-1-09	ongoing	Mrs. Wright
Strategy or activity to achieve the outcome (Who do what and when will they do it?) Cathy will be assessed by a speech pathologist by 2-15-09 and followed on an as-needed basis. **Criteria** (How will we know if we are making progress?) A follow-up report will be submitted.	I – Regional Center Speech and Language Clinic	1 hour play-based assessment	2-1-09	as needed	Sandy Drohman will make arrangements (funded by SARC)

Page __3__ of __6__ total IFSP

Figure 4–1 (continued)

117

INDIVIDUALIZED FAMILY SERVICE PLAN (IFSP) for Children Birth to Three Years   SANTA CLARA COUNTY

Child's name: _____Cathy Rae Wright_____

IFSP OUTCOMES

With the family, identify the goals they would like to work on in the next six months.
These should be directly related to the family's priorities and concerns as stated on page one.

OUTCOME: *Cathy will increase her weight in order to maintain health and continue a developmentally appropriate growth pattern*

	Service Type (Individual = I Group = G) Location	Frequency of sessions Length of each session	Start Date	End Date (anticipated)	Responsible Agency/ Group Including payment arrangements (if any)
	Kaiser Hospital Clinic	30 min. each month	ongoing	as needed	Mrs. Breez (Kaiser funded)

Strategy or activity to achieve the outcome
(Who will do what and when will they do it?)
Mr. and Mrs. Wright will continue to work with Mrs. Breez to improve Cathy's nutrition intake.

Criteria (How will we know if we are making progress?)

Strategy or activity to achieve the outcome
(Who will do what and when will they do it?)

Criteria (How will we know if we are making progress?)

Strategy or activity to achieve the outcome
(Who will do what and when will they do it?)

Criteria (How will we know if we are making progress?)

Figure 4–1 (continued)

INDIVIDUALIZED FAMILY SERVICE PLAN (IFSP) for Children Birth to Three Years   SANTA CLARA COUNTY

Child's name: _____ Cathy Rae Wright _____

IFSP OUTCOMES

With the family, identify the goals they would like to work on in the next six months.
These should be directly related to the family's priorities and concerns as stated on page one.

OUTCOME: Mr. and Mrs. Wright will join Parents Helping Parents in order to receive peer parent support and learn more about Cathy's condition.

	Service Type (Individual = I Group = G) Location	Frequency of sessions / Length of each session	Start Date	End Date (anticipated)	Responsible Agency/ Group Including payment arrangements (if any)
Strategy or activity to achieve the outcome (who will do what and when will they do it?) Sandy Drohman will provide all referral information to Mr. and Mrs. Wright and will accompany them to their first meeting if they desire.	G – Parents Helping Parents	(up to parent's discretion)			Sandy Drohman Mr. and Mrs. Wright Parents Helping Parents
Criteria (How will we know if we are making progress?) Mr. and Mrs. Wright will find satisfaction in increased support and knowledge.					
Strategy or activity to achieve the outcome (who will do what and when will they do it?) AIM Infant Educator will assist Mr. and Mrs. Wright in obtaining additional information about Cathy's condition.	I – Home	ongoing	2-1-09	11-10-09	AIM Infant Educator
Criteria (How will we know if we are making progress?) Mr. and Mrs. Wright will express satisfaction over the assistance received in becoming more informed.					
Strategy or activity to achieve the outcome (who will do what and when will they do it?)					
Criteria (How will we know if we are making progress?)					

Figure 4–1   (continued)

INDIVIDUALIZED FAMILY SERVICE PLAN (IFSP) for Children Birth to Three Years   SANTA CLARA COUNTY

Child's name: _____ Cathy Rae Wright _____

TRANSITION PLAN — This child's transition at __36__ months will be accomplished by completing the following steps:

1. At 30 months, Mrs. Wright will meet with the district program specialist to review placement options.
2. Mrs. Wright will visit the sites with Sandy Drohman.
3. Mrs. Wright will state her preference and will sign enrollment forms.
4. Mrs. Wright will attend the orientation with Cathy.

STATEMENT OF ELIGIBILITY — The IFSP team determines that assessment results demonstrate that the family and child are eligible for services under Part C of the *Individuals with Disabilities Education Act* — ☒ Yes or ☐ No.
Percentage of time child is in natural environment ____N.A.____ %.

FAMILY — I (We) had the opportunity to participate in the development of this IFSP. It represents my (our) concerns, priorities, and outcomes for my (our) child and family. I (We) ☒ do ☐ do not give permission for this plan to be implemented. I (We) understand that this IFSP plan is in effect through __11/15/10__ .

_____ Mrs. Martha Wright _____   __1/15/09__
Date   Parent(s)/Legal Guardian(s) Signature(s)   Date

OTHER IFSP PARTICIPANTS — The following individuals/agencies participated in the development of the IFSP either by attending the meeting or giving input by telephone or in writing and agree to carry out the plan as it applies to their role in the provision of entitled early intervention services.

Name, Title & Phone		Agency	Gave input by telephone or writing (Person receiving input initial here)	Date
Mr. and Mrs. Gary Wright		Parents		
Sandy Drohman	408-461-2192	Regional Center		1-15-09
Julie Maze	408-460-6190	Public Health Nursing		1-15-09
Margaret Breez	408-642-8316	Kaiser Nutritionist	SD	1-10-09
Rosalie Martinez	408-648-2941	AIM Infant Program		1-15-09

Notes for consideration at next review: _____ Consider relationship between Cathy and her older brother, John. _____

Page __6__ of __6__ total IFSP

Figure 4-1 (continued)

120

Developing Outcome Statements

The IFSP team is expected to develop outcome statements that will guide the choice of services to be delivered. It is important to remember that these statements should have a direct connection to the concerns and priorities expressed earlier by the family. These statements will document the changes families hope to see for their children or themselves as these changes relate to the developmental needs of their child. Outcome statements are to be functionally stated in the language of the family whenever possible. They should refer to practical activities that fit into a family's daily life and represent skills that enhance the child's ability to cope with daily environmental demands.

Phrasing the statements as "*in order to*" statements makes it easy to understand the functional purpose of the action to be encouraged. For example, parents who are eager for their child to learn to walk may not be satisfied with an outcome statement that is written as "Josh will pull to standing," unless an addition is made so that it reads, "Josh will pull to standing *in order to* begin the process of walking." This formula, long ago advocated by Deal, Dunst, and Trivette (1989), allows the result (product—walking) of the process (pull to stand) to be readily understood. That is, action A will be encouraged in order to realize outcome B. Activities or strategies should, then, flow directly from the outcome statements. For example, advice from a physical therapist should be sought to determine the most appropriate strategies to encourage Josh to pull to standing.

Figure 4–1 illustrates three outcome statements chosen by Mr. and Mrs. Wright for their daughter, Cathy. Others could have been included, but Cathy's parents decided that these three were of the highest priority at the time of the initial IFSP.

It is important to realize that the IFSP does not take the place of a **program plan.** The IFSP identifies *services* and desired *outcomes*. It does not identify a complete list of specific objectives, strategies, and activities to be used in bringing about the outcomes. Although not required by law, all service providers should prepare a written plan of specific

Photo by Krista Greco/Merrill

long- and short-term objectives (including teaching steps and strategies) for reaching each outcome. (See pages **132–135** for detailed information related to writing instructional objectives.)

SERVICE COORDINATION

P.L. 99–457 and now P.L. 108–446 mandate that a **service coordinator** be designated to ensure the full development of the IFSP for birth to 3-year-olds and their families. The law intends that professional assistance be provided to support optimal family functioning. Thus, service coordination is considered to be an integral part of the IFSP process.

Part C rules and regulations state that service coordination consists primarily of activities designed to assist and enable an eligible child and the child's family to receive the rights, procedural safeguards, and services that are authorized to be provided through each state's early intervention program. Service coordinators assume responsibility for the following:

- Coordination of the full IFSP process for each eligible child.

- Informing families of the availability of advocacy services.

- Inclusion of parents as full multidisciplinary team members.

- Inclusion of all professionals who should be involved with the family.

- If appropriate, acquiring an interpreter.

- Scheduling and facilitating assessments and IFSP meetings.

- Encouraging exchange of ideas and recommendations.

- Encouraging creative, integrated, and coordinated intervention options.

- Facilitating problem solving and conflict resolution.

- Serving as the single point of contact in helping parents obtain appropriate services.

- Facilitating the development of a transition plan to preschool services, when appropriate.

- Filing a copy of the IFSP transition plan documents in the child's record.

Service coordination is to be an active, ongoing process that involves helping parents to gain access to services identified in their IFSP, coordinating these services, and facilitating timely delivery of appropriate services throughout the duration of the child's eligibility. In many areas, early childhood special education teachers may be expected to become service coordinators. Those who have not had training in family systems theory, in understanding the requirements of federal and state legislation, and in local service delivery systems must seek this training before accepting such a responsibility.

Although specific service coordination activities are listed, it is understood that these activities are fluid, interrelated, and always individually determined in collaboration with families. Activities that are helpful to one family may be irrelevant or undesired by another. Even activities that are appropriate for a family today may not be suitable for that family tomorrow. Effectiveness of service coordination will depend on the competencies of the service coordinator, including his or her ability to actively involve families in helping to get their own needs met.

Who Can Become Service Coordinators?

Although the law does mandate the involvement of someone responsible for service coordination, it allows flexibility in the choice of service coordinator and in the model of service coordination implemented. It is the intent of the law that the person best qualified to meet the needs of the family and the child should become the family's service coordinator. Optimally, the service coordinator will be selected on the basis of the desires of the family and can be from any agency. Service coordinators will change as the needs and appropriate services for the family change. Parents do have the right to reject service coordination entirely.

Models of Service Coordination

In reviewing the breadth and depth of service coordination practices, Dunst and Bruder (2006) examined the three prevalent models of service coordination: (a) *dedicated and independent*, (b) *dedicated but not independent*, and (c) *blended*. The **dedicated and independent model** refers to a model where "the role of the service coordinator is dedicated to service coordination only, and the agency providing service coordination is independent from service provision" (Bruder, 2005, p. 34).

The **dedicated but not independent model** means that the service coordinator, like the first model, provides only service coordination. However, he or she works for the same agency or program providing early intervention services. Finally, in the **blended model**, the service coordinator provides both service coordinator and early intervention services. Harbin et al. (2004) found that 47% of all states and territories used a combination of models.

Dunst and Bruder (2006) endeavored to find out if different service coordination models were found to be associated with different service coordination practices. They found that when the service coordination is done by a coordinator who is independent from a program that delivers early intervention services, there is significantly less contact with program participants than when the service coordinator is from an agency that offers early intervention services.

The fact that independent but dedicated models are less efficient is explained by the need for independent coordinators to facilitate collaboration and integrate activities among more agencies than is true of the blended models. Given the fact that families often get relatively little time and attention from their service coordinators for a variety of reasons, it is up to the professionals who work with children on a daily basis to become well informed about local resources and participate in the networking discussed below.

PROMOTING ESSENTIAL INTERAGENCY COLLABORATION

Educational programs that serve young children with special needs can provide all the services that children and families require only through collaboration with other programs and agencies. **Community networking** describes the efforts involved in coordinating services among agencies. Community networking can reduce fragmentation, avoid duplication, and help families gain easy access to needed services.

As discussed above, families of children with disabilities under the age of 3 years will be assigned a service coordinator whose responsibility will be to facilitate interagency collaboration on behalf of families' needs. Older children or children whose disabilities are not severe enough to be deemed eligible for service coordination will look elsewhere for assistance in navigating the service delivery maze. The most appropriate professionals to be of assistance are the early intervention specialists and early education teachers with whom families are in daily contact.

Therefore, in order to develop efficient and effective interagency collaboration, programs must involve a variety of networking activities. Networking activities vary because of differences in resources or community needs and geographic and cultural factors. Early education specialists need to *develop a clear understanding of the needs of each child and family and a thorough knowledge of the available resources.* A personal evaluation of programs and personnel fosters a useful match between needs and services. Attention should be paid to the quality, breadth, and cost of services. Families will need help

in complying with referral procedures and support during waiting periods. Ideally, networking efforts will result in formal or informal interagency agreements that extend services to meet the special needs of children and their families.

Collaboration also includes involvement in activities that create awareness of the early education program and its contribution to the process of networking. Open houses, personal contacts, media coverage, brochures, presentations at meetings, and participation on community advisory councils develop public awareness. Even though networking activities will change with time, they remain essential to the delivery of a successful early intervention program.

DEVELOPING IEPS FOR PRESCHOOLERS

Federal guidelines require children who will receive any special education services to be seen for a diagnostic study by members of a multidisciplinary team before services can begin. The law does not specify the professionals to be included in the assessment phase of the IEP process. However, it is expected that choice of the members for a specific team will be determined by the characteristics and suspected disabling conditions of a particular child. For example, in all cases of suspected speech and/or language delays, the child should be seen by a speech-language pathologist. This pathologist should also be present at the subsequent meeting or "staffing," at which time the IEP is developed. In some cases, team members may participate through conference calls.

People expected to attend the meeting where the IEP document is developed include the following:

1. One or both of the child's parents.

2. At least one regular education teacher if the child is participating in a regular education program.

3. At least one special education teacher or, where appropriate, at least one special education provider of such child.

4. Any member of the school staff, other than the child's teacher, who is "qualified to provide, or

Photo by Scott Cunningham/Merrill

supervise the provision of, specially designed instruction to meet the unique needs of children with disabilities" (Sec. 614).

5. An individual who can interpret the instructional implications of evaluation results.

6. An administrator who has the authority to make commitments on behalf of the school district.

7. If a child has received early intervention services under Part C, the parent has the right to request that the Part C coordinator or representative be invitied to the initial IEP meeting.

8. Other individuals whose expertise may be desired by the parent or school.

The Interdisciplinary IEP Team Meeting Process

The interdisciplinary team, including the parents as valid members, considers the child's current strengths and the child's present level of performance. Priorities are chosen. Measurable **IEP annual goals** are specified, and how progress toward these annual goals will be measured is determined. The team, with critical input from the family, determines what supplemental supports, aids, and services will be received; where the services will be offered, and when the services will begin. These will be written on the program plan.

Referring Professional's Preparation.   In preparation for the interdisciplinary staffing, the teacher would write observations of the child in several different settings and circumstances. She would summarize any information gained from informal or formal classroom assessment and gather relevant samples of the child's work. She must be prepared to give evidence of the child's present level of functioning. Questions based on her concerns should be prepared.

Specialists' Preparation.   Whenever possible, the specialists who evaluate young children ask to see reports of observations made by others, including teachers and parents. Often a screening test is used as a preliminary to in-depth evaluations.

Each specialist will choose assessment procedures judged to be relevant to the suspected problems. During the diagnosis, it may become apparent that additional tests are needed. If one specialist

obtains information that suggests that additional specialists need to be included in the multidisciplinary diagnostic team, it is his or her responsibility to request the necessary additional diagnosis. The chairperson of the staffing in which the IEP is developed often is the person referred to in the law as the representative of the local educational agency. This person may be responsible for collecting all assessment information and being certain that no important aspect of the diagnostic process is overlooked. Professionals involved must be prepared to relate test results, their level of confidence in the child's performance, and recommendations for placement and services to the chairperson. *They should make every possible effort to translate their findings into information directly useful to program and activity planning.*

When participating in the interdisciplinary staffing, professionals should be prepared to speak in language that parents understand. They must remember that parents, as well as professionals, are to be included as active, vital members of the team.

Parents' Preparation.   Parents will be expected to organize any information they have received from previous examiners. They have the responsibility of honestly and accurately sharing information about their child's behavior and perceived strengths and concerns. Parents serve as the child's advocate.

Professionals can be very helpful in helping parents prepare information they wish to share as well as in developing a list of questions to be asked of specialists. Parents should be given any assistance they need to fully understand the program and services being proposed. In some cases translators or multilingual specialists will have to be included as part of the multidisciplinary team. It is especially important for professionals to understand exactly which intervention goals are important to each child's parents. A questionnaire or interview asking parents to identify those skills that they would *most* like to see their child accomplish in the coming year and behaviors that would reduce stress in the family, increase independence, and so on is an effective way to ensure parents' *active participation* in selecting

and prioritizing goals for their children. Parents' goals should take highest priority on the list of objectives to be achieved. For example, the parent may think the child's becoming independent in feeding is more important than making eye contact with the staff. It is more important that the child be accepted by significant others throughout the day than by those who work with the child at preschool. Although professionals tend to feel that they know what is most important for the child to learn and achieve, the needs and desires of the parents should take precedence whenever realistically possible. Initial understanding and genuine acceptance by parents of services to be offered can save many hours of discussion or even the necessity of changes later on.

Sending home a rough draft of goals and objectives for the family to review and react to prior to the IEP meeting is another way to solicit active parent participation in setting priorities. This approach may also help to relieve parental anxiety.

Cautions to Consider When Promoting Family Participation.   As Turnbull, Turnbull, Erwin, and Spodak (2006) point out, "Since the 1980s, the research literature has been fairly consistent in acknowledging that IFSP/IEP conferences often fail to honor partnership practices" (p. 258). In support of this statement, these authors go on to discuss the fact that IEP conferences usually do not allow enough time to plan appropriately, parents tend to have limited roles in meetings, conferences may be terminated at a set time even if the process is not complete, computer-generated IEPs are often developed prior to the IEP meeting, and parents often view the professionals as the primary decision makers. There is no doubt that IEPs developed from a commercially available computer program and inadequate time for discussion do not represent a family-centered approach to early education.

CONSIDERING DANNY

The following narrative gives insight into the background and proceedings of one child's multidisciplinary conference.

Background Information

Danny's parents are worried. Twice they have been asked to withdraw him from child-care centers. Now the private preschool that he has been attending has called them in for a conference. Both parents work, and they want the best possible placement for Danny. Several friends have told them that they know he would not be accepted in the public school kindergarten next year. He rarely talks, and when he does, it is very difficult to understand him. He is also stubborn. Many times when they tell him to do something, he acts as if he does not hear them unless they yell at him. They are worried that he might be placed in a special classroom.

October 21, 2007.   Danny has now been enrolled in a private preschool for 3 weeks. Ms. McLynn and Ms. Johnson are eager to discuss their observations with Danny's parents, the Dicksons.

Ms. Johnson: Thank you for coming. We are enjoying Danny and hope he is enjoying us. We have observed Danny in a variety of situations and would like to discuss our observations with you.

Mrs. Dickson: We are so pleased that Danny is coming to your program. We are grateful for the help you have given Danny and are eager to hear about how he is doing.

Ms. Johnson: Well, as you know, it is sometimes difficult for us to understand what Danny is saying, and it seems that often he doesn't understand us. When we try to tell him to do something, he just seems so confused. We can get him to pay attention by standing in front of him and talking directly to him. He also seems to have trouble with the names of things like colors and body parts.

Mrs. Dickson: We have also noticed some of the things you are talking about. His pediatrician examined him, as you suggested, and he said he is fine. He told us that many children don't learn to speak clearly until they are in school.

Mr. Dickson: Our friends the Joneses have a little girl who the psychologist said is very slow. She doesn't talk clearly either, and they put her in a special class. We really don't want Danny put in a class with children who have problems or can't learn. Danny isn't dumb.

Ms. McLynn: I agree with you, Mr. Dickson. Danny isn't dumb. But something is wrong. He misunderstands us most of the time, but we can't understand him. He doesn't know the names of lots of things the others know.

Ms. Johnson: We feel that we aren't helping Danny enough. He needs special kinds of help that we aren't trained to provide. We are hoping that you will agree to have specialists test Danny to help us find the best ways to work with him.

Mr. Dickson: I'm not sure. Are you sure that Danny needs all of this help? We can understand him.

Ms. Johnson: Yes, I believe you can understand Danny, and he is obviously bright in many ways. He does the most difficult puzzles easily and builds wonderful towns with blocks. We would just like to find out what is causing Danny's communication problems and how we should be working with him.

Mr. Dickson: Okay. Whom do we call?

As Mr. and Mrs. Dickson left the preschool, they still felt somewhat frightened. Mrs. Dickson remembered that one preschool teacher had said her son had a "dull expression" and another said that he seemed "bewildered." But when they spoke to friends and relatives, they all reassured them that Danny was just a late bloomer. In spite of their fears, they did call their local public school office and made an appointment for a diagnostic interview. They had to sign papers to release information from the preschool and to confirm that they agreed to the testing.

January 15, 2008.   An interdisciplinary team staffing conference is in progress at the Special Education Office. In addition to Danny's teacher from the private preschool and his parents, a school psychologist, nurse, social worker, speech-language pathologist, and supervisor of special education are present. The supervisor has reviewed the background information.

Mr. Dickson: I am eager to hear what the psychologist has to say, first.

Psychologist: Danny worked very hard and seemed to want to try everything. Because Danny seemed to understand so little speech and language, and I had a hard time understanding him, I gave him two kinds of tests. Well, really three. First, I tried a vocabulary test. For that test, I show pictures and name them. All Danny had to do was point to the picture that I named. There are four pictures on each page, and only one is correct. On that test, Danny responded by naming or pointing to a few pictures correctly. He often seemed confused. He couldn't identify as many pictures as most children his age. Then I attempted to use a standardized intelligence test that requires Danny to listen to me and answer questions and point to things, too. Again, he was unable to do most of the items that other 4-year-olds can do. So, next I used a nonverbal performance test. On this test, Danny had to listen to only a few directions and did not have to talk to me. He did have to watch me carefully and then imitate some of the things I did. And here he was more successful. He seemed to enjoy these activities. His confused expression disappeared, and he looked more interested. Danny was able to match the colors very well. He could do difficult puzzles, complete copying designs, and put pattern pieces together. When he finished, he grinned at me and seemed to want to do more.

Ms. McLynn: That's the way he is at school, too. He can color and draw better than most of the other children. He is quick to learn how to make things.

Speech-Language Pathologist: My tests indicate that Danny says most of the vowels correctly, although the short vowels, as in p*i*n, p*a*n, p*e*n, and p*u*n, aren't distinct. He can imitate the voiced consonants, for example, /b/, /d/, /g/, /m/, and /n/, and he uses them in some words, but he often omits them on the ends of words. He says b*aw* for b*all* and d*aw* for d*og*, for example. When he tries to make sentences, he leaves off /s/, /t/, and /z/ at the ends of words, so he cannot "signal" past tense, as

in hopp*ed* and look*ed*. He doesn't use plurals, as in car*s* and truck*s*.

When I asked him to listen to me say a sentence and point to the picture that showed what I had said, he was really confused. One picture page has a little boy looking into a mirror seeing himself and another picture where he is looking at a shelf. Danny had no idea what I wanted him to do. When I said, "He sees himself," he pointed to both pictures. Also, I recorded more than 50 things that he said while we played with some cars and trucks and a toy garage. He really enjoyed that. When I analyzed what he said, I found that he is using three- and four-word sentences, although the words are not clear. He tried to ask me for things, too.

Nurse: Danny responded very quickly and accurately to my vision screening test. I showed him just once what I wanted him to do. He was all business, paid close attention, and quickly demonstrated that he has good eyesight. But the hearing testing was another story! He wiggled and giggled. He said he heard the tones when the audiometer was off. At 25 decibels, the loudness level used for hearing screening, he heard 500 and 1,000 hertz in one ear, but he did not respond to the same loudness at higher frequencies. In the other ear, he did not answer correctly at all at 25 decibels. So, I referred him to our speech and hearing center for a complete hearing evaluation with more sophisticated equipment. The audiologist, a specialist in evaluating hearing and recommending needed remediation, reported that Danny exhibited a high-frequency sensorineural hearing loss in both ears.

Speech-Language Pathologist: Danny has problems hearing the difference between the high-frequency sounds in particular. He had trouble with other auditory processing tasks, too.

Mr. Dickson: But if he can't hear, how come he can hear us when he wants to? He can be sitting in front of the TV and just pay no attention when I tell him something. But if I get angry, he jumps right away.

Speech-Language Pathologist: When you get angry, you probably speak louder, and your tone of voice changes.

Mr. Dickson: You bet it does.

Speech-Language Pathologist: He can hear those changes because the vowels are in the lower frequencies, and he hears them almost as you and I do. He can hear the change in your tone of voice for the same reason. What he cannot hear is the consonants. All those years he must have been hearing things with the most important parts missing. For instance, with the reported hearing loss, he hears "Come to supper" as "um oo u er."

Mrs. Dickson: Why, that is exactly what he says when he tells someone it is time to eat!

Speech-Language Pathologist: So, you see, he has been saying what he has been hearing.

Mr. Dickson: So what do we do now?

Ms. McLynn: Is there someone who can help us to teach him what he needs to know? We really want to help Danny.

Speech-Language Pathologist: The first thing we must do is have the audiologist evaluate Danny for hearing aids. Then I can work with him regularly. I'll give his teacher many special activities to help him to learn in spite of his hearing loss. He can learn to use his hearing better, and he can learn to supplement what he hears through lipreading.

Mr. Dickson: I'm ashamed for all of the times I've punished him for not listening. But he always heard his brother's motorcycle when he was half a block away. And he was always the first to run outside to look for jet planes. He loves the stereo and sings right along with the tunes. You are telling me he can hear all that but not hear the speech sounds like /p/ and /t/?

Speech-Language Pathologist: Right. And I can teach him how to make those sounds and to recognize them when he sees them on people's lips, even if his hearing doesn't improve. Of course, we will expect that it will.

Ms. McLynn: We've noticed he seems to hear a man's voice best. Should he be placed in a man's class?

Speech-Language Psychologist: Not necessarily. But it will be helpful if you speak more slowly and in shorter sentences. Be close to Danny and be sure that you have his attention before you tell him something. Avoid having sources of bright light such as a window behind you when you talk to him. He will need to see your lips and mouth. Even though he is not dependent on lipreading, he will be taught to use visual as well as auditory clues. If the light is in his eyes, it is harder to see your lip movements.

Ms. McLynn: What should we do when we don't understand Danny?

Speech-Language Pathologist: Use all the situational cues available. Sometimes tell him to tell you again. If you still don't understand, ask him to show you. Encourage him to use gestures. When you do understand, let your face show your pleasure. Then say what Danny was trying to say. Look expectant. Be pleased if he repeats your model but don't insist. Make no corrections of his articulation at this time. You are striving to motivate him to talk more and to keep trying.

After the discussion, the members of the interdisciplinary team wrote the IEP. His parents agreed that it was an excellent plan. They were grateful for the care with which everyone had evaluated Danny. They felt that the specific suggestions met his needs very well.

REQUIRED CONTENTS OF THE IEP

The IEP is a written plan that must contain the following elements:

1. A statement of the child's present strengths and levels of educational performance (based on results of norm-referenced and criterion-referenced tests).

2. A statement of measurable annual goals based on the child's strengths and levels of performance. The goals must include academic (readiness)

and functional goals. Short-term objectives for meeting the annual goals are required if the child has significant cognitive delays.

3. A statement of the specific special education and related services and supplementary aids to be provided to the child and a statement of the program modifications or supports for school personnel that will be provided.

4. An explanation of the extent, if any, that the child will not participate with nondisabled children in the regular class.

5. The projected dates for initiation of services and the anticipated frequency, location, and duration of services.

6. The appropriate objective criteria and evaluation procedures to measure progress toward the annual goals.

7. Specific plans for provision of smooth transition into kindergarten.

8. Articulation of how families will be involved and the type and frequency of communication regarding the child's progress. Progress must be reported at least four times a year.

Although the precise written format may differ from area to area, the required content must be included.

Purposes and Limitations of the IEP

The **annual goals** included in the IEP describe what a child with disabilities can be expected to accomplish within a specified period. Usually the allotted time is one school year. However, the scheduled period may be as little as a few weeks or months.

There must be a direct relationship between the child's present level of educational performance and the goals and services to be provided. However, the IEP is *not* intended to be detailed enough to be used as a complete instructional plan. The written goals are expected to state skills that are most needed based on assessment of a child's level of achievement. There is

a definite assumption in the field that when quality goals are based on what is learned during assessment better child outcomes are produced (Pretti-Frontczak & Bricker, 2000). They are designed to target remediation of particular developmental lags or to accelerate learning. The intent is to focus attention and teaching effort on critical areas that are listed by priority and area of need.

The IEP is intended to serve as a basis for the subsequent development of a detailed, individualized instructional program that encompasses the complete curriculum. For example, although Danny's IEP focuses on his goals and objectives in speech and language, his complete instructional program would include social development, gross and fine motor skills, cognitive development, and school readiness activities. In all these areas Danny would be expected to participate and learn. Adaptations to meet his needs would be made in the process of instruction. Exhibit 4–1 offers some tips to assist in preparing for IEP meetings.

Considerations Beyond the IEP

Interpreters of the law recognize that special education teachers have primary responsibility for implementation of the IEP. These teachers are expected to monitor each child's progress. If at any time they feel that the plan is no longer appropriate, they are expected to request another meeting to review the IEP. Parents may also request a review of the individual program.

When children with special needs attend regular classes, even part time, their mainstream teachers should have copies of the IEPs. The special education teacher should explain the contents of each plan. This teacher should be available to serve as consultant to the classroom teacher. Consultations should include a mutual sharing of concerns and information, suggestions for behavior management, materials, and teaching strategies.

WRITING PROGRAM OBJECTIVES (BENCHMARKS)

The obvious reason for writing goals and objectives that serve as benchmarks is to develop educational plans that will be individualized and measurable for

Exhibit **4–1**

Preparing for the IEP: Meeting Tips for Early Childhood Special Education Teachers

Do your homework:

- Review child's progress and achievement of previous goals.
- Organize assessment data and other evidence of child's performance.
- Identify challenges and concerns.
- Communicate with team members regarding their assessment findings and recommendations; share your own observations and recommendations regarding the child. Keep in mind that in your role as the early childhood special education teacher, you will often be the team member who is most familiar with both the child and the family.

Meet with the family prior to the IEP meeting:

- Determine the family's concerns and priorities for their child.
- Help the family articulate their goals and requests in terms of the child's strengths and needs.
- Help them obtain copies of assessment reports.
- If the family has questions about reports, try to facilitate contact with team members prior to the IEP if possible.

Explain the IEP process to the family, including the following information:

- Each service provider on the team will present:
    - Present levels of performance.
    - Comparison with past goals.
    - Achievements.
    - Child strengths and needs.
    - Recommendations regarding new goals and least restrictive environment.
    - Services and supports required to meet goals.
    - While each team member can bring possible goals to the IEP meeting, they do not become formal IEP goals until the team (including the parents) agree.
        - If recommendations are made for placement in a special classroom rather than a typical early childhood setting, a detailed rationale must be provided.
- Parents have the right to invite a friend or advocate to attend the meeting with them.
- Prepare parents to express their concerns and desires or disagreements during the IEP meeting and to request clarification from team members if something is unclear.
- Parents have the right to request a reconsideration of the IEP at any time.

Remember: The IEP is a documented plan; the IEP meeting is a collaborative *process*.

children with special needs. However, there are even more compelling reasons. These reasons are contained in the following characteristics of a well-written behavioral objective:

1. What is to be taught is described precisely and accurately. Anyone reading the objective knows what to do and the conditions in which it is to be done.

2. What the children will be doing when the objective has been achieved is defined and described.

3. The time allowed to complete the task is stated. How well the child must perform (the criterion) is clearly identified. Because the task, the performance expected, and the criterion for success are clearly stated, accountability is facilitated.

The following two advantages are equally important, although their benefits may be less obvious:

1. After writing objectives and working with them, teachers often discover that they are able to analyze learning problems more efficiently. They recognize the critical importance of small changes in what they are doing. These seemingly small changes, sometimes referred to as *branching*, can make enormous differences in teaching success. In effect, practice in thinking in the manner required to write behavioral objectives enhances teaching skills.

2. Once a series of performance (behavioral) objectives has been developed, it can be used to teach other children with similar needs. A well-written file of objectives can be a tremendous time-saver in lesson planning.

Basics of Writing Behavioral Objectives

It is difficult to select the most efficient route to a destination unless you know what your destination is. Behavioral (or performance or instructional) objectives require that the teacher state the destination precisely. "Fuzzy" terms are appropriate in goals;

however, they are not allowed in behavioral objectives. For example, a correctly written *goal* might read, "To teach the colors red, yellow, and blue." But the *objective* related to the goal must contain the following three components:

1. What the teacher will *provide, restrict,* and *do.*

2. What the learner will be *doing* or *saying* when the objective has been achieved (a behavior that can be seen or heard).

3. *How well* or *how often* the learner must perform in this manner to convince the teacher that the task has been learned (within what time frame this performance must occur).

An example of a correctly written objective related to the goal "To recognize the colors red, yellow, and blue" might be "When the teacher points to any one of 15 different items (five of each color red, yellow, and blue) and asks 'What color is this?' the children will answer within 20 seconds, stating the color correctly on 80% of the trials." Exhibit 4–2 illustrates terms useful in writing goals and objectives.

The standard that must be achieved to accomplish this objective is 80% of the trials. This standard is referred to as the **criterion.** Eight of 10 (or 80%) correct performances is usually described as "proficiency" on the task. Ten of 10 or (100% accuracy) is defined as "mastery level." (The level required must vary with the needs of individual children. Some cannot be expected to reach 100%.)

The following is an example of an objective and goal related to a social skill:

Goal: Increase social interaction with peers.

Objective: When placed in a situation where she has the only items essential for cooperative play, Alisa will share spontaneously during at least five consecutive play sessions.

In some cases a time limit becomes part of the criterion for judging successful performance, for example, within 2 minutes.

Exhibit 4–2

Appropriate Verbs for Writing Behavioral Objectives

1. Goals

The verbs suggested in this category are useful for writing goals but are *not* appropriate for writing behavioral objectives:

To decrease	To discover	To improve	To practice
To develop	To demonstrate	To increase	To understand

2. Behavioral objectives

The verbs suggested in this category are useful for writing behavioral objectives and can be used to describe observable behaviors:

To answer	To follow	To name	To recall
To color	To hold (as directed)	To pick up	To say
To complete	To imitate	To place together	To sort
To cut	To list	To point to	To use
To draw	To look at		

Guidelines for Choosing and Writing Behavioral Objectives

Teachers will want to write objectives to meet particular needs. Norm-referenced tests and preschool curriculum guides suggest similar goals for all early childhood classes. However, each class and each program is unique and special.

The following procedure has been useful in writing objectives for preschool children. Each objective must contain the basic components, but the manner in which they are recorded may vary. Several different forms are suggested, although the process of choosing them and sequencing them remains the same.

1. *Identify a particular goal.* Goals should state in general what you want the children to learn. Examples of goals include to improve self-esteem, to express feelings, and to develop expressive language. Goals are not specific. They do not describe what teacher or child will do.

2. *Decide what you want the children to learn in relation to the goal.* Choose the most difficult task

you want them to be able to do. Visualize exactly what they will be doing when you look at them doing it and say, "Now they *know* that." Write a description of what you have visualized in your mind's eye. This will be the observable behavior.

3. *Think about what you will give them and tell them when you want them to perform this observable behavior.* This will become the part of the objective that identifies what the teacher will do, provide, or restrict. Often this section begins with "Given" or "When the teacher."

4. *Write what you have visualized in the form you have chosen.* At first, it seems helpful to write the objective in one long sentence that includes all the components. Later, you may prefer the shorter versions. Each must be complete. It is important to state a criterion or standard within each objective. Each criterion must be reasonable, and it must fit that particular objective.

5. *Begin task analysis.* So far, you have chosen a goal, decided on the most difficult of the objectives you want to achieve in relation to the goal, and written

all this in the form you have chosen. What you have written is the **terminal objective.** Next, think about what you would need to do if the children could not achieve this objective in the way you have written it. Assume that it was too difficult for some of them. But you do want all of them to achieve it at least by the end of their experience in your program. How could you make it a little bit easier? Write this slightly easier **en route behavior** (one of the objectives on the route to the terminal objective). Sometimes it is helpful to actually do the task yourself or carefully watch another do it to determine the en route objectives.

6. *Continue task analysis as suggested in the previous guideline.* Write en route behaviors that are simple and include so many prompts (cues) that you are certain every child you teach will be able to do at least the easiest one.

7. *Do not try to write every possible step.* Choose steps between objectives that you feel the majority of the children will be able to take. (Analyze the samples offered with this consideration in mind.) If you have a child who can perform a specific objective but seems unable to do any part of the next one in your sequence, you may need to plan another *branch.* That is, it may be necessary to insert additional objectives occasionally. Usually these need not be added to your sequence but should be recorded separately on the child's record. If you discover that you need this particular branch for a number of the children, add it to your sequence. (As noted earlier, keeping each en route behavior on a separate card makes it easier to add or delete objectives.)

8. *Assemble your objectives.* At first, putting the en route behaviors on individual cards makes it easier to arrange them in sequential order. Later, as your skill in task analysis grows, it becomes less necessary. However, if the en route behaviors are on separate cards, it is easier to insert additional steps for children who need tasks broken into tiny steps. After assembling the en route behaviors (objectives), it is helpful to actually do the task as outlined to verify the initial sequence and detect any missing steps.

Write the goal at the top of the form you have chosen. Beginning with the simplest one, write the objectives in sequence from the easiest to the most difficult. Remember, the most difficult one is your terminal objective; all the others are called en route behaviors—similar to en route destinations on a trip. The terminal objective is your final destination, and the other objectives are specific places you will proceed through on your way to this destination. When you are headed toward a particular place on a trip, it may be your "target" for that day or week. In the same way, you may refer to a particular objective for a certain child as a target behavior. This process of analyzing terminal objectives and discovering and sequencing en route behaviors is referred to as the process of **task analysis.**

9. *Identify the entry behaviors of each child.* Each of the children will enter your preschool or center with some awareness of the information or behavior you have chosen to teach. A few will be able to demonstrate the skills described in some of your terminal objectives the very first day. Others will be completely unaware of any facet of that particular target behavior. This is why you must analyze the terminal objective and write the en route behaviors. Attempts are then made to determine which of the en route behaviors each child can do (assessment). Dates must be recorded. When this is done, each child's entry behavior has been identified. Now you know where to begin.

10. *Provide a variety of equivalent practice.* Use many different materials and toys until you feel your criterion has been achieved. Don't rush. At first, some children will progress very slowly. When you feel confident that an individual has achieved criterion on the entry behavior (the objective this child was able to do when entering your class), record the date next to the name and begin working on the next objective in the sequence.

11. *Provide as much equivalent practice as necessary.* The sequence of the objectives is intended to be useful to you in planning for all the children. Some of them may learn quickly. Do not be surprised if some children move through a whole series of en route behaviors and right through the terminal objective in a very short time. Others may take days

or weeks on each en route behavior. For accelerated children, a variety of activities and materials should be provided. Maintain the same level of difficulty your written objective states as you provide this equivalent practice.

Your written objective describes particular materials to be used in checking for criterion performance (at least in some instances). But you should feel completely free to use any materials you choose in lessons, games, or spontaneous play. The intent is to provide each child with many successful experiences (equivalent practice) on each level. The critical task is to *maintain the appropriate level of challenge*. A well-planned sequence of behavioral objectives serves as a helpful frame of reference for working effectively and efficiently with individual children.

12. *Use the objectives you have written as the basis for daily lessons.* As soon as you have written your first goals and objectives, experiment with them. Use them as the basis for lessons with individual children. Try using them with a small group of children who are working on adjacent en route behaviors. Next, attempt working with a larger group, all of whom are working on two or three adjacent objectives. Gradually, as you feel comfortable with this new way of planning lessons, attempt to include one or two children who are working toward the same terminal objective but are working on widely separated en route behaviors.

13. *Evaluate your objectives continuously as you use them.* Writing a series of objectives becomes easier with practice. Trial and error can be an efficient teacher. However, failure by the children must be interpreted by the teacher as an indication that the objectives must be changed in some way. Asking the following questions can be helpful if problems occur:

 a. Could the children do any part of the task?
 b. Did they listen and look, or were the directions too long?
 c. What modality or modalities were involved in the teacher's directions, that is, visual, auditory, tactile-kinesthetic, or combinations of these?

Photo by Lisa Wadors

 d. Which modalities were required in the response?
 e. What distractors interfered?
 f. What additional cues might have helped?
 g. Did both the teacher presentation and the expected response allow for individual adaptations because of disabling conditions? For example, if the child had a visual impairment, were auditory and tactile-kinesthetic clues provided? If the child had a hearing impairment, were visual and tactile-kinesthetic clues available?
 h. Was the time allotted adequate?
 i. Was the content limited and specific to avoid misunderstanding?
 j. Were the related subskills well learned before the presentation?

In practice, children should be able to demonstrate proficiency performance or 80% accuracy on one objective before proceeding to the next. The new objective should be partially achievable on the

first try. That is, if the next en route behavioral objective is a total mystery to the children (or to any one child), more branches or tinier steps are needed. A well-written sequence allows for continued success experiences, although a limited amount of failure can be instructive. It can lead the children to use their mistakes as clues in the discovery of what they need to do differently. But for children who have experienced a great deal of it, failure must be kept to a minimum for a long time.

14. *Add new goals and objectives to the curriculum as the need for them appears.* Remember, your goals and objectives are your curriculum. You will want to add to them regularly. You will also want to delete or remove some from time to time. As you become accustomed to thinking in terms of what the children say and do (or do not do) as a result of your teaching, you will feel more effective as a teacher. Planning will be simplified. Individualizing lessons, based on the en route behaviors you have written, will be much easier. En route behaviors that do not work can be deleted. More steps can be inserted, if needed, for some children. Many children will be able to achieve each en route objective rapidly. When the steps are small enough for the slowest to "climb," many children will achieve each level within a brief time.

FACILITATING TRANSITIONS

Transitions mean change, and change normally means increased stress for children and families. As IDEA makes a major distinction between services required for infants and toddlers (birth to age 3) and preschoolers (3- to 5-year-olds), transition from program to program is inevitable. There is also an inevitable change as children and families move from preschool services to those provided by the public schools for school-aged children. Part C does recognize the need to assist families and to ensure continuity of services. It requires that plans for transition be spelled out in IFSPs and that service coordinators assist families during these vulnerable periods of change. Interagency coordination and

written agreements clarifying local transition procedures are being developed throughout the country. Exhibit 4–3 notes some of the unique issues and challenges related to transition.

Although stress may be unavoidable, it can be lessened through careful planning that should begin as early as possible. Service coordinators and other interested professionals should be certain that transition plans are made and implemented only in the context of a partnership with the child's family. Transitions are normal life events that require well-planned steps in order to effectively cope with the changes required. Parents who are taking a newborn home from the neonatal intensive care unit or are realizing they are leaving behind the comfort of the infant program may be feeling very anxious. Professionals, through the development of well-articulated transition plans, can help parents turn these anxious moments into opportunities for growth.

Steps in Transition to Center-Based or Public School Services

DEC Recommended Practices (Sandall, Hemmeter, Smith, & McLean, 2005) offers guidance to service coordinators and others involved in assisting families through what can be a difficult transition when children move from early intervention to preschool services at the age of 3. The following suggestions to service coordinators and other early intervention professionals acknowledge these guidelines and requirements as outlined in P.L. 108–446:

1. Plan ahead in order to allow adequate time for planning and preparation. Planning should begin when a child is 2 years, 6 months, old and must be completed by the time he or she is 2 years, 9 months, of age.

2. In their preferred language, families must be given information outlining the steps in the transition process, their role, and the role of other individuals who will be involved.

3. Placement options should be discussed with family members, and they should be assisted in realizing

Exhibit 4–3

Transition from Early Intervention (Part C) to Preschool Special Education (Part B): Unique Issues and Challenges

- The transition from early intervention to preschool services often occurs at a time when families are still dealing with significant emotional issues, such as ongoing grief and anxiety, clarification of diagnosis, difficulty obtaining services and dealing with bureaucracy, and impact on family members.

- In some cases this transition occurs just as families are beginning to develop important trusting relationships and partnerships with early intervention service providers. The transition may be experienced by the primary caregiver (usually the mother) as a loss.

- Part B preschool services are frequently much less family focused and less interdisciplinary. Families may perceive that they are losing services.

- A "transition plan" at 2 years, 6 months, is federally mandated and is crucial for a successful transition.

- During the 6-month period prior to the child's third birthday, the child is evaluated and the IEP document drafted. During this time the early intervention program staff and the receiving educational program—who will be responsible for implementing the IEP—*must* work collaboratively with each other and with the family.

opportunities to visit potential programs and to talk with the service providers and families who may be familiar with the programs under consideration.

4. Steps should be developed to prepare the toddler for changes in service delivery, including steps to help the toddler be successful in the new placement.

5. Service coordinators or other service providers should be knowledgeable of service options, tasks, time lines, roles, responsibilities, and related procedures as designated on interagency agreements.

6. Receiving programs should be prepared to facilitate and support the child who will be entering their program. Reciprocal follow-up between sending and receiving programs should be encouraged.

The Role of the Early Childhood Special Educator in Facilitating Transitions

Early intervention specialists are in a unique position to help families and children make the move from programs for infants and toddlers to programs

for preschool-aged children. Families who are coping with their children's special needs in a demanding environment can be especially stressed in times of transition. They have many questions and are faced with the unknown. Teachers and other early intervention personnel can encourage parents to visit and become familiar with possible new settings for their child. They can directly prepare children and families by first understanding the environmental expectations of the placement possibilities. Whenever possible, children can be exposed to new routines and requirements ahead of time. Exiting teachers can work directly with receiving teachers in person, via telephone, and through reports to smooth the way and provide reassurance and support to parents. Putting parents in direct touch with parents who already have children in the new environment can be invaluable. These same concerns and strategies should be used when children move from preschool programs into public elementary school programs and beyond. The focus of this chapter was on the process of developing individualized intervention plans and programs. Families were seen

as central to these planning processes and to the success of their implementation. Chapter 5 will address effective intervention strategies for realizing the outcomes, goals, and objectives detailed in the individual plans. Attention is given to describing generic instructional strategies while recognizing the importance of play as a primary context for learning.

Summary

Before intervention strategies can begin, either an individualized family service plan (IFSP) or an individualized education program (IEP) must be developed. In developing either document, it is essential to remember that the process itself is much more important than the documents. Families must be the primary decision makers in determining how they wish to be involved and what outcomes or goals and objectives should be included. Both processes do require multidisciplinary team assessment and involvement in determining services and strategies. This team considers the child's current development level in determining eligibility for services. Each process requires annual reviews.

Even though IFSPs and IEPs are similar in intent, currently there are some important differences. First, the IFSP is family focused, whereas the IEP is more child focused. Rather than functional outcome statements, the IEP includes goals and objectives. To date, only the IFSP process provides for service coordination and definite steps to smooth the stress of transitions. Readers may wish to watch closely to see if the IEP process becomes more like the IFSP process as families become used to a family-centered approach to service planning.

Discussion Topics and Activities

1. Consider the following problems. The IEP conference for David has concluded. The parents are pleased with the suggestions made by the multidisciplinary team. These include continued placement in your preschool class for 3-year-olds. An early childhood special education teacher has been assigned to help you plan activities for David. Test results indicated that David is lagging in all developmental areas. What questions will you want to ask the special education teacher when he or she visits you the first time?

2. Interview parents who have participated in an IEP or IFSP meeting. Try to find out how they felt about the experience. Did they feel comfortable? If not, what bothered them about the process? Ask them what advice they would give to a new early interventionist for making families feel welcome and a true part of the team. Share your findings with class members.

3. Consult your instructor about setting up an opportunity for you to sit in on an IFSP or IEP meeting. Try to determine just what the teacher and others do to make parents feel that their opinions are important and that they are essential to the decision-making process. Interview the early childhood special educator to ask for clarification if you have questions.

4. Ask your instructor for assistance in determining whom to contact in your local area to become involved in the Part C implementation process.

5. Compare the IFSP process with that of the IEP. Determine what would be necessary to carry over the family-focused approach into the IEP process.

6. Become thoroughly familiar with the local agencies that provide services to young children with special needs in your area. With a class member, visit at least one local agency to become familiar with how services are accessed, exactly what services are available, and what the eligibility criteria are. By collaborating with class members, develop a directory of services useful to parents as well as early intervention professionals.

chapter 5

Implementing Intervention and Instructional Strategies

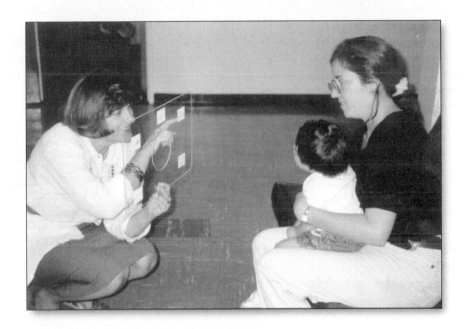

KEY TERMS

(Note: Terms are discussed within the text and/or defined in the glossary.)

activity-focused planning
alcohol-related
 neurodevelopmental disorder
antecedents
behavior analysis
behavior modification
consequences
contingencies
curriculum
ecologically relevant

eclectic model
effectance motivation
embedded learning opportunities
en route behaviors
equivalent practice
evidence-based practices
fetal alcohol spectrum disorders
high-preference items
high-preference inventory
mediated learning events

motivation
play
positive behavior support
positive reinforcement
progressive matching
reinforcers
scaffolding
social-transactional approach
successive approximations
zone of proximal development

- The content of curriculum must be functional and ecologically relevant.

- Curriculum content should also focus on the development of the underlying cognitive and psychoemotional processes that enable children to engage in self-directed learning and establish positive human relationships.

- Instructional strategies should be informed by meaningful assessments and reflect evidence-based practices.

- Identification of motivations is critical to successful intervention with infants and young children with special needs.

- Programs should use an "activity focus" by working on several objectives simultaneously in the context of a pleasurable and motivating activity.

- Adults play a crucial role in facilitating the development of infants and young children through responsivity to children's cues, use of communicative interactions, and social mediation of experiences.

- Creating a predictable environment through the use of routine and repetition is essential to children's learning and adjustment.

- One of the most important contexts for learning in the early education program is children's play.

- Careful arrangement of the physical environment is necessary to accommodate the physical needs of young children with disabilities.

- Thoughtful scheduling of daily activities through time-use plans provides for desired consistency and for a wide range of abilities and interests.

- Specific steps should be taken to prepare for the inclusion of young children with special needs.

- In addition to certain generic strategies, the early childhood special education professional must also have a thorough understanding of disabilities and at-risk conditions.

- The unique needs of all children must be considered and all should receive the services of a multidisciplinary team.

Up to this point, we have been concerned with issues preparatory to the delivery of direct intervention services such as the philosophical basis for inclusion of young children with special needs, history and legal precedents for early intervention, understanding and collaborating with families, assessment of child needs as mediated by family concerns, and the development of individualized service plans and programs. The purpose of this chapter is to suggest practical, generic instructional strategies that can provide the methodological foundation for intervention programs for all children. The overall approach presented in this chapter makes it possible to include children with disabilities or developmental delays in a wide range of early education programs. One such program is discussed in Exhibit 5-1.

CURRICULUM

Definition

Curriculum has been defined in various ways. Bowe (2004) defined curriculum as "a planned sequence of activities, including both content and process, through which educators change children's behavior. Curriculum is a vehicle for reaching goals and

Exhibit 5–1

A Child-Care Center Where Children with Special Needs Are Welcomed

Until recently, many public and private child-care centers were reluctant to accept children with special needs. They said that they were neither trained nor equipped to help them. Other centers accepted children with disabilities but simply took care of their physical needs.

Ms. Johnson and Ms. McLynn want to provide the best possible services for the children with special needs who come to their center. They begin by listening carefully to the parents' requests and descriptions of their children. Then they observe the children in their preschool environment.

These teachers find the following sequence helpful:

1. Before a child is enrolled, parents meet with the director and the teacher. Information, parent concerns, and available services are considered. The enrollment form includes questions about previous experiences as well as a health history. The child's developmental level is discussed.

2. For the first few weeks, the child is observed throughout the day. Special needs are identified. Ms. McLynn and Ms. Johnson discuss these with the parents at a second conference.

3. During this second conference, inquiry is made into what other services the child might be receiving and appropriate release of information forms are signed.

4. After a child has been evaluated and recommendations for intervention services and procedures have been received at an IEP conference regarding the individualized education program, Ms. McLynn and Ms. Johnson incorporate the suggestions and activities into the child's daily program.

5. Regular contact with parents and others working with the children is maintained through telephone conversations, conferences, and written reports.

This child-care center includes several children with disabilities during each session. If these children require a great deal of extra time and attention, an additional aide is provided.

Today this child-care center and others accept the challenge of including children with special needs. Wise teachers refuse to merely "love and take care of children." They are aware that the most critical years for learning occur before the traditional school entrance age of 5 or 6. As a result, they cooperate with parents and involved professionals by including children with special needs in their centers. They are careful to meet individual needs appropriately.

objectives as identified in individualized family service plans and individualized education programs—an ordered arrangement of individually selected learning experiences that respond to children's particular needs" (p. 156). This definition suggests that an acceptable early childhood curriculum is not simply a hodgepodge of objectives. It should provide a clear plan for programming that considers the needs of the child, parent, ethnic group, and general culture. Teacher styles and theoretical approaches influence its development.

Some time ago, Vincent (1988) aptly described curriculum as a "road map"—a tool that helps us know where we are going and how to get there. The desired outcomes for children and families are the destination. The instructional objectives and teaching strategies are the routes by which we get there.

Choice

Many types of curricula have been developed for infants and young children both with and without special needs. Curricula are based on various theoretical assumptions and have been designed in

a comprehensive way that may include criterion-referenced assessments; detailed, step-by-step behavioral objectives; and suggested activities and materials. These are often commercially available as packaged programs. It is important for early intervention professionals to understand, however, that such so-called self-contained curricula may or may not meet the needs of children in their particular programs. First, interventionists must clearly understand the nature of the children they are serving; they must identify their own as well as parents' educational goals for these children. Then they must examine the strengths and learning styles of children as well as their own instructional styles. A clear conceptualization of both the desired program outcomes and the best intervention strategies must be generated before a curriculum is selected. Early childhood special educators will find that packaged curricula need modifications and adaptations in order to meet unique needs of a particular group of children. They may also choose to design their own curricula.

To date, no one theoretical approach or curriculum has been found to be sufficient for children with disabilities. Programs that adapt curricula to meet the needs of children with a wide range of differences in skills learning styles, background, and potential require deliberate integration of facets from both early childhood education and special education. Early childhood specialists promote awareness of needs of the "whole child," whereas special educators promote awareness of unique needs of each child. These unique needs are considered in relation to environmental expectations. It is incumbent on the early childhood special educator to combine the best of both fields.

Linder (1983) pointed out long ago that most early childhood educational models can be described as falling on a continuum reflecting informal to formal structure. Exhibit 5–2 briefly illustrates this continuum, beginning with the most informal approach, often referred to as the child or normal development model, and ending with the most formal, behavioral approach. In between is what might be termed a cognitive/interactional approach based on the

Exhibit 5–2

| | **Informal** | | **Formal** |
	Child/Normal Development	**Cognitive/Interactional**	**Behavioral/Learning**
Role of the environment	Facilitate self-initiated involvement and child–child interaction	Facilitate active inquiry/ problem solving and learning from mistakes	Shape child's acquisition of specific behaviors
Role of adults	Encourages interaction with the environment and peers	Asks provocative questions; models, encourages exploration	Models, shapes, and reinforces desired behavior
Role of the child	Initiates own involvement	Explores, invents, problem solves, integrates concepts	Receptor and responder to information and reinforcement
Content of curriculum	All areas with emphasis on social emotional development	Key experiences that enhance cognitive development	Skills individually determined through assessment of deficits
Methodology	Play, centers, units	Centers arranged to maximize discovery; play	Objects, persons, and events are structured to reinforce behavior

theoretical orientation of Piaget and others that recognizes the dynamic nature of the interaction between the children's biological predisposition and the progressive changes in their environments. It is recognized that the brief description here does not do justice to any of the models involved. It is hoped that readers will be curious enough to search out a more in-depth explanation of each approach.

Considering Children with Special Needs

Bricker and Bricker (1974) were among the first to combine elements from a variety of approaches to develop an **eclectic model** for working with children with special needs. After careful consideration, these researchers felt that adherence to either a traditional maturational orientation or a behavioristic learning theory approach could not adequately account for the complexities of human behavior they would encounter. Therefore, they combined several key Piagetian concepts into a position they referred to as the "constructive interaction-adaptive" approach.

Anastasiow's (1978) discussion of their eclectic combination referred to it as the cognitive, learning model because it integrated the behavioral procedures for lesson strategies while also drawing on cognitive, psycholinguistic, and perceptual theories to diagnose the child's needs and to plan intervention programs. Exhibit 5-3 gives a glimpse into an eclectic approach that involves a combination of theoretical orientations in support of the inclusion of children with disabilities.

Philosophy of This Text

In practice, most programs for young children with special needs do combine elements of several curriculum models. The philosophy of this text is based on the following assumptions.

1. Curricula practices should be derived from **evidence-based practices** to the maximum extent possible. Authors of this text are in agreement with the definition of evidence-based practice proposed by Buysse, Wesley, Snyder, and Winton (2006). It reads, "a decision-making process that integrates the best available research evidence with family and professional wisdom and values" (p. 3). This definition recognizes that informed curricula decisions should build on a variety of sources of knowledge.

2. The content of the curriculum must include goals that are meaningful and relevant to each child within the context of his or her home and community. That is, they must be functional and **ecologically relevant.** Goals should be selected on the basis of their functional utility for the child in his or

---

Exhibit 5–3

Cognitive/Learning Perspective

Role of the environment	Structured but facilitative. Interest and activity centers.
Role of adults	Promote active exploration of the environment, play and peer modeling. Astute observer of children. Collect evaluative data daily and plan lessons accordingly.
Role of the child	Active explorer of the environment. Initiator of activities.
Content of curriculum	Goals derived from curriculum-based assessment. Maximize skill development in all areas. Foster spontaneous social and communicative interaction.
Methodology	Measurable behavioral objectives. Lessons in small steps using task analysis. Positive reinforcement of incremental progress. Use of play and embedded learning opportunities to encourage generalization of skills and functionality.

her immediate or next environment. In addition, curriculum content will also include the development of children's underlying cognitive and psychoemotional processes, which enable them to eventually engage in self-directed learning and establish positive human relationships.

3. As much as possible, intervention strategies should evolve around activities that target specific skills within the context of functional and normal daily activities (Squires & Bricker, 2006). Using functional behavior to enhance skills will promote generalization through the natural use of these skills. Educators must be prepared to provide direct instruction whenever needed.

4. The designing of specific behavioral objectives or benchmarks and **en route behaviors** will consider information related to the stages and processes of typical development. In addition, principles and techniques from the field of behavior analysis (e.g., task analysis) will be used as tools when necessary within the activity-based intervention.

5. Teaching strategies used to reach targeted goals will reflect a strong **social-transactional approach,** with the primary method of instruction being rooted in the quality of the social interactions between children and significant adults (e.g., teachers and caregivers) as well as between children and their peers.

GENERIC INSTRUCTIONAL STRATEGIES

A wide body of research and theoretical work in fields such as developmental and experimental psychology, child development, neuropsychology, and education has generated an extensive knowledge base from which we can develop a catalog of principles and strategies for early intervention. These strategies and principles are generic in that they apply not just to young children with special needs but to all children. They are based on several key principles that describe how children learn. Students wishing to develop expertise in the field of early childhood special education cannot hope to do so without under-

standing, first, how all young children learn and, second, how teaching strategies can be adapted and fine-tuned to meet the needs of children with special needs.

Motivation

One of the most powerful keys to learning is **motivation,** and it is one of the oldest notions in the field of psychology (Maslow, 1998). Motivation is an incentive or inducement to action. Human organisms behave and act on the environment for certain reasons. Young children with no disabilities are typically easily motivated; early childhood educators may not need to spend a great deal of conscious effort identifying and understanding the motivations of such children. For young children with disabilities, however, the identification of **high-preference items,** people, and activities is crucial to intervention success. If children are not paying attention and are not engaged, they are not likely to learn. It is very challenging for early interventionists to figure out what will attract and sustain a child's attention when it is difficult to "read" his or her cues, as is often true when children have multiple or severe disabilities. Klein, Cook, & Richardson-Gibbs (2001, p. 5) give the following examples of cues that may be missed or misunderstood:

- Children may not look directly at a toy or event. They may use peripheral rather than central vision, thus giving the impression of not visually attending.

- Children with special needs may not reach or point even though they are interested. This could be due to motor difficulties and/or visual impairment.

- Some children with special needs do not smile often or may have a rather flat facial expression. This may be characteristic of children with very low muscle tone or visual impairment, or it may be a symptom of an emotional disorder. Other children may lack a social smile but may smile unpredictably. This is sometimes a characteristic of children with autism.

On the other hand, Klein and colleagues (2001, p. 6) remind us of some of the unique ways of expressing interest and attention:

- Children may become very still and quiet when they are interested in something but may not be looking at or even facing the object.

- They may flap the arms and hands excitedly when interested in something.

- They may stiffen and extend the arms and legs or turn the head away even though they are interested. In other children, this reaction may be a sign of rejection or disinterest.

As a result of these kinds of difference, Klein et al. (2001) encourage early educators to conduct a **high-preference inventory** by interviewing caregivers and directly observing how children respond to the presentation of different activities, items, or persons and how they respond to the removal of such stimuli.

Effectance Motivation.   It is also important to view motivation as being of two types: external and internal. The techniques of behavior analysis and behavior modification rely primarily on externally provided motivators. These might include primary **reinforcers,** such as food and water, or socially conditioned reinforcers, such as praise or tokens. In addition to external motivation is **effectance motivation,** which is thought to be dependent on internal motivational factors as discussed below.

The classic theory of effectance motivation holds that all young children innately have an internal drive toward effectance or achievement (White, 1959). Children internalize or feel personally responsible for the mastery they have over their own behavior and the resulting effect on their environment. If free of disabling conditions, children can more easily feel pride in accomplishments they can attribute to their own effort or ability (Cook, 1986; Slavin, 2006). It is this personal feeling of control over oneself and pride in one's efforts that provides inducement to act (motivation).

The existence of an internal drive to have an effect on one's environment suggests the importance of encouraging young children to initiate interactions with both the animate and the inanimate world around them. For children without disabilities, the key to this type of motivation lies both in the opportunity for self-initiation and exploration and in the existence of a responsive environment. For children with special needs, teachers and caregivers must be able to read cues that are often ambiguous and that may occur infrequently. These cues must be perceived in order to identify situations in which a child with disabilities is attempting to act on the environment. It may also be necessary to manipulate the child's environment in ways that increase the likelihood that the child will initiate an interaction and experience success.

The teacher may have to, verbally and in other ways, call the child's attention to the fact that his or her actions really do make a difference. Only when the success of an action is attributed to one's own efforts can pride, resulting in motivation or the desire to try again, be realized (Cook, 1986). The following examples may help illustrate the importance of understanding children's motivations.

Johnny is a healthy, energetic, typical 4-year-old. Most of his interest is in large muscle activities. He loves being outside, riding tricycles, and climbing. One rainy day he wandered over to the cupboard where the play dough was kept, managed to precariously climb up on the counter, and opened the cupboard. Mrs. Hunt's first inclination was to reprimand Johnny for climbing, but instead she said, "What are you looking for? Can I help you?" She then realized that he was trying to get the play dough. This was uncharacteristic of Johnny because he typically had no patience for this kind of fine motor activity. So Mrs. Hunt decided to encourage his interest, and she provided him with the play dough. She also stayed close to him while he rolled it into balls and "snakes," assisting him and praising him occasionally. Thus, she was able to encourage participation in a new activity by taking advantage of Johnny's own drive to act on his environment.

Another child, Robert, has cerebral palsy. He has very limited movement in all four extremities. He cannot walk and is just beginning to reach and attempt to

grasp objects. Even though he has severe physical impairments, he has a great sense of humor and loves attention. During free-play time, he is placed prone on a bolster so he can watch two of his peers without disabilities, Maria and Jeff, playing with blocks. The teacher enters the group and begins to build a block tower just within Robert's reach. She demonstrates to Robert that if he reaches and contacts the block tower, he can knock it down. She pretends to be dismayed by the destruction of the tower. Robert beams. Now the teacher rebuilds the tower, and, without prompting, Robert reaches to knock the tower down again, thoroughly enjoying the game. Very shortly, Maria and Jeff want to get into the game, each building towers for Robert to knock down.

These scenarios demonstrate the use of motivation and the importance of having an effect on one's environment. In the first example, the teacher recognizes Johnny's interest in the play dough and responds to that interest, thus allowing him to have an impact on the objects and people around him. She then assists his development in a new skill area. In Robert's case, he becomes motivated by his effect on both the physical and the social environment. He experiences *effectance* by successfully making the tower fall down and also by initiating a turn-taking game (social interaction) with both his teacher and his peers. This is a result that is often difficult for young children with disabilities to achieve.

Behavior Analysis

The contributions of techniques of **behavior analysis** and **behavior modification** to the field of special education have been substantial. The ability to describe behavior objectively, analyze antecedent events and consequences, and shape children's behavior is a basic skill requirement for all educators. Although space does not allow a thorough presentation of the principles and applications of behavior modification in this text, early interventionists must acquire competence in the use of techniques such as successive approximations, the use of cues and prompts, and the provision of contingent reinforcement (see Walker, Shea, & Bauer, 2006).

Briefly, this approach is based on the principle that immediate consequences of a specific behavior can either strengthen or weaken that behavior. Consequences that are pleasurable are called *reinforcers*. Consequences that are unpleasant or aversive are called *punishers*. The use of punishers or aversive control is not appropriate for infants and very young children. However, the use of **positive reinforcement** can be very helpful in increasing the strength and frequency of certain behaviors. For example, giving a thirsty child a sip of juice each time he or she makes a sound might help increase vocalizations.

Whenever possible, the positive reinforcer should be a logical or "natural" consequence of the particular behavior rather than an artificial one. An example of a natural reinforcer for making the correct sign for a favorite toy would be providing the opportunity to play with the toy rather than receiving a piece of candy. Another example would be giving the child a glass of juice for saying "juice" rather than telling the child "Good talking."

Another key component of behavior modification is the planning and selection of specific cues and prompts. Again, whenever possible, the child should learn to respond to natural rather than contrived cues and prompts. Earlier behavior modification programs used highly structured programs aimed at so-called errorless learning. Teaching of specific skills was broken down into many small steps, beginning with highly contrived prompts that were to be faded gradually until the child could perform the behavior without prompts. Unfortunately, such procedures often produced children who were "cue bound"; that is, they continued to be extremely dependent on specific prompts. Generalization to other settings was difficult. For example, a child could be taught to say the word "cookie" in response to the prompt "Say cookie" but would not spontaneously request a cookie without a cue in another setting. Thus, more recently, emphasis has been placed on teaching children to recognize the appropriate situation in which to use the behavior and to respond to more natural cues such as an adult's expectant look or saying "Is there something you need?"

Still another key component of behavior modification is reinforcement of the child's **successive approximations.** This is a solid principle of learning based on recognition of the importance of starting with whatever the child can do and gradually encouraging closer and closer approximation to the correct behavior. For example, initially a child may be able to only swipe at a paper with a colored marker. Gradually the child can be reinforced for behavior that comes closer and closer to making a circle.

Positive Behavior Support.   Behavioral principles are also useful in our attempts to understand certain behaviors by carefully observing both the **antecedents** of the behavior (i.e., the events that occur immediately prior to the behavior) and its **consequences** (i.e., what occurs immediately following the behavior). For example, a child who has tactile defensiveness (i.e., is very sensitive to touch) may have frequent episodes of crying. Careful recording may reveal that these episodes are brought on by situations in which the antecedent event is the child's being crowded by other children. Observation may also reveal that the usual consequence of this crying is for the child's favorite adult to start talking to him. A simple intervention that may reduce the crying and increase the child's tolerance for crowding would be the following: When the favored adult notices the antecedent situation (crowding) occurring, she could approach the child *before* he begins to cry, commenting on how she is pleased he's having such a good time with the other children. Such a rearrangement of **contingencies** (i.e., what behavior or event follows or precedes what other behavior or event) both reinforces the child for participating and not crying *and* conditions the child to associate crowded situations with the pleasant experience of being talked to by a friend. This more recent, preventive approach to behavior management focuses on identifying the conditions that encourage positive behavior rather than focusing on reactions to already displayed negative behavior. The caregiver learns to predict the antecedents that help create negative behavior. By removing or revising these antecedents, the caregiver provides what is termed support resulting in positive behavior. Chapter 6 offers a more thorough discussion

on this more favored technique of behavior management, often referred to as **positive behavior support.**

Behavior management techniques can be powerful influences on children's behavior. It is extremely important that they not be used in isolation from a thorough understanding of the *whole* child. For example, one would not use behavior management strategies to control tantrums without also exploring all possible causes of these tantrums (e.g., medication effects, pain, or fear).

Social Mediation of Experience

The literature in the field of developmental and cognitive psychology is rich with both theoretical explanations and empirical descriptions of ways in which adults mediate (i.e., assist in making meaningful) the environment and the events that young children experience. Feuerstein, Rand, Hoffman, and Miller (1980) referred to these phenomena as **mediated learning events** or MLE, in which adults carefully enhance a child's understanding and mastery by translating events both physically and verbally as the child experiences them.

Another theorist, Vygotsky (1980), stated that cognition develops within a social context. He described the **zone of proximal development,** which is the realm of abilities that the child is able to exhibit while interacting with a significant adult but cannot perform independently. As sensitive adults interact with young children, they become aware of this zone and are able to facilitate development by providing just the right degree and type of support necessary to assist the child's progress toward independent mastery of a task. Bruner (1982) referred to this as **scaffolding,** or the providing of graduated cues to assist a child through problem solving. Such social mediation of the child's experience is important for all infants and young children regardless of their particular capabilities. Note the two examples that follow.

Jose is a highly gifted, somewhat rambunctious 3-year-old. He is trying to use three blocks to build a sort of archway for his truck to go under, but it is too narrow. He glances around briefly for a solution but quickly gives up and starts to move on to something

else. His teacher notices and says, "Gee, the space is too narrow, isn't it? The truck can't fit through there. The truck is too big. Hmm. What can we do?" While making these comments, the teacher finds a long piece of cardboard that, if substituted for the block across the top, will make it possible to widen the opening. She does not say this but simply offers the piece of cardboard to Jose. She waits, giving him the opportunity to discover the solution himself, which he promptly does. He pushes the truck through, and his teacher comments, "Oh, good. Now the opening is big enough for the truck to go through."

A second child, Min, has severe developmental delays and multiple disabilities. She is blind and nonambulatory. She is able to reach and grasp but does so infrequently. Her favorite activity is eating. She appears to be sensitive to food aromas because she becomes much more alert as lunchtime approaches and food carts are moved through the hallways. Her teacher helps Min organize and understand her experiences around lunchtime, mediating the environment around her. As the teacher notices Min becoming alert to the smell of the approaching food, the teacher says, "Lunch! It's lunchtime, Min. Let's get ready." The teacher first introduces Min's bib, encouraging her to touch and feel it, saying, "Here's your bib." The teacher puts on the bib, encouraging as much independence as possible by getting Min to push her arms through the holes. Next, as the cart enters the room, she taps its side so Min can hear it, then moves her close to it so she can feel it. The teacher says, "Good, our food cart is here. Now we can eat. I'll push you over to the lunch table."

In this way, the teacher is mediating what might otherwise be simply a confusing blur of sounds, smells, touches, and position changes. By doing this consistently, the teacher will eventually assist Min in understanding and anticipating these events.

Adult–Child Communication Strategies

As can be seen in the preceding examples, another critical factor in assisting children's learning is the use of language. How adults and older children talk

to infants and young children has a major impact on their development, particularly in the areas of language and cognition. These strategies will be discussed in some detail in chapter 8. However, it is appropriate to summarize them here as well.

1. *Use referential language.* That is, use the names of things and actions; be specific and concrete. For example, a child is enjoying rolling a ball down the slide. Teacher A might say something like "Wow! That's neat. Look at it go." Although this is an enthusiastic and positive response to the child's involvement, it is not referential. This comment would have a less positive effect on the child's language development than would teacher B's response: "Wow! The ball's rolling down. Down the slide. The ball's rolling down fast!"

2. *Use redundancy and repetition of key words and phrases.* It is not sufficient to refer to something only once. Language needs to be redundant, mentioning key concepts and events several times. In addition, repetition of key words and phrases is important. Redundancy and repetition are important to all children and even more important for children with disabilities. In the example above, the word "ball" is used two times, "down" is used three times, and "rolling" is used twice. Ideally, these three concepts would be introduced again during the play situation, in a slightly different context. For example, the teacher could roll a different ball down an inclined board, or the children could roll themselves down a hill and so on.

3. *Use routines.* Some degree of routine and predictability is important for all children. For children with special needs, the careful use of routines becomes an important teaching strategy. Repetition of key words and phrases within a familiar sequence of daily events facilitates language development. Both play routines and caretaking routines are effective strategies for encouraging many areas of children's development and will be discussed in more detail later.

4. *Provide comprehensive input.* The importance of comprehensive input was first described by MacNamara (1972). It is important for children to be tuned in to and understand what you are talking about, even if they don't actually understand all the words. Several strategies facilitate this. For example, adults can follow the child's lead and talk about what the child is paying attention to and experiencing. Originally, McLean and Snyder-McLean (1978) referred to this as "mapping language onto experience" (p. 193). Another strategy is to talk about concrete things that can be seen, felt, or heard. In this way, words can be associated easily with their referents.

5. *Match adult language to the child's language level.* For children who are just beginning to learn language, adult language input must be short, consisting of one- and two-word utterances and short, simple sentences. As the child's language develops, adult language can become more complex. MacDonald (1989, p. 173) referred to this as **progressive matching.** For example, John has just begun to use single words. As he is playing catch with his teacher, she says, "Catch. Catch the ball. Catch the ball, John." John's friend Theo, who speaks easily in simple sentences, joins the game. The teacher says, "Here Theo. Catch the ball, then throw it to John." In this way, the teacher models more complex utterances for Theo.

6. *Establish turn taking.* For very young children or children with severe disabilities, it may be necessary to first establish turn-taking skills before the strategies previously listed can be used effectively. Turn taking provides the social basis on which communication skills develop. In a child without disabilities, turn-taking skills are well established within the caregiver–infant dyad in the first 3 or 4 months of life. For some children, however, this may need to be established as a specific teaching goal. Several strategies can be used to establish turn taking: (a) imitating something the child is already doing, (b) engaging in a pleasurable activity and then interrupting that activity and waiting until the child makes some kind of response, or (c) physically prompting the child to take a turn. Chapter 8 will elaborate on other ways to develop communication skills.

Routines

Daily living routines are important in designing educational programs for young children. According to Rossetti (2001), "The EI [early interventionist] should

not feel the need to manufacture settings in which language might take place. Child-directed settings serve to maintain the child's interest, as well as increase the likelihood that newly learned skills will generalize to other settings. Adult-manufactured conversational opportunities need not be viewed as the goal. Rather conversational exchanges and opportunities that emerge as part of routine daily caregiving activities should be stressed" (p. 236). For infants, daily living activities may be referred to as *caregiving routines.*

Daily Living Routines.   Daily living routines are the kinds of routines that occur as part of carrying out the daily activities of life. Families may vary in the extent to which their lives are characterized by a predictable routine or schedule. Although some home environments may be quite predictable (e.g., wake up, eat breakfast, go to school, come home from school, have a snack, take a nap, play with Dad, eat supper, watch television, take a bath, read a story, go to bed), others may be chaotic and unpredictable. Some degree of predictability is thought to be important to young children. It helps them feel secure and gives them a sense of mastery and control over their

environment. As will be discussed in chapter 6, it facilitates both emotional and cognitive development.

Daily living routines are also important in the center or classroom for the same reasons that they are important at home. In addition, they provide useful contexts for teaching language and cognitive concepts. A familiar routine is a necessary background against which children with disabilities can experience novel and special events. For these children, such events can be attended to and processed more easily when they are experienced as different from the norm. On the other hand, when such events occur as simply one of many unexpected and unfamiliar events in a day, they are meaningless at best and probably confusing.

Play Routines.   Play routines provide another way to use repetition and routine in the classroom. Play routines can be designed specifically to teach language and concepts and social skills. A play routine often revolves around a pretend play theme, such as going shopping, going on a camping trip, finding something lost, hunting for treasure, and so on. The possibilities are endless. The purpose of a play routine is to provide a familiar activity sequence within which

Photo by Annette Tessier

to teach specific concepts, vocabulary, social behaviors, or pragmatic communication skills. The play routine requires a great deal of work and planning initially, but as the routine is repeated over and over, it becomes easier to implement while it also becomes more powerful as a teaching strategy. The complexity and content of the play routine will depend on the needs and characteristics of the children in the class.

Exhibit 5–4 demonstrates how the generic strategies discussed here can be incorporated into the medium of play, the context that is most normal to young children.

Exhibit 5–4

Use of Generic Instructional Strategies During Playtime

Event	Strategy
The children in Mr. Curtis's class have finished lunch. Mr. Curtis announces that it is time to clean up the tables and go to recess.	Signal for transition
The children are very familiar with this routine, so with little assistance they throw away their napkins and milk cartons and bring their cups and plates to the sink.	Use of routines
Andrea, a 4-year-old who has Down syndrome, heads out to the playground. On her way she notices the bottle of bubble soap on the shelf. She loves blowing bubbles and tries to grab the bottle.	
Miss Chinn, the aide, notices and asks, "Would you like to take the bubble soap outside?" "Okay. Can you get the bottle for us?"	Response to child's interest
Andrea reaches with one hand but has difficulty getting hold of the bottle. Miss Chinn gently moves Andrea's other hand toward the bottle, encouraging her to grasp with both hands.	Scaffolding
Andrea gets the bottle and carries it outside.	Child experiences success
Andrea's friend Alex notices that she has the bubble soap.	Peer interaction
He comes over and offers to help her get the top off. He blows some bubbles, then hands the wand to Andrea so she can try.	
The teacher approaches and sits down on the grass with the children.	Use of short sentences
He says, "Andrea, look at these bubbles. Many, many bubbles! Oops!	Repetition of key words
One popped. The bubble popped. Pop! Pop!"	
Andrea looks at Alex pointing to a bubble on the ground, saying	Child responds and is heard
"Buh!" Alex says, "Bubble. Right!" Then the bubble pops, and Andrea says, "Pop! pop!"	
Later that same day, Miss Chinn finds a balloon. She brings the balloon to Andrea, saying, "Let's blow up the balloon." Andrea does not seem interested at first, but she becomes intrigued as Miss Chinn starts to blow. She blows it up a little bit, then stops. She looks expectantly at Andrea.	Redundancy Generalization practice
Andrea waves her hand toward the balloon. Miss Chinn says, "Shall I blow some more?" Andrea says, "More."	Reading child's nonverbal cues
The aide finishes blowing up the balloon. Then she says, "I'm going to *pop* the balloon." "I'm going to *pop* it."	Responsivity Foreshadowing events
Andrea looks at her quizzically. Miss Chinn then takes a pin and pops the balloon. She says, "It popped!" Andrea claps her hands excitedly. She runs off to find her friend Alex at the sand table. She looks at Alex and says, "Pop!"	Social interaction Use of language to describe past events

PLAY AS AN IMPORTANT TEACHING CONTEXT

Skilled use of the strategies described here presents a significant challenge to the early childhood special education professional. There is no better context in which to use these strategies than the context of play. In fact, in many ways play is probably the single most important concept in early childhood special education. It is important both as a teaching context and as an end in itself. Play is an essential skill. Typical young children can often learn play skills with little guidance from adults. Many children with special needs, however, must be assisted in learning these skills. Thus, the teaching of play as a social skill is considered an integral part of the early education curriculum. This aspect of play will be discussed further in chapter 6.

Play is an ideal context in which to discover and mobilize children's motivations. It also creates a rich environment where teachers can use the interaction and mediation strategies described earlier.

Within the field of early education there is a strong historical precedent for a focus on play. Froebel, a German educator in the 1800s, believed that the principles of early education include the following:

1. Education should primarily protect and nurture.

2. It should not prescribe and control.

3. Play should constitute the heart of the curriculum.

4. Play is the means by which children gain insight.

5. Play is the means of mental development.

This is a strong endorsement of the role of play in education, and it has continued to influence the field of early education throughout its history.

It is equally important to apply this concept to the field of early childhood *special* education. This application requires some refinement. First, as mentioned before, some children with special needs do not engage in play easily. Thus, teachers must develop strategies not only for using play as a context but also for encouraging its occurrence. Second, it is

necessary to understand how the elements of play can be achieved for all children.

There are some 40 definitions listed in the dictionary for the word **play.** An operational definition that might be useful for our purposes would be the following: *play* is a situation in which an infant or child is actively engaged with his or her environment—either animate or inanimate—but for which there is not an intended or predetermined outcome or goal.

There are several key elements in this definition that parallel the principles and strategies discussed earlier and that demonstrate why play is such a powerful teaching and learning context. First, the child must be engaged. This suggests that, at the very minimum, there must be some information processing occurring; the child is paying attention to something. Furthermore, active engagement requires initiating and acting on the environment in some way. The term *environment* refers not only to the physical world of objects, space, and sensory stimuli but also (and perhaps more important) to the social environment. The social, or animate, environment consists of the people (and pets), communication, emotions, facial expressions, touches, and so on that impinge in some way on the infant's or child's experiences.

The element of play that perhaps most distinguishes it from other contexts or activities is the final element: there is no predetermined outcome or goal. In play, goals may emerge and unfold or arise spontaneously; outcomes are discovered through exploration and trial and error.

Given this definition of play, it can range from the simple exploratory behavior of the infant to the complex pretend scenarios of the preschooler. Playing peekaboo or putting blocks in a can may be play for one child, whereas pretending to be an alien from outer space is play for another.

Thus, play must be viewed as an important and necessary component of early childhood special education. It is, of course, not the only component. Routine daily living events are equally important contexts for learning. For busy parents, these contexts are possibly more important than play. There is also

an important place for more structured, traditional learning contexts, particularly as children reach preschool age or are enrolled in behaviorally designed programs that focus on particular skills or behaviors. But the hallmark of the competent professional in the field of early childhood special education will be the ability to unleash the full potential of play not only to facilitate learning but also to enhance the joy and quality of life for young children with special needs.

ARRANGING THE PHYSICAL ENVIRONMENT TO MAXIMIZE LEARNING

There is substantial evidence that the social environment, as reflected in the preceding discussion, has great effect on children's development. It is also important to consider how the *physical* environment can influence both children and adults in ways that will enhance children's opportunities to learn and to interact socially with one another. Generally, physical arrangements and facilities that are effective for typical young children will be suitable for children with special needs. However, some adjustments may have to be made, depending on the nature of the children's special needs. There may also have to be greater space within the classroom area to accommodate a larger number of adults, especially if active participation of family members is expected. A two-way mirror is helpful in allowing unobtrusive observation by families and teachers in training. The discussion that follows is meant to further highlight some of the unique considerations that might accompany integration of young children with special needs.

When integrating children who have physical challenges, ramps may have to be provided and enough space made available for children who need to maneuver equipment such as walkers or wheelchairs. Some may even need special positioning devices that take additional space within the classroom. Materials should be at eye level. Shelves and tables must be sturdy enough to support children who have difficulty standing and maintaining

balance. Sand and other activity tables should be set away from walls so that children may get to them from all sides. Tables with semicircular "bites" out of them and rims around the edges allow children to get closer to materials while also preventing items from rolling to the floor. In some cases, materials should be put on the floor. Nonslip floor coverings are necessary to prevent tripping or catching crutches. Adaptable equipment will be necessary to ensure full participation of all children.

For centers attended by children with visual impairments, room arrangements should be fairly fixed. Clutter must be eliminated. When changes must be made, it is important to assist children with visual impairments with adaptations to these changes. Routes from one area to another should be direct, minimize cross traffic, and be free of obstacles. Doors should be either fully open or completely shut. Sharp edges of tables should be padded. Auditory or tactile cues should be used to designate areas. For example, a carpet might mark the quiet corner and the bubbling of an aquarium the science center. Groups should be kept small and noise levels controlled to allow for maximal use of hearing.

Noisy, chaotic environments reduce opportunities for children with visual impairments to learn.

It is usually not necessary to make adaptations in facilities or equipment for children with cognitive, health, communication, or social-emotional differences. However, some children, such as those with autism, must have a well-organized and predictable environment in which to function (Magnusen & Atwood, 2006). Children who are experiencing difficulties in self-control or overactivity do require more clearly defined limits and greater consistency in caregiving in order to feel safe. Nevertheless, opportunities for as much natural social interaction as possible are essential to the success of an inclusive program.

Special Considerations for Infants and Toddlers

Some special concerns for infant and toddler environments are worthy of note. Health and safety issues are of primary importance. Floors need to be padded, sharp edges and table corners eliminated, and elevated areas be no more than 2 feet in height. Sinks and soap for hand washing and diapering must be conveniently located to encourage good hygiene. Diapering areas should not be located near food preparation centers. Carpets of short pile material will facilitate ease of cleaning. Storage areas that are easily accessible help avoid clutter and hazards in traffic areas.

Environments for infants and toddlers should be designed to encourage movement and interaction with one another. Movement can be facilitated by providing carpeted steps and ramps that lead to interesting play areas. Places to crawl through, such as tunnels, and cozy spaces to crawl into, such as a specially designed box or cubby, will motivate movement. Use of multiple elevations also encourages easier interaction between very young children and their caregivers by facilitating eye contact. Water beds set on the floor are effective movement motivators and can be comforting at the same time. Adult rockers and couches not only provide additional places for toddlers to climb into but also encourage adults' holding, reading, and talking to infants and toddlers. "Adopted grandparents" might be just the right people to provide needed encouragement to move and verbalize.

Providing choices for infants and toddlers whose disabilities may be confining is essential. They need incentives for body movement and a variety of toys. Toys and other interesting objects should be displayed clearly on shelves that are neutral in color so that the objects stand out. To avoid visual confusion, only a few toys should be visible at any one time. However, it is wise to keep some interesting toys in cupboards or on high shelves to encourage children's communicative behaviors as they request objects that they cannot reach.

Room acoustics can be optimized by use of absorptive materials on floors, walls, and ceilings to reduce resonance and ambient noise. Many children with and without disabilities (as well as many adults) find noisy environments distracting and disorganizing. This may be especially true of those who have visual impairments and those who are easily overstimulated. Constant background noise from radios and record players encourages children and adults to talk louder, thus increasing the overall noise level in the classroom. This, in turn, increases stress and fatigue. Of course, it is important that efforts be made to reduce environmental noise without inhibiting children's exuberance. Torelli and Durrett (2004) consider the environment to be a landscape for learning, as they discuss the fact that for mobile infants and toddlers, "exploring their physical environment comprises a great deal of the curriculum" (p. 11).

Before including young children with special needs, directors would be wise to assemble an advisory panel made up of a physical therapist, an occupational therapist, a child psychologist, a speech-language pathologist, a nurse, and an early childhood special educator. This committee can make recommendations for adaptations to be made in the physical setting and the program. Figure 5–1 illustrates one satisfactory environmental arrangement. Note that the library corner or block area may be conducive to "circle time."

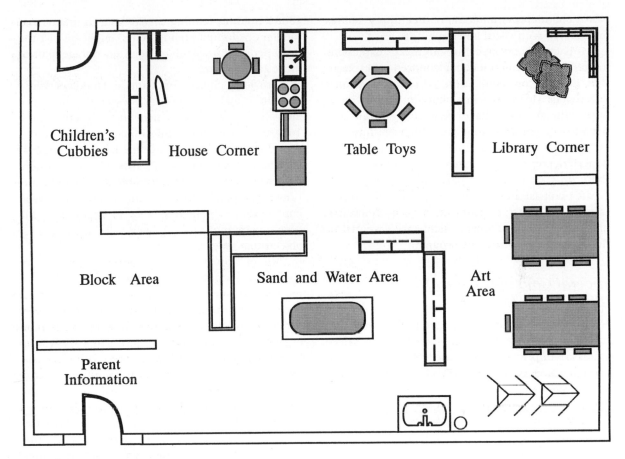

Figure 5–1   Room arrangement.
Source. Reprinted with permission from Teaching Research Division, Western Oregon State College.

EMBEDDING TEACHING AND LEARNING OPPORTUNITIES

When including young children with special needs in educational settings, early educators must select and schedule activities that allow for a wide range of abilities as well as interests. There is no special time for working on children's learning objectives. Interventions should be embedded within the daily activities and routines (Horn, Lieber, Li, Sandall, & Schwartz, 2000). **Embedded learning opportunities**, or those activities that originate out of natural play behavior, are very appropriate. For example, children can practice self-help skills in the dress-up corner, where they can learn naturally from their peers as the process of dressing and undressing occurs. In such an activity, each child's unique needs can be accommodated. One child can be encouraged to put on colorful socks while another is attempting to button a shirt and a third is tying shoes. All through the activity, children have the opportunity to socially interact. This is even more likely

if the teacher has contrived a purpose for the dress-up, such as "going out for lunch."

When scheduling center-based activities, balance is the key: there should be a balance of large-group, small-group, and individual activities; structured and unstructured activities; and active and passive activities. Activities should address all areas of children's development. Exhibit 5–7 illustrates such a balance.

Scheduled Plans Promote Desired Consistency in Routines

As discussed earlier, daily routines provide the consistency necessary to help young children feel secure and realize a sense of mastery and control over their environment. Scheduled plans are one means of regulating activities and providing for consistency through the establishment of daily routines. We acknowledge that teachers planning for a group of preschoolers rarely have the luxury of hours for planning on school time. Teaching young children is demanding work at best. It is important to develop efficient, effective ways to plan. This requires a well-organized curriculum.

The first step in planning is to ask the following questions:

1. How will the day be divided into the various activities?

2. How much time will be allowed for each activity?

3. Which routines and activities will be repeated daily (e.g., greeting the children as they arrive, circle time, bathroom routines, playtime, and outdoor time)?

4. How will themes be used to provide focus for the activities?

5. What use will be made of small and large groups for specific teaching?

6. Which activities must be repeated frequently over time to allow for increasingly complex skill development?

7. Who will have to follow these activity plans?

By answering these seven questions, a system appropriate for the classroom will emerge. First, consider question 7: who will have to interpret and follow your activity plans? Teacher aides and volunteers will need to understand what is being done and why, so while writing plans, you should consider the answer to question 7 continuously. Ms. McLynn's unique planning considerations are discussed in Exhibit 5–5.

Exhibit **5–5**

A Week's Plan and Individualized Activities

Ms. McLynn plans activities a week in advance. She is careful to choose things that the children are able to do and will enjoy.

Vocabulary, concepts to be emphasized, and gross and fine motor activities as well as music and stories are chosen in relation to a theme. For example, if the theme is "See signs of spring and learn about them," she will plan a walk to look at buds and spring flowers, plant seeds, do a craft (fine motor) activity such as making crepe paper flowers, and learn a song about spring.

Many of the objectives for each child require practice over time. Each day, Ms. McLynn chooses materials and games that promote these skills. This equivalent practice makes it possible for the children to do many different things at essentially the same skill level. They are not bored, even though they are practicing the same skills daily. The needed repetition never becomes meaningless drill.

Ms. McLynn found it difficult to include each child's individual objectives on the weekly lesson plan. She prefers to list the activity, such as "numerals and counting," on the plan. Then she uses her checklist and objectives to provide individualized

lesson targets for each child. This does not mean that she works with them one at a time. She conforms her directions and questions to each child on the basis of individual skills during the group activity.

Ms. McLynn's friend Ms. Watts has less experience in teaching young children with different individual needs. She prefers to have a separate page for each child. She writes the specific objective for each part of the weekly plan on each child's plan. Then she writes a comment each afternoon about the effectiveness of her planning. In this way she is learning to evaluate and adjust her planning. Each of these teachers chooses a theme and plans individualized activities within group lessons. However, they prefer different systems for organizing and record keeping.

In addition to the scheduled plan, a lesson plan form with spaces to write specific activities, strategies, and vocabulary for each day is also important.

Regardless of the materials used or specific activities, teaching will be guided by the specific objectives for each child. For instance, if the teacher chooses to teach colors this week by baking cookies and icing them with the colors being taught, he or she will conform to the objectives by asking some children to "Show me the blue icing" or "Use the yellow icing." For children who have demonstrated that they can *recognize* colors (e.g., "Show me") the teacher will be ready to ask, "What color did Joe use on his cookie?" This, of course, reflects individualizing because Joe is asked to *recall* the color, a more difficult objective than to merely recognize it when the color is named. When the teacher plans in this way, it becomes unnecessary to write objectives for each different activity because the teacher is providing **equivalent practice**. That is, the teacher is expecting each child to perform on the level identified on his or her individual plan.

Next, how the day will be divided and how much time will be spent on each activity (questions 1 and 2) should be considered. To avoid having to fill in a blank space each week with repetitive comments such as "Greet children individually" or "Take care of bathroom needs" or even "Sing the cleanup time song," it is helpful to write a schedule that can be used for many weeks. Any activities that are repeated daily should be included. Enough detail should be included so that a substitute will be able to have a clear picture of what is expected during each time segment. Exhibits 5–6 and 5–7 give examples of time-use plans.

However, some activities will involve cooking, whereas others involve dressing the doll, sorting different color toys, or choosing paper for a fine motor project. While teaching, the teacher is continually assessing the individual performances. He or she can be creative in the activities chosen but will not need to write each one in detail.

Exhibit 5–6

Example of a Daily Plan: Preschool Classroom

Time-use plan and description of daily routines for both morning and afternoon classes.

8:30 a.m. Greeting. Children are greeted individually as they arrive. Welcome by name, encourage to respond with eye contact, and use a smile and "Hello" or "Good morning." Help them only as much as necessary to hang up their coats and get ready for their special work. Ask whether they have brought a note from home. Some (as needed) go to the bathroom.

Active conversation with them about everything they are doing is a must because their primary need is to develop social, language, and cognitive skills about their everyday experiences. Encourage them to look into the mirror to see

whether they are neat and ready for school. During the first 30 minutes, children will appear to be playing, some alone and some in small groups of *their choice*. This open classroom is an important teaching time because children choose "lessons," games, or toys. Teachers, aides, and parents may play or work with them, but it is each child's option to choose what to do. Encourage children to choose carefully, complete an activity, and then return toys and games to the shelves. They are not required to share what they have chosen and may play alone if they prefer. It is important to enjoy conversation with children about what they are doing, although this will be a bit one-sided at first. Interactive conversation (which includes the adult's listening) is the optimum way to teach speech and language skills.

Concepts to emphasize are listed on the weekly theme page and on the *concept board* behind the teacher's desk. The intent of the concept board is to provide a "prompt sheet" for adults in the classroom to use these words continually in appropriate ways throughout the day. Contrive occasions for children to use these concepts correctly. Spontaneity is important. Repeated use is requisite.

8:45 a.m. Cleanup time. Children take turns ringing the bell to announce the end of play time. Sing the "cleanup" song. All participate in cleaning up and moving chairs to form a semicircle facing the bulletin board. Reward with praise those who arrive first with their work completed.

Circle time. Sometimes children sit on their own carpet squares on the floor or under a tree to allow for variety. The purpose of this period is to give children practice in participating, listening, and controlling themselves in a large group. This takes time. "Dailies" include a review of the weather, days of the week, the calendar, learning names, recognizing who is absent, and "show-and-tell." These activities not only help children become socially aware but also help develop their language expression, memory, and just plain everyday knowledge.

9:00 a.m. Small-group time. Children choose from activities previously set up by the teacher. These usually include a fine motor activity, language activity, problem-solving activity, and combination activity, such as cooking, which builds fine motor skills, language, and concepts. Some children may work individually with the teacher, aide, or therapist at this time. For children with special needs, choices may be narrowed to develop target behaviors such as cleaning up, toileting, and washing hands.

9:30 a.m. Snack time. A wide variety of nutritious foods are eaten to encourage conversation and understanding of differences, for example, in color, texture, taste, and shape. As children finish, they brush their teeth and select a book from the shelf.

9:50 a.m. Story time. Sometimes all children "read" to themselves. At other times, some read to themselves while others join an adult to listen to a story. When enough adults are available, several stories may be listened to in small groups around the room.

10:10 a.m. Movement time. Depending on the weather, movement activities may be inside the room, in the gym, or outside. Music may accompany such activities. The physical therapist may work with some children.

10:30 a.m. Music and art time. Music and fingerplay activities may be done in the group circle. Art activities are usually done in small groups. Sometimes parents will share special interests with children at this time. Choice is given, when possible.

10:50 a.m. Dismissal preparation. Children clean up and then join others in the circle. One at a time, children get their belongings and put on their coats while others exchange feelings about the day and sing the closing song.

11:00 a.m. Dismissal. Children are released to parents or bus drivers.

Note: Times suggested are approximate. Young children should not be rushed. Flexibility is necessary to capture "teachable moments" and to accommodate special events such as field trips.

Exhibit 5–7

Example of a Daily Plan: Infant Toddler Center

B. Ammons	D. Tison
Teachers	**Physical Therapist**
A. McKail/C. Rodriquez	M. Briggs
Assistants	**Speech Therapist**

DATE: September 20

Time	Daily Activities	Notes
9:00	1. Arrival	1. Staff will greet bus and assist children and parents in coming to classroom.
	2. Facilitated play • Puzzles • Blocks • House play • Mirror activity: old hats • Manipulative toys	2. • Optional areas: floor, table, and room areas. • Assistance given to individual children or small groups—encourage participation. • Objectives: language, socialization, fine and gross motor.
9:25	3. Transition	3. • Give signals/cues to end play. • Allow time to leave play areas. • Bring chairs to circle. • Assist in positioning children who need help.

9:30	4. Large-group circle
	  A. Music (with guitar)
	  "Good Morning"/"Buenos Dias"
	  "Where Oh Where?" (sing each child's name) "Wheels on the Bus"
	  B. Activity
	  "What's in the Box?" (balloons hidden in decorated box). Blow up balloon and pass around.
		4.
		  A. Parents may be encouraged to sit with the children.
		
		  B. Objectives: language concepts, social interaction, attention, motor activity, problem solving.

9:45	5. Outside play yard: facilitated and self-directed play: • Sandbox • Water play • Trikes, cars, wagons • Playground equipment (slides, ladders, swings, etc.)	5. • Objectives: gross motor, social interaction (encourage children with disabilities and those without to interact with toys, games, equipment); exploration through movement and space. • Parents are encouraged to participate.
10:15	6. Small-group activity (four or five children in each group). • Make pudding (choose flavor, open box, mix, taste)	6. Objectives: language concepts, choice, taste, social interactions, fine motor.
10:40	7. Cleanup Toilet	7. This is time for children to help clean up— wash pans and hands. As cleanup proceeds, two or three children go to "potty room." This is an important time for teaching self-help skills, language, and so on.

11:00	8. Lunch Cleanup	8. Good teaching opportunity: • Encourage self-help, language, socialization. • Attention to positioning and feeding techniques (as needed).
11:45	9. Closing: Large-group (three classes) music/activities	9. Parents, children, and staff join together in music, rhythms, rhymes, and relaxation. Bilingual songs and games.
12:00	10. Going home	10. Staff assists parents and children in going to bus.

Important Components Underlying Daily Program

1. Physical therapists and speech therapists work in classrooms throughout the morning.
2. Parents participate in classroom or observe through one-way mirror or socialize with other parents in parent room.
3. Bilingual interactions throughout morning activities.
   • Spanish/English
   • Chinese/English
4. Each child has individual goals within daily activities.
5. Signal transition times.

PROVIDING A VARIETY OF ACTIVITIES TO ACCOMPLISH ANY ONE OUTCOME OR OBJECTIVE

In choosing appropriate activities to achieve any one outcome or objective, educators are limited only by their imagination and creativity. For example, the following objectives might be chosen to achieve the goal "To learn the names of body parts":

Terminal Objective

When the teacher points to any body part (eyes, ears, nose, mouth, arms, hands, or feet) and says, "Tell me what this is called," Danny will name them correctly 80% of the time. Each body part will be checked on a doll, the child, and another child.

Individual (En Route) Objectives

1. When the teacher points to any of the body parts listed and says, "This is a _____," Danny will imitate the teacher's spoken model.

2. When the teacher points to any of the body parts listed and says, "Is this the _____?" Danny will name the part.

3. When the teacher says, "Show me your _____," Danny will point to his own named body part.

4. When the teacher asks, "What is this?" while pointing to his or her own, another child's, or a doll's features, Danny will name the features correctly.

The following list of activities could be used to provide equivalent practice on any of the objectives just described.

1. Bathing a doll
2. Dressing a doll
3. Washing hands and faces
4. Doing a puzzle (that includes body parts)
5. Drawing at the chalkboard
6. Drawing on paper

7. Making a jack-o'-lantern

8. Pasting features on a teddy bear made of construction paper

9. Singing a song ("Made up" chants are fun, such as "I touch my nose and blink my eyes. I clap my hands and say 'Surprise!'")

10. Making a gingerbread man

11. Telling stories and encouraging the children to act them out

12. Putting on puppet shows

As illustrated in the following dialogue, these activities will allow children to work on different en route behaviors while participating in an activity together.

The Activity: Bathing a Doll

Equipment: Aprons, warm water, soap, washcloths, towels, a doll bathtub, and a dirty doll.

Teacher: Sally, will you help me wash our doll? She is so dirty. Look at those hands and feet. (Pointing.)

Sally: I get the water and soap.

Danny: Wa-er (water).

Teacher: Get the towel, Danny.

Vicky: Where? (Grabbing the doll.)

Teacher: Hold her very carefully, Vicky. Be gentle. (Pointing to the arm.) See, her arm is all wet.

Danny: Dere no (nose). (Pointing.)

Teacher: Right Danny, that's her nose.

Danny: Wha da? (What's that?)

Teacher: That's her ear. (Pointing.) Can you find her other ear?

Danny: Dere (There).

Teacher: Right!

Using the objectives, the teacher can individualize any activity by applying the expected level of performance (criterion) requirements to the activity.

Evaluating the Effectiveness of Each Activity

The usefulness of any activity is determined largely by its appeal to children. In addition, the activity should lend itself to repetition with minor variations.

(Children enjoy a meaningful amount of repetition.) Each activity should be chosen to develop skills in ways that are a challenge but do not overwhelm the least capable child in the group. Participation is a prerequisite for effective learning with young children. "Just watching" is a useful beginning for some very shy or young children. With gentle encouragement, these children can be helped to become full participants.

Using an Activity to Achieve More Than One Objective

Squires and Bricker (2006) suggested an "activity focus" for program planning that builds on Bricker's (1998) early work. This approach suggests that programs must be built around activities that are *appropriate* and *motivating*.

Most activities can be used to achieve several objectives at the same time. For example, learning to follow two- and three-stage directions is an important skill. Counting and learning colors and other concepts are goals included in every preschool curriculum.

In bathing the doll, teachers might say, "Get the blue towel. It is under the sink" (emphasizing color and the preposition *under*). She might say, "Take off both socks. See, one sock is on her foot, and the other is on the floor" (emphasizing one-to-one correspondence, foot, and the preposition *on*).

Of course, most preschool teachers do many of these things spontaneously and without much conscious planning. However, when the program includes children with special needs, this important emphasis on specific skills cannot be left to chance. These children require explicit examples, meaningful repetition, and a variety of related experiences. One experience is inadequate. The ability to generalize from one experience to the next must be conscientiously nurtured.

PREPARING THE WAY FOR SUCCESSFUL INCLUSION OF YOUNG CHILDREN WITH SPECIAL NEEDS

The following suggestions are based on the belief that teachers play the central role in the development of programs to successfully include children with special needs. The tone of the classroom is set through the teacher's attitudes and actions; therefore, teachers are strongly encouraged to acknowledge their own fears and apprehensions before initiating an inclusive program. It helps to remember that every child is more like others than different from them. Understanding that all children can have adjustment problems because of their stage of development makes it possible for teachers to recognize that some deviant behavior is just plain normal. Learning something about each specific disability will alleviate many fears and make the teacher feel less helpless. Preparation and planning will go a long way in smoothing the transition for children, families, and staff. The following suggestions are general and can be considered only in light of each specific situation:

1. *Meet with the child's parents before including him or her in the program.* Besides seeking vital parental support, you can explore special interests, specific problems, and solutions. Unpleasant times may be avoided through preventive advice. Some teachers find it helpful to have the child visit the classroom either as a guest for a short time during the day or after the other children have departed. Arranging such a visit before a regular day of enrollment relieves the fears of many children.

2. *After the brief visit just described, phase children in slowly.* A parent may need to be present in the beginning. Adding only one child with special needs at a time will allow you the opportunity to give as much individual attention as necessary.

3. *Prepare already enrolled children in advance.* Be honest in dealing with children's questions. It is extremely important to understand and deal with the fears and concerns of the children who are not disabled.

4. *Be honest in dealing with children's questions.* Give short, truthful answers. Avoid making a big production about introducing the child or explaining his or her differences. Remember, children are more alike than different. To the child who asks, "Why does Susie talk so funny?" you can reply, "Susie had an operation so that she can learn

to talk just like you. Perhaps you will be able to help her make new words while you are playing with the puppets today."

5. *Deal with fears and concerns of parents.* In general, parents of young children tend to favor inclusion. However, they often do have concerns as to whether children will receive adequate attention in integrated programs and question the adequacy of staff training. Parents of children with disabilities also express concern that integrated settings may result in social rejection of their children. Staff must be adequately trained to deal with fears and concerns of parents. Facilitating meetings between parents of children with and without disabilities can be helpful. Parents also appreciate receiving information from clear, relevant, and readable materials that address their concerns and questions.

6. *Give all parents support and encouragement.* They will need it. They especially want to be kept informed of their child's progress. Be positive and encourage them to participate as much as possible.

7. *Be positive.* Focus on the attitudes and behaviors you wish to see in children. Be what you want to see expressed.

8. *Be realistic.* Do not expect too much or too little. Go slowly. Get to know the child well. By thoroughly understanding the child's developmental strengths and weaknesses, you can be realistic.

9. *Do not be afraid to be structured.* Young children need clear, firm guidelines for behavior. Identify specific safety rules. Tell and show the children what to do from the first day when safety and cleanliness are involved.

10. *Develop guidelines for classroom behavior with the children whenever possible.* Keep the rules simple and few in number. Do not expect the child with special needs to understand and follow all rules immediately. Tell other children that they must help the new child learn by showing him or her how to behave.

11. *Highlight the strengths of the child with special needs.* These need to be real. For example, a child may know how to operate a computerized communication device or may be artistic or good at drawing detailed designs (e.g., child with autism). Express enthusiasm and pleasure as each milestone

(no matter how small) is achieved. Be genuine. Do not exaggerate.

12. *Be sure the child with the disability is not always the recipient of assistance.* Create opportunities for him or her to help others.

13. *Seek to change the environment, not the child.* Be creative in designing strategies to support participation in all activities.

14. *Train staff to facilitate peer social interactions.* As social interaction between children with and without disabilities does not happen automatically, staff must be trained to facilitate this interaction. Resources in the form of consultants and curriculum guides such as those described at the end of the chapter are helpful. Assigning "special buddies" for all children is a very effective technique for seeing that children with disabilities become socially included. The typical peer buddies should be trained so that they will understand how the child with a disability communicates—how to read that specific child's cues. The typical peer can be given definite strategies for initiating and responding to the child with the disability. Other useful strategies such as small-group "cooperative learning" activities and physical proximity control are discussed in chapter 6.

15. *Most of all, do not expect too much of yourself or of the situation.* Progress takes time.

CONSIDERATIONS FOR ADAPTING CURRICULA FOR CHILDREN WITH SPECIFIC SPECIAL NEEDS

It must be remembered that a child with disabilities is first a child. The suggestions given here are designed to help teachers, parents, and other caregivers meet those special needs that can get in the way of a child's opportunity to experience the best possible childhood. These ideas are suggestions to be accepted, rejected, or modified to meet each child's unique needs. Of course, only some of the many possible considerations are included here. Numerous others can be found in appropriate sections throughout this text. We hope they will serve as a stimulus to the development of many other successful adaptations.

Health Impairments

Common chronic health problems include allergies, anemia, asthma, cancer, cystic fibrosis, juvenile diabetes, epilepsy, heart defects, hemophilia, pituitary problems, juvenile rheumatoid arthritis, muscular dystrophy, and sickle cell disease. No attempt will be made here to describe each of these problems in detail. A number of them are defined in the glossary. For more details, readers are referred to medical and nursing reference books. The suggestions made here are appropriate for almost any child with chronic health impairment regardless of its specific nature.

Caregivers must work closely with health care providers not only to ensure coordination of care of the primary disorder but also to assist in the maintenance of general health. Remember that children with health impairments are more prone to common illnesses such as colds, ear infections, or diarrhea than are typical children. Children with chronic health needs usually miss more school, spend more time convalescing at home, and are hospitalized more frequently than are children with most other disabling conditions. Repeated separation and trauma create emotional and physical stress.

Much greater responsibility is placed on parents, who must continually monitor the child's health, chauffeur the child to and from appointments, endure the anxieties of medical routines, and sometimes perform daily therapy. In addition, some chronic health problems are life threatening. Caregivers must, then, be more sensitive and supportive than usual.

Specific Strategies for Working with a Child with Health Impairments.

1. Find out as much as possible about any health problems experienced by children in your program. Read widely and personally visit health care agencies. Ask questions and record answers. Pay attention to the role of diet, medication, possible side effects of medication, physical restrictions, and behaviors indicating that a chronic illness is becoming acute.

2. Consult the child's parents and the primary care physician in planning the child's program. Become aware of what may cause a health crisis such as a seizure or insulin reaction. Caregivers must be completely prepared to deal with any such health-related crisis. They must know what warning signs to look for, what accommodations are appropriate, and how to follow through on emergency measures.

3. Prepare classroom aides and other children for the possibility of crisis events so that no one will be frightened and everyone will receive appropriate care. Perhaps a curriculum unit can deal with emergencies, including fire protection, earthquake procedures, and so forth. Then the child who has a health impairment is not made to feel different.

4. Prepare a list of typical classroom activities. Ask the parents and the physician to note which activities should be avoided and to suggest adaptations so the child can participate as fully as possible.

5. Encourage the child to be as independent as possible.

6. Some children fatigue rapidly. Arrange the class schedule so that vigorous activities are followed by less strenuous ones. Do not restrict a child unless there is a clear physical or emotional danger.

7. Help children understand the implications of their health problems. Be open and encourage them to discuss or act out (in play) their fears and anxieties. Children who understand what foods they can or cannot eat, what activities they must avoid, and so on can begin to make decisions for themselves and thus feel more in control of their lives.

8. Develop a plan for keeping in touch with children who must be absent for long periods. Telephone calls, cards, and tape recordings can go a long way toward helping children cope with isolation.

Hearing Loss

A hearing loss ranges from mild (hard of hearing) to profound (deaf). Specialists (audiologists, otologists, and speech-language pathologists) can assist

caregivers in understanding the degree to which development of communication skills will be affected by the disabling condition. Parents should be consulted to determine how much hearing capacity the child does have and which teaching methods and communication system (oral vs. total communication) to use with those who have more severe impairments. Early developmental milestones will be similar to those of the hearing child. The impact of a hearing impairment is most obvious in language development. Cognitive ability is hindered only to the extent that performance depends on language comprehension and use. Children with hearing impairments may exhibit inappropriate behavior due to lack of understanding or resulting socialization problems.

Specific Strategies for Working with a Child with a Hearing Loss.

1. Seat the child up close for good visibility of teacher, activity, or other children.

2. Experiment to find out or ask parents how close a speaker must be for the child to hear.

3. Provide the child with experiences that make use of residual hearing.

4. Speak at normal speed and volume without exaggerating lip movements.

5. Avoid speaking with your back to the child or with a bright light behind you. Don't inadvertently cover your mouth when speaking. Realize that moustaches and beards do interfere with visibility of lip movements. Lipstick may enhance visibility.

6. Use normal vocabulary and sentence structure. Be prepared to repeat, rephrase, point out, or demonstrate if the child does not understand.

7. When seeking the child's attention, be certain to use his or her name. Teach the child to attend to your face and do not give any directions until the child is obviously attending.

8. When teaching the child, use visual and tactile aids. Model the desired behavior whenever possible.

9. Learn to change a hearing aid battery and/or cord.

10. Encourage speech in group activities by allowing time for the child to start and finish speaking.

11. Work closely with the audiologist and speech and language specialist in planning programs for any child with a hearing impairment.

12. Adaptations made for children with speech and language delays will also be effective with children with hearing impairments.

Difficulties in Learning

Children with learning impairments are those who may be at risk for the development of learning disabilities or who for some reason learn "differently." Such children may exhibit excessive motion, find it difficult to attend or concentrate, lack coordination, experience difficulties in visual or auditory processing of information, have poor memories, or have difficulty in abstract reasoning and in making generalizations. Such disabilities are often difficult to detect and accept because they may be invisible.

Specific Strategies for Working with a Child with Difficulties in Learning.

1. Be consistent in the use of behavior management techniques to increase or decrease movement. Structure and consistent classroom organization helps those children feel secure and respond appropriately to their environment.

2. Present content in short segments using a multisensory approach (audio, visual, or manipulative). Provide for as much overlearning or repeated practice as necessary.

3. Analyze tasks. Break them down into as many small steps as needed for success. Use short sentences and simple vocabulary.

4. Use concrete examples when presenting new concepts. Choose functionally important concepts, not just those next on the developmental scales.

5. Praise the child's progress, no matter how small.

6. Concentrate on each child's strengths, not weaknesses.

7. Be patient when it is necessary to show a child how to do something many times. Don't expect children to generalize easily.

8. Give directions one at a time until a child can handle more than one. Provide physical help if necessary.

9. Consult with speech and language specialists in planning the child's program. Suggestions for the children with hearing impairments, visual impairments, and speech and language impairments are also useful for those with learning disabilities.

10. Help parents understand that such children are not just "dumb" or stubborn. Encourage the establishment of consistency and opportunities for multisensory learning experiences at home. Help parents recognize their children's small successes.

Physical Disabilities

Orthopedic impairments (of the bones, joints, or muscles) may be the result of conditions such as arthritis, cerebral palsy, muscular dystrophy, spina bifida, and spinal cord damage. Characteristics will vary by the nature and severity of each condition. Children with physical disabilities acquire information and manipulate the environment through other sensory modes. Children who are severely involved communicate and signify learning through breathing changes and eye blinks.

Of course, the most obvious developmental disabilities are in the motor area. Such children may attain motor milestones at a different rate or in a qualitatively different way than typical children. Some will never attain certain milestones. Certain aspects of language and cognitive development will be delayed because of motor impairment. For example, inability to grasp and manipulate the environment contributes to delayed problem solving. Alternative responses using adaptive equipment may be necessary to enhance cognitive development.

Delays in postural control and inability to use the muscles necessary to imitation may hinder development of communication skills. Speech itself may be directly affected. Children with physical disabilities who are unable to cuddle with their caregivers may not receive the positive interaction so necessary to all aspects of early development. Frustration may be a major part of life for both children and parents.

Specific Strategies for Working with a Child with Physical Disabilities.

1. Review the suggestions made for working with the child with health impairments.

2. Proper handling and positioning of the child is extremely important. The child needs to feel comfortable and well balanced to be able to concentrate. Consult the parents and physical therapist in order to determine appropriate positions. For example, a prone position over a bolster will allow the child to make visual contact with the environment. A side-lying position may assist arm and leg movements. Each child's position will usually need to be changed every 20 to 30 minutes.

3. Arrange activities and the environment so that minimal movements will produce effects on the environment.

4. Use adaptive equipment that allows the child to interact with the environment as much as possible. Consult specialists in making the most appropriate physical adaptations to the classroom and its equipment.

5. Become proficient in the use of wheelchairs, crutches, braces, artificial limbs, and other mechanical aids.

6. Consult speech and language specialists in order to identify a successful response mode for the child. Special language boards will need to be constructed for some children.

7. Work toward realizing the goal of maximum physical and social-emotional independence for each child. Positive self-regard may be the key to future motivation and self-fulfillment.

8. Do not underestimate a child's capabilities; do be realistic.

Visual Disabilities

Legally, a person who is partially sighted is one with corrected visual acuity between 20/200 and 20/70. The term *partially sighted* is used when there is enough usable vision for learning with the help of correction. A person who is legally blind has corrected visual acuity no better than 20/200 in his or her better eye. Such a person sees at 20 feet what those with normal vision see at 200 feet. Vision loss may result from common refractive errors (nearsightedness or farsightedness) or from impairments such as amblyopia (lazy eye), cataracts, cornea damage, detached retina, glaucoma, and retinitis pigmentosa.

Many of the children enrolled in mainstreamed programs will have some functional vision. Visual impairments do affect other areas of development. Delays have been noted in motor milestones that require self-initiated mobility, such as elevation of self by arms, raising to a sitting position, or running. Delay in the use of the hands results in delay of concept development.

Depending on the severity of vision loss, there may be a corresponding delay in language development due to the inability of the child to discern facial expressions, including the movement of lips and decreased stimulation. The ability to visually associate concrete objects with verbal labels is highly critical to early language development. Many children with severe visual impairments also experience difficulty with personal and possessive pronouns. In general, both cognitive and language development are hindered by lack of stimulation.

Specific Strategies for Working with a Child with Visual Disabilities.

1. Consult with the child's parents and vision specialists to determine just what the child can see. Many children can at least see shadows, color, and sometimes large pictures.

2. For some children, peripheral vision may be best. Therefore, do not assume that a turned-away head means inattention.

3. Be aware of lighting conditions and their effect on the child.

4. Orient the child to the classroom layout and materials location. Give a new orientation whenever changes are made.

5. Areas of the classroom can be identified by different floor coverings, different mobiles, and so on.

6. Provide the child with a rich variety of tactile, manipulative, and auditory experiences.

7. Facilitate auditory localization, reaching for sound, and auditory discrimination skills.

8. Try to keep the general noise level down, as a child with visual impairments relies heavily on auditory cues.

9. Encourage independence both by your actions and in the way the room is arranged. For example, giving the child the cubby at the end of the row will make it easier to find. Experiment with bright, shiny, and lighted objects of various sizes and shapes.

10. Encourage children to identify themselves when they approach a child with severe visual impairments.

11. Be alert to the need for physical prompts. When teaching new self-help skills, work from behind the child and gradually reduce the help given.

12. Before beginning a new activity, simply say what is going to happen.

13. Consult with specialists to develop aids for the child who is partially sighted. For example, black pen marks on the edges of paper will help the child know the boundaries of the drawing pad.

14. Be creative in finding ways to help the children develop a positive concept of self.

Autism Spectrum Disorders

Autism spectrum disorders (ASD) range from a severe form called autistic disorder to a milder from called Asperger syndrome. No two individuals with ASD seem to have identical symptoms. A symptom may be mild in one child and severe in another.

Children classified with ASD vary widely in abilities. Some may demonstrate near- or above-average intellectual and communication abilities, whereas others may be severely developmentally delayed and may never develop spoken language skills. Therefore, ASD is used to refer to the broad range of subtypes and levels of severity that fall on this spectrum of pervasive developmental disorders (PDD). However, the term *autism* is often used either specifically to refer to autistic disorder or more generally to ASD.

Difficulty relating to others, socially and emotionally, is a hallmark of autism. Children with autism often demonstrate restricted or absent pretend play. They frequently engage in repetitive, stereotyped behaviors (e.g., hand flapping) or ritualistic behaviors (e.g., sequentially touching certain objects on entering the classroom every day) and may become agitated in response to change. For the official diagnostic criteria on autism, refer to the *Diagnostic and Statistical Manual of Mental Disorders* (American Psychiatric Association, 2000).

On the other hand, children on the spectrum tend to display strengths in rote memory, visual memory, and processing and are likely to pursue their special interests. Some of the specific strategies noted below seek to build on these strengths.

Specific Strategies for Working with a Child with ASD.   According to the National Research Council's report published in 2001 in which a committee of experts was charged with the task of integrating the scientific, theoretical, and policy literature, "There are virtually no data on the relative merit of one model (of intervention) over another" (Lord & McGee, 2001, pp. 171–172). Nevertheless, there are a number of intervention approaches that are showing positive changes in children who receive intensive services from an early age currently in use. It is important to note that these different interventions tend to focus on different aspects of the disorder and on different developmental domains. Because of the variability in the targeted skill areas, the underlying theoretical assumptions, and the strategies employed, the selection of a particular approach (or combina-

tion of approaches) should depend on the needs and characteristics of the child with autism and the needs and preferences of families. Although it is not appropriate to discuss each approach in detail in this text, Exhibit 5–8 presents a glimpse at the highlights of current intervention models.

In addition, the following strategies reflect those that are necessary for the successful inclusion of children with autism regardless of the model or theoretical approach that is followed:

1. Collaborate with the child's family, as typically they are well informed about their child's disorder and their child's unique characteristics. This will also help ensure smooth transitions between home- and center-based or school programs.

2. Interview the child's parents to determine those objectives and activities that their child really likes (high preference) and those that he or she really dislikes. These may include unusual fixations, either positive or negative. Understanding the child's fears and cravings helps in understanding the child's behavior.

3. Create a well-organized, predictable environmental space. Establish clear, visual boundaries and minimize distractions. This may be the single most important strategy. Classroom areas must be well marked, and the daily schedule should be consistent and transitions between activities clearly signaled by visual and/or auditory cues. Activities that are regular and routines that are familiar provide predictability for all children and are especially important for children who have autism.

4. Capitalize on strengths in visual processing and special interests by individualizing visual work schedules with the use of objects, photographs, and icons.

5. Use visual aids whenever possible. Handing a child four place mats with the outline of the plate and silverware automatically tells the child that he or she is expected to set the table for four people, and the mats show exactly where to place items.

Exhibit 5–8

A Glimpse at Current Interventions in Autism

Assumptions/Targets	Strategies	Advantages
Applied Behavior Analysis[1] *(also referred to as Discrete Trial, Behavior Modification, or Intensive Behavior Intervention)*		
Focuses on acquisition of skills Rewarded behavior will be strengthened or repeated	Intensive (25–40 hours per week) Tasks are analyzed Rewards for each step	New skills are learned Adapted to individual child
Treatment and Education of Autistic and Related Communication Handicapped Children (TEACCH)[2]		
Focuses on academics Highly structured, routinized environment is essential Relies on visual cues	Highly structured Visual learning (schedules, sequenced charts)	Child gains independence Adapted to individual child Less parental stress
Picture Exchange Communication Systems (PECS)[3]		
Focuses on development of communication Relies on visual cues	Communicates by exchanging pictures for desired objects or activities	Initiated by the child Facilitates functional communication Can teach simple language structures
Floor Time (Greenspan)[4]		
Focuses on social-emotional interactions with significant others Targets turn taking and affective responses	Follows child's lead in play Encourages "circles of communication"	Increases social interactions Heightens child's effect
Social Stories[5]		
Focuses on social behavior Deals with difficulties with perspective taking	Teaches social routines using scripts or stories	Easy to individualize Improves social skills
Sensory Integration[6]		
Focuses on modulating and integrating sensory information Addresses child's overarousal or underarousal	Physical or occupational therapist directs various sensory activities	Increases sensory discrimination and tolerance of stimuli Improves motor planning and self-regulation

[1] Koegel and Koegel (2006).

[2] Mesibov, Shea, and Schopler (2004).

[3] Bondy and Frost (2002).

[4] Greenspan and Weider (2006).

[5] Gray (2006) and Gray and White (2002).

[6] Ayres (2005).

6. Unplanned changes can cause behavioral outbursts in children who have autism. Often these behaviors can be minimized through simple redirection with verbal prompts (e.g., "We're going to go outside in a minute" instead of simply saying, "Let's go, everybody").

7. Reduce the noise level of the classroom to the extent possible by using area rugs and wall hangings made of sound absorbent materials. Use a quiet voice when speaking. If possible, use incandescent and natural lighting rather than fluorescent.

8. When touching the child, use firm pressure rather than a light touch. If touch is annoying to the child, firm pressure, especially if applied to the chest and back, can even be soothing. Always provide some anticipatory cue so the child knows he or she is going to be touched and is not startled by the contact.

9. Be absolutely consistent about consequences for unacceptable behavior. Even more important, try to determine exactly what triggers the behavior and change the environment to reduce the likelihood of reoccurrence. Remember that behavioral approaches to management are not inconsistent with sound developmental approaches and can be especially effective for children with autism or ASD.

10. Verbal and visual cues are powerful tools to communicate with and help children with autism participate in regular everyday activities (e.g., pointing to the cubby and saying "Hang it on the hook" to a child who needs to hang up his coat or allowing children to point to pictures to indicate their wants or needs).

11. Sequence cards that illustrate a series of connected actions or activities can help the child with autism. These may be semipermanent or changed frequently, depending on individual children and programs. Such pictures will help a child know what to expect next.

12. Work closely with team members from other disciplines. Children with autism and ASD frequently have unique needs across several areas of development. A behavior specialist may help determine the cause of and interventions for certain disruptive behaviors.

13. Work with in-home program personnel to maximize the impact of intervention provided in more than one setting. This is especially important when working with private agencies whose programming efforts need to be coordinated to minimize confusion for the child.

Fetal Alcohol Spectrum Disorders

One substance that is clearly related to an identifiable long-term outcome is alcohol. Although some specific symptoms of fetal alcohol exposure, such as malformations of the face, occur only during certain periods of vulnerability, the developing brain is susceptible to alcohol damage throughout pregnancy (Streissguth & O'Malley, 2000). Chasnoff (2001) discussed the cluster of physical and mental deficiencies that are present from birth in children born to women who are chronically alcoholic. The criteria for **fetal alcohol spectrum disorders** (FASD) fall into the categories listed below. In order for a diagnosis of FASD to be made, a child must demonstrate symptoms from all three categories:

1. Deficiency in both prenatal and postnatal growth. As FASD children grow older, they continue to be small for their age, and their head size continues to be small.

2. Facial malformations such as microcephaly, short palpebral (eye) fissures, frontonasal alterations, thin upper vermilion (lip) border, flat midface, and hypoplastic maxilla and/or mandible (jaw).

3. Central nervous system effects, such as cognitive disability, motor problems, tremulousness, and/or hyperactivity.

A child who exhibits some of these features but not enough to be diagnosed with fetal alcohol

syndrome is referred to as having **alcohol-related neurodevelopmental disorder** (ARND). Children with ARND may have minimal to moderate facial characteristics or none of the characteristics at all. They do, however, tend to have behavioral difficulties that have a negative impact on learning. The impact may not be apparent until a child reaches the second or third grade.

Many children with FASD or potential for ARND are not formally identified in their early years because they do not show the classical facial characteristics or do not test out as developmentally delayed on standardized tests. Nevertheless, they may present regulatory problems that may make them in need of early intervention services. For example, as an infant they may show early signs of difficulty regulating and controlling their behavior. They might be described as restless and difficult to comfort. They may easily become overstimulated and agitated.

During the preschool years, regulatory difficulties may persist. Some children continue to be easily overstimulated and often have difficulty modulating their behavior. For example, giggles can turn into uncontrolled laughter, pleasant moods into sullen ones, independence into extreme dependence. Particularly in the area of social-emotional development, these children may show delays and exaggerated reactions to events. For example, they often display more difficulty with transitions within the school day (e.g., changes in routine and changes in staff) than is expected for children their age. Such children may eventually be labeled as having learning disabilities or attention deficits.

Specific Strategies for Working with a Child with Prenatal Exposure to Alcohol.   There are several strategies that can be very helpful in working with young children who have been influenced by prenatal alcohol exposure. The strategies are useful for many children with special needs:

1. Be aware of the kinds of situations and events that trigger inappropriate behaviors:

   - Inconsistent, unstructured environments
   - New situations
   - Overstimulation
   - Internal changes, such as illness or extreme fatigue

2. When misbehavior occurs, attempt to understand what triggers the behavior as well as what consequences may be maintaining the behavior.

3. Increase predictability and consistency in classroom routines. Prepare children for what comes next.

4. Avoid making cognitive and social demands that are far beyond the developmental level of the child.

5. Provide extra support during new or difficult tasks; teach in small steps.

6. Reduce unnecessary stimulation, especially background noise.

7. Respect children's play and work space by keeping unnecessary interruptions at a minimum.

8. Limit the number of rules; communicate them clearly and enforce them consistently.

9. Expect setbacks and regressions, as this is a common problem for many children prenatally exposed to alcohol. They are inconsistent in their ability to perform skills they have previously been taught. Also, be aware that home events, particularly family or neighborhood violence, caregiver changes, and dependency court dates, can have a major impact on children's behavior and learning.

10. Be vigilant! *Safety* is an issue with children with increased activity level, poor impulse control, and trouble understanding cause and effect. Take nothing for granted. Reteach safety precautions continuously. Use of the above strategies, over time, strengthens children's self-control and sense of mastery over the environment.

The principles and strategies described in this chapter are powerful and effective for all children. They represent some of the basic competencies of all early educators. Because this is a text in early

childhood special education, there are additional skills and methods that must be mastered by the early childhood special education professional. These include environmental manipulations, use of special methods and adaptive devices for children with specific disabilities, microanalysis of children's behavior and of teaching effectiveness, and, especially, parent–professional partnership in the design

and implementation of programs for children with special needs. These will continue to be addressed throughout the remaining chapters of this book.

Having focused on strategies common to all high-quality early education programs and on specific adaptations for those with unique needs, in the next chapter we will discuss techniques for promoting healthy emotional and social development.

Summary

Curriculum is a clear description of what we teach (goals) and how we teach (strategies). Goals and strategies are to be developed in accordance with a clearly defined philosophy based on assumptions about human nature and how young children learn. The philosophy of this text assumes that goals must be functional and ecologically relevant. Strategies will be built on what we know about each child's development and the most appropriate techniques for helping each child reach his or her goals. Instruction is thought to be rooted in the social interactions between children and significant others in their environment.

A wide body of research has contributed to the catalog of principles and strategies that make up what can be called generic instructional strategies.

The strategies that can be adapted and fine-tuned to meet the needs of children with special needs have been outlined. No matter the strategy, play is seen as the most natural and important teaching context.

It is important not only to arrange the social environment but also to consider how the physical environment can influence both children and adults in ways that will enhance children's opportunities to learn and to interact socially with one another. Considerations special to arranging the environment for infants and toddlers were worthy of note.

Time-use plans promote desired consistency through routines and assist the staff in accommodating special needs within their daily activities. Finally, numerous specific suggestions were made for adapting curricula for children with unique special needs.

Discussion Topics and Activities

1. Observe a teacher in an early intervention program. Describe how he or she uses each of the generic strategies discussed in this chapter.
2. Visit a center where children with special needs are included. Observe the children during play activities. Follow a particular child and note the materials, physical arrangement, and number of children. Try to determine whether the child is really engaged in the play activity. Make a hypothesis or two as to why the child is or is not engaged. Discuss your observations with your classmates.
3. Observe an inclusive preschool program and make a sketch of the physical environment. After comparing it with the drawing in the text, determine the strengths and weaknesses of the observed layout.
4. Develop a time-use plan for a program involving infants and toddlers. Include prompts for accommodating children with special needs within the overall daily plan.
5. Develop a file or notebook where you can add additional suggestions for adapting curricula for children with specific special needs.

Promoting Emotional and Social Development

Photo by Annette Tessier

KEY TERMS

(Note: Terms are discussed within the text and/or defined in the glossary.)

affect attunement
affective domain
attachment
bonding
distal communication
ecological perspective
hyperresponsive

hyporesponsive
logical connection
logical consequences
natural consequences
observational learning
positive behavior support
primary provider

reactive attachment disorder
reward-to-punishment ratio
self-regulation
temperament
transactional model

- A strong, positive attachment to a primary care-giver appears to be the key to the development of a healthy personality.

- A healthy environmental climate is conducive to the prevention of social and emotional problems.

- Specific intervention strategies should be employed to assist young children in the development of positive social skills.

- Play is not only an important context for development but also a critical social skill that can be facilitated.

- Children with behavioral difficulties can be positively managed through careful environmental planning and positive behavioral support.

- Children who have been abused and neglected need consistency, predictability, and an opportunity to become attached to a primary care provider.

The promotion of social and emotional development means helping children to become emotionally secure and to develop a healthy sense of self. Numerous attempts have been made to describe the attributes of a healthy personality. The work of early theorists such as Erik Erikson, as well as the more recent work of Stanley Greenspan and Daniel Stern, provides useful foundations for the understanding of infant and child emotional development. From the initial attachment to a primary caregiver in infancy through the establishment of mutually responsive interaction patterns and communicative strategies, the emotionally supported preschooler achieves a strong and healthy sense of self and the ability to express and understand a wide range of emotional experiences and ideas.

With this emotional strength and healthy autonomy, the young child begins to develop effective social skills. For many children, preschool is their first experience in a group setting. They may need assistance in handling this new experience. All children are in the process of learning to recognize and to cope with their feelings in environments that require that they also learn to regulate their own behavior. Typical social skill development is illustrated in Appendix A.

This chapter aims to help professionals and parents understand how adults can assist children in becoming emotionally and socially well adjusted. We present techniques for dealing effectively with emotional and behavioral needs. We recognize the influence of the environment and emphasize the importance of play in the creation of a secure, growth-producing early education experience.

BECOMING EMOTIONALLY SECURE

Understanding emotional development and the growth of personality in infants and young children must begin with a careful look at the process of attachment. The infant's strong, positive feeling for a primary caregiver provides the seed from which all aspects of development can grow. For children with special needs—children with disabilities as well as those at risk due to factors such as maltreatment and prenatal drug exposure—the establishment of a strong caregiver–infant attachment relationship may be threatened. It is important for early education professionals to understand the nature of the attachment process and to be able to facilitate its development.

Attachment

Over the years, the development of an attachment bond between the child and the caregiver has been thought by developmentalists to be perhaps the

most pervasive early social and emotional event in the child's life (Greenspan & Weider, 2005). **Attachment** is the term Bowlby (1982) used to describe the bond of affection that develops between an infant and his or her primary caregiver. He found the infant to be biologically predisposed to turn to the caregiver for a sense of security when venturing out. Infants are thought to become securely attached to their caregivers when their caregivers have been there to provide comfort and reassurance during times of distress. Historically, attachment was commonly assessed using the Ainsworth Strange Situation paradigm (Ainsworth & Wittig, 1969). In the "strange situation," the infant's responses to a series of separations and reunions with a stranger and parent are carefully observed. The paradigm consists of the following seven 3-minute episodes:

1. The mother brings the infant to the playroom and puts down the infant.

2. A stranger enters the room and attempts to play with the infant.

3. The mother leaves the room.

4. The mother returns and the stranger leaves.

5. The mother leaves the infant alone.

6. The stranger returns.

7. The mother returns and greets and picks up the infant.

As a result of early studies conducted by Ainsworth (1973) and associates, three categories of attachment were defined. Group B infants greeted parents in an unambiguous manner on reunion. For example, the child might smile, greet, approach, or establish physical contact. These infants were considered to be *attached.* Group A infants demonstrated pointed avoidance of the caregiver on reunion, characterized by aborted approach, averted eye gaze, or ignoring. These infants were labeled *insecurely attached-avoidant.* Group C infants could not be comforted by caregivers, and on reunion they directed angry, resistant behavior at the parents

through behaviors such as pushing away, kicking to be put down, or refusing a toy. These infants were described as *insecurely attached-resistant.* A fourth group of infants who are disorganized and demonstrate *both avoidant and resistant behaviors* was added to the categories (Lyons-Rich, Connell, Zoll, & Stahl, 1987).

Ainsworth (1973) described the insecurely attached infant as a child who becomes greatly distressed when separated from the caregiver; at the same time, this child is not easily comforted by the caregiver. It is as if the child's sense of trust has been disturbed or never fully developed. More securely attached children, on the other hand, fuss less when left and cease crying more quickly. There is an interesting parallel between Thomas, Chess, and Birch's (1968) descriptions of easy and difficult children (discussed later in this chapter) and Ainsworth's description of securely and insecurely attached children. Some children, then, may be predisposed by temperament to influence the attachment process negatively or positively.

Over two decades ago, Connor, Williamson, and Siepp (1978) offered a glimpse of the importance of the reciprocal relationship between the young child and the primary caregiver: the baby signals his need for some kind of caretaking by crying or fussing, the mother responds by picking up the child, and the child responds in turn with some kind of bodily reaction, such as cuddling. The baby's bodily adjustments signal to the mother that he is ready for the next step, be it diapering, feeding, bathing, or just cuddling and stroking. The baby responds to the caregiving by quieting, which reinforces the mother's caregiving. The importance of such a chain of cues and responses is readily apparent. Any breakdown in the signaling and response system may affect the whole bonding and attachment process. Fraiberg (1974), in her classic research on blind infants, notes that their mothers frequently have difficulty feeling attached because of the lack of eye contact and delay in the development of the infant's social smile. Other disabilities and difficult temperament can delay the attachment process. Children with cerebral palsy may not be able to give warm reinforcement to the

caregiver because cuddling may be more difficult. Children with hearing impairments cannot respond with eye contact and other attachment signals when the mother uses her voice. Resultant attachment patterns, then, are an end product of a complicated interactional process. Not only do the child's innate mannerisms influence the response of the parents, but, of course, the adult's natural tendencies help determine the child's view of self and environment. The self-esteem of one affects and is influenced by the other.

One of the goals of many early intervention programs is to encourage and support the development of a strong affectional bond between caregivers and children, especially in those instances when disabling conditions adversely affect attachment. Educators can help parents become tuned in to the child's cues so that their responses can produce an enjoyable response in the child. When parents can learn to understand unclear or confusing cues from their child who has special needs, they have a chance to respond in appropriate ways, allowing them to develop higher parental self-esteem. Bromwich (1997) developed a process of identifying the level of mutually positive and pleasurable interactions between parent and child. Teachers can use such an observation technique as they plan intervention strategies that may include modeling of recognition, sensitivity, and responsiveness to young children's signals and cues.

Erikson's Stages of Psychosocial Development

In his classic developmental outline, Erikson (1993) discussed three stages of psychosocial development thought to be characteristic of the young child. Each stage includes the solution of a problem involving conflicting feelings and desires. The resolution of the central problem of each state creates a favorable disposition for adjustment at the next developmental stage. Table 6–1 presents Erikson's stages of personality development along with adult behaviors that can help children come to a healthy solution of each stage's problems of conflicting desires and feelings.

Sense of Trust Versus Mistrust.   The first year of life was considered by Erikson (1993) to be the crucial time for the development of a sense of trust. During this time, an environment characterized by consistency and dependability fosters the development of

Table 6–1   Adult behaviors to promote child's personality

Erikson's Stage	Appropriate Adult Behaviors
1. To promote sense of *trust*	Be consistent and sensitive in caretaking.
	Play trust-building games (playful repetition such as peekaboo).
	Provide prompt relief of discomfort.
	Provide genuine affection.
	Establish climate of stability and predictability.
	Avoid showing favoritism.
	Provide for choice making.
2. To promote sense of *autonomy*	Allow opportunities to explore.
	Forbid only what really matters.
	Couple firmness with tolerance.
	Avoid shaming.
	Let child set pace, try developing skills.
	Be accepting of individuality.
3. To promote sense of *initiative*	Provide leeway for imagination.
	Encourage role-playing (pretend play).
	Serve as an appropriate model.
	Hold punishment to a minimum.
	Talk about feelings and dreams.
	Answer questions.

trust in those responsible for the child's care. The quality of caregiving is more important than the quantity of food or love given. Caregiving that is basically consistent and sensitive to an infant's needs promotes a view of the world as dependable and safe. Negative, inconsistent, or insensitive caregiving, by contrast, stimulates a fearful, suspicious view of the world.

The child's development of a sense of trust (or mistrust) in the world is only one of the personality attributes developed during infancy. Erikson also discussed the importance of children's perceptions of their ability to control their own body movements. Through actions such as continuous repetition of grasping and holding objects, children learn that they can depend on their bodies to do their bidding. It is not difficult to imagine the frustration experienced by children with physical disabilities during their quest to develop a sense of trust in their own bodies. A curriculum that incorporates specialized body movement activities encourages even children with disabilities to become more trusting in their body control.

Interventionists who provide an atmosphere of consistent, sensitive caring help to further a young child's development of trust in the environment. Conversely, helter-skelter experiences in the program can make a fearful child even more fearful or a basically secure child question his or her relationship to others. A trustful atmosphere is easily developed through establishing reasonable, enforceable rules of conduct, the regularity of a basic schedule of activities, and sensitive, immediate responses to children's needs.

Sense of Autonomy Versus Shame and Doubt. From the end of the first year of life through the second and third year of life, most children are busy exploring their environment and trying to establish some independence. Children who are primarily trustful usually do not hesitate to join the "terrible twos" if encouraged to develop skills at their own pace. Children of this age who are given opportunities to make simple choices, to exercise their expanding sensorimotor abilities, and to experiment with

their newfound verbal skills will become confident enough to assert themselves appropriately.

Children who are shamed (e.g., being called a "bad boy") or told "no" continuously will begin to doubt themselves and their abilities. They may react by defiance or act ignorant of authority. Children who are not allowed to make choices when they are young may become overdependent and fearful when they need to make major life choices. Some children may withdraw into their feelings of worthlessness, whereas others may strike out aggressively.

Interventionists can assist children in developing autonomy with a reasonable degree of self-control by creating opportunities for young children to explore, to make decisions, to ask questions, and to exercise appropriate self-restraint. Curricula and room arrangements that provide centers with materials to manipulate and activities from which a child can choose ideally promote autonomous, confident behavior. Establishing firm, reasonable guidelines for classroom exploration and conduct encourages autonomy while not letting children become overwhelmed by their need for independence and by their lack of mature judgment. Children of this age who are readily propelled by their more mature large muscles may be easily frustrated when their smaller muscles do not react so efficiently. Interventionists must lend assistance that does not create conditions for loss of self-esteem. Children with disabilities may need special incentives to venture into the activities so easily enjoyed by children without disabilities.

Although controls and gentle firmness are essential protections for young children, these controls must have meaning. In this regard, Erikson (1971) suggested that the most constructive rule an adult can follow is "to forbid only what really matters and, in such forbidding, to be clear and consistent" (p. 126).

Sense of Initiative Versus Guilt. Children who have developed a basic trust in their environment and in themselves and who have experienced a growing self-confidence in their ability to explore and experiment are ready to develop a sense of initiative. Around 4 or 5 years of age, children experience a heightened period of imagination and fantasy.

It is a time for reaching out and intruding both physically and verbally. Children with healthy personalities and healthy bodies vigorously try out their developing ideas of themselves. They are great imitators, as evidenced by their "superhero" play and their use of any and all four-letter words.

Children of this age are also beginning to develop what is termed a *conscience*. Because they often have difficulty separating fantasy from reality, they may feel guilty about merely thinking unkind thoughts. Teachers who are aware of this tendency try to avoid overreacting to a child's characteristic statement of "I hate you." When difficulties occur in the home such as death or a divorce, children need to be helped to realize that their actions or thoughts did not cause the unpleasant event to happen. This is also an age of nightmares and dreams. These children need extra comfort and reassurance in separating fantasy from reality.

Teachers who allow leeway within secure guidelines for children's developing sense of initiative can contribute significantly to their motivation to achieve. This motivation is important to the next stage of industry versus inferiority, and it is necessary to the development of self-esteem and the desire to try out the freedom to explore, to imagine, to question, to help plan, to make choices, to participate in meaningful activities, to create, and to engage in role-playing behavior. Teachers of young children with special needs must be aware of the need to teach some children to explore, to play, and to attempt what may be difficult. Children whose abilities or environments are limited may have to be helped directly if they are to develop feelings of trust, autonomy, and initiative. Usually these qualities develop spontaneously in children without disabilities through nurturing environments.

Greenspan's Model of Affective Development

Stanley Greenspan has been an important contributor to the understanding of infant–child emotional development. His work has been particularly important because he has addressed the specific needs of infants and young children with disabilities and developmental differences, including children with autism (Greenspan, 1990; Greenspan & Weider, 1998, 2005). Like Erikson, Greenspan proposed a "developmental structural model" of the stages of emotional growth (Greenspan, 1992) that are summarized here. Greenspan's model parallels Piaget's stage theory of cognitive development in many ways.

There are six basic stages represented in Greenspan's model. It should be noted that in more recent writings, the last three stages (complex sense of self, emotional ideas representation, and emotional thinking) are each divided into two substages. In most cases, the second substage simply represents greater elaboration of the particular emotional capacity being addressed. Thus, for the sake of simplicity, only the six basic stages are described below.

Self-Regulation and Interest in the World.   During the period from birth to approximately 3 months, healthy infants develop the ability to regulate their internal states in ways that allow them to take in and attend to the world around them. Through sight, vision, sense of touch, and smell, infants experience their environment. This experience is best achieved when they are in a calm, alert state.

Babies who are neurologically overresponsive and are easily overstimulated may experience great difficulty maintaining a calm, alert state. As a result, such babies will have less opportunity to take in the world around them. They may not develop a natural interest in their world if that world is painful or irritating.

Babies who are hyperirritable will need special handling techniques that assist them in self-regulation and maintenance of a calm, alert state. For example, swaddling them, placing them in a tucked and flexed position, applying firm pressure to the chest, using deep pressure massage (rather than light stroking), and rocking can be helpful in calming **hyperresponsive** infants. Some premature babies, babies who have been exposed to certain drugs prenatally, and babies who have experienced certain neurological insults may benefit from the use of such techniques.

Some infants may be **hyporesponsive;** that is, they are difficult to arouse. They have trouble becoming fully awake and maintaining an alert state. They

are sleepy and passive. Such babies may respond more to certain types of sensory stimulation than to others. For example, a baby might remain sleepy through parents' exhaustive efforts to interest him or her in their sounds and funny faces. Such a baby might be more aroused by touch and kinesthetic stimulation (movement and position). Thus, it may be possible to assist the baby in reaching an alert state by massaging or tickling and frequently changing his or her position. Once in an alert state, the baby may find voices and faces more interesting.

In summary, during this early stage of development, infants must be supported in their efforts to achieve a calm, alert state and to experience the sensations provided by the world around them without being overwhelmed.

Falling in Love (Attachment).   During the period from approximately 2 to 5 months, infants who have been successful during the first stage in regulating internal states (homeostasis) will begin to be very familiar with their primary caregiver. In addition, they begin to associate sensations of the primary caregiver—face, voice, odor, touch—with pleasurable sensations of being cuddled and fed. As a result, as Greenspan said, the babies "fall in love" (Greenspan & Greenspan, 1985, p. 16). This is the essence of infant attachment. The reciprocal of this experience for a caregiver, as an infant responds to the caregiver's presence and behaviors, is what is called **bonding.** As a caregiver bonds with the infant, he or she becomes more responsive to the infant, both behaviorally and affectively, and, in turn, strengthens the infant's attachment. As discussed earlier, the development of attachment and bonding progresses over time and is dynamic and interactive. Each partner influences the other in powerful ways.

Infants who have disabilities such as blindness or deafness or who have difficulty responding in positive ways to caregivers' behaviors (e.g., infants who are born very prematurely or who have been affected by prenatal exposure to drugs) may be in some jeopardy during this stage. For example, an infant who is hyperirritable may cry or turn away when his mother brings her face close or talks to him. He may look at her only fleetingly

and may avert his gaze when she smiles. Such an infant may have difficulty developing a preference for the human world, which is an important outcome of this stage of attachment. According to the **transactional model,** understanding how infants and their parents influence each other over time is essential to the development of appropriate recommendations for treatment. "The treatment may simply involve augmenting the parents' ability to see the normal in the abnormal— for example, to recognize that preterm babies, although different in size, have cognitive and social-emotional needs and patterns of development similar to full-term babies" (Sameroff & Mackenzie, 2003, p. 18).

Intentional Two-Way Communication.   From approximately 3 to 10 months of age, as their behavior consistently elicits feedback from significant caregivers, one can observe the gradual development of intentionality in infants. They learn that they can do things that have an effect on the environment and particularly that they can use actions to communicate with the social world. Caregiver responsiveness to this intentional communication is crucial to infant development.

Specifically related to children's healthy emotional development is a type of caregiver response referred to as **affect attunement.** By the time infants reach 9 or 10 months of age, the nature of their caregivers' interactions begins to include mirroring of the infant's affect (emotional state). Parents no longer simply imitate or respond to the baby's behavior but also accurately reflect the baby's feelings. When the baby is happy, Mother smiles and reflects this feeling. When the infant is crying and upset, Mother may furrow her brow and frown, saying, "Oh, poor baby." When the infant is startled or surprised, Mother may pull back quickly, with her eyes opened wide, saying, "Oh, my goodness!" In this way, the infant can begin to learn that it is okay to express a wide range of emotions. As caregivers match and reflect their emotions, infants also learn to recognize emotions in others. Most important, they learn that not only their behavior but also their feelings can influence others.

It is extremely important that adults learn to read the affective cues of infants with disabilities. For example, an infant with severe motor impairment

may have difficulty giving clear cues of joy or sadness. Parents may be extremely frustrated by not being sure whether the child finds an experience pleasurable. Sometimes only the greatest extremes of emotions, such as anger, can be understood easily. Early interventionists from several fields may need to work together as a team with parents to help make this kind of emotional communication clear so that parents can respond appropriately. Failure to do this enhances the risk that the infant will give up and become passive and withdrawn. Such a reaction will significantly interfere with the child's ability to fully realize the next stage of emotional development—an organized sense of self.

The Emergence of an Organized Sense of Self.
The period from 9 to 18 months (the transition from infancy to toddlerhood) is an important period of development in which infants achieve a clearer sense of themselves as individuals who are separate from others. They begin to be able to move away from caregivers by using **distal communication.** That is, they can crawl across the room and look back at Father, who, in turn, smiles and vocalizes to them. In this way, toddlers learn that they can be separated from caregivers but still experience their love and support. Thus, they eventually learn that it is safe to be separated by physical space and that they, themselves, are separate beings.

Children with certain disabilities may need special assistance during this stage. For example, a child who is blind may need to be assisted in learning to communicate distally and in learning that he or she has a separate identity. A toddler who has been in neglectful environments or who has had multiple placements may have been thwarted at every stage of emotional development. If the toddler's social environment has been unresponsive and he or she has not been successful in expressing and understanding a wide range of emotions, development of a sense of self will be significantly threatened.

As toddlers develop a sense of self, they become increasingly able to associate and use more complex chains of behavior around emotional events. For example, when their mothers return home, toddlers

do not simply smile, but they smile, vocalize, toddle over, and reach their arms up to be held. They initiate and carry out these behaviors in competent ways. Their sense of ways of interacting in various circumstances begins to be internalized and organized. Their self-image is forming.

Emotional Ideas (Representation).
From 18 to 30 months of age, toddlers become increasingly able to represent ideas and experiences internally (mentally). By 24 months, the toddler can create a mental image of basic feelings and needs (e.g., happiness, sadness, anger, fear). By 30 months, the child can mentally represent and express a wider range of needs and emotions as well as two or more emotions in one play episode or expression (e.g., baby's tired, baby hugs mommy). The emotionally healthy toddler develops a clear mental image of what these basic emotions feel like as well as what they look like in other people. For example, the infant can create a mental image of his own feeling of fear or anger as well as create images of Mommy or Daddy when they are angry or happy.

During this period, toddlers are becoming much more independent. They develop a more sophisticated

understanding of themselves as emotional beings and of the emotional characteristics of significant others. That is, not only can they see themselves as "sometimes naughty and sometimes nice," but they also know that although mommies are sometimes happy and sometimes sad, they are still the same person.

Emotional Thinking.   From 30 to 48 months, the child begins to understand and think about the logical connections between ideas. For example, the child understands causal relationships such as "The girl is sad because her mother is angry," "If I kiss my baby sister she will be happy," and so on. The child learns that certain ways of behaving will make Mommy mad and others will make her happy. Children who have not experienced consistent reactions to their behavior or who have not been allowed to express a range of emotions will be hampered in this stage of development.

During this stage, children's participation in pretend play plays an important role in their development of emotional thinking. Pretend play is also a critical educational and therapeutic activity. Through pretending, a child can act out his or her own range of emotions as well as practice elaborated relationships between mothers and fathers, parents and children, brothers and sisters, and so on. Pretend play can provide the child with the opportunity to learn to say "I'm really mad at you!" rather than hitting someone to express anger.

Children can also act out their own emotional crises and frustrations. Children from abusive and neglectful environments may learn important coping strategies by playing out themes of abandonment or violence. For these children, as well as children with severe emotional disorders, it will be important for the early educator to work in collaboration with mental health professionals in determining appropriate intervention strategies.

BUILDING A HEALTHY ENVIRONMENT

Early education specialists have shifted their focus away from a skill-based approach to a more interactional view recognizing the importance of the child–environment fit. This **ecological perspective** recognizes the need to create a healthy environmental climate conducive to preventing emotional and behavioral problems. Such a climate not only can prevent the occurrence of problems but also can be the major factor in resolving conflicts that develop between children and their environment. The following sections discuss characteristics that most researchers consider essential to optimum growth during the early childhood years. These are highlighted in Figure 6–1.

Structure and Consistency

Werner (2000) discusses the tendency for adaptive behavior to be "associated with a more responsive and nurturant atmosphere and a more organized and predictable environment, which clearly defined and consistently enforced standards, rules and responsibilities" (p. 126).

Consistency means predictability. In instructing parents and teachers in techniques for effective child management, predictability can be equated with the feeling of being safe. The pioneer expert on motivation, Maslow (1968) recognized the expectation for safety as a basic bodily need. When we cannot predict what will happen next, we are usually constantly ready to defend ourselves. "If our predictions come true, we feel safe. If they don't come true, it is upsetting—we become angry. If we can't make any successful predictions at all, we are in a constant state of turmoil" (p. 7).

From a practical point of view, caregivers must be consistent for children to learn the rules of conduct for social acceptance. Children are as baffled by inconsistent rules as we would be if we were trying to learn the rules of baseball and the batter sometimes ran to third base instead of first base after a hit. If it is sometimes all right for a child to jump up and down on the sofa and if other times a reprimand results, the rule the child learns is to "try and see."

Instead of the "terrible twos," we should call toddlers the "testing twos." Given consistent responses to their testing, they learn the rules and usually try to function within them. At the same time, consistency fosters their understanding of the basic relationships between cause and effect.

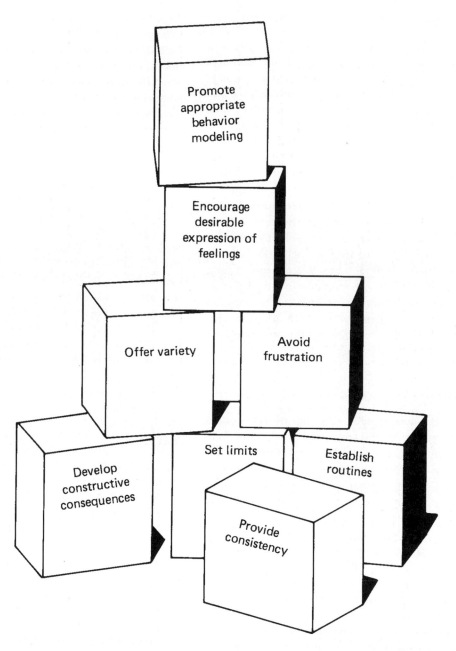

Figure 6–1   Building a healthy environment

Routines

To develop Erikson's sense of trust or the feelings of being safe, professionals must plan carefully. Routines or schedules that allow children to predict within reason what will happen next help them relax and handle transitions from one activity to another with relative ease. Although schedules should not be so rigid that teachers cannot take advantage of "teachable moments," children can be prepared for changes in routine and for the times between activities when movement, a change of pace, or grouping is required.

Misbehavior often results when children do not know when or how to change to the next activity. Children should be given a signal, such as a flick of the lights or a soft word, that they will soon need to stop the activity in which they are engaged. Young children need time to become uninvolved just as they need time to become involved. Teachers should discuss obvious changes in the daily schedule with children so that they can develop the understanding that change can be predicted.

Limits

Reasonable limits or directions help provide consistency. Developmentally appropriate and clear directions or limits not only contribute to children's emotional needs for security but also create conditions for bodily safety. Although children have a strong need to be autonomous, they lack the cognitive judgment to control their own behavior enough to avoid harming themselves or others at times. Behavioral limits offer children guidelines they can imitate and internalize in their development of appropriate self-regulation. As pointed out earlier, teachers must establish a delicate balance between necessary limits and the freedom to explore.

Only limits that are absolutely necessary to a positive learning environment for both children and teachers should be established. Too often teachers and parents establish so many limits or rules that none can be learned or enforced consistently. Teachers should remember that if children are to follow a rule or a direction and have no choice, they should not be given a choice. Inadvertently, adults sometimes make the mistake of saying something such as, "It is time to go home. Wouldn't you like to put on your coat?" What if the child replies "No"?

In a well-quoted text on child management, Smith and Smith (1976) suggested that a good rule or direction should fulfill the following three requirements that are still applicable today:

1. *It must be definable.* Rules have to be at the developmental level of the children both in vocabulary and in expectations. They must state specific behaviors that are expected or not allowed. For example, we often hear parents or teachers tell children to "be good." What does "be good" mean to the child or to the adult? To the child it may mean not running in the building because that is what he or she got into trouble for yesterday. To the parent it may mean eating all his or her lunch because the parent has noticed many leftovers in the lunch pail. Rules or expectations must be clearly stated in behavioral terms. If teachers want children to stay within a certain area while sitting on the carpet, then they should mark the area with a piece of tape so the child knows exactly what the limits are. Concrete, visual aids help young children learn rules of conduct just as they help them develop cognitive skills.

2. *It must be reasonable.* Teachers must judge the developmental level of children before rules can be established. It is not reasonable to expect many two-and-a-half-year-olds to share to the extent that many parents and teachers would like them to. A constant reference to developmental norms is necessary. It must be remembered that children with developmental delays require extra patience as they learn to adapt to limits that others may adapt to more easily. For example, some children may be able to listen to a story for only 5 minutes, whereas other children may still be engrossed 20 minutes later.

3. *It must be enforceable.* Teachers and parents must assume that not all children can or will adhere to all limits. Some rules will be broken. For limits or rules to help children feel safe and trustful, any established rule must be enforceable. When children

observe that teachers cannot or will not do anything about a broken rule, they cannot predict what will happen and become anxious. Children seek and enjoy limits. Some will break a rule just to see whether they can indeed predict what will happen. This is generally called "testing the limits," and it happens in every classroom. As suggested earlier, teachers should see a certain amount of this as typical in children's establishing predictability. Teachers should react firmly, consistently, and calmly. This reaction will define for children the consequences of their behavior. It will tell them what will happen if rules are broken. Seeking to avoid the consequences will motivate them to control their behavior. They feel secure when others are helping them develop self-restraint. Of course, only developmentally appropriate rules can be enforced. If a special circumstance causes a teacher to change the rules or limits, a discussion with the children will help them to understand the need for flexibility within consistency.

Constructive Consequences

An effective means of helping children develop social responsibility is through the use of natural and logical consequences. **Natural consequences** occur when an adult does not interfere at all and a child learns from what naturally happens in a situation. For example, children who do not cooperate when games are played soon learn that other children avoid playing with them. If a child does not eat the prepared snack, becoming hungry may help him or her to learn to eat when food is available. **Logical consequences,** conversely, are those developed by adults who find that natural consequences either are not readily available or are harmful. These usually help to keep or to restore order and avoid chaos. For example, children who insist on throwing sand must be removed from the sandbox. Consequences that help children to learn to control their own behaviors must be both logical and immediate. If a consequence does not bear any logical relationship to the misbehavior, then it will be difficult for the child to learn the logical relationship between cause and effect. A consequence that occurs long after the

misbehavior will not be associated with it by the child. If the child cannot remember what it was that caused the consequence, then he or she will not make the link between cause and effect. This is one of the reasons why the threat "Father will punish you after he gets home" does not work.

Logical Connections

A **logical connection** between an act and its consequences provides a number of advantages to establishing and maintaining a healthy relationship between children and their environment. Children who are denied the use of materials after being careless with them are less likely to see the teacher as arbitrary than when they are told to sit in the corner for being careless. Children will only feel "picked on" if ordered to sit in the corner. Removing the materials, however, can be seen as necessary to the protection of the other children. A logical connection also helps children to focus on the behavior to be changed, making it easier to interpret the misbehavior as the cause of the consequence.

A child who is also given some control over the extent of the consequence will be more likely to feel the ability to do something about terminating or preventing such consequences in the future. For example, children who are asked to remove themselves from the group for being disruptive and told they may return when they feel they can control themselves have an opportunity to take part in their own rehabilitation. They can learn not only that disruptive behavior will cause removal but also that self-control can earn the chance to return. Conversely, children who are told to sit in the time-out area for 20 minutes or until the teacher comes for them feel that immediate self-control will not help and that only the passage of time changes events.

Variety

Careful planning to include a change of pace during the day is essential to motivating children to learn. A variety of both individual and group activities consistent with the children's developmental level should be included. Young children need to have

active involvement interspersed with quiet activities. Children whose senses or physical mobility are limited will fatigue more quickly and need an opportunity for rest. Others may need additional opportunities to move freely to release inner tension.

By nature, young children generally have short attention spans. (Of course, there are exceptions.) This needs to be considered carefully when planning the daily schedule. If children's attention wanders and they are bored or frustrated, they become restless. This restlessness can become contagious, influencing the behavior of a number of children. This is one of the reasons why learning theorists recommend that practice of any kind be distributed over time.

Finally, a change of pace also means including activities that are just plain fun and full of laughter. Most adults are guilty of being in too much of a hurry or so intense that they miss the occasional opportunities to laugh with children or to turn a mistake into a learning experience. Even shoes on the wrong feet often appear funny enough for a chuckle and for encouragement to try again rather than the usual response of "Your shoes are on the wrong feet."

Avoiding Frustration

Teachers who are astute observers of children are able to plan and implement a therapeutic environment. They are alert to individual signs of frustration and stress. Understanding the developmental level of each child makes it possible to plan appropriate activities. Even the best-matched activities, however, can produce frustration in a tired, hungry, or sick child. Teachers should quickly recognize warning signs such as fussing, crying, nail biting, sighing, fidgeting, thumb sucking, and tantrums. Usually a prompt change of activity will reduce the frustration and thus *prevent* disruptive behavior.

Frustration can be avoided by teachers' reducing clutter and noise. (It has been found that high levels of noise are related to stress and increased behavior problems [Schneider, 2002].) Directions should be simple, activities need to be meaningful and relatively short, and the teacher should be available in case the child needs help. Teachers should analyze

tasks and break them into manageable subskills that are appropriately sequenced. Efforts, regardless of outcomes, should receive recognition. Competition should be avoided. Activities that guarantee success can make not only a child's day but also the day of the teacher.

Transition times can be periods of frustration for children if not smoothly organized. Distractible children can become unruly if left to wander or wonder. Withdrawn children may become fearful. Routines for transition times must be explicitly taught. As discussed earlier, signals such as flickering the lights help children wind down from one activity to get ready for the next. Hurrying young children only frustrates the teacher who forgets that preschoolers have not developed the inner time clocks that often become the bosses of adults. Scheduling major activities to end at natural breaks during the day makes transitions smoother. For example, it is easier to gain children's cooperation in cleaning up art materials if they know lunch will follow.

Encouraging Desirable Expression of Feelings

In spite of an appropriately planned schedule of activities, consistency, and well-defined limits, unpredictable things do happen. Children need to learn to cope constructively with feelings that arise from interpersonal situations. Anger, jealousy, depression, fear, and other unpleasant feelings are common interpersonal emotions. Teachers choose either to provide an opportunity for helpful expression or to insist on at least temporary suppression. The success and choice of teachers' approaches often depend on how well they can handle their own unpleasant feelings. Teachers who have confidence in their abilities to handle negative feelings and have carefully created a trustful relationship with their children can handle stressful situations in ways that promote emotional growth (Snowman & Biehler, 2004).

Sensitive teachers find many opportunities to help children accept and express their feelings appropriately. Practically any unpleasant experience in the classroom can be a source of discussion. Young

children cannot assimilate long lectures explaining feelings or behavior. Short statements or a warm physical touch will help a child know that having feelings is all right. A simple acknowledgment of feelings and inquiry about coping behaviors will help a child understand and express emotions appropriately while feeling accepted. For example, the teacher might say, "It is okay to be mad when Johnny rips your paper, but I can't let you hit him. Can you think of another way to let Johnny know how angry you are?"

Numerous well-written books are available that help children learn to cope effectively with their developing feelings. Even difficult topics such as death and divorce are subjects of sensitive presentation. Puppets, role-playing activities, art activities, punching bags, and imaginative, unstructured play also give children opportunities to work through their feelings acceptably. Exhibit 6–1 illustrates a lesson that can be planned to help children learn to understand, label, and constructively express their feelings.

Promoting Appropriate Behavior Modeling

Young children with disabilities often learn new and more adaptive behavior through imitating their peers without disabilities. The modeling effect is a strong argument for integrating children with and without disabilities in early education programs. In fact, one of the most important advantages of group instruction is the opportunity for **observational learning** (Noonan & McCormick, 2006). This form of learning has often been referred to as modeling and consists of imitation of another's actions. This form of learning cannot be left to chance.

The teacher's responsibility is to understand the dynamics of learning through observation and imitation and to ensure that appropriate models of desired behavior are available. A number of variables help determine whether a child will reproduce the observed behavior. Researchers have found that simply placing children with and without disabilities together does not necessarily result in the desired peer imitation. Children are more likely to imitate or model their more competent peers and those they observe receiving direct reinforcement from their teachers and others in their environment. As Allen and Cowdery (2005) state, "Teachers make it happen" (p. 311). Teachers are in a position to be very obvious when they dispense reinforcement for desired behavior. They can encourage children to clap for one another, they can put or have another child put happy-face stickers on the paper of a child who has completed tracing his or her name, and they can distribute snacks to the first child who is seated and waiting patiently.

FACILITATING SOCIAL SKILLS

The development of positive social skills is critical to the successful inclusion of children with special needs in community-based settings. Social skills are also essential to the emotional well-being of young children, as such skills enable them to develop friendships and self-esteem. (Appendix A outlines the developmental sequence of social skills.) It has been found that "children with disabilities in inclusive preschool classrooms do not participate in social behaviors as much as their peers without disabilities, and they are more likely to be socially rejected" (Lau, Higgins, Gelfer, Hong, & Miller, 2005, p. 208). Early childhood educators understand the importance of their role in helping young children with disabilities establish appropriate and effective relationships with their peers. They provide modeling, direct instruction, praise, token reinforcement, and social integration activities. In addition, they also structure the environment to facilitate peer mediation in the facilitation of full social participation of young children with disabilities. Examples of this environmental structuring follow.

Use of Environmental Structuring

1. *Keep the groups relatively small* (from two to four children) when structured learning activities are involved. Small groups make it possible for teachers to facilitate ongoing positive social interactions without interrupting them.

Exhibit 6–1

Teaching Thoughtfulness

Goal

To create daily opportunities to nurture thoughtfulness in children.

How to Begin

1. *Be* what you wish to see children express. If you want them to be thoughtful, be thoughtful yourself.
2. Notice nearly every expression of *that* quality. Call attention to the child who expresses it in a spontaneous way. Do not make a major production of it. Rather, touch the child gently or hug lightly. Say, "That was thoughtful. You helped Susie with her coat." You may think that the other children are not paying attention, but they are. In no time they will try to figure out ways to get you to tell them how they are being thoughtful. And, of course, they will be learning the subtle meaning of "thoughtful."
3. Avoid calling attention to thoughtlessness. Ignore it.

After a Few Days

1. Reduce the frequency with which you call attention to the target quality. Continue to do all the things suggested above, just less often.
2. Make up short stories about children who are thoughtful. Use puppets, flannel boards, or Polaroid pictures. Catch a child expressing thoughtfulness. Paste the picture on one page and write a brief story below it telling what happened: "Susie couldn't get by. Tommy moved his chair. Then she could get through. That was thoughtful."
3. Read stories and comment about examples of thoughtfulness as you read. ("Little Red Riding Hood was thoughtful. She shared her cookies with her grandma.")
4. Occasionally, with puppets and stories, mention lack of thoughtfulness (or whatever quality you are focusing on at the time). Then ask the children to suggest a thoughtful thing to do. Be careful. At this point, do not lecture. Do not try to relate it to something they should have done.

Note: Remember, you are not only nurturing thoughtfulness but also helping the children learn the names of their feelings and actions. All too often adults tell children to "be thoughtful" or "That was a thoughtless thing to do." Children may not have the slightest idea what they are talking about. Labeling the good behaviors makes it easier for children to express them spontaneously and purposefully.

From Then On

1. Continue to call attention to examples of the qualities you wish to see expressed. Of course, as these qualities increase in number, it becomes impossible to call attention to each of them constantly. It also becomes unnecessary. There seems to be a special magic to the expression of positive qualities. If a once-established quality seems to be diminishing, however, merely begin to call attention to it again and do so on a regular basis.
2. Introduce new targets regularly. Watch them expand. You may discover quickly that even some of the naughtiest children express some of the target qualities from the first day. You may not have noticed before.

Photo by Scott Cunningham/Merrill

2. *Assign seats around tables or at group time* to encourage interaction. In inclusive environments, typically developing children can be seated next to children with special needs.

3. *Provide materials appropriate to the skills or interaction desired.* Children must learn to use play materials before they can be expected to play with them in cooperative situations. Children who become frustrated because they do not have the skill to use a material may become disruptive or withdraw.

4. *Promote selection of materials that facilitate cooperative interaction.* Some materials are more conducive to positive social interaction than others. Promote the choice of social toys (blocks, balls, and puppets) rather than isolated toys (crayons, modeling clay, and puzzles). Simple table games such as Lotto or Candyland, with specific rules, may be more conducive to cooperative play than more unstructured play materials such as sand, crayons, or puzzles. Children with disabilities who have not developed imaginative play may need to move gradually from structured to unstructured play when positive inter-personal relationships are a high-priority goal. Teachers will need to observe carefully to determine

which materials are most conducive to fostering the desired behavior. See Appendix F for additional ideas.

5. *Make sufficient materials available to promote cooperation and imitation.* When children outnumber the materials available, cooperative play obviously is dependent on children's willingness to share. If sharing is not one of the priorities for the play activity, then abundant materials should be available. Imitation is also not immediately possible and cannot be reinforced if children must wait to use the materials.

6. *Plan definite activities that require cooperation.* In their classic work, Hewett and Taylor (1980) described a number of tasks that require at least two children to communicate and cooperate to reach a mutual goal. Each one's actions are indispensable to the other. For example, the pan-sorting task requires one child to sit on each side of a screen. Each has three different-colored pans and a number of objects. One child is the dispatcher, who describes what he or she is doing as objects are placed in the pans (e.g., "I am putting the yellow car in the red pan"). The other child attempts to follow these directions to imitate the actions of the dispatcher. Such an activity is particularly helpful to children who have difficulty cooperating

Photo by Lisa Wadors

and paying attention long enough to follow directions. Of course, the more verbal the children, the easier the task. Remember, some children must be taught how to imitate or to model the behavior of others.

Use of Typical Peers as Mediators of Social Skills

Several authors described strategies for using peers as mediators of social skill development. With peer-mediated strategies, coaching is provided to a peer in order to promote social interaction skills rather than prompting the child with disabilities (Rosenberg & Boulware, 2005). Such strategies include asking a peer to demonstrate a skill or activity for the child with special needs and training or prompting children (both with and without disabilities) to *initiate* interactions with one another. It is ideal to coach peers who have higher-level social skills than the children with special needs. Peers are taught to share, request to share, assist, and compliment the attempts at social interaction made by children with disabilities.

ENCOURAGING DEVELOPMENTAL PLAY BEHAVIOR

Although research on the significance of play for children with disabilities is limited, the contention that play is an important contributor to their development is widely accepted. Recognizing the critical role of play in the enhancement of every aspect of a child's development, researchers are now investigating play behavior from a variety of viewpoints.

The Importance of Play

The importance of play has been noted in the early literature as far back as Plato and Aristotle. Freudians view the repetition of experiences in play as a means of gaining mastery over painful events. Eriksonians consider play to be a method by which children organize and integrate life experiences. Piagetians see play as an essential means of mastering one's environment. Play develops creativity and increases the child's repertoire of responses. The importance of play as a context for teaching and learning was discussed in chapter 5.

In addition, the crucial role of play in the development of skills leading to social competence is receiving considerable attention (Pierce-Jordan & Lifter, 2005). Teachers are directed to become social engineers who can help young children play appropriately with others as a means to ensuring the development of acceptable social skills.

The importance of creating an environment that promotes spontaneous and appropriately directed

play cannot be underestimated. Early childhood educators have long realized the need for play activities as a part of all preschool curricula. The issue of accountability, however, has jeopardized the role of spontaneous play in some classrooms. Teachers feel pushed to judge the value of a play activity by what is learned. Perhaps the challenge now is to create a three-way balance among less structured creative activities, freedom of choice, and directed tasks designed to remedy developmental deficits.

The Nature of Play

Piaget (1963) placed play into three broad categories. First, *practice play* accompanies the sensorimotor stage of cognitive development. Practice play is characterized by the exploration and repetition involved in mastering an activity. The game of taking things out and putting things in is typical practice play.

Symbolic play describes the second type of play, which occurs during the preoperational stage of cognitive development. Preschool children involved in symbolic play can be seen using one object to represent or symbolize another. A child might attribute the qualities of a camera to a small wooden block and go around "taking pictures." The child's increased verbal ability allows imitating and reenacting experiences, thus facilitating pretending and dramatic play. The third kind of play is referred to as *games with rules,* which require more complex communication and cooperation. Whereas some children may engage in rule-oriented play during preschool, interest in this behavior is thought to heighten during the concrete operational stage of cognitive development near 7 years of age.

Development of Social Interaction Skills Through Play

A review of the literature readily suggests that investigators have shifted their focus from emphasis on the cognitive competence of children with disabilities as a predictor of future functioning to concern for social development. Despite the good intentions of inclusion, we find again and again that children who are typically developing do not regularly include children with disabilities in their play. In their research, Brown and Bergen (2002) found that children with disabilities were included only when an adult was present. Special programming strategies are necessary to increase interaction and promote social skill development of children with special needs. They are just less adept at developing the interpersonal skills typical children may acquire through usual play behavior. To understand the developmental levels of social play behavior, we will discuss a variation of the classic work of Parten (1932). Parten's six levels of social participation provide a sequence for reference, but they need more empirical support to be followed without caution. At least they do provide guidelines for observation and selection of intervention strategies. The following discussions of each level elaborates on the work of Bailey (1978):

1. *Unoccupied behavior.* At this level there is no interpersonal interaction. The child may watch anything that attracts his or her attention. Some children will engage in self-stimulating behavior. Even at this level, children should be placed near other children and reinforced for manipulating a toy and staying within the social environment.

2. *Solitary independent play.* Again the child plays alone and with toys that are probably different from those being used by other children. He or she may be within speaking distance of other children but is unlikely to interact with them. Teachers should encourage involvement with toys even if the child is not interacting with others. Toys must be carefully chosen and reinforcement given for appropriate use. Encouragement of appropriate use of toys and objects not only will help children enhance their cognitive skills but also will make them better prepared to become socially integrated.

3. *Onlooker behavior.* On this level, children are definitely observing the play of others and may even engage in conversation with them. As a step toward actual involvement with others, adults should place children where they can clearly observe them and should encourage any attempts at interaction. One promising approach to increasing the social interaction of

young children with disabilities has been to teach peers without disabilities to be the initiators of social exchanges (Chandler, 1998; Morris, 2002). Considerable success has been reported when peers are trained to use behavioral procedures to elicit social responses during play from young children with a variety of disabilities (Odom et al., 1999). However, generalization to new settings has been a problem. Thus, Guralnick and Neville (1997) suggested that an effective procedure might involve play with an untrained peer without a disability who possesses the "natural" initiations to which the children with disabilities might respond.

4. *Parallel activity.* Behavior on this level includes independent play among children that uses toys like those used by the other children. To move children toward complete involvement, the teacher should encourage the children without disabilities to share toys with the children who have disabilities and to ask for toys from the children with disabilities. In this way the children without disabilities act as initiators of involvement. Children with disabilities should be placed clearly within the group and not on its fringes.

5. *Associative play.* On this level, children are playing with other children. There is borrowing, lending, sharing, engagement in similar activities, and interest primarily in association rather than activities. To facilitate such involvement, teachers must deliberately structure the environment. They must provide toys and objects such as blocks, dress-up clothes, and games that encourage interaction. Space must be adequate, as crowding tends to lead to disruptive play. Peers without disabilities should be reinforced for conversation and sharing with playmates who have disabilities. Children with disabilities may need extra reinforcement and redirection if they begin to wander from the group.

6. *Cooperative or organized play.* On the final level of Parten's continuum, children play in a group that is organized in some way. There are common goals and a division of labor. All members usually feel part of the group even though it is led by one or two players. Typical activities include building structures during block play and dramatization. The teacher's role in facilitating cooperative play centers around preparation of the environment and providing appropriate space and "social" toys requiring cooperative interaction between two or more children.

Some Ways to Get Children to Play.   Education usually emphasizes structured, teacher-directed play because some children do not appear to learn readily

Photo by Lisa Wadors

through spontaneous play. There is increased recognition of the environmental factors that can impact on children's involvement in play (Taylor, Peterson, McMurray-Schwarz, & Guillou, 2002). For example, inappropriate toys and play materials may contribute to the limited play behavior of children with disabilities. Toys that are not durable fail to withstand rough treatment, and toys such as dolls designed for symbolic play are not developmentally appropriate for some children. Children who still need to engage in practice play must be provided with toys strong enough to accommodate repeated use. Children who lack attending skills, imitation skills, or communication skills cannot be expected to share or take turns. Developing these abilities takes time and is taught deliberately through modeling and reinforcement. Teachers need to assess a child's developmental strengths and weaknesses to encourage the most appropriate play activities.

Once the teacher notes that a child has begun to explore the environment and effectively uses a variety of different toy objects, it is time to encourage the development of more sophisticated and sustained toy play and play that requires more social interaction.

Exhibit 6–2 suggests some guidelines to enhance productive free-choice play.

Imagining and pretending may be difficult for many children. Granting this freedom to be somebody else or something else is often a good way to lead a withdrawn child out of his or her shell. Dress-up clothes, an assortment of hats (firefighter, cowboy or cowgirl, train conductor, or nurse), and old costumes left from Halloween are appealing. Pretending to be animals during story times and participating in musical activities allow many children to romp and move freely. With freedom of movement comes greater ease in being around other children.

A large box with holes for windows provides a sense of protection. As the children crawl in and out, they discover new ways of looking at things. Looking through the window in the box restricts the view in unexpected ways. Moving becomes purposeful. Seeing what is inside intrigues some children. If the box is large enough, a small carpet and a place for a snack will encourage some children to enter.

Teachers may want to tell short stories using a flannel board or pictures. Then, as the teacher provides simple props and withdraws from the center of

Exhibit 6–2

Setting the Stage for Productive Free Playtimes

A. *Arrange the play area thoughtfully.*

1. Provide adequate space indoors and out. Avoid crowding.

2. Arrange small play spaces separated by shelves or other dividers. Puzzles, books, and other things to do alone should be available.

3. Prepare larger spaces for cooperative play with blocks and other building materials.

4. A play kitchen in a corner encourages group play. Provide some full-sized pans and spoons and child-sized equipment.

5. Maintain the same basic room arrangement over time but vary the play materials available. Have a storage area where toys may "rest." Sometimes allow the children to choose what will be stored and what will be available.

6. Include clay and easels but monitor their use.

7. Puppets, dolls and dollhouses, and barns and animals should be regularly available. These imagination stimulators require setup space, whether used alone or with a group.

8. Remove toys that appear to encourage an activity or noise level incompatible with the best interests of all the children. In small areas, large cars and trucks usually generate too high an activity level for safety.

9. Plan to alternate indoor and outdoor play whenever possible. Outdoor areas should provide safe climbing and running spaces as well as tricycles and structures for crawling in, over, and under.

10. Be alert for special needs. Provide special equipment for children with physical disabilities.

B. *Establish rules or guidelines from the beginning.*

1. Keep the rules simple and limited in number.

2. Telling children rules is important but not very effective. They will need to learn the guidelines by observation and experience. But the teacher should have the rules firmly in mind.

3. Rules should be designed to establish thoughtful, kind, and courteous behavior. The following are some we have found useful:

    a. The child who chooses a toy first may decide whether he or she wants to play alone or with others. The child's decision will be respected.

    b. Sharing is not required, especially if the item to be shared belongs to a particular child. Sharing is, however, encouraged.

    c. Children wanting to join an established group must be invited to join. The newcomer may ask to play but cannot move in without a welcome.

    d. Good manners are modeled and expected. "May I," "please," and "thank you" are routinely used by teachers. Children absorb these courtesies quickly.

    e. When a child or a group is finished with an item, the item must be returned to its place on the shelf before a different toy or game is chosen.

    f. Sometimes children like to just watch for a while. This wish is respected. A rocker and a beanbag chair are often used by watchers.

    g. Just as child newcomers may not barge into an established group, so adult (teacher or parent) newcomers must ask permission and be accepted.

C. *Some attitudes for teachers and parents during free play.*

1. Respect the children's ability to choose an activity suited to their present learning needs. By providing a range of materials and possible activities, the teacher allows the self-knowledge of each child to function.

2. Trust each child to use good judgment. Interfere only if real danger or unkindness is imminent. Anticipate and prevent trouble rather than punishing it after the fact.

3. Be aware of what is happening throughout the room. Even when attending to a particular child, the teacher must be alert to everyone and everything. Evidence of this awareness from the beginning leads children to follow the rules consistently.

4. Avoid overprotecting the child who lacks assertiveness. By "making" more aggressive children share, the teacher rewards the child who fails to assert him or herself for this lack of assertiveness. Rather, suggest to the quiet ones that they ask for a turn. If they begin fussing, remove the object of the argument for a time. Explain that they will have to find a way to resolve the problem.

5. If an unacceptable behavior persists, reevaluate the whole situation. If things are being thrown in the wrong place, find a place where it is appropriate to throw and move the throwers there. If loud noises inside are a problem, be outside more often.

6. Avoid making children self-conscious. Calling everyone's attention to a mistake or a mess is unkind.

7. Avoid comparisons. Respect uniqueness consistently.

---

the activity, children usually accept the suggestion to "play the story."

Role-playing is a form of pretending and imagining. An apron and play kitchen equipment make it possible for children to be Mom or Dad. A plastic hammer or a wrench enables a child to be a carpenter or a garage mechanic. Some children pretend to be their big brothers and sisters.

Much insight into fears and frustrations can be gained by encouraging role-playing without evaluating it. Of course, the insights gained may not be pleasant. Judgment about how to use such knowledge requires compassion, understanding, and wisdom.

Puppets are therapeutic and fun for most children. A box with a "stage" cut out, an old television with the insides removed, or a table with a curtain becomes the puppet theater. Of course, a real puppet stage can be constructed by a willing parent. The puppets can be made from socks or sewn from a simple pattern. Commercial puppets are enchanting, although most are expensive. Children enjoy merely playing with the puppets, but if a teacher puts on the first show, they will have a better idea of how to be puppeteers.

It is not unusual for withdrawn children to say their first words with a puppet on their hands. Often they will find it necessary to use the puppet for days whenever they want to talk. A change of puppets should be offered with care. If a particular puppet is effective, the teacher should not rush into expecting the child to assume many roles with other puppets. Some children require prolonged encouragement before they can venture out.

Peers and play often draw children out of their shells. Suggesting that one child help another by picking up a spilled puzzle leads to later spontaneous kindnesses. Some children notice the needs of other youngsters more completely than most adults believe. Consider this experience of Lance and Carla:

Lance was enrolled in kindergarten, but over a period of several months he stood quietly and firmly in one corner of the room. The kindergarten teacher was patient and experienced, but with 32 other children, the situation was overwhelming to Lance. Because of Lance's continued withdrawn behavior, his parents placed him in a preschool. When he entered school, his eyes were unsmiling, and his lips were taut. For several days the other

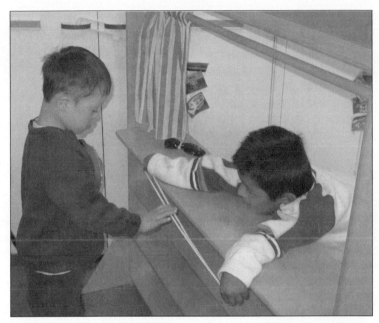

Photo by Lisa Wadors

children played around him. He refused snacks, special treats, and all efforts to involve him in play. Then Carla took over. She was 4 years old. She walked right up to Lance and said, "I like blocks. Play with me." Without further ado, she pulled Lance abruptly to the floor, pushed the blocks to him, and began to build. Smiling and chatting away (definitely a monologue), she told him all about the wonderful house she was building. Lance stared emotionless, but Carla was not disturbed. After a while Carla said, "Help put the blocks back. We'll do a puzzle." Lance did not move. A few minutes later Carla announced, "Lance likes grapes." The teacher did not discover how Carla knew of Lance's liking for grapes but promised to bring the fruit the next day.

The following day, Carla asked for some grapes "for Lance." Carrying the grapes with one hand and dragging Lance with the other, she moved to the puzzle corner. She said, "We'll do a puzzle first." With the grapes plainly in sight but out of Lance's reach, they began a puzzle. "When we finish, we eat grapes," said Carla. Lance smiled and slowly pushed a puzzle piece to Carla. He also ate grapes with Carla.

Carla's mothering continued for weeks as she ignored Lance's rebuffs. She regularly told everyone, "Lance is my friend," and busily planned things to do with him. She alternately insisted and cajoled. Frequently, when Lance ignored her, she walked away, only to return as if nothing had happened a few minutes later. Carla literally planned and executed therapy for Lance. No doubt, Carla's natural inclinations accomplished more than many well-planned teacher-directed lessons.

Facilitating Play and Social Skill Development in Children with More Severe Disabilities. Children with obvious or more severe disabilities may have had little opportunity to play with other children. Some may have spent a lot of their short lives in hospitals, whereas others may have been overprotected by parents who fear their child might experience ridicule or rejection. Of course, many disabling conditions by their very nature make it difficult for children to play in ways that lead to social skill acquisition. For instance, children with severe hearing, speech, or cognitive impairments may not have the language necessary to make their needs known

or to engage in appropriate verbal interchange. Children with physical disabilities or lack of behavior control may have problems making friends because their behavior or necessary adaptive equipment has become a barrier to social interaction. Therefore, caregivers must make special efforts to facilitate effective involvement of children with more special needs.

Some time ago, instructors from Texas Tech University (1984) listed the following target skills for special consideration when working with children with more severe disabilities:

1. Start and sustain play with other children.
2. Follow another child's lead or model.
3. Pretend in creative dramatic play.
4. Share materials and take turns.
5. Let other children know what they think and feel (p. 104).

Several strategies for developing these skills have already been discussed. Of course, it is necessary to begin by carefully observing to find out what social skills each child already has and which ones need to be developed. In addition, the transdisciplinary play-based approach to assessment presented by Linder (1993) and discussed in chapter 3 provides comprehensive guidelines for assessing children's social skills through everyday play routines.

Physical Prompting and Fading. Sometimes children with more severe disabilities do not become involved because they do not know how to play with the available toys or respond to others. When they do not react, there is no play behavior for the caregiver to reinforce and encourage. The caregiver, then, may have to physically guide the child through the desired response. For example, if the game is to roll a ball from one child to another, the caregiver or a trained peer may manually guide the child's hand until the child can approximate the behavior on his or her own. The guiding hand should be gradually removed as the approximation becomes closer and closer to the desired behavior. If during this fading or gradual removal of the physical prompting the child

becomes upset or apparently is not ready to continue alone, the fading should be discontinued temporarily. Such an approach can be very effective with children who experience severe physical, visual, hearing, or mental impairments. It is much easier for these children to follow directions illustrated through physical prompting.

Initiating and Sustaining Play. Sometimes physical prompting is not enough. Children may need to be given the words they need to initiate and sustain play behavior. When a child doesn't seem to have the words to invite another to play, the caregiver must supply them for the child. For example, when Danny wanted Brad to help him build a road in the sand, he kept looking and motioning to him. Brad, who often does not follow nonverbal cues, did not respond. Then Ms. McLynn said, "Danny, go and say to Brad, 'Come help me build the road.'" Danny modeled Ms. McLynn, who, in turn, reinforced both Danny and Brad as both began to build a road. When another child began to step on the road, Ms. McLynn said to Danny, "Say, 'Stop!'" Danny again modeled Ms. McLynn, and the children played on.

HELPING CHILDREN WITH EMOTIONAL AND BEHAVIORAL CHALLENGES

No matter how consistent and positive a teacher and the environment are, there will be children who continue to need additional help as they strive to develop a healthy, well-adjusted personality. There will also be behaviors that we perceive to be challenging just because our unique set of past experiences, values, instructional practices, and institutional guidelines lead us to perceive certain behaviors to be challenging. Or, as Tomlin (2004) states, "'Difficultness' (often) lies in the eye of the beholder, rather than in the behavior of a given child" (p. 33). Perhaps further understanding of the "normalness" of individual temperamental traits will help us be less stressed and more tolerant in the face of challenging behaviors.

Individual Temperament

"Temperamental predispositions are necessary, but not sufficient, building blocks for the child's developing personality" (Sturm, 2004, p. 5). As these constitutionally based building blocks are influenced by experience, they evolve into the features of individual personalities. Temperamental traits determine how a child typically interacts with his or her environment.

Current writers often turn to the pioneering work of Thomas, Chess, and Birch (1968, 1970) when they discuss concepts of temperament or early-appearing patterns of observable behavior. Through intensive parent interviews and observation of children, Thomas and colleagues identified nine characteristics of temperament that they clustered into three basic types describing approximately 65% of the children studied. The other 35% just did not show a basic constancy of temperament or style of behavior.

They described the *easy* child as one whose behavior is low in intensity and who is adaptable, approachable, predictable in bodily functions, and positive in mood. This kind of child easily makes parents believe they are good at parenting. Obviously, such a child (who accounted for approximately 40% of the sample studied) would be a pleasure in the classroom.

The second type of temperament is that of the *difficult* child, who made up approximately 10% of the sample studied. This type of child is often negative in mood, adapts slowly to change, has unpredictable biological functions, and often exhibits intense reactions to environmental demands. Such a child not only requires that teachers and parents exercise extra effort and patience to keep the child's self-esteem intact but also behaves in such difficult ways that the self-esteem of involved adults is often threatened. When adults are unable to provide firm guidance by building the environment discussed throughout this chapter, they may experience a sense of helplessness when such children appear unhappy or out of control. The threat of becoming burned-out caregivers is very real. This possibility is even more acute in the case of at-risk children who have exhibited early developmental delays. When children are unable, because of disabling conditions or prematurity, to give forth the early social signals necessary to establish early attachment, their difficult behavior later on is even more of a threat to parents who may already be feeling uneasy about their parenting skills.

The third type of child discussed by Thomas et al. is the *slow-to-warm-up* child, who accounts for approximately 15% of the sample. Such a child typically exhibits negative responses to new situations but, given time and patience, eventually adapts. Patience and understanding of the child's tendency to withdraw seems to be the key to helping this child become well adjusted.

The stability of these temperamental traits is thought to be dependent not only on characteristics of the child but also on the dynamic interplay between the child and his or her primary caregivers. As Blackwell (2004) states, "In other words, an adequate understanding of temperament must be one in which the child is regarded within the context of her environment" (p. 38).

It is the responsibility of caregivers to influence the child–environment interactional process so that difficult temperamental traits can be modified toward healthy adjustment to environmental demands now and in the future (Pelco & Reed-Victor, 2003). Therefore, the following sections suggest some practical methods of giving additional assistance to children whose behavior interferes with learning or can be described as disruptive or harmful.

Children Who Lack Self-Control

Children who lack sufficient self-control are usually thought of as aggressive, hostile, overactive, impulsive, or hyperactive. Such children find it difficult to follow classroom limits. Some, such as hostile and aggressive children, may deliberately strike out at others or damage equipment. Others, such as hyperactive or impulsive children, may merely be unable to control extraneous movements. Although these behaviors are certainly challenging, it is important to remember that any behavior that continues over time is "working" for the child exhibiting such behavior. Such behaviors have a purposeful, communication function. Strain and Hemmeter (1997, p. 4)

suggest that such behaviors may be attempting to communicate messages such as the following:

1. "You're asking me to do something that is too difficult."
2. "I don't understand what you want."
3. "I want a certain thing, and I want it now."
4. "I'm bored; pay some attention to me."

It is our responsibility to try to recognize what the child is trying to communicate and assist them in learning socially acceptable ways to communicate their thoughts and needs. We are further encouraged to try to prevent undesirable attempts at communication by anticipating needs and preventing such behavioral episodes. Efforts at prevention include making sure activities are developmentally and individually appropriate and requests are clearly understood, using highly desirable toys and activities, and providing positive feedback.

It is only when aggressive behavior occurs with high frequency; involves extreme behavior, such as destruction of property or cruelty to animals or behavior that is dangerous to other people; or increases after 3 years of age that we should consider that serious problems exist that need a specialist's intervention.

Some children with challenging behaviors may be labeled as having attention-deficit disorder (ADD) or attention-deficit hyperactivity disorder (ADHD). ADHD is characterized by the inability to maintain normal levels of attention, by extreme impulsivity, and by high levels of activity. Whereas many young children normally exhibit these behaviors, children with ADHD exhibit inappropriately high degrees of these behaviors (Wolraich, 2006). The onset of ADHD is before the age of 7, and it occurs more often in boys. Degrees of severity differ, and symptoms can be exacerbated or ameliorated by environmental factors. Early intervention specialists should be careful not to automatically ascribe the ADHD or ADD label to every child who exhibits extreme problems with behavior control. Only through complete, multidisciplinary diagnosis is the diagnosis of ADHD warranted.

Any diagnosis involving attention span is especially difficult with young children, as many adults have unreasonable expectations. The literature has not been consistent in indicating what length of attention is normal in everyday contexts. Ruff and Capozzoli (2003) hypothesized that two systems are responsible for attention in the first 3 years and that they are important at different times. During the first year, infants give most of their attention to novelty. As they develop neurologically, they start coordinating attention and activity, and their actions follow intentions. It is not until closer to 4 years of age that children can readily stay focused on a task and resist distraction. Tomlin (2004) discusses the importance of the development of cognitive skills such as self-talk in providing the mechanism that helps children develop the capacity to attend. She reminds us that "it is useful to consider the ability to persist with tasks and give sustained attention to activities and situations as a developmental skill that is at least partially dependent on cognitive abilities and is influenced by situational factors, such as what else is going on at the time and the type of activity" (p. 32).

If, after a thorough diagnosis, children are found eligible for additional community resources through special education by being referred as learning disabled, seriously emotionally disturbed, or otherwise health impaired, parents can be helped to realize that these labels are necessary evils to obtain funding for available additional services, such as family counseling or behavior management consultation. However, as noted throughout this book, labels usually do more harm than good. The basic problem for the classroom teacher or parent is the same—helping the child control his or her own behavior. Many of the same techniques for behavior control can be used effectively with all children who have these problems. Some children, however, will need individualized help. We will begin with those techniques that will be useful with a number of children and then follow with special considerations.

Prevention Through Environmental Preparation.
Teachers need to prepare the child's environment. Children who are hyperactive, anxious, or angry often find it almost impossible to sit still, to take turns, or to

wait for explanations. They may constantly squirm, turn, or wiggle. Such children may be easily overstimulated if they have difficulty filtering out extraneous sounds or sights. Teachers must take care to limit the noise level in their classrooms and the visual stimuli surrounding these children. Centers that have minimal space or are associated with different activity or noise levels may create too much confusion. The inability to filter out extraneous stimuli and to control impulses may be the reason some of these children can be so difficult for parents to handle when shopping in department or grocery stores.

Concentration can be improved by providing a quiet place to work free from distraction. Ample equipment and materials should be available so that these children do not have to do too much waiting or sharing. Teachers should limit the use of toys or games with many small pieces to manipulate that can create frustration. They must space tables far enough apart so that extraneous movements will not bother others. They should eliminate toys, such as guns and soldiers, that elicit aggressive behavior. They should place impatient children in a position to receive snacks or working materials relatively early in the waiting time. As these children show signs of increasing their capacities for self-control, waiting time can be increased.

Scheduling. As discussed earlier, predictable routines are essential to supporting young children's socially acceptable behavior. Schedules must be reasonably consistent in order for children to learn expected routines. By knowing what to do and when to do it, children are less likely to exhibit challenging behaviors. Predictability in type of activity, rather than sameness, is the key.

Carefully Consider Curricular Implementation. Teachers must carefully consider curricular implementation. When children are appropriately involved in activities with materials or people, they usually are demonstrating appropriate behavior as well. Children who find it difficult to concentrate may fall behind in developing preacademic skills and may be labeled as learning disabled later on. Sometimes their speech is so fast that words and thoughts become a jumble, resulting in excessive use of gestures. Children's frustrations may develop into aggressive behavior and a loss of self-esteem from being ashamed of their lack of self-control. To avoid these frustrations, directions must be extremely clear and given one by one, often with visual aids. Teachers should analyze tasks and present them in sequential steps so that they can reinforce success intermittently and frequently. Materials and activities must be interesting. Using the child's name often while working with a group helps the child focus his or her attention. A calm voice is a must. A raised voice will only create anxiety and heighten the child's level of activity.

Unstructured free playtimes or transition times can be especially difficult for impulsive children. Choices for these children may have to be limited. When transitions are clearly signaled and structured to minimize waiting time, opportunities for disruptive behavior are decreased. It helps to establish definite procedures for transition times, such as those suggested in Exhibit 6–3. A teacher or paraprofessional will need to stay with the most challenging children until they have become involved in their new activities. In their classic work, Hewett and Taylor (1980) described "order tasks" that can be especially useful in "helping children learn to adapt to routines, follow directions, complete assignments, and control their behavior" (p. 189). These are tasks that usually involve eye-hand coordination and are simple enough to complete so that children can readily realize success. Examples include picture puzzles, pegboard designs, and bead stringing. When children are losing control during either free play or work time, they can be directed to these order tasks to help them gain composure acceptably and nonpunitively.

Using loud, lively CDs during music time can be upsetting for children who have difficulty with control. Some activity records require children to be able to process auditory information quickly to participate. For children who lack self-control, these records may be inappropriate or can be used for only

Exhibit 6–3

Daily Activity Transition Techniques

A. *When children are playing (free-play or free-choice activities):*

1. Five minutes before cleanup time, quietly say, "It's almost cleanup time." Speak to small groups and individuals—do *not* make a group announcement.

2. Have a child ring a bell to signal "Cleanup time, now."

3. Sing a "cleanup song."

4. Move among the children, helping them find containers and properly sorting and replacing toys. As children learn where things belong, teacher assistance should be reduced.

   SUGGESTIONS: Early in the year, have a limited number of toys and games available. As the children learn to replace those correctly, add new ones and remove some things. Avoid clutter. Provide variety, that is, puzzles, games, blocks, beads, or coloring materials. Have a specific container for each kind of toy. Provide a particular place to which each container is returned as the children clean up.

B. *Transition from circle time or a group activity to another directed activity such as a small-group lesson, snack time, or individual lessons:*

1. As the activity in progress draws to a close, tell the children, "It's almost time for _____."

2. Establish brief eye contact with each child—a look and a smile at the same time. Then say, "Listen for the directions. It is _____'s turn."

3. Give each child in turn specific directions for moving to the next lesson or activity location. For example:

   Teacher: Matt, clap your hands two times, touch your ear, and walk backward to the table for a snack. (Others watch as Matt follows the directions. The directions are given in one long sentence. Matt must wait until the teacher finishes speaking before he begins.)

   Teacher: (To Danny, who has a learning problem): Danny, jump two times. (Danny's directions are shorter and spoken more slowly.)

   When the teacher gives specific directions for going to the table or the next activity location, children learn to listen to and follow directions while being able to "let off a little steam." The transition occurs in an orderly way and enhances a sense of appropriate behavior.

---

a very short time. Teachers must remember that many behavior problems are simply children's responses to overstimulation or frustration. Why create or accentuate such problems?

Teachers can use visual aids to help children control themselves. Carpet squares or pieces of tape on the floor give them a definite, visual, and tactile space in which they are to keep themselves. Having a definite location for their belongings is also important to all children. It helps them control their things and themselves. While on field trips, overactive children should be in small groups and close to adults. If they are verbally engaged, they usually have better body control. Similar-style name tags for groups of two or three help these children feel a manageable sense of belonging to a small group.

Maintain Physical Proximity and Touch Control. An adult's physical proximity or a gentle touch will help some children maintain control over

their behavior. This is especially useful when young children are placed in situations that require extra efforts at control. Many publicly supported early childhood programs are placed within elementary schools. As a result, children may be expected to stand and walk in lines and to control their behavior in ways that usually are not expected until they reach kindergarten age. Teachers may even need to take the hands of some children to help them maintain the needed control. This should not be done as a punishment for misbehavior but should be done before problems arise, as a help to the child. If the teacher uses hand-holding as a punishment, the teacher might become an aversive stimulus, and the child might feel less worthy.

Use Signal Interference to Prevent Loss of Self-Control.   Signal interference can be very effective with impulsive children if teachers have observed carefully to see what usually "sets off" such children. Sometimes patterns in behavior are obvious, such as excessive frustration or activity just before a snack, during circle time, or near the time to go home. Environmental factors such as overstimulation, lack of sufficient movement space, or lack of time to complete a task might be a part of the patterns. Nonverbal (and sometimes verbal) signals, such as a nod or a wink, can be especially effective if used in the beginning stages of misbehavior and with children who are capable of understanding them and can remember why the signal is being given.

Signals must be used before a child becomes so emotional that he or she is unable to stop the behavior. A warm relationship between the teacher and the child contributes to the effectiveness of this approach. As children mature, they can be taught to understand their own signs of impending loss of control. They can then be encouraged to signal the teacher that they need a time-out or a change in activities.

Pick Your Battles.   Teachers and parents should pick only the most disruptive and aggressive behav-

ior as targets for control. Those who work with very young children must be willing to tolerate a high level of activity. Otherwise, their negative reactions will exacerbate the child's behavior.

Do Not Permit Aggressive Behavior.   Not permitting aggressive behavior should be the first rule toward helping children control the expression of unacceptable, possibly harmful behavior. From the very beginning, adults must make it perfectly clear that hitting, kicking, pushing, and shoving will not be allowed. Then teachers and parents must act swiftly in the face of the expression of such behavior to demonstrate consistently and firmly what the consequences of such actions will be. Children thus learn that such acts will not be tolerated, as they lead to nonpunitive but effective consequences. Firm consistency helps children develop trust in themselves and in others.

Despite the teacher's best efforts toward preventive discipline, aggressive acts do occur and must be dealt with immediately. The key to dealing with aggressive children is for the teacher to be nonaggressive. Nonhurtful discipline, such as a time-out, is considered by many to be effective. Children learn that aggressive behavior will not be tolerated of anyone, not even of the teacher. They also learn that the teacher can be trusted to be nonhurtful. If teachers are to give attention, they should give it to nonaggressors. That is, the teacher should give attention to the victim rather than to the aggressor. Throughout this chapter, other examples of nonaggressive methods of behavior control are discussed. These merit consideration.

Deescalate Play Behavior.   Children need to be helped by active adult participation to deescalate their play when it gets out of hand. To illustrate the need to help children refocus their play when they become too involved, one can describe the all-too-familiar building blocks scene. Children begin innocently making block towers, and one child accidentally knocks against or otherwise destroys a child's product. Then hostility erupts, and aggression occurs.

Involved adults should not only try to environmentally prevent or catch the behavior before it escalates but also return children to positive playfulness by not making judgments and reading intent into every aggressive act.

Use Time-Out Effectively. Although *time-out* has long been used to deescalate behavior, disadvantages of this technique are being noted. These include the opportunity for the distressed child to damage the area of time-out, to make distracting noise, to leave the area, or to forget that he or she is being punished. There is also concern that it might be too much to ask a very young child to regain control by him- or herself and appropriate behavior cannot be taught when a child is in isolation. If time-out is being used, Klein, Cook, and Richardson-Gibbs (2001) offer the following important considerations:

1. Make sure the child understands exactly what behavior will result in a time-out.

2. Warn the child, calmly, only once.

3. Be sure the child is within the teacher's view at all times.

4. Keep the time-out very short.

5. Be positive at the end of the time-out; praise the child for being in control of him- or herself.

6. Help the child choose and engage in another activity.

Consider the Value of Time Away. It is generally agreed that everyone needs a break when a child has lost control. Therefore, Miller (2007) recommends *time away* instead of time-out. Time away acknowledges that everyone needs a breather once in a while. When a child loses control, the caregiver can suggest that the child go off by him- or herself until he or she feels better and wants to be cooperative. This action should not be considered to be punishment but a brief respite instead. The time-away area should be a pleasant place near a window or a book or puzzle corner. Giving the child something to do will facilitate

self-control. There should be a rule that only one child be in the area at any time, and children should be encouraged to take themselves there when they feel the need for quiet time. Whenever possible, an adult should be available to provide support to the child.

Deal Consistently with Temper Tantrums. Temper tantrums that are only bids for attention may go away when they are consistently ignored. If the tantrums persist, then the child becomes a candidate for the six-step time-out process just outlined. Nonthreatening statements are preferred, such as "It seems that you are unable to play with us right now. I hope you will be able to work with us after some time in the 'thinking corner.'" Once the child is back and participating appropriately, reinforcement should be given for the constructive behavior in progress.

Mutual cooperation with parents is essential to establishing firm, consistent guidelines. The adult reactions should not be punitive or display anger when firmly redirecting the child. Above all, adults must be certain that a tantrum does not result in the child's getting his or her own way if that way is inappropriate. The child's day should be programmed so that numerous opportunities exist for the child to get attention in constructive ways.

Help Overactive Children Feel Good About Themselves.   Many children who overact are angry underneath and expend energy covering up feelings of inferiority or fears of being vulnerable. Possibly the primary objective for such children is to help them see themselves as worthwhile people capable of developing self-control. Experience has shown that when these children begin to feel like responsible individuals, their need for negative behavior is diminished.

Healthy young children enjoy pleasing adults whom they can trust. When these children misbehave, teachers should ask themselves whether something they are doing or not doing is causing the problem. Have the children been allowed to change activities frequently enough? Is too much being demanded? Are the children being allowed to constructively express their feelings verbally and physically by pounding clay or knocking down tenpins? Is the reward-to-punishment ratio at an optimum level? The teacher's responsibility is to prevent children from losing control of their behavior. Loss of control creates shame, guilt, and lowered self-esteem.

The curriculum needs to be reviewed periodically to ensure realistic developmentally and individually appropriate expectations. Experts caution educators to beware of stressing academics to the detriment of social and emotional development. It is suggested that early educators avoid emphasizing academics during the preschool years. Instead, they are encouraged to concentrate on certain prerequisite skills, such as listening, being able to relate past experiences to present activities, and using and respecting the tools of learning.

Finally, helpful teachers will (a) express their acceptance of children's feelings, negative and positive; (b) reassure overactive children that one of the teacher's jobs is to protect children from harming others or themselves; (c) exhibit confidence in children's abilities to improve self-control; and (d) demonstrate that children will be allowed greater opportunities to control their own behavior as they exhibit increased self-restraint and appropriate expressions of feelings.

A Word About Medication: Caution

Perhaps the most controversial method of handling children who lack sufficient self-control involves using psychotropic drugs. The use of psychotropic drugs with preschoolers is increasing. Methylphenidate hydrochloride (Ritalin) and dextroamphetamine sulfate (Dexedrine) appear to be used most often with preschool-aged children (Rappley, 2006). However, there is evidence to suggest that side effects may be stronger and different from those observed in older patients. It should also be noted that that the Food and Drug Administration guidelines for methylphenidate-based products do not recommend use in children younger than 6 years (Kollins & Greenhill, 2006).

Considering the diagnostic difficulties involving young children and lack of sufficient treatment studies, a cautious approach to the use of stimulant medication is definitely warranted. Medication should *never* be used as the only treatment. Its use should be considered only when the hyperactivity is extreme and when medication is part of a well-designed and well-monitored, multimodal management program.

Children Who Are Reluctant to Participate

Children who are reluctant to participate are rarely a bother to teachers and classmates. Shy or timid children are easily overlooked. Research suggests that social withdrawal in early childhood is a risk factor for maladjustment (Nelson, Rubin, & Fox, 2005). Special attention is important for children whose behavior ranges from timid and inhibited to completely withdrawn; otherwise, their needs may go unnoticed. Such children usually separate themselves physically, avoid group activities and verbal interaction, seem afraid to try new tasks, sometimes appear disinterested, and may seek comfort through self-stimulation (e.g., rocking, twisting their hair, or thumb sucking). These children lack the very behaviors that would normally bring them into social

contact, such as looking, talking, approaching, and playing with others. Teachers often find themselves responsible for helping these children develop approach and responsiveness behaviors.

In addition to lacking social contact behavior, some of these children may be preoccupied with self-stimulation or with daydreaming and fantasy (Miller, 2007). By being so absorbed in their imaginations or their repetitive acts of sensory stimulation, they miss social cues. This lack of attention prevents them from the social learning available to children who are not isolated either physically or emotionally. Children who also experience language delays are at an even greater disadvantage. Even if they are paying attention, they may not be able to understand directions or to ask necessary questions. They have or take few opportunities to demonstrate what they know and understand. Skill and patience are absolutely necessary to help these children develop the trust they so desperately need.

Prepare the Child's Environment.   Throughout this text, the importance of thoughtful preparation of the environment is stressed as a means of preventing behavioral challenges. For reluctant or inhibited children, on the one hand, the teacher needs to establish a climate of safety, predictability, and consistency. On the other hand, the teacher needs to extend an acceptance of his or her responses, however limited, and provide nurturance, nourishment, and individual attention regardless of the quality or quantity of the child's initial output. By focusing on reducing stress and creating a nonthreatening atmosphere, the child may become more actively involved (Nelson et al., 2005).

Children who are reluctant to participate will appreciate a small, safe place into which they can retreat. The place must not be like the time-out area. The child should be able to view the classroom activities from the safe place. Many inhibited children learn a great deal from watching others. Through watching, they may develop the confidence necessary to attempt a new or different task.

As the child becomes more trustful, the "watching chair" can be moved closer to the ongoing activity. At an intermediate point, identical play materials can be placed within the child's reach. The teacher should not coax the child. No attention should be given to the child unless he or she attempts the activity either alone or with the others. If this occurs, then positive reinforcement should be given quietly and inconspicuously. The teacher must know what the child enjoys. A smile, rather than a public announcement of the child's participation, would probably be more appropriate.

These children will feel more secure if materials are kept in the same place day to day. They want a definite place for their own objects, including crayons and coats. The teacher should not force them to share until they are ready to do so. Consistency in routines and procedures helps them predict and therefore feel more comfortable. The children must be prepared in advance for any new or strange situations such as visitors, field trips, or tornado drills.

Promote Peer Assistance.   Seating nonparticipating children near relatively quiet but competent children can do wonders in promoting peer assistance. Experience has shown that extremely shy children often respond to another child much more quickly than to an adult. Caring, concerned children who do not move too loudly or quickly are excellent models, and they do not threaten the insecure child. Such children can be prompted to invite the reluctant child to participate without begging for involvement. As noted earlier in the story of Lance, sometimes the best approach is for the child or perhaps the teacher to ask for help, for example, "Johnny, will you please help me clean up this paint" or "Please hold the picture." Help can begin with an independent activity such as passing snacks and can graduate to a cooperative activity such as two children going to get the juice. Helping others gives the child an easy basis to establish relationships; at the same time, self-esteem can be enhanced.

Consider Curricular Adaptations.   Like most children, inhibited children need a predictable schedule that includes both group time and individual

time. Group size can be increased as the child builds confidence. Some children who are unwilling to express themselves in conversation will join in a song because they feel less conspicuous. They may sit on the edge initially. The teacher should not rush them. In the beginning, peripheral involvement such as holding pictures rather than naming them can be encouraged. Many of these children will participate physically before they will participate verbally. If a story is being read and followed by questions, call on the reluctant child last and then do not coax. Teachers must remember that the child must set the pace.

Many young children will interact with pets before they will interact with people. Letting such children take care of pets helps them feel that they are contributing to the welfare of the pets and to the classrooms. Their involvement also gives them a chance to receive the approval they seek.

Socially isolated children often respond to the social learning principles of modeling and imitation. Teachers should therefore seriously plan opportunities for these children to observe positive, pleasant social interaction as discussed earlier.

Individual attention is sometimes the key to getting reluctant children to participate in instructional activities. Teachers should approach them calmly, speaking slowly and clearly, and state exactly what they expect. They should present activities that they are reasonably certain are interesting to the child. Teachers must try to couple their attention to the child with something pleasant. They should help children to be reminded of good things when they see or think of their teacher. If the child refuses to become involved, then the teacher should merely place the materials nearby and let the child watch. This procedure should be followed at snack time as well. The teacher should not become anxious if the child does not eat. The more uncomfortable attention the child receives, the less he or she is likely to eat.

An effective strategy for facilitating engagement includes the following. Begin by standing close to the reluctant child. Then suggest that he or she join a group: "Tim and Laura could use someone to help build a bridge. Why not give them a hand, Bob?" At this point, the teacher should move away, returning

to give positive attention if the child acts on the suggestion. Teachers then may wish to give additional suggestions if they seem to facilitate involvement.

Provide Opportunities for Expressing Feelings.
As mentioned earlier, the expression of a full range of emotions is essential to healthy emotional development (Greenspan & Weider, 2005). Inhibited, withdrawn children typically experience many unexpressed emotions. Special encouragement thus must be given to self-expression. Drawing, painting, puppetry, clay, water play, fingerpainting, and music can provide opportunities for this expression. Of course, these children must not be forced, and their efforts must be rewarded without regard to their products. As trust develops, teachers can gradually encourage verbal expression by asking questions such as "Is the girl in your picture very upset or unhappy today?" Like active listening, this approach helps children feel understood and accepted. They can attribute their unpleasant feelings to the object in the drawing and thus find these feelings to be less threatening.

Pictures, especially photographs of the children themselves, are especially useful when talking about feelings. Pictures that show clear facial expressions, definite gestures, or obvious effects of the child's actions on others should be chosen. Such pictures help the child to perceive how another may feel and to discover cause-and-effect relationships. Guided discussion should focus on describing what is happening, what will happen, and how those in the picture might feel.

Help Reluctant Children Feel Good About Themselves. Above all, teachers must be conscious of the need to help reluctant children feel good about themselves so that they may find the courage to develop the social contact and attention skills critical to healthy social involvement. The teacher should begin with step-by-step presentations of noncompetitive tasks that can be achieved by the child. Nonthreatening rewards for effort coupled with a trusting relationship developed through dependability

are essential. When children participate little, it is extremely difficult to manipulate the environment to ensure an optimal reward-to-punishment ratio. Avoiding punishment may be the most efficient means toward helping the child build confidence and trust in the beginning.

Because a child's inhibited, withdrawn pattern can be a developmental pattern later associated with serious disturbance, it is imperative that teachers work closely with parents, counselors, and psychologists. When a child's severe reluctance persists after a couple of months of consciously structuring the environment and creating nonthreatening opportunities for involvement, the teacher should not hesitate to seek help. After giving the child a reasonable time to become adjusted, considering the child's age and previous experiences (or lack of them), the teacher takes careful observational notes. The teacher should study these carefully to see whether any progress is being made, and he or she should discuss minimal progress with the school psychologist or with some other mental health worker to determine whether additional evaluation or a change in programming is necessary.

USE OF REINFORCEMENT

Research suggests that lack of achievement may be related to children's failing to link acceptable performance with their own efforts or abilities. They may instead attribute their successes to chance, task ease, or powerful others (Cook, 1986). Given this tendency of some children to attribute successful performance to external causes, teachers must be extremely careful in phrasing their praise.

Give Credit Where Credit Is Due

The praise must describe in specific terms the behavior that the teacher wishes to have repeated either by the child being praised or by those who are watching at the time. Furthermore, the praise must give the child credit for his or her efforts or abilities. Consider these statements: "Danny, you should feel happy. You listened carefully to my directions and then tried to do

exactly what you were asked to do." If the teacher had said, "Thank you, Danny for being good," Danny would have no idea of what behavior to repeat in the future if he wished to "be good." By being specific, Danny learned that carefully following directions and trying to do what was asked of him is considered to "be good." Such explicit statements point out to others what behavior is expected at the same time Danny is helped to realize that his efforts are important. Note that effort rather than outcome was emphasized.

Young children, and especially young children with special needs, must be encouraged to focus on effort rather than on outcome. After all, they may be able to control their efforts even though successful outcomes are sometimes out of reach. Consider this statement: "Danny, I'm so glad you have a new hearing aid. You were able to follow my directions." Danny now feels that he could succeed because of the hearing aid, not necessarily because of his effort. He may or may not put forth effort in the future, especially once his hearing aid is no longer a novelty.

Ignore Minor Disruptive Behaviors

Some irritating behaviors will disappear if they receive no attention or reward from anyone. Teachers must be astute observers. Even though a teacher may ignore a behavior, it does not mean that other children are not giving attention to it. Simply ignoring the behavior will not work in such a situation. The child is getting attention of some kind and is possibly modeling inappropriate behavior for other children.

Some children will use troublesome four-letter words, stick out their tongues, or tap their tables merely to get a reaction from the teacher. Observant teachers usually guess when this is the case. Ignoring behavior can be effective as long as the teacher realizes that the child may go on until some kind of attention is given. The answer is to find a way to give the child positive attention. This can be done by directing the child into an activity while simultaneously ignoring the undesired behavior. Depending on the child, ignoring alone may just bring on more disruptive behavior.

Minimize the Use of Negative Consequences

Punishment is thought to only decrease the rate at which inappropriate behaviors occur and can also produce negative side effects, such as fear, tension, and withdrawal. Any aggressive acts by an adult also provide undesirable models for children to imitate.

To minimize negative side effects of any form of punishment, teachers and parents must make careful efforts to control each child's **reward-to-punishment ratio.** Rewards are considered to be any action or statement that builds a child's self-esteem or anything that makes the child feel good about him- or herself. Punishment may refer to any action or statement that decreases a child's self-esteem or makes him or her feel less worthy.

Long ago, Kirkhart and Kirkhart (1972) offered valuable "food for thought" when they clearly pointed out the importance of the reward-to-punishment ratio in the development of a healthy personality: a reward-to-punishment ratio of five rewards for every one punishment is about optimal in guiding and directing a child's behavior. However, when the ratio falls down to only two rewards for every one punishment, neurotic symptoms begin to develop, especially those of inferiority and inadequacy and a generalized fear of failure. They further stated that predelinquent behavior is often observed in children whose reward-to-punishment ratio falls to 1:1 or below.

Observations of classrooms readily suggest that many teachers are unaware of the reward-to-punishment ratio they are using. This is especially a problem when a child does very little that merits reward and functions as if negative attention is better than none at all. To control the reward-to-punishment ratio, teachers must plan carefully to ensure that such children are attempting tasks for which their efforts can be rewarded.

Preventive observation is essential. When a teacher sees children begin to lose control or interest because of frustration, fatigue, or hunger, the teacher must quickly change the child's activity. The reward-to-punishment ratios can approach optimal levels by preventing punishment and by increasing reward.

Teachers can develop special nonverbal signals such as a nod or a wink to be given as reminders to children who seem about to misbehave. Then immediate reward or reinforcement can be given when a child increases the effort to control his or her behavior.

Punishment in the form of *logical and natural consequences* can have an informative effect if used wisely. Punishment that is part of rule setting in the classroom can be a natural consequence predicted by those who do not follow classroom rules. When linked directly to their behavior, they can see the relationship between their causative act and the resulting effect.

If children know that hitting others or otherwise fooling around during circle time will cause them to be asked to leave the activity, then they will see the punishment as justified and directly caused by their behavior. They will not see the teacher as arbitrary or themselves as unresponsible for the outcome. They will know how to prevent the punishment in the future if the teacher has specifically stated why they were punished. The teacher might say, "Vicky, you must take a time-out. You have hit Susie and we cannot hurt others."

Walker, Shea, and Bauer (2006) provided the following guidelines to those who find it absolutely necessary to use punishment:

1. Specify and communicate the punishable behavior to the children by means of classroom rules for behavior.

2. Post the rules where the children can see them and review them with the group frequently.

3. Provide models of acceptable behavior.

4. Apply the punishment immediately.

5. Apply the punishment consistently, not whimsically.

6. Be fair in using the punishment (what is good for Peter is good for Paul).

Of course, these rules have to be adapted for use with very young children. Picture symbols might be used instead of words when listing the rules. Walker and colleagues also listed 14 reasons why teachers should avoid using either physical (spankings) or psychological (derogatory statements) punishment. Basically, other forms of behavior management are more effective and avoid damaging effects. More important, punishment bruises the already fragile developing self-images of children.

Punishment that is in any way derogatory or demeaning should be avoided at all costs. Only punishments that are logical, natural, and unattached to the child's person or personality should be used. Table 6–2 illustrates the importance of this suggestion. Acceptable punishments, when kept to a minimum and used as a last resort, include deprivation of privileges (including time-out) and compensation for

Table 6–2   Logical consequences versus punishment

The Behavior (What Happened)	Logical and Natural Consequence	Punishing the Personality
Child spills milk	Child cleans up spill	"You are so clumsy." "Don't you ever watch what you're doing?" "You messed up again."
Child grabs another child's toy	Child returns the toy	"You're a brat again." "Must you be so bad?" "You're always the selfish bully."
Child "forgets" to hang up coat	Child hangs up coat	"Can't you remember anything?" "How many times have I told you . . . ?"
Child yells loudly in supermarket	Child says softly, "Let's practice a soft voice." Child returns to market and practices being quiet	"Shut up; you're a bad girl." "Good girls are quiet in public." "I'll never take you to the store again."

intentional wrongdoing, such as picking up deliberately spilled puzzle pieces. It should be remembered, however, that any form of punishment should be administered with firm kindness to avoid becoming derogatory or demeaning.

POSITIVE BEHAVIOR SUPPORT

The use of negative consequences to modify or eliminate certain behaviors reflects a traditional "behavior modification" approach. This approach focuses on adding or changing the consequences of the child's behavior (e.g., responding to the child's biting with a brief time-out or removal from the play area). More recent approaches to encouraging the appropriate behavior and managing challenging behavior focus on (a) understanding the *antecedents* of behavior as possible triggers of inappropriate behavior, (b) analysis of typical *consequences* of the behavior (i.e., what usually happens as a result of the behavior), (c) identifying the *function* of the behavior, (d) determining those contextual conditions that might best support the positive behavior of a particular child, and (e) identifying appropriate *replacement* behaviors. This approach, defined by Koegel, Koegel, and Dunlap (1996), is referred to as **positive behavior support.**

According to Fox, Dunlap, and Cushing (2002), the positive behavior support approach determines the function of a particular behavior and its relationship to specific antecedents and consequences. Through careful observation of the child in daily environments and working in partnership with the child's family, a positive behavior support plan is generated. Rather than manipulating the consequence, a positive behavior support approach focuses more on changing the antecedent conditions and on teaching appropriate communication and social skills as *replacement behaviors.*

Factors such as low frustration tolerance, emotional lability, lack of impulse control, and tactile and auditory hypersensitivity are common characteristics of children with disabilities. As a result of these characteristics, certain antecedent situations may be more likely to trigger unacceptable behaviors in children. Although any child, regardless of whether he or she has a disability, can develop patterns of behavior that are disruptive or are considered unacceptable, the characteristics of certain disability conditions may increase the likelihood that a child will develop a behavior problem.

Using Behavioral Analysis to Understand Disruptive Behavior

In preventing and managing a behavior that is truly disruptive (e.g., screaming) or potentially harmful (e.g., biting, hitting, or self-injurious behavior), it is helpful to use a systematic, functional behavior analysis procedure to determine the function or purpose of that behavior. Any given behavior may have different functions. *The type of behavior does not tell you the function of the behavior. The same behavior in two different children may have two completely different functions.*

There are a limited number of possible reasons why a child might engage in unacceptable behavior. Possible functions of challenging behavior include the following:

1. *To escape something unpleasant.* In some cases, the child may be trying to escape an *internal state.* For example, the child may be in some kind of discomfort or may feel extremely stressed or anxious because of physiological or biological factors rather than external conditions.

More often, the child is trying to escape *environmental* conditions that cause stress, anxiety, or discomfort. For instance, a child with very sensitive hearing (often the case in children who have autism) may experience discomfort in a noisy room. Analysis of antecedent conditions and events are critical to understanding the escape function of a behavior. Common environmental conditions that

may cause stress or discomfort for some children are the following:

- Noisy or highly resonant acoustic environment
- Too many children in close proximity
- Cluttered or disorganized physical environment
- Confusing, unpredictable environment and schedule
- Large, open spaces with no boundaries

Some children may be trying to escape a specific task or activity he or she dislikes. For example, the child may hate brushing his teeth or may dislike the tactile sensation of certain materials such as fingerpaint or sand.

Some "escape" behaviors are obvious like running away or refusing to stay seated. Just as often, however, the behaviors are less easily interpreted. Consider the following list of behaviors that are frequently caused by a need to escape:

- Tantruming
- Throwing objects
- Hitting or biting
- Self-injurious behavior (e.g., biting own hand)
- Self-stimulatory behavior (e.g., hand flapping or rocking, which often serves to block out the environment)

2. *To get attention.* Frequently, the primary motivation of unacceptable behavior is to gain attention and interaction from a caregiver or significant adult. An effective general strategy that can significantly reduce behavior problems is to *make sure you connect with each child on an intimate, one-on-one basis, frequently throughout the day.* This means being at the child's eye level, patiently listening to both his or her words and feelings. A young child's seeking interaction and attention from a significant adult should not automatically

be considered inappropriate or atypical. It is the particular *way* in which the child obtains attention that may be problematic. For children who often engage in inappropriate behavior to get attention, an effective strategy is to provide the child with some brief special attention before the child engages in the inappropriate behavior. It is also helpful to immediately attend to the child when he or she engages in an appropriate behavior ("catch them being good"). The following are common attention-getting behaviors:

- Running away
- Leaving an activity
- Picking on peers
- Tantruming
- Removing clothing
- Destroying property
- Turning water/lights on or off

3. *To gain access to something the child wants.* In this case the child engages in unacceptable behavior to *gain access* to a toy, activity, or area he or she finds pleasurable. Engaging in a negative behavior to obtain an object is usually fairly obvious. Gaining access to something less tangible may not be obvious. For instance, a child who frequently runs away may be running away not to escape or to gain attention but because she loves being outside. The child may turn the lights on and off not because he wants the teacher's attention, but because he loves the visual effect of the lights going off and on. Careful observation of the behavior, the antecedents, and the consequences can help accurately determine the function of a behavior.

Designing Positive Behavior Support Plans

Understanding Problem Behaviors as Communication. Often problems occur in children who cannot express themselves verbally. Many children with disabilities have limited language skills and frequently

express strongly felt needs in nonverbal ways. All too often these nonverbal communications are inappropriate and are then identified as behavior problems.

An important step in reducing problem behaviors is to determine what the communicative function of the behavior is. It may be helpful to view the child's behavior as an attempt to communicate the need to escape, the desire for attention, or to request a desired object or activity, as described above. Once this is determined, a more appropriate communicative behavior can be trained. This new behavior is referred to as replacement behavior, as mentioned earlier.

Exhibit 6–4 depicts a step-by-step approach adapted from Klein et al. (2001) for designing and implementing a positive behavior support plan. By following this approach and providing support for positive behavior, interventionists are truly intervening and are more likely to prevent or reduce negative behaviors while promoting those that are positive.

Exhibit 6–4

Positive Behavior Support Procedure

Step 1: Conduct an "A-B-C" analysis to carefully observe the behavior over a period (at least 1 week).

A is for "antecedent":

What happens just before the behavior occurs?

B is the inappropriate behavior:

What does the child do?

C is the "consequence":

What happens immediately following the behavior?

Step 2: Carefully describe the unacceptable behavior.

What does the child actually do? Describe the sequence:

Child looks at teacher.

Child begins to scream.

As teacher approaches, child runs toward door.

When does child do it?

Where does the behavior occur?

Who is usually present when the behavior occurs?

Step 3: Hypothesize about why this behavior occurs.

Is the cause internal? (e.g., medication, illness, fatigue, low threshold)

Is the child trying to escape?

Is the child trying to get attention?

Is the child trying to obtain a desired object or activity?

Step 4: Determine a possible communicative value of the behavior.

Is the child using this behavior to try to tell us something? For example:

"I'm in pain."

"Let me out of here!"

"Please touch me (look at me, talk to me, come close to me)."

"I would rather play with the Legos or be outside on the swing."

Step 5: Identify possible behavior "triggers."

Use information from step 1 regarding the antecedent. What sets off the child's behavior?

Step 6: Plan environmental changes or changes in antecedent events to reduce triggering behavior. For example:

Place certain items out of reach.

Keep other children a certain distance away.

Change acoustic characteristics of room to dampen sound.

Step 7: Identify replacement behavior, if appropriate. For example:

Child will make sign for "Stop" rather than hitting.

Child will point to card that says "Quiet Zone" when he or she needs "time away."

Child will sign "All done" when he or she is full rather than dumping food on the table.

Step 8: Carefully plan with staff what the consequence will be if the behavior still occurs occasionally. For example:

Teacher will remove child from the play area.

All adults will move away from the child. (If an extinction procedure—for instance, ignoring—is used as a consequence, the frequency or intensity of the negative behavior may initially increase before it begins to decrease.)

Step 9: Monitor frequency and intensity of behavior to make sure it is decreasing.

Note: Teachers must realize the behavior is not going to suddenly disappear overnight using this procedure. Thus, it is important to periodically measure the behavior (i.e., how many times per day the behavior occurs or how long the behavior episode lasts) to determine if it is gradually decreasing. Often teachers think the procedure is not working and abandon it too quickly.)

SPECIAL CONSIDERATIONS FOR WORKING WITH CHILDREN WHO HAVE BEEN ABUSED AND NEGLECTED

Child maltreatment or abuse and neglect is thought to be a leading cause of disability and developmental delay in young children. At least half of all young children in foster care placement exhibit delays or disabilities (Dicker & Gordon, 2006). Probably the single most important intervention strategy for children who have been abused and neglected is the establishment of a predictable and safe environment. Over a period of time, a responsive, predictable environment may provide the child with the support

necessary to enable him or her to explore the physical environment as well as relationships with others. Earlier discussions of classroom routines, both in this chapter and in chapter 5, provide important suggestions for designing and implementing predictable environments. Programs that depend primarily on children's own self-direction or that require children to accept major responsibility for their use of time may provide too much freedom and ambiguity for children who have been maltreated.

Current research suggests that severe maltreatment can result in what is termed **reactive attachment disorder** (RAD) (Haugaard & Hazen, 2004). The primary feature of children with RAD is inappropriate social relating. These children either are indiscriminate in seeking affection or, at the other extreme, are reluctant to seek or accept affection. Haugaard and Hazen state, "The goals of intervention with children who have RAD are to give the child (a) a source of emotional security, (b) opportunities for corrective social experiences, and (c) better social skills" (p. 158). Therefore, for children with attachment disorders, it is extremely important to assign a **primary provider**—one person who is consistently available to the child to greet the child, to assist with self-help skills, and especially to be available in moments of frustration and loss of control (Hanson & Spratt, 2000). By experiencing repeated and consistently warm responsiveness, the child can learn to obtain comfort from a social relationship.

It is also important for children to learn how to influence people and events in appropriate and effective ways. Other important program goals for these children will be to assist them in learning self-control and how to express and understand a wide range of emotions. Children who have been maltreated will often engage in disruptive behavior that interferes with the learning of others. Both punishment and sympathy should be minimized and coercion and power struggles avoided. When negative consequences are necessary, they should be predictable, consistent, mild, and brief.

Discipline should be carried out in an affectively neutral environment so that positive expressions are not paired with negative consequences. Children who have been abused and neglected often receive mixed messages from caregivers. For example, a parent may be physically abusive one moment and overly solicitous the next, or the parent may assume a false sweetness to induce the child to comply or perform some task. Thus, a teacher should not apply a discipline strategy such as removal from an activity while at the same time saying something positive such as "You know I love you very much."

In addition, staff members should be clear and consistent in their expression of such emotions as happiness, sadness, or fatigue. This will assist the child who has been maltreated in understanding human emotions and will provide models for the child's expression of his or her own emotions.

Cicchetti and Toth (1987) emphasized the importance of a **transactional model of intervention** for maltreating families. In a transactional model, all elements of the system (e.g., child, family, and environment) are viewed as exerting reciprocal influences on one another. A transactional model does not isolate one element of the system, such as the child, for intervention. Rather, such a model attends to all components of the dysfunctional family system, including child, family, and environmental characteristics. Thus, it will be necessary for the classroom teacher to work in close collaboration with other team members and social service agencies to meet the many needs of the child who has been maltreated and his or her family. Exhibits 6-5 and 6-6 provide information on recognizing signs of physical abuse and following up after a case of abuse has been reported.

As thoroughly discussed in this chapter, children who have developed healthy self-concepts through nurturing environments will develop more readily in all areas. The next chapter will outline the concerns and techniques most essential to the promotion of motor and self-help skills.

Exhibit 6–5

Recognizing Signs of Physical Abuse

1. Be alert for signs of sadness or anger as well as bruises, burns, and cuts. Listen to what the children say. Be especially alert for changes in behavior that cannot be explained by impending illness or a happening at school. Begin *at once* to record specific details of your observations. Be certain to make a written note of the date, time, and manner of observation. These may be necessary if a report must be made to authorities. Keep these confidential and under lock and key.

2. Cigarette burns are usually round. Small, round burns should always be investigated.

3. Bruises on legs and buttocks can be the result of falls. The frequency and the severity of the bruises are useful criteria. Even clumsy children stay unbruised most of the time. If the child is nearly always bruised, be suspicious.

4. Black eyes do result from bumping into things. So do bumps on heads. Again, the severity and the relative frequency of the bruises dictate the degree of teacher concern.

5. Little children usually "tell all," but even 3-year-olds can be frightened into lying about how they were hurt. It is not unusual for parents to tell little ones that if they say that Mommy and Daddy hurt them, a big bad person will come and take them away. When this happens, the children's explanations are usually and obviously "dictated." If the story changes, be suspicious.

Exhibit 6–6

Follow-Up

1. After a report to the proper authorities has been made, the teacher should seek help and guidance from the principal or the director of the school. Next steps with the parents should not be decided by the teacher alone. Home visits should be discontinued at least for some time. This is a needed safety precaution for both the teacher and the parents.

2. On subsequent visits, after conferences with persons who are competent to advise the teacher on what to do and how to do it, the teacher should not go alone to the home. An aide should accompany the teacher and should be alert to what is said. Confidential notes made by the teacher after the meeting should not become part of the child's file but should be kept in the teacher's personal possession. These can be destroyed when the need for them is ended.

3. Regardless of the nature or severity of the case, if the child continues to attend school, it is the teacher's responsibility to continue to try to encourage the parents to participate in parent meetings and volunteer at school. The teacher should have the help of persons trained and skilled in helping these parents. If the school or center does not offer this service, the teacher should insist on receiving it from some public or private source. Skill in teaching does not imply that the teacher must be all things to all people. Trying to be so can result in disaster.

Summary

This chapter provided an overview of the essential elements of a home and school climate conducive to developing healthy personalities. Some of Erikson's growth stages were reviewed to emphasize the interaction between forces within the child and conditions from without. These necessitate early warmth and consistency in caregiving, encouraging autonomy within reasonable guidelines, and developing initiative tempered with gentle direction.

More recent theory proposed by Greenspan has described five major stages of emotional development: self-regulation, attachment, intentional communication, an organized sense of self, and emotional thinking. Greenspan stressed the importance of a responsive environment and the infant's need to learn to express and recognize a wide range of human emotions. Using a Piagetian framework, such cognitive milestones as intentionality and pretend play assume important roles in affective growth.

The essential blocks that build a growth-producing environment were illustrated and described. Teachers were urged to prevent inappropriate behaviors by building security through the use of a number of behavioristically oriented principles, including establishing limits, routines, variety, constructive consequences, avoidance of frustration, behavior modeling, and opportunities for appropriately expressing feelings.

Some children arrive at preschools and child-care centers with behaviors and emotional characteristics that interfere with learning. They may be too active or too withdrawn. They may be impulsive. Some are overly dependent on adults for direction, whereas others refuse all directions from their teachers. Techniques for working with unique ways of behaving were suggested. These range from effectively using time-out to using puppets and play. Throughout, the role of positive reinforcement and appropriate modeling of behavior was emphasized. Enhancing self-esteem is an ever-present goal.

Guidelines were offered to assist teachers in creating an environment that fosters the development of spontaneous play behavior considered to be essential in the development of emotional well-being. The procedure for developing positive behavior support plans give caregivers a systematic approach to behavior management.

The final section addressed the characteristics and needs of children who have been abused and neglected.

Discussion Topics and Activities

1. Make a list of necessary center limits or rules. Be certain that each is definable, reasonable, and enforceable. Role-play the explanation of these limits to determine whether they are indeed definable.

2. List and discuss any special adaptations that will have to be made in classroom structure and management for children with disabilities.

3. Develop a workable classroom schedule that provides a balance between active and passive involvement, experiences that require visual attention, those that necessitate auditory attention, and group and individual activities. Exchange constructive criticism with classmates.

4. Make a chart of as many natural and logical consequences for behavioral difficulties as you can think of. Keep the chart handy. Observations in classrooms should help you expand your list. A review of any of the current books on behavior management will convince you of the importance of these alternatives to punishment.

5. Role-play how you would deal with a parent who insists that his or her child should settle arguments by fighting.

6. Try to identify toys that might be frustrating to some children. Make a list of these toys and the types of children who might have difficulty with them.

7. Develop a repertoire of techniques to effect smooth transitions. Role-play some of these with classmates.

8. Study one of the many excellent texts on behavior management techniques. Conduct a behavior management project to increase or decrease a designated behavior. Report the results of your project in graphic form to your classmates.

9. Participate with colleagues in the development of a positive behavior support plan.

10. Visit a school supply center or obtain catalogs from toy companies. Develop a list of "social" toys and a list of "isolate" toys. Share with your classmates in the development of a master list for all to keep.

11. Observe children engaged in pretend play. Describe the range of emotions expressed.

12. Observe the caregiver–infant interaction of three dyads.

Helping Young Children Develop Motor and Self-Help Skills

Photo by Lisa Wadors

KEY TERMS

(Note: Terms are discussed within the text and/or defined in the glossary.)

adaptive behavior (skills)	forward chaining	hypotonicity
adaptive equipment	functional independence	laterality
athetoid movement patterns	gross motor skills	movement education
branching	handedness	occupational therapist
cephalocaudal pattern	handling	orthosis
chaining	hyperresponsiveness	physical therapist
fine motor skills	hypertonia	positioning
fluctuating muscle tone	hyporesponsiveness	prosthesis

proximo-distal pattern
quadriplegia
reverse chaining
self-regulation

sensorimotor observations
sensory defensiveness
sensory integration
spasticity

symmetry
vestibular defensiveness

Key Concepts

- Infants learn from the sensations of movement, which come primarily from active rather than passive movements.

- Motor development follows a highly predictable sequential and overlapping pattern.

- Physiological maturation and environmental factors influence the rate and quality of physical and motor development.

- Assessment of motor skills is a team effort using a variety of approaches.

- Therapeutic intervention should encourage functional behaviors, including gross and fine motor skills, and their use in daily living.

- Positioning and handling are important considerations in normalization of muscle tone, prevention of deformity, and stabilization of the body.

- Adaptations of materials and environmental considerations should be a vital concern in program planning for children with motor impairments.

- Various strategies and aids are useful in teaching self-help skills. Including parents in the design and implementation is vital.

NIKKI

Nikki was born 2 months premature, weighing in at 2 pounds, 2 ounces. She remained in the neonatal intensive care unit for 8 weeks, during which time she experienced a life-threatening infection. As she recovered, it was clear early on that she sustained some brain damage with neurological impairment. Hearing and vision appeared to be within normal limits, but movement on the left side was limited. She was eventually diagnosed with cerebral palsy (CP) with spastic hemiplegia (involving the arm, trunk, and leg on the left side). She was followed in the CP Clinic at Children's Hospital and received home visits from a physical therapist who helped her parents with positioning and activities to maximize Nikki's gross and fine motor skills. Specific "exercises" were recommended to encourage use of her left arm and

leg. Most of the therapy was embedded into daily living routines and play time. As she began to walk, she was fitted with an AFO (ankle-foot orthotic brace), which provided support and better balance.

At age 2, Nikki was referred to an early intervention program that had both home- and center-based components. The team worked closely with her parents to develop strategies for interaction that would (a) maximize use of her left side, (b) maximize use of reciprocal movements (i.e., right and left together), and (c) motivate self-help activities (eating, dressing, and toileting). Nikki's father is a musician, and he uses music to get Nikki to move and "dance." He ties bells, balloons, or ribbons on her left wrist or ankle to make sound and increase awareness. The teachers at school are also doing similar activities with Nikki as well as with other children in the program. When Dave, Nikki's father, visits the class, he brings his

guitar and encourages all the children to "get their groove on."

As Nikki is getting ready to transition to an inclusive preschool program, a teacher and therapist from the program will help the staff of the receiving class make adaptations (as needed) for Nikki's success.

Working with young children to develop motor skills requires a special kind of planning. Infants and young children need to learn about their bodies. They need to develop balance and coordination. It is important for them to discover themselves in relationship to space. Care must be taken to help children develop an inner awareness of the difference between the two sides of the body because moving through space requires both sides of the body to act as a team.

Coordination of movement skills contributes to children's development of confidence and trust in themselves and their bodies. This sense of bodily trust has long been considered to be important to the emergence of healthy personalities (Erikson, 1993; see chapter 6). These are just some of the reasons that sensorimotor activities have held a dominant place in early education. For many children with motor problems or delays (cerebral palsy, cognitive delays, orthopedic disabilities, and so on), movement experiences are often limited. Additional instruction, therapeutic intervention, and encouragement are essential to minimize the disability and maximize children's potential in all aspects of development.

Motor skills are usually divided into at least two general categories. **Gross motor skills** refer to activities that involve the use of the large muscles of the neck, trunk, arms, and legs. Included are basic body movements such as lifting the head, rolling, crawling, creeping, walking, running, leaping, jumping, hopping, galloping, and skipping. Large muscle strength and endurance are also important in climbing, pushing, pulling, hanging, and lifting.

Fine motor skills involve more precise movements of the small muscles, especially those of the eyes, speech musculature, hands, fingers, feet, and toes. Movements such as blinking, focusing, sucking, grasping, releasing, pinching, and writing are considered to be fine motor activities. Many fine motor skills, including cutting, copying, stringing beads, and pasting, require the eyes to direct the hands. These activities are referred to variously as those that require perceptual-motor, visual-motor, sensorimotor, ocular-motor, or eye-hand coordination.

This chapter reviews normal motor development, including gross and fine motor skills and perceptual-motor integration, and suggests activities to enhance development. Identification and problems of atypical motor development are emphasized, with suggestions for intervention. Special efforts are taken to encourage the integration of movement skills with other areas of the curriculum as well as in day-to-day functional activities.

THE DEVELOPMENT OF MOTOR SKILLS

Babies learn from the sensations of movement, which come primarily from active rather than passive movements. In this developmental process, the ability of the higher centers to mature is in part dependent on sensory information brought to them. Sensory input (such as tactile, proprioceptive, visual, or auditory) is sent through the nervous system and integrated at appropriate levels of the brain and spinal cord. As messages are received and processed, responses are sent back in the form of motor acts. Voluntary motor activity is controlled by upper brain centers located in the cerebral cortex, whereas involuntary or unconscious muscle movements (e.g., digestion of food, eye blinking, and reflex movements) are controlled by lower brain centers, that is, the cerebellum and parts of the brain stem.

In general, the development of motor skills proceeds according to the laws that govern the physiological maturation of the child, with the development of movement patterns progressing from simple arm or leg actions to highly integrated total body coordination.

The rate of development is thought to depend not only on the quality of environmental stimulus but also on the stage of brain development. No distinction is usually made in the motor abilities of boys and girls in infancy and early childhood because the differences are not very great. During the late preschool years, girls appear to perform better on tasks requiring manual

dexterity, whereas boys are more adept when using large (gross) muscles. The extent to which this difference may be culturally determined is still being questioned. Parents' expectations and interactions with infants often differ according to the gender of the child. These expectations are reflected in play activities.

Environmental factors such as amount of sleep and exercise, quality of medical care, and adequacy of nutrition may influence the rate and ultimate degree of physical and, thus, motor development. In addition, childrearing practices that vary among cultures also should be taken into account when viewing differences in motor skill development. In general, a child's potential for motor skill development is considered to be the result of genetic origin and specific environmental influences.

By the time a child is 5 or 6 years of age, many motor behaviors have been established and require only refinement and mastery at a higher, more complex level. During these early years, motor development follows a highly predictable sequential and overlapping pattern. Although the rate varies at which typical children progress, the sequence remains fairly constant. The literature on motor development contains many descriptions and timetables for the stage and age at which motor abilities are attained. Variation in developmental rate is well documented. It is not unusual to hear mothers compare walking age variations from 8 to 18 months. See Appendix A for a summary of typical gross and fine motor development.

Sequential Trends of Motor Development

There are seven basic principles that govern the sequence of motor development:

1. *Cephalocaudal pattern.* Muscular development proceeds from the head to the foot. For example, infants have voluntary control over their heads before lower parts of their body. Similarly, children can usually throw before they can catch.

2. *Proximo-distal pattern.* Growth and development tend to proceed from the spine (proximo) to the outer extremities (distal). That is, voluntary

movement begins in the shoulder, then moves on to the elbow area, wrist, and finally the fingers.

3. *Mass-to-specific pattern.* Body movement of young infants is undifferentiated, involving the total body. Later, specific patterns of movement develop out of these generalized mass movements. When learning new skills, it takes time for children to inhibit the unwanted extraneous movements.

4. *Gross-motor-to-fine-motor pattern.* Children usually gain control over large muscle activity before fine or small muscle activity. In addition, a child must gain differential control. That is, movement of muscles on one side of the body should occur without similar movement on the other side of the body, unless desired.

5. *Maximum-to-minimum-muscle-involvement pattern.* Like the mass-to-specific pattern, body movement becomes increasingly more efficient. With practice, children learn to eliminate unnecessary expenditures of energy. Where it once took a whole bodily effort to catch a ball, children learn to catch with the use of just one arm and hand.

6. *Bilateral-to-unilateral pattern.* Children progress from undifferentiated use of both sides of the body to unilateral preference, referred to as the *establishment of laterality.*

7. *Orderly development pattern.* Children differ in the rate of their development but do tend to follow a similar pattern if environmental conditions are adequate and no organic deficits are present.

Helping Parents Understand

In teaching or talking to parents about various aspects of child development, early interventionists often find themselves caught up in lengthy, detailed descriptions of developmental domains. As a result of parents' requests for jargon-free explanations of sequential development, Lacy (1981) put together a manual describing development from the view of the growing infant. *Dear Mom and Dad* includes extensive recommendations for parent–child activities and is included in Figure 7–1 as a summary of early motor development.

Dear Mom & Dad

a baby's Letters to her Parents

Project Hope

(Gross Motor Development)

Dear Mom and Dad,

I'm sure that one of the first things you noticed when I was born was that I came out moving and haven't stopped yet! Those early movements weren't really planned out by me, though. A lot of that thrashing about was because of my immature nervous system and getting into certain positions was because of reflexes. Remember how you used to put me on my back to change me and I would jump? Well, that was my startle (Moro) reflex. And also that position on my back where I looked like a fencer (head turned toward bent arm and leg-- opposite ones straight)? Well, that was my ATNR reflex. I really began to notice things around me with my senses before I could act on them with my body, and that was frustrating--let me tell you!

As I did get going, though, I developed from my head down to my toes and from the center of my body to the outside muscles--"head down" and "inside out" is how I remember it. You see, my control was first with eye muscles, then with facial, on to neck, and finally down to trunk, legs, and feet. So I could focus my eyes and make faces, then balance my head before my body, and after that drag my body on the ground before creeping on hands and knees, and finally pull up to stand before walking. The sideways growth showed up in arm-waving, then batting, then using wrist, hands, and finally individual fingers to manipulate objects. (I'll tell you more about arms and hands later.)

In those early months, my physical performance depended a lot on whether I was crying, sleepy, active, or alert. I really wasn't tuned in too much back then. But you kept on trying just the right activities for my abilities, giving me opportunities for new growth by the way you placed my body, praising and encouraging me, but always you found out very early that the way I felt about myself (my self-concept) depended so much on how well I could move

Infant Development Program

Figure 7–1 Summary of early motor development
With gratitude to Virginia McDonald, Ann Lacy, and Project Hope, Department of Education, San Diego County, California.

my body by myself. So, you used a "hands-off" policy
when you could, helping me to crawl or walk with a towel
around my waist, etc. Then I really began to feel that
I could make things happen in my new world.

Well, that whole first year seemed to be a time of learning more and more about how to use my body. My social
growing and use of objects and language weren't quite as
important to me yet. But I was really doing some learning
as I thought out and planned all of those movements. A
couple of things were going on all at once. First of all,
I began to take in (integrate) those reflexes that I mentioned earlier, and also some others and started doing
motions that I had control over. At the same time, I was
gradually changing from being sideways to being upright
as I got control over my head and trunk and then arms and
legs. This ability to move and choose my actions and to
move toward being vertical in my second year affected all
parts of my life. It helped me to explore more with objects and try out new experiences through my senses (fine
motor and cognitive), I could see people better and get to
know them (visual and social), and my inside breathing organs were in a better position to help me talk (language).
The best part of all was being able to move about by myself and have many more chances to explore things that had
been out of reach or range--and just be more independent
on my own.

As I learned each new step, you must have wondered why I
sometimes did things so slowly--and also the same thing
over and over. Well, I went slowly because I really
needed to concentrate on my new accomplishments. (Sometimes I even wanted to give up eating and sleeping, too,
to concentrate on my new physical miracles.) And the
reason I practiced so much is that I wanted to make sure
that each movement really became a part of me so that I
wouldn't forget it. Sometimes I tried a new movement,
like standing, only once and then dropped it for awhile
(maybe even two months) because my new independence
frightened me.

No, it wasn't all easy. I went along first wanting to
take on the world, then needing to slow down or stop, and
sometimes even drop something I had learned. I know you

(continued)

could tell, Mom, as I often cried, clung to you and acted difficult, that sometimes this new independence brought by a new movement was a little scary; I needed to slow down and come back to you for some reassurance. You probably came to realize that my shakiness and unsureness was sure to pop up right before a new "motor milestone." Thanks, Mom and Dad, for understanding and going along with my difficult times of wanting to move away from you and then being scared and returning for the comfort and love only you could give.

Thanks, too, for finding that nice balance between freedom and limits. It must have been hard for you to give me the chance to explore and learn, while also teaching me about rules and dangers. But you did a great job of protecting me and also giving me a nice environment to want to learn about. And best of all, you watched my own individual signals and trusted me. From the top of my head to the bottom of my toes and from the inside out, I thank you.

Love,

Your Growing Child

Infant Development Program

Figure 7–1 (continued)

Reflexive Development

Early motor activity of infants is structured by a variety of primitive and automatic reflexes. Primitive reflexes are evident in early infancy at or soon after birth. It is not known whether these reflexes are the framework for further motor maturation or must be inhibited for the development of coordinated voluntary control. There is a wide range of variation in reflex responsiveness among infants as well as within the same infant, depending on the behavioral states of the child being observed. These reflexes are expressions of the immaturity of the infant's nervous system and provide a basis for assessing the integrity of the developing neuromuscular system early in life.

Although the teacher may have difficulty understanding the complexities of neurological development, it is important to have some idea of how coordinated movement evolves and what factors may interfere with normal functioning. Appendix C summarizes major reflexes and potential problems. Concerned early interventionists may consult a physical or occupational therapist who is specifically trained to assess reflexive behavior.

Developing Gross Motor Skills

Gross motor skills refer to the involvement of the large muscles of the neck, trunk of the body, arms, and legs. Early childhood affords the time and practice for emerging skills to become accomplished before rapid bodily changes begin to occur. Children develop postural control and learn to walk, run, catch, and jump with relative skill. The extent to which children become proficient in these skills is dependent on muscle development as well as opportunity for muscle use. However, it must be remembered that even in the most optimal situations, large and uneven growth spurts do occur. To provide the stimulation needed, safe environments free from obstacles and full of encouragement are needed.

Proficiency in gross motor skills is influenced by changes in body proportions. The 2-year-old's head accounts for about one fourth of the child's height. By the time the child is 5 years old, it accounts for only about one sixth of the total height (Blasco,

2001). As children become less top heavy, their ability to balance themselves develops. Children entering kindergarten have usually experienced an increase in muscle tissue, creating a larger potential of muscle energy available for movement.

Developing Fine Motor Skills

Fine motor skills involve small muscles. Most fine motor skills, as far as preparation for manual control is concerned, involve hands and fingers. (See Figure 7–2 for progression of change in manual control.) Coordination of hands and fingers is often described as requiring strength, flexibility, and dexterity. The coordination of eye-hand movement is referred to as a visual-motor skill.

Handedness.   When observing children engaged in fine motor activities, the question of "handedness," or hand preference, usually arises. Preschool teachers can relax, for research indicates that it is usual to find children frequently interchanging the use of hands throughout early childhood. Hand dominance is often not achieved until the age of 6. Even then, some children develop functional ambidexterity. The fact that children tend to use their right hands more often in taught activities such as cutting and throwing suggests the influence of our cultural bias.

Practice Payoff.   Long before a baby can walk, her mother may report, "Sally picked up a raisin today." Surprised that the child could pick up something so tiny, mothers become more alert about leaving beads and other nonedibles around. Later, this ability to see small things and pick them up will become the foundation for grasping and holding crayons, pencils, and other small objects.

Although merely having things available to pick up is all that is necessary for most young children to learn important fine motor skills, they must have opportunities to practice. Building with small blocks, manipulating small toys, and using crayons, chalk, and scissors all lead to the improvement of essential skills.

Snap-together beads, geoboards, puzzles, beads for stringing, button and lacing boards, and large nuts

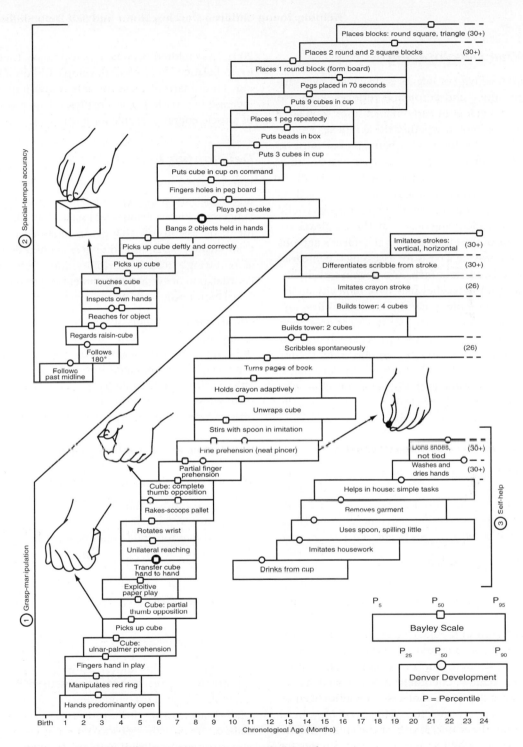

Figure 7–2   Progressions of change: Manual control
Source: From *Movement Skill Development* (p. 32), by J. Keogh and D. Sugden, 1985, Upper Saddle River, NJ: Merrill/Prentice Hall. Reprinted with permission.

Table 7–1   Typical motor skills activities

Gross Motor Development

Eye-Foot Coordination	Eye-Hand Coordination	Body Awareness	Balance
Kicking	Climbing	Crawling in and out of things	Standing on tiptoe
Climbing	Hanging	Crawling through and around things	Walking the balance beam
Jumping	Striking balloons		Riding wheeled toys
Hopping	Throwing	Moving like an animal	Walking around tire edges or sandbox rails
Dancing	Catching	Mirroring activities	
Walking the balance beam	Using tools	Playing "Simon Says"	Moving and carrying some-thing without spilling it
Jumping over ropes	Block building	Steering wheeled toys	Walking with bean bag on head or shoulder
	Rolling balls		
	Pounding		
	Stirring		

Fine Motor Development (Eye-Hand Coordination)

Cutting	Lacing	Outlining with stencils or templates
Coloring	Geoboards	Copying
Drawing	Tracing	Pasting
Sewing	Painting	Building block towers
Puzzle building	Paper folding	Stacking
Bead stringing	Copying designs	

Self-Help Skills

Dressing (buttoning, zipping, snapping, buckling)
Eating
Personal hygiene (brushing teeth, washing hands)
Toileting

and screws offer interesting and challenging fine motor practice for young children. Even cooking activities help children develop skills such as stirring, cutting, pounding, and rolling while learning a variety of concepts. A sample list of typical motor skill activities is found in Table 7–1. A chart of normative expectations can be found in Appendix A.

Developing Eye-Hand Coordination.   Encountering sensory stimulation of a particular kind for the first time, children *receive* (sense) the stimulation. Subsequent encounters usually result in their *perceiving* (interpreting) the stimulus. If any of the senses are impaired, even slightly, children may not be able to sense the initial stimulus accurately. If they do not receive an accurate first impression, later interpretations of that stimulus will be wrong or confusing to them. Thus, for infants and young children, any limitation in movement may interfere with development

of perceptual skills and have an adverse effect on other kinds of learning and social skill development (Greenspan, 2001).

Therefore, we encourage the development of perceptual-motor skills as tasks in and of themselves and in association with language and concept development. There is no doubt that functionally and developmentally appropriate curriculum for young children contain numerous activities that promote perceptual-motor development as part of the daily routine. Puzzles, marking pens, scissors, buttoning and unbuttoning, and self-feeding are just a few of the daily activities that embed the development of eye-hand coordination within their very nature.

Individualizing a Visual-Motor Activity.   By writing the goal and objectives for cutting with scissors on one page, as illustrated in Table 7–2, the teacher has a helpful one-page reference to guide

Table 7–2   Example of using goals and objectives to individualize an activity

Given (the teacher will provide or restrict)	The child will	Criterion
Goal: To develop cutting skills.		
Terminal objective: Blunt-tip scissors; paper with a 3-inch straight line, a 3-inch curved line, and a 3-inch-diameter circle; and directions to cut on the line and cut out the circle.	Cut as directed.	Cut within $\frac{1}{4}$ inch of lines within 5 minutes.
En route objectives (least to most skilled):		
1. Tongs, 5 cotton balls, 4-inch bowl, teacher's guidance in placing fingers and thumb and forefinger in cutting position, and help in opening and closing tongs.	Open and close tongs around cotton ball, lift it to bowl, and release it into bowl, accepting teacher's assistance as needed.	Keep fingers in correct position and accept help.
2. Same as above, except restrict teacher's help to verbal directions, encouragement, and reminders.	Same as above.	Keep fingers in correct position and complete action (no time limit and no penalty for "dropped" cotton).
3. Same as above.	Same as above.	Maintain correct position, lift and drop cotton into bowl (no more than one ball outside bowl within 2 minutes).
4. Blunt-tip scissors and strips of construction paper 1 inch wide and 11 inches long.	Cut paper.	Cut at least 10 pieces within 5 minutes.
5. Same as above, with heavy black lines marked on paper at 1-inch intervals.	Cut paper on lines.	Cut within $\frac{1}{4}$ inch of lines, one cut per line (no time limit).
6. Blunt-tip scissors and construction paper 3 inches wide and 11 inches long, with heavy black lines at 1-inch intervals the width of the paper.	Make three cuts per line.	Cut within $\frac{1}{4}$ inch of lines, severing each piece within 10 minutes.
7. Same as terminal objective (except longer time criterion).	Cut as directed.	Cut within $\frac{1}{4}$ inch of lines within 10 minutes.
8. Same as terminal objective.		

Note. Adaptations for children with physical disabilities include squeeze scissors instead of traditional scissors. For some children, scissors with four finger holes may be useful because they allow the teacher to cut with the child. Children with visual impairments should be provided buff-colored paper with a heavy brown line for necessary contrast.

him or her in planning the lesson to be useful to a group of children with widely varying skills. The terminal objective is an appropriate skill for a 5-year-old, whereas lifting cotton balls with the tongs can be accomplished by most 3-year-olds.

However, some 5-year-olds with developmental delays may find it difficult to learn to use the tongs. They may require help and physical guidance as well as encouragement and verbal guidance for many days

or weeks before they can proceed to the second objective. By being included in the activity with children who can do the more difficult tasks, they observe and discover that they also can learn.

It is critical to remember that one of the reasons for the sequence of carefully planned en route behaviors is to provide each child with a task until criterion is reached. It is possible to develop difficult skills gradually and without the pain of failure. Beginning

by expecting each child to "cut on the line" guarantees failure for many of them.

To teach five or more children to cut on the line, it is necessary to provide each one with the materials needed, demonstration at his or her level of performance, and continued encouragement. In this way, no one fails; rather, each child succeeds. Most will recognize the challenge of the next step and be eager to try it.

In addition to the usefulness of the clearly written behavioral objectives to the teacher, as the lesson is planned and conducted, these same objectives help in pinpointing necessary **branching** or smaller steps.

The basic set of goals and objectives should be designed to be useful guides in teaching the majority of the children. But some children will need even smaller steps. By analyzing the existing objectives, the teacher can identify what these more precise steps should be.

The format of the page of objectives is helpful in analyzing the task. If the child is not succeeding, where is the breakdown? Should a change be made in what the teacher is providing or restricting? Or is the quantity of work or time allowed inappropriate?

Sometimes the en route behaviors become more difficult because the task changes. At other times only the time limitations change. By evaluating the task, the criterion, and what the teacher does or does not do, it is possible to establish a much better sense of successful teaching for the teacher as well as the children.

Throughout all of the activities, teachers attempt to help children establish independence, accuracy, patience, and persistence. These qualities can be nurtured more successfully when en route behaviors are clearly stated.

Recording Progress.   Figure 7–3 illustrates an easy way to record children's progress when a group includes children with varying skill levels focusing on the same goal. By placing the en route (expected behaviors) down the left side of the page and the names of the children across the top, it is easy to record progress and to identify each child's current en route behavior. The teacher (or aide) simply records the date and level of accomplishment for each item. Some prefer to include only the date of achievement. Then the next item on the list becomes the current en route behavior to be practiced.

CURRICULUM DOMAIN: Fine motor

Goal: To learn cutting skills

Key: + = Skill already established
  ☐ = Current target behavior
  ☒ₓₓ = Date achieved

	Meg A.	Mary C.	Danny D.	Bobby J.	Vicky M.	Eric R.
Tongs and cotton balls	+	+	+	+	+	+
1-inch snipping	10/03	9/03	10/03	+	☐	+
1-inch snipping on heavy line	☐	10/03	10/03	+		+
3-inch cutting on heavy straight line		☐	☐	10/03		+
3-inch cutting on heavy curved line				☐		10/03
Cutting out 3-inch-diameter circle, heavy line						☐

Figure 7–3   Recording progress in group with varying skill levels

ATYPICAL MOTOR DEVELOPMENT

Atypical motor development or motor differences can occur for a variety of reasons. Brain damage, orthopedic problems, progressive diseases, genetic defects, developmental delays, and sensory impairments can potentially interfere with motor skill acquisition.

Deviations in movement patterns affecting the young child usually originate in the prenatal or perinatal period. Neuromuscular dysfunction originating in the central nervous system, specifically cerebral palsy (CP), is the most common motor disability among children of all ages. *Cerebral palsy* is a general term given to nonprogressive brain lesions. It generally causes complex problems in all aspects of development (Batshaw, 2002). Abnormal movement patterns seen in children with CP are related to primitive reflex retention and problems of motor coordination and muscle tone. A continuum of motor dysfunction due to insult

to the brain may include on one end a child with clumsy and awkward movements and on the other a child with CP who has such severe impairments that any coordinated movement is next to impossible. In between are varying degrees of movement problems.

As suggested by Howard, Williams, and Lepper (2005), a diagnosis of CP is not very useful for the early interventionist unless it is paired with a description of the degree of involvement or the extent a child is affected motorically. Descriptions of the general characteristics of children with mild, moderate, and severe CP are found in Table 7–3.

Although the severe form of CP affects many other developmental areas, it is important to be cautious not to equate the degree of motor disability with cognitive deficits. According to Batshaw (2002), studies show that central nervous system insult is not an accurate predictor of cognitive growth and later academic performance.

Table 7–3   Diagnostic criteria for severity of cerebral palsy

Degree of Involvement	Characteristics
Severe	1. Total dependence in meeting physical needs 2. Poor head control 3. Deformities, present or potential, that limit function or produce pain 4. Perceptual and/or sensory integrative deficits that prevent the achievement of age-appropriate motor skills
Moderate	1. Some independence in meeting physical needs 2. Functional head control 3. Deformities, present or potential, that limit function or produce pain 4. Perceptual and/or sensory integrative deficits that prevent the achievement of age-appropriate motor skills
Mild	1. Independence in meeting physical needs 2. Potential to improve quality of motor and/or perceptual skills with therapy intervention 3. Potential for regression in quality of motor and perceptual skills without intervention

Source: Best, Heller, and Bigge (2004). Adapted by permission of Pearson Education, Inc., Upper Saddle River, New Jersey.

Problems in Muscle Development

Muscle characteristics of tone, control, and strength are significant concerns in development and eventual intervention. Causes of problems vary from central nervous system damage and genetic disorders to nonspecific delays in development (Batshaw, 2002). Hanson and Harris (1986) discussed the deviations in muscle development that require consideration when programs are planned.

1. *Deficits in muscle tone.* The degree of tension in the muscle at rest defines muscle tone. Three types of muscle tone deviation are noted. The first, **hypotonicity,** describes low tension or flaccidity in muscles. The "floppy" child usually demonstrates generalized weak, flabby muscles and often hypermobile joints, especially in shoulders, hips, and ankles. The child with Down syndrome or Prader-Willi syndrome or those classified as having ataxic CP are good examples of floppy children. The hypotonic child is usually less active than his or her peers and may become fatigued easily by motor activities.

Motor milestones such as sitting, creeping, and walking are usually delayed because of the affected child's generalized low muscle tone. Other areas affected may be the chest and face muscles. Because of low muscle tone, breathing tends to be shallow. The child may also have difficulty sustaining sounds when attempting to cry, babble, or talk.

Conversely, the child with **hypertonia** has too much muscle tone. Another name for hypertonia is **spasticity.** A high percentage of children with CP have spasticity. The affected muscles are characterized as feeling stiff and rigid. For instance, when the child tries to passively extend the flexed arm, it feels "locked," and a slow, steady pressure at the elbow is necessary to perform this motion. In children with spastic hemiplegia, one side of the body is affected. In spastic diplegia, the legs are primarily affected, but trunk and arms may also be involved. In spastic quadriplegia, all four extremities and trunk are involved.

Children with hypertonia are frequently delayed in achieving motor milestones. They often have difficulty assuming and maintaining postures that go against gravity, such as sitting, creeping, and standing. Breathing may also be impaired because of decreased movement of the ribs and chest. If facial and oral muscles are involved, as is often the case in spastic **quadriplegia,** articulation, chewing, and swallowing

also may be affected (Klein, Cook, and Richardson-Gibbs, 2001).

Fluctuating muscle tone can be seen in children who are generally hypertonic or hypotonic. Usually in these cases, an attempt at voluntary movement sets off increased muscle tone. However, when the child is resting, muscles may be hypotonic. The incoordination of contraction and relaxation may be seen in **athetoid movement patterns,** which are repetitive, poorly coordinated voluntary movements. The most common type of motor disability in which fluctuating tone occurs is athetoid CP.

2. *Deficits in muscle control.* Writhing movements, tremors, and fluctuating muscle tone are abnormal motor characteristics that interfere with voluntary movements. As the child with CP tries to do something, for example, not only fluctuating tone but also uncoordinated movements and abnormal posture caused by increased or decreased tone are present. Involuntary facial movements (mouth opening and closing and the tongue moving in and out) are often related to general muscle tone fluctuation throughout the body. Attempts at fine motor activities tend to increase problems in overall coordination in some children with CP.

3. *Deficits in muscle strength.* There may be differences in muscle strength among and within children. Certain degenerative diseases such as muscular dystrophy have a progressive effect on muscle strength. Paralysis of muscles related to spinal cord damage such as spina bifida or traumatic injuries often cause permanent loss of strength in certain muscle groups. The inactivity of a child wearing a cast for a broken bone will cause losses of strength and muscle tone that quickly return to normal with exercise and movement.

ASSESSMENT OF MOTOR ABILITIES

In educational planning or therapeutic intervention, it is important to assess the young child in all developmental areas and to determine how the absence or delay of motor abilities will affect overall learning and social interactions. No matter what type of assessment approach is used (observation checklist or standardized tests), the information should be translated into optimal learning experiences.

As emphasized throughout this text, the responsibility for assessing the child should be a team effort. The parent, teacher, physician, and allied health professionals all contribute information essential in identification, diagnosis, and remediation of motor problems. As with all assessment, care must be taken not to apply diagnostic labels until all pertinent information is obtained. The high-risk premature infant, for example, is too often given an early diagnosis of CP based on symptoms characteristic of an immature but developing nervous system. Imagine the effects of that incorrect diagnosis on the parents!

Early education program staff often become coordinators and synthesizers of assessment information. Information from parents on early developmental milestones, family history, and current behavior, plus hospital records and diagnostic assessment from medical specialists, add up to a more comprehensive view of a child's physical development.

Infants and Toddlers

Probably the earliest assessment of motor development is performed routinely at 1 minute and at 5 minutes after birth. The newborn baby is assessed for appearance (color), heart rate, reflex irritability, activity, muscle tone, and respiratory effort to determine whether further medical assistance is needed. A practical scoring system usually used to assess these attributes is the Apgar score (Apgar & James, 1962). Table 7–4 shows the five criteria and point values used to measure the effect of loss of oxygen and damage to the circulation in newborns. Each characteristic is rated 0, 1, or 2 (2 being best). These are added together to obtain an overall score that varies from 0 to 10. The 5-minute score has been shown to predict future developmental progress quite accurately (Batshaw, 2002).

More extensive observation of the newborn may be accomplished through the Newborn Behavioral Observation System (Nugent, Keefer, O'Brien, Johnson, & Blanchard, 2007). This system is based on years of research utilizing the Brazelton Neonatal Behavioral Assessment Scale originally published in

Table 7–4   Apgar scoring system

Points	0	1	2
Heart rate	Absent	Below 100	Above 100
Respiratory effort	Absent	Slow, irregular	Normal respiration
Muscle tone	Limp	Some flexion	Active motion
Gag reflex	No response	Grimace	Sneeze, cough
Color	Blue all over; pale	Blue extremities, rest of body pink	Pink all over

1973 (Brazelton, 1996). The 18 items of the Newborn Behavioral Observation system identify the newborn's strengths as well as the challenges the infant will encounter in his or her new environment. It takes less than 10 minutes to administer and offer parents the opportunity to learn about the kinds of caregiving techniques and stimulation that are appropriate for their infant.

When infants or young children lack obvious or visible impairments, it is much more difficult to detect possible problems related to motor development. Usually a parent or early educator detects the more subtle behaviors that can be observed over time and are not seen in a short office visit with a medical specialist. Some of the behaviors that should be noted and considered as indicators of the need for referral include the following:

1. Delayed motor milestones. (Although delay is an important indicator, typical developmental variations must be kept in mind.)

2. Abnormal posturing of arms and legs during rest or activity.

3. Tremor of hands or arms when performing a task.

4. Significant difference in skill between right and left arms or legs.

5. Early hand preference (before 13 months of age).

6. Poor balance and equilibrium.

7. Difficulties in eye tracking.

8. Poor coordination in gross or fine motor activities.

9. Poor motor control of tongue, lips, or mouth muscles (e.g., drooling).

10. Inability to inhibit movements, as shown by jerking, mirroring, or fidgeting.

11. Poor visual-motor integrative skills, often seen in drawing.

12. Weakness or extreme fatigue during movement activities.

The more of these signs a child displays, the more likely he or she is to have some type of neurological dysfunction. Any of these behaviors should be noted and communicated to the child's primary care physician. In addition, various medications can cause side effects that may appear to be symptoms of neuromotor or attentional problems. Early childhood program staff and parents should know about the possible side effects of any medication a child may be taking.

Severe Motor Impairments

Young children with severe motor impairments present some difficult assessment problems, especially if cognitive or communication skills are also being evaluated. Because many assessment tasks require both fine and gross motor skills, the child with severe motor problems is penalized for inability to perform on standardized items. An understanding of primitive reflexes and abnormal movement patterns helps the educator place the child in the *best position* for achieving optimum voluntary motor responses. A physical or occupational therapist can provide ways to help the child improve motor performance and demonstrate skills in other developmental areas.

Videotaped records of a child's behavior and performance in informal play settings can also be

---

Exhibit 7–1

Example of Five Basic Steps in Facilitating Motor Development

BEHAVIOR: Child Rolls from Back to Stomach

1. **Decide which behavior you want to teach.**

   Debbie will roll from back to stomach without assistance.

2. **Decide on the cue you will use to prompt the child.**

   Say, "Roll over, Debbie," while physically assisting her. Favorite toys are lying out of reach in the direction Debbie will roll to encourage rolling.

3. **Decide on consequences to follow the behavior.**

   Debbie will play with the toy obtained by rolling.

4. **Break the behavior into small steps and order the steps (task analysis).**

   a. When Debbie is lying on her back, physically bring her arm across her chest and, by bending her at her knee, gently roll her all the way over from back to stomach.

   b. Debbie is physically rolled over one half of the way. She rolls the last half of the way on her own.

   c. Debbie rolls on her own from back to stomach.

   d. Debbie rolls on her own from back to front.

   Note: The verbal cue "Roll over, Debbie" is used during each step.

5. **Decide how well Debbie must do the behavior.**

   a. The number of seconds you will wait following the cue. Debbie will roll within 30 seconds of the cue.

   b. The number of times Debbie should perform correctly. Debbie will perform correctly 8 out of 10 times. When Debbie does this 8 out of 10 times for 3 days in a row, she can go on to the next step.

---

helpful in understanding the qualitative aspects of his or her ability. The evaluator may require several sessions to properly assess the child's strengths. Because the child's psychological and physiological state can drastically influence muscle tone and coordination, movement abilities may differ considerably from day to day.

General Considerations for Assessment of All Young Children

Effective observation of motor skills requires observers to keep in mind that the *process* of or *approach* to motor tasks is significant. How a child goes about trying to catch a ball is much more revealing than whether the ball is caught. There is a great difference in ability between (a) the child whose eyes are following the path of the ball and whose hands are working together to attempt a catch and (b) the child who seems not to be looking at the ball and whose hands hang loose or do not seem to work together. Although neither one may actually catch the ball, their differences in attempts must be carefully noted and considered. They are clearly at different levels developmentally. A child's lack of experience in activities such as climbing stairs or using scissors also influences performance. The child's level of excitement or fear of strangers and/or new tasks could be further inhibitors to motor processes.

Because the quality of performance is dependent on physiological maturation and experience, assessment for the purpose of developing instructional objectives must depend on individually referenced criteria. Although comparison with group norms can provide the early childhood educator with a general frame of reference, it cannot determine whether individual progress is adequate in light of changes that take place within that individual. For example, a 3-year-old who has the body height and weight of a 2-year-old cannot be expected to perform balance tasks with the ease of most 3-year-olds. Considering lack of balance to be a weakness and including objectives to teach balance would be inappropriate until a shift in bodily proportion takes place. In short, educators are expected to combine knowledge from normative tests with observation of individual differences and develop a set of *criterion-referenced* objectives.

Developmental Task Analysis.   Once a teacher has used a developmental checklist derived from normative expectations and has observed very carefully while considering individual levels of maturation, interests, and experiences, program activities can be determined. The checklist may include only broad curriculum objectives that may be stated more as goals, or it may contain a more specific task analysis that breaks each broader goal into teaching steps. The checklist then becomes a teaching as well as testing or assessment tool.

In using task analysis as an observational tool to establish appropriate motor goals and objectives, a sample formula may be helpful for both interventionists and parents. Hanson and Harris (1986) suggested five basic steps as illustrated in Exhibit 7–1. The section "Development of Adaptive Behavior Skills" later in this chapter provides applications of task analysis.

Play-Based Assessment

This approach provides many opportunities to observe a wide range of infants and young children in both structured and unstructured play activities. It is especially useful in observing movement behav-

iors. Linder (1996, 2000) has developed observation guidelines for sensorimotor development that encompass categories of (a) general appearance of movement, (b) muscle tone/strength/endurance, (c) reactivity to sensory input, (d) stationary positions used for play, (e) mobility in play, (f) other developmental achievements, (g) prehension and manipulation, and (h) motor planning. The **sensorimotor observations** are integrated into the overall transdisciplinary play-based assessment, which includes cognitive, language, and social development. Bricker (2002) also utilizes play as a means for curriculum-based assessment and, in addition, describes strategies for setting up play centers within a classroom to facilitate the assessment process.

THERAPEUTIC INTERVENTION

What is the purpose of therapeutic intervention? Who should provide the therapy? How is it used in home- or center-based intervention programs? Early childhood educators ask these critical questions when planning for children with physical limitations.

Therapists and teachers have shifted the focus from *developmental* goals to **functional independence.** Work on functional motor goals should begin as early as possible, especially for young children with severe disabilities. Examples of functional goals might include picking up Cheerios, turning a doorknob, and holding a crayon. Such skills enable the child to be more independent or to better interact with his or her environment. Too often professionals persist in trying to "normalize" the muscle tone and movement patterns of young children with severe brain damage. They must relinquish responsibility for trying to "fix" this brain damage and instead work toward setting realistic functional goals for the child, the parents, and themselves.

In planning intervention for an individual child, the therapist should look carefully at the child's functional level, considering activities for daily living, interactions within home and community environments, skills needed to support other developmental areas (i.e., positioning for problem-solving activities or social interaction), and types of assistive devices needed to enhance performance. After reviewing this information, teachers have a better picture of the functional level and the type of motor goals to be initiated for the child. Exhibit 7–1 illustrates the basic steps to facilitating motor development.

Role of Therapists

As part of the team approach in early childhood special education, the therapist must help teachers and parents understand the objectives and techniques for the development of functional motor skills. In consultation with physicians, the occupational or physical therapist will provide the expertise for implementing gross and fine motor activities and offer advice on positioning and use of therapeutic devices

(braces, wheelchairs, and so on) as well as facilitating the development of feeding and other adaptive skills. He or she will also work with families in both home and school settings to help integrate the therapy prescriptions into the daily routine of the child's care.

In working with infants and young children, there is considerable overlap in the roles of physical and occupational therapists. In institutional programs or in working with older children and adults, the **physical therapist** is usually concerned with large muscle movement and gross motor activities, whereas the **occupational therapist** is more often involved in evaluation and treatment of perceptual-motor (fine motor) functioning and activities of daily living.

Current best practice in the field is to have the therapist actually work in the center beside the teacher or in the home with the parents. In this way the therapist also demonstrates how the therapeutic activities can be integrated into the daily routine of the classroom or the home. In addition, the therapist can observe and participate in classroom or home activities that may lead to better understanding of other developmental concerns.

Therapy must be an integral part of the early childhood special education program, with the teacher understanding the rationale and serving as a promoter and translator of therapeutic objectives in the child's daily program. Regular staffings or dedicated meeting time is an essential element for a successful therapy program in a center-based early intervention program. Ongoing staff training in the classroom or in special meetings should be a significant part of the therapist's responsibility.

Approaches to Therapy

There are a number of widely differing therapeutic techniques to improve motor performance of young children with physical disabilities, including exercise, skill instruction, use of adaptive devices, drug therapy, and often surgery.

Proper positioning, inhibition of abnormal reflexes, and facilitation of active movement are major concerns in working with a child who has CP

or other neurological disorders. Among several techniques for dealing with these, physical therapists continue to utilize the Neurodevelopmental Treatment Approach (NDT) originally developed by Bobath and Bobath (1984) as part of their treatment regime. Although skillful use of the NDT approach requires extensive training and results are inconclusive, the basic principles and practical application can be used by both teachers and parents under guidance of physical therapists.

One therapeutic approach that continues to have significant influence in the field of early intervention is sensory integration. Even though sensory integration has become a very popular approach to working with young children with disabilities, it remains controversial. There is much anecdotal evidence of its positive effect in working with a variety of disabilities, particularly with autism. However, there is as yet no widely accepted body of research demonstrating its effectiveness. In the following section, a brief explanation of important components is included.

Sensory Integration

The theory and therapeutic techniques of sensory integration were developed by Dr. Jean Ayres (1979, 1994, 2005). Sensory integration is the ability to take in, filter, and process incoming information from all the senses (Howe, Brittain, & McCathren, 2004). Information from the sensory systems (touch, movement, smell, taste, vision, and hearing) are integrated with stored information (e.g., prior experience, memories, and knowledge) and then organized into responses. Difficulty processing and organizing sensory information can result in "sensory integrative dysfunction." Ayres (1994) describes sensory integrative dysfunction using the following analogy: "Good sensory processing enables all the impulses to flow easily and reach their destination quickly. Sensory integrative dysfunction is a sort of 'traffic jam' in the brain. Some bits of sensory information get 'tied up in traffic,' and certain parts of the brain do not get the sensory information they need to do their jobs" (p. 51).

Many of the sensory integration activities are designed to provide tactile (touch) and vestibular (balance) stimulation. The therapist uses multisensory approaches that enhance the nervous system's abilities to organize and interpret sensory input in order to improve motor output effectiveness. Swings, rotary equipment, scooters, and other play equipment are used in the child's therapy. Sensory integrative dysfunction may include the following.

Attention and Regulatory Problems. Some children may have difficulty screening out or inhibiting their response to extraneous nonessential sensory information, such as background noises or visual stimuli. Such children may be easily distracted and have difficulty inhibiting their attention to these irrelevant stimuli. Therefore, they have difficulty maintaining attention to appropriate information. Some children may also have problems with **self-regulation.** That is, they may overreact to stimuli and have difficulty calming themselves once they are in a highly aroused state.

Sensory Defensiveness. Most early interventionists are familiar with children who demonstrate "tactile defensiveness" or hypersensitivity to touch. These children resist touching or handling common materials and textures. In addition, children may also be highly sensitive to other sensory stimuli, resulting in visual defensiveness (e.g., avoiding direct eye gaze or hypersensitivity to light or flashing lights) or vestibular defensiveness (intolerance of movement or unstable surfaces). Children can also be highly sensitive to oral sensations (e.g., certain food textures or temperatures), to olfactory stimuli (e.g., negative reactions to strong odors), or to auditory stimuli (e.g., avoidance of certain sounds or inappropriate behavior in the presence of too many people talking at once).

Sensory defensiveness may result in social withdrawal, avoidance of certain objects (e.g., vacuum cleaners), foods, sounds, and social experiences. Children's motor movements may be greatly inhibited by fears such as walking up or down steps or on uneven surfaces. This can result in an insistence on certain routines and behavioral rigidity (e.g., insistence on wearing certain clothing and eating certain

foods or insistence on highly predictable, "safe" daily schedules).

Activity Level as Possible Indicators of Sensory Integrative Dysfunction. Listed below are possible variations in activity level that may indicate problems in this area. These are offered because, as Dunn (2001) states, "Sensory processing knowledge adds a level of awareness about the conditions necessary for the child to negotiate the demands of the day successfully" (p. 615):

- Child does not explore environment; avoids manipulating objects or moving around

- Child is disorganized and lacks purpose

- Child lacks variety in play activities; engages in repetitive, stereotypic play

- Child appears clumsy, has poor balance, trips often; may lack protective responses

- Child has difficulty calming herself following rigorous physical activity or after becoming upset

- Child seeks excessive amounts of sensory input (e.g., excessive spinning, bumping into others, or jumping)

Careful observation of children's behavior is critical. As Howe and colleagues (2004) point out, it is useful to consider that a child's response to sensory input can be viewed as one of two generalized responses: **hyperresponsiveness** and **hyporesponsiveness.** Those who respond in a hyperresponsive manner may avoid stimuli as they have a lower tolerance for it. Children who respond in a hyporesponsive manner may be slow to respond to stimuli and make seek more of it. Understanding these general categories will make it easier to appropriately respond.

Therapeutic techniques are based on complex theories of neurology and require very specific training to design and implement. Individuals who are most likely to have attained clinical competence in this area are physical and occupational therapists. Some advocates of "SI" therapy, as it is called, may be overzealous in their claims of broad applicability of this therapeutic approach in treating a wide range of behavioral, educational, personality, and movement disorders. Although still controversial, sensory integration therapy appears to have significant promise in alleviating or managing certain attention and regulatory disorders.

Positioning and Handling

Although it is often important to encourage movement, there are times when the young child should remain in a static position. For infants and young children with motor impairments, one area of significant concern is positioning and handling. In order to modify excessive or insufficient muscle tone and to control the predominance of abnormal reflexes, certain positions and specific handling techniques should be integrated into the child's home and school or center activities.

Positioning is the placement of the child in carefully selected positions (e.g., side-lying, sitting, standing) in order to normalize muscle tone, prevent deformity, and stabilize the body. Careful positioning will also allow a child to function more efficiently during toileting, feeding, play, and other functional activities. For example, if a child's trunk is not stabilized for sitting, control of arms and hands for self-feeding and playing with toys may be compromised.

Handling, according to Copeland and Kimmel (1989), is a dynamic process with goals of normalizing muscle tone, preparing the child for movement, and facilitating movement. Use of hands on an appropriate key point of the body can control or inhibit undesirable postures and movements. In addition to specific activities for the positioning and handling of individual children, Hanson and Harris (1986) have suggested the following general guidelines to consider in planning intervention:

1. *Key points of control* refers to parts of the body nearest the center of the body, including the *head and neck,* the *shoulder girdle,* and the *legs.* These are the key points to think about whenever you move, carry, or position a child. Paying close attention to these points will aid in normalizing muscle tone as well.

2. *Symmetry* of the child's body means that both sides of the body are positioned similarly so that one side is a mirror image of the other. Symmetry is also a consideration in developing muscle tone as well as in inhibiting primitive movement patterns.

3. *Midline positioning* is important. Many young children with motor impairments are unable to bring their hands together at the midline (the middle of the body). Activities using hands in midline will help develop motor and self-help skills. Side-lying positioning is one way to facilitate midline activities. Hanson and Harris (1986) have offered specific techniques and equipment to encourage activities at the midline.

4. Use only *minimal support* when positioning and handling the child. Providing too much support will not allow children to use the muscle control they have already developed. For example, if a child has adequate trunk control to sit independently, a corner chair with a high back is not necessary. Using such a device will only inhibit trunk muscles and not provide the practice needed to develop strength and endurance.

Based on these guidelines, Copeland and Kimmel (1989) suggested asking the following questions during assessment:

1. Is the head at midline and can the child visually focus on the desired target (e.g., toy, object, playmates)?

2. Is the trunk symmetrical and well aligned with the rest of the body?

3. Are the lower extremities properly aligned? If seated, kneeling, or standing, are the lower extremities bearing weight equally?

4. Are the upper extremities properly aligned and in functional positions for weight bearing or manipulation of objects?

5. Does this position promote the development of tightness, contractures, deformity, or pressure sores? (p. 48)

Whenever possible, parents and professionals should consult with the therapist to determine the child's individual needs for positioning and handling. There are also several excellent resources that give detailed guidelines and activities. Some of these include Best, Heller, and Bigge (2004); Forney, Alberto, Schwartzman, and Goeckel (2000); and Klein et al. (2001).

Proper Lifting

In using correct lifting and carrying techniques, especially with young children who have severe motor impairments, the early interventionist or parent has an opportunity to provide support as well as therapy. When a young child is lifted correctly, abnormal reflexes are not stimulated, and the child appears more normal and actually is under less stress. Some important steps in lifting and carrying are as follows:

1. Speak to the child, telling her what you are going to do and where you are going.

2. Wait for some response and encourage the child to assist in the process (e.g., "You need to help. Give me your hand.").

Figure 7–4   Proper and improper lifting techniques
Source of drawings: From *Positioning for Infants and Young Children with Motor Problems* [videotape manual], pp. 8–11. Courtesy of the University of Colorado School of Nursing, Marilyn Krajicek, Director, First Start.

3. Praise the child for any attempts to help.

4. Lift the child gently.

To protect yourself from injury, practice the following:

1. Bend your knees and keep your back straight.

2. Avoid twisting; approach the child straight on.

3. Keep the child's body as close to yours as possible.

4. Do not try to carry the child by yourself if she is too large or too heavy.

5. Give the *least* amount of help needed.

Proper and improper lifting techniques are shown in Figure 7–4.

Adaptive Equipment for Gross and Fine Motor Activities

Appropriate early intervention program planning for children with motor problems may involve a diverse array of equipment. Children may require *prostheses* (aids designed to function as limbs), *orthoses* (aids for assistance), *mobility devices* such as walkers and wheelchairs, positioning aids, or *academic aids* to help function in a classroom. Best et al. (2001) have illustrations of adaptive equipment.

It is especially important for teachers of children with severe disabilities to learn about and use **adaptive equipment.** Basically, the value and purpose of this type of assistance are to (a) help maintain normalized muscle tone, (b) inhibit primitive reflexes, (c) allow the child to use voluntary movements, (d) provide optimal positioning to interact

more effectively with the environment, and (e) encourage independence.

Equipment to aid in positioning is now commonly found in almost every program serving children with special needs. The wedge, the bolster, the prone board, and modified chairs are used in a variety of ways as required. These types of equipment can be purchased commercially or made by a skillful teacher or parent. The choice of adaptive equipment should be made in consultation with a therapist, who can also help the teacher to identify its purpose, explain its use for a particular disability, and describe any special precautions to be observed while the child is using the equipment. (Inappropriate use of adaptive equipment can often do more harm than good.)

DEVELOPMENT OF ADAPTIVE BEHAVIOR SKILLS

Adaptive skills (toileting, feeding, grooming, and dressing) make up a large portion of the young child's daily living tasks. Providing for skill development and necessary adaptations are major considerations in early intervention programs. For children with delayed or limited motor skills, the normal unfolding of adaptive skills is seriously compromised. Integration of functional activities that provide optimum opportunities for learning require an ongoing team effort. The role of positioning, handling, and therapeutic approaches provide much of the framework for development to occur.

Certain motor skills, including a child's ability to control parts of his or her body, are important precursors for adaptive skill development. For example, the ability to pick up an object and bring it to the mouth is required for finger feeding and usually appears around the seventh or eighth month (Noonan & McCormick, 2006). Although there are differences in when adaptive skills are acquired, development appears to follow a developmental sequence. Knowledge of the steps in the adaptive domain is essential. This provides the basis for determining where to begin instruction and what prerequisite skills are needed. Table 7-5 presents the major milestones for adaptive skills.

Use of Task Analysis

Task analysis of adaptive skills is a process of breaking down a skill area into its component parts, as noted in Exhibit 7-1. Task subskills offer the specific information from which to assess and plan a developmental program for use by both parents and early interventionists. For example, when teaching self-feeding, the steps may be broken into single teaching units (Klein et al., 2001, pp. 208–209):

1. The child grasps the spoon handle firmly.
2. She rotates her wrist to place the spoon into food.
3. She scoops food onto the spoon.
4. She rotates wrist and arm to bring the spoon to her mouth without spilling.
5. She opens her mouth.
6. She places the spoon in her mouth.
7. She closes her lips around the spoon.
8. She transfers food to her mouth.
9. She removes the spoon.

The number of steps and substeps may depend on the child's cognitive level, the amount of physical mobility, and response to praise or rewards.

If the goal is too difficult or requires participation beyond the young child's physical abilities, a **partial participation task analysis** may be an alternative. In this approach, steps are broken down into even smaller increments. This is to encourage the child with more limitations to participate in a meaningful way. Snell and Brown (2000) present a useful illustration of tooth brushing to describe partial participation task analysis. The child's participation involves opening her mouth for the caregiver to brush one quadrant of her teeth and swallowing a drink of water after each quadrant is brushed.

A unique feature of task analyzing adaptive skills involves the use of **chaining.** Chaining is based on the fact that one step must be accomplished before the next step can be performed. For assessment purposes, **forward chaining** (beginning with step 1) yields the most useful information. **Reverse chaining** is more

Table 7–5 Developmental sequence of adaptive skills

Age in Months	Eating Skills	Toileting Skills	Dressing and Grooming
0–3	• Oral reflexes (e.g., sucking) present at birth • Coordinates sucking, swallowing, and breathing		
3–6	• Brings hand to mouth holding object • Begins to hold bottle with some assistance • May eat some solids—sucks from spoon • Begins to swallow from cup • Basic chewing begins to appear		
6–9	• Can hold bottle and bring it to mouth • Can hold and eat cracker • Uses tongue to move food in mouth • Eats infant food		
9–12	• More control over lips, tongue, and jaw • Holds spoon • Finger feeds	• Pays attention to acts of eliminating	• Holds arm out for sleeve
12–18	• Brings spoon to mouth • Drinks from cup with some spilling • Chews appropriately	• Indicates discomfort over soiled pants • Begins to sit on potty	• Takes off shoes and socks • Tries to put on shoes
18–24	• Sucks with straw • Scoops food, feeds self • Chews with rotary jaw movement • Uses cup with fewer accidents	• Communicates need to go to toilet	• Finds large armhole • Attempts to brush teeth
24–30	• Holds fork and begins to spear food	• Bladder trained during day	• Removes pull-down garments • Buttons large front button
30–36		• Becomes more routine and sets time for elimination • Uses toilet independently	• Attempts to wash hands • Uses toothbrush • Opens front and side buttons • Closes front snaps

useful for teaching a skill. With reverse chaining, the last part of the task is done first. Consider this example:

1. Child puts on sock when just above heel.
2. Child puts on sock when just below heel.
3. Child puts on sock when toes started in.
4. Child puts on sock when handed to her with heel in correct position.
5. Child puts on sock (heel in correct position).

Smiles and praise for each success combined with "you put your sock on" encourage self-help and builds language.

Dressing, toileting, and feeding are each a complex set of adaptive skills that are critical to independence. Therapeutic and instructional procedures are emphasized in the next section.

Dressing

When at all possible, training should be done at appropriate times and in natural settings. Training should be done as often as possible in the child's home and during times when dressing and undressing normally occur. This will involve active family and staff participation in defining the goals, teaching procedures, establishing several types of reinforcers, and designing an easy data-keeping system.

As with all other adaptive areas, children with motor impairments have more difficulty learning dressing skills unless adaptations can be made. It definitely requires a team effort. Some suggestions made by Finnie (1997) are the following:

- Training plans should begin with the easiest garments and follow the normal sequential development of accomplishing undressing before learning to put on clothes.

- Clothes used for training should be several sizes larger than the child's normal size for ease of manipulation and putting on and off. (This method has been found to be more successful than practicing with dressing form boards.)

- Children who have difficulty conceptualizing may benefit from dressing or performing dressing or grooming tasks in front of a mirror.

- Children who have poor balance can perform many dressing skills while lying down. The child, for example, may begin by side-lying to put on pants and gradually turns as pants are raised to waist level. This positioning is especially useful when there is excessive motor tone.

- Children can sit in a corner or use a corner chair to provide more stability while dressing.

- If the supine position on the caregiver's lap, changing table, or floor does not reduce extensor tone, the child may be placed prone over the caregiver's lap. Lower and upper extremity dressing can be done in this position. (Always consult with the therapists.)

- Simple changes to a child's clothes may be the determining factor of the success level in self-dressing: use of Velcro in place of snaps or buttons, elasticized waistbands, adding a metal ring through a zipper's tab to make it easier to grasp and pull, tube socks to eliminate the need of getting the heel positioned correctly, and slip-on shoes or shoes with Velcro closures.

- For all young children, use the opportunity to verbally label and discuss each step of the process.

Toileting

Independent toileting skills are often an area of concern and frustration for both parents and child (and, yes, for the early interventionist). Children achieve bowel and daytime bladder control between 2½ and 3 years of age. Children with more severe developmental delay may not be ready until 5 years of age (Snell & Brown, 2000). This does not suggest that younger children with developmental disabilities cannot be toilet trained. It does, however, point out the need for a coordinated team effort and consistent follow-through for both home and center programs.

Prerequisites to training include neuromuscular control and the child's awareness of discomfort when she eliminates in her diaper. Then the child's pattern of elimination must be established. One way of doing this is to check the child every half hour to determine whether she is dry or wet or has had a bowel movement. Over time, perhaps 7 days, a pattern of elimination may emerge if eating habits and activity levels have remained constant. This pattern guides the trainer in designing the implementation.

Other prerequisite skills that speed toileting control are the ability to walk with or without assistance, the ability to indicate a need to use the toilet, the ability to remain in a sitting position for at least

5 minutes, and the ability to comprehend and follow instructions.

While the child is learning the prerequisites, Noonan and McCormick (2006) suggest that toileting needs are most easily managed through "timed toileting." This involves placing the child on the toilet for a few minutes at a time until elimination occurs. If the child uses the toilet, provide reinforcement. If the child does not eliminate, remove her from the toilet without consequences. To further increase awareness of the toileting process each time the child eliminates, the trainer can label the process by saying, "Megan, you did number one (or two)," using whatever label the parents and teacher feel are appropriate. (Terminology should be consistent.)

When children have difficulty in maintaining trunk control while sitting on a potty chair, adaptation can be made to existing chairs by adding back and side supports or hip and shoulder straps or using a commercial potty seat that has these features. Fear or discomfort in sitting on a potty seat or potty-chair will certainly make this process more of a "combat zone" than a natural, pleasurable experience. Relaxation can be achieved when the child feels secure with feet either on the floor or with some type of footrest.

Supportive adults willing to work through the ups and downs of the training period are essential. Potty time, as well as diaper changing, is an opportune time to engage in language development activities, including nursery rhymes and songs.

Feeding

An integral part of many early intervention programs is the consideration of teaching adaptive skills related to feeding, eating, and drinking. Mealtime is the natural time for teaching and reinforcing feeding skills as well as a time when prespeech skills can also be facilitated. For young children with special needs, teachers, therapists, and parents need to coordinate efforts at all meals to reinforce newly learned skills and develop others. The family dinnertime provides the best opportunity to integrate language, socialization, and motor skills learned during the day. Because of time and attention required by the parent to perform the task of feeding, parents can consider feeding the child with a disability before the regular dinnertime. Then, during the meal, the child can be given dessert or a toy so that she may continue to participate and interact with the family without placing demands on parents' mealtime. As the child becomes more independent, this schedule would probably change.

For infants and young children with severe disabilities, individualized plans for feeding must be a necessary part of the team's recommendation. This is especially true when there is a neuromotor disability, such as CP. Strategies may be needed to minimize the effects of oral-motor problems, including proper positioning and use of adaptive equipment. Positioning is critical in feeding the child with motor problems. If proper positioning techniques are not used during feeding, many children with abnormal muscle tone will have problems with gagging, choking, or swallowing. Everyone who feeds the child must have an understanding of the child's movement patterns in order to respond appropriately to changes that may occur from day to day and hour to hour. Whenever possible, ongoing consultation with the occupational therapist or physical therapist can offer important assistance in this process. Figure 7-5 shows the most usual positions for feeding: lap, arm, or chair.

In addition, the following suggestions are adapted from Best et al. (2004), Hooper Umansky (2003), Klein, et al. (2001), and Morris and Klein (1998).

Feeding Positions.
- Positions in which a child can be fed will depend on age, physical size, postural tone, and movement patterns (see examples in Figure 7-5).
- Unless an infant is still being bottle- or breast-fed, she should be positioned as upright as possible.
- The child's head should be tilted slightly forward to encourage normal swallowing.

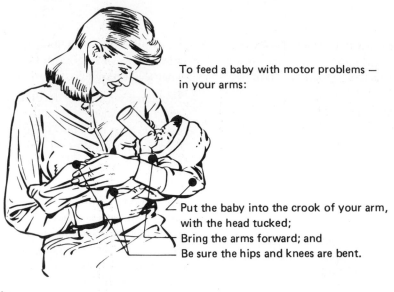

To feed a baby with motor problems —
in your arms:

Put the baby into the crook of your arm,
with the head tucked;
Bring the arms forward; and
Be sure the hips and knees are bent.

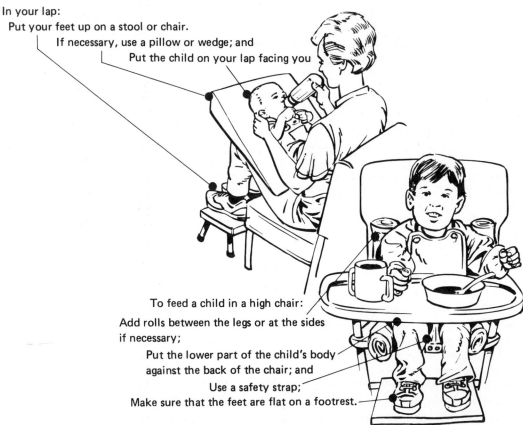

In your lap:
Put your feet up on a stool or chair.
If necessary, use a pillow or wedge; and
Put the child on your lap facing you

To feed a child in a high chair:
Add rolls between the legs or at the sides
if necessary;
Put the lower part of the child's body
against the back of the chair; and
Use a safety strap;
Make sure that the feet are flat on a footrest.

Figure 7–5　Most common positions for feeding
Source of drawings: From *Positioning for Infants and Young Children with Motor Problems*
[videotape manual], pp. 8–11. Courtesy of the University of Colorado School of Nursing, Marilyn
Krajicek, Director, First Start.

- Hand pressure on the back of a child's head while feeding may elicit a primitive reflex that causes the child's body to extend and, thus, should be avoided.

- While sitting in a highchair or adapted seat, the child's legs should be relaxed and feet flat on the footrest or on the floor.

- The food and trainer generally are positioned in front of the child unless oral-motor intervention is required.

Sucking and Swallowing.

- For bottle feeding, use nipples with regular-sized holes. Larger holes in a nipple may cause choking if there is difficulty swallowing.

- When the child begins to suck on the nipple, "tug" gently at the nipple as if to pull it out. This can encourage the child to suck a bit harder. Also try thickening the liquid with a small amount of rice cereal for more suck resistance.

- A downward stroke on the cheek stimulates sucking.

- If there are problems with jaw control, assist by holding the child's chin in a cupped hand.

- Assist lip closure by placing index and second fingers above and below the child's lips using a "scissors" motion to close lips. If assistance for jaw closure is needed, support the jaw with the baby finger.

- If there is a lack of normal swallowing, close the child's mouth (supported if necessary); stroke downward under chin.

- Encourage mouthing and sucking of toys, hands, and pacifiers during nonfeeding times.

Self-Feeding.

- When beginning to teach chewing, use foods that a child can digest easily.

- Place small amounts of food between the child's teeth on the inside of the mouth. Use lip and jaw control as necessary to keep the mouth closed. This should stimulate a chewing response.

- From pureed or baby foods, gradually introduce textured foods (e.g., bits of dry cereal, toast, soft cheese, diced potato, and so on).

- Problems with finger feeding may require that the trainer place a hand over the child's and assist getting food into the mouth. Reduce support from hand, to wrist, to elbow, and finally to no support. Use the same routine when a spoon is introduced.

- For a hypersensitive bite reflex, use a small, rubber-coated spoon for feeding. Place spoon on front third of tongue and apply downward pressure. Remove spoon at 45-degree angle and avoid scraping food off with teeth. Food should be removed with lips.

- Children with severe eating and drinking problems are at risk for choking. Food may easily obstruct airways. If a child is coughing, the airway is not totally obstructed. Allow the child to cough and assist the child to lean forward.

- Safety reminder: Avoid bacon, peanuts, popcorn, hot dogs with skin, grapes, raw carrots, or any small, round food, such as candy. These foods are easy to choke on.

- A nonslip rubberlike material, purchased by the roll, can be used for placemats under plates, toys, and so on to keep them in place.

Drinking.

- Offer broths or semisweet liquids (warm or cool) for the beginning stages of cup training. Milk and sweet liquids seem to impede the process.

- Place the rim of the cup on the child's lower lip. Placing the cup between the teeth causes abnormal swallowing.

- Use of a cutout cup helps to observe lip closure and avoids bending the child's head back.

- A wide range of cups and eating utensils are available from several adapted equipment companies. Consult with therapists on selection of most appropriate items for individual children.

ADAPTING THE ENVIRONMENT

Because most disabling conditions require children to work extra hard to use the learning resources in their environment, most programs for children with special needs attempt to identify obstacles to learning and facilitate children's involvement in the learning process.

The Classroom or Center

The integrated early education classroom is a dynamic system that includes both physical and social components. Physical components include the actual classroom space, the arrangement of activity areas within the space, the furniture and fixtures, the play and work materials, the activities of the program and their sequence, the number of adult participants, the number and types of children (with and without disabilities), and the grouping of staff and children. Social components are the behaviors of adults and children in the classroom setting.

The classroom environment can facilitate movement and independence by providing opportunities for children to determine their own behavior and manage some of their own materials. Even a child with the most severe disabilities needs a chance to have some effect on the environment. Accessible bathrooms, drinking fountains, and play materials will encourage independence and learning. Some time ago, Rogers-Warren (1982) suggested a useful checklist that continues to help teachers accommodate young children with physical disabilities in the classroom:

- How does the setting appear at a child's level? Are there interesting things to see and touch, such as windows, mirrors, mobiles, aquariums, and toys?

- Is there room for a wheelchair-bound or awkwardly mobile child to negotiate in and out of spaces and turn around?

- Are shelves and tables at a comfortable level for a child's height? Is there a place (preferably more than one) that can accommodate a child in each activity area?

- Are shelves, tables, sinks, and other fixtures sturdy enough to hold the weight of a minimally mobile child who may need support?

- Are prosthetic devices (such as a standing cuff) easily accessible in the areas where children might gain practice standing or sitting without an adult's assistance while engaged in an activity?

- Are some of the materials and toys accessible to a child without assistance even if she is minimally mobile?

- Is the sound level and acoustic arrangement of the room satisfactory for a child with a hearing impairment or a hearing aid? Are there some special quiet areas for children to work with minimal noise distraction?

- Does the environment contain sufficient contrasts to attract the notice of a child with a visual impairment? Do color and light contrasts corroborate texture and height contrasts?

- Are the cues (use of color, change of levels, dividers) that designate different areas clear and consistent?

- How much of the environment is designed for self-management or self-engagement? How frequently do children use these opportunities? Does a child need training to use these opportunities?

- Does the arrangement of the room allow for quiet places and social places to meet the changing moods and needs of children? (pp. 29–30)

In an effort to make integrated classrooms appropriate for the young child with motor impairments, activities involving movement should allow the child to be involved as much as possible without accentuating the inability to move well. For example, the leader can combine sitting activities with floor locomotion activities such as rolling or combat crawling. (These movement activities are enhanced by music or rhymes.) If a child is unable to perform movements voluntarily, an adult should assist in motoring the child through the activities.

The Home

In home-based programs, the primary learning environment is the home and its surroundings. Although program staff may have little control over the child's home, the home interventionist may recommend ways to make the home safe and facilitate learning. Burns, cuts, falls, electrical shock, and poisoning are some of the major home hazards. An interventionist who reviews such hazards with the family and explains what to expect from children at different ages promotes safety concerns. Other things that the home interventionist may wish to explore with parents are the following:

1. The kinds of toys and objects in the home that stimulate exploration and learning.

2. Toys that are age and developmentally appropriate and can be adapted to accommodate special needs.

3. The level of visual and auditory stimulation in the home.

4. Modification to the environment that may allow the child greater independence and freedom of action.

5. Adaptive equipment, such as chairs, prone boards, and self-help aids, should be included in home-based programs to encourage opportunities for social interaction and participation in family life.

Exhibit 7-2 describes a model therapeutic home-based program.

Thus, **movement education** as a critical component of early intervention and preschool programs should also be viewed as a means of providing growth in self-image, concept development, language development, perceptual discrimination, socialization, and recreation. This section will highlight adaptations in movement education, including the significant role music and imaginative play in young children's development.

Movement Skills and Music

Music, even without movement, enhances any program as it allows everyone to participate. As Humpal and Wolf (2003) point out, it levels the playing field. It offers varying levels of involvement ranging from listening or observing to joining as an active participant. Dancing, marching, imitating, and imagining are often more enjoyable with music and partial participation does not detract from the positive experience.

It should be recognized that most commercially prepared CDs and tapes move a bit too fast for preschoolers, at least at first. If so, sing the songs without accompaniment and say the directions first. Gradually, as the children's ability to listen and move quickly grows, accompaniment can be added. Keep in mind that young children with mild hearing losses or perceptual problems may find recorded voices difficult to understand.

Rhythm bands, whether they include real instruments or pans with spoons, are exciting to children. Banging on something is an excellent way to develop awareness of body movement. The music may not be concert hall quality, but it certainly pleases the performers. Learning to make different kinds of noises by stamping feet loudly and tiptoeing quietly leads to other kinds of body awareness.

A number of books are available to assist teachers in movement skills activities with the accompaniment of music. Because it is difficult to define dances or other rhythmic activities in terms of age, teachers must carefully think through their children's developmental characteristics. Even the most appealing jingle can frustrate children if the accompanying movements are too difficult (Palmer, 2001). For children with special needs, beginning with the most simple and gradually working up to the more

Exhibit 7–2

Model Therapeutic Home Program

Because therapeutic intervention for young children with significant physical disabilities must include more than a once-a-month clinic visit or prescribed routines in a center-based program, emphasis on the integration of occupational and/or physical therapy into a functional home-based program seems critical to the provision of consistent, ongoing therapy. Part C of the Individuals with Disabilities Education Act emphasizes natural environments as the most appropriate context for early intervention services. In keeping with this emphasis, it is essential that the therapist and family work together to identify the times and contexts within which to apply therapeutic methods and work on therapeutic goals that are relevant for the child and realistic for the family. By assessing the family's typical routine, the therapist and family can identify naturally occurring teaching opportunities within the child's home and community.

An example of embedding home programming recommendations into existing family routines can be seen in the case of Frankie R.:

Frankie is a 2-year-old boy with severe CP (spastic quadriplegia). He is enrolled in a home- and center-based early intervention program where he receives physical therapy on a weekly basis. The therapist and Frankie's parents identified several goals for home and center. Two of the goals included in the family plan are the following:

1. To increase range of motion in shoulders and hips.
2. To establish symmetry and head control while sitting.

5:30 P.M.: Television, relaxing with Dad

Method: Position Frankie straddling Dad's leg, side-lying on the couch, or prone-lying over Dad's lap.

Rationale: Mr. R. agreed that these procedures would not conflict with his need to relax and also would provide an opportunity for him to interact with Frankie. The physical therapist indicated that both goals were being addressed.

7:00 P.M.: Bath with Mom or Dad

Method: Stretch Frankie's shoulders and hips while bathing and drying him; also stretch his trunk by hip and shoulder rotation. Facilitate head control and reaching by playing in the water and touching body parts.

Rationale: The warm water and terry-cloth towels tend to help Frankie relax, and, while he is undressed, this is a good opportunity to work on range of motion. Bathtime provides a natural motivation to maintain head control and to move arms in the water. It is also an excellent time for communication.

Adapting this type of model for all home activities allows the maximum benefit from parent-identified activities that, with minimal intrusion, can be used to provide practice of important developmental skills.

Movement Education

Whenever infants and young children move any part of their bodies, there is potential for two kinds of learning to occur: learning to move and learning from moving. The relationship between movement and cognitive development has long been recognized. The classic cognitive theorist Piaget (1952) supported the belief that the child's first learning experiences are motoric. This realization emphasized the importance of movement for young children and allows them to explore and experience the world.

difficult songs or games is appropriate. Reluctant children may need a personal invitation to join by offering them your hand. If they do not accept, they should not be forced to join.

Movement Skills and Imagination

Children often need help in imaging things since some have had little opportunity to pretend. They enjoy pretending to be engineers on trains, bus drivers, animals, and robots. Dress-up clothes add to the fun but are not necessary. Stories and flannel board materials can lead to stimulating ideas. Pretending to put out a fire with an imaginary hose is almost as exciting as the real thing and much safer.

Children discover the motions people make through seeing a combination of real people, videos, and pictures. Then they take turns pretending. Gradually, they become more creative. The fireman has to put out a fire on the roof, so he stretches up high. Next, the fire is in the basement, so he aims the hose down low. A robot, walking with stiff legs, may move very slowly. Then, as someone turns the controls, he moves faster or even more slowly. Although the teacher may need to suggest ways to move at first, the children's use of imagination improves quickly.

Adaptations in Movement Education

Parents and early childhood educators are adept at using prompts (cues) when assisting children who are having difficulty developing motor skills considered to be age or developmentally appropriate. If a child does not respond to a normal verbal direction and modeling of desired responses, the verbal direction is repeated and accompanied by gestures. If there is still no response or an inadequate one, the verbal request can be accompanied by physically helping the child to perform the act. Positive reinforcement is given at whatever level the act is attempted. Of course, physical or gestural prompts are removed (faded) as soon as possible. Other adaptations are included in the following list and noted in Exhibit 7–3.

1. When planning weekly lessons, incorporate some degree of movement education into each

day's plan, alternate vigorous activities with more relaxing ones, and intersperse activities in a group with activities alone or with a partner.

2. Vary body positions in on-the-floor activities as well as during activities that involve locomotion with the goal of giving attention to all attributes of movement.

3. Allow time for children to concentrate on their own bodily actions by using equipment and music with some but not all activities.

4. Provide for those with perceptual or linguistic delays by allowing for repetition and modeling when giving directions using simple vocabulary. Move from simple to complex and do not expect transfer from one activity to another.

5. Breaks tasks into simple, sequential steps and provide possible reinforcement at the accomplishment of each step. Avoid trying to cover too much or continuing an activity for too long.

Exhibit 7–3

A Gross Motor Activity with Adaptations

Goal

To develop body image; to increase awareness of moving in different directions (directionality).

Objectives

Given directions to move forward, backward, and sideways, each child will do the following:

1. Do as directed when the teacher prompts (physically, with gestures, or with additional words, as needed).
2. As a member of a group, follow the teacher's spoken and gestured signal.
3. As a member of a group, follow spoken directions (no gestures).
4. Throughout this lesson, stop and remain still in the exact position he or she was in at that moment when asked to "freeze." (This condition helps children learn to inhibit unnecessary movements.)

Procedure

Begin with children sitting in a line facing the teacher. Then the activity may proceed according to the following steps (of course, variations will be determined by the individual needs of the children):

1. "Susie, come stand here" (point to a masking tape *X* on the floor).
2. "Good, now walk forward" (physically prompting and gesturing Susie).
3. "Right, you walked forward. Thank you. You may sit down. Tommy, it's your turn. Come stand on the *X*."
4. "Tommy, can you walk backward?" (Gesturing—but because Tommy begins to move backward, no physical prompting is needed.)
5. "Tommy, you did that just the right way. You walked backward."

Procedural Notes

The teacher's enthusiasm and encouragement are of critical importance. The lessons will be individualized as each child's movements are observed. Physical prompts, gestures, and demonstrations will be faded as quickly as possible. Children will be encouraged to verbalize their understanding of their body movements through natural conversation as the activity progresses. Other considerations include the following:

1. Initially each child should be given a brief individual turn. Children will learn from watching. Begin with the child who is most likely to succeed with little or no help. This child serves as a model for the others to follow.
2. Next, pair two children at a time to follow the directions. The children may be given the same or two different directions, depending on their stage of development. (Keep the activity moving.)
3. As soon as possible (but for some children this may take several days), have groups of three to five children moving at the same time.
4. To add variety, a 4/4 march or dance rhythm can be introduced with records, with a drum, or by singing. A square dance calling format can be included with the help of another adult. Guide children as needed, using modeling or prompting as well as calling the directions.
5. New directions should be introduced following this same sequence, before incorporating them into the dance.

Lesson Adaptations

1. For the child with a hearing impairment:
    a. Be sure the child can see your face and gestures.
    b. Place a child without a hearing disability on either side.
    c. Let this child feel the drum or other musical instrument as the rhythm is played. It sometimes helps to set record players on the floor and let the child perform with bare or stocking feet.
2. For the child with a visual impairment:
    a. Use physical prompts until the verbal prompts can be followed. (Fade physical assists as soon as possible.)
    b. Assign a sighted partner. Holding hands will be helpful.
    c. Be certain the space used is free from tripping and falling hazards.
3. For the child with a motor impairment:
    a. Encourage as much participation as possible.
    b. Use supports (e.g., walkers and crutches) as needed.
    c. Have an adult push a wheelchair, if necessary.
    d. Assign the child to be caller or drum beater.
4. For the child with learning delays:
    a. Continue the prompting as needed.
    b. Place excellent models beside the child.
    c. Give directions slowly and one at a time.
    d. Repeat directions as often as necessary (with kind enthusiasm).
    e. Demonstrate patience if the child cannot do what she could do the day before.
    f. Socially reward each small step of progress.

6. Be conscious of each child's fatigue and attention levels. Maintain eye contact and do not allow outside distractions.

7. If a child has a visual impairment, be sure to use his or her name when verbally directing his or her activities.

8. Use of visual cues such as "stop" and "go" signs in red and green not only serve as attention getters but are essential to assist those with hearing impairments. Avoid standing in front of a window to minimize the potential for glare when children look to you for direction. Be sure to get every child's attention before beginning to give directions.

9. Be creative as you include children with physical disabilities. Many activities can be done from a sitting position as well as a standing position. For example, children can touch their "heads, shoulders, knees, and toes" while sitting. Rather than run under a parachute, peers may be just as happy pushing their disabled peer's wheelchair under the parachute.

10. To keep control, encourage only those activities that do not go beyond the level of movement or noise that can easily be tolerated by the teachers and aides.

The purpose of the next chapter is to convey the complex nature of the development of communication skills. Focus will be on the importance of helping young children develop functional communication skills that will enable them to initiate and influence social interaction.

Summary

Professionals who work with children with a wide range of abilities and disabilities in various early intervention settings should understand physical and psychological factors that may interfere with the typical developmental process. Because infants are now in many programs, knowledge of the beginning behaviors is critical in planning intervention and assisting parents effectively. All early educators should study the development and interrelationship of the nervous system and motor skills.

The young child with a motor delay requires a team approach involving the physician, therapists, nutritionists, parents, and teachers to meet special needs at home and school. Observations and team planning ensure consistency and selection of appropriate intervention strategies. Mutual understanding of therapeutic and educational goals serves to strengthen motor skill development.

Adaptations of materials and environmental considerations should be a concern for all early education programs but more specifically when children who are medically fragile or have motor delays are included. Finding ways for these children to interact, respond, and develop will require more than the few activities usually listed in curriculum guides. Gross and fine motor skills, adaptive skills, and movement experiences must be an integral part of each child's day-to-day home and school activities. Its relationship to other aspects of development makes movement an essential component of an effective early education program.

Discussion Topics and Activities

1. Thoroughly review at least three developmental checklists. Pay special attention to the sequential order of the motor skills. Adopt a checklist that seems to be complete or compile your own. Observe a typical child and a child with a disability or children of two different ages. Were you able to detect differences in skill development? If not, your checklist needs to be broken into smaller steps.

2. Now take a major skill such as throwing and break it into subskills. Sequence these skills. After your task analysis is complete, try to teach the skill to a friend or a child. What subskills did you leave out? Did the order of your skills need to be changed? With adults, skipping is a good skill to analyze.

3. Interview or ask a physical and occupational therapist to visit class. Ask for information, for example, about positioning techniques, adaptive equipment, and special teaching procedures. Be certain to ask the therapist to explain his or her view of motor development.

4. Investigate the relationship between motor skills and body awareness. Begin a file of activities specially designed to teach body awareness and contribute to self-esteem.

5. There are several suggestions in the literature that instruction in perceptual skills may not be defensible. Research this matter. Discuss and debate the issue with classmates.

6. Try to explain the sequential trends of motor development to another person, deriving and using specific examples. If you can explain them clearly to another, then you probably understand them well.

7. Research and discuss the various disabling conditions, such as cerebral palsy, muscular dystrophy, and visual impairment, that have an impact on motor skill development. If possible, invite a member of the community who has experienced difficulties from such an impairment to discuss ways teachers can be of assistance.

8. Plan a motor activity. Be creative. Consider parachutes, isometric exercises, and dances. Teach this lesson to your classmates. Discover the fun some movement activities can create. Do your lesson with children.

9. Design a playground that would be suitable for children with a variety of disabling conditions.

chapter 8

Nurturing Communication Skills

Photo by Barbara Schwartz/Merrill

KEY TERMS

(Note: Terms are discussed in the text and/or defined in the glossary.)

augmentative and alternative
   communication system
cochlear implant
content
echolalic speech
form
illocutionary behaviors
interactive model
grammatical morphemes
high-preference items
   and events
joint reference (attention)

milieu teaching
modeling
motherese
morphology
pause-and-wait strategy
Picture Exchange Communication
   System
phonology
pivotal response
   treatment
pragmatics
preference inventory

prelinguistic communication
profound hearing loss
progressive matching
reference
residual hearing
semantics
semantic relations
spoken English
syntax
telegraphic language
use
verbal routines

- Communication and language are very complex skills that are best understood as occurring within a context of social interaction.

- Communication skills develop in predictable stages beginning at birth; the foundation of language is laid during the first year of life.

- The development of language during the preschool years consists not simply of more words and longer sentences but of pragmatic skills that enable the child to communicate effectively and appropriately in a variety of social contexts.

- The focus of communication intervention must be on the development of functional communication skills that enable the child to *initiate* social interaction and influence his or her environment.

- Key adult behaviors that facilitate communication skills are listening and responding to children's communication attempts and carefully mapping language onto children's experiences.

- The learning of a second language proceeds in much the same fashion as the acquisition of the first language, and, like the first, the second language is best learned in interactive social environments.

- All children can communicate. For young children with severe and multiple disabilities, alternative modes of communication can be established.

- For children with hearing impairments, teachers must be aware of both the role of residual hearing and the use of manual communication as well as new technologies such as the cochlear implant.

In recent decades, probably no aspect of child development has received more attention than the area of communication. Similarly, a great deal of interest has been generated regarding intervention strategies to facilitate the development and acquisition of speech and language skills. Much has been learned about which techniques and strategies best support the efforts of young children with disabilities to communicate with those around them.

This chapter will consider several interesting areas of research and apply them to the design of early childhood curricula for children with special needs. We must first review some basic terminology used to describe the various subskills of language. (Note: for more thorough description of speech and language acquisition and the processes of development of communication skills, see Hulit & Howard [2006] and Owens [2004].)

THE SUBSKILLS OF LANGUAGE

The complexity of language is impressive. Language is often referred to as the most complex human function. In order to manage this complexity in discussing language, it is helpful to use the conceptual framework originally described originally by Bloom and Lahey (1978) and more recently by Loeb (2003). This framework defines three dimensions of language: **content, use,** and **form.** Each of these dimensions includes several traditional linguistic subskills, such as **semantics, syntax, morphology, phonology,** and **pragmatics.** These are described in the sections below.

Content, Use, and Form

The *content* of language is its vocabulary and meaning (semantics), that is, what it is about. *Use* refers to the purpose or function of language—what it is used

for. The *form* of language refers both to its syntactic and morphological structure (i.e., the order and forms of words) and to the phonological form (i.e., the particular sounds, or phonemes, and the sound sequences that occur in spoken language). Every utterance can be analyzed according to these three dimensions. Take, for example, the child who, hoping for a second helping of ice cream, looks at his mother and says, "Is there more ice cream?"

- The content of this utterance refers to the existence of a frozen, sweet dairy product called "ice cream."
- Its use, or purpose, is to obtain a second helping.
- The structure of the utterance is a five-word interrogative sentence.

This theoretical framework is helpful in making clear the multidimensional and complex nature of language.

Semantics

Learning the *meanings* of words (**semantics**) is very dependent on interactions with adults who make their meaning clear. For example, talking about the ocean to a child who has never seen one will result in little understanding of *ocean*. Young children do not learn word meanings through vicarious experiences. Things they see must be named while they are looking at them and touching them. Activities must be described while they are happening. Then children must have the opportunity to experiment with the words to discover whether they have learned what each really means.

Lahey (1988) described several **semantic relations** typically expressed in children's early two-word combinations. These include meanings such as *recurrence* (e.g., "more juice" or "'nother birdie"), *disappearance* (e.g., "cereal gone" or "no dollie"), *appearance* (e.g., "that Mommy" or "there ball"), *rejection* (e.g., "no want!" or "don't wash!"), *actions* (e.g., "baby fall" or "push Daddy"), *locations* (e.g., "cookie 'frigerator" or "doggie bed"), *possession*

(e.g., "Teddy mine!" or "Mommy shoe"), and occasional *descriptors* (e.g., "cereal hot" or "pants dirty").

Syntax

Learning the rules for correct word order in sentences is one aspect of **syntax.** Syntax includes knowing that it is correct to say "We are going to the ball game" rather than "game ball we are going to." Of course, children learning to utter syntactically correct sentences are really just trying to communicate. They are not consciously practicing the rules they are learning. But as they learn, children everywhere develop language in a similar sequence. Between ages 10 and 14 months, most typically developing children use single words to communicate. By age 2, they string two or three words together, and by age 4 they have mastered most of the syntactic rules and are creating grammatically correct sentences that follow the rules of the language they have been hearing and practicing.

Morphology

Children must also learn the rules for changing the *form* of individual words (rules of **morphology**). For example, they discover when to add *s*, when to add *es*, and when to change the word *man* to *men*. They discover how to form possessives and how to use number and tense in verbs (e.g., *he walks, they walk, he walked, he is walking*, or *we walked*). Children learn comparatives (*long, longer, longest*) and how to add prefixes and suffixes to alter meaning. They use pronouns as possessives (*his* or *hers*), as subjects (*I, he*, or *they*), and as objects (*him* or *her*).

As they learn these rules of morphology, children make many interesting mistakes. They overgeneralize, saying, "We wented" and "The mans." However, their errors are logical and confirm that they are not just imitating what they are hearing. They are learning rules. Exceptions to the rules, such as irregular verbs and irregular plurals, will be learned in time. Often very young children can be heard using irregular nouns and verbs correctly (*men, ran*, or *fell*). As they begin to internalize language rules, they may change to rule-governed forms (*mans, runned*, or *falled*).

Then the adult models around them must help them discover these exceptions to the rules all over again.

Phonology

Learning the rules of the sound systems of speech and language **(phonology)** involves not only the individual speech sounds, or *phonemes*, but also discovering that pitch and rhythm changes make a difference. The intonation patterns (*prosodic* or *suprasegmental features*) are learned very early. Babies just a few months old babble in ways that sound almost like the patterns adults use. A conscientious listener can hear questions and statements in the intonation patterns of babies long before words can be heard. Careful listening will also detect exclamations!

As they near 6 months of age, many babies begin to babble in syllables that include some of the phonemes of the adult system. Their production is usually somewhat wide of the mark. By 1 year, they have learned to use some sounds accurately some of the time, and the first words begin to appear. However, the accuracy of children's production is highly dependent on being able to hear the sounds they are trying to produce clearly, accurately, and often. They do not need to hear the sounds in isolation or even in syllables. Hearing them in words and connected speech

(phrases and sentences) appears to be enough. But they do need to hear the phonemes, and they do need lots of opportunity to practice them. Most children learn to produce nearly all of the 44 phonemes of English by the time they are 4 years old.

Pragmatics

Learning how to use language in appropriate ways within various contexts is crucial to the successful development of communication skills (Prutting & Kirchner, 1987). Linguistic **pragmatics** refers to rules and conventions that govern how language is used for communication in different situations. Pragmatic communication skills also include many nonverbal behaviors (Hulit & Howard, 2006).

Speakers and listeners follow a set of unconscious guidelines as they talk to each other. These include behaviors such as looking at each other and looking away and waiting for the speaker to pause before the listener begins to speak. These behaviors require attention to subtle cues. Facial expressions and body language appropriate to particular circumstances must be learned. The situation, the specific topic, the relation of listener to speaker, and many other variables determine *what* is said as well as *how* it is said. Children who have not acquired these

Photo by Anne Vega, Merrill

pragmatic skills stand out as "different" in preschool groups almost as much as those whose speech is unintelligible. But it is more difficult for parents and teachers to pinpoint how and why they are different.

The following are ways in which the situational context influences how a person communicates: (a) the people present, (b) what was just previously said, (c) the topic of conversation, (d) the task that communication is being used to accomplish, and (e) the times and places in which the communication occurs. Observation suggests that young children readily use these contextual clues to enable themselves to understand much more than words alone.

The acquisition of pragmatic skills begins to develop well before children's first words. Hulit and Howard (2006) describe various prelinguistic communication acts, such as pointing and reaching, combined with vocalizations and directed eye gaze. These behaviors, which typically emerge in young children around the 10th month, lay an important foundation for later language development.

CONTRIBUTION OF SOCIAL INTERACTION THEORY TO UNDERSTANDING EARLY COMMUNICATION DEVELOPMENT

Social interaction theories maintain that language is learned primarily through social interactions (McCormick, Loeb, & Schiefelbusch, 2003). An important shift of interest has been away from the child in isolation and toward the dyad (significant pair of individuals) in this case the parent-child or teacher-child dyad. The contributions of conversation and interaction to children's development of communication skills and the role of early caregiver–infant and caregiver–child interactions in children's development are well established (Sachs, 2001).

Another shift of focus in the study of children's development of communication has been toward the study of the purposes of children's communicative behaviors and the functional uses of communicative behavior within social contexts. These areas of emphasis have generated information and theories with important implications for the field of early

childhood special education. Several theories have evolved that reflect some aspect of this social interaction focus. Tannock, Girolametto, and Siegel (1992) described an **interactive model,** which suggests that parent responsiveness and the use of **motherese** are critical factors in the development of communication. This model also proposes intervention strategies based on the theory. These include following the child's lead, using strategies such as increased wait time to encourage communicative initiation and turn taking, and certain language modeling techniques, including describing what the child is doing, repetition of key words and phrases, and syntactically and semantically expanding the child's utterances. Bates and McWhinney (1988) described the "functional" model. This theory suggests that grammar develops as a function of communicative use and meaning and within the context of communicative interactions.

A third theory of this type was proposed earlier by Nelson (1986). Nelson's theory is based on the notion of the existence of a "rare event learning mechanism." In the course of children's interactions with others, on occasion they will be particularly attentive to certain language inputs and to mismatches between their current grammatical skill and the adult's model. At such points, children's cognitive processes of selective attention, storage, retrieval, and hypothesis testing are all activated, and the learning of new language structures takes place. Again, it is within the context of meaningful interactions with more competent speakers that this occurs.

A fourth theory is a familiar one. This is Vygotsky's (1978) theory of adult social mediation of children's learning experiences. This theory, which is applicable to all learning, not just language development, suggests that more capable adults or peers provide assistance to the child within social interaction contexts. When this assistance is provided within the "zone of proximal development," it provides the necessary "scaffolding" (Bruner, 1983) to enable the child to master a particular skill and achieve independence.

More recent research has focused on the importance of "joint reference" (i.e., the caregiver's and child's focus of attention is on the same object or event at the same time; Campbell & Namy [2003]). By

6 or 7 months of age, the typically developing infant will begin to respond to caregiver signals to focus attention on a particular object. By 1 year, most infants are able to take control and direct adults attention to something of interest. Adults enhance the establishment of **joint attention** and **reference** by following the child's lead and commenting on something the child is attending to, pointing at, or commenting on. Some children with disabilities (e.g., autism) may have difficulty responding to the caregiver's attempts to establish joint attention. See Mundy and Crowson (1997) for a review.

These social interaction approaches have provided a much greater understanding of the precursors of language development occurring during the child's first year of life. In addition, research and theories related to the effect of caregiver input and social interaction on children's development have important implications for intervention strategies and the design of early intervention curricula (Rossetti, 2001).

STAGES OF DEVELOPMENT OF COMMUNICATION SKILLS IN YOUNG CHILDREN

Early childhood special educators must thoroughly understand the development of communication skills in typically developing children. Several available texts provide detailed descriptions of typical communication development within each of the five subskills previously defined (see, for example, Owens, 2000). Table 8-1 also provides development information for the major language subskills.

The following section will briefly describe the major accomplishments in communication skills development from birth to 3 years of age. Because space does not allow a detailed description of this process, the section is intended only as a review.

Prelinguistic Communication

It is important for early childhood special educators to recognize that the infant begins the process of learning to communicate long before the onset of true or conventional speech and language. Literally from the moment of birth, communication takes place between infant and caregiver. Research in the areas of mother–infant interaction and developmental pragmatics has suggested that the communication patterns established during the first year or two of life are crucial to children's later development in several areas, including language, cognition, and social skills. (See, for example, Kelly & Barnard [2000] and Landry, Smith, Swank, & Miller-Loncar [2000].)

During the first few months of life, the infant's communications are not really intentional. Nevertheless, they can be easily understood by those around the infant. For example, crying, smiling, cooing, looking, and eventually reaching are behaviors that often have great meaning for the infant's caregivers, even though the infant may not be doing them "on purpose." A term often used to describe these kinds of communicative behaviors is *perlocutionary* (Hulit & Howard, 2006).

These perlocutionary behaviors are responded to and interpreted by caregivers as though they *were* intentions. As the infant gains greater control, voluntary behaviors eventually become *intentional* communicative acts. By 9 or 10 months of age, most children are engaging in a variety of intentional (but still unconventional) behaviors, such as pointing, use of directed eye gaze, and use of vocalizations to get attention, to exclaim, or to accompany their own actions or expression of wants and needs.

Prelinguistic Functions.   These types of intentional communicative behaviors are often referred to as **illocutionary behaviors.** In his now classic work, Halliday (1975) described several categories of communicative functions that infants may use even prior to the acquisition of first words:

1. The *interactional function* is also referred to as the "you and me" function. By using this function, the infant is attempting to elicit interaction and attention from others in his immediate environment. For example, an infant may look at mother, clap his hands, and vocalize in an attempt to play "pattycake." Or he may wake from his nap and call from his crib in order to get some company.

2. The *instrumental function* is also referred to as the "I want" function. Here the infant uses

Table 8–1   **Normal language development: Expected sequence and approximate age norms**

Age in Months (Approx.)	Pragmatics	Phonology	Grammar Morphology-Syntax	Semantics
1	Gazing, crying, "comfort sounds"	Begins to play with pitch change		
3	Laughs, smiles when played with; looks at speaker; sometimes responds to a speaker by vocalizing	Vocalizes two or more syllables		
6	Babbles and smiles at a speaker; stops (begins turn taking) when someone speaks	Babbles four or more syllables at one time; plays at making noises; labial (/p/, /b/, /m /) consonants emerge; vowels		
8	Plays "peek-a-boo" and "pat-a-cake"; listens to adult conversations; turns toward speaker; understands gesture	Intonation patterns for questions and commands; jargon includes vowels and consonants (five or more of each)	No real words, but vocalizing sounds as if forming a sentence or question	Recognizes names of some common objects
10	Follows simple commands; enjoys clapping to music; begins to "send message" by pointing	Uses a varied jargon, with pitch and rhythm		Says first words; tries to imitate words
12	Responds to manner and attitude of speaker (e.g., joy, anger, or hurry)	Consonant-vowel and consonant-vowel-consonant jargon	Holophrasic speech (one word stands for a whole sentence)	Uses two or more words; learns new words every few days
12 to 18	Follows one- and two-step directions	Imitates noises and speech sounds	Some begin to use two-word sentences	Recognizes and points to many familiar objects; learns new words almost daily
18 to 24	Jargon and some echolalia; "dialogue" uses speech to get attention; "asks" for help	Uses /p/, /b/, /m/, /h/, /t/ and vowels	Two- to three-word sentences, but omits articles and most modifiers; begins to use personal pronouns; telegraphic speech	Says 10 to 20 words at 18 months, but some say as many as 200 words by 24 months; understands many more
24 to 36	At 2, speech is not used for social control, but at 2½ demands and attempts control By 3, language is linguistically and contextually contingent, and 70% of speech is intelligible, although	Many begin to use additional consonants; add /f/, /k/, /d/, /w/, /g/; vowels 90% intelligible	By 2½ grammatical morphemes begin to appear: *-ing* (present progressive); *-s* and *-es* (plurals); *-ed* (past tense); *a, an, the* (articles); *my* and *'s* (possessives); auxiliary verbs; prepositions	Recognizes names and pictures of most common objects; understands 500 words

Age in Months (Approx.)	Pragmatics	Phonology	Grammar Morphology- Syntax	Semantics
	articulation errors are still common. Short sentences (three to four words) are common. All vowels are correct, but /r/, /s/, /ch/, /j/, /v/, /l/, /x/ are often incorrectly spoken. Vocabulary ranges to as many as 1,000 words. Sentence types include agent-action, action-object, and agent-object			
36 to 48	Social control; whispers; tells name; "explains" what happened; asks questions, sustains topic; systematic changes in speech depend on the listener; some role playing; metalinguistic awareness (ability to think about language and comment on it); "hints" at things through smiles and gestures as well as words	All vowels correct; although many children articulate most consonants accurately, articulation errors on the following are still within normal range: /l/, /r/, /s/, /z/, /sh/, /ch/, /j/, /th/; pitch and rhythm variations similar to adults, but this age enjoys extremes— yells and whispers	Expands noun phrases with tense, gender, and number; conjugates "to be" correctly; uses pronouns, adjectives, and plurals; near age 4, begins using longer and more compound and complex sentences; begins to interrelate clauses (uses *and, because, when,* and *then*)	Vocabulary grows rapidly; actively seeks to learn new words; likes to experiment and makes many charming errors; continues process of differentiating lexical types; knows between 900 and 1,000 words
48 to 60	Seeks information constantly; "why" is a favorite; becomes aware of behavior listeners attend to; begins to grasp relevance	Begins to use stress contours, pitch changes purposefully; articulation errors still common, but diminishing; nonfluency not unusual; blends difficult	Uses comparatives (*big, biggest*); uses all sentence types, including relative clauses; grammar approximates that of adults	Size of vocabulary varies widely with experiences; many know 2,000 or more words

Sources: Adapted from Prutting and Kirschner (1987).

communicative behaviors to obtain something he wants from the environment, such as food or a favorite object. For example, an infant's looking toward his bottle, pointing, and saying "Uh" is an instrumental communicative behavior.

3. The *regulatory function* is the "Do as I tell you" function; it is used by the infant to control others'

behaviors. For example, an infant may be requesting someone to push him in his stroller or pick him up.

4. The *personal function* is called the "Here I come" function. The infant uses this function to simply express some emotion or to accompany his own actions. For example, an infant tastes a

bite of ice cream and says, "Mmmm," or drops something and says, "Uh oh!"

5. The *heuristic function* is an important function because it sets the stage for the infant's use of communication to obtain information from adults in his environment. This is referred to as the "Tell me why" function. By use of strategies such as a vocalization with questionlike rising intonation or raised eyebrows, the infant learns to solicit additional information, such as a label or explanation, from people nearby.

6. The *imaginative function* may be used by some infants during this prelinguistic stage of communication development. The imaginative function is referred to as the "Let's pretend" function; it accompanies the older infant's pretend play activities (e.g., car sounds).

The Onset of Language

Somewhere around 1 to 1½ years of age, the infant learns his first "real" words. After this point, communication becomes symbolic and conventional. The toddler continues to use all the communicative functions just described, but now many of these functions are expressed using recognizable words such as *peek, bottle, up, oh oh, whaddat,* and *night night.* In addition, a new function is now added to the toddler's repertoire: the *informative function.* Halliday (1975) called this the "Let me tell you" function because the child can now truly share information via symbolic language behavior.

Around this same time, the child also begins to move toward a new stage of cognitive development: the *preoperational stage.* Now the infant becomes increasingly able to represent things mentally. As a result, he can also use his newly found symbolic behavior to refer to things that are not immediately present in the environment and, very shortly, to events that happened in the past.

Thus, the onset of conventional speech and language skills also typically coincides with several other exciting milestones in the infant's development. The infant's communication is no longer tied to the here and now. In addition to using social interaction and manipulating his environment to meet his basic wants and needs, he can now share his experiences with others.

It should be noted that the speech of a toddler at the early one-word stage is often unintelligible to anyone not involved with the toddler on a regular basis. Some words may even be idiosyncratic, bearing little phonemic relationship to the conventional word (e.g., "da" for bottle). Real words may also be combined with jargon or strings of unintelligible speech sounds (often consonant–vowel syllables, such as "da" or "tee"). The toddler may sound as though he is uttering whole sentences, although he really is not.

Combining Words

Sometime around 20 to 24 months, when the infant has learned approximately 50 to 100 words, he will begin to put them together. Often his first combinations will be words he already uses. For example, instead of saying "juice" or "more" to get another glass of juice, he will say "more juice." Just why the infant begins to combine words in this way is not clear. For many years, child language acquisition research focused on this process of learning to produce longer and longer utterances that conform more and more closely to adult language.

The *structure* of language refers to the way in which words are combined into sentences (syntax) and the various forms of words (morphology). The young child must learn to say "I want juice" rather than "Want juice I" and "The boys are running" rather than "The boys is run." There is much literature from the 1960s and early 1970s that described in some detail the evolution of children's grammar. Although teachers of young children need not be familiar with all the specific details of children's grammatical development, it is important that they know the major stages of language structure development as described in the following paragraphs.

1. *Telegraphic language.* When children begin to combine words, they are most likely to use words

that have the most meaning. In earlier writings on child language acquisition, these utterances were called **telegraphic language** because they appeared to omit unessential words. Utterances such as "Baby like bottle" are typical of children in this stage.

2. *Grammatical morphemes.* Around 2 years of age, children begin to include **grammatical morphemes** in their utterances. Words such as *the* and *an*, word endings such as plural *-s*, present progressive *-ing*, past tense *-ed*, and others are gradually included. As a child first begins to use grammatical morphemes, she may often use them incorrectly. For example, she may say "The boy runned" or "an apples." The teacher should be aware that incorrect use of grammatical morphemes nevertheless represents a more sophisticated stage of grammatical development than the earlier telegraphic stage in which grammatical morphemes were omitted altogether.

3. *Simple sentences.* Gradually, by the age of 3, children learn to produce sentences that resemble simple ones used by adults. These sentences will contain a subject and a predicate and will include the necessary grammatical morphemes, although still not always in the correct form. The 3-year-old says, "I want some milk, please," or "Let's go outside," or "My dollies is mad!" The 3-year-old has also learned to make sentence transformations, that is, to ask questions ("Do you have my doll?") and give commands ("Give me my doll!"), as well as to make simple declarative statements ("This is my doll.").

4. *Complex language.* By the age of 4, young children can easily combine words into sentences and produce them intelligibly. In addition, they can produce complex sentences such as "I don't want to go to the store if I can't buy a new toy." Perhaps even more important is their increasing linguistic flexibility.

Children's increasing skills in structure and vocabulary enable them to combine these skills with their emerging pragmatic skills. They can now adjust the structure and content of their language according to the nature of the situation and the age and status of the listener. For example, to his 2-year-old sister, the

4-year-old might say, "Give me the ice cream!" But when talking to an older adult, he would change the structure of his language (e.g., "Could I have some more ice cream, please?").

The 4- or 5-year-old child is also capable of carrying on a conversation: the child can take turns, extend the topic, and return the conversational floor to his partner. The following dialogue demonstrates these conversational strategies, which are so crucial to the young child's development of social skills:

Danny: Did you see *The Simpsons* on TV last night, Erin?

Erin: No, 'cause I watch *Sabrina.*

Danny: Bart got in trouble.

Erin: How come?

Danny: He played a trick on his teacher.

Erin: I like *Sabrina* better than *The Simpsons.*

Finally, the 4- or 5-year-old child can engage in *narrative forms*, that is, stories or explanations that have a beginning, a middle, and an end. The child is now able to use language not only to manipulate the environment and obtain social interaction but also to express emotions and to share experiences and ideas with others. Language and cognition now become inextricably woven together as a means of problem solving and learning about the world.

It is hoped that the 4-year-old has acquired the kinds of linguistic skills that will also support academic achievement. These autonomous or literate-style language skills are discussed in chapter 9. The child's words and sentences can now stand alone. He can tell a story or describe a situation clearly and successfully to a listener who has no previous knowledge or shared reference regarding the event being described.

Many of the milestones described in this section will be communication goals for young children with special needs. Strategies for helping children develop these communication skills will be described later in the chapter.

NECESSARY CONDITIONS FOR THE DEVELOPMENT OF COMMUNICATION SKILLS

Because of the tremendous complexity of speech and language skills, several necessary conditions must exist in order for these skills to develop typically.

First, the peripheral sensory system must be intact. Hearing is of greatest importance, of course, for the development of language. In addition, vision and oral sensation must function well.

The central nervous system must also be intact. Speech and language development depend on the ability not only to receive incoming auditory information but also to process, organize, and store it. Of particular importance in the development of speech production (i.e., articulation skills) is the motor system. The production of speech involves incredibly precise coordination of many muscles and muscle groups making up the speech production mechanism, including those involved in movement of the tongue, lips, jaw, velum, larynx, and muscles of respiration. The production of speech sounds in the rapid sequence necessary for the production of intelligible speech requires synergistic split-second timing and smooth control of these muscles. For children with motor impairments such as those associated with many forms of cerebral palsy, the production of speech is extremely difficult.

Cognitive abilities are crucial to the development of language skills. The content of a child's language is dependent on what the child is able to represent, organize, understand, and recall of the world around him.

Communication is first and foremost a *social* phenomenon. Communication development during the first year of life (and many of the precursors of language) depends on the infant's or young child's interest in the caregiver's social cues and seeking the attention of—and interaction with—others in his environment. The child who lacks this drive toward social interaction, as, for example, in many cases of autism, will most likely be significantly impaired in the development of communication skills.

Finally, the environment itself must be responsive to the infant's and young child's needs, and the linguistic input provided by caregivers must be appropriate to the infant's ability to process information. As mentioned earlier in this chapter, early caregiver–child interactions can enhance children's later development. These interaction strategies are also important to teachers in the field of early childhood special education, and they should be incorporated into the daily activities of the classroom. We will discuss these interaction strategies in more detail later in this chapter.

Characteristics That Can Interfere with Language Development

Characteristics of common communication disorders are summarized in Figure 8-1. The following sections discuss these disorders in more detail.

Hearing Loss.   Hearing loss can interfere with both speech and language development. Even mild or intermittent hearing impairments, such as those associated with otitis media, can interfere with the learning of speech and language. Children who are hearing impaired can be taught to speak and to understand language, but the task is not an easy one and requires the help of parents and highly trained specialists. Frequently, children with severe and profound hearing loss will need to use sign language as their primary mode of communication. Although children who are deaf are eventually identified, lack of language development in children with mild hearing losses frequently goes undetected.

Children with mild hearing losses cannot hear all phonemes with equal clarity. The distorted speech pattern they hear is inconsistent and incorrect. Roberts and Burchinal (2001) discussed the possible long-term effects of mild, intermittent hearing loss from otitis media on language and literacy development. If a child fails to develop normal communication skills at expected ages, regardless of what other factors seem to be involved, the child's hearing should be checked and regularly rechecked by a competent audiologist. If any hearing deficit is detected, the causes should be discovered and treated. If this is

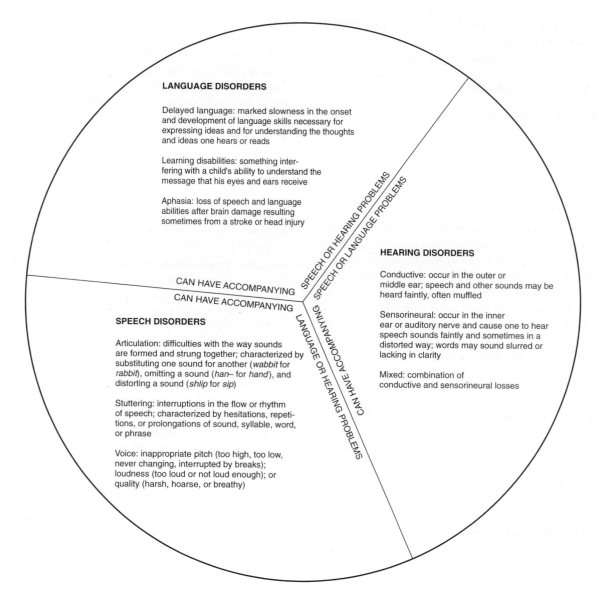

LANGUAGE DISORDERS

Delayed language: marked slowness in the onset and development of language skills necessary for expressing ideas and for understanding the thoughts and ideas one hears or reads

Learning disabilities: something inter-fering with a child's ability to understand the message that his eyes and ears receive

Aphasia: loss of speech and language abilities after brain damage resulting sometimes from a stroke or head injury

CAN HAVE ACCOMPANYING

CAN HAVE ACCOMPANYING

SPEECH OR HEARING PROBLEMS

SPEECH OR LANGUAGE PROBLEMS

LANGUAGE OR HEARING PROBLEMS

CAN HAVE ACCOMPANYING

HEARING DISORDERS

Conductive: occur in the outer or middle ear; speech and other sounds may be heard faintly, often muffled

Sensorineural: occur in the inner ear or auditory nerve and cause one to hear speech sounds faintly and sometimes in a distorted way; words may sound slurred or lacking in clarity

Mixed: combination of conductive and sensorineural losses

SPEECH DISORDERS

Articulation: difficulties with the way sounds are formed and strung together; characterized by substituting one sound for another (*wabbit* for *rabbit*), omitting a sound (*han–* for *hand*), and distorting a sound (*shlip* for *sip*)

Stuttering: interruptions in the flow or rhythm of speech; characterized by hesitations, repeti-tions, or prolongations of sound, syllable, word, or phrase

Voice: inappropriate pitch (too high, too low, never changing, interrupted by breaks); loudness (too loud or not loud enough); or quality (harsh, hoarse, or breathy)

Figure 8–1 Characteristics of common communication disorders
Source: From public information materials of the American Speech-Language-Hearing Association (1991). Reproduced with permission.

not possible, parents should receive guidance, and the child's language development should be monitored and directed by a speech-language pathologist or a trained teacher of children who are deaf.

The family, taking into account input from pro-fessionals, must make a decision as to what com-munication methods will be used: speech, sign, or a combination of the two. Children who are unable to

hear normally during the first years of life may be disabled in all aspects of language and speech development. The longer the hearing impairment is undetected and untreated, the more serious will be the effects on the development of communication.

Specific Language Impairment. There is a lack of consensus regarding the nature of specific language impairment (McCormick, Loeb & Schiefelbusch (2003b). Leonard (1998), for example, has suggested that specific language impairment simply represents the lower end of the normal continuum of language ability (Leonard, 1998). On the other hand, Tallal et al. (1996) suggested that auditory processing disorders—and particularly difficulty processing rapidly presented stimuli—may be the cause of specific language impairments in some children. While there is no current consensus on the role of processing speed, parents and teachers may wish to avoid presenting stimuli too rapidly. Rapid speech rates may be difficult for some children to process. Chaotic noisy environments may be overwhelming. As a result, these children may eventually develop the habit of "tuning out" their environments, which can cause additional learning problems.

Visual Disabilities. Although visual disability does not produce the same degree of interference as hearing disability, it does affect concept and vocabulary development (Fazzi, 2002). If the child cannot see clearly, it is difficult to recognize the things and events being discussed. Children who are blind, by virtue of their disability, have a different *experiential* base (Rogow, 2000). They need some assistance in mastering certain aspects of language development, particularly in the area of vocabulary and concept development and nonverbal pragmatic skills. Like children with a partial hearing loss, children who are partially sighted may have special needs that often go unnoticed. In her classic work, Fraiberg (1977) offered specific and useful information to aid early identification and intervention for children with visual impairment. Appendix D lists warning signs of possible visual disability.

Cognitive Disabilities. Children with slower-than-average cognitive development need thoughtfully planned and carefully provided individualized opportunities and challenges. Children who have moderate and mild retardation will often be able to learn to talk and understand speech and language in the expected sequences, although at a slower pace. It is especially important to provide these children with a language-nurturing environment that gives input that is developmentally appropriate to their language and cognitive level.

The child with more severe retardation poses very different problems and challenges for the early childhood special education teacher. When there is severe impairment of cognitive and perceptual processes, the impact on the development of communication skills is great. In many children who have severe or profound retardation, rule-governed symbolic language skills may not develop. However, it is important to recognize that these children, too, must have some means of communication. We will discuss young children with severe and multiple disabilities in a later section.

Emotional Problems. Atypical language development or the refusal to communicate at all may result from emotional problems. Although these problems require the skillful and caring therapy of persons especially trained to help children and their parents, much can be done to support mental health in a preschool environment. Chapter 6 offers a number of classroom support strategies for children with emotional or social problems. Cooperation among therapists, parents, and teachers is especially critical in this area.

Autism. The core identifying characteristics of children who have autism is the atypical development of social skills and language. Current theories regarding etiological factors in autism suggest that its basis is neurological; for example, there may be differences in how the child's central nervous system responds to incoming stimuli. These differences can result in information-processing deficits and problems of sensory regulation and integration (Wetherby & Prizant, 2000). Many children with autism are particularly sensitive to tactile and auditory stimuli, which can interfere with the development of communication skills and contribute to behavior problems.

In addition, problems with social perception and responsiveness may also contribute to difficulty establishing joint attention and the development of functional uses of communication. Eventually, there are signficant limitations in pragmatic skills (Mundy & Crowson, 1997; Wetherby & Prizant, 2000).

Lack of Parent–Child Interaction.   Lack of appropriate interaction limits communication development. Some parents may not be aware of the importance of talking to young children. Some parents may think it silly to talk to their infant or toddler before he or she learns to talk.

It is often assumed that people who speak a language, children as well as adults, instinctively know how to talk to infants and young children. This is not always true. Later in this chapter, suggestions for teaching parents and others how to talk to their children will be given. In any case, when a child is not talking, be alert to help parents create a language-nurturing environment.

Parents can learn to use everyday experiences to teach communication skills. Cooking, cleaning, and gardening are excellent experiences for children. Conversation during these activities becomes an excellent language-teaching time. Washing the car or working with tools provides additional excellent opportunities to foster speech and language learning. But parents need encouragement, effective examples, and thoughtful reminders if they are to make their child's language-learning environment stimulating.

Characteristics That Can Interfere with Speech Development

Structural Abnormalities.   Craniofacial deformities of any kind interfere with speech skill development. A child who cannot imitate and reproduce speech sounds will be less skilled in using language as well. For example, if deviant oral structure precludes placing tongue and teeth in the correct position to pronounce /s/, as in *boys* and *shoes*, the child cannot use the language rule "Add /s/ to form plurals."

Hypernasality, often associated with cleft palate, also interferes with speech production. Only three English speech sounds are intended to have this characteristic nasal quality: /m/, /n/, and /ng/ (as in *ring*). When most of the sounds of speech are nasalized, listeners usually characterize the speech as unintelligible. Conditions other than cleft palate can cause this. If a child seems to be "talking through the nose," the causes should be discovered and corrected.

Motor Problems.   Normal control of the muscles necessary for speech is needed for correct articulation. This develops so spontaneously in most children

that its significance is not recognized. Playing the violin skillfully is far less complex than pronouncing a word correctly. (To appreciate this muscular achievement, shut your lips lightly and focus on the movements of your tongue as you say, "Look at Larry's new green coat.")

Cerebral palsy interferes with muscle coordination. It also can create problems with respiration, which, in turn, affects speech. Injury, other physical problems, and certain drugs also interfere. Teachers will want to work closely with therapists when children have problems of this kind. For some children with severe motor disorders, some form of augmentative technology will be critically important to ensure development of communication skills.

Voice Disorders.   The effect of a cleft palate and/or lip may result in a nasal voice even if a surgical repair was accomplished early in the child's life. Children who have frequent respiratory infections may lack nasal resonance. Children who scream a lot may be hoarse. All these problems deserve skillful attention and remediation from professionals.

Stuttering.   Stuttering is a disturbance in the rhythmic flow of speech. When a speaker repeats a sound or syllable, prolongs it more than is typical of other speakers, or blocks (completely halts the speech flow), many people describe this as stuttering. Some individuals who stutter develop patterns of grimaces and gestures in an effort to avoid disturbing their flow of speech. These are sometimes referred to as *secondary characteristics*, that is, motor behaviors that become conditioned responses over time.

Stuttering usually begins between the ages of 2 and 4 years, although it may happen later. All speakers normally repeat, hesitate, and sometimes prolong sounds. This is especially true of young children. They are in a hurry. Finding the right word is difficult for little children, and this is reason enough for them to hesitate and repeat. These behaviors are common and are referred to as *developmental disfluency* (Hulit, 2004).

Some speech-language pathologists believe that calling attention to the perfectly normal disfluencies

of young children may result in more repetitions. Telling children to slow down or to think before they speak may cause them to stumble even more. Then parents become even more anxious, and so do their children. Guitar (1998) provides guidelines for dealing with children's stuttering.

NURTURING SPEECH, LANGUAGE, AND CONCEPTUAL SKILLS

There is a large body of information available to the early childhood special education professional regarding ways of facilitating the development of communication skills in young children. Some of this information will be presented in the following sections.

The Important Role of Caregiver–Child Interaction

The importance of the early caregiving environment—and particularly caregivers' use of responsive communicative interactions—has been well established. Research (e.g., Landry, Smith, & Miller-Loncar, 1997; Mahoney & Perales, 2003) has clearly demonstrated the impact of certain kinds of caregiver–infant and caregiver–child interactions on the development of young children. For example, a longitudinal study reported by Coates and Lewis (1984) demonstrated a positive relationship between mothers' interaction behaviors with their infants at 3 months and the children's school achievement and cognitive skills at 6 years of age. As many studies of this type have found, maternal responsivity appeared to be the strongest factor in the development of the young child.

Particularly important to the development of children's language skills are caregivers' uses of certain communicative interactions, which will be described in the following section. For more detailed understanding of this important area, students are referred to descriptions of several intervention programs designed to assist parents of children with special needs in developing and refining these skills (e.g., Klein & Briggs, 1987; Klein, Chen, & Haney, 2000; Mahoney & Perales, 2003; Weitzman & Greenberg 2002).

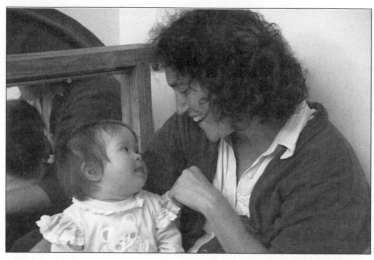

Photo by Scott Cunningham/Merrill

Figure 8-2 gives examples of the kinds of interactions often targeted for infants and very young children.

The caregiver–child interactions described in the following sections are equally important for teachers and early interventionists in other disciplines. Early interventionists must not only develop the ability to recognize and encourage the use of interactive behaviors between parents and children but also, just as important, demonstrate and consistently use these strategies themselves.

Encouraging Conversation.   The early literature on mother–infant interaction described several specific strategies mothers use to encourage and maintain a dialogue with their infants. These include behaviors such as (a) use of rising intonation "yes/no" questions (e.g., "Wanna eat now?" or "Is baby tired?"), (b) pausing expectantly after each utterance to give the infant a turn, and (c) imitating the infant's vocalizations or responding to the infant's vocalizations as though they were intelligible (e.g., "Oh yeah?," "Is that right?," "No kidding!," and so on). Cross (1984) referred to this communicative style as "motherese."

Responding Contingently to Child's Behavior.
Maternal responsivity has frequently been found to be a robust correlate of later development in young children. Particularly important for the early childhood special educator is a sensitivity to all communicative attempts on the part of the child. For example, a child with severe disabilities who is nonverbal and rarely initiates interaction or attempts to get attention should receive *immediate* attention for any communicative effort, including gestures, changes in body position, vocalizations, and so forth. The child who communicates only by crying or pulling the teacher's sleeve should receive an enthusiastic response for making a grunting sound or pointing to get a drink of juice because this is a new behavior for the child. MacDonald (1989) described an interaction strategy called "upping the ante," in which the teacher or parent encourages a slightly more sophisticated response than the one the child typically uses.

Modifying Interaction in Response to Negative Cues.   Another important aspect of maternal responsivity, albeit a more subtle one, is the ability to change or terminate interaction with an infant in response to such cues as gaze aversion, changes in body tension and facial expression, or lack of response from the infant. Interventionists, too, must be able to read children's cues of disinterest, overload, or distraction. Continuing a particular cue or

OBSERVATION OF COMMUNICATIVE INTERACTION (OCI)
Mother-Infant Communication Project

Infant's Name _____ Birthdate _____ Age _____

Setting _____ Date _____ Adjusted Age _____

Observer _____

	Rarely/Never	Sometimes	Often	Optimally	Not Applicable
1. Provides appropriate tactile and kinesthetic stimulation (e.g., gently strokes, pats, caresses, cuddles, rocks baby).	1	2	3	4	N/A
2. Displays pleasure while interacting with infant.	1	2	3	4	N/A
3. Responds to child's distress.	1	2	3	4	N/A

    a. changes verbalization.
    b. changes infant's position, attempts to distract.
    c. provides positive physical stimuli (e.g., patting, rocking).
    d. avoids negative physical or verbal response.

	Rarely/Never	Sometimes	Often	Optimally	Not Applicable
4. Positions self and infant so eye-to-eye contact is possible (e.g., facing and 7 to 12 inches away).	1	2	3	4	N/A

    a. attempts to make eye contact.
    b. reciprocates eye gaze.

	Rarely/Never	Sometimes	Often	Optimally	Not Applicable
5. Smiles contingently at infant.	1	2	3	4	N/A

    a. consistently returns infant's smile.
    b. smiles in response to infant vocalization.

	Rarely/Never	Sometimes	Often	Optimally	Not Applicable
6. Varies prosodic features.	1	2	3	4	N/A

    a. uses higher pitch.
    b. talks more slowly.
    c. exaggerates "intonation."

Figure 8–2   Communicative interaction checklist
Source: From "Facilitating Mother–Infant Communicative Interaction in Mothers of High-Risk Infants," by M. D. Klein and M. H. Briggs, 1987, *Journal of Childhood Communication Disorders, 10*(2), pp. 95–106. Reprinted with permission.

prompt, such as "Show me the doll," when the child is clearly not attending to the stimulus is wasted effort and may eventually teach the child to "tune out" as a generalized strategy to overwhelming or meaningless stimulation.

Using Communication to Teach Language and Concepts. Much has been written about the maternal language patterns that are typical of middle-class mothers as they interact with their young children. Some of these communicative interaction strategies appear to be correlated with later language development. Caregivers and professionals should use these interaction strategies in response to the infant's or toddler's interest and attention as demonstrated by the child's eye gaze, gestures, and vocalization or words (Meadows, Elias, & Bain, 2000). These interaction strategies include the following:

1. *Commenting* on what the infant or child appears to be attending to (e.g., "Oh, you hear that doggie barking, don't you?"), also referred to as "parallel talk" (McCormick et al., 2003).

2. *Repeating and recasting* one's own words or phrases in different ways in order to emphasize

7. **Encourages "conversation."**   1   2   3   4   N/A

    a. uses rising intonation questions.
    b. waits after saying something to infant, and looks expectantly, providing infant turn.
    c. imitates child's vocalizations, or words.
    d. repeats own sounds, words, or phrases (e.g., "Here's the bottle. Bottle.").
    e. answers when infant vocalizes (e.g., "Oh, yeah?" , "Okay.", "Is that right?").

8. **Responds contingently to infant's behavior.**   1   2   3   4   N/A

    a. touches or responds with facial expression within 2 seconds after infant vocalization.
    b. vocalizes within 2 seconds after infant moves arms, head, etc.
    c. vocalizes within 2 seconds after infant vocalization.
    d. stops own activity or verbalization in response to interruption by infant's vocalization or movement.
    e. responds vocally to infant from a distance of more than 2 feet.

9. **Modifies interaction in response to negative cues from infant.**   1   2   3   4   N/A

    a. changes activity.
    b. reduces intensity of interaction.
    c. terminates attempts at interaction.

10. **Uses communication to teach language and concepts.**   1   2   3   4   N/A

    a. interprets infant's behavior appropriately (e.g., "Oh, you're hungry, aren't you.").
    b. re-casts own sentences (e.g., adult says, "Shall we turn on the light? Turn on the light. There's the light.").
    c. comments on infant's attention to immediate environment and *labels* objects (e.g., "You see the doggie? That's the doggie.").
    d. matches infant's vocalization, or word with slightly more elaborate language (e.g., baby says, "Ball," and adult says, "That's a ball." or "Big ball.").

important words (e.g.,"*Doggie*. That's the *doggie*. Hear the *doggie*? *Doggie*!").

3. *Matching* the child's vocalization or word with a slightly more elaborated response, thereby interpreting the utterance (e.g., the child says "buh" and the teacher says "Bottle, yes bottle"). This is also referred to as "progressive matching" by MacDonald (1989).

4. *Expanding* the utterance syntactically (e.g., the child says "cookie" and the teacher says "That is a cookie") or *semantically extending*, that is, adding meaning to the utterance (e.g., the child says "doggie" and the teacher says "Yeah, that's a *big* doggie!").

CLASSROOM STRATEGIES THAT FACILITATE COMMUNICATION

The social interaction theory of language development and knowledge about the stages and major achievements of language acquisition generate a useful approach to early language intervention. Before describing some of the strategies suggested by this approach, let us consider three important principles related to the development of communication skills:

1. *Interaction* is the first key to the development of communication skills. Infants and young children must learn to experience the pleasures of turn taking and reciprocal interaction.

2. True communication skills must be *functional* for the child. The ability to provide rote answers to stereotyped questions is not really communication. Infants and children must have opportunities to *initiate* communication. Observation of early childhood special education classrooms reveals that children are too often placed in a respondent role; that is, they are taught to respond to specific prompts and cues provided by the teacher. Communication used only in this way cannot be a learning tool for children. They must be encouraged to initiate interaction, to use language and other communicative behaviors to appropriately manipulate the environment, to ask questions and obtain information, and to solve problems. Children must learn to use language for purposes other than simply answering questions.

3. Language develops best in a *responsive environment*. The teacher who is most sensitive to the infant or child's communicative intentions will be most successful in facilitating language development. Many specific ways of responding are suggested by the literature describing motherese (the speech and language characteristics typical of mothers' communication with infants and young children described earlier).

Beginning Where the Child Is

An understanding of appropriate practices in nurturing receptive and expressive language suggests that teachers should attend to children's levels of development. Thus, if 4-year-old Sean does not yet try to tell adults anything, one thing to nurture is the "telling" of things as very young children do. If Susie cannot produce any speech sounds distinctly, she may need to be encouraged in simple vocal play and babbling. If Tommy does not try to ask for things, perhaps he should be expected to make some kind of sound before he is given what he wants.

Developmental scales of speech and language can be checked to determine whether a child has a developmental lag. Speech and language pathologists can assist as questions arise. Table 8–1 can be used as a basis for constructing a checklist for evaluating language

development. However, instructional objectives for language development should also be based on the *functional needs of the child*. They should not be limited to items on a developmental checklist.

Conversing with the Child

Conversations about familiar things that interest young children are a critical tool in helping them to learn communication skills. Children's first verbal labels or names are of objects, people, events, and actions they know and can associate with. Unless they are truly interested and can make associations, they will not attend, and attention is a prerequisite for learning anything.

Choosing What to Talk About

Communication skills develop around objects and events that interest children. For the really reluctant talker, food can be a good place to begin. For example, while sitting around a table with other children, the teacher can cut an apple into pieces and describe such things as the name of the fruit; the smooth, red skin and small, black seeds; the sharp knife; and how the apple will taste. Pragmatic skills also can be nurtured in this "social situation" (e.g., turn taking and use of polite requests).

Any game, dollhouse, play kitchen, or toy barn can be used as the conversational focal point. At first, the teacher should join the children in an ongoing activity with toys they have chosen, following the children's lead. Later, when rapport has been well established, the teacher may choose the activity. Introducing variety is important, but at first, joining into the children's choice of things to do is best. The following are general suggestions for engaging in conversations with young children:

1. Listen attentively. Even if the sounds children are making are unintelligible, look at them with interest and listen.

2. Speak clearly and not too fast, especially if the child has very limited language ability. Use natural or slightly exaggerated intonation patterns (prosodic features), emphasizing key words.

3. Avoid long and complex sentence structures. Recast words and phrases (e.g., "Where's your *ball*? Oh, there it is! There's your ball.").

4. Avoid one-sided conversations that usually result from the adult asking too many questions. Questions asked one after another do not constitute conversation. In fact, too many questions result in no conversation. But *good* questions can facilitate learning.

5. Talk mostly about the here and now. Make sure references to the past and future are very clear and contrast them with references to the present. For example, "Today it's raining, but *yesterday* it was sunny," or, "*After* we finish our snack, *then* we will go outside."

6. Use a calm and pleasant tone of voice. Bring fun to every conversation.

7. Use words the children are interested in because they can see or understand what they refer to as you talk. Tell them the names of actions as well as things.

8. Pause between sentences. Don't be in a hurry.

9. As the children understand and speak more, gradually make your sentences longer and use a larger vocabulary.

10. For children who have mastered simple sentence structure, model complex relationships through more complex sentence structure. For example, "Oh look, now the sand sticks together *because* we mixed it with water" or "*If* we put one more block on top, *then* what will happen?"

Listening

Adults should listen to children with great interest. This is especially true if the children have not developed speech and language skills at the expected rate. Communication on their part requires a great deal of effort. The reward most likely to accelerate the growth of speech and language is an interested listener. Presenting an alert facial expression, remaining quiet, and giving the child your patient, undivided attention are important strategies.

Developing Pragmatic Skills

Pragmatic skills are the social skills of language. Taking turns during a conversation, refraining from interrupting, and saying the appropriate thing cannot be learned in isolation. Children require social experiences and are dependent on social interaction. By modeling correct pragmatic skills, adults can direct attention to courteous and effective ways of conversing. Also, role-playing is a very useful strategy for helping children develop such pragmatic skills as use of polite forms, initiating conversations, and topic extension.

Expanding Skills

Ideally, children's language skills are expanded through increasingly complex conversations using more complex sentences and vocabulary. MacDonald (1989) referred to this strategy as "progressive matching" (p. 174). Exhibits 8–1 and 8–2 suggest ways to promote children's syntactic development.

FACILITATING COMMUNICATION IN CHILDREN WITH SEVERE AND MULTIPLE DISABILITIES

Children with severe and multiple disabilities demonstrate very few communicative behaviors. Many of these children may never develop the use of intelligible speech. Some may never be able to use any formal symbolic system of communication such as signing or graphic symbols. Nevertheless, these children *can* learn to communicate using nonverbal, nonspeech systems of communication.

In planning communication instruction programs for children with multiple disabilities, it is perhaps easiest to consider two types of children. The first group includes those who have the cognitive skills necessary for the development of language (i.e., some formal system of symbolic communication) but do not have the fine *oral-motor skills* required for the production of intelligible speech. The largest number of children in this group would be those with severe forms of cerebral palsy but without mental retardation.

Exhibit 8–1

Some Ways to Promote Syntactic Development

Tony uses many two- and some three-word sentences, and he loves to talk. Both his parents and his teachers have many conversations with him throughout the day. They *listen* to him with obvious interest. Some of the time they *expand* what he has said. When he says "Falled down," they may say "Your big tower fell down. That was noisy." They do this in a way that suggests "You're right, it fell down," never in a manner that indicates "Now, say it the right way."

As the adults do things while Tony is present, they may use *self-talk*. They talk about what they are feeling and doing—as they do it. "Time for supper. I'll take the plates to the table now. The meat and the green beans are almost ready, and it's time to make the salad. I'll cut the carrots first." Of course, the speaker pauses after each sentence and *listens* if Tony starts to say something.

Sometimes his teachers and parents use *parallel talk*. They talk about what Tony is doing. "Tony, you put the toys on the shelf just the right way. I like the way you are picking up those blocks. You put the biggest ones on the bottom."

When Tony says something incorrectly, they rarely correct him directly, but they do use *corrective echoing*. If he says "Her throwed dat ball," they might say "You saw Susie. *She threw* the ball." And although they may exaggerate the "she" and the "threw" slightly by saying them slowly, they are really just confirming that they understood.

Exhibit 8–2

Arrival Time to Build Language Skills

The Scene: Children are arriving, and the teacher and aide are greeting them individually.

The Teaching Strategy: A warm greeting and a brief conversation with each child are designed to make each child feel welcome and expected. Modeling, expanding what the children say, and listening to them are some of the strategies to be used to promote communication skills. Direct correction of articulation errors or grammatical mistakes will be avoided.

Ms. McLynn: Good morning, Sally. I am so glad you brought your doll. Do you want to take her coat off?

Sally: Me do. Coat dirty.

Ms. McLynn: I know you can take her coat off. Her coat *is* dirty, isn't it? We can brush the dirt off.

Sally: Wed shoes. (Pointing to her new shoes)

Ms. McLynn: I like those new red shoes. They are shiny.

Timmy: Hey, looka dat! Dat nose wiggles.

Ms. McLynn: I see our rabbit. She *is* wiggling her nose!

Nancy: Ms. McLynn, my mommie said that she couldn't come today but she will call you afterwhile. She has to go to the supermarket 'cause we're having company tonight.

Ms. McLynn: I'm glad you told me she couldn't come. Would you like to pretend that you are at the supermarket too? We have lots of things in our store too.

The second group of children are those with disabilities that produce a poor prognosis for the development of any formal symbolic system. The group includes children with severe and profound cognitive disabilities and some who demonstrate multiple sensory impairments (e.g., a child with deafness, severe visual and motor impairments, and moderate mental retardation). For such children, the goals of intelligible speech production and any formal symbolic system of communication, such as sign language or graphic symbols, may be unrealistic. However, they *can* learn to use specific behaviors in functional ways to communicate basic wants, needs, and feelings.

A classroom teacher who is unfamiliar with children who have severe multiple disabilities is often initially overwhelmed with the apparent difficulty of working with such children, especially in the area of communication skills. Again, although space does not permit a thorough description of intervention

strategies for this group of children, several keys to facilitating communicative behaviors are presented in the following sections. In addition, the strategies included in Exhibits 8-2 and 8-3 can encourage communication in *all* children regardless of the nature of their disabling conditions.

Verbal Input Strategies: Communicating with Children with Severe Disabilities

Respond to Child's Behavioral Cues. Many of the input strategies discussed earlier are also appropriate for children with severe disabilities. When an infant or young child demonstrates a low response rate (i.e., just doesn't seem to "do much"), the teacher's immediate and consistent *response* to the child's cues of interest and attention—and to any attempts to communicate—becomes crucial. Teachers must be more vigilant with such children and be ready to respond with appropriate communicative input (for strategies for working with infants and young children who have limited intentionality and multiple disabilities, see Klein et al., 2000).

For example, let us consider a child who has severe motor and visual impairments. The child's voluntary behavioral repertoire consists of moving his head from side to side and a few vocalizations. He does not appear to understand any verbal input, but he does respond to sudden loud sounds, to the sound of his mother's voice, and occasionally to food odors as lunch is prepared. The teacher must be very alert to cues from this child that he is recognizing and processing some incoming stimulus. For example, if another child in the classroom drops her tray on the floor, the child with severe disabilities is startled and begins moving his head from side to side. The teacher should provide some verbal input appropriate to the situation and its meaning to the child. In this case, the teacher might say something like, "Oh oh! That was loud, wasn't it? That was a loud crash! Maria dropped her tray." In this way, the teacher comments on the most salient aspect of the situation (in this case the sound because the child cannot see well), repeats his comment in a slightly different way, and semantically

extends his own comment by adding information about the source of the sound.

Use Repetition and Predictable Schedules. Repetition, redundancy, and responsiveness are important input strategies in working with infants or young children with severe disabilities. Certain key words and phrases should be used repeatedly to make significant the events of the day. Certain verbal cues should always be associated with certain actions and events. In this way the teacher establishes **verbal routines,** which are important as children begin to learn to decode language. Classroom strategies that build on the child's focus of attention can establish "joint action routines" in which the adult engages jointly in an action with the child while associating key words and phrases with the activity.

For example, the greeting activities that begin the classroom day should include parts that are always repeated. The transition from music time to lunch should always be accompanied by many predictable cues, such as "OK, who knows what time it is now? It's lunchtime. It's time to eat," followed by a sequence of predictable events (e.g., chairs moved, bibs put on, table set, and so on). After lunch, the input might be, "OK, we're all done. All done eating. Let's go outside. We'll play outside." Tables are cleaned, chairs pushed in, coats put on, and so forth, while appropriate verbal input strategies accompany these key events.

Techniques for Teaching Communicative Behaviors: "Output Strategies"

Careful verbal input (in response to cues provided by the child that indicate interest and attention or attempts to communicate) is an important key to facilitating communication development. However, for children with severe disabilities, the adult's use of input strategies is not enough. For these children, it is also necessary for caregivers and teachers to create the opportunities and the need to communicate. Some of the strategies for doing so are described as follows.

mere
objec
respc
or wi
effec

Ide
Be

Whe
tive
the t
can
seve
that
eye
beh

dete
use

1.

Using Structured "Milieu Teaching" Techniques to Shape Specific Communicative Behavior

Milieu teaching is a term used to refer to a variety of semistructured behavioral techniques that are used in the natural environment to teach specific communication skills. Milieu techniques include three basic elements: (a) arranging the environment in ways that increase the need for a particular type of communicative behavior, (b) identifying specific target behaviors, and (c) applying specific teaching procedures (McCormick et al., 2003b). Some authors have described sequential communication training steps to be used in the natural environment, such as "*mand*-model technique" (Halle, Alpert, & Anderson, 1984), "incidental teaching" (Warren & Kaiser, 1986), "time-delay procedure" (Peck, 1985), and, more recently, "pivotal response treatment" (Koegel & Koegel, 2006). Detailed descriptions of several of these procedures can be found in Beukelman and Mirenda (1998). Appendix H describes a common sequence of steps used in milieu approaches.

Although the strategies and approaches described in this section have been most frequently reported in association with children with more severe disabilities, they can be equally effective with children who have mild to moderate disabilities. Some specific strategies for encouraging young children to talk are given in Exhibit 8–3.

Facilitating Social Communication Between Children with and Without Special Needs

In order for successful social interaction to take place between a child and his peers, two components must be in place. First, the child must be able to *respond* to a peer's initiation in an appropriate way. Second, the child must be able to *initiate* interaction in a way that is likely to obtain a positive response.

Some children with disabilities may lack these skills, and they may need direct instruction related to these important social communication behaviors.

Familiar procedures of modeling, prompting, and reinforcement are used. The teacher first talks to a small group of children about appropriate play behaviors, demonstrating "good" and "bad" social behaviors and familiarizing the children with classroom behaviors related to playing together cooperatively. Both children with disabilities and those without can then be taught to initiate (e.g., "Jose, can you ask Mary to help you with the tower?") and respond appropriately (e.g., "Jose, Mark is sharing his cookie with you. Tell him 'Thank you.'") in actual play situations. Initially, children's appropriate social behavior may need to be reinforced externally by the teacher (e.g., saying, "Jose, that was very nice of you to say 'Thank you' to Mark," giving the child a sticker for being polite and so on). However, these contrived reinforcers should be discontinued as quickly as possible. The goal ultimately is for the natural consequence of the child's appropriate interaction and communication to be its own reward. It should also be noted that it is equally—if not more—important to train typical peers how to initiate and sustain communication with their classmates who may have social communication needs in ways that will encourage genuine communication and friendship.

AUGMENTATIVE AND ALTERNATIVE COMMUNICATION SYSTEMS

For many children with severe and multiple disabilities, the development of an **augmentative and alternative communication system** (AAC) will be necessary (Beukelman & Mirenda, 1998). Such a system involves the use of nonspeech communication strategies. Examples of these include signing, pointing to pictures, use of electronic communication boards and computerized speech synthesizers, and so on. The system can "augment" existing communication skills and behaviors or may provide an "alternative" to speech production for a child who has no means of communication.

In recent years, AAC has come to be associated in many people's minds with high-technology equipment such as adapted computer keyboards that can be activated by a touch or laser beam to produce a communication printout or synthesized speech.

(For a list of resources related to AAC technology, see Appendix I.)

It is important to understand, however, that AAC can include both high-tech and low-tech systems and is often multimodal. Low-tech systems are nonelectronic. They include strategies such as simple adaptations of manual signs, use of photos or black-and-white line drawings arranged on a communication board or in a communication book, and letters of the alphabet printed on a card.

Particularly for very young children, it is important to begin training with very simple, low-tech strategies and devices. It is easy for the early intervention professional to be somewhat in awe of the many computer hardware components and the hundreds of software programs designed for young children. However, for many children, low-tech strategies and devices are more appropriate for their individual needs. Even for those children who will eventually benefit from computerized systems, early training in simple strategies such as touching pictures or directed eye gaze will make the transition to high-tech devices much easier. Early interventionists should not wait to see whether efforts to teach speech to the child with multiple disabilities are going to be successful before beginning augmentative communication instruction. Teaching nonspeech communication strategies does not appear to interfere with speech development. Such instruction may actually facilitate vocalization and speech development. In addition, many of the skills necessary for successful use of an AAC system are also beneficial for children who do not have severe disabilities, for example, use of pictures or line drawings as representations of real objects and activities and use of computer keyboards.

The development of an AAC system for a particular child requires a team approach. Ideally, such a team might include the parent, early childhood educator, occupational or physical therapist, and speech-language therapist. In addition, if high-tech devices are being used, a technician would also be an important member of the team.

Although space does not allow a thorough discussion of the strategies and procedures for developing an AAC system, the following briefly outlines the sequence of necessary steps.

Steps in Developing an AAC System

1. *Determine the child's communicative needs and opportunities.* Together with the child's family, it is important to determine in what situations and for what purposes the child currently needs or attempts to communicate. (If the child does not *attempt* to communicate, then the primary goal becomes creating motivation necessary to encourage communicative attempts.)

2. *Determine the child's current communicative repertoire.* If the child does attempt to communicate, how does he do it? What does the child do to express wants and needs, express emotions, or share information? What movements can the child voluntarily control? Does he use his eyes, vocalizations, or gestures, such as reaching or pointing?

3. *What are the barriers to successful communication?* Determine why the communication is not successful. Are vocalizations unintelligible? Are hand gestures poorly controlled? Is the child trying to refer to things that are not immediately present, such as something that happened yesterday?

4. *Determine the best "indicating response" to be used.* What behavior does the child have the best control of? For many children with severe physical disabilities, eye gaze may be the only reliable voluntary movement. Other children may be able to touch or point to a picture successfully. Some children may not be able to use their hands but may have sufficient head control to point with a head stick (pointer) mounted on a headband or may be able to move the head to activate a switch.

5. *Determine the best "symbol system."* The symbol system will depend largely on the child's cognitive level. Some children will need to begin with the actual object, moving step-by-step to more abstract representations, whereas others may be able to begin immediately with black-and-white line drawings of very concrete objects.

6. *Design the "display."* Once the indicating response and the symbol system have been determined, it is then necessary to determine how the symbols will be displayed. For the child who cannot walk but who can point to pictures, a common display would be a

communication board mounted on a wheelchair. For a child who uses eye gaze as an indicating response, the most common display would be pictures arranged on a clear Plexiglas frame called an "E-tran" board. For a child who is mobile, the display might be a picture book or laminated cards on a large ring.

7. *Design training steps.* Teaching a child to use an augmentative communication system requires careful planning of training steps. Exhibit 8–4 is an example of the training steps used to teach a young child with cerebral palsy to use directed eye gaze. More detailed information on the development of AAC systems can be found in Beukelman and Mirenda (1998) and Light and Drager (2002).

Classroom Strategies That Facilitate Augmentative Communication Skills

Several activities that facilitate the development of low-tech augmentative communication skills can be built into the everyday activities of an early childhood program. These activities can be both fun and meaningful for all children, not just for the child with severe disabilities. Examples of these include the following:

1. *Use of switch-operated toys.* Battery-operated toys can be included among the play materials in the classroom. The switches can be adapted to be more easily operated by children with severe motor impairments. Cause-and-effect toys can be adapted with pressure switches, large toggle switches, heat-sensitive touch switches, and so on. Such switches are intriguing to all children and facilitate the learning of cause-and-effect relationships. In addition, for the child with severe motor impairments, they provide the motivation and opportunity to practice the fine motor movements required for eventually activating various communication devices.

2. *Use of computers.* It is important for all children to become comfortable with keyboard operations and monitor displays. Hundreds of software games and activities are available that are interesting and appropriate for very young children. These should be included in the early childhood classroom, and every effort should be made to familiarize the child with disabilities with the operation of the keyboard and the relationship to the monitor display. This is a particularly good activity for peer interaction and modeling.

3. *Use of picture representations and symbols.* An important skill in the development of a successful AAC system is the ability to recognize that pictures and abstract symbols have representational meaning— that they stand for some real object or activity. Many young children, with and without disabilities, have not acquired this understanding. Obviously, this symbolic representation skill is necessary for the eventual development of literacy (see chapter 9) as well as for the development of AAC systems.

Thus, whenever possible, functional use of pictures and symbols (including printed words) should be demonstrated in the classroom:

- Black-and-white line drawings can be pasted on cupboard doors and boxes indicating their contents.
- Bathroom signs should be similar to the adult bathroom sign.
- Lunch menus should be posted and referred to.
- Children can choose a favorite toy by choosing the appropriate laminated card or by pointing to a picture on a grid that corresponds to that toy.

Visual discrimination and matching skills can also be encouraged by use of picture matching games and name recognition. (For more cognitively advanced children, shapes and letters could be matched.)

4. *Conversation starter strategies.* Many communication training strategies rely on teaching the child to request something. While this is an important starting point, it is equally important to find ways to assist children who cannot speak in sharing information and experiences with others. These strategies are very important because it is easy to overemphasize the communicative function of requesting. This is because it is relatively easy to teach a child to request wants and needs; thus, this is the communicative

Exhibit 8–4

Training Angie to Use an AAC System

Angie was a 2½-year-old girl with spastic cerebral palsy. There was severe involvement of all parts of her body. She was unable to sit unsupported, reach or grasp, or bring her hands to midline. She also had some difficulty with head control. She was unable to produce speech sounds, though she occasionally vocalized. One day her mother mentioned to her early interventionist that Angie had recently begun to stare intently at things she wanted. Together, the early interventionist and parent, in consultation with a speech-language specialist trained in augmentative methodology, planned the following intervention.

1. *Carefully describe current communicative behavior.* In Angie's case the most reliable communicative behavior was "directed eye gaze."

2. *Identify high-preference and low-preference objects and activities.* Angie loved to eat, so favorite foods were identified as high-preference items, especially strawberry yogurt, ice cream, and orange juice. One low-preference activity identified was having her face washed, which she had always hated.

3. *Establish "indicating response."* The logical indicating response in Angie's case, since she really had no other consistent communicative behavior, was the use of eye gaze. Angie's mom began to give her lots of practice using her eyes to track her glass or spoon before giving her a bite or drink.

4. *Offer choice of a high- or low-preference item.* Angie's mom or her teacher would hold up two items: a glass of juice and a washcloth, saying, "Which would you like Angie: juice or washcloth?" Whichever item she looked at for more than a fleeting glance was the one she received. Initially, she would occasionally stare at the washcloth. She immediately got her faced washed a bit, even though her mom knew this was not what she really wanted. This step was necessary to help her understand the communicative nature of her eye gaze. Quickly she learned to scan the items quickly to look for the item she wanted and then fix her gaze on that item.

5. *Offer choice of two high-preference items.* The next step was to offer her a choice of two high-preference items. This represents a true communication situation. Her communication partner really does not know which of two foods she wants. Her eye gaze communication puts her in control of the choice.

6. *Pair pictures with items.* Next, the objects, such as a glass of juice and a bowl of yogurt, were paired with pictures. In Angie's case, black-and-white line drawings of a glass and a bowl were used. (Photos of the objects could have been used, but Angie's mom felt she could learn to recognize the line drawings easily, and they were easier to produce than photos by simply using a magic marker on a 3-by-5-inch index card.) The name of the item was printed at the bottom of the picture.

7. *Fade objects.* Gradually, the items were removed from sight, and only the pictures were presented. Angie learned that the picture *represented* the object. This was the beginning of Angie's comprehension of symbols, which is an important cognitive skill for the use of an augmentative communication system.

8. *Reduce picture size and design display.* Now the pictures could be made somewhat smaller and placed on a see-through Plexiglas board that could be attached to her wheelchair. The teacher and occupational therapist experimented to determine the best position of the board and how far apart the pictures needed to be to reliably tell what Angie was looking at.

9. *Add vocabulary; expand system.* From this point on, it was a fairly easy matter to add new pictures representing key vocabulary (e.g., "bathroom" and "TV") and whole sentences (e.g., "What's your name?"). Eventually, Angie developed better control of her hands and arms and learned to activate an adapted keyboard to produce synthesized speech.

function that is most often emphasized in work with children with severe disabilities. However, it is critically important for young children to have ways of sharing information with others. Beukelman and Mirenda (1998) describe three conversation starter strategies:

> *Collections* Children can be encouraged to collect things of interest to them, such as bracelets, toy cars, pictures of friends, and so on. Both teachers and peers can be encouraged to notice and comment on the items in the collection as well as new additions to the collection. Again, this is an activity that all children can enjoy. For the nonspeaking child, it provides an excellent communicative context in which others can easily participate.
>
> *Remnant Books* Remnant books provide a way for the nonspeaking child to share past experiences. For example, a child may save various scraps and reminders—"remnants"—from a weekend trip to the zoo. The teacher and parent should help the child construct the book. The remnant book might have a postcard with a picture of the zoo, a ticket stub with the price of admission, a hamburger wrapper from lunch, photos of the most interesting animals, and a parking ticket next to a drawing of the family car. The book should be easily accessible so that the experiences can be shared at any appropriate time.
>
> *Topic Setter Cards* For children who have difficulty initiating conversations, topic setter cards may be useful. A simple line drawing or symbol that has meaning for the child is drawn on an index card. On the back of the card facing the prospective communication partner there is a message. For example, "What's your favorite TV show? Mine is *Power Rangers*."

Using the Picture Exchange Communication System

In recent years, a simple low-tech system of picture communication has become popular, particularly for developing early communication skills of children with autism who do not have functional oral language. The Picture Exchange Communication System (PECS; Frost & Bondy, 1994) uses behavioral techniques to teach the child to use pictures to obtain desired objects or activities or to make comments. The system begins with careful observation of the child in order to determine high-preference objects and activities. Whenever a highly motivating activity or object is identified, a photo or black-and-white line drawing is produced and placed on a card or in a binder with Velcro.

Unlike more typical AAC picture systems, the child does not *point*. Rather, the child is taught to remove a Velcro-attached picture from a book or binder, approach another person, and hand the picture to the person. The person receiving the picture responds with appropriate language and gives the child the desired object or activity. Careful physical prompts (not verbal prompts) are provided until the child learns the following sequence:

1. Finding the correct picture
2. Removing the picture
3. Approaching the adult
4. Handing the adult the picture
5. Waiting for the adult's response/compliance with the request

A significant advantage of the PECS system is that it requires *social interaction* for the communication to be successful. Eventually, the child may learn to combine sequences of pictures to represent word combinations and sentences.

WORKING WITH CHILDREN WITH HEARING LOSS

A preschool teacher whose class includes a child with a hearing loss must work in close collaboration not only with the child's parents but also with specialists trained to work with infants and young children with hearing loss. These specialists may include an audiologist (if the child wears a hearing aid), a speech pathologist trained to work with children with hearing loss, or a teacher of the deaf.

A very important decision for every family of a child with a significant hearing loss will be the selection of a primary communication modality: speech or manual sign (or a combination of both).

The signing, or "manual communication," approach is strongly endorsed by members of the deaf community as well as by many teachers of students with hearing impairments who believe that manual communication is the most easily and naturally acquired language for children with significant hearing losses. While the early introduction of signs enables the child who is deaf to achieve major *language* milestones without delay, the process of teaching *speech* skills is often slow and tedious (Hunt & Marshall, 1994).

There are several different systems of sign language. American Sign Language (ASL) is the system preferred by most members of the deaf community. ASL is a language in its own right. Its structure does not correspond to the structure of English: rules of word order are different, and there are no signs for grammatical markers, such as *-ing* or *-ed*. Because of the belief that ASL does not facilitate the learning of spoken English and literacy skills, other sign systems have been developed that more closely match the grammar and vocabulary of the English language. These systems can be signed simultaneously with speech. Examples of such systems (referred to as "manually coded English") are Signing Essential English (SEE I) and Signing Exact English (SEE II). Another interesting system is called "cued speech." This system manually supplements speech production through the use of hand signs made near the mouth; these signs provide supplementary information about the vowels and consonants being spoken (Hage & Leybaert, 2006).

Proponents of the oral approach believe that the individual with a hearing loss must be given the skills to function comfortably in a hearing world. Approaches that emphasize speech (sometimes referred to as "oral" or "oral English" approaches) stress the importance of teaching the child with a hearing loss to produce intelligible speech and to be able to understand the spoken language of others. Within this approach, some emphasize the use of both auditory (via the use of a hearing aid to maximize the use of the child's residual hearing) and visual (e.g., lip-reading) input. Ling (1984) advocated a "unisensory" approach that relies only on auditory cues in an effort to maximize the child's ability to use auditory information and residual hearing. In recent years, technological improvement in the **cochlear implant** has greatly increased the use of oral approaches in promoting understanding and use of spoken English in children who have even severe to profound hearing loss.

The controversy over which approach is best has raged for over 200 years and continues to be an emotionally charged debate. Overall, the research

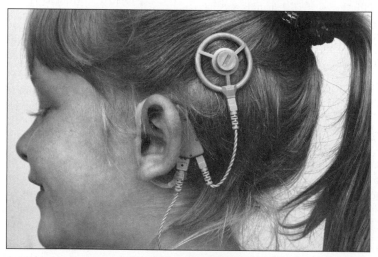

Photo by Michael Newman/PhotoEdit, Inc.

findings on efficacy are mixed. One consistent find-ing has been that for deaf children of deaf parents the early use of ASL clearly facilitates language develop-ment. Adults who are deaf and who identify strongly with the deaf community are proponents of the notion that children who are deaf should be viewed not as deficient or having a pathology but as mem-bers of a different culture that has its own language, traditions, values, and literature. Most individuals within the deaf community view ASL as their natural native language (Stokoe, 2001); spoken English is an optional second language.

The decision regarding the language modality to be used with the child who is deaf or hard of hearing must be made by the parents. If parents have already made this decision, it is the responsibility of the early childhood professional to understand and support that approach. In those cases where parents are in the process of trying to decide which approach is best, the early childhood professional can direct them to specialists who can give them accurate and reliable information about the characteristics of each approach.

Specific Strategies for Working with Children with Hearing Loss

The following are general suggestions for early inter-ventionists or early childhood professionals whose classes may include a young child with a hearing loss. Additional suggestions were included in chapter 5.

1. For children learning to sign, ask parents to teach you signs used at home; teach parents new signs introduced at school.

2. Teach signs for key words to *all* the children in the classroom.

3. Be sure that windows or other light sources are not behind you or shining into the eyes of the child. In order for the child to read lips or signs, the light must be on the speaker or signer, not in the child's eyes.

4. As often as possible, include adults and older children with hearing loss in your classroom. It is important for all young children (not just the child with a hearing loss) to observe role models who wear hearing aids and/or use sign language. Such an individual might sign and speak a story or song or simply assist with daily routines.

5. Include in your classroom books that include the signs for key words in the story. (Many such materials are available from Gallaudet University Press in Washington, DC.)

6. When the child does not appear to understand, repeat the sentence or say it in a slightly different way. Then add visual cues (e.g., gestures, facial expressions, or pointing to an object or picture).

Facilitating Comprehension of Speech

Use the following suggestions to facilitate the devel-opment of the child's ability to comprehend speech:

1. Don't talk too fast. You may need to slow your speech rate slightly, but be careful not to dis-tort the rate and rhythm of your normal speech pattern.

2. Do not exaggerate lip movements or pause after each word. This will not make lip-reading easier and provides inappropriate speech mod-els for the child. However, do avoid mumbling, chewing gum, or keeping your hands in front of your mouth.

3. Stand or sit still. It is hard for children to focus on a moving target!

4. Don't ask, "Do you understand?" Children will often say "yes" regardless. Rather, discover how much has been understood by asking questions or giving directions and observing the child's responses.

5. If the child does not appear to understand, repeat the sentence or say it a different way. Then add visual cues such as facial expression, gestures, or pointing to an object or picture.

6. Be aware of the child's potential for use of resid-ual hearing. Help the child learn the meaning of

various sounds in the environment by drawing his attention to them, for example, the sounds of musical instruments or the sound of a timer bell.

7. Perhaps most important, follow the suggestions made in this text for nurturing the development of speech and language in all children.

Hearing Aids

It is critical that the early childhood professional be aware of the child's potential for the development of **residual hearing.** Even children with the most severe losses usually have some hearing and with assistance can eventually learn to use this hearing. The *meaning* of sounds must be learned and does not happen automatically.

The past decade has produced unprecedented changes in both early identification of young children with hearing loss as well as major advances in biomedical technology (Ackley & Decker, 2006). In the past, the average age of diagnosis of a hearing loss was 24 months, well beyond a critical developmental period for learning to recognize sounds of speech. Increasingly, states are implementing comprehensive early hearing detection and intervention programs in which all newborns are routinely screened. In addition, major advances in technology have resulted in improved instrumentation for assessment, thus increasing the reliable identification of the incidence of as well as the type of hearing loss.

Equally significant has been improved amplification technology, such as digital, programmable circuitry resulting in major improvements in the performance of hearing aids. As a result, hearing aids can be programmed to match specific characteristics of the child's hearing loss and minimize the effects of background noise.

Ideally, the young child with a hearing loss will have been fitted with a hearing aid in infancy in order to maximize the use of residual hearing. The challenge of supporting the very young child's use of a hearing aid is an important one. With the assistance of the audiologist, the teacher and parent must work together to ensure optimal use of the hearing aid. *Ensure that the child wears the hearing aid consistently in the center*

and help the family to expect the same at home. Also, consult with the audiologist to determine the types of sounds the child can most easily perceive.

The following suggestions may be helpful in encouraging the child's use of a hearing aid:

1. Check the batteries daily; have extra batteries on hand.

2. Cover the controls on the hearing aid so they remain set at the proper levels; keep cords from being twisted.

3. Keep earmolds cleaned (do not clean with alcohol); keep the receiver away from water or extreme heat; avoid dropping the receiver.

4. Work with parents to teach preschool children to care for and insert their own aid as part of their daily self-care routine.

5. At home have a special place where the aid is always kept, away from pets and siblings.

6. For infants and very young children, behind-the-ear aids may need to be taped on.

7. Be aware of the acoustic characteristics of your classroom and the child's home environment. For optimal use of amplification, the acoustic environment must be appropriate, that is, relatively free of extraneous noise (such as background music, playground or hallway noise, and so on) and reverberating surfaces. When speech sounds are reflected off hard surfaces, they are more difficult to comprehend. Dampen noise by use of carpets, wall hangings, acoustic tile, and so on.

Cochlear Implants: Amazing Advances in Technology

Increasing numbers of children with severe sensorineural hearing losses are being treated via cochlear implants (Nicholas & Geers, 2006). A cochlear implant is a surgically implanted electrical device that directly stimulates the auditory nerve, thus bypassing the damaged nerve fibers in the cochlea. A cochlear implant consists of four components: a microphone, a signal processor, a receiver, and the surgically implanted electrodes. A cochlear

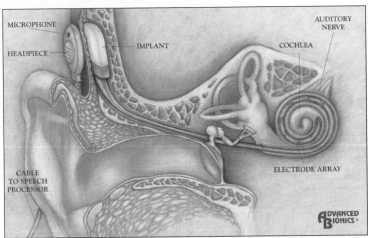

Courtesy of Advanced Bionics

implant does not restore hearing; however, with intensive auditory training, children can develop significant auditory skills and in some cases spoken language development within normal limits.

The improvements in cochlear implant technology have been very dramatic, making it possible to program many more channels of discrete stimulation, thus more closely mimicking the neural input frequency band of the normal ear. Some research has demonstrated that the language development of children with cochlear implants is superior to that of children with hearing aids (e.g., Tait & Luttman, 1994). This is particularly true for children with profound hearing loss who are identified early. Prior to the development of cochlear implants, the achievement of intelligible speech in children with profound hearing loss was very limited—even when the mode of communication was oral plus conventional amplification (hearing aids) (Yoshinaga-Itano, 2006). Currently, there remains some controversy around the use of this technology, though children with significant hearing loss are receiving cochlear implants at younger and younger ages. As of the publication of the current edition of this text, there appears to be a growing consensus that earlier implantation results in superior speech development. Nicholas and Geers (2006) conclude that there is research evidence that children who receive cochlear implants prior to age 2 years have a greater chance of achieving normal spoken language development than children receiving the device after age 2.

Supporting Spoken English

Regardless of the mode of communication, Yoshinaga-Itano (2006) recommends the following to support the child's development of **spoken English:**

- Frequent assessment to ensure that intervention strategies are, in fact, promoting age-appropriate expressive language skills.

- A team-based approach to ensure that amplification is fitted at the earliest possible age and that it is adjusted to the specific characteristics of the child's hearing loss.

- Incorporation of auditory skill development into families' daily routines and meaningful opportunities to teach listening skills (e.g., doorbell, telephone, or car pulling into driveway) and use of specific sounds for certain events (e.g., "oh oh" for something falling, "up up up" for lifting the child up, or "whoo whoo" while moving the toy train).

- Further, for young children with **profound hearing loss,** "early cochlear implantation and a high quality early stimulation program results in expectations that are similar to those for early-identified mild-to-severe hearing loss and the use of conventional amplification" (p. 323).

Children with Intermittent Hearing Losses

Often young children have hearing losses that come and go. Fluid in the middle ear, wax in the ear canal, and frequent colds, no matter how mild, may result in a hearing loss that comes and remains a while. Usually, physicians are unaware of this condition unless parents report it to them, and parents are unaware because the child is not complaining. However, they often report that "Johnny has been so stubborn this week. He doesn't come and do what I tell him unless I yell at him." Or they may say, "Sandy has been so grumpy all week. She won't listen. She just pretends not to hear me." It is important to recognize that these mild, intermittent hearing losses may affect children's language development and learning. Roberts and Burchinal (2001) summarize the effects of otitis media with effusion, or middle ear fluid, which results in a fluctuating hearing loss. There is at least some evidence that these intermittent hearing losses can affect both language development and early literacy skills, although Roberts and Burchinal also point out that the early interaction patterns of parents and children are more important factors than the history of otitis media.

WORKING WITH CHILDREN WITH VISUAL DISABILITIES

It is important that early intervention professionals work collaboratively with specialists in visual disabilities. This collaboration can provide the early interventionist with important information describing the nature of the child's functional vision and ensure that optimal adaptations are made. It is wise to involve orientation and mobility specialists as well as those who specialize in teaching children with visual disabilities (Pogrund & Fazzi, 2002). The following suggestions may be helpful in facilitating communication skills in children with visual disabilities:

1. Use the strategies already described in this text.

2. During vocalizations, touch the child to let him know you are there listening. Converse or interact with the child verbally just as you would with any other child of the same language development level.

3. Use auditory and tactile cues to help the child *anticipate* what will happen next; for example, before you wash the child's face, touch his hand with the washcloth and say, "Let's wash your face now."

4. Talk about and describe the child's actions as well as your own and others' actions as it happens.

5. Be certain the child uses vision to the maximum extent possible and then combine looking with touching and talking.

6. Be certain that children with visual impairments see and feel all parts of an object and understand the relationship of parts to the whole and to the context in which it is used.

7. Spatial relations are difficult to demonstrate. Place the child in various positions and encourage touching and manipulating. Sometimes use toys to demonstrate concepts such as on–off, up–down, and in–out.

8. Use language and the auditory modality to facilitate children's beginning understanding of directionality and distance, for example, say, "I'm across the room, far away." "Now I'm coming closer!" so the child can hear the difference in your voice as you approach.

9. Avoid "bombarding" the child with too much talk. Use key words and descriptions but don't describe every possible object and action. Pause frequently and avoid talking too rapidly.

10. Teach the child to localize sounds and recognize their source, direction, and distance.

WORKING WITH CHILDREN WITH AUTISM

In establishing communication intervention goals and strategies for children with autism, professionals first may want to consider the possible need to manage problems of tactile defensiveness and auditory

sensitivity. Assistance should be sought from occupational or physical therapists in designing strategies to reduce and manage tactile sensitivity. In addition, staff members should work with parents to identify and understand the child's aversions and sensitivities to certain sounds or other sensations.

We have mentioned previously the challenges associated with establishing joint reference, which is a prevalent characteristic in young children with autism spectrum disorder. This social perceptual difficulty also interferes significantly with the development of language (Girolameto, Verbery, & Tannock, 1994). Important intervention goals related to communication interaction include turn taking, social initiation, and the development of instrumental and regulatory functions of communication—that is, using gestures and words to express wants and needs and to influence the behaviors of others (see Prizant, Wetherby, & Rydell, 2000).

The use of traditional modeling approaches to language instruction that rely on elicited imitation may be problematic because children with autism often develop so-called **echolalic speech** (i.e., the immediate or delayed exact repetition or "parroting" of another person's speech). Although they may respond easily when the teacher models a cue such as "say 'cookie,'" generalizing the response to functional and meaningful spontaneous use of the word *cookie* is often extremely difficult. Techniques that may be more helpful include a combination of modeling and environmental manipulation techniques, such as those presented earlier in the discussion of strategies for children with severe disabilities. Children with autism often handle visual or graphic information more easily than auditory or verbal information. One successful approach to developing communication behaviors is the use of the Picture Exchange Communication System described earlier in this chapter. This approach has several advantages for children with autism (Frost & Bondy, 1994):

- It focuses on *functional* communication.
- It *requires* social interaction and exchange.
- It relies more on visual information than on auditory.

- It provides an acceptable "replacement behavior" for children whose communicative behaviors have become disruptive and inappropriate.

Ogletree and Oren (1998) stress the importance of designing communication intervention programs for children with autism that are both structured *and* functional rather than one or the other. They point out that historically, approaches have emphasized one or the other. For example, Lovaas's "discrete trial" approach (McEachin, Smith, & Lovaas, 1993) has been criticized because of its lack of generalization across partners and situations, its emphasis on the child as a respondent rather than an initiator, and its focus on specific language forms rather than on functional communication skills. On the other hand, an incidental teaching approach described by McGee, Morrier, and Daly (1999) and the similar pivotal response training approach described by Koegel and Koegel (2006) can be very effective with young children.

A combined approach is both structured and functional. In this type of approach, functionality is established by working with the child within meaningful contexts such as play and daily routines and identifying high-preference, motivating activities. In addition, a communicative need is established through strategies such as delay of an expected event, placing desired items out of reach, and use of "environmental sabotage," such as forgetting to give the child a spoon or putting a lid on too tight. When the child indicates a desire for an item, then structured direct teaching steps are used, including expectant waiting, verbal prompts, modeling, and so on.

There are many approaches and therapies recommended for children with autism. Unfortunately, there is no "magic bullet" or cure, and there is disagreement among professionals as to the most effective communication intervention. There are, however, certain strategies and considerations that are well established. Children with autism have great difficulty communicating regardless of their cognitive abilities. Often they are extremely hypersensitive to auditory and tactile stimuli and may handle visual or graphic forms of communication better than auditory or verbal. They are

often easily overwhelmed by changes in daily routines and have great difficulty learning in chaotic, noisy, unpredictable environments. Predictable daily schedules, with ample visual cues signaling transitions, will create an environment in which the child's energy and attention can be made available for learning. Behavioral techniques that provide repetition and clear cues and predictable consequences can be used within natural daily activities to teach functional communication and social interaction skills. For a diagnostic description of autistic disorder, refer to the *Diagnostic and Statistical Manual of Mental Disorders* (American Psychiatric Association, 2000).

WORKING WITH CHILDREN WHO HAVE LANGUAGE DIFFERENCES

The English spoken by the majority of people in the United States is usually called standard American English. Realistically, there is little question that people who speak standard English have advantages in school and in the job market. Ideally, speakers of non-standard dialects can also learn standard English. Similarly, children from different language backgrounds should be encouraged to develop both their native language and English as a second language. As will be described in chapter 9, in the discussion of literacy, there are also important differences in how families *use* language.

Because demographics in the United States are changing so dramatically, it is imperative that professionals working with young children be prepared to respect and celebrate diversity while at the same time preparing children to succeed in the mainstream.

Dialectal Variations

The United States is an increasingly diverse society. As a result, there are increasing numbers of children whose dialect is not "standard American English." In 1979, a federal judge in Michigan's Eastern District Court ruled that the Ann Arbor School District must develop a plan for teaching standard English to dialect speakers while respecting differences in dialect (Bountress, 1980). This decision was in response to African American parents' contention that their children were experiencing academic difficulties as a result of teacher insensitivity to the students' dialects. "The best recommendation appears to be that the teacher should respect the black child's dialect just as she respects the Mexican or Puerto Rican child's Spanish, yet while doing this, also make it possible for him (or her) to learn standard English" (Hendrick, 1980, p. 239).

There is growing awareness of various social dialects, and attempts are being made to assist children in the development of both their native dialect and standard English. Early on, Adler (1979) was an avid proponent of "bidialectalism," which is an approach to the teaching of standard English while maintaining the native dialect. According to Adler, "The espoused goal of such programs is to increase language skills *in general*—to teach children to use standard English in appropriate contexts while respecting and maintaining the native dialect" (p. 125). The intent is to teach children to be competent in any social situation by being able to use whatever form of language is appropriate to the participants and the setting.

English as a Second Language

The same degree of respect is necessary for children who are learning English as a second language. In addition to learning the vocabulary, grammar, and syntax of the new language, these children must discover acceptable social behaviors in the new culture. Learning two sets of social–language interactions as well as two languages can result in confusion and discomfort.

More and more programs expect either the teacher or an assistant to be bilingual. When this is not possible, teachers should study the basic social differences and hold conferences with parents and others who can explain the cultural expectations. For example, one difference often noticed is the degree to which speakers of different languages expect or avoid eye contact. Teachers who do not understand social differences may accuse the Indian or Puerto Rican child of not paying attention when actually the child is avoiding eye contact in an effort to show respect to adults. This is only one of many pragmatic differences that are influenced by culture.

Learning a New Language

Richard-Amato (1988) emphasized the notion that second language learning must be an *interactive* process. It should be clear that the strategies already described in this chapter can make important contributions to children's learning a second language.

The most efficient way to help children learn a second language uses conversations about the things they are interested in throughout the day. Krashen and Terrell (1983) and Tabors (1997) contended that the same principles that undergird the fostering of language in all children should be the basis of teaching. They emphasized that the dialogue between teacher and child should be in situations that maintain the child's interest and attention. However, they pointed out some important differences in the way the teacher might use the same situation with a first and a second language learner. The teacher may help the child who is already using the language (first language learner) to think and speak beyond the immediate situation. Such a child can be reminded of similar past events or helped to anticipate future similar situations. On the other hand, a child who is learning a new language may initially need to focus on present situational cues to understand what is being said. The teacher should use language that makes the meaning clear for each specific time and place.

As we have emphasized throughout this chapter, consideration of each child's unique needs is necessary, whether the child is a first or a second language learner. The communication strategies discussed earlier related to children with disabilities will also be important for children learning English as a second language (Bunce, 2003; Klein & Chen, 2001).

COLLABORATIVE CONSULTATION WITH SPEECH AND LANGUAGE SPECIALISTS

Nurturing the development of communication skills in young children requires a team approach. Major contributions can be made by a qualified speech and language specialist who has received training in early intervention. The speech-language specialist can make a particularly important contribution in the area of assessment, using both formal and informal measures.

In the field of communication disorders, some emphasis has been placed on the use of collaborative consultation models (Montgomery, 1992). A collaborative consultation model differs from a more traditional "expert" model of consultation (see chapter 10) in which the consultant assumes the role of a professional who provides information or services that the teacher does not possess. The collaborative model emphasizes the parity between the teacher and the speech-language specialist, who work as a team and contribute different skills and information to the processes of assessment, planning, and intervention as well as solving specific problems. The following are examples of the types of collaboration that might occur in such a model.

As part of the assessment, the speech-language specialist would carefully interview the classroom teacher regarding the child's communicative behavior and observe the child in the classroom. Communication goals and objectives would be generated as a team, involving the parents, who meet with the teacher and the speech-language specialist together. Innovative teaching strategies and activities might be demonstrated in the classroom by the speech-language specialist, who would receive feedback and suggestions for adaptation from the classroom teacher.

Although some professionals might argue that cognitive skill development precedes development of language skills, we chose to discuss the development of communication skills first. It is fitting, then, that the next chapter will concentrate on techniques for encouraging the development of cognitive skills and literacy. Understanding of the dynamics of language development will assist in obtaining insight into children's developing mental capacity as they journey toward becoming literate beings.

Summary

Communication, language, and speech are highly complex skills that develop as a function of many underlying processes, including cognitive, fine motor–perceptual, and especially social interaction. There is perhaps no area of development as crucial to the young child with special needs as communication skills. The early education teacher, in close partnership with parents, can have a major impact on this area of development. For the child who has less severe disabilities, providing language input finely tuned to the child's perceptual and cognitive level, in a style that follows the child's lead and within a context of social interaction, can greatly facilitate communication skills development.

For the child who has more severe and multiple disabilities, in addition to these input strategies it will also be necessary to structure the environment in ways that encourage the child to communicate his or her basic wants and needs. Once this important motivational factor has been provided, specific communicative behaviors can be shaped. Often these are not conventional speech or language behaviors. Nevertheless, they can be used in functional ways and can form the basis of augmentative communication systems.

With careful planning, the strategies that facilitate communication can be incorporated into all classroom activities. Furthermore, monitoring of children's communicative behaviors within a variety of *naturally occurring contexts* can provide the most meaningful assessment of progress.

Discussion Topics and Activities

1. Using a good-quality tape recorder, record conversations of mothers and young children. Look for mothers who have more than one preschool-aged child. Record the verbal interactions with each child alone. How are they similar? How do the conversations differ?

2. Analyze the children's responses to the mother's speaking pattern. Consider length, grammar, and syntax, using tapes made for activity 1.

3. Record your own conversations with children 1 year, and 2, 2½, 3, and 4 years of age. Attempt to interact intuitively with these children. Then analyze what you have done in response to the feedback from the children.

4. Bring the tapes to class. Listen to them and critique the appropriateness of the adult's utterances with the children. Consider vocabulary, length of sentences, speed, pauses, interest to the children, and the effect on the children's vocalizations.

5. Record a 15-minute conversation with one 4-year-old and an adult as they make cookies or do something similar. Play the tape for the class. What *new* concepts were introduced?

6. Record the conversations of several 4-year-olds as they play together. Analyze the speech and language used from the frame of reference of each of the subskills of language.

7. Write two dialogues: one to demonstrate appropriate conversation communicative interaction with a typical 2-year-old and one demonstrating a conversation with a typical 4-year-old.

8. Select a child who has severe and multiple disabilities. Conduct interviews with the child's teacher and parents to try to identify three high-preference activities or objects. Systematically present each to the child and observe his or her behavior. Also, observe the child's behavior as you take the object away or as you interrupt an enjoyable activity. What behavior can you identify that could be used by the child as a communicative system?

Encouraging the Development of Cognitive Skills and Literacy

Photo by Annette Tessier

KEY TERMS

(Note: terms are discussed in the text and/or defined in the glossary.)

alphabetic principle
accommodation
adaptation
assimilation
attention
autosymbolic play
classificaton

cognition
concrete operations
deferred imitation
discrimination
emergent literacy
formal operations
intentionality

literate-style language
means–end behaviors
mental representation
metacognitive
metalinguistic
object permanence
perception

phonemic awareness
phonics
phonological awareness

referential language
schema
seriation

symbolic ability
trial-and-error exploration
whole language approach

Key Concepts

- Understanding the development of thinking and reasoning, from the infant's first reflexes to the 5-year-old's problem-solving strategies, is critical to the effectiveness of the early childhood special educator.

- The three cognitive processes of attention, perception, and memory work together to enable the child's development of cognitive skills.

- The most significant single contribution to the understanding of children's cognitive development has been the theory of Jean Piaget.

- The early childhood special education professional must master techniques that facilitate critical cognitive skills, such as intentionality, means–end discovery, trial-and-error exploration, object permanence, and imitation in infants and toddlers with special needs.

- Critical cognitive skills for the preschool child include symbolic representation (particularly pretend play), problem solving, cognitive sub-skills related to academic readiness, and expansion of referential language skills.

- Early childhood special education professionals must be able to use specific strategies for adapting learning environments for infants and young children who are cognitively delayed.

- Preschool programs should be designed to support emergent literacy within naturalistic daily activities to develop children's appreciation of and interest in the nature and purposes of writing and reading and to develop important precursors of literacy, including rich vocabulary and interest in stories and books. In addition, the curriculum should target the development of concepts of print, phonological awareness, and the alphabetic principle.

- Children's home culture and experiences with literacy and literate oral language styles such as narrative will vary.

Kim: When we talk on the phone, how does our words get to the telephone pole wires and to our house?

Mom: Well, that is hard to explain. Our voice travels by what we call sound waves.

Kim: Oh, it must be like on the ocean. Our talk rides like a surfer.

As this interaction between mother and child demonstrates, cognitive development of young children is evidenced in their attempts to use what they know to solve new problems. New information is taken in and related to what was learned earlier. New knowledge and old knowledge are adapted to solve problems more efficiently. Cognition can be thought of as the individual's attempts at making sense of his world.

WHAT IS COGNITION?

Cognition is defined in the *Oxford English Dictionary* as "the mental action or process of acquiring knowledge through thought, experiences and the senses." Decades ago, Piaget (1954) referred to the development of cognition as the child's construction

of reality. These simple definitions belie the great complexity of human cognitive processes. How the young child develops the ability to mentally represent and understand the world around her is by no means simple. Understanding the evolution of thinking and reasoning, from the infant's first reflexes to the development of complex problem-solving strategies, is critically important to our effectiveness as educators of young children. Many children with special needs have cognitive impairments that interfere with the development of the conceptual and reasoning skills necessary for mastery of academic skills. The early childhood special education professional can recognize these challenges and provide the support necessary for the achievement of important cognitive skills.

BASIC COGNITIVE PROCESSES

Three basic processes related to information processing are important to the development of cognition: attention, perception, and memory. Infants must be able to pay attention to the world around them; they must also be able to receive, recognize, and discriminate stimuli. Eventually they must be able to organize and interpret those stimuli and store them for later retrieval.

Attention

Attention is the focusing of the individual's perceptual processes on a specific aspect of the environment. Learning cannot take place unless the individual is able to focus attention on the important elements of a task or situation. Attention is basic to many cognitive tasks and is a prerequisite for effective intervention. Attention in the form of concentration requires that the developing child learn to master two somewhat contradictory skills: (a) the ability to focus on those aspects of her environment that are relevant and have the greatest functional value to the task at hand and (b) the ability to ignore the multitude of irrelevant stimuli around her. *Selective attention* begins almost at birth, and the kinds of stimuli and the way babies look at them change in predictable ways. When a child attempts to attend and respond to too

many irrelevant stimuli, the child may be labeled as distractible.

Perception

Perception is the process of receiving and interpreting sensory information. Perceptual abilities are dependent on the sensory systems of touch, taste, proprioception, smell, hearing, and vision. These systems actually develop in utero, thus enabling the newborn infant to begin the processes of perceptual development at birth. Each sensory system (tactile, visual, auditory, olfactory, and gustatory) is associated with a different mode of perception. For perception to occur, some information must be stored in the nervous system. Sensations are then interpreted in the context of stored information.

The interpretations or perceptions of individuals may differ, depending on what is stored and on the strength of the perception modality, such as visual and auditory, which develop unevenly. Thus, one child may perceive more accurately through the visual channel, whereas another may gather information more efficiently through the auditory channel. As stated earlier, young children may find it easiest to interpret physical cues, followed by visual and finally verbal cues. Unfortunately, most teachers tend to teach predominantly through talking and expecting responses to verbal directions. Teachers who attempt to match teaching input to the developmental needs of their children will contribute greatly to the progress of children with perceptual disabilities, who usually have difficulty interpreting and obtaining accurate meaning from their environment.

Discrimination Abilities. **Discrimination** is the perception of the similarities and differences among related stimuli. This is an important aspect of information processing. For example, the young infant's ability to discriminate change and novelty in the repeated presentation of a stimulus increases attention. Later, children who learn to visually discriminate characteristics such as shape, size, distance, and color while in preschool will be prepared for the subtle discriminations between printed letters, numbers, and words necessary to success in kindergarten and first grade.

Likewise, children who learn to perceive the differences and similarities in pitch, loudness, rhythm, melody, rate, and duration of sound will likely be successful in learning to read by phonetic methods. Most prereading activities, by design, assist children in developing discrimination skills. For example, when a child is asked to find a picture illustrating a spoken word, she is discriminating among details in the picture while also practicing sound discernment, association, and memory skills. A majority of the activities discussed in this book, found in early childhood methods books and highlighted in Appendix F, give children practice in developing perceptual efficiency and accuracy.

Memory

The third basic cognitive process is memory. Memory is the process by which information that is received through attention and perception is stored in the central nervous system. Long ago, Atkinson and Shiffrin (1968) suggested the following model of memory:

1. Incoming sensation is perceived briefly (about 1 second).

2. If attended to, it will be placed in short-term memory, which can store information for 10 to 15 seconds.

3. Depending on a number of factors, some information will be placed in long-term memory, where it can be stored indefinitely.

Very young children have few memory strategies and may need repeated experiences of the same event or information before it can be stored in long-term memory.

The ability to learn is highly associated with memory. The most common kinds of memory include long term, short term, sequential, auditory, visual, rote, recognition, and recall. When assessing a child's difficulties in memory, several important questions must be considered. Are environmental conditions such as noise, excitement, emotional upset, or interpersonal problems interfering with retention? Is the content to be remembered meaningful, concrete, and short

enough to be developmentally appropriate? What kind of response is required? Is it immediate or delayed? Does it require recognition or recall or a motor or vocal response?

In reality, the three processes of attention, perception, and memory are interdependent. Individuals cannot pay attention if they are unable to perceive incoming stimuli, they cannot store information that they are unable to perceive, they cannot further develop perceptual skills of recognition and interpretation if they are unable to store the information in memory, and so on.

DEVELOPMENT OF COGNITIVE SKILLS

The Developmental Theory of Piaget

The most prominent cognitive theorist to influence the fields of child development and early education was Jean Piaget, a Swiss scientist interested in epistemology, or the study of human knowing. He was neither a learning theorist nor a maturationist. Rather, he combined these two views and believed that human cognitive development is a product of the interaction between the environment and the infant's biological capacities.

Two now classic concepts developed by Piaget's theory are the **schema** and the process of **adaptation.** The schema can be defined as a psychological structure that provides the individual with a template for action in similar circumstances (Piaget & Inhelder, 1969). Schemata (or "schemes"), which are initially infant reflexes, gradually become differentiated, combined, organized, and under the child's control. They also eventually become internalized; that is, they become mental processes. This occurs through adaptation, a twofold process comprised of **assimilation** and **accommodation.**

During the assimilation part of adaptation, experiences are taken in by infants or young children through the application of existing schemata. For example, the infant applies her "sucking schema" to her thumb. However, not all experiences can be assimilated to existing schemata. For example, if the

infant tries to apply her existing sucking schema to the corner of her blanket, she will not be successful. The infant must change, or "accommodate," her existing schema in order to adapt to this new situation. Thus, through the complementary processes of first using existing schemata and then modifying them to adjust to new experiences, the infant adapts to the world around her. In Piaget's view, this is the process of learning.

In addition to his important theory of cognitive development, Piaget also contributed an important research methodology that included naturalistic observations of infants and young children combined with presentation of situations in which to test his hypotheses. Information related to the sensorimotor and preoperational periods was based on his observations of his own children. His descriptions of the development of mental operations was based on his observations of schoolchildren.

Piaget described several stages in the development of cognition. Each stage of development builds on the previous one. This is referred to as the "spiral of knowing" (Gallagher & Reid, 1981, p. 35). As children mature and interact with their environment, they construct and reconstruct reality through the processes of assimilation and accommodation in accordance with their cognitive capabilities at each stage.

The Sensorimotor Stage.   The most creative and rapid period of human development is between birth and 18 months of age. The sensorimotor stage is divided into six substages. The first five of these stages lay the foundation for the beginning of representational thought—the mental representation of objects and events. The sixth stage, with its full achievement of object permanence, marks the transition from sensorimotor "knowing" through patterns of action to mental knowledge and symbolic ability.

Sensorimotor Substage 1: Use of Reflexes (0-1 Month).   During the first month of life, the infant interacts with her world primarily through reflexes. As the nipple touches her lips, she sucks; she "roots," or turns automatically to the side of the cheek that is touched; sudden loud sounds or loss of support elicit a startle, or "Moro," reaction; and so on.

Sensorimotor Substage 2: Primary Circular Reaction (1-4 Months).   During the second substage, the infant's reflexive behavior leads accidentally to new experiences. For example, the infant discovers her thumb and assimilates this experience to her existing nipple-sucking schema. She accommodates to the new object (her thumb) and thus *learns* to suck her thumb. Such primary circular reactions are always centered on the infant's own body.

Sensorimotor Substage 3: Secondary Circular Reactions (5-8 Months).   During this substage, the infant becomes increasingly interactive with events and objects in the external environment, outside her own body. Secondary circular reactions are those behaviors in which the infant engages in order to repeat an interesting event. For example, the infant accidentally hits a mobile hanging above her crib, which provides the visual experience of seeing the mobile move. The infant then tries to hit the mobile again to re-create this experience.

Sensorimotor Substage 4: Intentional Adaptations (8-12 Months).   During this substage, the infant begins to use and coordinate her secondary circular reactions in order to achieve a specific goal. This represents a major milestone in the development of cognition: the development of intentionality. Now the infant can look at the mobile and use the "looking-and-swiping" schema acquired through her secondary reactions of substage 3 and *intentionally* activate the mobile. She now has the goal in mind *before* she engages in the behavior. She has discovered the means–end relationship.

Also during this stage, the baby demonstrates the earliest ability to search for hidden objects. However, she will search in the place in which she last discovered the object. For example, an interesting object is covered with a blanket, and the infant is assisted in rediscovering the object. In full view of the infant, the object is then hidden under a box. Despite observing this, the infant will again search for the object under the blanket. She does not engage in a

systematic search based on where she sees the object disappear.

Sensorimotor Substage 5: Discovery of New Means (12–18 Months).   In substage 5, rather than simply repeating a behavior in order to re-create an interesting event, the infant searches for novelty through tertiary circular reactions. She systematically changes her behavior and observes the effect. This is sometimes called trial-and-error exploration. The following is a familiar example of this type of behavior. An 8-month-old infant, sitting in a highchair, drops and then tosses her food onto the floor, first from one side of the tray, then from the other. Although parents may interpret this as willful naughtiness, it is actually evidence of the growing cognitive abilities of the infant. It enables her to learn about cause and effect. Through such trial-and-error behavior, the infant discovers new means, or strategies, for achieving goals. For example, the child learns that she can crawl *around* a barrier to reach something on the other side if she is unable to crawl *over* it.

Continued development of the concept of object permanence can also be seen during this substage. Now the infant will more systematically search for the object at the place where she sees it disappear. However, if the infant does not see the object being moved, she will not search for it.

Sensorimotor Substage 6: Rudiments of Representational Thought (18–24 Months).   Substage 6 marks the end of the sensorimotor period. By the end of this substage, the toddler has mastered the full concept of **object permanence.** She clearly understands that objects exist whether or not she can see them. She will search systematically for an object even when she has not seen it disappear. This important cognitive capability now frees the infant from her dependence on sensorimotor actions for discovery and understanding. It frees her from the "here and now" world and enables her to develop memory skills.

The 18- to 24-month-old toddler now has the capacity for **mental representation**—the ability to think. This mental representation ability is particularly evidenced in two types of behavior observed toward

the end of substage 6: deferred imitation and pretend play. The ability to imitate something observed at an earlier time reflects the toddler's mental representation and memory for that event; deferred imitation also provides a mechanism for learning.

The ability to act out previously experienced events through pretend play (e.g., putting the doll to bed or pretending to serve breakfast) also is clear evidence of the ability to think about and remember such events. Like deferred imitation, pretend play provides important contexts in which to learn.

The Preoperational Stage.   The second major stage of cognitive development in Piaget's theory is called the preoperational stage. This term simply reflects the fact that although preschool children are clearly more capable than sensorimotor infants, they are not yet able to perform the mental operations required of logical thinking and reasoning. Piaget was more intrigued with what the preoperational child could *not* do than with the important achievements of this period. In Piaget's later writing, this stage was divided into two periods: the preconceptual and the intuitive.

The Preconceptual Period (2–4 Years).   A major accomplishment during this period is the development of **symbolic ability.** The child learns that one thing can represent another thing. This symbolic ability is evidenced both in her pretend play and in increasing language development. The child can now use a block as a truck, or she can *imagine* that a cloud is a bear floating in the sky. Language becomes freed from the immediate context. Words as symbols can now be used to describe and share experiences that occurred in the past.

The Intuitive Period (4–7 Years).   During this late preoperational stage, the child begins to demonstrate certain precursors of the next cognitive stage. For example, she can now categorize objects on the basis of certain features (e.g., the red balls and the blue balls or forks and spoons). However, children are still unable to focus on more than one feature or dimension at a time.

Piaget was very interested in the mental operations that children could *not* perform during this

stage. The classic "conversation experiment" demonstrates the child's inability to decenter: Two identical beakers are filled with equal amounts of water. The water from one of the beakers is poured into a narrower, taller beaker. When asked whether the tall beaker now contains more or the same amount of water as the short, wide beaker, the child invariably responds "more" despite repeated demonstrations of pouring water back and forth. According to Piaget, the preoperational child lacks the ability to attend to both height and width and centers only on height (tallness). She also lacks reversibility of thought and cannot realize that the width of the shorter beaker would compensate for its lack of height and vice versa.

The lack of ability to decenter is also observed in the preschooler's egocentrism. She has difficulty taking another person's perspective and views the world in relationship to herself. She does not understand that someone else may not be able to see what she can see, and her language is often insufficiently referential. This inability to take the perspective of others relates to the recently developed concept of "theory of mind." (See Tager-Flusberg [2000] for a discussion of this topic relative to children with autism.)

During the intuitive period, the preschool child experiences a gradual shift in the ability to perform mental operations. Also during this period, the child's thinking becomes more elaborated, as is particularly demonstrated in dramatic play episodes. The preschooler can orchestrate long and complex interpersonal sequences that provide opportunities for practicing social routines and solving problems. Another characteristic of children during this period is their inability to think logically. Children's thought is sometimes referred to as *transductive*. Although truly logical thought is either inductive (proceeding from the specific to the general) or deductive (from the general to the specific), young children's thought often proceeds from the particular to the particular, with no logical connection. For example, a 4-year-old trips as she comes in the door and announces, "I just ate a whole candy bar so I can't walk too good!" Although the child cannot think logically at this stage, she clearly recognizes that events have causes and perceives the need for explanations.

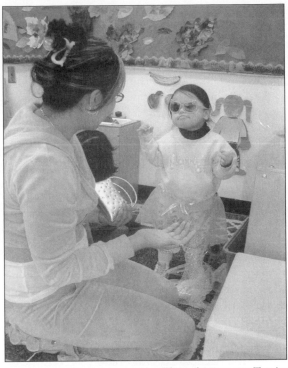

Photo by Annette Tessier

The Stages of Concrete Operations and Formal Operations. Once the child moves into the stage of **concrete operations** (which extends from the ages of 7 to 11 years), she has achieved the mental flexibility necessary to perform the operations required in reading and mathematics and the ability to think logically. In the conversation experiment described earlier, the child at this stage has no difficulty understanding that volume of liquid is the same regardless of the height of the beaker. The child no longer centers on only one dimension. This significantly enhances her problem-solving capability. The child in this stage of cognitive development is able to decenter and to consider many dimensions of an object or a problem simultaneously.

The final stage of **formal operations** is achieved somewhere between 11 and 15 years of age. The young adolescent is now capable of performing the mental operations mastered during the concrete operations stage on more abstract material. She can now think about complex moral dilemmas that often have

more than one "right" answer, depending on the situation. She can also think scientifically, using processes of the scientific method, such as hypothesis testing.

The developmental theories of Piaget and his associates are complex, and their development spanned a time period from the early 1930s to the 1970s. Because these works have been addressed here in the briefest manner, the student of early childhood special education is encouraged to examine texts such as Piaget and Inhelder (1986), Piaget (1977), Gallagher and Reid (1981), and Bell-Gredler (1986).

Alternate Views of Cognitive Development.

Although the theory of Piaget continues to provide the cornerstone of our understanding of the intellectual development of young children, several theorists have offered alternative or supplementary views of development. For example, neo-Piagetian theorists (Case, 1985) have suggested that Piaget's stages of development are domain specific—that subareas of development such as drawing, language, and mathematics may have their own developmental schedules. Bidell and Fischer (1989) discussed the roles of cultural and social interaction on cognitive development, an approach that is consistent with the social-constructivist views of Vygotsky (1986).

DEMONSTRATION OF COGNITIVE SKILLS THROUGH THE DEVELOPMENTAL STAGES OF CHILDREN'S PLAY

One of the easiest ways to observe the development of children's cognitive skills is through the observation of their play. The stages of cognitive development can be readily observed using the following taxonomy: simple manipulation, exploratory play, functional play, and symbolic play.

Simple Manipulation

Simple manipulative behaviors such as mouthing, poking, waving, banging, or throwing are examples of secondary circular reactions that are typical of sensorimotor substage 3. As the infant reaches substage 4, around 8 to 10 months, these sensorimotor schemata

become combined and under her intentional control. She now clearly *intends* to bang or throw. For example, the infant notices a ball and purposely moves toward it, picks it up, and throws it.

Exploratory Play

As the infant moves into the fifth substage of sensorimotor development, she engages in trial-and-error exploration. She notices some blocks and a can. She picks up the can and bangs it on the floor, then puts it on her head. She picks up the block and puts it in the can. She dumps the block out of the can. She is also capable of inventing new means to achieve her goals. For example, she can't reach a ball that has rolled under the sofa, so she takes her mother by the hand to solicit her help.

Functional Play

By the end of the fifth substage, the child can demonstrate appropriate object use. She pushes the truck, pounds with the hammer, dials the telephone, combs her hair, and so on. She may also demonstrate autosymbolic play, pretending to engage in some familiar activity such as sleeping or eating.

Symbolic Play

By the end of the sixth substage, the child has achieved the ability to represent objects and events internally and to engage in symbolic behavior. Symbolic play develops through several stages from the end of the sensorimotor period through the preoperational period.

Initially, the child engages in pretend play activities in which she is the actor, engaged in some highly familiar activity such as going to sleep. During the next stage, she focuses the pretend play activity on some inanimate recipient of her actions, such as a doll or teddy bear. Now she pretends to put the doll to bed or pour coffee for the bear. Next, the doll will be the agent, not just the recipient, of the child's actions (i.e., the doll washes herself or puts the teddy to bed).

After 24 months, there is a gradual increase in the preoperational child's ability to use nonrealistic objects to represent real objects as symbolic skills

improve. Eventually, after 36 months, the child uses imaginary objects or people. There is also an increase in the length and complexity of pretend play sequences in the preoperational period. After 24 months the child can play the roles of different individuals and reenact events from the past. After 36 months the child begins to plan pretend scenarios in advance and organize who will do what. Play sequences begin to look more like a story, with a beginning, a plot that evolves (e.g., a problem to be solved or a special occasion), and an ending. By this stage, language becomes an essential element of play.

By age 4 or 5 the child begins to act out possible *future* scenarios (i.e., "what would happen if . . . ?" situations) and can act out multiple roles (e.g., play the mother who is also a doctor).

FACILITATING THE DEVELOPMENT OF COGNITIVE SKILLS IN INFANTS AND TODDLERS

Several cognitive milestones are particularly important targets for early intervention. Certain disabling conditions may begin to interfere with children's achievement of these important cognitive skills early in infancy. For example, a child who is blind may have particular difficulty with the achievement of object concepts and object permanence. A child with motor impairments may have difficulty discovering means–end strategies, and her opportunities to practice trial-and-error exploration will be limited.

The following section describes several key cognitive milestones during the period from birth to 3 years of age and provides suggestions for facilitating these cognitive skills. In addition, the reader is encouraged to review earlier chapters that have described generic strategies such as scaffolding (chapter 5), communicative interactions (chapters 5 and 8), and naturalistic milieu approaches to intervention (chapter 8). These strategies are particularly effective in the development of cognitive skills. Many of the specific suggestions in this chapter reflect those approaches.

The reader is also again reminded that teaching must be activity based. That is, intervention goals and objectives are integrated and incorporated into pleasurable, developmentally appropriate *play* activities. They are *not* isolated as bits of behavior to be learned.

Intentionality

As discussed earlier, somewhere around 8 to 10 months of age typically, developing infants achieve the ability to do things intentionally. They no longer must discover things by chance in order to repeat them. They can now perform an action on purpose. Achievement of **intentionality** is a prerequisite to almost every other skill. The ability to deliberately act on the environment is an important key to continued development.

Some children with severe disabilities may need assistance in the development of intentionality. For such a child, the importance of intentionality cannot be overemphasized. Learning that the individual can produce a behavior volitionally and that such behavior has an effect on the world around her is a major accomplishment. The following strategies are examples of ways to facilitate this important cognitive milestone.

1. *Increase motivation by use of high-interest objects and activities.* Begin by taking a careful inventory of high- and low-preference objects, people, and activities. It will be necessary to interview caregivers to obtain a good understanding of the child's likes and dislikes. Once these are identified, they may be used to create the need or desire to act on the environment in some way.

2. *Create the desire or need to perform intentional acts.* The following are examples of strategies:

   a. Place a high-preference object within the child's view but out of reach.

   b. Begin a pleasurable activity, then abruptly stop it. Wait for the child to do something in an attempt to continue the activity. For example, push the child in the swing, then stop the swing. Wait for some kind of signal from the child that she wants to continue, then resume the activity.

c. Engage in an unpleasant activity, such as washing the child's face, then discontinue the activity if the child indicates rejection (e.g., pushes your hand away).

d. Interpret even unintentional cues such as head turning or arm waving as intentional; respond as though the child did it purposely. For example, if the child inadvertently moves her arm toward a toy, respond by handing the child the toy.

e. Adapt favorite toys, tape players, television sets, and so on so that they can be activated by a switch requiring only minimal movement from the child.

3. *Allow ample time for the child to initiate a purposeful behavior.* Some children appear not to demonstrate intentional behavior simply because they have learned that there will not be enough time to organize a response. Adults frequently anticipate children's needs or perform actions for them, interfering with their initiation of intentional acts.

Means-End Behavior

As infants learn to act intentionally on their environment, they discover that these actions have certain effects on objects and people. As they become familiar with these causes and effects, they are able to engage in an action intentionally in order to bring about a desired end and, when necessary, to modify that action to create new means to achieve the desired end. For example, a child may use a stool to help her climb onto a counter so she can reach the cookies, or she may pull at mother's hand and take her to the counter to get the cookies.

These kinds of behaviors are important manifestations of the child's ability to cognitively associate certain events with their consequences. Children with disabilities often need assistance with both understanding these relationships and engaging in **means-end behaviors.** It may be necessary to structure the environment carefully in ways that clearly demonstrate cause and effect and

consistently reinforce the child for attempts to achieve certain goals.

Simply constructed toys and devices that produce an interesting response to a specific type of manipulation can be effective. These include infant toys such as a busy box, a jack-in-the-box, and an easily activated musical toy.

Equally important is the contribution of a responsive social environment. Caregivers who respond quickly to an infant's signals of discomfort or to an older child's bids for attention will support the development of means–end behaviors.

Trial-and-Error Exploration

The ability to systematically explore objects and space is crucial to the development of the child's ability to learn from experience and develop problem-solving skills. Systematic manipulation of objects and modification of the individual's own actions, referred to as **trial-and-error exploration,** lead to self-directed learning and the discovery of new behaviors and solutions.

In attempting to assist children in learning these exploratory strategies, teachers must understand that they are teaching a *process* rather than a specific behavior. For example, a jar containing pieces of candy is offered to a child. The jar has a tightly fitted lid. To teach the child to take off the lid would simply require task analyzing this skill and teaching it step-by-step until the child had mastered unscrewing the lid. On the other hand, encouraging trial-and-error exploration requires a different approach. It is necessary for the teacher to use several of the generic strategies described in chapter 5. The teacher must assist the child in initiating different attempts to open the jar and reinforce *persistence,* not just success. The teacher must be able to read the child's cues of boredom or frustration and know when to finally scaffold successful unscrewing of the lid. Other opportunities must be created later on in which to generalize this trial-and-error process.

The following example demonstrates a way of encouraging trial-and-error behavior as a problem-solving strategy.

Nathan is sitting at the snack table with several peers without disabilities. Each child is handed a fruit roll in a wrapper as a special treat. The children eagerly tear open their wrappers. Nathan has motor coordination difficulties and typically cannot manage such a task. He has become accustomed to seeking help in such situations, so he hands the package to his teacher. This time, the teacher does not immediately open the package. She hands it back to him and says, "I'm sorry Nathan, I can't help right now. I'll help in a few minutes." She signals to the aide to sit next to Nathan. Nathan fiddles briefly with the wrapper, then looks at the aide, who says, "Well, try it this way." She turns it around and hands it back to him. He tugs at one end of the wrapper unsuccessfully. The aide says, "Boy, that's hard to do, isn't it?" He pulls at the other end of the wrapper, again to no avail, then bangs it on the table. At this point the aide takes the package and makes a small tear in one corner. She hands it back and points to the torn corner. Nathan pulls at that corner and opens the wrapper. The teacher then approaches Nathan, saying, "Well, you got that
unwrapped all by yourself, didn't you!" It is hoped that this child has learned something about the value of trying different solutions and the importance of persistence.

Object Permanence

The achievement of the concept of object permanence is critical to the child's continued development of important mental processes including memory and mental representation. Throughout the first year of development, children learn about the existence and properties of objects. As they continue through the sensorimotor period, they eventually discover, by the end of the second year, that objects and people continue to exist even when they are out of sight and their removal was not observed.

At this point, which marks the end of the sensorimotor period, children have the ability to represent objects and events internally. They can conjure mental pictures in their minds; they no longer must see an object to know it exists. This is obviously important for the development of memory skills.

There are many simple ways in which object permanence can be demonstrated for young children. Perhaps one of the first such activities introduced to infants is the game of peekaboo, a simple way to demonstrate that a person continues to exist even when the infant cannot see the person's face. Other ways to demonstrate object permanence include searching for something missing from its expected storage container, playing hide-and-seek, or hiding cookies in your pocket and asking children to guess what you have.

Deferred Imitation

The ability to re-create an action observed at a previous time reflects the development of important cognitive skills. It requires an understanding of object permanence, the beginning development of memory skills, and the ability to mentally represent a sequence of events. **Deferred imitation** eventually plays an important role in the development of pretend play and language development.

The development of imitation skills, both immediate and deferred, may be encouraged by using the following sequence:

1. Begin by imitating the child's behavior, encouraging turn taking, and then encouraging the child to continue the game. Children who have no disabilities will happily see this as a sort of "Simon Says" game.

2. Next, introduce a variation of the behavior to see whether the child will attempt to follow suit.

3. Once the child can do this easily, you can be the initiator of the imitation game rather than imitating the child's behavior first. (Over the years, many programs have been developed that teach imitation at this level, using modeling, physical prompts, and reinforcement techniques.)

4. When the child has acquired a generalized imitative response (i.e., the child will attempt to imitate novel behaviors in addition to those that have been trained) and has developed the concept of object permanence, it may be possible to teach *deferred* imitation. The length of time between presentation of a model and imitation of the model can be increased gradually. For example, at recess, children can pretend to "walk like a duck." Later, you can say, "Can you remember what we did at recess?" This requires the child to use both memory and imitation skills.

FACILITATING THE DEVELOPMENT OF COGNITIVE SKILLS IN PRESCHOOLERS

Symbolic Representation

As children enter the preoperational stage of cognitive development, two major achievements reflect emerging symbolic skills: (a) increasing use of language to represent objects and events that are not present in the immediate environment or that occurred in the past and (b) the ability to engage in symbolic, pretend play. The topic of language, which was discussed in some detail in chapter 8, will be

addressed later in this chapter. Much has already been said about play in this text. Play is important as a context for teaching (chapter 5), as an end in itself in the development of social skills, and as means for facilitating healthy emotional development (chapter 6). Through symbolic play, children express their understanding of the world around them and the interrelationships of people and events. In addition, symbolic play provides an important context within which to experience and express emotions, both one's own and those of others.

In this chapter we have discussed symbolic play as an important cognitive milestone. The ability to allow one thing to stand for something else, such as a block representing a car or a tissue representing a blanket, is evidence of the child's developing symbolic representation skills. Other evidence of symbolic skills can be observed in drawing, language, mental images, and eventually in reading, writing, and mathematics.

It is important for the early childhood special educator to be aware of the importance of facilitating play skills in general and pretend play in particular. As we discussed earlier in this chapter, symbolic play moves through various stages. The first is **autosymbolic play,** in which children themselves are the actors. These play episodes reenact highly familiar activities such as pretending to eat or go to sleep, and they incorporate materials that are real (e.g., a pillow) or that closely resemble real objects (e.g., a small plastic spoon or tiny cup from a tea set). For children who are functioning developmentally at the end of the sensorimotor period, these are the kinds of activities that can be modeled both by the teacher and by other children. The use of play routines discussed in chapter 5 can be helpful in establishing this early type of pretending.

The simple level of pretending can also be encouraged in group activities. For example, the teacher can say, "Let's pretend to be a snake" or "Let's pretend to swim." For children with special needs, it will be important to select pretend activities that represent very familiar activities or concepts. Children cannot pretend to do or be something they have never experienced.

Gradually, the teacher should introduce pretend play scenarios that involve other actors, such as dolls and stuffed animals, as well as other children acting out familiar roles in relationship to one another. The classroom should include dramatic play centers that include materials that encourage pretending, such as dress-up clothing, a toy stove, a sink and cupboards, dishes, brooms, telephones, dolls and doll beds, and so on.

Also, the teacher should gradually encourage the use of objects that are more and more abstract. For example, instead of toy cars that crash and have to go to the Fisher-Price garage for repairs, wooden blocks can be used for cars and an upside-down box can become a garage. The ability to use the same blocks for a fence and the box for a doll bed represents the emergence of the kind of mental flexibility (i.e., reversibility and understanding of transformations) that is a hallmark of the next stage of cognitive development, the stage of concrete operations.

The following example demonstrates the facilitation of symbolic play skills in a child with severe disabilities.

Jason and Monique love to play house in the dramatic play center. Andrea, who has many autisticlike behaviors, loves to sit in the rocking chair in the classroom and rock. The teacher decides to move the rocking chair into the dramatic play area and suggests to Jason and Monique that maybe Andrea could be the mother today: she could help put the baby to bed by rocking her. After rocking for a while, while Jason and Monique are "cooking," Andrea is encouraged to put the doll in her own bed. Now it is time for everyone to go to sleep. Jason and Monique lie down with their pillow, and they encourage Andrea to do the same. The baby then wakes up crying in the night, and, because Andrea is the mother, she must rock her back to sleep.

A scenario such as the one just described could also be worked into a play script that is repeated several times. In this way, Andrea could be assisted not only with pretending but also with language development and cooperative play.

Problem Solving

As preschoolers face increasing demands to develop greater and greater independence, the cognitive skills that enable them to engage in problem solving become increasingly important. Typical preschoolers often have little difficulty *recognizing* problems to be solved; they may need help only with generating more effective solutions. Children who have disabilities or are at high risk, however, may need assistance not only in the development of problem-solving strategies but also in recognizing that a problem exists and that they have the capability to solve that problem through their own focused efforts.

Problem solving is distinctly different from academic learning. Academic skills represent external knowledge that must be taught; problem-solving opportunities during early childhood encourage the child to create new mental relationships by interacting with the environment. Meaningful problems stimulate children's mental activity as they relate new understandings to previous ones.

Conditions Necessary for Problem Solving to Occur. It is all too easy to structure activities with young children so carefully that they never have the opportunity to solve problems or to realize the relationship between cause and effect. Alert parents and teachers often prevent problems so consistently that young children seldom have the chance to recognize a problem, let alone solve it. Yet everyday activities at home and at school can offer many opportunities to teach children these important skills. Even if problem-solving opportunities are readily available, children will respond only when the following conditions are met.

Freedom from Fear of Failure. Taking risks is natural to young children. That is why they must be watched so carefully. But taking risks in trying new things requires courage for some children. This is especially true if their early explorations resulted in pain or punishment. Sometimes the punishment has been a part of their disability. The child with visual impairments may be physically insecure and may resist exploring. Some children with disabilities may

be overprotected, and abused children may be excessively wary. Children who have had limited opportunities to play, to use a variety of different toys and materials, and to discover need help in freeing their natural talents and curiosity.

Opportunities to Experience Cause and Effect.   Young children readily learn the relationship between cause and effect through inquiry and experimentation. Teachers and caregivers must take time to listen to and act on children's questions. Safe conditions, inside and out, should allow for experimentation. Noise and mess often are a sign of cognition in action. Children learn when they can dig and pile up things. Pouring and stirring with sand and water teach new concepts. The opportunity to discover is controlled in part by what there is to discover. But the freedom to "do it myself" must be taught to some.

Encouragement and Reinforcement.   Encouragement and reinforcement are also necessary for cognitive learning. Cognitive learning is disrupted if children fear punishment. The natural consequence of making a mess should be cleaning it up, never a teacher's scolding or saying "I warned you not to do that." Encouraging experimentation may merely require making the materials available, but some children need to be told repeatedly that it is all right to play with particular things that were (and perhaps are) forbidden at home. Both these children and their parents need to understand that some things are appropriate at school and not at home.

Teachers should be alert to provide social and tangible rewards for progress in expressions of curiosity and resilience and for the learning achievement. Just as structured, sequential lessons are needed for children to learn to recognize shapes and colors, so prompting and supporting are needed for children to learn qualities such as curiosity, experimentation, and problem solving.

Problem-Solving Skills to Be Nurtured.   In speaking of the problem-solving skills to be nurtured, Cook and Slife (1985) concluded that most research about problem solving suggests that the five steps are practically a universally endorsed process: (a) recognition

of the problem, (b) analysis of contributing factors, (c) consideration of possible solutions, (d) choice of optimal solutions, and (e) evaluation of feedback to determine results. Not only is problem solving a natural logic, but the motivation to overcome obstacles appears to be natural as well.

Children basically enjoy solving problems. Deciding where to have a snack or the best place for playing with clay presents opportunities to talk about why one place is better than another. This is the beginning of problem solving. "Staging" or contriving problems to solve is a useful addition to those problems that occur spontaneously. Having too few cartons of milk at snack time creates the need to count the children before going to get the milk. Losing pieces of puzzles can become the occasion to talk about how this problem could be avoided in the future. Children can then be helped to see that puzzles should not be put away unless they are finished and complete. Discovering that the taller children can reach things whereas others cannot leads to problem solving, an arithmetic lesson, and a lesson on concept comparatives (e.g., Who is tallest? John is tall, but Timmy is taller. Bill is the tallest child in the class.).

Although problem solving itself is considered to be a cognitive (thinking) skill, it involves language learning, social awareness, and motor activities. The alert teacher sees the distinct opportunities to develop many skills from the simplest situations.

WORKING WITH CHILDREN WHO HAVE COGNITIVE DISABILITIES

Identifying and labeling infants and preschoolers as having mild to moderate cognitive delays or learning disabilities is difficult to do with accuracy prior to formal schooling. However, some young children will clearly demonstrate significantly delayed or impaired cognitive functioning early in life. The primary identifying characteristic of these children is significantly slowed development of cognitive skills, hence the older term *mental retardation*. In the 1980s and 1990s, the term *developmental delay* was commonly used to refer to this disability. (Note that parents often find the term misleading because it implies that the

child will eventually "catch up" and that development is just proceeding at a slower pace.) We will use the term *cognitive disability*. It should be noted that today there are also differing views of "intelligence." The notion that intelligence—or even cognitive ability—is some single measurable ability is no longer widely accepted (Gardner, 2006). Rather, it is believed there are many types of ability or "intelligences," such as verbal, motor, social, musical, and so on.

For purposes of our discussion here, we are referring to those cognitive processes and skills described by Piaget and, in this section, to children who, very early in life, demonstrate significant difficulty with the kinds of skills discussed in this chapter. These cognitive challenges can be caused by many factors, including genetic disorders (e.g., Down syndrome), prenatal insult to the fetus from toxic substances (e.g., alcohol) or viral infections (e.g., rubella), perinatal complications (e.g., anoxia), and postnatal influences such as head injury, asphyxia (e.g., near drowning), and poisoning (e.g., lead poisoning). Although these factors do not always cause significant cognitive impairment, it is a possible outcome. We are referring to global developmental or cognitive deficits, not impairments of specific neurological processes.

Characteristics of Children with Significant Cognitive Disabilities

The following are characteristics commonly associated with children who have significant cognitive disabilities.

1. One of the most obvious and defining characteristics of children with retardation is their slower rate of development. Children with mental retardation learn at a slower pace. Often learning can be enhanced by repeated, systematic instruction.

2. Depending on the degree of mental retardation, children may experience significant difficulties with the kinds of basic cognitive processes described earlier in the chapter. They may experience short-term memory deficits and difficulty attending to relevant stimuli.

3. Children with significant mental retardation experience particular difficulty with language development. Whereas for most developmental domains the child will be functioning at a level similar to his or her mental age (i.e., cognitive level), language development may be below the child's mental age.

4. Many children with retardation process information more slowly than their normally developing peers and require more time to produce a response.

5. Children with significant mental retardation often do not demonstrate learned skills spontaneously and have difficulty generalizing skills to new situations.

Adapting Instruction

In light of these learning characteristics, several strategies can be effective in assisting young children who have significant cognitive impairments. These are summarized in Exhibit 9-1. These adaptations are easily incorporated into any preschool program. Peers without disabilities can often benefit from them as well. For example, during activities designed to facilitate classification skills, familiar, functional materials can be used, such as forks, knives and spoons, or different-colored socks. Another simple adaptation is to remind all staff to speak more slowly and increase the length of pauses. This adaptation will make it easier for all children to understand, and it will provide ample time for children to organize their ideas and communications. Particularly important are the use of repetition, creating a predictable environment, and facilitating active learning by teaching the child to initiate.

FACILITATING COGNITIVE AND INFORMATION-PROCESSING SUBSKILLS RELATED TO ACADEMIC ACHIEVEMENT

For the preschool child, one of the greatest concerns regarding the development of cognition has to do with the cognitive skills that will ultimately support

Exhibit 9–1

Special Considerations for Children Who Need Extra Time and Spaced Practice

1. *Provide concrete, multisensory tasks.* Preschool-aged children naturally learn more easily when tasks are three-dimensional and concrete rather than abstract.

2. *Find the child's most efficient mode of learning.* Observe carefully to determine each child's strongest mode of learning. If it is visual, then use visual cues to assist auditory directions. If auditory, then accompany visual tasks with auditory assists. If motoric, then use movement as much as possible to teach language and cognitive skills.

3. *Monitor pacing.* Children who must work extra hard to concentrate or to process information usually tire easily. The amount of effort exerted should be varied to allow for occasional rest times, quiet activities, or soft music. Children who process information more slowly should receive less information or should receive it over a longer time.

4. *Provide repetition.* Some children need to try things again and again or need to have something repeated several times before it can be grasped. Intermittent practice helps children remember skills they have learned.

5. *Plan for modeling and imitation.* Some children do not acquire information incidentally. If a specific response is desired, plan experiences in which the behavior is demonstrated and positively reinforced. Once the child imitates the desired behavior, be certain to give the expected reinforcement.

6. *Task analyze.* Tasks must be broken into simple, short steps that can be sequenced from the easiest to the most difficult.

7. *Give explicit directions.* For some children it is necessary to give nearly all directions slowly and in small steps. One step can be completed before the next direction is given.

the learning of academic skills of reading, writing and mathematics, and classroom language skills. Many of the mental operations and thinking skills that evolve throughout the preschool years will be critical to school performance and the development of academic skills. This section addresses the teaching of these cognitive subskills.

However, it is important to realize that the development of academic skills—and literacy skills in particular—does not depend on levels of cognitive development alone but also on the social and linguistic experiences of the child. Thus, to truly understand academic readiness and to develop strategies for facilitating academic skills in young children, it is also necessary to understand the role of the social context of the young child's family and culture (Gee, 2001).

The reader is reminded also that the early caregiver interactions described in chapters 5 and 8 play a critical role in children's later development of cognitive and academic skills. The preschool years can be viewed as a period of preparation for the formal

academic achievement that must take place in the early elementary school years: reading, writing, and mathematics. In addition, there is a fourth area that is now realized to be crucial to children's academic success. It is referred to as *school language.*

Significant debate exists regarding to what extent academics should be stressed during the preschool years. Preschool programming approaches often reflect one of two polar views. One view suggests that academic skills should be directly taught in preschool programs emphasizing learning the alphabet, sound–letter relationships, counting, and reading and writing numbers and letters. At the other end of the continuum are programs that stress that neither academics nor academic readiness skills are appropriate for the preschool classroom. These programs emphasize self-directed play and exploration and exclusively child-centered activities.

In light of the continuing concern regarding the lack of school preparedness of millions of young children from impoverished environments who are

at risk for a variety of biological and social reasons, there is probably an important middle ground somewhere between the two views. There is much that can be done within a child-centered program to enhance the child's cognitive, social, and linguistic foundations for the development of academic skills. It is our position that the early childhood special educator must understand the nature of these academic foundations and be able to design educational environments and programs that facilitate those skills. Equally important, these programs must be child centered, developmentally appropriate, engaging, and supportive of children's creativity, exploration, unique learning styles and sense of self. (See Exhibit 9–2 for an example of an adapted approach to "Calendar Time" that promotes cognitive development while realizing that understanding of time is a highly abstract concept.)

Basic information-processing skills such as attention and memory, as well as certain mental operations such as seriation, categorization, one-to-one correspondence, and logical thinking, form the cognitive bases for academics. The following sections provide developmentally appropriate classroom strategies for facilitating these processes and concepts.

Facilitating Children's Engagement

Assessing Problems of Attention. To help young children develop appropriate capacities for focused engagement, the teacher must identify the factors that may be contributing to lack of attention. *However, as discussed in chapter 5, the most fundamental factor in establishing attention and engagement in children is to identify high-preference activities that are intrinsically interesting and motivating to each child.* The teacher must also be certain that the child has no health problems and no interference with normal vision or hearing. Obviously, many young children with special needs do have physical problems that affect their concentration. The guidelines in chapter 5 offer some assistance in developing an environment most responsive to particular special needs.

Assuming that their attention expectations take into consideration each child's special needs, teachers will want to assess whether tasks match the child's abilities and are broken into manageable steps, directions are clear, vocabulary is at an appropriate level, and the amount of stimulation is reasonable.

Stimulus Selection. Teachers should analyze the amount and complexity of stimuli to which the child is being asked to respond. Some distractible children may not be able to attend to a very colorful puppet with a very high voice while seated on the floor in a large group far away from the teacher. The same puppet might get a totally different response in a small group with two or three children seated at a table with a volunteer aide who uses a soft voice. Decreasing the amount and complexity of impinging stimuli will make it easier for the child to separate relevant from irrelevant stimuli.

When children have difficulty figuring out what stimuli are relevant, using novelty in the form of concrete objects, touch, and movement can help focus and sustain attention. It is believed that infants first learn to interpret stimuli received through the sense of touch (tactually). Then around the age of 3 or 4 months, they integrate information presented visually and auditorally as well. Even so, for many children, touch continues to help isolate the relevant features of a stimulus and increase the child's ability to focus on them. When trying to teach children how to walk across a street safely, giving each child a teddy bear to "instruct" in role-plays might be an effective means of focusing attention and recall.

Duration of Attention. Initially the amount of time required for a task should be in keeping with the child's natural ability to sustain attention. Then, using positive reinforcement and in some cases a timer, the *time on task* requirement can be increased. Remember that often children do not sustain attention because the task itself is inappropriate. For the very young child, learning tasks need to have visually concrete (obvious) beginnings and endings. Because some children just do not know how to start an activity and have poor visual organizing skills, they are easily distracted. Through careful structuring of environmental

Exhibit 9–2

Making Calendar Time Meaningful for All Children

Calendar time is an almost universal activity in preschool programs. Because of the abstractness of concepts of time, children with special needs often have difficulty relating to this activity. The following is an example of how calendar time might be made more meaningful for children with cognitive disabilities.

1. Rather than presenting the entire calendar month, highlight only the current week. Each day should be a different color, with Saturday and Sunday easily distinguishable from the days of the school week (e.g., they might be pastel, whereas the weekdays are primary colors).

2. Identify one activity for each school day that is done only on that day. For example, Monday is "Pudding" day, Tuesday is "Walk-to-the-Park" day, Wednesday is "Popcorn" day, Thursday is "Hat" day, and Friday is "Cleanup" day.

3. Each of these days has a special symbol or picture representing that activity. The symbol is placed on a cardboard square of the same color as the corresponding day on the calendar and with the name of the day printed on the bottom.

4. Introduce the calendar activity by saying, "Who knows what day it is today? Right! It's Monday. What do we do on Monday? We make pudding. It's Monday, and we're going to make pudding. Who can find the Monday card?"

5. Teach the children to learn to recognize the appropriate day-of-the-week card by relating the activity symbol to its matching color and word.

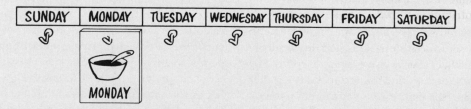

(For children with severe disabilities, show a duplicate of the activity card during the actual activity. This will help with symbolic representation and memory.)

6. At the end of the day, again say, "What day is it today? It's Monday and we made pudding." Then foreshadow a *future* event by saying, "Who knows what day it will be tomorrow? It's Tuesday. And what do we do on Tuesday?" Encourage the children to find the Tuesday card but do not hang it on the calendar until the next day.

7. At the beginning of the next day, begin by asking, "Who knows what day it was *yesterday*? What did we do?" Point to the Monday activity card already placed on the calendar the previous day and review the Monday activity. This facilitates children's learning of past tense.

SUNDAY	MONDAY	TUESDAY	WEDNESDAY	THURSDAY	FRIDAY	SATURDAY

MONDAY   TUESDAY

8. Repeat steps 4, 5, and 6 for Tuesday and so on.
9. As the week progresses, have the children mark the sequence of days and the passage of time as the activity cards fill up the calendar. As the week comes to a close, briefly review the week's events and talk about weekend plans.

   With this activity, a child who has severe cognitive disabilities can work on matching and eventually associate the activity symbol card with the activity and a particular day of the week. Children without disabilities can learn the days of the week; use language to describe past, current, and future events; and learn to read the names of the days of the week.

demands, teachers can help children have productive contact with early learning materials.

When environmental demands do not exceed children's response capabilities, frustration can be avoided and involvement sustained. Puzzles exemplify a type of material that often places inappropriate demands on children. Teachers are surprised at the difficulty level of many puzzles supposedly designed for young children. Even though puzzles do have concrete beginnings and endings, their difficulty level may be conducive to only limited involvement. Perhaps an appropriate puzzle is just not available when the child decides to visit the puzzle corner. She may then wander around or try to take another child's puzzle. This child's so-called attention deficit may be related more to the characteristics of the activity than to those of the child.

Active Looking and Listening. An excellent activity in which to encourage active looking, listening, and thinking is through cooking activities. For example, nearly all children (and adults) love to make cookies or popcorn. Children are presented with the steps of a recipe: first demonstrated verbally with actual ingredients and utensils and then with a large written display including both print and pictures.

The teacher demonstrates each step of the recipe, then children participate in each step (with as much active hands-on participation as possible). Each child should be encouraged to describe what he or she is doing and, later, what was done. Children can count and measure and practice scooping and pouring. They can observe and describe the properties of the ingredients used. They can anticipate/predict how the ingredients might change as they are heated—that is, "cooked" or "baked." They can observe the final product to test their predictions and review the process. Finally, they can eat and savor their snack! Demonstrated and talked about, cooking is a literacy lesson, a language lesson, a fine motor lesson, a science lesson, and a math lesson all rolled into one. Further, children's attention and engagement are easily maintained. Exhibit 9–3 discusses why snack time is a perfect activity in which to embed cognitive skill development.

Exhibit 9–3

Snack Time: A Perfect Time to Develop Concepts

Most early education centers focus on teaching children how to enjoy a wide variety of foods. They stress good nutrition and encourage social manners. In addition, snack time provides a unique opportunity for developing concepts. Although different foods are eaten, the routine remains essentially the same each day: arranging the table, deciding how much food is needed, and discussing the qualities of the food. Eating is a multisensory experience that should not be taken for granted.

Unlike nouns, concept words cannot be taught directly, as they are not objects with names. Instead, concepts must be experienced and appropriate concept words applied to the experiences. Snack time provides an ideal opportunity for many children to become directly involved in concept-related experiences. For example, a child's glass may be *full* or *empty,* the grapefruit is *larger* than the apple, there are *not enough* straws, but there are *more* on the table. Through lively conversations, observations can be guided, comparisons made, and concept words practiced. Meaningful questions readily bring light to number, size, and placement concepts.

Of course, snack time is not the only time to focus on concept development. It is just one of the best and often overlooked times. The ability to attend is greatly enhanced when touchable favorite foods can be smelled, seen, and tasted. Even children who are very easily distracted become intently involved when they have good things to eat.

Structuring Learning Experiences

Young children who have not yet developed adequate attention, concentration, perceptual, or memory skills may not be making effective contact with their learning environment. By structuring the curriculum, teachers can help these children become active problem solvers and effective learners. Attention must be given to the scheduling of a structured, isolated, small-group instructional session by restructuring the periods of the day traditionally called "free-play time" or "center time." In an inclusive early education class, there might be 4 or 5 children with disabilities in a group of 20. Even though there may be only one or two teachers, aides are usually available so that one adult can be involved in each of three small groups. Ideally, each group would contain a mix of children with and without disabilities. The children without disabilities function as models and often spontaneously assist a child who is having difficulty with a particular task.

Many activities such as puzzles, cutting, and drawing are easily adapted. Children can work side by side with puzzles of differing difficulty level or can cut with scissors designed to accommodate different levels of skill. If necessary, a particular child may be seated closest to the adult at the table so that sufficient opportunities for reinforcement and prompts are available.

Photo by Lisa Wadors

Another approach includes having half the class group come to the work area while the other half continues in free play. The second group comes to the work area after the first group has completed a designated number of individually prescribed tasks. In this way children who need extra support always have peer models available.

Supporting Children's Planning Skills.   Many young children with special needs have difficulty *planning*. They need to learn how to begin a task, stay with it, and recognize when it is completed. They may see a task as endless and fail to recognize when they should take pleasure in a product or in the process of learning to learn. To promote successful contact with the task and recognition of accomplishment, it may be best to begin with learning tasks that have a visually concrete beginning and ending. Functional activities such as picking up all the blocks after play time, putting them in their proper container, putting the top on, and returning them to the shelf can be broken down into small units that are gradually combined as children develop increasing attention and concentration skills.

Arranging Materials.   The following suggestions will be helpful to the child who has difficulty organizing her own work area. Such a problem is common to children who have delays in perceptual development.

1. Limit materials to only those needed to complete the task.

2. Arrange initially needed materials before the child arrives or ask the child to bring the red tub (which contains necessary materials) to the center. This prevents distractible children from having to wait and possibly beginning to lose interest.

3. Be certain that all materials are within the child's reach and at eye level.

4. Put loose materials in a container to avoid spills and their resulting distraction.

5. Use visual supports and guidelines such as the placement card holders that come with some visual matching cards to help the child develop necessary organization skills such as left–right progression.

EMERGENT MATH AND SCIENCE

According to a 2000 joint statement by the National Association for the Education of Young Children and the National Council of Teachers of Mathematics, as we become "more aware of the importance of early experiences in learning to read and write, a similar awareness with respect to mathematics is critical" (p. 1). No doubt the same can be said with regard to early science instruction. Research conducted by Gelman and Brenneman (2004) concludes that young children may be capable of far more complex scientific thinking than is commonly assumed. A recent report from the National Research Council (2005) examined the topic of math and scientific development in early childhood. It is important for early childhood educators and special educators to realize that many of the early cognitive skills described by Piaget can be enhanced and utilized in early childhood classrooms to prepare children for successful learning in math and science. Indeed all children—including children with special needs—are fascinated by the world around them. Children love engaging in hands-on exploration and experimentation with every kind of "flora and fauna" and are sensitive to interesting changes in space (e.g., "big," "round") and quantity (e.g., "one," "lots") and similarities and differences (e.g., "more," "bigger"). The inherent appeal of elements associated with math and science should not be underestimated. For many toddlers and preschool children with disabilities, activities associated with pre-math and scientific inquiry may be more engaging and more accessible than language and literacy. Teachers must not overlook the possibilities of accessing these skills *through* science and math.

In the past, activities related to classification (grouping), including sorting and matching, categorization, and seriation (ordering); concepts of space, time, and number; and comparisons (similarities, differences, and opposites) were common in early childhood curricula. Classroom strategies for several of these are presented below.

Classification, Seriation, and Concept Development

Matching (a form of discrimination) and then putting things together that are the same or alike is among the first of the expected skills. Identical things are matched, whereas things that are alike in some way are *grouped. Sorting* is also a form of discrimination followed by separating according to differences. Both matching and sorting activities are described within the broader context of **classification** (distinguishing characteristics of things, then sorting, matching, or otherwise grouping them). Note that the ability to understand the concepts of "same" and "different" is essential to performing on tests and following directions. Teachers should carefully teach the verbal labels of "same" and "alike" and "different," "not the same," and "not alike." As children learn to classify, they are encouraged to begin with concrete, multisensory objects. Attention must be called to the various *attributes* (features or characteristics) of the objects. It is a pleasure to watch children as they move from the concrete to the abstract or from the simple to the complex in their thinking. For example, very young children are dominated by what they see, hear, smell, or touch. This is known as being "perceptually dominated." They will describe an orange as something that is orange in color, round, or rough (depending on the words within their vocabulary). Later they will be interested in its function and will classify it as "something to eat." Finally, it will become part of a whole class labeled "fruit."

In general, expectations move from the concrete to the abstract, from the simple to the complex, and from the here and now to the remote in time and space (Hohmann & Weikart, 2002).

Seriation (ordering according to relative differences) is thought to be preliminary to understanding number concepts. Practice in seriation helps children coordinate relationships as they begin to understand size, position, and time comparisons. Teachers begin with highly dissimilar objects and move gradually toward the discrimination of finer and finer differences.

Making comparisons to see what goes together and what does not enhances thinking skills. *Grouping* and *regrouping* in many different ways require flexibility of thought. This flexibility is basic to successful reasoning, judging, and problem solving.

Once critical preacademic skills are identified as preschool objectives, the next step is to embed them into meaningful and engaging activities within the curriculum. The following sections present suggestions for teaching and developing necessary preacademic skills in young children. Exhibit 9-1, presented earlier in the chapter, can help teachers implement their curriculum with children who need extra time and spaced practice.

Facilitating Classification

Classification activities should not simply teach children to group or sort by similar features but should also encourage children to organize (group or sort) the same information in different ways. This will encourage more flexible thinking. Most preschool curricula emphasize teaching colors, shapes, and sizes. Initial classification of things by these attributes should include a wide range of items. As children become adept at sorting things by color, they should be introduced to colored shapes. As they learn to sort by shapes, they can be provided with shapes of different sizes and thicknesses.

Children with special needs may first enjoy functional sorting with and matching familiar objects such as shoes, cups, cars, and so forth before they can sort more abstract features such as shapes, colors, and size. Matching socks of different colors and sizes is as useful as more elaborate teaching activities. Sorting colored balls into two boxes can be both a learning experience and a useful cleanup activity. The teacher should encourage children to think of *their own* criteria for grouping. In this way the teacher can reward their tendencies toward divergent or creative thinking.

Using Attribute Blocks. A good set of attribute blocks includes red, yellow, and blue circles, squares, rectangles, and triangles. Each shape is provided in two sizes and two thicknesses. Children can sort them into several identical plastic boxes with low sides to make it easy to see them. At first the children are taught to put all the red shapes together, mixing

all the shapes in the same container but keeping the color constant. The blocks are mixed together on the floor in a pile, in equal amounts of red, yellow, and blue. The teacher begins by saying, "Let's put all the red ones here" and then picks up three or four red blocks one at a time, saying, "This one is red" each time. Next, a child is directed to "Find another red one" and place it into the correct box. The process is continued until all of the blocks have been sorted according to color.

After a few days of doing this, circles and squares are contrasted. Again, blocks of all three colors and both shapes are mixed in a pile on the floor. The teacher sets the stage in the manner just described, except that now *shape* is the criterion.

As soon as the children are secure in this classification, multiple criteria can be introduced. Using the identical materials and boxes, they sort the blocks according to color *and* shape. Blue squares can be placed in one box and yellow circles in another. Later, big blue squares and little blue squares may be segregated. Yellow circles and yellow triangles should be sorted before thin yellow circles are segregated from thick yellow circles.

Adapting Instruction.   Individualizing behavioral objectives is important because as in all teaching activities, the teacher's skill in making the activity interesting and enjoyable is important. There should never be a sense of solemnity or serious importance with games. It is critical for the teacher to be alert to support each child at her success level. If the lesson includes children of more than one skill level (and it should), all of the suggestions made for individualizing within the group should be followed.

A well-organized set of performance objectives enables the teacher to move forward or backward in providing the appropriate challenge while avoiding the overwhelming obstacle of failure. For example, the teacher may hand a red circle to Willie and say, "Let's put this big red circle with the other big red circles here" as she points and guides Willie's hand to the right box.

But she may say to Susie, sitting next to Willie, "Susie, what should go into this box?" as she points to the box with big red circles. Susie likely will respond,

"Big red circles." In this way, each child is challenged, but no child fails. They also learn from each other.

Attending to Relevant Features

The attribute blocks can be used to develop the understanding of *rules*. During the beginning sorting activities, the teacher can say, "My rule (criterion) in this box is everything yellow," or "My rule in this box is only circles." After several sessions using the term *rule*, the teacher may ask, "What is my rule in this box?" as she points to a box with blocks of one characteristic. If the children seem puzzled, the teacher can simply answer the question, "My rule in this box is _____," and then call one child to "follow the rule" and choose a block to add to the box.

The teacher should continue to use the term *rule* and to assist any child who does not grasp the idea. Usually several children will begin to understand and use the word correctly. They provide continued practice for the others. For those who grasp the idea quickly, a new dimension can be added. By providing them with an assortment of blocks and boxes, the teacher can encourage the children to make up a rule and make the teacher figure out their rule. But this is difficult for many children long after they can quickly identify the teacher's rules. The teacher should be patient. Continuing to play with the blocks in this manner leads to a firm grasp of an important principle: the same things can be sorted (categorized or classified) in different ways.

Grouping the Same Things Using Different Rules.   Awareness of grouping the same things using different rules is necessary for reading. After all, the same letters can be grouped in many different ways. Children must recognize that they can group things according to one category, such as animals, food, things that go (transportation), and toys, and then that these things can be grouped in other ways. As soon as children grasp the idea of primary categories, they should be introduced to sorting each category into subclassifications. Foods divide into fruit, meat, and vegetables. Animals can be classified as farm and zoo, tame and wild, or pets and nonpets. Clothing can be sorted into things for the head,

things for the feet, things to wear outdoors, and things to wear inside. Each of these cognitive skills requires knowing the names of things, the uses of things, and the ways in which they can be sorted. Remember, these are readiness activities for true *hierarchical* grouping that occurs later.

Encouraging Flexibility in Thinking.   Teachers should encourage flexibility in thinking. Sorting toys into different storage containers at different times is one useful way of doing this. For example, a class had been keeping toy animals in a box with pictures of animals on it and Lincoln Logs in their special box. One day, two boys insisted that Lincoln Logs belonged with the animals. Their reasoning: "We plan to use the logs to make a fence in our zoo tomorrow." Because teaching children to think in flexible, creative ways is a major goal, the logs stayed with the animals—that is, until someone else decided they were just right for the farm. Then they sorted the zoo animals and the farm animals separately with no direction from the teacher. The logs moved to the farm.

Children enjoy the challenge of sorting anything if the teacher is enthusiastic and excited when they grasp new ideas. For example, a teacher laminated a large piece of cardboard and divided it into four sections. Pictures were chosen from categories the children had been studying. At first, the cardboard merely took the place of the boxes used in the first lessons. (For some children, it is useful to actually place the boxes on the cardboard at first.) Then, when they recognized that the task was the same (sorting according to categories), the boxes were removed. The teacher continued to refer to the divisions on the cardboard as boxes.

Later, the children will need to know that rectangles and squares in their kindergarten workbooks are called boxes. These earlier experiences help them bridge the gap between real boxes and boxes on paper. Children who learn less quickly than some of their peers will benefit from a larger variety of materials. Not only does this help them see more relationships, but it also lessens the likelihood of boredom in doing the same thing in the same way over a longer period.

Problem Solving in a Montessori Classroom

A visit to a Montessori classroom would reveal an array of attractive materials. Each would emphasize teaching one dimension. Each would be "self-correcting" in that the material would reveal the error, allowing the child to correct herself by further experimentation. For example, the knobbed cylinders shown in the picture fit snugly in only one corresponding hole. Focus between the ages of 3 and 6 would be on self-directed concentration.

Facilitating Seriation

Introducing children to serial ideas such as first and last should be done in the context of everyday activities, especially those that involve whole-body movement. *First* and *last* may refer to place in line or when one does something. These concepts are critical for young children entering kindergarten. Most of the problems involved in lining up or being allowed to do something are caused by children's lack of understanding and experience with these terms.

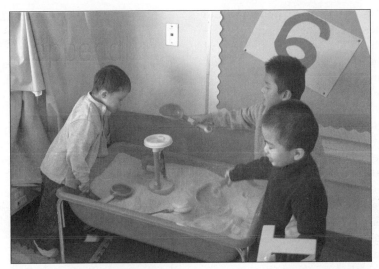

Photo by Lisa Wadors

Understanding the concept (cognition) and using the correct label (language) cannot be separated. Without the concept words, one cannot talk about the concept. Without the idea, the word is useless.

Montessori cylinders and "nesting" toys are typical seriation materials. Hardware stores often provide sample paint cards that can be used to seriate from dark to light. The teacher should not overlook using household measuring cups or variously sized nails.

Facilitating Concept Development

Learning abstract concepts such as "many," "different," "whole," "taller," "tallest," "in front of," and so on is often a special challenge for children with disabilities. Providing children sufficient experiences with the many concepts they must learn and the association with the words is a challenge. Merely keeping track of the concepts requires a system. A system for teaching concepts includes the following features:

1. Identify the concepts to be taught.

2. Plan a large number of activities and experiences that make explicit the idea of each concept.

3. Use the associated concept word throughout many class sessions as the need for the word occurs. That is, grasp the moment most likely to demonstrate the concept meaning to the child and use the word at that moment.

4. Provide many experiences involving a particular concept close together but in natural, spontaneous ways. For example, if grasping the idea of "first" is the target, play many different games requiring lining up in serial order. Focus on "first" in moving from one activity to another in the room. Lining toy animals in a row, identifying the animal that is "first," and then turning all the animals around to discover that the one that was first is last helps to make the concept clear.

5. Provide for contrived uses of the concept word by the children. That is, create the occasions when spontaneously using the target word throughout the day is appropriate.

6. When most of the children use the word some of the time and most of them appear to understand it, establish a system for regular review. Of course, if the concept words are used frequently because they are needed and useful, the review is spontaneous and effortless.

Each playgroup or classroom will want to focus on many of the same concept words. Needs are quite universal. An examination of teachers' manuals for kindergarten and first-grade reading and arithmetic yields a large number of necessary concept words. These should be introduced through real-life and play activities at least 2 years before the children encounter them in school. "Put your finger at the top of the page" is a much harder direction to under-

stand if children have not learned about "the top shelf" or "the top of the page" in a book as someone reads a story. A review of the Boehm Test of Basic Concepts (Boehm, 2001) will be helpful in selecting target concepts.

Teaching Number Concepts.   Exhibit 9–4 presents early pre-number and number concepts. Some pre-number concepts are included in the skills described

---

Exhibit 9–4

Number Concepts

Pre-number skills

Sorting and classification

- Describing attributes
- Sorting/classification
- Attribute games

Patterning

- Pattern replication using objects
- Describing pattern
- Complete pattern using objects
- Translate pictured pattern to objects
- Create a pattern

Relations

- Comparing two objects (bigger/smaller; same as)
- Comparing substances (more/less than; same as)
- Ordering objects (smallest to largest and so on)
- Equivalence sets of objects: one-to-one correspondence

Spatial relations

- Understanding self in space
- Relation of self to objects (near, far, under, outside, and so on)
- Relation of objects to other objects

Time relations

- Understanding time periods have beginning and end
- Order events sequentially
- Concepts (first, last, before, after, next, yesterday, today, tomorrow)

Conservation

- Understanding that quantity and volume remain unchanged if arranged differently (e.g., viewing liquid in different-shaped containers)

Number skills

- Counting
- Rote counting
- Rational counting: identifying group by cardinal number (e.g., "There are *three* ducks")
- Ordinal number (e.g., "first, second, third)

Source. D. Keane, personal communication (2007).

above. In teaching numbers and counting, it is common to teach rote counting from 1 to 5 or 10. Many children with disabilities learn this verbal pattern fairly easily. However, repeated rote counting without matching number to each item counted (as evidenced by pointing or touching the item) may interfere with actual understanding of number concepts. While stacking and counting blocks, for example, the teacher should assist the child in actually picking up and placing each block as he or the teacher says each number. Also, counting to see how high the blocks can be stacked helps demonstrate the usefulness of number as a way of measuring quantity (e.g., "Oh wow! You stacked *nine* blocks this time!"). This approach supports the development of *rational counting,* that is, identifying the number of things in a group (the *cardinal* number). This can then lend itself to the development of understanding *ordinal* numbers (first, second, third, and so on).

Avoiding Stereotyped, Labored Teaching of Concepts.   It is important to understand that regardless of specific behaviors identified as required school readiness skills, teachers must understand and be able to support the child's development of flexible, analytical, logical thinking. The examples above support this process. Teachers should provide frequent opportunities for children to learn the concepts through experiences appropriate to a particular setting. (See Exhibit 9–3 for an example.) They should not leave the learning of important concepts to chance. The basic procedure that should be followed is outlined here:

- Identify the concepts.
- Use them.
- Make meanings clear.
- Monitor use over time.

DEVELOPMENT OF LITERACY

The previous section considered certain cognitive subskills related to academic readiness. In this section, we consider social and linguistic factors related to literacy.

Nearly two decades ago, Morrison (1991) suggested that literacy had become the "hot topic" among early educators (p. 91). This is even more true today. Debates about the best instructional approaches to literacy have intensified in recent years. This is at least partly in response to the fact that millions of Americans are functionally illiterate. It is also related to the growing numbers of children who enter school without the necessary prerequisite communication skills and early experiences that prepare children to participate in formal literacy education.

A term that reflects the emphasis on the relationship of early experience to literacy is **emergent literacy.** "Emergent literacy refers to the developmental precursors of formal reading that have their origins early in the life of the child" (Whitehurst & Lonigan, 2001, p. 12). Literacy is not simply an accumulation of the specific skills related to reading and writing but rather evolves through both social and cognitive processes that begin at birth. Literacy evolves gradually as a function of exposure to and interaction with print materials and exposure to other children and adults who are *using* print, that is, "literacy events." Examples of literacy events include the following:

1. Daily living activities, such as making lists for grocery shopping; reading labels and recipes; going to various public services offices such as the departments of welfare, employment, and motor vehicles; and paying bills.

2. Entertainment, such as reading newspaper movie listings, television guides, and books; doing crossword puzzles; and reading subtitles or credits on films or videos.

3. Religious activities, such as attending Bible study groups, singing hymns, and reading daily devotions books.

4. Work-related activities, such as writing checks, reading instructions, following delivery instructions, and stocking shelves.

5. School-related activities, such as doing homework or playing "school."

6. Interpersonal communications, such as writing and reading notes, letters, and birthday cards.

7. Storybook time, in which children are read to, primarily for their entertainment.

8. Literacy techniques and skills, which include activities in which reading or writing is the specific focus of the interaction. Such activities are often initiated by the child (e.g., the child asks "What is this word?" or "How do you make a *T*?").

Van Kleeck (1990) pointed out that mere exposure to literacy materials and experiences is not sufficient for the development of literacy. Rather, it is the adult–child interaction around such events that is important.

The Precursors of Reading and Writing

Increasingly, researchers in the area of literacy development acknowledge the relationship between certain early skills and experiences and the development of reading and writing (e.g., Hart & Risley, 1999; Palakian, 2004; Snow, Burns, & Griffin, 1998; Strickland & Shanahan, 2004; Whitehurst & Lonigan, 2001). The best early predictors of eventual competency in literacy appear to be speech and language abilities, particularly vocabulary, and **phonological awareness** and familiarity with the **alphabetic principle.** (In chapter 8 we addressed the social interactions and language inputs and experiences that are important to language development. Thus, these same early caregiver interactions have later impact on literacy.)

Writing.   Several developmental domains relate significantly to the beginning development of children's writing skills. The development of fine motor and visual-motor skills is obviously critical to the child's ability to eventually use pencils and markers to draw the abstract forms that make up letters of the alphabet. Specifically, the following are important:

- Children's early experiences with art materials such as paints, crayons, and markers.

- Adult encouragement and assistance in controlling print tools to make lines and circles.

- Noticing similarities and differences in shapes and configurations.

Photo by Annette Tessier

Also important is the cognitive skill of representation:

- Recognizing that pictures represent real things.

- Attempts to use drawings as representation.

- Adult assistance in learning to draw faces, body parts, and houses, flowers, grass, sky, and so on.

Early social experiences are also critical in the emergence of writing. Particularly important is the opportunity for involvement in adults' functional uses of writing, such as making a grocery list or writing a letter.

Reading.   Certain experiences and achievements are also critical to the eventual development of reading. In the area of language development, the following are important:

- The development of oral language, particularly the development of narrative (e.g., storytelling) skills.

- The development of a rich vocabulary.

- Phonological and phonemic awareness and skills such as sound segmentation and rhyming.

Early exposure to literate events in the home is also critical to learning to read:

- Exposure and access to children's books.

- Being read to on a regular basis.

- Observation and participation in adults' functional uses of reading (e.g., reading recipes, correspondence from friends and relatives, reading menus in restaurants, and so on).

- Adults' attention to the alphabetic principle (e.g., reference to printed words and letters in storybooks, naming letters, teaching letter sounds, and so on).

Exhibit 9–5 presents an example of the sequence of development of emergent literacy skills for one child.

Watson, Layton, Pierce, and Abraham (1994) discuss the importance of including activities and materials that can facilitate the development of emergent literacy for all children, including those with speech and language impairments. They describe a preschool classroom that is designed to address the following literacy goals throughout the day. These are discussed in the following sections.

Print Awareness.
- Recognizes environmental print (e.g., fast-food logos on napkins, empty food containers and wrappers, stop signs, bathroom signs, and so on)

- Understands functional uses of print (e.g., daily attendance, lunch menus, job assignments, treasure hunts, letter-writing center, pretend mailbox, and so on)

Concepts of Book Print.
- Recognizes parts of a book (cover, pages, back)

- Understands book orientation (turning pages from front to back, top and bottom of page, reading left to right)

- Understands vocabulary labels related to print (e.g., "letter," "word," "sentence")

Exhibit 9–5

Sample of Emergent Literacy: Sequence of Emergence of Reading and Writing for One Child

Writing

1. Scribbles with marker and crayon
2. Makes lines and circles
3. Draws a face
4. Adds arms and legs to face
5. Draws a house
6. Pretends to write letters to friends using wavy lines
7. Practices making letter-like forms
8. Includes some real letters
9. Writes own name
10. Writes other words (e.g., "Dear Mom")

Reading

1. Enjoys looking at books
2. Listens carefully to story while looking at pictures
3. Holds book right side up; turns pages from front to back
4. Talks about picture
5. Retells favorite stories by looking at pictures
6. Recognizes environmental print (*McDonald's* and *Coke* logos)
7. Tries to rhyme words; likes books with rhyming words
8. Pretends to "read" storybooks
9. Recognizes repeated printed words in familiar book
10. Recognizes own printed name
11. Associates "mm" and sound to initial letter in "Mom."

Story Sense.

- Recalls main story elements (e.g., characters, main event, ending [resolution])
- Can retell well-structured story (e.g., maintains main story elements in sequence)

Vocabulary Development.

- Demonstrates steady increase in vocabulary
- Enjoys learning to understand and use new words throughout all activities of the day
- Can define and discuss meanings of words

Phonologic Awareness.

- Can separate spoken words (e.g., knows that "I love you" contains three separate words)
- Can identify the beginning sound ("onset") of a word and separate the beginning sound from the rest of the word ("rime")
- Can segment spoken words into syllables (e.g., can break up word "elephant" into "el-e-phant")
- Can break syllables into phonemes, or sounds (e.g., "pup" has three sounds: "p-uh-p")
- Can hear and produce syllables and words that rhyme

Alphabetic Understanding.

- Can name letters
- Understands that letter combinations/sequences represent words
- Understands that individual letters represent speech sounds (phonemes)

Speech/Print Match.

- Can follow print while listening to familiar story
- Has some sight vocabulary
- Can make initial sound–letter association (e.g., knows that printed word "door" starts with "d" sound, though child does not recognize entire word)

Control of Reading/Writing.

- Tries to read and write
- Identifies letter names
- Can write some letters given the sound
- Uses invented spelling (i.e., makes up spelling; writes words like they sound, e.g., "bk" for "book," "luv" for "love")

Watson et al. (1994) made several specific suggestions for including literacy-rich activities and materials into each component of the preschool classroom. (See also Hemmeter, McCollum, & Hsieh, 2005; McCathren & Allor, 2005.) The following are just a few of these suggestions:

1. *Opening Circle Time.*
   - Have children find their own mats for circle time by identifying their name on the mat or their own picture symbol.
   - Assign children to daily jobs by hanging name tag next to duty assigned (e.g., "Jon— Pass out cups").

2. *Story Time.*
   - Repeat stories frequently.
   - Select stories with concepts that are developmentally appropriate to child's cognitive level and interest.
   - Select books with rhymes and predictable phrases.
   - Provide extra copies of the book in the reading corner for individual use.
   - Make sure books used in circle time are large enough and have pictures and print that are easily seen and recognizable from a distance.
   - Encourage child's *active* participation in storytime, both motorically and cognitively (e.g., invite children to act out parts of the story; ask children what they think will happen next). Use "dialogic reading" strategies (Whitehurst & Lonigan, 2001) in which the child comments and asks questions and the adult responds.

- Ask children to find letters in words that are also in their own name or a friend's name. Or count certain letters on a page (e.g. "How many letter *B*s can we find in this sentence?").

3. *Literacy-Rich Centers.*
   - Art and writing center: Provide drawing and writing tools, stationery, envelopes, blank pages, and albums for making books and so on.
   - Role-playing center: In addition to usual dress-up materials and housekeeping toys, also include pads and pencils for shopping lists, a mailbox and envelopes, TV guide, cookbooks, checkbook, and so forth.
   - Book and library center: Include books with cassette tapes, copies of books read in circle time, predictable books, newspapers, and magazines. Make sure seating is comfortable and inviting for both adults and children.

4. *Snack Time.*
   - Make alphabet soup.
   - Read labels on food containers.
   - Follow recipes.

5. *Outdoor Activities.*
   - Play "Simon Says" using large word cards or pictures. Combine name card with action card to encourage reading two words at a time (e.g., "Sandra—Jump" or "Everyone—Run").
   - Label storage areas (e.g., "BIKES," "BALLS").

6. *Closing Circle/Music Time.*
   - Have a picture representing favorite songs on a large poster. Children choose closing songs by pointing to the appropriate picture.
   - Send notes home with children for parents to read.
   - Have children find their own art project to take home by looking for their name.

Early exposure to literacy activities is equally important to children with and without disabilities. Some time ago, a study by Katims (1991) found that preschool children with mild to moderate disabilities benefited significantly from the addition of three types of literacy activities to the classroom: (a) classroom library with familiar and predictable books, (b) frequent group storybook reading, and (c) a classroom writing center.

Relationship Between Oral Language and Literacy

Much has been written about the relationship between oral language skills and literacy (e.g., Catts & Kamhi, 2005; Dickinson & Tabors, 2001) as well as the nature of the school discourse style, or school language, that is required for successful performance in schools. Young children need to be familiar with certain types of language, sometimes referred to as **literate-style language,** in order to learn to read and write. This type of language is more decontextualized than language that is used in the home. Language used in the home often has a great deal of shared understanding among speakers. Such language does not depend solely on the *words* used in the communication but also on gestures, facial expression, and intonation as well as the shared knowledge and experience of the speakers. The examples in Exhibit 9-6 demonstrate two types of communication style: *interpersonal language style* typical of that used in the home or with close friends and *literate style,* which is the type required in the classroom and serves as the basis for the development of reading and writing. In addition, school classrooms require certain kinds of communication skills. These include answering questions, using language to "show and tell," raising hands before speaking, using language to talk about language and thinking, and so on.

The Nature of School Language

To be successful in school, children must be able to demonstrate certain kinds of communication skills. Some of these skills are linguistic, and some are social or pragmatic.

Exhibit 9–6

Demonstration of Literate and Interpersonal Language Styles in a 4-Year-Old

Interpersonal Style

Kisha: (Spilling chocolate milk on her dress) *Oh darn!*

Mother: Oh oh. Take it off.

Kisha: Should I put some of that stuff on it?

Mother: Good idea.

Kisha: Hope it's not ruined.

Literate Style

Kisha: (Returning from a visit to her grandmother's) *Hi, Mom!*

Mother: Did you have a good time? Tell me all about it.

Kisha: Well, Grandma took me shopping at the mall. We went to the new Disney store there. They have the same stuff as in Disneyland. I saw a really cute Minnie Mouse doll, but it was awful expensive, so Grandma couldn't buy it for me. I did get a silver necklace, though. It has lots of things on it, like Mickey and Minnie and Pluto and even Goofy. After the mall we had supper at McDonald's.

In the first example, language is characterized by short utterances and frequent use of pronouns. There is little specificity or explicitness because it is not necessary. Mother and child both share the same reference—the spilled milk and the stain on the dress.

In the second example, Kisha is engaging in a narrative; she is describing past events, much as she would tell a story. Her narrative has a beginning, a middle, and an end, and it represents the sequence in which events actually occurred. She is using explicit and specific language, which is necessary because her mother has not shared her experience. This type of language use is said to be more *decontextualized* because there are fewer contextual cues. It is also referred to as *autonomous* language because the words and sentences must stand alone without the assistance of shared context or visual props.

It is also important to note that in the second example there is clearly an expectation on the mother's part that Kisha will "perform" the narrative account of her experiences. This helps prepare Kisha for the kinds of academic performances that will be required of her in school.

Certain kinds of interactions required in classrooms may be unfamiliar to some children. The following are examples:

- Children are required to raise their hands before speaking.
- Children are expected to answer questions individually, addressing the group at large. (Many children may be more accustomed to demonstrating their understanding through action rather than words.)
- Children are expected to respond very quickly.
- Teachers ask questions that are "test questions"; that is, the teacher already knows the answer and is using the question to evaluate the child's knowledge. Such a format is unfamiliar to many children.

The linguistic skills required are those that have been alluded to earlier in the chapter, including the following:

- The child must use and understand language in the classroom that is often decontextualized (i.e., not embedded in the immediate context). For

example, the teacher often gives instructions using only words, or the child is asked to describe a past event.

- Vocabulary is expected to be specific and precise.

- Syntax and grammar are used to carefully mark the relationships among sentences (e.g., "if," "but," "because," and so on).

- Narratives are expected to reflect sequence accurately and be coherent.

These literate language skills are built on the symbolic, referential language concepts that emerged during the preschool years. In turn, reading and writing skills, which must be learned in the primary grades, will be based on literate-style language. Many children do not have the kinds of early language experiences that prepare them for success in the early grades. In part this may be due to cultural differences. The following section addresses some of the ways in which children's early experiences with language and literacy may be different from what is expected in the classroom.

CULTURAL DIFFERENCES IN EARLY LANGUAGE AND LITERACY EXPERIENCES

Bunce (2003) discussed the impact of cultural and linguistic differences on early language development and school achievement. Infants and young children are exposed to a wide variety of early experiences related to language use and reading and writing. Some of the most important research related to cultural differences in these early experiences was reported by Heath (1983) in her book *Ways with Words*. Using the classic ethnographic research method of participant observation, Heath carefully observed families in two communities in the Piedmont area of Appalachia. Heath provided detailed descriptions of the interactions between adults and young children in a working-class White community and in a rural African American community. She compared these interactions with the types of interactions that are typical of what

she referred to as White middle-class "mainstream" families.

Differences in Children's Early Use of Narrative

Of particular importance, according to Heath, are differences found in the types of narratives that young children are encouraged to use. Narratives are important both because they are believed to form the foundation for learning to read and write and because children are expected to be able to perform certain types of narratives when they enter school.

Heath (1986) summarized the kinds of narratives most common among different cultures as follows.

1. *Recounts.* A recount is a report of an experience from the past. It is commonly parent initiated (e.g., "Jenny, tell Daddy about your field trip"). Recounts are the most common form of narrative required in the public school. Unfortunately, they are the least common form of narrative in nonmainstream cultures. In middle-class mainstream families, however, children are encouraged not only to produce recounts frequently but also to use literate-style language—that is, language that is precise, highly referential, and in proper sequence.

2. *Eventcasts.* An eventcast is a description of a current activity. It describes situations or activities that are immediate or obvious, such as "I'm building a tower" or "Mommy's making pudding now." This type of communication is also common in mainstream families and in public schools (e.g., "John, tell us what the boy in the picture is doing"). However, it is very uncommon in many nonmainstream cultures, in which it is often considered ridiculous to talk about the obvious. Consider the effect of the following classroom scenario on a child who is not accustomed to the use of eventcasts. Paul is making a ball out of a piece of clay. The teacher notices and says to Paul, "Oh Paul, tell us what you're making!" Whereas a middle-class child might easily launch into a detailed description of what he was doing, Paul is somewhat bewildered and probably not sure he understood the teacher's question. He might even be concerned

that describing such an obvious thing would be insulting to her.

As children get older, they learn to use eventcasts in **metalinguistic** and **metacognitive** ways. In other words, they use language to reflect on language or thinking (e.g., "Let me think about how to do that" or "Oops! I said that wrong"). This is an important school language behavior, and it is useful in learning how to learn.

Somewhat related to eventcasts is the kind of response required by the typical classroom test question format—the familiar teacher–student interaction consisting of a question–reply–evaluate sequence that predominates in school classrooms. The following is an example:

Teacher: Sean, what is the first word?

Sean: Trucks.

Teacher: No, that's wrong.

In this format, the child is being asked to answer a question that the adult already knows the answer to. For many children this is bizarre.

3. *Accounts.* Accounts are similar to recounts in that they tell about a past event. However, accounts are initiated by the child rather than by an adult. Accounts are often accompanied by communication strategies designed to get and hold the listener's attention (e.g., "Hey, ya know what?"). Although these types of narratives are much more common in nonmainstream families than are recounts and eventcasts, they are discouraged in many public school classrooms and are often punished as interruptions or off-task behavior.

4. *Stories.* According to Heath (1986), the most common type of narrative among nonmainstream families is the story. Stories are often handed down from generation to generation, or they may evolve over a period within the child's early experience. Stories may begin with an adult teasing a child about a particular event. Stories evolve and change over time, and eventually some parts may be fictionalized. Stories contain strong elements of performance; the narrator's style is important, and listener participation

in the story is often expected. Needless to say, such language activities do not follow the rules of school language, and they may be viewed as lying or attention-getting behavior.

Cultural Differences in Early Caregiver–Infant Interaction

Long before children learn to use narratives, important cultural differences can be observed in how parents interact with their infants and young children (e.g., Westby, 1985). These differences can determine whether young children have opportunities to learn literate-style language prior to school entry.

Typically, middle-class caregivers are verbally responsive to their infants and young children. This may not be the case in certain other cultures. Although caregivers from other cultures may be responsive physically through touch or through facial expression, they may not respond verbally. Westby (1985) pointed out many such differences among non–middle-class cultures.

Middle-class caregivers are also more likely to use highly referential language than are caregivers who are members of some nonmainstream cultures (Snow et al., 1991). **Referential language** is characterized by use of frequent labels and precise vocabulary with clear referents. Thus, typical middle-class communication practices expose children to both a large quantity of language and the quality of language that facilitates eventual development of literate school language skills. Examples of these different kinds of caregiver–child interactions are presented in the following dialogues:

Sample 1

Jason, 12 months old, sitting in his high chair, starts to whine.

Mother: Jason, what's wrong?

Jason: (Looks down at the floor)

Mother: Oops! Your cookie, huh? You dropped your cookie. (Mother picks up the cookie) Yuk. This cookie's all dirty. See, it's dirty 'cause it was on the floor.

Sample 2

Alice, 12 months old, sitting in her high chair, starts to whine.

Mother: (Looks up at Alice)

Alice: (Looks and reaches toward the floor.)

Mother: (Picks up the cookie and hands it to Alice)
   Here it is.

In both these examples, the caregiver is responsive to her infant's cues. However, in the first example the mother is both verbally responsive and referential. She uses the word *cookie* several times and uses other key words that specifically refer to the key features of the experience—*dropped, dirty,* and *floor.* In the second example, although the mother is responsive, her language is limited. When she does verbalize, it is nonreferential in that she does not explicitly name the object *(cookie)* or the location *(floor).* Instead, she uses the words *here* and *it.*

Cultural Differences in Uses of Print

Cultural differences can also be observed in children's early experience with reading and writing. Even though reading books for pleasure or information and using writing for communication are common in middle-class homes, they may not be common in some nonmainstream homes.

In the 21st century, teachers will increasingly encounter children whose native language is not English. It is important to realize that the native language of the child is often not the only difference. Many factors can create a serious mismatch between teacher and child. The ways in which nonmainstream families provide early language and literacy experiences for their children are not wrong; they are simply sometimes different from those expected in our school systems. It is particularly important that teachers of young children with special needs understand these differences and be aware of educational strategies that can help children make a successful transition to public school settings.

STRATEGIES FOR FACILITATING EMERGENT LITERACY

In early childhood programs, the major goals related to the development of literacy range from development of a rich vocabulary and literate-style oral language skills and an awareness and understanding of the functions of reading and writing to the learning of subskills of literacy (e.g., phonological awareness, learning the alphabet, and beginning to learn sound–letter associations). These skills will provide the foundation for reading and writing as well as the skills necessary for successful teacher–student interaction in the classroom.

In order to help children achieve the necessary foundation, teachers must begin by determining which kinds of language and literacy activities are already familiar to the children in their classes and then building on these experiences. As Heath (1986) stated, educators must find ways "to use what children do with language in their homes and communities to extend and enrich the school's repertoire of narrative genres" (p. 93). In addition, teachers must help young children understand the *value* of reading and writing. The following are examples of such strategies. (See also Exhibit 9–7 for an example of embedding emergent literacy goals into a preschool science project.)

• *Demonstrate the functional uses of print.* This is one of the most powerful strategies teachers can use in the classroom. It includes such activities as reading the daily menu to see what will be served for lunch, listing on the board the names of children who are present or absent, writing notes to themselves as reminders to do something later, writing notes to other teachers, and so on. In these activities, children are *not* expected to read; more important, they are developing an understanding of the *functions* of reading and writing. As they observe the power of the printed word, children develop a fascination with decoding the mysterious symbols.

• *Work with parents to identify the ways in which print is used in each child's home.* This might include such activities as reading the television guide, reading recipes, reading food labels at the grocery store, reading comic books, and so on. Similar activities and materials can easily be incorporated into the classroom.

Photo by Krista Greco/Merrill

• *Incorporate literacy events into children's play.* Treasure hunts are exciting ways to demonstrate the use of print. Again, children are not expected to actually read the clues but to experience their effectiveness in leading to the treasure. Other examples of play activities include playing postal service (letters are "written," placed in the mailbox, and delivered), going to the grocery store with a shopping list, and pretending to read a bedtime story to a doll. Reading recipes during cooking activities and writing notes that have been dictated by children to take home to parents are other good activities.

• *Play games that require referential language to facilitate literate-style oral language.* For example, two children can be separated by a screen. The child who is "It" draws a picture and instructs the other child to draw the same thing (e.g., "Make a big circle and color it blue. Now put two black eyes on it"). The object of the game is to see how closely the pictures match. The same format can be used in playing with different shapes and colors of blocks or setting up a dollhouse. For children with severe disabilities, the game can be made simpler by using familiar objects and performing very simple tasks, such as selecting objects such as a cup and a shoe to be placed in a box, then comparing to see whether both children end up with the same objects in the box.

• *Structure other activities that facilitate literate language style.* These might include helping children explain the rules of a game to someone else, go to the school office and deliver a verbal message, describe an exciting event to a student who was absent, and play the "telephone" game. Simpler versions might include having children feel objects in a sack and guess what they are or playing "Simon Says." These activities facilitate the use of specific autonomous language. For children who are less verbal, they demonstrate the functional uses of language for the purpose of sharing information and regulating others' behavior.

• *Read stories to both large and small groups and to individual children.* The importance of doing this cannot be overestimated. The stories selected must be meaningful to the children. They should be short, and they should be repeated often. Stories should also include props, such as a flannelgraph board, or actual objects to highlight important story points. Involving children's actions at key story points is also important. Including props and actions will make story time more interesting for all children. As stories are repeated, pause at key points to allow the children to fill in the familiar phrases. Familiar storybooks should also be available to children during free-play time so they can "read" the stories to themselves or to a friend or doll. (This will necessitate having several copies of favorite books available.)

Exhibit 9–7

Supporting Emergent Literacy Through Science: Planting Seeds

Planting seeds is a common early childhood theme or unit lesson. Many features of this activity make it inherently engaging for young children. It is a hands-on activity involving familiar and interesting sensations and material such as digging in dirt and pouring water. And it usually involves being outdoors. Once the seeds are planted, it offers an on going opportunity to observe changes and make predictions. It provides a great science lesson (e.g., the transformation of a seed into a plant, identifying the different parts of the plant, comparing different kinds of plants, and so on) and opportunities to develop pre-number skills and early math concepts (e.g., How many new plants have emerged? Which one is biggest? How many inches tall is it? How many days since the seed was planted?). The possibilities are limitless.

While this activity is typically intended to support science-related goals in the curriculum, a creative teacher can easily embed the components of emergent literacy into this activity. Consider adding the following elements to the seed-planting project:

1. First, books and discussions are provided related to plants, growing things, and seeds.
   (book reading; concepts of print)

2. As children are outside at recess or on a "discovery walk," the teacher points out different plants (grasses, flowers, and so on) to make sure that children's expressive and receptive vocabularies include key words.
   (vocabulary development)

3. Children can draw the various plants they have observed or even take pictures.
   (emergent writing)

4. The teacher introduces the planting project so that children can anticipate the activity.

5. Seed packets are supplied. Children are encouraged to not only look at the picture of the plant on the package but to read the labels as well.
   (functional print)

6. Three types of seeds are provided: beans, mums, and daisies (one vegetable and two types of flowers).

7. The key words related to the project are printed on cards—Seeds, Plants, Beans, Flowers, Mums, and Daisies—and placed on a bulletin board.
   (print-rich classroom)

8. Children say the words and analyze sounds and segments:
   a. /sss/ plus /eeds/ rhymes with beads!
   b. "Dai-sies," "Flow-ers," each have two syllables
   c. "Mums" starts and ends with same sounds as "Moms"
   (phonological/phonemic awareness)

9. The word cards (with no pictures) are placed on the bulletin board in a hierarchical configuration:

Seeds

Plants

Beans   **Flowers**

Mums   **Daisies**

10. The soil is prepared in a small space outdoors. Children check to make sure the garden location will get plenty of sunlight. Three sections are marked off for planting the three different types of seeds.

11. Children participate cooperatively making small holes, pinching just a few seeds, placing them in the holes, and covering them with soil.

12. As the children place the seeds in the soil in each section, the empty seed packets are attached to a stake to make three signs representing where the different seeds are planted.
    (functional print)

13. Children are assigned responsibilities for watering.

14. As the plants begin to emerge, each week the children observe each section of the garden to see which plants are growing.

15. Key words are reinforced. New words are added in response to children's questions and comments.
    (vocabulary enrichment)

16. On the bulletin board, each week a mark is made under the name of each plant as new seedlings emerge. Numbers of plants are tallied periodically:
    a. How many bean plants?
    b. How many mums?
    c. How many daisies?
    d. How many flowers?
    e. How many plants altogether?
    (inquiry, observation, documentation, counting, addition, hierarchical classification)

17. The teacher points to each word, saying, "Which plant is this?"
    Over time she draws children's attention to the following:
    a. The letters in each word
    b. Letters the words have in common
    c. Letters that match letters in children's names

d. The sounds of the initial letter in each word

e. Long words and short words

(alphabetic principle)

18. Children may also document the growth of plants by taking photos

a. of the seeds, the soil, and placing seeds in the holes, and

b. watering the seeds, the first shoots, new leaves, measuring the height of plants, and so on.

19. A book is then made of the photos. Children generate a phrase or sentence for each page.

(narrative, grammar, concepts of print)

20. As the garden matures, new words are added to the vocabulary list, such as water, leaves, stems, pick, prune, and bouquet.

(vocabulary and knowledge enrichment)

Whole-Language Versus Phonological Approaches to the Development of Literacy

Early childhood special educators must be aware of changes in trends in teaching reading and writing in the primary grades. During the 1980s and 1990s, the field was dominated by a **whole-language approach** (Goodman & Goodman, 1986). In this approach, reading, writing, speaking, and listening are viewed as interactive and interdependent. The following are examples of common activities in a whole-language approach:

- Language experience stories that children dictate to the teacher based on shared experiences. Stories are written by the teacher on flip charts so they can be read again and again by the class. Students may copy the stories for their own reading later on.

- Choral reading of familiar stories or poems. Choral reading can play the same positive role that singing favorite songs plays for younger children. Choral reading combines this pleasurable repetition and predictability with written words.

- Use of predictable storybooks that include repetitions of sentences and key words.

- Journal writing and writing picture captions on students' own pictures.

Teaching Phonological and Phonemic Awareness

It is certainly the case that social-linguistic skills and experiences identified in whole-language and emergent literacy approaches are very important. However, the child's ability to discriminate and recognize the sound segments of words (phonological and phonemic awareness) and early learning of sound-letter relationships (alphabetic principle) are also necessary subskills in learning to read. (For a discussion of developmentally appropriate practice in teaching reading and writing, see Neuman, Copple, & Bredekamp, 2000; for a review of the research literature, see Neuman & Dickinson, 2001.)

Phonological awareness refers to the ability to recognize and discriminate certain sound segments of language including phonemes, syllables, and words and the realization that these segments can be separated, linked, and moved around. Phonemic awareness refers more specifically to the ability to perceive and manipulate phonemes (i.e., the smallest linguistic units, such as the three phonemes in the word *pin*: /pIn/). Children must ultimately learn the relationships between phonemes and letters of the alphabet in order to learn to read (i.e., sound-letter association). Learning to read by focusing on these sound-letter associations is referred to as **phonics.**

Many children have not developed this kind of sound awareness by the time they enter school. Adams (1990) reported that 25% of middle-class children—and a much higher proportion of children from less "literacy-rich" environments—have not developed these skills by first grade. Needless to say, children with auditory-based learning disabilities also have difficulty with sound awareness.

Early childhood programs can make a significant contribution to the development of these skills. The following are examples of activities (adapted from Adams, Foorman, Lundberg, & Beeler, 1998) that can support the development of phonemic awareness.

- **Develop listening skills.** Children must first learn to *listen* (i.e., to concentrate and actively process auditory information). A wide variety of simple sound awareness games can be helpful in developing children's ability to listen.

  1. With eyes closed, ask children to identify different *environmental* sounds (e.g., running water, guitar, bell, drum, scrunching paper). Increase the difficulty of the game by asking children to identify the location of the sound and then to identify the *sequence* of two or three sounds.
  2. Ask children to imitate or identify "soft" or "quiet" sounds versus "loud" sounds.
  3. Select a child to be "It." While he closes his eyes, an item with a subtle noise, such as a ticking clock or a timer, is hidden somewhere in the room. The child then has to listen carefully and try to find the item.
  4. Ask children to listen carefully and try to identify softly whispered words.

- **Help child perceive "onset and rime."**

  1. Bring to child's attention the beginning sound and the rest of the word (e.g., "pat" = /p/ plus /at/; "top" = /t/ plus /op/).

- **Develop rhyming skills.** Learning to produce and recognize words that rhyme is a first step in phonological awareness.

  1. Use ample nursery rhymes, poetry, and rhyming books in group activities. Allow children to fill in the rhyming words and to make up new rhymes.
  2. See how many words or nonsense syllables children can generate to rhyme with a certain word (e.g., "What rhymes with *bike?*").
  3. Complete rhyming pairs (e.g., *pie-sky, pin-fin, wig-?, fire-?,* and so on).

- **Develop the concept of a "word."** Children do not automatically know what a word is.

  1. Ask children to list different words (e.g., "How many color words can you think of?").
  2. Say a short sentence (e.g., "John ate pizza"). Ask children to listen carefully and count the words. Explain that there are three different words.
  3. Help children identify "long" versus "short" words (e.g., *cat* vs. *refrigerator*).

- **Teach recognition of syllables.** Children must be taught to recognize that words are made up of syllables.

  1. Ask children to count and say syllables in a word (e.g., *re-frig-er-a-tor*).
  2. Clap hands to each syllable in a word.

- **Synthesize words by combining syllables.** Help children listen to individual syllables in a word and synthesize them into the correct word.

  1. Say "Who can figure out what word I'm saying": *tel-e-vi-sion?*

- **Listen for initial sounds in single-syllable words.**

  1. Listen to the word *pin*. What is the first *sound* in the word? What other word starts with the "puh" sound?
  2. Which word starts with "puh": *cow, hat,* or *pig?* (Note that many of the activities listed above can be readily adapted for children with disabilities. Use of repeated rhymes that include movement and identifying the sources of environmental sounds, for example, can be highly motivating activities even for children with severe disabilities.)

Finally, another critical emergent literacy skill—and an important predictor of reading achievement (Whitehurst & Lonigan (2001)—is referred to as the "alphabetic principle." According to Moats (2000), this includes naming the letters of the alphabet and understanding that each alphabet letter is associated with a particular sound and that printed words are made up of sequences of letters/sounds. It is acknowldeged that the alphabetic principle must be *taught.*

As early childhood teachers help children become more aware of the functions of print and more sensitive to the phonological and phonemic elements of words, they must also make specific and frequent references to letter names and their associated sounds. They must motivate and activate the child's interest in identifying letters and sounds in words. This will provide important support for the child's eventual realization that he can use sound–letter associations to sound out words—indeed, *to read!*

Summary

All preschool and child-care teachers share the responsibility of developing cognitive, active learning, and problem-solving skills together with academic readiness in young children. This task is especially important for teachers of children with developmental delays or disabilities. This chapter focused on practical ways to identify and teach these skills.

Piaget's stages of cognitive development were reviewed, as were ways of observing cognitive development through children's play. Strategies for facilitating early cognitive skills were described, as were later skills related to problem solving and academic readiness.

Cognitive skills in preschoolers can be enhanced readily within a seemingly natural environment of play and curiosity. Elements from the major theories of child development help in devising strategies to stimulate problem-solving skills and academic readiness.

By giving children the freedom to explore and opportunities to learn from failure while remaining free from anxiety, early educators can easily incorporate problem-solving skill development into the curriculum. Examples and rationales are provided to illustrate how children can develop the skill to identify and define problems, consider alternative solutions, choose among alternatives, and evaluate results with flexible judgment. The relationship between problem solving and academic readiness becomes apparent as concepts and abstract images are translated into words that facilitate movement through the stages of problem solving.

The section on emergent literacy describes the importance of encouraging children's appreciation of the purposes of reading and writing as well as the importance of developing phonologic and phonemic awareness. Also important is the development of literate-style language skills, which are necessary for school success. Teachers must be aware of the many cultural differences in children's early language and literacy experiences. These differences will significantly influence children's social adjustment and academic success in school.

If a preschool is to be successful in preparing children for the transition to kindergarten and beyond, it must identify the preacademic skills relevant to any local school district. In addition to "pays attention" and "follows directions," the curricula of most early childhood classrooms provide readiness activities involving classification (including sorting, matching, categorization, and seriation), colors, shapes, space, time, numbers, opposites, and letters. Suggestions for promoting a child's awareness of various attributes or relevant features necessary for generating and following rules used to manipulate concepts are included. Finally, special consideration is given to the needs of those who have cognitive skill deficits or potential for giftedness or who will be making a transition to a new environment.

Discussion Topics and Activities

1. Think of several ways to create the need to solve a problem. Design situations appropriate for a 2-year-old and a 4-year-old.

2. Observe a preschool classroom and identify ways in which functional uses of print can be incorporated into the existing schedule and activities.

3. Think of ways to involve a child with severe cognitive impairments with peers without disabilities in a pretend block play activity in which children are building streets and houses.

4. Design some preschool lessons that will encourage children to experience cause-and-effect relationships. If possible, carry these out with children. What improvement could be made in your lesson design? Did you get the results you desired? Discuss the children's involvement with classmates. Perhaps a recording of the children's responses will help you analyze the children's reactions in greater detail.

5. Why is it important to maintain a balance between social-emotional and intellectual activities in the preschool? This is a critical issue that is receiving attention nationally and should be thought through periodically. Recognize your own philosophy and investigate its implications for young children.

6. Role-play your answer to a parent who insists that reading per se should be taught in preschool. Ask colleagues for constructive criticism.

7. Visit and observe a local kindergarten class. Be alert to the behavioral and academic expectations. Compare these expectations with the "exit" goals of preschool classrooms you have observed. Discuss what you learned with classmates.

8. Collect samples of environmental print—for example, McDonald's cups, Coke cans, pizza boxes, airline ticket envelopes, and so on.

9. In the seed-planting activity described in Exhibit 9-7, for each step of the activity, give examples of challenges that might be experienced by a child with a particular disability and how you would adapt the activity or scaffold the child's response to ensure his or her participation and learning.

Teaming: Collaboration, Problem Solving, and Consultation

Photo by Anne Vega/Merrill

KEY TERMS

(Note: The terms are discussed in the text and/or defined in the glossary.)

affective conflict
coaching
collaboration
collaborative consultation model
conflict resolution
coteaching

expert model of consultation
itinerant
itinerant consultant model
modeling
nonverbal communication
   behaviors

observation
paraeducator
progress monitoring
resistance
substantive conflict
verbal conversational strategies

- Toddlers and preschoolers who have disabilities are increasingly served in nonspecial education (inclusive) community-based settings.

- A variety of service delivery models are used to support children with disabilities in early childhood settings.

- Successful inclusion support requires establishing collaborative relationships with early childhood educators.

- Successful collaboration and conflict resolution depend on skills in communication and problem solving.

- In order to provide effective support, inclusion support specialists must develop competencies in a wide range of knowledge and skill areas.

- Two common inclusion support service delivery models are coteaching and itinerant consultation.

- Paraprofessionals are critical to the effective support of children with disabilities in inclusive environments.

- Early childhood educators must develop skills in supervision and support of paraprofessionals in the classroom.

- Use of paraprofessionals as one-to-one assistants presents specific challenges.

Earlier chapters in this text have focused on understanding the needs of infants and young children with special challenges and disabilities and have delineated the theories and strategies that are useful for supporting children's learning and adaptation across all developmental domains as well as for supporting their families. As important as these areas of knowledge and skill are, training in the area of early childhood special education cannot be complete without an appreciation of the skills and dispositions necessary to engage in effective collaborative teaming with other key players in children's lives. This chapter will examine three broad areas: collaborative teaming and problem solving, models of inclusion support, and management of paraprofessionals.

The information presented here provides only an introduction to a substantial body of knowledge and practice. The ideas and strategies presented are deceptively simple; however, they are difficult to implement effectively without a great deal of practice and patience. Effective collaboration is both an art and a science.

COLLABORATION, PROBLEM SOLVING, AND SHARED DECISION MAKING

Three important components of effective collaboration will be considered. Friend and Cook (2003) define **collaboration** as a style of interaction. Thus, a major component of skillful collaboration is effective communication. Becoming aware of one's own communication style, reading the communication cues of others, and mastering the communication skills and styles that are necessary for effective collaborative consultation and teaming can be a major challenge. Second is problem solving. Truly collaborative problem solving and shared decision making don't occur

just because a group of people have agreed to work together. An effective team—even a friendly team—must have a step-by-step process in place for solving problems and making difficult decisions. A third important component of collaboration involves the skills related to **conflict resolution.** Sometimes teaming and problem-solving processes cannot proceed because of significant conflict and resistance. Insights into the sources of conflict and resistance and the knowledge of strategies to manage and resolve conflict are essential skills for the early childhood special educator.

Communication Strategies: The Key to Successful Teaming

Increasingly one of the greatest challenges faced by early childhood special educators working in roles that require collaborative teaming and consultation is the need to develop effective communication skills and to understand the problems and barriers that can arise from certain communicative behaviors. The suggestions in Appendix F related to both verbal and nonverbal communication have been adapted from a variety of sources. Effective collaborators are aware of their own verbal and nonverbal communication in ways that encourage collegiality and consensus building. Effective teaming and collaboration also require the ability to read the communication cues of others in order to understand their perspectives and concerns. Sometimes a person can be well meaning, only to be undermined by his or her own communicative behaviors or interpersonal style or inability to listen to others.

In order to become aware of their own communication behaviors, early educators must carefully examine their own communication styles via videotape, self-reflection, or feedback from a colleague. Then they can seek to eliminate interfering behaviors from their professional repertoire. There are several common barriers to effective communication that can undermine communicative effectiveness. These can lead to less effective communication or even breakdowns in communication. For example, giving advice too quickly or too emphatically, false

reassurances, not paying attention, making abrupt topic shifts, or asking unrelated questions can quickly undermine collaboration and problem solving. Another common barrier to consensus building is trying to arrive at a "quick fix"—arriving at a solution too quickly and not taking the time to insure genuine buy-in from team members.

Nonverbal Communication Behaviors.   Particularly important are **nonverbal communication behaviors** that speakers are often not even aware of. The old saying "It's not what you say but what you do" holds a great deal of truth when it comes to effective communication skills. Surprisingly, nonverbal communication can often have a greater effect (both positive and negative) than what the speaker actually says!

The impact and meanings of nonverbal communication are culturally determined. The positive or negative impact of a particular behavior or expression will be influenced by the conventions and rules of social interaction in any given group. The successful collaborator will have a good understanding of other peoples' cues and will develop a keen awareness of the impact of her own nonverbal behavior. Amazingly, body language can either inflame or diffuse conflict; thus, it is important to learn to avoid sending certain negative messages with nonverbal behaviors and to use other nonverbal behaviors to help deescalate potential conflicts. Equally important is learning to read the body language of others to better understand their perspectives and feelings. Of course, it is also possible to use body language to reduce tension and resistance. There are several nonverbal elements that facilitate positive interaction: facing the speaker with arms open and relaxed, mirroring the speaker's affect and movements, and providing nonverbal acknowledgment of what is being said by smiling and nodding. These acts of nonverbal communication tend to reduce conflict in mainstream American culture.

Verbal Conversational Strategies.   Verbal communication behaviors can also have negative or positive effects on group processes and the establishment of relationships. For example, simply talking too much or interrupting can significantly interfere with collaborative efforts. Also, rather than focusing

on defending one's own position, it is important to sincerely focus on understanding and reflecting on the meaning of what each person says. Perhaps one of the most effective conversational strategies is simply to stop talking and listen! Other effective strategies include use of restatements, reflection, use of "I" messages, and so on. Detailed information and examples related to effective communication strategies are included in Appendix F. These communication efforts and skills can have very positive benefits for children and families. *It is important to note, however, that these specific strategies will not be effective in the absence of a genuine concern for the best interests of the child and family and a genuine respect for the contributions of all the individuals involved in the inclusive setting.*

Problem Solving and Conflict Resolution

Problem solving and shared decision making are critical processes of effective teaming. Using collaborative strategies within a problem-solving process can also be a way to reduce conflict on an ongoing basis, particularly when problem-solving techniques are routinely incorporated when making difficult decisions. Even though such a process may admittedly be time consuming, it can be very helpful in resolving difficult issues. It will be most effective if the whole team is familiar with the process and agrees to use it in those situations where there are significant differences of opinion or when important decisions need to be made. It should also be noted that there will be some cases where use of the problem-solving process is not appropriate (Friend & Cook, 2003). For example, the problem may be outside the responsibility of the team, or there may be a general lack of willingness and commitment on the part of the team to tackle the problem.

One Problem-Solving Approach.   There are many problem-solving approaches discussed in the literature on consultation and conflict resolution. The approach presented here is adapted from Kurpius (1978) and Heron and Harris (2001). It is intended as a simple but systematic way to approach situations

that are interfering with the effectiveness of the team process. The following steps are recommended in this problem-solving process. (They are demonstrated in greater detail in the case of Paulo presented in the next section.)

- **Identify the problem.** Objectively describe and agree on the behavior or the situation that is problematic. *Failure to agree on just what the problem is often leads to failure to solve the problem.* One helpful strategy in problem identification is to identify the discrepancy between the current situation and the desired situation. (For example, the current situation is the child bites other children once or twice each day. The desired situation is that he not bite anyone at all.) Then phrase the problem in the form of a question: "What strategies can we implement to reduce the frequency of biting?"

- **Generate potential solutions.** It is important for team members to understand that the "right" solution is not yet known. Brainstorming possible solutions, with all ideas being placed on the table without being judged, can be a productive process in generating ideas.

- **Discuss and select a solution to implement.** The team agrees to try a particular solution. Generally the person who will actually have to carry out the plan should have the opportunity to select the solution to try.

- **Implement the solution.** Write an action plan regarding who will do what and by when.

- **Evaluate the outcome.** Determine what worked and what didn't work. Recycle the process and select another solution if necessary.

Dealing with Conflict: Perspective Taking and the Process of Conflict Resolution

Often, because there are many players and many perspectives and sometimes because successful inclusion is truly challenging, conflicts will arise. The inability to successfully resolve conflict will seriously

undermine the consultative process and will make it more difficult to implement the problem-solving steps presented earlier. The following sections briefly describe conflict and outline conflict resolution strategies.

The Nature of Conflict.   Conflict is inevitable in any true team process. Teams of individuals bring very different backgrounds, goals, values, and perspectives to a planning and decision-making process where there are seldom definitive solutions or "proven" techniques. The more complex and intensive the child's needs are, the greater the variance will be in the range and configuration of optimal support.

According to Ellis and Fisher (1994), conflict may be either "substantive" or "affective":

- Substantive conflict arises from intellectual differences and is content based. It comes about because individuals naturally differ about priorities, intervention strategies, curriculum, philosophy, best practices, service delivery procedures, and so on. This type of conflict is inevitable and when managed properly can make a healthy contribution to the team process.

- Affective conflict is based on emotional clashes between individuals. Such factors as personality clash, paranoia, fear of loss of status or control, grief, and so on can create the most difficult conflict. Frequently there are affective components in substantive conflict. This kind of conflict can be the most challenging.

Sources of Resistance.   Often an important component of conflict is **resistance.** Individuals may resist participating and cooperating in the problem-solving process or in implementing solutions. This in turn causes conflict. There are many possible sources of resistance. In the early childhood inclusion situation, the following are common:

- **The "If it ain't broke don't fix it" attitude.** Sometimes an individual simply believes the situation is as good as it can be and there is no reason for change or problem solving.

- **Fear.** Individuals may be fearful of change. Job responsibilities may change. The individual may feel incompetent to take on a new role. The most common example is the early childhood educator teacher who has little or no training with young children with disabilities. Often the teacher simply fears not knowing what to do. This is seldom a comfortable situation for anyone. An individual who fears failure or incompetence should not be viewed as a "bad" person.

- **Social resistance.** Many individuals find a great deal of comfort and social support in their jobs. Anything that threatens this feeling of security and comfort can create anxiety. In the inclusive situation, such as a day-care setting, one of the benefits of these often very low-paying jobs may be social camaraderie and support. Inclusion may result in several other professionals (often more highly trained) intruding into this comfort zone.

In order to understand resistance, the inclusion consultant must be able to take the perspectives of other key players. For example, in many communities early education programs are understaffed. Including a child with even a mild disability requires some kind of adaptation and increased workload (if the child's needs are really being met). Early childhood staff may resent that they are being asked to meet the needs of children with disabilities with no additional resources or income.

A lead teacher in an inclusive setting may be used to being in control of the "domain": the center or classroom environment, the children, and the staff. She may feel a significant loss of status if bombarded by advice and suggestions from therapists, special educators, and parents.

Dealing with Resistance.   Hoskins (1996) has suggested several specific considerations that may be helpful in understanding and dealing with team members' resistance. The first step is to try and identify the fears and concerns that are the source of the resistance, as mentioned above. The next step is to

try to understand how these fears are influencing the individual's behavior (e.g., doesn't return phone calls, becomes aggressive and emotional at team meetings, doesn't follow through). Next, try to determine what the "resistor" wants (e.g., to feel respected, to maintain authority) or seeks to avoid (e.g., feeling humiliated, admitting a lack of expertise, taking on extra work). Finally, help the resistor achieve what she wants while still achieving the group's goal (e.g., give credit for good ideas, acknowledge validity of concern).

In order to be effective in dealing with resistance and supporting the collaborative group process, team members must be willing to let go of their own needs to control, to be given credit for having the best ideas, or to be acknowledged for being proven "right." In our competitive American culture, this is often one of the most difficult strategies to master. Most of us have a deeply ingrained need to win—to be better than the next person, to stand out from the crowd. Collaboration requires letting go of these needs.

Conflict Avoidance. Resistance can lead to conflict. Everyone has experienced the frustration and emotionality that arises out of conflict. Almost everyone (with the exception of those few individuals who "love a good fight") will vigorously seek to *avoid* conflict. However, sometimes avoidance of conflict can be as deleterious as conflict itself. The following are examples of avoidance:

Withdrawal (e.g., "Just leave me out of it").

Compromising in such a way that no one is happy.

Accommodation (e.g., "Okay, just do whatever you want").

Majority rule (e.g., "Let's take a vote").

In any situation in which there is a need for relationship building and ongoing collaboration, conflict avoidance will usually undermine the consultation process.

Conflict avoidance is often an unsatisfactory approach in inclusion support. It may worsen conflicts and damage relationships over time.

Conflict Resolution Strategies.   So the key question is, How *does* one manage and resolve conflict? Several strategies can offer immediate short-term solutions.

- **Pause and take a breath.** In any situation where either you are experiencing strong emotions related to conflict or you observe it in others, it is important to do nothing and say nothing for a short period. Take a deep breath. Don't be impulsive. Assess your own emotions. Try to listen carefully to the concerns of others before speaking.

- **Try to state the issues or sides of the conflict in a neutral way.** State, for example, "Let me see if I can summarize the two different ideas here: Mrs. Rivera, you are fearful that your daughter is going to be hurt; that there are too many children and the staff cannot really protect her every moment. Janice, you seem to feel that Mom is being somewhat overprotective and her concerns are not really warranted. Am I right?" This approach allows individuals to restate their position if you have not captured it correctly or to acknowledge that your statement is correct. Either way it can be a nonconfrontational method encouraging and valuing honest expression of differences.

- **Assess your own role honestly.** Be aware of your own role in the conflict whenever you are not truly neutral (which will probably be most of the time!). Say, for instance, "You know, I have to admit I have some of the same concerns about whether the staff are really able to monitor the situation carefully enough. I get frustrated when I think they're ignoring her."

- **Attempt to move the group toward a problem-solving approach.** Ideally, when conflicts are full blown, an attempt should be made to use the same problem-solving approach described earlier to resolve the conflict. However, because of the emotions that are often involved, getting

to this point may require significant skill on the part of the consultant.

- **Use your sense of humor.** Humor can sometimes diffuse and deescalate a tense situation.

Although these strategies may offer some short-term management of conflict, longer-term ongoing strategies must be incorporated. There are certain behaviors and practices that, over time, will create a collaborative atmosphere, such as the following:

- Clarifying issues before misunderstandings can occur.
- Encouraging all players to express opinions as a general operating procedure.
- Focusing on needs (e.g., child's needs, teacher's needs, parents' needs, etc.) rather than focusing too quickly on solutions.
- Facilitating open discussion by expressing your *own* feelings and biases (e.g., "I have to admit I'm really uncomfortable with this").
- Giving feedback that values others' opinions (e.g., "Oh, I see where you're coming from on this").

- Encouraging members of group to see others' perspectives. They don't have to agree, just acknowledge or understand. Supporting the notion that understanding many different perspectives results in a better understanding of the situation and generates better solutions.

Also critical to establishing a collaborative relationship and preventing conflict is **establishing trust.** In Exhibit 10–1 there are suggestions for establishing trust.

Finally, an important longer-term strategy for dealing with conflict is for the team to incorporate a systematic problem-solving process and be willing to use it when necessary (it is hoped before a conflict crisis arises). The problem-solving process described earlier in this chapter will be applied to the case of Paulo next. It provides examples of perspective taking, resistance, and effective conflict management.

Problem-Solving Case Study: Paulo

The following case sets up a typical challenge faced by key players within an inclusive setting. Critical to resolving such a problem is the process of

---

Exhibit 10–1

Establishing Trust in Collaborative Team Problem Solving

- Listen to understand, with unhurried attention. Use phrases such as "Correct me if I'm wrong . . ." or "Let me see if I understand what you're saying . . ."
- Keep your word.
- Learn what matters to people and try to respect that.
- Share yourself honestly.
- Share your expertise without dominating the conversation.
- Solicit others' opinions.
- Trust others; trusting others often results in them trusting you. (Don't push others to trust you more than you trust them.)

Source: Adapted from Bridges (1991) and Margolies and McCabe (1988).

perspective taking. Adults who are given the responsibility of implementing and evaluating effective intervention and educational programs for children like Paulo may have very different perspectives on what is best.

The "Problem" with Paulo.

Paulo has recently been enrolled in a neighborhood child-care program. The family has arranged for a one-to-one assistant for him. Marie, an early childhood special educator, is the inclusion support specialist assigned to Paulo. Paulo has autism. He has little communication ability, and his speech-language pathologist believes that these tantrums are related to his inability to communicate. Therefore, she has introduced an alternative communication procedure known as the Picture Exchange Communication System (PECS; Frost & Bondy, 1994). This system uses specific procedures to teach the child to select and give the adult a picture (or pictures) in exchange for a desired object or activity. The inclusion support specialist is teaching Evelyn, the one-to-one assistant, to implement the procedure. She believes that if the rest of the staff would also learn the PECS procedure, two important objectives could be achieved: Paulo would have a functional communication system, and his disruptive behavior would decrease.

The early childhood staff are fairly skeptical of the effectiveness of the PECS procedures being recommended. They believe Paulo's tantrums are increasing and are frustrated about whether Paulo can be successfully included in their center. The team has reached a crisis point.

Possible Perspectives of Key Players in Paulo's Case.

It is clear that the members of this team bring different perspectives to the table. The following section describes these perspectives.

Inclusion Support Specialist. Marie, the special educator on the team, strongly believes that Paulo's behavior problems are related to his lack of functional communication. She wants Paulo to be successful in this setting. She is highly invested in teaching Paulo to use the PECS procedure but believes this will require the cooperation of the staff

and time to train them. She believes she knows how best to support Paulo, but she is frustrated at the staff's lack of commitment to learning the PECS procedure and their narrow concern about how to control his disruptive behavior. She believes they are moving toward a single agenda: to have him removed from the program. She feels Paulo's mother expects her to be able to solve this problem as well as teach him to communicate. Marie is starting to feel like her credibility is on the line.

Paulo's Mother. Mrs. Johnson, Paulo's mother, does not think he belongs in a special education class, but she realizes his behavior is jeopardizing his inclusive placement. She has an additional burden in that she needs to work and needs child care for Paulo. She is worried that she has seen little progress. It was her understanding that Marie would know how to help Paulo, but now she's not so sure. Mrs. Johnson is beginning to sense some negative feelings from the teacher, Jenny, and suspects she dislikes *Paulo*.

Early Childhood Teacher. Jenny is a very committed early childhood teacher. She enjoys her work and accepted Paulo willingly into her classroom. However, she has little experience with children with special needs. She was definitely not prepared for the challenges presented by Paulo. She is amazed that even with the one-to-one assistant, he is totally disrupting the classroom. She feels overwhelmed and is beginning to dread going to work each day. She feels pressure from Marie to implement the communication training procedures. Though she knows Marie is the "expert," Jenny can't see how the procedure will reduce his temper tantrums. She's beginning to see reactions from the other children in the class. Jenny also feels guilty about Paulo's mother. She knows how badly Mrs. Johnson wants *Paulo to stay in the program.*

Child-Care Administrator. Ms. Murillo, the child-care program administrator, understands that legally there is increasing pressure on the center to enroll children with special needs. She is resigned to doing this and is interested in putting mechanisms into

place to support these children. However, she had no idea what would be involved and how time consuming it could be. She hopes Paulo is an unusual case. She is amazed at how much effort is being expended for this one child. She is increasingly concerned about the effect it is having on Jenny, the best teacher at the center. Ms. Murillo is aware that the pressure on Jenny, and Jenny's feeling that she is being critiqued and falling short of other people's expectations could lead her to resign. Ms. Murillo is also starting to feel some resentment toward Marie. Mrs. Murillo's limited experiences with school district personnel and therapists have not been particularly positive. She believes they look down on child-care staff. She feels generally frustrated that she has to manage the child-care program on such a meager budget. It is unfair.

One-to-One Assistant.   Evelyn has worked with just one other child. He was nothing like Paulo. She is increasingly unhappy with this job. The PECS procedure is complicated, and she's not convinced it will work. She realizes the ECE teacher thinks she should be able to control Paulo's tantrums. She also gets the impression that Marie isn't satisfied with how she's doing the communication training. She sees her only once a week. She's starting to feel paranoid that she's not pleasing anyone. She's also not sure who her boss is. A job at Starbuck's is sounding better all the time.

Speech-Language Pathologist (SLP Consultant). The SLP, while not involved in Paulo's support on a regular basis, is very confident that her insights and recommendations are valid and should be implemented. She is surprised that Maria, the special education itinerant, is having such a difficult time getting the staff to implement the PECS procedure.

Factors That Contribute to Conflict.
Differing Perspectives.   Although all the team members portrayed in the scenario above are interested in supporting Paulo, they come to the table with very different perspectives as described above. Successful collaboration requires that none of these perspectives

be viewed as "wrong." It is important that inclusion support professionals respect and value the perspectives and ideas of others and that they develop effective strategies for determining the nature of each perspective.

Sources of Resistance.   A major source of conflict is people's resistance to change or resistance to ideas different from their own. The seeds of this resistance often lie in the different perspectives reflected by the team. These differences are common in the field of early childhood inclusion. In the case of Paulo, the special educator believes so passionately in her approach that she resists the ideas of others. Ms. Murillo, the administrator, may resist Marie's suggestions for the staff because she feels her authority is being challenged. Jenny, the teacher, may resist any suggestions that don't deal with the immediate issue of Paulo's behavior because she feels her competence and control of her classroom are threatened.

Solving Paulo's "Problem".   A step-by-step description of how the problem-solving process was used by Paulo's team follows:

Step 1. Preparation

Marie, the special education itinerant, assumes the role of convening a meeting to try to resolve the impasse that is beginning to form. Before the meeting, she touches base briefly with each of the key players.

Step 2. Entry (as First Meeting Begins)

At the beginning of the meeting Marie attempts to build rapport and diffuse tensions by bringing refreshments and talking about the pleasant weather and commenting on the display of children's artwork. She acknowledges that the team members have limited time and she asks the group if they will agree to some problem-solving "ground rules" to help keep the discussion on track. The focus at this point in the process is not on solutions but on establishing a process for the discussion and for shared decision making.

Step 3. Defining the Problem

One of the biggest mistakes in problem solving is bypassing the steps below in an attempt to rush too quickly to the solution!

First, each team member must state what he or she thinks the problem is. Often conflict arises because people view the problem very differently or focus on totally different issues. This step helps the team understand one another's perspectives. If there are disagreements about what the problem is, some consensus must be reached before the team can move on to possible solutions. It is also important for the individual who is facilitating the process or the person who is viewed as having the most influence over the group to avoid presenting her perceptions first. In the case of Paulo, Marie listens to everyone's view of the problem, then states her view last.

Before the group can proceed, they must reach some consensus about what the problem is—that is, what needs to be solved or fixed? Marie realizes she is clearly in the minority. She believes the primary problem to be solved is Paulo's lack of a communication system, whereas all the other team members believe the immediate problem is his disruptive behavior. It would be counterproductive at this point for Marie to attempt to persuade the group that her view is correct. Thus, the group agrees that the problem at hand is Paulo's temper tantrums.

Step 4. Determining Possible Solutions

This phase needs to be conducted as a brainstorming session: Marie suggests that everyone contribute their ideas, no judgment or criticism can be made, and all ideas are acceptable. Each suggestion needs to be recorded, preferably on chart paper or on a board so all can see. Although Marie is facilitating the meeting, she asks for a volunteer to record the ideas. It is important that every effort be made to ensure that all key players be true participants in the process. Marie must not overinvest in what she believes is the best solution. In Paulo's case some ideas suggested by team members are totally unacceptable to Marie, such as the use of time-out and calling his mother to take him home. Nevertheless, all ideas must be placed on the table.

After several solutions have been suggested (behavior analysis, PECS, time-out, removing the child from the room, and calling his mother to take him home), the person who gets to choose a solution to try should be the person who will actually be responsible for implementing it. In Paulo's case, it is Jenny, the classroom teacher. Marie asks Jenny to choose a solution to implement. Because the situation had previously been at an impasse, even if Marie does not think the solution is the best one, she supports Jenny's preference in favor of the group process. It is also helpful if the group understands that the selected solution may or may not work and that

another solution can be tried. It is not a contest to see who has the "right" idea. Once a solution is agreed on using the collaborative process just described, the resistance may begin to dissipate, making way for emerging trust.

Jenny chooses the strategy of asking Evelyn to remove Paulo from the group when his behavior becomes extremely disruptive. She will return him to the group when he is calmer. Marie does not feel this will be a successful strategy and had previously been resistant to this idea because of her strong belief that communication training is the best solution. But she supports Jenny's desire to give it a try. Mrs. Johnson, Paulo's mother, then suggests a limited implementation of the PECS procedure during snack time. Jenny agrees after Evelyn suggests that she would be happy to take responsibility if it is limited to snack time.

The process has become much more collaborative. Rather than Marie trying to convince the group that she has the right solution, the entire group generates a plan that everyone can agree upon.

Step 5. Action Plan

It is important not to leave the meeting without an action plan (see the action plan form in Appendix H) that describes the details of the solution agreed on. Marie records who will do what, when, how often, and so forth. Marie also sets a date in 3 weeks for a quick follow-up meeting to determine how the plan is working.

Step 6. Follow-up

At the follow-up meeting the team evaluates the effectiveness of the action plan. Which elements worked? Which didn't work? What are the next steps? Marie admits that, to her surprise, Paulo's tantrums have decreased in both frequency and intensity. Jenny comments that having the option of removing Paulo from the group if necessary has made her life much easier. She feels more in control of the situation. She also admits

she has been fascinated with how quickly Paulo has caught on to using the PECS cards at snack time.

Members of the team must not feel responsible for or blame another team member for a solution that is not effective. It simply means that another approach must be tried. Almost always, important things will be learned from attempting the first solution. This will, in turn, increase the likelihood of success of a second try. It is critical that when a solution does not work, team members avoid "I told you so" reactions. Any notion of individual "winners" and "losers" will undermine the collaborative group process. When a solution works and the child benefits, everyone wins.

A truly collaborative process and relationship requires a sharing of power and the establishment of parity among all team members. (Note that this does not happen over night!)

Step 7. Recycling Problem-Solving Steps, if Necessary

If the solution was not effective, if the problem has worsened, or if there is a new problem, the problem-solving steps should be executed again. Over time, the problem-solving process becomes second nature. In addition, certain features of the process continue to enhance the development of collaborative relationships and mutual trust and respect among team members.

MODELS FOR SUPPORTING CHILDREN WITH SPECIAL NEEDS IN INCLUSIVE SETTINGS

Children with disabilities who are served in typical, community-based group settings are supported in a variety of ways. Currently there are no generally accepted standards or guidelines for whether, when, and how inclusion support is to be provided for children from birth to age 5 (Guralnick, 2000). The "individualized" aspect of the individualized education plan (IEP) and the individualized family service plan (IFSP) remains, regardless of where the child is

served, and a "one size fits all". approach to inclusion support would be inappropriate. The ideal support model for a given child probably depends on several factors, including the needs of the child, the preferences of the family, and the characteristics of available settings.

Klein, Richardson-Gibbs, Kilpatrick, and Harris (2001) describe a variety of service delivery models for support within these settings. These include itinerant direct teaching, itinerant collaborative consultation, team teaching, inservice training of the early childhood teacher, reverse mainstreaming model with a special educator as the teacher, and use of a paraprofessional as a one-to-one assistant (with or without supervision). Also, for various reasons, some children are placed in early childhood settings with no support. The features and advantages of these service delivery models will be considered.

No Support

There does not appear to be agreement among decision makers as to whether a young child with a disability placed in a community-based setting *always* needs some kind of support. For example, the early childhood staff may be considered highly skilled and quite capable and willing to make whatever modifications are necessary for the child to participate. Another example might be a case where parents feel that their own communications with the staff are sufficient to support the child in a given setting. (There are also cases where a child and the staff need support, but the support simply is not available or hasn't been appropriately requested.) A challenge in these situations is determining who is responsible for progress toward achieving the child's IEP goals.

Use of One-to-One Assistant

Many issues have emerged around the use of one-to-one assistants (also known as "shadow aides," "inclusion support aides," "therapeutic companions," "coaches," and so on). In this model a specific adult is assigned to a particular child for the purpose of providing some specific assistance or support to the child that the existing program staff cannot readily

provide. Issues include lack of training; need for supervision, roles, and responsibility; and the possible deleterious impact on children's independence and peer interactions (Giangreco, Edelman, Broer, & Doyle, 2001). In some cases, the one-to-one assistant is the only support. In others, the one-to-one assistant is trained for a specific role and works under the supervision of an early childhood special educator or other professional. It has been our observation that in a quality early childhood setting, when appropriate support and consultation are provided by a specialist in a collaborative spirit, the need for one-to-one assistance can often be eliminated or significantly reduced to a short-term basis.

Staff Inservice Models

A variety of projects have targeted the training of early childhood program staff as the primary vehicle for ensuring support for a young child with special needs. In these cases, staff are provided with training related to the kinds of strategies that are often helpful in working with young children with disabilities. In some cases this inservice training is provided in conjunction with other models of support.

Itinerant Consultation Model of Inclusion Support

One of several models of inclusion support is the itinerant approach. As stated earlier, an **itinerant** is an individual who travels from one site to another providing support for children with disabilities at each site. A typical itinerant caseload might be 15 to 20 children, depending on the number of targeted children at each site and the distances from one site to the next. Frequency of visits typically range from once a week to once a month.

As Dinnebeil, McInerney, Roth, and Ramaswamy (2001) pointed out, some itinerants simply engage in the same kinds of direct instruction activities they used when they were teachers in specialized settings. They may provide the direct intervention either on a pullout basis or within the inclusive classroom. Although there is often some communication with the early childhood staff, there is little interaction

with children without disabilities, and the primary focus is on children with disabilities. This *itinerant direct instruction* role (also sometimes referred to as an "itinerant teacher") tends to isolate the children with disabilities from the rest of the class and unfortunately may further the belief of the early childhood staff that the children must receive specialized services in order to be included.

Another itinerant model—one that in most cases is more appropriate as an ongoing support model for young children in inclusive settings—is an **itinerant consultant model.** The consultant role is a relatively less familiar role for most early childhood special educators than is a direct teaching role. Wesley, Buysse, and Keyes (2000) and Wesley, Buysee, and Skinner (2001) have reported that early childhood special educators may not be comfortable in the role of consultant.

The traditional role of the special education teacher in a special education preschool classroom or early intervention center-based program is *very different* from the role of an itinerant consultant. As a consultant, the early childhood specialist does not have direct responsibility for the teaching and learning of the children in a classroom. Instead, she has a more *indirect* responsibility for assisting children within a larger group of typical peers *via her relationships with other adults.* In addition to the skills and knowledge required for working with children with specific needs in a traditional special education class setting, additional skills are needed to successfully engage children with disabilities with their typical peers in inclusive environments. Furthermore, because the implementation of these teaching and support strategies will be carried out by the early childhood staff, the ability to work effectively with a variety of other adults, in a variety of settings, is also essential.

The next section defines consultation and discusses two types of consultation: *expert* and *collaborative* consultation models (Friend & Cook, 2003; Heron & Harris, 2001).

What Is "Consultation"?   According to Brown, Pryzwansky, and Schulte (2006), consultation is an indirect method of solving problems in which the consultant and the consultee work together in some way to define the problem and bring about a solution or resolution. In this definition, consultation is "triadic" in that the consultant works with the consultee (e.g., early childhood teacher) who works with the client child. Klein et al. (2001) have suggested that itinerant consultation in early childhood special education combines elements of *both* collaborative and expert consultation. The purpose or nature of the consultation must determine the type of consultation approach used.

Expert Consultation Model.   In many situations consultation is provided using an expert model, sometimes referred to as "clinical consultation." In this approach the consultant is viewed as the expert who uses her expertise to evaluate a problem and provide recommendations to the consultee. Traditionally, an expert consultation model implies a hierarchical relationship between the consultant and consultee. The goals of this approach are for the consultant to provide an expert evaluation of the child's situation and authoritative recommendations as to how staff might effectively work with the child. Generally, the outcome is to increase the consultee's (staff's) ability to manage (support, teach) the client (child). This approach is best used when there is a need for high-quality technical expertise and for which there is a "best" solution to the problem (Heron & Harris, 2001).

In the field of special education, the notion of an expert consultation approach often carries with it a negative connotation of a consultant who presents herself as superior and who may not respect the skills of the regular education teacher. As a result of negative experience with traditional expert models of consultation, there is increasing emphasis on the collaborative approach where all players have "parity" in the process and are seen as having equal—though perhaps complementary—skills. However, Klein et al. (2001), reporting on their experiences in Project Support, have found in many instances that the early childhood staff had little or no training related to working with children with special needs

and in many instances were eager for the inclusion support specialist to provide expertise. In addition, as Friend and Cook (2003) point out, regular education teachers in K–12 may sometimes prefer an expert model, perhaps because of the time demands of true collaboration. Of course, this "expert" role can—and should—be implemented using a respectful approach that values and seeks the contributions of other key players and works toward a collaborative problem-solving relationship.

Collaborative Consultation Model.   The preferred consultation approach in education today is the **collaborative consultation model** (Idol, Nevin, & Paolucci-Whitcomb, 2000). This model is best used when a group commitment is needed for the successful performance of the child and when more than one solution may resolve the problem. For example, if there are a number of possible approaches to reducing the tantrums of a child in a preschool setting, it may be necessary to assess the preferences, skills, and philosophies of all the individuals who are involved in working with the child before obtaining a commitment to a particular intervention plan. Because a collaborative consultation approach involves a group, there are two dimensions to consider in this type of consultation: the development of a resolution to the problem (the task) and the social dynamics and effects of effective group interaction (social dimension).

A key feature of collaborative consultation is the reciprocity and mutuality that must exist between the consultant and the consultee. According to Heron and Harris (2001), collaborative consultation is an interaction in which each person contributes particular expertise to solving specific problems. This also implies that effective consultation must be an *ongoing process.* The effective consultant must collaborate in the processes of assessment, planning, implementation, and evaluation.

Each player (in our case, the early childhood inclusion support consultant and the early childhood teacher or caregiver) brings something of equal value to the problem-solving process. Although their contributions may be quite different, the collaborative

process produces solutions that could not have been generated by either party independently (Idol et al., 2000). The process may often require the leadership and facilitation of the itinerant consultant, but the problem solving must occur as a result of mutual contribution and reciprocal interactions.

According to Friend and Cook (2003), collaboration must include parity in the relationship, shared goals, shared accountability, trust and respect, shared resources, and shared responsibility for decision making. Critical prerequisites to successful collaboration include effective communication skills and the ability to engage in interactions that support the processes of "shared problem solving" (p. 79).

Early Childhood Special Education Consultation Model.   The early childhood special education itinerant consultation model presented here draws heavily from the collaborative consultation literature yet maintains the need for the consultant to possess expertise in the areas of early childhood special education and early intervention. The features of each component of the model are presented in the following box.

This combined approach suggests that the effective inclusion support specialist must come to the task with significant expertise to offer but must share this expertise in ways that enhance the collaborative relationships among key players as they pursue the common goal of enhancing the learning and development of the child with special needs.

Responsibilities of the Inclusion Support Specialist in an Itinerant Consultant Role

Some of the greatest challenges faced by an itinerant consultant are the complex and changing demands. These demands and expectations may be different for each child and each setting. The consultant will have responsibilities to many different individuals: to the early childhood staff, to the child and family, to peers without disabilities, to the other team members, and to program administrators. These responsibilities may vary considerably from one site to another.

Early Childhood Special Education *Expert* Consultation Features

- Provides high-quality technical expertise.

- Consultant has knowledge and skills related to defined problem (i.e., is not just a mediator).

- Consultant is able to clearly explain nature of child's disability and is able to communicate family's perspective and priorities.

- Consultant clearly defines own role and ongoing recommendations, both verbally and in writing.

- Consultant carefully observes and evaluates problem.

- Consultant makes recommendations for solving the problem.

- Consultant effectively demonstrates and coaches staff in use of teaching and intervention strategies.

Early Childhood Special Education *Collaborative* Consultation Features

- Consultant facilitates reciprocal, trusting relationships among key players.

- Consultant models open, effective communication processes.

- Each person's unique skills and contributions are valued.

- Goal or problem must be carefully defined and agreed on.

- Consultant guides team in systematic problem-solving process.

- Consultant is aware of and respects values, perspectives, and time demands of early childhood program.

- Consultant is aware of sources of resistance and conflict and effectively engages in conflict resolution.

Photo by Barbara Schwartz/Merrill

Examples of some of the possible roles and responsibilities related to other stakeholders in the inclusion support process are described below. (Several forms in Appendix H can be helpful in planning specific roles and activities.)

To the Community-Based School or Child-Care Staff.

- Listening to concerns of teachers and staff and incorporating staff insights and expertise into recommendations for meeting child's needs.

- Providing information to individual staff members or to group staff meetings (e.g., information about specific disabilities, IEP processes, transition planning, and so on).

- Continuing ongoing reciprocal interactions and information sharing with teachers regarding all areas of child's development and attainment of specific IEP or IFSP goals or outcomes (e.g., responsiveness to activities in the classroom, development of play or self-help skills,

socialization with peers, fine and gross motor skill levels).

- Modeling or coaching effective teaching strategies for staff to observe and replicate.

- Videotaping classroom activities to use for supportive feedback and demonstration of instructional strategies (if requested).

To the Child.

- Observing and assessing child's needs within the school setting on an ongoing basis.

- Working individually with child, as necessary, to encourage achievement of specific goals (e.g., participation in group activities, smooth transitions from one activity to another, appropriate and effective communication with peers and teachers).

- Creating or obtaining adapted equipment for child's use in classroom to increase success in all areas of curriculum (e.g., photographs or line drawings to increase communication, various equipment to meet needs of children with disabilities such as orthopedic, vision, or hearing).

To the Family.

- Providing ongoing discussion and feedback to parents regarding child's progress.

- Serving as liaison between working parents and early childhood staff.

- Assisting parents with decisions regarding placement transitions.

To Typical Peers.

- Assisting early childhood staff in dealing appropriately with peers' reactions to a child with a disability.

- Working with typical peers to encourage their interaction and effective communication with the child with special needs.

- Occasionally using specific peer coaching strategies to teach peers to use specific interactions with the child with special needs.

To All Team Members.

- Arranging times for classroom visits that best meet the needs of staff and child (ability to be flexible and creative when scheduling visits).

- Participating in team meetings (IEPs or IFSPs) to share information about child's development.

- When appropriate, serving as a liaison between specialized service providers (e.g., therapist) and early childhood staff.

- Assisting in coordinating other services to ensure appropriate levels of support for child (e.g., assisting in obtaining services of and supervising one-to-one aide, if needed; responding to requests of team members for assistance in areas such as speech and language, health needs, and so on).

- Providing timely and ongoing reports of results of consultation services to agencies (e.g., school district or community-based program administrator).

- Modeling and facilitating collaborative team interactions and effective problem solving and shared decision making.

Unique Collaborative Challenges for Inclusion Specialists

Important challenges faced by the itinerant consultant are the number of key players and the unique characteristics in each different inclusion site. Because of the many players involved in the inclusion support process, several people will be directly influenced by the itinerant consultant. Conversely, these individuals can have a strong effect on the itinerant.

Early Childhood Staff. Possible issues involving the staff of a child development setting may relate to their philosophy and attitude toward early childhood education and special education. The itinerant support provider may encounter viewpoints that she disagrees with, including selection of curriculum or attitudes toward inclusion of children with certain kinds of disabilities.

Another issue may arise from the variation in training of the early childhood staff. Training and knowledge in both child development and special education will vary from site to site. In those sites where staff are well trained in early childhood education and child development, it will be easier to establish true collaborative partnerships; the staff and the special education itinerant readily share their expertise in a reciprocal way. When the early childhood staff are less well trained, even in the foundations of early childhood education, the establishment of a collaborative relationship may present more of a challenge.

Another challenge may relate to the staff's expectations of the itinerant. Consultants have tended to operate under the assumption that early childhood teachers automatically understand the consultant role and approach (Wesley, 2002). Clearly defining roles and responsibilities is always an important first step. The staff may have had past experiences with consultants, both positive and negative. Their past experiences will affect how they perceive the inclusion support itinerant.

Finally, how the itinerant communicates with the staff from the beginning can reassure teachers that they are not being observed and critiqued. Rather, the itinerant is there to observe the child and to support both the staff and the child in that setting. *It is critical that the itinerant consultant convey to the early childhood staff that she is there to support them.* The best way to support the child with special needs is to support the staff.

At the beginning of a new relationship between the itinerant consultant and the staff, it will be impossible to make a priori judgments about what kinds of supports the staff may need. This will be revealed only through the processes of communication, observation, and collaboration.

Families.   The consultant may find that there are possible issues around family expectations and family needs. As noted above, it is essential that the itinerant clarify what she can and cannot do as an inclusion support specialist. Helping families understand the role of the inclusion support specialist will help the family decide what other services they might need.

The family will also have expectations of the early childhood staff. If the child has attended a special education class in the past, the family may have similar expectations for the inclusive setting (e.g., low teacher-to-child ratio, frequent individualized interaction with the teacher, and so on). Prior to placement in the inclusive setting, if possible, the inclusion support itinerant can help the family understand what the center's philosophy is, how many children are in the class, and what the adult-to-child ratio will be.

The family will also have certain expectations for their child in the early childhood setting. For example, if they are used to special education settings, the expectations they have for their child's program may be more focused on meeting IEP goals, therapy support, one-to-one instruction, and so on. Some families may be more interested in their child's opportunities for social participation in the inclusive setting. It is very important that these expectations be clarified early on.

As the child's placement in the inclusive setting continues, other family needs and concerns may arise for which the inclusion support itinerant can be of great assistance, including providing the following:

- Specific information about the child's disability

- Emotional support

- Help with transitions to preschool or kindergarten

- Information regarding special education law, service systems, parent's rights, and so on

- Information regarding special education–regular education interfaces

- Access to other (noneducational) support services for children with disabilities

Child.   For the inclusion itinerant to adequately support the child with disabilities in the regular education setting, certain challenges often emerge. For example, the itinerant will need to address how to meet diverse needs across different settings (especially if a child has significant, multiple disabilities).

For example, how will the things learned at the center or within a certain therapy setting be transferred to the home environment?

Another significant challenge may occur in the area of **progress monitoring** and accountability. The specialist may need to help the team determine who will coordinate assessments, take responsibility for achievement of goals or outcomes, and collect data on the child's progress. These have not been issues in traditional self-contained classrooms because the special educator had complete responsibility and control.

Behavioral issues often present special concerns for early childhood staff. Sometimes particular behaviors not previously identified as serious behavior problems take on new significance when the child is placed in the early childhood setting. In other cases, a child may develop behavior difficulties while attempting to adjust to the new setting. If a child's problem behavior in group settings is not addressed immediately and effectively, a child with serious or challenging behaviors could potentially be dismissed from the school. Such a situation creates a great deal of frustration and disappointment for everyone. The inclusion support itinerant must be prepared to prevent or quickly manage behavior challenges. For children already identified as having a *significant* behavior disorder, a management plan should be addressed even before the child's placement.

Sometimes, as with any child, behavioral issues may emerge over time. A child may do well at first, then problem behaviors may begin. Regular visits to the center and good communication with the staff and the child's family will greatly assist the itinerant in applying the old adage, "A stitch in time saves nine."

A Note on Disability Specialists and Therapists in Itinerant Service Delivery Roles

This discussion of appropriate itinerant roles and practices is also relevant to many disability specialists and therapists who provide on-site services to children. A brief description of the roles various specialists

play is found in Table 10–1. Each specialist is typically focused on one particular developmental area. Even though the role of these specialized service providers is not necessarily to support and monitor the overall achievement and well-being of the child or the quality of the child's daily participation in the inclusive setting, the model of service delivery used is an itinerant model: either a direct service or a consultant model or a combination of the two. Thus, much of the discussion here, including the specific strategies described in the next section, can also be applied to these very important members of the team.

Specific Support Strategies Provided by Itinerants

The itinerant consultant must view inclusion support as a shared venture, that is, a collaborative partnership with the early childhood staff. Within that context, the following are examples of specific support strategies and activities used by itinerant consultants. It should be noted that these same strategies are often used by coteachers as well.

Providing Information. Obviously a significant portion of the itinerant consultant's job is to provide information to the early childhood staff. It is important to realize that not all information is wanted or useful and therefore may not be ultimately beneficial for the child.

The following guidelines are suggested for providing information to staff:

- Always follow up on staff requests for information. If you don't have the information, attempt to obtain it.

- Provide information in the most efficient, unobtrusive ways possible.

- Ask the staff for their preferences for receiving information—for example, do they prefer brief discussion during your visit or after the visit? In the classroom or outside the classroom? Verbally or in writing? On NCR forms or in a notebook? During a team meeting, via e-mail, or on the phone?

Table 10–1   Roles of specialists on intervention teams

Specialist	Description
Audiologist	Conducts screening and diagnosis of hearing problems and may recommend a hearing aid or suggest training approaches for children with hearing disabilities.
Early childhood specialist	Conducts assessments and implements individualized programs for young children with special needs; is concerned with all aspects of the child's development that impact on learning and successful daily living.
Early interventionist	Any professional who is a primary service provider for infant and toddlers with special needs and their families.
Neurologist	Conducts screening, diagnosis, and treatment of brain and central nervous system disorders.
Nurse	Oversees the overall medical well-being of the child and family. May initiate preventive procedures as well as take responsibility for specific treatments such as management of a gastrostomy tube.
Nutritionist	Conducts an evaluation of a child's eating habits and nutritional status; provides advice about normal and therapeutic nutrition and information about special feeding equipment and techniques to increase a child's self-feeding skills.
Occupational therapist	Conducts evaluation of children who may have difficulty performing self-help or other preschool activities that use arms, head, hand, and mouth movements; suggests activities to promote self-sufficiency and independence.
Ophthalmologist	Conducts screening, diagnosis, and treatment of diseases, injuries, or birth defects that limit vision.
Orthopedist	Conducts screening, diagnosis, and treatment of diseases and injuries to muscles, joints, and bones.
Otolaryngologist	Conducts screening, diagnosis, and treatment of ear, nose, and throat disorders; is sometimes known as an ENT (ear, nose, and throat) physician.
Pediatrician	Specializes in the diseases, problems, and health care of children.
Physical therapist	Conducts an evaluation of a child's muscle tone, posture, range of motion, and locomotion abilities; plans physical therapy programs aimed at promoting self-sufficiency primarily related to gross motor skills such as walking, sitting, and shifting position; helps with special equipment such as wheelchairs, braces, and crutches.
Psychiatrist	Conducts screening, diagnosis, and treatment of psychological, emotional, developmental, or organic problems; prescribes medication; is alert to physical problems that may cause nervous disorders.
Psychologist	Conducts screening, diagnosis, and treatment of children with emotional, behavioral, or developmental problems; is primarily concerned with cognitive and emotional development.
Social worker	Provides counseling or consultative services to individuals or families who may be experiencing problems.
Speech-language pathologist	Conducts screening, diagnosis, and treatment of children with communication disorders.
Technology assistant	Assists with development and maintenance of adaptive equipment and devices.

Source. Adapted from *Head Start: Mainstreaming Preschoolers Series,* by Project Head Start, 1978, Washington, DC: U.S. Department of Health and Human Services, Office of Human Development Services, Administration for Children, Youth and Families.

- Offer mini-inservices on topics of interest or importance to staff.

- Determine the best way for staff to provide you with information or observations and to ask questions. Information *must* flow in both directions.

Observing.   **Observation** is an important activity for the itinerant consultant. She must carefully observe to understand the rules, routines, and culture of the classroom. She must observe the child's behavior in different activities and with different individuals. She must also observe how others interact with

the child, and antecedents and consequences of the child's inappropriate behaviors.

Modeling.   In a **modeling** strategy, the itinerant demonstrates a particular strategy while a staff member watches. For example, she may demonstrate how to fade a hand-over-hand prompt or how to scaffold a difficult task to provide just the right amount of assistance for the child. It is important to note that simply modeling a procedure may not be sufficient to enable the staff to actually carry it out on their own. Modeling is best used in combination with coaching. That is, the inclusion specialist would demonstrate the procedure, then step back and encourage the staff member to do it. (It will be difficult for early childhood programs with limited staff to incorporate intensive complex procedures on a daily basis. Unrealistic expectations may result in staff feeling guilty or resentful.)

Coaching.   **Coaching** can be an effective technique to assist staff members in learning specific strategies that may be helpful in supporting or teaching the child. However, coaching requires a positive trusting relationship between the itinerant and the staff member. Coaching may be more effective following ample use of modeling, described above. The itinerant observes the staff member and the child in the particular activity of concern (e.g., free play or snack time) and makes direct suggestions in real time as the activity proceeds. This is an example of an expert consultation approach and can be threatening if not done carefully.

Using Developmentally Appropriate Activities.
Sometimes the early childhood staff may not realize that a child's disruptive behavior or reluctance to participate may be due to the fact that the child is developmentally younger than the other children in the class. In this case, the materials, curricular objectives, and behavioral expectations in the class may be inappropriate for the child. Beginning with **developmentally appropriate** expectations and activities may ease the challenge of certain activities or situations in the classroom. The following is an example:

Tina and the Blocks

Tina is reluctant to engage in any interactions with the other children. She tends to isolate herself and sometimes engages in repetitive self-stimulatory behaviors. Marie, the itinerant consultant, notices several very large blocks piled in one corner of the room where other children are playing with smaller blocks. Marie moves to the corner and begins to pile up the large blocks. Tina is intrigued by this simple activity, and she approaches Marie's large tower and immediately knocks it down. Tina claps with excitement. A little boy in the vicinity joins in the activity piling the blocks again. When the tower is precariously tall, Tina knocks them down again. The typical peers clap and shout along with Tina. They continue taking turns in this thoroughly enjoyable game.

Admittedly, this game is developmentally much younger than might be considered appropriate for the typical peer. On the other hand, it is appropriate for Tina and provides for her an entry into a turn-taking game with peers the same age.

Using Direct Instruction.   Occasionally, even in a consultation model, direct intervention may be necessary to work on a particular skill to enable the child to fully participate in a particular activity. The itinerant may spend time directly teaching the child a skill or may implement a specific behavioral consequence over a period. Generally, however, because the itinerant is not consistently present in the classroom, this strategy may have less-than-satisfactory effects.

Adapting Curriculum or Materials.   As Guralnick (2000) has pointed out, it is not feasible to assume that an existing program can or should totally modify its curriculum in an effort to accommodate the needs of one child. In some cases, however, the itinerant may suggest relatively unobtrusive adaptations. The following example demonstrates such an adaptation with Tina:

Tina Learns to Pretend

The typical children in the class are participating in a tabletop activity that supports the school readiness

goals of sorting, grouping, and matching. The materials include various figures (e.g., animals, adults, and children) and cars and small colored blocks of different shapes. Because Tina has Down syndrome and is developmentally younger, she is not interested in the activity and tends to simply push the small figures around the table, annoying the other children. When Marie, the itinerant consultant, notices this, she places two large, flat blocks on the table. She takes one of the figures and lays it on the block, saying, "Look. This boy is sleepy. He's sleeping on his bed. Night night!" Tina immediately focuses her attention. She shuts her eyes and pretends to sleep, and says, "Night. Go sleep." The itinerant prompts her to take another figure. Tina immediately places the figure on the second block and says, "Her night night." At this point a typical peer next to Tina places a dog figure on the bed and says, "This doggie's tired too! He wants to go to bed."

Here Marie has demonstrated for the staff that by introducing a more cognitively appropriate (and consequently more engaging) adaptation, she can encourage a pretend play activity, which is an appropriate developmental objective for Tina.

Another example of an adaptation is a simple physical adaptation:

Good Positioning for Tina Encourages Participation

Tina is smaller than the other children and the chairs in the classroom are too big for her. Tina's feet do not touch the floor. Although she is able to sit in the chair without her feet flat on the floor, she is less stable and is more likely to fidget and swing her feet. This may interfere with her ability to focus on the activity at hand and may even interfere with her fine motor skills. Marie suggests that taping together phone books to place under Tina's feet might stabilize her and make it easier for her to maintain a solid sitting position. The staff were unaware that the size of the chairs might be contributing to Tina's fidgeting, and they were appreciative of this suggestion.

It is important for the itinerant to offer to make these adaptations herself rather than simply telling the teachers how to do them. In many cases the early childhood staff do not have the time or the resources to make modifications, even if they are simple. In an itinerant model, staff "buy-in" of suggested procedures or adaptations is critical. The itinerant is in the classroom on a limited basis, for relatively short periods. If staff do not become invested in a particular strategy, if the strategy is too difficult, if they don't have sufficient resources and time to implement it, or if they don't think it makes sense, then it is likely that the procedure won't be used consistently or appropriately. In other words, the expert consultant approach without good communication and a strong, collaborative relationship will probably not be effective.

Adapting the Environment.   There are some instances where adaptation of the environment will be critical to a child's successful inclusion. Take, for example, a child who is partially sighted or blind. Creating clear, well-marked pathways from center to center will be essential. For the child who is blind, marking key materials and areas of the room with different textures or braille labels will provide important cues and—together with collaboration with an orientation and mobility specialist—will contribute to the child's independence.

Coaching Peers.   The research on early childhood inclusion suggests that, particularly for children with more severe disabilities, typical peers will need some assistance in learning how to relate and establish friendships (e.g., Odom, 2000). Thus, coaching peers is another useful strategy that the itinerant can demonstrate for the staff. Tina has very limited communication ability. She is able to select photo representations of desired objects or play activities. Marie is coaching two little girls who have taken an interest in Tina to use the photos for communication. Because Tina has been trained previously to use this communication strategy, it results in a very positive (and genuine) engagement among the girls.

Assisting Staff in the Classroom.   It is important that the itinerant consultant sometimes be available to

Photo by Scott Cunningham/Merrill

provide assistance in the classroom. This can be valuable to the staff when they are shorthanded. It also provides an opportunity for the itinerant to participate with the other children while at the same time observing the child with a disability from a distance.

Involving Parents.   Parents are essential to the successful inclusion of a child with a disability in a community-based setting. Early childhood staff may not be accustomed to facilitating active involvement of the family in the day-to-day progress or activities of the child in the center or ensuring clear and consistent communication. The itinerant can provide crucial assistance in involving the parents in ways that best meet the family's needs. In some cases families may prefer that the itinerant consultant serve as a liaison between the parents and the early childhood staff. She should communicate with the family via phone calls and provide them copies of her written notes after each visit. It is also important that family members be viewed as important team members and that they be invited to attend all team meetings.

The itinerant can provide assistance to the family in many different ways. For example, she may need to help parents understand the difference between the early childhood setting and a child's special education setting (i.e., limitations on resources, differences in philosophy, curriculum, and so on). She may need assistance determining if

the child needs a one-to-one assistant. The itinerant also may need to serve as a liaison between the parent and the early childhood staff. It is also important that the itinerant clarify with the parents what the expectations are for the setting: Is it primarily to provide a safe child-care environment? Is the goal to provide social interaction opportunities with typical peers? Or is the family assuming that all the child's IEP goals and therapeutic needs can be met in the early childhood program?

Coordinating and Meeting with the Team.
Although admittedly difficult to schedule in many early childhood programs, the itinerant must recognize the importance of regular meetings, including as many of the key players as possible. (Key players might include teachers and paraprofessionals, one-to-one assistant, program administrator, inclusion support specialist, therapists, and family members.) Such meetings are often difficult for early childhood programs whose budgets may not allow for the necessary time allocations. However, some kind of regular meeting schedule can often prevent many problems and may actually save time in the long run. It should be assumed that from time to time problems and conflicts are inevitable. In this event, it is important to have a systematic way of addressing them.

It is important to ask the early childhood staff for their suggestions and preferences for when and where meetings might best be conducted. It is also

important for the itinerant to be realistic and not have expectations for the early childhood staff that cannot be met.

One of the challenges of serving children in inclusive settings is the increased number of key players and the need and difficulty of coordinating the services and communication among them. Even when the special education services are housed within one agency or program, placement of a child in a community-based program by definition results in the need for coordination between two agencies. The more intense or complex the child's needs, the greater the coordination challenge. In addition, when there are a number of specialists and therapists involved in attempting to provide services on-site, a stressful situation can sometimes result for the early childhood program staff (and perhaps the child). Thus, the need to coordinate the activities of these service specialists becomes a significant priority. In many cases, however, there is no single individual who has the responsibility for coordinating the team. The early childhood special education inclusion specialist may be in the best position to understand all the service delivery needs of the child and family and, thus, in the best position to coordinate them. It should also be noted that genuine and effective team collaboration takes effort, skill, and practice.

Building a collaborative relationship within an itinerant model does not occur automatically, even when all parties are friendly, willing participants. It is an ongoing and continuously evolving process. Certain itinerant practices will enhance this process, whereas others will impede or undermine it. Appendix H provides specific itinerant support procedures and practices that may enhance these relationships. (Also included in Appendix H are useful forms for planning and monitoring IEP goals and support strategies.) Ideally, the itinerant consultant will develop mutually satisfying relationships with the key stakeholders at each site. Over time she can contribute to increasing the knowledge, skill, and comfort level of the early childhood staff in ways that enhance their own confidence, acceptance, and enjoyment of the child with special needs.

COTEACHING APPROACHES TO INCLUSION SUPPORT

Much of the previous discussion related to itinerant consultant service delivery can also be applied to another common inclusion support model: that of coteaching. But there are also some important challenges and strategies that are particularly characteristic of coteaching support arrangements.

Coteaching Defined

In a coteaching approach to inclusion support, an early childhood educator and a special educator share the classroom responsibilities. Gately and Gately (2001) give the following definition: "[Coteaching is] the collaboration between general and special education teachers for all of the teaching responsibilities of all students assigned to a classroom" (p. 41).

Friend and Cook (2003) list the following definitive characteristics of coteaching:

- Two or more professionals
- Joint delivery of instruction (a coteacher is not just an "extra pair of hands")
- Student with diverse learning needs
- Shared classroom space

The roles and responsibilities of each coteacher in this model will depend on several factors, including child needs, teacher preferences, classroom configuration, the nature of the activity, and the availability of other staff.

Challenges of Coteaching

There are a number of unique challenges associated with coteaching. First, individuals must *work closely* with one another on a daily basis. (Experienced coteachers often describe the relationship as being similar to a marriage!) This requires team members to become aware of their own work style. For example, one teacher may be highly organized and may have difficulty with change, whereas another may be creative and easily bored. Persons who have a strong

need to be the leader rather than a follower and need to feel in control may have difficulty sharing the leadership and working collaboratively.

Coteaching partners must often negotiate their differences in teaching *philosophy and values,* such as their attitudes toward inclusion, their knowledge and understanding of the characteristics of specific disabilities, or their beliefs about the most effective strategies and accommodations for children with special needs. Probably more important than any other single factor is that *coteachers must value and respect one another's philosophy and skills.* When this mutual respect is lacking, the effectiveness of the strategies suggested in this text will be significantly weakened.

Another significant challenge of coteaching is the need for *planning time.* Successful coteaching cannot occur without careful planning, as well as time to debrief and evaluate. In most cases, finding sufficient time for these planning activities (especially for hourly child-care staff) will require the support and involvement of program administrators.

Components of Effective Coteaching

There are four critical components of coteaching. The first is *adequate planning*, including adequate time, as mentioned above, and the development of appropriate planning procedures. Another is the design of appropriate *coteaching structures* (i.e., who does what in which activities). Another component (essential for all effective teamwork, not just a coteaching approach) is an ongoing commitment to effective *collaboration and conflict resolution*. Finally, obtaining *administrative buy-in and support* is essential. Each of these will be discussed briefly.

Planning and Evaluation. Many coteaching activities and strategies can be used to effectively support children with disabilities. There are two areas that the coteaching team must plan for. They must plan the specific adaptations and supports that are likely to be needed by the child to ensure maximum participation and achievement of IEP goals. In addition, they must plan who will do what (i.e.,

specific coteaching structures). Although some support activities become routinized, others will vary depending on the activity and the needs of the child and the available personnel.

Coteaching teams should plan together (professionals and paraprofessionals) and plan the role of each adult. For daily routine activities, teams may wish to assign standing responsibilities and simply revisit them periodically to make sure the team is happy with their assignments. For atypical events (such as a field trip, a special presentation in the classroom, daily art activities, and so on), potential challenges need to be identified and specific adult roles and responsibilities planned and written down. (In some cases, peer roles can also be planned, such as assignment of a peer buddy.) This will help maximize the learning and participation of each child with special needs without hovering over children and providing *too much* support. The following are some of the critical steps that should be included in planning:

1. Identify a *consistent* time to meet. Consistency is a key, even if the meeting is for a short period or every other week rather than every week. If it is impossible for all team members to attend every meeting, rotate participation.

2. Begin the meeting by reflecting on the events and experiences since the previous meeting: What worked? What went wrong? What should be changed? What new understanding can be gleaned related to the child's needs or learning style?

3. Plan activities in detail: What activities and strategies will be continued with no change? What are new activities? When are they scheduled? Who will do what? What materials are needed?

4. Plan accommodations and teaching strategies to both support the child's full participation and reach the child's IEP or IFSP goals—within the daily schedule and daily routines or within a specific activity. *Do not lose sight of specific IEP goals for each child. Participation in daily activities is not enough.*

5. Plan or revise coteaching structures based on each child's needs, the nature of the activity, resources available for support, and teacher styles and preferences (i.e., what roles or tasks does each adult do best and enjoy the most?).

6. When planning a new or unique activity (e.g., visiting Santa), plan for possible challenges or negative reactions for each child. (See the example of Elijah later in this chapter.) How will they be handled?

7. Evaluate the plan. Carefully debrief results and revisit plans during next the meeting.

The form presented in Exhibit 10-2 may be helpful in conducting efficient planning meetings.

Specific *roles* of each adult in the classroom need to be planned to maximize learning and participation of each child. In addition to planning each staff member's role in a certain activity, it will also be necessary to plan for the implementation of certain teaching strategies to help children master specific skills and reach IEP goals. It will also be necessary to plan for specific accommodations as necessary to ensure the child's fullest participation in classroom activities. See Exhibit 10-2.

Designing Coteaching Structures.   Different ways of configuring the coteaching roles and responsibilities are referred to here as structures. It is important to realize that there are no limits on the types of structures that can be designed. Also, as mentioned earlier, some structures may be routinized, whereas others need to be specifically planned for certain activities or children. The types of coteaching structures, or configurations, are determined by the needs and creativity of each inclusion team. The following are examples of common coteaching structures.

One Teaching—One Supporting.   The easiest coteaching structure is the one teaching–one supporting structure. In this case one teacher (usually the early childhood teacher) leads the activity while the early children special education teacher provides assistance to children with disabilities as needed. This coteaching structure is clearly the easiest because it requires the least planning and collaboration. The disadvantage of this structure is that often the special educator plays the role of a teaching assistant rather than a true collaborating teacher. Decisions about the nature of supporting activities or accommodations lack careful planning. Although this structure may be effective in encouraging some level of child participation, and immediate troubleshooting, it may be less effective in meeting specific and challenging IEP goals.

Complementary Teaching.   In complementary teaching the special educator provides highly specialized support to one child, teaching very specific skills. These skills are carefully selected to eventually enable the child to participate in the activity independently. Complementary teaching can be best used when the required assistance is not so intrusive as to require the intensive teaching strategies of preteaching described below. The special educator task analyzes the required skill and teaches the skill by using various decreasing prompt strategies during the activity. The prompts are faded, and the strategy eventually leads to the child's ability to perform independently. The following is an example:

Joshua was not able to clear his table setting after snack and tended to wander and engage in disruptive behavior. Usually an adult would provide total assistance to Joshua to try to encourage him to participate in learning to clear his table. But there had been no improvement in his ability to perform the task independently. The special educator and the early childhood teacher discussed the need to prioritize teaching Joshua this skill. Using a complementary teaching structure, the special educator was assigned to provide direct instruction to Joshua each day after snack. By using such teaching strategies as backward chaining, hand-over-hand assistance, and decreasing prompts, Joshua quickly learned to clear his table and throw waste materials in the trash.

Preteaching.   Another example is preteaching. Occasionally there will be an activity that requires skills too difficult for a particular child to learn within the context of the activity via complementary teaching. Or it may be necessary to prepare a child to participate in a new activity or some novel event. In this case the team may design a structure in which the special education teacher provides direct, one-to-one

Exhibit 10–2

Coteaching Planning Form: Assignment of Roles and Responsibilities

Date: _____ **Child:** _____

Members Present: _____

_____

I. Review of previous period:

What worked?

What went wrong?

What should be changed?

II. Evaluation of IEP progress:

Goals:

#1

#2

#3

#4

#5

#6

III. Planning for the next period (Who will do what, when?):

A. Regular procedures to continue:

B. Special events, new activities coming up:

Possible challenges for this child:

Specific support strategies (Who will do what?):

Any preparation/preteaching necessary?

IV. Date of next meeting: _____

instruction on the skill briefly each day until the child is sufficiently independent to be able to participate within the activity with minimal prompts and cues. An example might be working with a child to learn to set the table a few minutes each day before children come in for snack until the child can do it quickly and independently at the typical time. Consider the following example:

Elijah Gets Ready for Picture Day

The annual "picture day" is coming up in 1 month. Elijah has great difficulty handling flashing lights, strangers, and changes in routine. Picture day will pose a significant challenge for Elijah! His teachers meet with Elijah's mom to develop a preteaching plan. The early childhood special education teacher will develop a small-group Picture Day play script with pretend cameras. Several children play picture day during free play over the next few weeks. In addition, the teacher develops a simple program to help Elijah learn to sit still on a stool and tolerate the flash of a camera. She uses successive approximations. She does this each day, just before snack, which is Elijah's favorite activity. At home, Elijah's mom begins to mention picture day frequently to Elijah, using positive affect and counting the number of days until the day the pictures will be taken. Use of this preteaching structure not only helped prevent a disaster on picture day but also introduced a very popular pretend play scenario in which Elijah was a willing participant.

Station Teaching.   Station teaching is used to support children's learning and participation in centers. In this coteaching structure, the special education teacher is strategically assigned to the center that will pose the greatest challenge for certain children. For example, if several children need assistance and support for development of fine motor skills, the art center may be the most logical center to which to assign the teacher. Or, if there are children who experience particular behavioral challenges in more open-ended activities, the early childhood special education teacher assigned to the block area or the dramatic play area. She can share specific strategies or techniques with other adults so over time they will feel comfortable implementing the interventions themselves. The following is an example of station teaching:

Halloween Mask Center

Three centers are planned for the week of Halloween. One is fingerpainting with the colors orange and black. The second is a story listening center with a Halloween story on tape, and the third is a craft activity making masks out of paper plates and feathers. Of the three centers, the mask-making activity requires the greatest task sequencing, task persistence, and fine motor skills. Two of the children with special needs will need considerable encouragement to participate in the activity. In addition, both children have IEP goals related to improving fine motor skills. Thus, the early childhood special education teacher is assigned to this "station." She carefully plans the support techniques and accommodations that will assist each child in participating as fully as possible and in making progress toward IEP goals.

Supporting the Achievement of Specific IEP Goals

Obviously, improvement of social skills in daily activities is a common and important IEP goal for many children in inclusive settings. Social skills can be readily supported simply by supporting full participation and peer interactions in daily activities. However, some IEP goals will require careful planning and implementation of a variety of teaching strategies (and perhaps collaboration with other disciplines) to ensure their achievement. Modifying certain behaviors (e.g., encouraging a child to wear eyeglasses or a hearing aid), making progress toward mastery of specific skills (e.g., learning to recognize one's name in print), and achievement of certain developmental milestones (e.g., self-feeding) will require consideration and design of specific teaching strategies, including the embedding of teaching opportunities and practice within daily activities referred to as Lieber, "*embedded learning opportunities*" (Horn, Lieber, Li, Sandall, & Schwartz, 2000; Horn, Lieber, Sandall, & Schwartz, 2001). (For an annotated bibliography related to embedded learning opportunities, see Pretti-Frontczak, Barr, Macy, & Carter, 2003). Early childhood special educators not only must be able to identify and plan opportunities in which IEP goals can be addressed, but they must go one step further and design specific teaching or adaptation strategies that will move the child closer to mastering each goal. The Objectives-by-Activity Matrix in Exhibit 10–3 is an example of such planning for embedded learning opportunities.

Exhibit 10-3

Embedded Learning Opportunities Objective-X-Activity Planning Matrix

Child's Name ___LISA (L)___   DATE: ___

Goals Adaptations/Strategies

Goals	Social	Language	Motor	Pre-Academic	Self-Help/Independence
Goals	Increase tolerance for proximity to peers. Acknowledge peers using social communications.	Increase functional communication (requests). Increase use of spoken vocabulary.	Develop motor planning and accuracy to increase efficiency and independence in play and daily routines.	Enjoy looking at books. Develop alphabetic principle; understand relationship of print to language.	Move through daily routine without prompts. Use utensils and cup for self feeding without assistance.
Activity:					
Arrival Transition cue: Natural cue to play area	T greets L and provides imitative prompt for L to say "Good Morning" to peer.	T uses pause-and-wait strategy to encourage L to request help taking off her backpack.	T uses physical scaffolding to help L hang jacket and backpack on hook.	T says, "Find your cubby," directing L's attention to name/picture card on the cubby.	T uses backward-chaining procedure to help L motor plan her sequence of entering room, placing items in cubby, and walking to play area.
Free Play Transition cue: Lights on/off for clean up	T helps L tolerate proximity of peers by inviting peer to sit on mat at a comfortable distance from L, commenting to L, "It's great to have a friend to play with isn't it!"	T uses violation of routines strategy by placing L's favorite musical toy out of sight. When L approaches teacher and vocalizes her distress T immediately says, "Oh my. Let's find your music box!"	If L has difficulty activating a toy she has selected, T provides (then fades) physical prompts.	T directs L's attention to labels on Lego bins and plastic dinosaur bins, encouraging choice.	T waits for L to select toy.

Goals	Social	Language	Motor	Pre-Academic	Self-Help/Independence
	Increase tolerance for proximity to peers. Acknowledge peers using social communications.	Increase functional communication (requests). Increase use of spoken vocabulary.	Develop motor planning and accuracy to increase efficiency and independence in play and daily routines.	Enjoy looking at books. Develop alphabetic principle; understand relationship of print to language.	Move through daily routine without prompts. Use utensils and cup for self feeding without assistance.
Activity:					
Circle Transition cue: Let's line up for recess (T points to door)	T allows L to remain outside the circle until all children are settled, then moves her closer to the group, prompting her to "show me where you'd like to sit."	T uses verbal imitative prompt for L to request her favorite song, "Little Red Caboose," by saying, "Train song" (L already uses the word "train" when playing with the train in the block area).	For songs with motions, T provides physical prompts as needed. During active dancing activity, L is allowed to move away from the circle if she prefers.	T makes sure L's favorite storybook is one of the story choices during circle time. T does not ask L to come to the front of the circle but places three name cards directly in front of her, asking her to "find your name; LI-SA," exaggerating the /l/ sound at the beginning of the word, saying, "Lisa begins with L."	T prompts L to move toward circle area only if necessary. T waits until all other children are seated. If L still does not move toward the circle area, T directs L's attention to table closest to circle, if necessary taking her to that spot. (see "Social" goals)
Outside Transition cue: T rings bell to go inside	T prompts J (typical peer) to invite L to play on teeter-totter (L's favorite outside equipment), reminds L it requires two people.	T asks L before going outside, "Where do you want to play?" If no response, T prompts, "teeter-totter or water table?"	T scaffolds L getting on teeter-totter by first waiting to see what L does, then saying, "First grab onto the handles." T pauses. "Next, put your leg over." Use physical prompts only if necessary. Reduce prompts over time.	T points out interesting letters on playground equipment, particularly letter L. Also writes L's name in sand, then goes to paint easel later and uses hand-over-hand to help L paint her name.	(see "Motor" goals)

Activity					
Snack Transition cue: Children clean up table; sing good-bye song	T places L and J with two other peer volunteers at small four person table. (Over time, small table is moved closer to rest of class at large table.)	L's favorite snack, grapes, are in the cupboard. If L eats at least two bites of less preferred food, T says, "What would you like for dessert?" If L does not respond or points, T says, "Apples or grapes?" If L still does not respond, T busies herself with another child briefly.	T scaffolds fine motor tasks (e.g., opening milk carton, removing wrapper from cheese and crackers, peeling banana, taking sandwich from baggie) as appropriate, using verbal and physical prompts; decrease prompts over time.	T reads labels to identify juice versus milk. Points out letters on labels that match L in L's name. Prior to lunch, T should take L to look at printed lunch menu.	(see "Motor" goals)
Departure	T asks peer J to hold L's backpack while L puts on her jacket. T provides imitative prompt for L to wave good-bye to friend J. If L does not respond to imitative prompt, provide physical prompt.	As L gets on bus, T says, "See you tomorrow," using exaggerated intonation. Then says to L, "Tell me, 'See you tomorrow,'" repeating exaggerated intonation pattern. T does this every day, in same way. If L vocalizes in any way, T says, "Right! See you tomorrow!"	T uses backward chaining to assist L's motor planning to walk to cubby, take jacket off hook, put on jacket, remove backpack from cubby. T uses scaffolding to help L put on jacket.	T gives cue, "Find your cubby Lisa." Points to wrong name printed on other child's cubby, saying "Does this say Lisa? Nope, the first letter is P—must be Paul's." T shows L a note to take home to mother, saying, "Ask mommy to read this, okay?"	(see "Motor" goals)

Communication and Collaboration in Coteaching Models

Coteaching arrangements can place intense pressure on teachers to develop collaborative relationships. Good communication skills and the ability to solve problems and resolve conflicts are critical skills in successful coteaching. Teaming and coteaching can place great demands on individuals' communication and problem-solving ability. On the other hand, conscientious efforts to work collaboratively can create a sense of "family" and a satisfying work environment.

It is helpful for all members of the team to be aware of their own temperament, communication style, and preferences. They must also be able to articulate their own program philosophies and understand how they are similar to or different from those of their coteaching partner or other team members. Some of the personal characteristics and interpersonal skills that are important to successful teaming and coteaching include the following:

- Open communication

- Self-awareness

- Satisfaction and enjoyment of one's role

- Mutual respect and acceptance of each team member

- Team spirit and empathy

- Flexibility

- Willingness to share the spotlight

- Ability to work within clearly defined roles

- Professionalism

- Commitment to planning and evaluation

Note: There is often a natural tendency in coteaching models for the special educator to focus primarily on the children who have disabilities and for the early childhood teacher to focus on the typical children. It is extremely important that the special educator and her coteaching partner each take ownership for all children in the classroom.

Problem Solving and Conflict Resolution in Coteaching Models

Problem solving and conflict resolution are discussed in more detail in another section of this chapter. However, some problem-solving considerations are particularly important in coteaching situations. First, it is important to develop a general agreement that problems must be solved, not avoided. The intensity of day-to-day contact in a coteaching model requires that problem-solving strategies be used as a matter of course. Checking on the degree of congruence or difference should become part of the daily routine. It is also important to understand that conflict is inherent within any group process. Expecting that disagreements will occur, finding ways to encourage team members to express their disagreements, and dealing with them on a regular basis is much more effective in team building than trying to avoid conflict.

Second, team members need to realize that personal friendships may make communication and problem solving more difficult rather than easier in some cases. When real differences occur between friends, there may be a tendency to avoid any interactions that may jeopardize the relationship. This may interfere with effective problem solving.

A third point is the realization that genuine problem solving can be time consuming, especially during the early phases of team building. It takes time to analyze a problem and understand others' perspectives. Rushing to find solutions often results in failure to solve the problems. In turn, this failure can interfere with team building.

Administrative Issues

An important factor in successful early childhood inclusion using a coteaching model (or any model for that matter) is administrative support (Hanson et al., 2001). Many of the coteaching strategies and practices described above require collaborative processes that are very time consuming. If there is no administrative support for this planning time, the

collaborative team process is significantly at risk. Furthermore, in some administrative situations administrators from two agencies may be involved (e.g., a state-supported preschool program and a local school district). Klein et al. (2001) have described several factors that may enhance administrator support for early childhood special education inclusion practices and structures:

- **Establish clear, open lines of communication with administrators.** It is important to understand that administrators may be dealing with "fear of the unknown." Early childhood special education inclusion may still be relatively new in some areas, and it is different from K–12 inclusion. Administrators bear the ultimate responsibility for program success and should be clearly informed of practices and challenges. Administrators also should be given credit and appreciation for their support.

- **Encourage "thinking outside the box."** Because of the nature of their job demands, administrators are often conservative. Staff who understand the two points listed above will have greater success in encouraging administrators to be creative, to join in the problem-solving process, and to risk trying entirely new ways of doing things.

Stages of the Coteaching Relationship

Effective coteaching relationships do not develop quickly. Depending on personalities, values, preferences, habits, and so on, it may be a slow process. Gately and Gately (2001) describe three major phases of the coteaching relationship.

The beginning stage is characterized by guarded, careful communication. Communications are fairly superficial, and partners determine boundaries (e.g., certain topics or issues may be considered off limits). The early childhood teacher may feel intruded on, whereas the early childhood special educator teacher may feel detached or excluded. They struggle to determine their roles. Coteaching partners may

get "stuck" in this beginning stage. Their communication continues to be guarded until some crisis or stressor results in confrontation.

The next stage is referred to as the compromising stage. As the relationship develops, communication becomes more open and interactive. There is a give-and-take in the relationship, and an acceptance that compromise is necessary. Partners are willing to give up certain ideas or preferences to achieve or gain agreement on other issues.

Eventually the team reaches a more collaborative stage. This stage is characterized by open, honest communication; humor; and a high degree of comfort. In this stage there is true collaboration, with each partner contributing equally. Boundaries and role definition become somewhat blurred: teachers no longer refer to "your kids" and "my kids." At this stage there is often mutual admiration and respect for one another. (In truly collaborative teams, this comfort and respect is extended beyond the coteachers to paraprofessionals and staff.)

It is important to add that effective coteaching relationships are not free of problems and disagreements. The beauty of effective teams is that they can usually deal with these potential conflicts as a matter of course, in collaborative ways, before they become crises.

EFFECTIVE TEAMING WITH INTERDISCIPLINARY SPECIALISTS

There are few situations in early intervention or early childhood special education that do not require working as a member of a team. Many stakeholders and key players are involved in meeting the developmental and educational needs of young children with disabilities. Effective teamwork will increase the likelihood that the contributions of each of these individuals will be used in appropriate and efficient ways and will enhance the development of the child with special needs and the satisfaction of the family. On the other hand, lack of effective teaming results in insufficient access to key players' input—or, worse, confusing and perhaps even harmful service delivery.

We have discussed a variety of service delivery structures for involvement of family members, early childhood teachers, special educators, and paraprofessionals in effective inclusion support. However, children with unique or intensive needs will also require input, support, and evaluation from a variety of specialists. These include discipline-specific therapists (e.g., occupational therapists, physical therapists, and speech-language pathologists) and disability-specific specialists (e.g., visual impairment specialists and deaf and hard-of-hearing specialists). The roles of many were noted in Table 10–1.

Incorporating this input into the inclusive setting and coordinating their efforts can be a significant challenge. There are a variety of ways in which specialists may provide services to children in inclusive settings. Typically, the specialist works as an itinerant. In this model, itinerant specialists may work directly with the child or in a consultation role, working primarily with the staff, or a combination of these two models. Communication with the specialist is critical. There is little evidence that working directly with a child for an hour each week can be effective if the specialist's intervention strategies and goals for the child are not understood and incorporated into daily routines. Further, specialists' own efforts are enhanced only via their collaboration with other key players in the child's life.

Each specialist visits the center according to her own availability and scheduling. Ideally, the ways in which the services of specialists are organized should be carefully planned and coordinated. Specialists should meet regularly with the team at the center. However, this may be unrealistic. One possible model for using and coordinating the input from a variety of specialists in an inclusive setting is for the early childhood special education coteacher or itinerant to serve as a sort of "conduit" of their input. She assumes the primary responsibility for working with the specialists and conveying information to other staff and to families. Because the well-trained specialist coteacher is likely to be familiar with the strategies used by specialists, this model can be quite efficient and can facilitate communication across team members even when meeting together as a group is difficult.

WORKING WITH PARAPROFESSIONALS

The Individuals with Disabilities Education Act and its amendments have recognized an important role for paraprofessionals in addressing the shortage of personnel by requiring that states develop training for paraprofessionals. The shortage of service providers is further complicated by the recognition that cultural competence is essential to providing of family-centered practices. "Since paraprofessionals often live in the communities where they work, they may provide cultural perspectives or speak the primary language of non-English speaking students" (Giangreco, Yuan, McKenzie, Cameron, & Fialka, 2005).

In addition, the frequent use of one-to-one assistants to support children in inclusive settings has further increased the use of paraprofessionals in early childhood special education. Realizing this, a number of states have integrated paraprofessionals into their service delivery system and have established new occupational categories for paraprofessionals. The remainder of this chapter provides guidelines for effectively developing and using paraprofessionals in the center or classroom.

Paraprofessionals increasingly play crucial roles in early childhood service delivery, regardless of the setting (Appl, 2006). They are essential members of any early intervention or preschool education team. However, the supervisor–supervisee relationship between the paraprofessional and the early childhood educator or early childhood special educator presents a unique set of challenges, somewhat different from the challenges of teaming and collaboration described earlier.

Who Are the Paraprofessionals?

Paraprofessionals are individuals who by their assistance extend the capacity and effectiveness of teachers and other interventionists. By definition, paraprofessionals do not have the training and expertise of professional teachers, and they receive less in monetary compensation (Hans & Korfmacher, 2002).

Various terms have been used to refer to those who participate in early intervention programs but lack the full training and certification necessary to function as fully as teachers or clinicians. Terms such as *teacher aide, early intervention assistant, paraeducator, special education program aide,* and *instructional* or *therapist assistant* are common. Throughout this chapter, the term *paraprofessional* or *teacher assistant* will generally refer to all those who provide assistance within early education programs but who are not fully certified or credentialed.

Designing and Defining Jobs

Designing and defining jobs is the starting point for effectively using paraprofessionals (French, 2003). There are two primary reasons why job design is the appropriate point of departure. First, careful consideration of job design elements provides the criteria for recruiting and selecting paraprofessionals, especially paid teacher aides. Second, people work more effectively when they know what they are supposed to do and how and when they are supposed to do it. Job design, thus, frames the expectations that are so important to job functioning and role relationships.

Because this responsibility falls on teachers, it clarifies in their minds the purposes, tasks, and conditions in which paraprofessionals are to be part of the classroom team. Similarly, a clearly defined set of tasks, responsibilities, and relationships establishes for paraprofessionals the framework within which they are expected to work.

Framework of Activities, Interactions, and Sentiments. Job design refers to specifying the content and relationships of any job, be it the job of teacher assistant, volunteer, teacher, principal, or director. Properly conceived, job design considers both the jobholder as a person and the performance contributions expected on behalf of the organization (or classroom). A simple way of thinking about job design characteristics is to borrow concepts from a classical study of group dynamics in which Homans (1992) conceived of any work group (e.g., teacher, paraprofessionals, and pupils) as a social system. Homans identified three features common to any

small work group: activities, interactions, and sentiments. With slight modification, the following are the basics for defining essential job design elements in centers and schools:

1. *Activities or tasks.* This feature defines the content of what a jobholder is to do. What is the scope or breadth of tasks? To what degree are they to be standardized and routinized instead of creative? How often are they to be performed? What results are expected? How are results to be recognized (by both the paraprofessional and the teacher)?

2. *Interactions or role relationships.* This defines with whom the jobholder is expected to interact, how often (or under what conditions) this is to happen, and the quality of that relationship. What relationship is the paraprofessional to have with the children? With other staff members and parents? What are the paraprofessional's responsibilities and limits of authority relative to the teacher? How much autonomy or self-initiative freedom is given the paraprofessional for certain types of tasks? To what extent is teamwork instead of individual action expected?

3. *Sentiments or values and attitudes.* Sentiment defines the conditions under which work is to be performed and sources of satisfaction available to the jobholder. By calling attention to sentiments, the teacher is forced to anticipate and build on essential questions that affect the quality of the paraprofessional's involvement in the classroom, such as the following: What personal rewards are meaningful to the paraprofessional? How is the paraprofessional expected to view sensitive issues such as discipline methods and toilet habits? What values and attitudes held by the paraprofessional will contribute best to the program's objectives and be compatible with those of the teacher?

Developing Job Task Descriptions. Since each paraprofessional brings different skills and expectations to the job and each teacher's or classroom's needs are different, the paraprofessional's job description must be designed to reflect the unique interaction desired. A clear understanding of paraprofessional roles and responsibilities is essential to ensure that

paraprofessionals are being used appropriately. "The appropriateness of tasks depends on the paraeducator's training, knowledge and skill, as well as the level of supervision and the clarity of instructions provided by the teacher" (Warger, 2003).

The job task descriptions should be expressed in writing, with each participant keeping a copy for reference and review. These should be rewritten at least once each year following performance evaluation and at any time there is a significant change in assignment. This job description typically conveys more than a trite list of "responsible for" statements. As previously suggested, a written job description provides both the criteria for screening candidates (in the case of teacher assistants) and a picture of the job for the candidate. For a starting point in creating a useful statement of job task design, the supervisor should think about the ways in which a teacher assistant or a volunteer can be useful. One of the easiest ways to develop such a list of task possibilities is to jot down ideas as they occur during the day. Some of the ways paraprofessionals could be useful are included in Exhibit 10–4.

Once the teacher has identified desirable tasks, it will be necessary to clarify (a) who is to conduct the activity, (b) how often it is to be performed, (c) the manner in which it is to be performed (if standardization or consistency is desired), and (d) how all concerned can recognize successful performance.

Visualizing Role Relationships.   After the teacher has defined activity areas, she should think carefully about the role visualized for the paraprofessional. Will the paraprofessional be a creative contributor to the

Exhibit 10–4

Possible Paraprofessional Tasks

- Preparing the room, including setting up centers, organizing materials needed for special projects, and locating daily supplies.
- Greeting the children and assisting with all routines.
- Supervising activities in the classroom and on the playground.
- Nurturing appropriate behavior, including dealing with misbehaviors acceptably and effectively.
- Directing specific activities planned by the teacher.
- Assisting children with eating and toileting programs.
- Helping children with assistive technology.
- Charting behaviors during the implementation of behavior management programs.
- Helping to order or build adaptive equipment.
- Following specialists' instructions in helping to position or transport children.
- Providing appropriate prompts to help ensure positive social integration.
- Preparing, cataloging, and filing intervention games and materials.
- Setting up media equipment.
- Showing videotapes, slides, and special materials.
- Contacting parents to set up conferences.
- Helping with end-of-the-day routines, including cleanup.

children's learning or merely the person behind the scenes who prepares materials? Will she be encouraged to suggest activities or be relegated to doing only what the teacher has planned?

The answers to such role relationship questions reflect the philosophy and style of the teacher. Figure 10–1 depicts the extreme views of interaction that teachers have of themselves in relation to support personnel. A teacher who wants to be the boss and run a tight classroom or center ought to be aware of this philosophy. Such a situation will definitely restrict the range of freedom and autonomy given to paraprofessionals (and may also interfere with the development of collaborative relationships).

It is helpful if the teacher thinks carefully about her role-relationship philosophy and leadership style before developing specific guidelines for the paraprofessionals who may be assisting her.

Translating Sentiments into Policy Guidelines.
Few dedicated teachers work without some form of lesson plan or curriculum guide. Similarly, the teacher plans in advance the essential performance tasks expected of paraprofessionals and clarifies intended relationships. For optimum effectiveness, however, the teacher should also plan for and codify the *affective* behavior expected of paraprofessionals. This means in part explaining (in writing when possible) not just the duties of the paraprofessional but the affect and tone of their interactions with children as well as the level of intrusiveness versus responsiveness that is expected.

Particularly important are guidelines for responding to unacceptable child behavior. For example, if a child spits at another child, what is considered an appropriate response? Gentle redirection? A stern facial expression? In saying "Jason, I see you're angry at Philip," there is not necessarily a clear "right" or

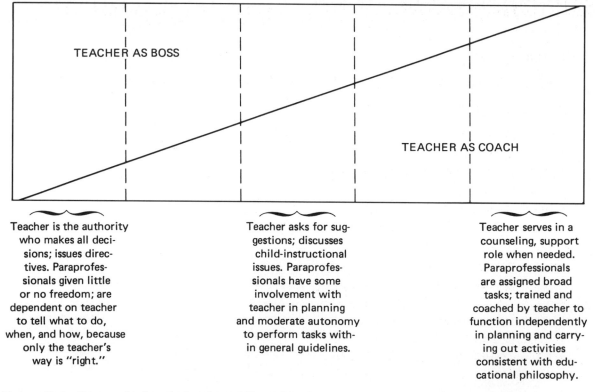

TEACHER AS BOSS

TEACHER AS COACH

Teacher is the authority who makes all decisions; issues directives. Paraprofessionals given little or no freedom; are dependent on teacher to tell what to do, when, and how, because only the teacher's way is "right."

Teacher asks for suggestions; discusses child-instructional issues. Paraprofessionals have some involvement with teacher in planning and moderate autonomy to perform tasks within general guidelines.

Teacher serves in a counseling, support role when needed. Paraprofessionals are assigned broad tasks; trained and coached by teacher to function independently in planning and carrying out activities consistent with educational philosophy.

Figure 10–1   Range of role relationship philosophies between teacher and paraprofessionals

"wrong" response, but there may be certain expectations that have become part of the culture within a given setting. It is important that the paraprofessional understand these kinds of affective expectations. Clarifying roles includes not only clear expectations regarding the scope of work but also the nature of the paraprofessional's authority to act. Exhibit 10–5 features examples of written guidelines for interacting with young children.

Because they serve as a frame of reference for feedback, job design guidelines not only help in redirecting a paraprofessional's behavior when necessary but also stimulate job satisfaction. The paraprofessional knows when she has done a good job or has handled a difficult situation successfully and consistently within the program's standards. Guidelines also permit teachers to reinforce appropriate behavior. To the extent they allow the paraprofessional to make discretionary choices, the guidelines can help her feel more "professional" about being involved in the learning process.

Communicating Expectations

The socialization process of building an effective working relationship is genuinely a mutual responsibility. Both people have to learn about each other. In

---

Exhibit 10–5

Child Interaction Guidelines for Paraprofessionals

1. *Create a pleasant atmosphere.* Tense children cannot become effectively involved. Help them feel comfortable by being warm and enthusiastic. If you relax and enjoy yourself, the children will feel this and follow your example.

2. *Your voice is your asset.* A soft, confident voice elicits a child's attention more quickly than a high or loud one. First gaining eye contact with a child and then speaking directly and softly to him or her will be more effective than shouting across the room.

3. *Be positive.* Instead of saying "Don't spill your milk," it is better to say "Hold your glass with two hands." "Good builders put their tools away carefully" is a better statement than "Don't throw your tools."

4. *Labels are for jelly jars, not for children.* Labels and phrases such as "naughty boy" or "bad girl" make children feel ashamed and unworthy. Children with these feelings cannot learn.

5. *Keep competition out of the classroom.* Nothing is to be gained from fostering competition among young children. Discourage children when they say "I can draw better than Susie" by saying "Each can draw in his or her own special way."

6. *Choices are for choosing.* When it is time to clean up, do not ask the children whether they want to clean up. Instead say, "It is time to clean up now." If you do not intend to accept no for an answer, do not give them a choice. Give them a choice only when you really want them to choose.

7. *Sharing is not simple.* Preschool-aged children are just learning to share. If they are playing with something, in their minds the toy belongs to them at that moment. Children should be encouraged to ask whether they can have a turn and to tell others when they are through playing with something.

8. *Keep your eyes on the children.* Children must be within the visual range of supervising adults at all times. They need and deserve alert supervision, which is not possible when the responsible adult is engaged in adult conversation. If too many children are entering any one play area, redirect some to other areas.

9. *Do not dominate children's activities.* Children should be allowed to use their active imaginations as they experiment with ideas and materials. Unless you are teaching a specific lesson, stay in the background with supportive but not suppressive comments.

10. *Prevention is perfect.* Be alert so you can redirect behavior that can become a problem. Remember that children should not be allowed to hurt themselves or others.

the process of communicating (verbally, in writing, and through behaviors), they begin to expand their clarification of mutual role relationships. At its very essence, *a role is a set of expectations about what is appropriately to be done and what is to be avoided.* For paraprofessionals, the role can either be reasonably well defined and stimulating or ambiguous, conflicting, and stifling with unpleasant jobs and oppressive supervision.

Both the teacher and the paraprofessional must communicate their expectations. The relationship between teacher and paraprofessional can make the experience rich and fulfilling or miserable and tedious. Perhaps more important, negative relationships can interfere with program effectiveness.

If only one teacher and one teacher assistant are involved, the orientation may take place in a pleasant corner of the classroom, or it can take place at a restaurant during a planned lunch hour. The number of people involved will influence where the meeting takes place and how it is conducted, but it should not influence what is discussed.

Stressing the importance of communicating common goals, Carroll (2001) identified several key items to be addressed immediately as paraprofessionals are oriented to a new position. She suggests putting together a packet that includes the following:

- Start and end times
- Bell schedules
- Parking permits
- A map of the building
- Emergency procedures
- Attendance policies
- Confidentiality policies
- A schedule of students and staff with his or her schedule highlighted

One could add to this list the importance of professional conduct. The paraprofessionals who are expected to behave as professionals will usually do so. This includes being prompt, appropriately dressed, and respectful of all aspects of confidentiality regarding children's characteristics and behaviors.

Discovering and Using Special Skills and Talents

To make the orientation truly an opportunity for two-way communication, the resourceful teacher should encourage new paraprofessionals to reveal their special interests, skills, and talents. Asking about previous work experience is important.

Parenting and homemaking skills, however, are equally important in preschools and child-care centers. Very few skills cannot be adapted to useful and interesting classroom activities. Everything from sports to needlework fits in somewhere. Hobbies can be the source of exciting lessons. Baking, gardening, sewing, and cleaning can be the basis for science and mathematics lessons.

One effective method of discovering the special skills and talents of paraprofessionals is to develop a simple questionnaire that can be filled out by potential assistants. Many teachers ask parents to complete the questionnaire to encourage parent involvement. Others use the questionnaire with hired teacher assistants and with volunteers. The questionnaire in Figure 10-2 was designed to incorporate the needs of an early childhood center while allowing the respondents some latitude of choice.

Once the special interests, skills, and talents of the paraprofessional are known, the teacher may plan to adapt activities to them. A teacher assistant in one class loved to garden. An outdoor garden provided lessons in many concepts. Children learned about *straight, front,* and *back* rows. They learned about plants that grew *taller* and things that were *shorter.* They discovered the *shortest* stem and the *longest* vine. That garden was the basis of science lessons and nutrition themes as well as a source of beauty and joy.

Another teacher assistant was particularly interested in puppets. She made sock puppets for each child and taught them basic skills. Puppet shows enlivened nutrition lessons and language lessons. Puppets sang the opening song and learned to say "please" and "thank you." Puppets helped with everything, and the teacher assistant felt proud of her accomplishment.

When the teacher gives special thought and care to matching classroom responsibilities with the paraprofessional's skills and talents, everyone benefits. Ideally a teacher assistant will be ready for anything, and many of them are. But even when paraprofessionals are willing to do "anything and everything," relationships and performances are better when interests are allowed to blossom.

Defining the Teacher's Responsibilities to Paraprofessionals

Relationship building is a two-way process. We have stressed the importance of the teacher's responsibility for mentoring and guiding the paraprofessional. A few of the commonly accepted responsibilities for teacher leadership and guidance are summarized in Exhibit 10-6. However, this genuine caring must not interfere with the teacher's awareness of her role as the person on whom ultimate responsibility rests. A tug-of-war for the affections of the children or their parents is destructive and dysfunctional. Differing philosophies of what is best for children lead to subtle and disruptive experiences. Refusal of the paraprofessional to accept the teacher's responsibility and authority may lead to termination.

Just as the teacher avoids embarrassing or criticizing the teacher assistant or volunteer in front of parents and other adults, so must the paraprofessional avoid undermining the teacher. It is the teacher's responsibility to make this clear from the beginning. The teacher must be alert to recognize any overt or covert attempts to interfere with behavior management or teaching methods. Such interference should be dealt with immediately. If free and open discussion of the importance of consistent attitudes and management of children is established in the beginning, future problems will be minimized.

Being an Appropriate Role Model

Teachers must be appropriate role models. Saying one thing and behaving in a different way is inexcusable. What teachers *do* speaks louder than what they *say.* Also, teachers must be clear about their intent to demonstrate a particular procedure and their expectation that the paraprofessional will practice and learn the procedure. The teacher should explain what will be done and why it will be done. Sometimes a particular procedure should be written and available for reference. This is important for new activities.

Name _____

	Mom	Dad	WOULD YOU LIKE TO:
1.	[ ]	[ ]	Read a story to some of the children?
2.	[ ]	[ ]	Lead a song or some other musical activity?
3.	[ ]	[ ]	Help children create something in art?
4.	[ ]	[ ]	Bring the family pet to visit the center?
5.	[ ]	[ ]	Help set up or supervise a field trip?
6.	[ ]	[ ]	Make a book of a child's story?
7.	[ ]	[ ]	Work puzzles or play games?
8.	[ ]	[ ]	Share your hobby with the class? Hobby:
9.	[ ]	[ ]	Show children how to use simple carpenter tools?
10.	[ ]	[ ]	Bring a guitar (or other instrument) and demonstrate?
11.	[ ]	[ ]	Help cut and paste pictures?
12.	[ ]	[ ]	Teach the children something about your occupation?
13.	[ ]	[ ]	Conduct a simple science experiment?
14.	[ ]	[ ]	Wear clothing from another country and tell about it?
15.	[ ]	[ ]	Bring necessary materials and plant some seeds?
16.	[ ]	[ ]	Demonstrate rug weaving, leather tooling, or other crafts?
17.	[ ]	[ ]	Make jam or churn butter?
18.	[ ]	[ ]	Decorate a bulletin board?
19.	[ ]	[ ]	Sew dress-up and/or doll clothing?
20.	[ ]	[ ]	Construct special toys or equipment?

And if none of these appeals to you, what would you like to do?

Figure 10–2   Samples from a parent volunteer checklist

Exhibit 10-6

Some Responsibilities of Teachers to Paraprofessionals

1. To exert active leadership and guidance to build a team of coordinated helpers.

2. To create an atmosphere in which paraprofessionals feel accepted and motivated to perform effectively.

3. To provide ample structure and direction so paraprofessionals know what is expected of them.

4. To hold an orientation session with new paraprofessionals to discuss program goals, procedures, and policies and what to expect of children with special needs.

5. To plan work in work in advance of the workday and to build variety into the tasks paraprofessionals are assigned to perform.

6. To provide adequate information so that paraprofessionals can carry out their tasks and to provide feedback so they know how they are performing.

7. To have on hand the resources paraprofessionals will need to carry out assigned tasks; to show them where to find materials, how to set up an activity, and how to operate any special equipment; and to make known any restrictions or special requirements to accommodate particular children.

8. To assign tasks within the range of competency of a paraprofessional while providing increased responsibility and autonomy as performance indicates increased competence.

9. To provide opportunities for regularly scheduled meetings between the teacher and the paraprofessionals. Such meetings will allow for adequate planning and avoid waiting for a crisis to force communication. Impromptu meetings should not become substitutes for regularly scheduled meetings.

After the teacher completes a specific demonstration of a strategy or directing an activity, the teacher assistant will want to practice the skill on her own. It is helpful for the teacher to suggest that she would like to observe the paraprofessional's use of the strategy when the paraprofessional feels ready, for example, "Tomorrow when you feel ready for me to watch you, let me know."

Part of a teacher's responsibility as a role model is to build up, not undermine, the desire and productive energies of paraprofessionals. Just as the teacher's responsibility toward children is to help them become more fully functioning independently rather than dependently, the same applies to paraprofessionals. But development of the independent skills and motivation of paraprofessionals does not occur through abandonment. A disorganized teacher

whose actions reveal that she has given little thought to how paraprofessionals are to serve confuses and discourages those who seek to help. Perhaps one of the most effective ways in which a teacher can help develop the skills and motivation of the paraprofessional is through the eyes of someone working in the paraprofessional role. Exhibit 10-7 presents such a perspective in a sensitive but strongly worded message from a practicing paraprofessional.

Allowing for Sufficient Planning Time

The teacher assistant who provided the message for Exhibit 10-7 wrote about the implications of the teacher's planning (or failure to plan) on the motivation of assistants. Another facet of paraprofessional

Exhibit 10–7

Advice from a Paraprofessional to Teachers

Note: The comments that follow were written by an experienced teacher assistant. She has worked with a number of different teachers and has strong feelings about teacher actions that made her work effective and rewarding and those that interfered with her own effectiveness.

Treating your assistants as if they have no common sense will get you little help. Most aides are more intelligent than they are given credit for. Don't give them only menial chores but also things that are more gratifying. Give them air to breathe and expand themselves, and they will be more help to you as the teacher than you can imagine. One time I worked for a teacher just 1 day a week. Often when I came she said, "Oh! Are you here today? I didn't know you came this week." Really made me feel welcome and useful. Sometimes she just said, "I don't have anything for you to do today. Go see if any of the other teachers have something for you to do." So, planning ahead is important. Teachers complain of "having too much to do," and then they don't make good use of the assistant's time because they didn't plan.

Treat your assistant as an intelligent person. Aides can do much more than set up snacks and wash dirty faces. If you tell them what to do and why and then show them how, they can be really good teachers. Don't expect them to plan the lessons, but with a little help, they can teach little children very effectively. Answer all questions as soon as possible, and answer them as you would any other adult. Don't "talk down" to them. Your college degree doesn't give you the right to belittle their ability to understand. Tell why you do something, and if they don't understand the first time, tell them again in another way. Show them how to do something the right way yourself. Don't just tell them and leave.

Compliment your assistant sometimes, but not too much. Too much flattery is insulting. But a genuine "I like the way you showed Susie how to button her coat" helps to make it all worthwhile.

Let your assistants learn from their mistakes. Don't "catch them" every time. Just look the other way for a while. Give them a chance to change by themselves. But if they are really doing something wrong, or they are stuck in the same way, suggest, "Sometimes it helps to do it this way." And then show them or tell them again.

Never embarrass them in front of the children or parents, or anybody for that matter. If you must correct them, wait until you can do it when you are alone. Smart teachers know how to make suggestions look and sound like compliments. "You really are teaching Tommy how to wash his hands. Do you think he is ready to learn to use the brush?" is a lot better than "Don't you remember, I told you that you should teach the children to brush their fingernails when they wash their hands."

Listen to the assistants' comments. Let them have the satisfaction of suggesting things to you sometimes. An occasional "Oh, I'm so glad you suggested that" is better than a hundred insincere things. Ask your aides' opinions sometimes and then listen.

Do remember, you are the teacher. You are responsible. You are in charge. Assistants need to know "their teacher" knows what to do. They need to respect all that education you've had. Give them a chance.

by Robbie Crane
Alton, Illinois

motivation and effectiveness comes from the teacher and the teacher assistant prioritizing planning time. Many federally funded programs in the early days allowed for whole days for teachers and teacher assistants to plan together each week. Money was available for regular evaluation and planning sessions. Few programs today include this necessity. Time for planning is a luxury.

As with everything else, teachers must do what they can. Day-to-day planning may need to be squeezed

into very small time segments. The time after school, lunch periods, and so-called breaks become the scarce moments for planning. These daily time constraints make it necessary for the teacher to do overall planning before the school year begins. Necessary planning before the school year starts includes designing record-keeping systems, choosing basic activity plans, organizing the classroom, scheduling activities, preparing materials, and assigning responsibilities. The paraprofessional's responsibilities within the daily schedule should be written out. There is rarely enough time before and after school for such comprehensive planning, no matter how dedicated the teacher and the teacher assistant may be.

Over time, however, teacher assistants should be encouraged to plan some of the specific activities. The teacher identifies the goals and objectives, but the "equivalent practice" can be suggested by paraprofessionals. For example, one teacher assistant raised tropical fish. With her help, the children planned an aquarium. They learned colors as they chose the stones for the bottom. They discovered water temperature as they planned for the fish. Feeding the fish developed measuring skills and a sense of responsibility.

During the months that the aquarium served as an excellent teaching tool, the teacher and the teacher assistant discussed many different ways in which it could be used. More than half of the excellent teaching ideas that evolved originated with the teacher assistant. The teacher continued to pinpoint specific objectives that could be achieved, but it was uniquely successful because of the teacher assistant's knowledge and enthusiasm to take charge of this project.

Providing Constructive Feedback: Coaching and Mentoring the Paraprofessional

Just as routine planning time boosts effectiveness, so also does regular and constructive feedback and coaching from teacher to paraprofessional. The

teacher must build in feedback about how the teacher assistant is doing. This is especially critical for paraprofessionals who are inexperienced in working with young children with special needs. Informal feedback should not be the occasion for a great deal of discussion. It should be specific, clearly stated, and timely. The teacher should identify strengths, behaviors, and attitudes to be changed or developed. The more straightforward the feedback, the more effective it will be.

Avoid focusing on personalities. Focus on the task behaviors and the procedures that are changeable. For example, telling the teacher assistant that she is disorganized is not helpful. Explaining why the crayons and scissors should be placed within the reach of each child instead of at the end of the table, however, will help her understand precisely how to become more organized and efficient. The teacher should discuss why specific things are important or how a certain strategy might work better for a particular child's learning style. If necessary, she should reteach and demonstrate again. It is especially important for the teacher to evaluate and provide suggestions to the teacher assistant with no other adults or children present or within hearing distance. The teacher's goal is to support and develop the teacher assistant's skills. It is important not to exaggerate the negative effects of a particular behavior. Rather, state what is wanted, why it is desirable, and how it can be achieved.

The teacher should not forget to reward effort and abilities as part of success. Things that are easy for the teacher may be difficult for an inexperienced teacher assistant. The teacher should not expect everything to be learned at once! Time is needed for practice. Recognition by way of "thank yous" for regular role-appropriate behaviors is as important as special rewards for exceptional success. But such spontaneous or informal feedback opportunities do not eliminate the need for periodic formal evaluation of paraprofessional behaviors. It is also essential that the early childhood special education teacher be willing to acknowledge contributions and strengths of the paraprofessional that the teacher herself may not have. Every paraprofessional—even

if inexperienced—brings his or her own special knowledge and insights to the team.

In addition to providing ongoing feedback and encouragement to the paraprofessional, the experienced professional will engage in mentoring and staff development. Providing interesting written materials, encouraging attendance at conferences and workshops, and observing other classrooms, coaching the paraprofessional in learning difficult or unique teaching methods or procedures are examples of teacher activities that extend beyond good supervision. This mentoring relationship can often enhance the collaborative problem solving and team processes in the classroom.

PARAPROFESSIONALS AS ONE-TO-ONE ASSISTANTS

Increasingly, as mentioned earlier, paraprofessionals are being used as one-to-one assistants in inclusive settings. They are sometimes referred to as a "shadow aide." The assignment of a one-to-one assistant exclusively to a specific child can have definite drawbacks. The early childhood educator often assumes that the assistant has been well trained to work with the designated child, when usually this is not the case. Another disadvantage is that the child often becomes very attached to the assistant because of the intensity and exclusivity of the relationship and may avoid interacting with peers and other adults. Also, when peers try to approach a child with a disability, at times the paraprofessional unintentionally interferes with the peers' efforts to be friendly or helpful to the child with disabilities (Causton-Theoharis & Malmgren, 2005).

In some situations, such as in the case of a child who is extremely aggressive, self-injurious, or medically fragile, it is necessary to assign a one-to-one assistant, or the child would have to be removed from the program. However, it is important to remember that the use of a one-to-one assistant may be just as restrictive as a segregated special education setting.

Giangreco and colleagues (2005) discussed the use of paraprofessionals in K–12 educational settings.

Research suggesting that the unnecessary proximity of instructional assistants to children with special needs in general education can actually impede children's progress is cited. The following areas of concern related to the "hovering" of instructional assistants were noted: (a) the general educators tended to avoid assuming responsibility and ownership for the education of students who have one-to-one assistants, (b) the assistant tended to separate the child from the rest of the group, (c) the prolonged close proximity with assistants fostered dependency of the child on the adult, (d) the excessive proximity sometimes interfered with peer interactions, (e) the unrealistic instructional expectations or lack of training of the assistants led to inadequate academic instruction of the children under their care, (f) students who had difficulty communicating often found their assistant speaking and making decisions for them, (g) the student's gender became secondary to that of the assistant in such matters as toileting, and (h) students may express their embarrassment/discomfort abut having a paraprofessional by displaying inappropriate behaviors.

Even though cited research typically involves older children, the results present many cautions for early childhood special educators. Authors recommend reconsideration of the growing tendency to assign one-to-one assistants. They also recommend that whenever feasible, assistants should be hired for groups of children rather than individual children. They urge the development of definite guidelines to ensure the fading of prompts, the use of natural supports such as peer support, avoidance of excessive proximity (hovering), clarification of role responsibilities, and additional training of both the paraprofessional and her supervisor (Giangreco & Doyle, 2002; Giangreco et al., 2001).

Supervision of One-to-One Assistants in Inclusive Settings

When a child is assigned a one-to-one assistant, one of the most serious issues is supervision. In community-based inclusive settings, one-to-one assistants may be employed by a different agency or school

district than the early childhood teacher or the special educator. As a result, the responsibility for training and supervision of one-to-one assistants may be unclear. Lack of clarity on this issue can be a potential source of conflict in the inclusive setting. Determining who is responsible for employing the assistant may or may not indicate who will provide supervision. Whereas some one-to-one assistants have developed skills in providing appropriate support, many have had little or no training.

Another issue that must be clarified is the role of the one-to-one. Who determined that this level of support was needed and for what purposes? What are the one-to-one assistant's specific duties? Early childhood specialists teachers will want to know their role in terms of training and supervision. Will they have time? Do they have the knowledge and expertise? Do they want the added responsibility of supervising another adult in their classroom?

Guidelines for Use of One-to-One Assistants

The following are suggested as guidelines for the use of one-to-one assistants in in early childhood settings:

- Clearly define the purpose of the one-to-one assistant.

- Make it clear to the one to one assistant that she should provide *only* the degree of intervention necessary to support the child's learning and participation and ensure the child's safety.

- The one to one assistant must not interfere with the child's opportunity for interactions with other children and must not become a constant barrier or buffer between the child and her environment.

- The use of a one-to-one assistant must not interfere with the child's development of independence.

- Avoid stigmatizing the child as the only child in the class who requires an attached adult.

- Put the specific daily responsibilities and activities of the assistant in writing.

Successful Use of a One-to-One Assistant

James was a 30-month-old child with developmental delays. Mealtimes were very challenging for James because of occasional choking. He was also sometimes aggressive toward other children. He was fully included in a large day-care setting, and both his mother and teacher were concerned that the staff ratio and skill level did not provide adequate support for him in this environment. The decision was made to employ a one-to-one assistant for James. Initially, there were problems because the one-to-one assistant hovered over him every moment, even though he had choking episodes only when eating, and his aggressive behavior was unpredictable.

In a team meeting including the mother and the assistant, it was decided that the only time close proximity of the assistant was necessary was at mealtimes. A careful functional behavioral analysis revealed that the aggressive behavior occurred only when other children were crowding James. Rather than shadowing the child all day, the assistant simply watched for and managed those situations that typically triggered the aggressive behaviors.

Within 6 months, James was no longer choking, and the staff had learned how to prevent aggressive behavior, significantly reducing the need for one-to-one assistance. At this time, the use of the assistant was terminated.

- In consultation with parents, gradually decrease the intensity and proximity of the assistant.

- Gradually include more and more children in the target child's space.

- Whenever possible, view the one-to-one assistant as a temporary assignment.

- Encourage the child's attachment to other staff. The assignment of a one-to-one must not discourage the other staff from interacting with or taking responsibility for the child with a disability.

- The use of a one-to-one assistant must not become even more restrictive than a segregated setting!

EVALUATING PARAPROFESSIONAL SERVICES

Evaluating paraprofessional services is a critical step in developing improved and successful programs for young children. Informal daily feedback helps create an atmosphere in which the paraprofessional feels secure, worthy, appreciated, and professional. More formal periodic evaluations not only help ongoing personnel development but also can strengthen program development.

Typically, the first evaluation is not too long after initial employment to focus on and correct misunderstandings and confused expectations. (It may be helpful to begin with a 1-month probationary period. This, of course, can be extended or dropped, depending on the results of this initial evaluation.) Such a clarification serves the interests of both parties because an effective evaluation acknowledges that the teacher, as well as the paraprofessional, can learn from the experience. The time between subsequent evaluations is lengthened to 3 or 4 months. For an experienced teacher assistant, once a year may be adequate.

Using Self-Evaluations

One formal technique is to allow paraprofessionals the opportunity to evaluate their own contributions and feelings. If the paraprofessional feels comfortable in sharing this self-evaluation with the supervising teacher, chances for growth and development can be enhanced. Perceptions of self-performance are tested against the teacher's observations and expectations. The teacher has the opportunity to provide constructive feedback, to offer encouragement, and to coach. The self-evaluation process may be open ended, or it may be guided by a checklist such as the one illustrated in Figure 10–3.

As noted in the directions in Figure 10–3, using recent critical incidents is typically a practical technique for clarifying role behaviors and learning. By contrasting a successful event with a not-so-successful one, a problem-solving approach can emphasize conditions necessary for future success rather than belabor criticism of a past problem. When a teacher assistant or volunteer has not been doing something believed necessary (e.g., has failed to listen to children), the teacher can probe the consequences of such behavior. The teacher should be prepared to provide an example of when such a failure or neglect led to an inappropriate consequence. Then both the teacher and the teacher assistant should work toward a plan of action for reducing the frequency of the undesirable behavior.

Teacher-Initiated Evaluations of the Paraprofessional

Teacher-initiated evaluations of assistants are necessary because some people see their own behaviors in a more positive light than do others. Thus, the self-evaluation conference potentially must deal with distortions in perception between the teacher assistant and the teacher. As long as the primary reason for evaluation is personal and team improvement, however, the dangers of conflict due to differing perceptions are reduced. An evaluation initiated by the teacher overcomes the potential clash between views, especially when the teacher uses a form or checklist. However, teacher-initiated evaluation can generate anxiety and defensiveness on the part of the person being evaluated. Success in either case hinges on the manner in which the teacher handles the conference.

It is better for the teacher to focus on specific behaviors rather than on generalities such as dependability or interpersonal relations. To do this effectively, the teacher needs to take the time to describe specific behaviors of the teacher assistant that are helping and hindering performance effectiveness.

Check the appropriate box for each question as it applies to you. On the back of this page, note briefly two examples (contrasting if possible) of recent experiences for each question.

HOW OFTEN DO I . . .	Usually	Some-times	Seldom
1. Follow directions of the classroom teacher?	[ ]	[ ]	[ ]
2. Observe closely techniques used by the teacher and put them into practice when working with children and groups?	[ ]	[ ]	[ ]
3. Offer my services to the teacher when there is an apparent need for help?	[ ]	[ ]	[ ]
4. Plan for assigned tasks with children rather than wing it on a hit-or-miss basis?	[ ]	[ ]	[ ]
5. Observe closely to realize individual children's likes, dislikes, interests, and limitations?	[ ]	[ ]	[ ]
6. Allow children time to think and act on their own before giving directive help?	[ ]	[ ]	[ ]
7. Find opportunities for giving children choices in daily activities?	[ ]	[ ]	[ ]
8. Really listen to what children have to say?	[ ]	[ ]	[ ]
9. Acknowledge children's successes and appropriate behaviors and minimize failures or inappropriate behaviors?	[ ]	[ ]	[ ]
10. Accept suggestions and criticisms without becoming emotionally upset?	[ ]	[ ]	[ ]

Figure 10–3   Self-evaluation worksheet for paraprofessionals

An easy technique for organizing a face-to-face evaluation conference is for the teacher to list a select few behavioral descriptions under the following three focal areas:

1. To enrich your performance, consider increasing or doing more often the following.

2. To help maintain your performance, keep doing the following things much the same as you have been doing them.

3. To avoid diminishing your performance, decrease or stop doing the following.

The teacher and the teacher assistant then discuss each of the behaviors to be increased, decreased, or maintained. Specific incidents are used to interpret and demonstrate why the change (or maintenance) would be helpful. The lists for each category should not be too long. The objective is to identify a few important behaviors that conceivably could be changed with concentrated effort. The teacher encourages commitment to some plan of action for changing, but improvement of the assistant's performance may mean that the teacher has to change also if she is part of the cause of the problem.

The key to a meaningful evaluation is not what is written but rather the discussion of the recorded comments between the teacher and the teacher assistant. The conference is the basis for developing objectives or intended targets of change (and behavior maintenance) in the future. In a "management by objectives" fashion, any objectives and action plans agreed on by the teacher and the teacher assistant can be briefly written, dated, and signed by both. Each subsequent review considers progress toward attaining the previously formulated objectives. Collectively, these periodic evaluations are the basis for the year-end evaluation required for teacher assistants in most school districts. As a psychological benefit, however, the periodic conferences reduce the chances that the teacher will take the teacher assistant for granted, and they encourage professional-like involvement.

Paraprofessional's Evaluation of the Teacher

Teachers who are dedicated to developing an effective use of paraprofessional services find it valuable to evaluate themselves as responsible models of instructional excellence and supervisors of paraprofessionals. If teachers and the paraprofessionals have developed a relationship of trust and professionalism, teachers can gain much from the paraprofessionals' evaluative feedback. Teachers need to know when their directions are not clear, when they are expecting too much, and when they have been unappreciative or unresponsive. Most teachers do not wish to be negative or ineffective. They are human, however, and do err from time to time. Everyone will benefit if a two-way communication of constructive feedback and positive reinforcement is in effect.

Because the objective of an assistant's evaluation of the teacher is to improve their role relationship and team performance, the process needs to be kept simple. Teacher assistants need to be given an opportunity to capture their thoughts on paper, however, before any face-to-face meeting. This provides the teacher assistant the security of having reflected on and organized thoughts about the quality of the role relationship. A time should be scheduled, and the teacher assistant should be requested to bring in some written comments or feedback. A most effective way of promoting such preparation is to use a simple three-part variation of the technique mentioned in the previous section. Such an evaluation form is presented in Figure 10–4.

If both the teacher and the teacher assistant use a variation of the same three "increase, decrease, or continue" role behavior issues, the process is enhanced. The simplicity of this single-page sheet enables the teacher and the teacher assistant to think in parallel terms, considering what each of them can do to help the other so they both benefit. The concept of increasing, decreasing, or maintaining certain behaviors is easily understood. Not using scales, scores, or rating points reduces the

A TECHNIQUE FOR AN AIDE'S EVALUATION OF TEACHER

To (Teacher): _____

From (Aide): _____

Date: _____

1. You could help my performance and our team effort if you would increase or do more often the following things:

2. I could do a better job of helping you if you would decrease or stop doing these things:

3. To help maintain good performance, keep doing these things much the same as you have been doing:

Figure 10–4 Technique for an assistant's evaluation of the teacher

defensiveness or anxiety of either party. The conference focuses on the three levels, inviting objectives and strategies for dealing with the specific identified behaviors.

Preventing Paraprofessional Burnout

The tendency toward extreme disillusionment with one's job—professional burnout—is common among paraprofessionals. Several reasons for disillusionment were first identified by Frith and Mims (1985) over 20 years ago. Later, Mueller (1997) conducted a survey of 758 paraeducators in Vermont and found the same factors implicated in paraeducator burnout. Therefore, it is safe to assume that the following factors continue to be relevant today:

1. Stagnation due to lack of opportunity for professional advancement.

2. Inadequate training, which keeps some paraprofessionals from actively becoming involved in the professional team.

3. Poor organizational structure due to undefined role descriptions and unclear understanding of lines of authority.

4. Poor salaries for those who do not have the opportunity to climb a career ladder.

5. Lack of recognition when highly competent paraprofessionals are a threat to those in a position of supervisory responsibility (pp. 225–227).

Even though teachers may not be in a position to implement a career ladder, they can provide opportunities for paraprofessionals to feel valued and needed. We have discussed the importance of clear job descriptions, the need to discover and incorporate special skills and talents to help the paraprofessional feel like a contributing member of the team, and some helpful ways to show appreciation. Even these basic strategies will go a long way toward preventing burnout for those paraprofessionals who have become creditable members of early education teams.

The effectiveness of paraprofessionals, whatever their role, is greatly dependent on not only their skills but also their motivation. Since paraprofessionals work more because of a desire to help young children than for tangible rewards, the jobs they are expected to do should allow for the growth of their abilities.

Summary

This chapter has dealt with a wide range of topics related to providing support for young children with special needs in inclusive settings. Central to effective inclusive support are the processes of teaming and collaboration and problem solving and conflict resolution. Two common approaches to inclusion support are itinerant consultation and coteaching.

The role of the paraprofessional is expanding via the use of one-to-one assistants. Paraprofessionals are valuable resources for extending the teacher's care and development of young children. The extent to which this potential is realized depends primarily on how the teacher communicates expectations and develops a working relationship with paraprofessionals.

As we attempt to meet the needs of young children with disabilities in community-based early childhood settings and as the numbers of key stakeholders and service providers increase, the approaches and strategies described in this chapter will be more and more critical to ensuring that the wealth of knowledge and skills can be implemented in effective ways and can truly enhance the development and well-being of young children with disabilities and their families.

Discussion Topics and Activities

1. In the case of Paulo presented in this chapter, do you think it is an overstatement to refer to this situation as a "crisis"? Why or why not? Do you agree that sometimes conflict can be useful? Why or why not?

2. What are some examples of sources of resistance that you have observed in your own work? Can you think of a situation in which understanding another's perspective led to successful resolution of some problem?

3. In using a problem-solving process, do you think there is some disadvantage or negative impact to agreeing to an intervention solution that you believe will not succeed?

4. It is often suggested that some people's personalities do not allow them to be effective as a collaborative consultant. Effective collaboration requires the ability to put aside your own views and have faith in the group process. Individuals with strong ego needs or the need to control or who have difficulty dealing with ambiguity or giving credit to others and so on may not be the best candidates for this work. Do you think your own personality is well suited to the role of collaborative consultant?

5. What are the various ways in which specialists and therapists can serve children who are in inclusive settings (e.g., off-site, consultation, direct service, use of paraprofessionals, staff training, and so on)?

6. You are an itinerant consultant for a child-care center. Tony, the child you are supporting, has limited language skills but is very social and motivated to communicate. You make a simple communication board for him to be used during free-play time. It allows him to choose the center or toys he prefers. You notice on your subsequent visits, even with reminders, that the staff do not use the communication board. What can you do?

7. Videotape an actual team meeting. Develop a checklist to analyze each of the following components: physical configuration of the team, body language, verbal behavior (conversational strategies), and decision-making strategy used. Rate the team's "potential for success" in avoiding and managing conflict.

8. Role-play an interview with a prospective assistant. Be alert to questions that help you get to know something about the individual's talents, skills, interests, motives, and biases. Think ahead and be prepared to be explicit about what you will want the teacher assistant to do or not do. Observers may give constructive feedback to the participants by sharing their reactions and what they learned from watching the interaction.

9. Generate for discussion a list of situations in which you believe the assignment of a one-to-one assistant would be essential. For each situation, solicit ideas from classmates about alternatives to a one-to-one assistant.

10. Develop a set of general instructions or guidelines for a newly hired one-to-one assistant who will be assigned to a child who tends to run away (including out the door of the classroom as well as into the streets when on a walk).

11. As an itinerant, how would you approach the issue of a child in a poor-quality child-care setting where little attention is given to social participation but that provides a single, working parent with safe child care?

12. Consider each of the following possible challenges of team coordination: Who has the responsibility for monitoring progress on the child's IEP? Who convenes the team? Are some members of the team more "essential" than others in terms of team meetings? What if family members cannot attend or do not choose to attend team meetings? How are specialized services (e.g., therapists, behavior specialists, psychologist, and so on) coordinated? What would you suggest as a standard agenda for every team meeting?

13. In a coteaching model of inclusion support, what are some strategies to ensure that both

teachers share equally in the responsibilities for all children in the class?

14. How might each of the following different situations influence the coteaching support plan:

    a. A child who is in a wheelchair versus a child who tends to run away.

    b. Teacher preference for direct instruction versus another teacher's preference for following child's lead in play contexts.

    c. The presence of several senior volunteers in the classroom versus a shorthanded staff.

References

Chapter 1

Banet, B. A. (1979). A developmental approach for preschool children with special needs. In S. J. Meisels (Ed.), *Special education and development.* Baltimore: University Park Press.

Barnard, K. E., Morisset, C. E., & Spieker, S. (1993). Preventative interventions: Enhancing parent-infant relationships. In C. Zeanah (Ed.), *Handbook of infant mental health* (pp. 386–401). New York: Guilford Press.

Beller, E. K. (1979). Early intervention programs. In J. D. Osofsky (Ed.), *Handbook of infancy research.* New York: Wiley.

Bijou, S. W. (1977). Practical implications of an interactional model of child development. *Exceptional Children, 44,* 6–14.

Bloom, B. S. (1964). *Stability and change in human characteristics.* New York: Wiley.

Bredekamp, S. (1993). The relationship between early childhood education and early childhood special education: Healthy marriage or family feud? *Topics in Early Childhood Special Education, 13*(3), 258–273.

Bredekamp, S. & Copple, C. (Eds.). (1997). *Developmentally appropriate practice in early childhood programs.* Washington, DC: National Association for the Education of Young Children.

Bricker, D. D. (1988). Commentary: The future of early childhood special education. *Journal of the Division of Early Childhood, 12,* 276–278.

Bricker, D. D. (2000). Inclusion: How the scene has changed. *Topics in Early Childhood Special Education, 20,* 14–19.

Bricker, D. & Veltman, M. (1990). Early intervention programs: Child-focused approaches. In J. P. Shonkoff & S. J. Meisels (Eds.), *Handbook of early childhood intervention* (pp. 373–399). New York: Cambridge University Press.

Brown v. Board of Education, 347 U.S. 483 (1954).

Bruder, M. B. (2000). Family-centered early intervention: Clarifying our values for the new millennium. *Topics in Early Childhood Special Education, 20*(2), 105–115.

Caldwell, B. M. (1973). The importance of beginning early. In J. B. Jordan & R. F. Dailey (Eds.), *Not all little wagons are red: The exceptional child's early years.* Reston, VA: Council for Exceptional Children.

Carta, J. J., Atwater, J. B., Schwartz, I. S., & McConnell, S. R. (1993). A reaction to Johnson and McChesney Johnson. *Topics in Early Childhood Special Education, 13,* 243–254.

Childress, D. C. (2004). Special instruction and natural environments: Best practices in early intervention. *Infants and Young Children, 17*(2), 162–170.

Copple, C. & Bredekamp, S. (2005). *Basics of developmentally appropriate practice.* Washington, DC: National Association for the Education of Young Children.

Dinnebeil, L. A., McInerney, W., Roth, J., & Ramaswamy, V. (2001). Itinerant early childhood special education services: Service delivery in one state. *Journal of Early Intervention, 24,* 36–45.

Dunn, L. M. (1968). Special education of the mildly retarded—Is much of it justifiable? *Exceptional Children, 35,* 5–22.

Fenichel, E. (Ed.). (2002). Perinatal mental health: Supporting new families through vulnerability and change. *Zero to Three, 22*(6, entire issue).

Foley, G. M. & Hochman, J. D. (1997–1998). Programs, parents and practitioners: Perspectives on integrating early intervention and infant mental health. *Zero to Three, 18*(3), 13–18.

Furth, H. (1970). *Piaget for teachers.* Upper Saddle River, NJ: Prentice Hall.

Gotts, E. E. (1973). Headstart research, development and evaluation. In J. L. Frost (Ed.), *Revisiting early childhood education.* New York: Holt, Rinehart and Winston.

Greenspan, S. I. & Weider, S. (2003). Infant and early childhood mental health: A comprehensive developmental approach to assessment and intervention. *Zero to Three, 24*(1), 6–13.

Gronlund, G. (2006). *Make early learning standards come alive: Connecting your practice and curriculum to state guidelines.* St. Paul, MN: Redleaf Press.

Guralnick, M. J. (1990). Early childhood mainstreaming. *Topics in Early Childhood Special Education, 10*(2), 1–17.

Guralnick, M. J. (1997). *The effectiveness of early intervention.* Baltimore: Brookes.

Guralnick, M. J. (2000). An agenda for change in early childhood inclusion. *Journal of Early Intervention, 23*(4), 213–222.

Hanline, M. F. & Daley, S. (2002). Mom, will Kaelie always have possibilities? *Phi Delta Kappan, 84*(1), 73–76.

Hanson, M. J. & Lynch, E. W. (2004). *Understanding families.* Baltimore: Brookes.

Harris, K. C. & Klein, M. D. (2002). Itinerant consultation in ECSE: Issues and changes. *Journal of Educational and Psychological Consultation, 13*(3), 237–247.

Hebbeler, K. M., Smith, B. J., & Black, T. L. (1991). Federal early childhood special education policy: A model for the improvement of services for children with disabilities. *Exceptional Children, 58*, 104–111.

Horn, E., Lieber, J., Sandall, S., Schwartz, I., & Li, S. (2000). Supporting young children's IEP goals in inclusive settings through embedded learning opportunities. *Topics in Early Childhood Special Education, 20*(4), 208–223.

Hunt, J. M. (1961). *Intelligence and experience.* New York: Ronald Press.

Itard, J. M. G. (1962). *The wild boy of Aveyron.* New York: Appleton-Century-Crofts.

Jerugim, L. (2000). *A personal perspective on raising a child with developmental problems.* Unpublished manuscript.

Karnes, M. B. & Zehrbach, R. R. (1977). Alternative models for delivering services to young handicapped children. In J. B. Jordan, A. H. Hayden, M. B. Karnes, & M. M. Wood (Eds.), *Early childhood education for exceptional children.* Reston, VA: Council for Exceptional Children.

Kelly, J. F. & Barnard, K. E. (2000). Assessment of parent-child interaction: Implications for early intervention. In J. P. Shonkoff & S. J. Meisels (Eds.), *Handbook of early childhood intervention* (pp. 258–289). Cambridge: Cambridge University Press.

Kirk, S. (1958). *Early education of the mentally retarded.* Urbana: University of Illinois Press.

Klass, C. S. (2003). *Home visitor's guidebook.* Baltimore: Brookes.

Klein, M. D., Chen, D., & Haney, M. (2000). *Promoting learning through active interaction: A guide to early communication with young children who have multiple disabilities.* Baltimore: Brookes.

Klein, M. D. & Harris, K. C. (2004). Consideration in the personnel preparation of itinerant early childhood special education consultants. *Journal of Educational and Psychological Consultation, 15*(2), 151–167.

Klein, N. K. & Gilkerson, L. (2000). Personnel preparation for early childhood intervention programs. In J. P. Shonkoff & S. J. Meisels (Eds.), *Handbook of early childhood intervention* (pp. 454–486). Cambridge: Cambridge University Press.

Knitzer, J. (2000). Early childhood mental health services: A policy and systems development perspective. In J. P. Shonkoff & S. J. Meisels (Eds.), *Handbook of early childhood intervention* (pp. 416–438), Cambridge: Cambridge University Press.

Lally, J. R., Torres, Y. L., & Phelps, M. C. (1994). Caring for infants and toddlers in groups: Necessary considerations for emotional, social, and cognitive development. *Zero to Three, 14,* 1–8.

Lazar, I. & Darlington, R. (1979). *Lasting effects after preschool* (OHDS 79-30179). Washington, DC: Office of Human Development Services Administration for Children, Youth and Families.

Lazar, I. & Darlington, R. (1982). Lasting effects of early education: A report from the Consortium for Longitudinal Studies. *Monographs of the Society for Research in Child Development, 47*(Serial No. 195).

Lord, C. & McGee, J. P. (Eds.). (2001). *Educating children with autism.* Washington, DC: National Academy Press.

Mahoney, G., Boyce, G., Fewell, R. R., Spiker, D., & Wheeden, C. A. (1998). The relationship of parent-child interaction to the effectiveness of early intervention services for at-risk children and children with disabilities. *Topics in Early Childhood Special Education, 18*(1), 5–17.

Mahoney, G. & Perales, F. (2003). Using relationship-focused interventions to enhance the social-emotional functioning of young children with autism spectrum

disorders. *Topics in Early Childhood Special Education, 23*(2), 77–89.

McWilliam, R. A. & Scott, S. (2001). A support approach to early intervention: A three-part framework. *Infants and Young Children, 13*(4), 55–66.

Meisels, J. J. (1985). The efficacy of early intervention: Why are we still asking the question? *Topics in Early Childhood Special Education, 5*(2), 1–11.

Miller, P. S. & Stayton, V. (1998). Blended interdisciplinary teacher preparation in early education and intervention: A national study. *Topics in Early Childhood Special Education, 18*(1), 49–58.

National Association for the Education of Young Children. (1987). Position statements on developmentally appropriate practice in early childhood programs. *Young Children, 41,* 3–29.

National Association for the Education of Young Children. (2002). *Early learning standards: Creating the conditions for success.* Retrieved August 11, 2006, from http://www.naeyc.org/. . . positions/pdfposition_statement.pdf

Noonan, M. J. & McCormick, L. (2006). *Young children with disabilities in natural environments.* Baltimore: Brookes.

Odom, S. L. (Ed.). (2002). *Widening the circle: Including children with disabilities in preschool programs.* New York: Teachers College Press.

Ozonoff, S., Rogers, S. J. & Hendren, R. L. (Eds). (2003). *Autism spectrum disorders.* Washington, DC: American Psychiatric Publishing.

Public Laws 85–926, 88–164, 90–538, 92–424, 93–380, 94–142, 95–568, 98–199, 99–457, 101–336, 101–476, 102–119, 105–17, 108–446. Washington, DC: U.S. Government Printing Office.

Rapport, M. J., McWilliam, R. A. & Smith, J. (2004). Practices across disciplines in early intervention. The Research Base. *Infants and Young Children, 17*(1), 32–44.

Reynolds, A. J., Temple, J. A., Robertson, D. L., & Mann, E. A. (2001). Long-term effects of an early childhood intervention on educational achievement and juvenile arrest—A 15-year follow-up of low-income children in public schools. *Journal of the American Medical Association, 285*(18), 2339–2346.

Sandall, S., Hemmeter, M. L., Smith, B. J., & McLean, M. E. (2004). *DEC recommended practices: A comprehensive guide for practical application in early intervention/early childhood special education.* Longmont, CO: Sopris West.

Sandall, S., McLean, M. E., & Smith, B. J. (2000). *DEC recommended practices in early intervention/early childhood special education.* Longmont, CO: Sopris West.

Scheuermann, B. & Webber, J. (2002). *Autism: Teaching does make a difference.* Belmont, CA: Wadsworth/Thomson Learning.

Schweinhart, L. J. & Weikart, D. P. (1988). The High/Scope Perry Preschool Program. In R. H. Price, E. L. Cowen, R. P. Lorion & J. R. McKay (Eds.), *14 ounces of prevention* (pp. 53–65). Washington, DC: American Psychological Association.

Shearer, D. E. & Shearer, M. S. (1976). The Portage Project: A model for early childhood intervention. In T. D. Tjossem (Ed.), *Intervention strategies for high risk infants and young children.* Baltimore: University Park Press.

Shonkoff, J. P. & Meisels, S. J. (Eds.). (2000). *Handbook of early childhood intervention.* Cambridge: Cambridge University Press.

Shonkoff, J. P. & Phillips, D. A. (Eds.). (2000). *From neurons to neighborhoods: The science of early child development.* Washington, DC: National Academy Press.

Simpson, R. L. (2005). *Autism spectrum disorders: Interventions and treatments for children and youth.* Thousand Oaks, CA: Corwin Press.

Skeels, H. (1942). A study of the effects of differential stimulation on mentally retarded children: A follow-up study. *American Journal of Mental Deficiency, 46,* 340–350.

Skeels, H. (1966). Adult status of children with contrasting early life experiences. *Monographs of the Society for Research in Child Development, 32*(2).

Skeels, H. & Dye, H. A. (1939). A study of the effects of differential stimulation on mentally retarded children. *Proceedings of the American Association on Mental Deficiency, 44,* 114–136.

Swan, W. (1981). Programs for handicapped infants and their families supported by the office of special education. *The Communicator, 7*(2), 1–15.

Talbot, M. E. (1964). *Edward Seguin—A study for an educational approach to the treatment of mentally defective children.* New York: Columbia University Teachers College.

Wasik, B. H. & Bryant, D. M. (2000). *Home visiting: Procedures for helping families.* Thousand Oaks, CA: Sage.

Wesley, P. W. & Buysee, V. (2004). Consultation as a framework for productive collaboration in early

intervention. *Journal of Educational and Psychological Consultation, 15*(2), 127–150.

Wolery, M. & Wilbers, J. S. (Eds.). (1994). *Including children with special needs in early childhood programs.* Washington, DC: National Association for the Education of Young Children.

Zigler, E. (1978). The effectiveness of Head Start: Another look. *Educational Psychologist, 13,* 71–77.

Chapter 2

Banks, J. B. (2002). Childhood discipline: Challenges for clinicians and parents. *American Family Physician, 66*(8).

Barber, P. A., Turnbull, A. P., Behr, S. K., & Kerns, G. M. (1988). Family systems perspective on early childhood special education. In S. L. Odom & M. B. Karnes (Eds.), *Early intervention for infants and children with handicaps* (pp. 179–198). Baltimore: Brookes.

Beach Center on Disability. (2001). *Family Quality of Life Survey.* Lawrence: University of Kansas.

Bernstein, V. J. (2002, Summer). Supporting the parent-child relationship through home visiting. *IDA News, 29*(2), 1–8.

Bill, P. (2000). *Father's involvement is important.* Minneapolis: Pacer Center.

Boyd, D. (1950). *The three stages.* New York: National Association for Retarded Children.

Carter, B. & McGoldrick, M. (Eds.). (1999). *The expanded family life cycle: Individual, family and social perspectives.* Boston: Allyn & Bacon.

Chao, R. & Tseng, V. (2002). Parenting of Asians. In M. H. Bornstein (Ed.), *Handbook of parenting: Social conditions and applied parenting* (pp. 59–93). Mahwah, NJ: Lawrence Erlbaum Associates.

Collins, W. A., Maccoby, E. E., Steinberg, L., Hetherington, E. M. & Bornstein, M. H. (2000). Contemporary research on parenting: The case for nature and nurture. *American Psychologist, 55,* 218–232.

Cook, R. E., Tessier, A., & Klein, M. D. (1996). *Adapting early childhood curricula for children in inclusive settings* (4th ed.). Upper Saddle River, NJ: Merrill/Prentice Hall.

Dabkowski, D. M. (2004). Encouraging active parent participation in IEP team meetings. *Teaching Exceptional Children, 36,* 4–39.

Eldridge, D. (2001). Parent involvement: It's worth the effort. *Young Children, 56*(4), 65–69.

Finn, C. D. (2003). Cultural models for early caregiving. *Zero to Three, 23*(5), 40–45.

Gonzalez-Mena, J. (2001). *Multicultural issues in child care.* Mountain View, CA: Mayfield.

Guthrie, A. C. (2000). Fathers' involvement in programs for young children. *Young Children, 55*(4), 75–79.

Hanft, B. E., Rush, D. D., & Shelden, M. L. (2004). *Coaching families and colleagues in early childhood.* Baltimore: Brookes.

Hanson, M. J. & Lynch, E. W. (2004). *Understanding families—Approaches to diversity, disability, and risk.* Baltimore: Brookes.

Hanson, M. J. & Zercher, C. (2001). The impact of cultural and linguistic diversity in inclusive preschool environments. In M. Guralnick (Ed.), *Early childhood inclusion: Focus on change* (pp. 413–431). Baltimore: Brookes.

Holzman, M. (2004). *Public education and black male students: A state report card.* Cambridge, MA: Schott Foundation for Public Education.

Johnson, C. P. & Kastner, T. A. (2005). Helping families raise children with special health care needs at home. *Pediatrics, 115*(2), 507–511.

Kübler-Ross, E. (1969). *On death and dying.* New York: Macmillan.

Kunjufu, J. (2005). *Keeping black boys out of special education.* Chicago: African American Images.

Lamorey, S. (2002). Evil eyes, prayer meetings and IEPs. *Teaching Exceptional Children, 34*(5), 67–71.

Lavin, J. L. (2001). *Special kids need special parents.* New York: Berkeley.

Lessenberry, B. M. & Rehfeldt, R. A. (2004). Evaluating stress levels of parents of children with disabilities. *Exceptional Children, 70*(2), 231–244.

McWilliam, R. & Scott, S. (2001). A support approach to early intervention: A three-part framework. *Infants and Young Children, 12*(4), 55–66.

Moore, M. L., Howard, V. F., & McLaughlin, T. F. (2002). Siblings of children with disabilities: A review and analysis. *International Journal of Special Education, 17*(1), 49–64.

Moses, K. (1987, Spring). The impact of childhood disability: The parents' struggle. *WAYS,* pp. 6–10.

Pacer Center. (2000). Father's involvement is important. *Fact Sheet.* Minneapolis: Author.

Pacer Center. (2001). Tips for parents from siblings' viewpoints. *Early Childhood Connection.* Minneapolis: Author.

Poyadue, F. (1998). *Helping families travel an unchosen path.* Santa Clara, CA: Parents Helping Parents.

Public Laws 94–142, 105–17, 107–110, 108–446. Washington, DC: U.S. Government Printing Office.

Purcell, M. L., Turnbull, A., & Jackson, C. W. (2006). Linking early childhood inclusion and family quality of life. *Young Exceptional Children, 9*(3), 10–19.

Sameroff, A. J., & Fiese, B. H. (2000). Transactional regulation: The developmental ecology of early intervention. In J. P. Shonkoff & S. J. Meisels (Eds.), *Handbook of early childhood Intervention* (2nd ed.), pp. 135–159. New York: Cambridge University Press.

Santelli, B., Poyadue, F., & Young, J. (2001). *The parent to parent handbook: Connecting families of children with special needs.* Baltimore: Brookes.

Shea, T. & Bauer, A. (2002). *Parents and schools: Creating a successful partnership for students.* Upper Saddle River, NJ: Merrill/Prentice Hall.

Smith, T. B., Oliver, M. N., & Innocenti, M. S. (2001). Parenting stress in families of children with disabilities. *American Journal of Orthopsychiatry, 71,* 257–261.

Smith, T. E. C., Gartin, B. C., Murdick, N. L., & Hilton, A. (2006). *Families and children with special needs.* Upper Saddle River, NJ: Pearson.

Turbiville, V. P. & Marquis, J. G. (2001). Father participation in early education programs *Topics In Early Childhood Special Education, 21*(4), 223–232.

Turnbull, A. P., Summers, J. A., Brotherson, M. J. (1983). *Working with families with disabled members: A family systems approach.* Lawrence: University of Kansas, Kansas University Affiliated Facility.

Turnbull, A. P. & Turnbull, H. R. (2001). *Families, professionals, and exceptionality: A special partnership.* Upper Saddle River, NJ: Merrill/Prentice Hall.

Vacca, J. & Feinberg, E. (2000). Rules of engagement: Initiating and sustaining a relationship with families who have mental health disorders. *Infants and Young Children, 13,* 51–57.

Varias, L. (2005). Bridging the widest gap. *Education Update, 47*(8).

Wasik, B. H. & Bryant, D. M. (2000). *Home visiting.* Thousand Oaks, CA: Sage.

Zeanah, C. H. (Ed.). (2000). *Handbook of infant mental health* (2nd ed.). New York: Guilford.

Chapter 3

Alper, S. & Mills, K. (2000). Nonstandardized assessment in inclusive settings. In S. K. Alper, D. L. Ryndak, & C. N. Schloss (Eds.), *Alternate assessment of students with disabilities in inclusive settings* (pp. 54–74). Austin, TX: PRO-ED.

Bondurant-Utz, J. A. (2002). *Practical guide to assessing infants and preschoolers with special needs.* Upper Saddle River, NJ: Merrill/Prentice Hall.

Bricker, D. D. (2002). *Assessment, evaluation, and programming system for children.* Baltimore: Brookes.

Conroy, M. A. & Paolini, S. (2000). Assessment of infants and young children with disabilities. In S. K. Alper, D. L. Ryndak, & C. N. Schloss (Eds.), *Alternate assessment of students with disabilities in inclusive settings* (pp. 199–219). Austin, TX: PRO-ED.

Gargiulo, R. & Kilgo, J. (2005). *Young children with special needs.* Clifton Park, NY: Thomson Delmar Learning.

Grisham-Brown, J. (2000). Transdisciplinary activity-based assessment of young children with multiple disabilities. *Young Exceptional Children, 3*(2), 3–10.

Guralnick, M. J. (2000). *Interdisciplinary clinical assessment of young children with developmental disabilities.* Boston: Brookes.

Jarrett, M. H., Browne, B. C., & Wallin, C. M. (2006). Using portfolio assessment to document developmental progress in infants and toddlers. *Young Exceptional Children,* 10(1), 22–32.

Jones, J. (2004). Framing the assessment discussion. *Young Children, 59*(1), 14–18.

Linder, T. W. (1993). *Transdisciplinary play-based assessment.* Baltimore: Brookes.

Linder, T. W. (2000). Transdisciplinary play-based assessment. In K. Gitlin-Weiner, A. Sandgrund, & C. Schaefer (Eds.), *Play diagnosis and assessment* (pp. 139–166). New York: Wiley.

McLean, M., Wolery, M., & Bailey, D. B. (2003). *Assessing infants and preschoolers with special needs.* Upper Saddle River, NJ: Prentice Hall.

Meisels, S. J. (1996). Charting the continuum of assessment and intervention. In S. J. Meisels & E. Fenichel (Eds.), *New visions for the developmental assessment of infants and young children* (pp. 27–52), Washington, DC: Zero to Three.

Meisels, S. J. (2001). Fusing assessment and interventions: Changing parents' and providers' views of young children. *Zero to Three, 21*(4), 4–10.

Meisels, S. J., Dombro, A. L., Marsden, D. B., Weston, D. R., & Jewkes, A. (2002). *The Ounce of Prevention Scale.* Ann Arbor: University of Michigan, School of Education.

Mindes, G. (2003). *Assessing young children*. Upper Saddle River, NJ: Merrill/Prentice Hall.

National Association for the Education of Young Children. (1988). Position statement on standardized testing of young children 3 through 8 years of age. *Young Children, 43*, 42–47.

National Association for the Education of Young Children & National Association of Early Childhood Specialists in State Departments of Education. (2004). *Young Children, 59*(1), 51–52.

Neisworth, J. & Bagnato, S. (2000). Recommended practices in assessment. In S. Sandall, M. McLean, & B. Smith (Eds.), *DEC recommended practices for early intervention/early childhood special education* (pp. 17–28). Longmont, CO: Sopris West.

Neisworth, J. & Bagnato, S. (2005). DEC recommended practices: Assessment. In S. Sandall, M. L. Hemmeter, B. J. Smith, & M. E. McLean (Eds.), *DEC recommended practices: A comprehensive guide for practical application in early intervention/early childhood special education* (pp. 45–69). Longmont, CO: Sopris West.

Noonan, M. J. & McCormick, L. (2006). *Young children with disabilities*. Baltimore: Brookes.

Pretti-Frontczak, K. & Bricker, D. (2000). Enhancing the quality of individualized education plan (IEP) goals and objectives. *Journal of Early Intervention, 23*(2), 92–105.

Provence, S., Erikson, J., Vater, S., & Palmeri, S. (1995). *Infant-Toddler Developmental Assessment: IDA*. Chicago: Riverside.

Puckett, M. B. & Black, J. K. (2007). *Meaningful assessments of young children*. Upper Saddle River, NJ: Merrill/Prentice Hall.

Salvia, J. & Ysseldyke, J. E. (2007). *Assessment in special and inclusive education* (10th ed.). Boston: Houghton Mifflin.

Shea, T. M. & Bauer, A. M. (2002). *Parents and teachers of children with exceptionalities: A handbook for collaboration*. Boston: Allyn & Bacon.

Spies, R. A. & Plake, B. S. (2005). *Buros mental measurements yearbook*. Lincoln: University of Nebraska Press.

Twombly, E. (2001). Screening, assessment, curriculum planning and evaluation: Engaging parents in the process. *Zero to Three, 21*(4), 36–41.

Wieder, S. & Greenspan, S. (2001). The DIR approach to assessment and intervention planning. *Zero to Three, 21*(4), 11–19.

Wolery, M., Brashers, M. S., & Neitzel, J. C. (2002). Ecological congruence assessment for classroom activities and routines: Identifying goals and intervention practices in childcare. *Topics in Early Childhood Special Education, 22*(3), 131–142.

Wolery, M., Strain, P., & Bailey, D. (1992). Reaching potentials of children with special needs. In S. Bredekamp & T. Rosegrant (Eds.), *Reaching potentials: Appropriate curriculum assessment for young children* (pp. 92–111). Washington, DC: National Association for the Education of Young Children.

Chapter 4

Bruder, M. B. (2005). Service coordination and integration in a developmental systems approach to early intervention. In M. J. Guralnick (Ed.), *The developmental systems approach to early intervention* (pp. 29–58). Baltimore: Brookes.

Deal, A. G., Dunst, C. J., & Trivette, C. M. (1989). A flexible and functional approach to developing individualized family services. *Infants and Young Children, 1*(4), 32–43.

Dunst, C. J. & Bruder, M. B. (2006). Early intervention service coordination models and service coordinator practices. *Journal of Early Intervention, 28*(3), 155–165.

Hanson, M. J. & Lynch, E. W. (2004). *Understanding families*. Baltimore: Brookes.

Harbin, G. L., Bruder, M. B., Adams, C., Mazzarella, C., Whitbread, K., Gabbard, G., et al. (2004). Early intervention service coordination policies: National policy infrastructure. *Topics in Early Childhood Special Education, 24*(2), 89–97.

Noonan, M. J. & McCormick, L. (2006). *Young children with disabilities in natural environments*. Baltimore: Brookes.

Pretti-Frontczak, K. & Bricker, D. (2000). Enhancing the quality of individualized education plan (IEP) goals and objectives. *Journal of Early Intervention, 23*(2), 92–105.

Public Laws 99–457, 105–17, and 108–446. Washington, DC: U.S. Government Printing Office.

Sandall, S., Hemmeter, M. L., Smith, B. J., & McLean, M. E. (Eds.). (2005). *DEC recommended practices: A comprehensive guide for practical application in early intervention/early childhood special education*. Missoula, MT: Division for Early Childhood, Council for Exceptional Children.

Turnbull, A., Turnbull, R., Erwin, E., & Spodak, L. (2006). *Families, professionals, and exceptionality*. Upper Saddle River, NJ: Merrill/Prentice Hall.

Chapter 5

American Psychiatric Association. (2000). *Diagnostic and statistical manual of mental disorders* (4th ed.). Washington, DC: Author.

Anastasiow, N. J. (1978). Strategies and models for early childhood intervention programs in integrated settings. In M. J. Guralnick (Ed.), *Early intervention and integration of handicapped and nonhandicapped children* (pp. 85–111). Baltimore: University Park Press.

Ayres, A. J. (2005). *Sensory integration and the child: 25th anniversary edition.* Los Angeles: Western Psychological Services.

Bondy, A. & Frost, L. (2002). *A picture's worth: PECs and other visual communication strategies for autism.* Bethesda, MD: Woodbine House.

Bowe, F. G. (2004). *Early childhood special education: Birth to eight.* Clifton Park, NY: Delmar Learning.

Bricker, D. (1998). *An activity-based approach to early intervention.* Baltimore: Brookes.

Bricker, W. A., & Bricker, D. D. (1974). An early language training strategy. In R. L. Schiefelbusch & L. L. Lloyd (Eds.), *Language perspectives—Acquisition, retardation and intervention.* Baltimore: University Park Press.

Bruner, J. (1982). The organization of action and the nature of the adult-infant transaction. In E. Tronick (Ed.), *Social interchange in infancy: Affect, cognition and communication* (pp. 23–35). Baltimore: University Park Press.

Buysse, V., Wesley, P. W., Snyder, P., & Winton, P. (2006). Evidence-based practice: What does it really mean for the early childhood field? *Young Exceptional Children, 9*(4), 2–11.

Chasnoff, I. J. (2001). *The nature of nurture: Biology, environment and the drug-exposed child.* Chicago: NTI Publishing.

Cook, R. E. (1986). Motivating children to succeed. *Santa Clara, 28,* 7–10.

Feuerstein, R., Rand, Y., Hoffman, M., & Miller, R. (1980). *Instrumental enrichment.* Baltimore: University Park Press.

Gray, C. (2006). *The new social storybook: Illustrated edition.* Arlington, TX: Future Horizons, Inc.

Gray, C. & White, A. L. (2002). *My social stories book.* New York: Jessica Kingsley.

Greenspan, S. J. & Weider, S. (2006). *Helping children relate, communicate and think with DIR Floortime approach.* Cambridge, MA: Da Capo Press.

Horn, E., Lieber, J., Li, S. M., Sandall, S., & Schwartz, I. (2000). Supporting young children's IEP goals in inclusive settings through embedding learning opportunities. *Topics in Early Childhood Special Education, 20,* 208–223.

Klein, D., Cook, R. E., & Richardson-Gibbs, A. M. (2001). *Strategies for including children with special needs in early childhood settings.* Albany, NY: Delmar/Thomson Learning.

Koegel, R. L. & Koegel, L. K. (2006). *Pivotal response treatments for autism: Communication, social and academic development.* Baltimore: Brookes.

Linder, T. (1983). *Early childhood special education program development and administration.* Baltimore: Brookes.

Lord, C. & McGee, J. P. (2001). *Educating children with autism.* Washington, DC: National Academy Press.

MacDonald, J. (1989). *Becoming partners with children: From play to conversation.* San Antonio, TX: Special Press.

MacNamara, J. (1972). Cognitive basis of language learning in infants. *Psychological Review, 79,* 1–13.

Magnusen, C. L. & Atwood, T. (2006). *Teaching children with autism and related spectrum disorders: An art and a science.* Philadelphia: Jessica Kingsley.

Maslow, A. H. (1998). *Toward a psychology of being.* New York: Van Nostrand Reinhold.

McLean, J. & Snyder-McLean, L. (1978). *Transactional approach to early language training.* Upper Saddle River, NJ: Merrill/Prentice Hall.

Mesibov, G. B., Shea, V., & Schopler, E. (2004). *The TEACCH approach to autism spectrum disorders.* New York: Springer.

Rossetti, L. M. (2001). *Communication intervention: Birth to three.* Albany, NY: Singular/Thomson Learning.

Slavin, R. E. (2006). *Educational psychology. Theory and practice.* Boston: Pearson Education.

Squires, J. & Bricker, D. (2006). *Activity-based approach to developing young children's social and emotional competence.* Baltimore: Brookes.

Streissguth, A. & O'Malley, K. (2000). Neuropsychiatric implications and long-term consequences of fetal alcohol spectrum disorders. *Seminars in Clinical Neuropsychiatry, 5,* 177–190.

Torelli, L. & Durrett, C. (2004, Winter). Landscape for learning: The impact of classroom design on infants and toddlers. *Connections,* pp. 11–13.

Vincent, L. (1988, March). *Curriculum development.* Inservice training for early childhood special

education teachers. Los Angeles Unified School District, Los Angeles, CA.

Vygotsky, L. (1980). *Mind in society: The development of higher psychological processes.* Cambridge, MA: Harvard University Press.

Walker, J. E., Shea, T. M., & Bauer, A. (2006). *Behavior management: A practical approach for educators.* Upper Saddle River, NJ: Merrill/Prentice Hall.

White, R. (1959). Motivation reconsidered: The concept of competence. *Psychology Review, 66,* 297-333.

Chapter 6

Ainsworth, M. D. (1973). The development of infant-mother attachment. In B. M. Caldwell & H. Riciutti (Eds.), *Review of child development research* (Vol. 3, pp. 1-94). Chicago: University of Chicago Press.

Ainsworth, M. D. & Wittig, B. A. (1969). Attachment and exploratory behavior in one-year-olds in a strange situation. In B. M. Foss (Ed.), *Determinants of infant behavior* (Vol. 4, pp. 129-173). London: Metheun.

Allen, K. E. & Cowdery, G. E. (2005). *The exceptional child—Inclusion in early childhood education.* Clifton Park, NY: Thomson/Delmar Learning.

Bailey, E. W. (1978). Ongoing data collection in the classroom. Seattle, WA: Western States Technical Assistance Resource.

Blackwell, P. L. (2004). The idea of temperament: Does it help parents understand their babies? *Zero to Three, 24*(4), 37-41.

Bowlby, J. (1982). *Attachment and loss: Vol. 1. Attachment.* New York: Basic Books. (Original work published 1969)

Bromwich, R. (1997). *Working with parents and infants: An interactional approach.* Baltimore: University Park Press.

Brown, M. & Bergen, D. (2002). Play and social interaction of children with disabilities at learning/activity centers in an inclusive preschool. *Journal of Research in Childhood Education, 17*(1), 26-37.

Chandler, L. (1998). Promoting positive interaction between preschool-age children during free play: The Pals Center. *Young Exceptional Children, 2*(2), 14-19.

Cicchetti, D. & Toth, S. L. (1987). The application of a transactional risk model to intervention with multi-risk maltreating families. *Zero to Three, 7*(5), 1-8.

Connor, F. P., Williamson, G. G., & Siepp, J. M. (1978). *Program guide for infants and toddlers with neuromotor and other developmental disabilities.* New York: Teachers College Press.

Cook, R. E. (1986). Motivating children to succeed. *Santa Clara, 28,* 7-10.

Dicker, S. & Gordon, E. (2006). Critical connections for children who are abused and neglected. *Infants and Young Children, 19*(3), 170-178.

Erikson, E. H. (1971). A healthy personality for every child. In R. H. Anderson & H. G. Shane (Eds.), *As the twig is bent.* Boston: Houghton Mifflin.

Erikson, E. H. (1993). *Childhood and society.* New York: Norton. (Original work published 1963)

Fox, C., Dunlap, G., & Cushing, L. (2002). Early intervention, positive behavior support, and transition to school. *Journal of Emotional and Behavior Disorders, 10*(3), 149-158.

Fraiberg, S. (1974). Blind infants and their mothers: An examination of the sign system. In M. Lewis & L. Rosenblum (Eds.), *The effect of the infant on its caregivers.* New York: Wiley.

Greenspan, S. I. & Greenspan, N. T. (1985). *First feelings: milestones in the emotional development of your baby and child from birth to age four.* New York: Viking Penguin.

Greenspan, S. I. (1990, September). An intensive approach to a toddler with emotional, motor and language delays: A case report. *Zero to Three, 1*(1), 20-26.

Greenspan, S. I. (1992). *Infancy and early childhood: The practice of clinical assessment and intervention with emotional and developmental challenges.* Madison, CT: International Universities Press.

Greenspan, S. I., & Weider, S. (1998). *The child with special needs: Encouraging intellectual and emotional growth.* Reading, MA: Addison-Wesley.

Greenspan, S. I. & Weider, S. (2005). *Infant and early childhood mental health: A comprehensive developmental approach to assessment and intervention.* Arlington, VA: American Psychiatric Association.

Guralnick, M. J. & Neville, B. (1997). Designing early intervention programs to promote children's social competence. In M. J. Guralnick (Ed.), *The effectiveness of early intervention* (pp. 579-610). Baltimore: Brookes.

Hanson, R. F. & Spratt, E. G. (2000). Reactive attachment disorder: What we know about the disorder and implications for treatment. *Child Maltreatment, 5,* 137-145.

Haugaard, J. J. & Hazan, C. (2004). Recognizing and treating uncommon behavioral and emotional disorders in children and adolescents who have been severely maltreated: Reactive attachment disorder. *Child Maltreatment, 9*(2), 154–160.

Hewett, F. M. & Taylor, F. D. (1980). *The emotionally disturbed child in the classroom* (2nd ed.). Boston: Allyn & Bacon.

Kirkhart, R. & Kirkhart, E. (1972). The bruised self: Mending in early years. In K. Yamamoto (Ed.), *The child and his image* (pp. 121–177). Boston: Houghton Mifflin.

Klein, M. D., Cook, R. E., & Richardson-Gibbs, A. M. (2001). Preventing and managing challenging behaviors. In *Strategies for including children with special needs in early childhood settings* (pp. 79–100). Albany, NY: Delmar/Thomson Learning.

Koegel, L. K., Koegel, R. L., & Dunlap, G. (Eds.). (1996). *Positive behavior support.* Baltimore: Brookes.

Kollins, S. H. & Greenhill, L. (2006). Evidence base for the use of stimulant medication in preschool children with ADHD. *Infants and Young Children, 19*(2), 132–141.

Lau, C., Higgins, K., Gelfer, J., Hong, E., & Miller, S. (2005). The effects of teacher facilitation on the social interactions of young children during computer activities. *Topics in Early Childhood Special Education, 24*(4), 208–217.

Linder, T. (1993). *Transdisciplinary play-based assessment: A functional approach to working with young children.* Baltimore: Brookes.

Lyons-Rich, K., Connell, D. B., Zoll, D., & Stahl, J. (1987). Infants and social risk: Relations among infant maltreatment, maternal behavior and infant attachment behavior. *Developmental Psychology, 123*(2), 223–232.

Maslow, A. H. (1968). *Toward a psychology of being.* New York: Van Nostrand Reinhold.

Miller, D. F. (2007). *Positive child guidance.* Clifton Park, NY: Thomson/Delmar Learning.

Morris, S. (2002). Promoting social skills among students with nonverbal learning disabilities. *Teaching Exceptional Children, 34,* 66–71.

Nelson, L. J., Rubin, K. H., & Fox, N. A. (2005). Social withdrawal, observed peer acceptance, and the development of self-perceptions in children ages 4 to 7 years. *Early Childhood Research Quarterly, 20,* 185–200.

Noonan, M. J. & McCormick, L. (2006). *Young children with disabilities in natural environments.* Baltimore: Brookes.

Odom, S. L., McConnell, S. R., McEvoy, M. A., Peterson, C., Ostrosky, M., Chandler, L. K., et al. (1999). Relative effects of interventions supporting the social competence of young children with disabilities. *Topics in Early Childhood Special Education, 19,* 75–91.

Parten, M. B. (1932). Social participation among preschool children. *Journal of Abnormal and Social Psychology, 27,* 243–269.

Pelco, L. E. & Reed-Victor, E. (2003). Understanding and support differences in child temperament. *Young Exceptional Children, 6*(3), 2–11.

Piaget, J. (1963). *Play, dreams, and imitations in childhood.* New York: Norton.

Pierce-Jordan, S. & Lifter, K. (2005). Interaction of social and play behaviors in preschoolers with and without pervasive developmental disorder. *Topics in Early Childhood Special Education,* 25(1), 34–47.

Rappley, M. D. (2006). Actual psychotropic medication use in preschool children. *Infants and Young Children, 19*(2), 154–163.

Rosenberg, N. & Boulware, G. (2005). Playdates for young children with autism and other disabilities. *Young Exceptional Children, 8*(2), 11–20.

Ruff, H. & Capozzoli, M. C. (2003). Development of attention and distractibility in the first 4 years of life. *Developmental Psychopathology,* 39, 877–890.

Sameroff, A. J. & Mackenzie, M. J. (2003). A quarter-century of the transactional model. *Zero to Three, 24*(1), 14–22.

Schneider, M. (2002). *Do school facilities affect academic outcomes?* Washington, DC: National Clearinghouse for Educational Facilities.

Smith, J. M. & Smith, D. E. (1976). *Child management.* Champaign, IL: Research Press.

Snowman, J. & Biehler, R. F. (2004). *Psychology applied to teaching.* Boston: Houghton Mifflin.

Strain, P. S. & Hemmeter, M. L. (1997). Keys to being successful when confronted with challenging behaviors. *Young Exceptional Children, 1*(1), 2–8.

Sturm, L. (2004). Temperament in early childhood: A primer for the perplexed. *Zero to Three, 24*(4), 4–11.

Taylor, A. S., Peterson, C. A., McMurray-Schwarz, P., & Guillou, T. S. (2002). Social skills interventions: Not just for children with special needs. *Young Exceptional Children, 5*(4), 19–26.

Texas Tech University (1984). *The special child: Student laboratory manual.* Lubbock,TX: Home Economics Curriculum Center.

Thomas, A., Chess, S., & Birch, H. G. (1968). *Temperamental and behavior disorders in children.* New York: New York University Press.

Thomas, A., Chess, S., & Birch, H. G. (1970). The origin of personality. *Scientific American, 223,* 102–109.

Thomas, A., Chess, S., & Korn, S. J. (1982). The reality of difficult temperament. *Merrill-Palmer Quarterly, 28,* 1–20.

Tomlin, A. M. (2004). Thinking about challenging behaviors in toddlers: Temperament style or behavior disorder? *Zero to Three, 24*(4), 29–36.

Walker, J. E., Shea, T. M., & Bauer, A. (2006). *Behavior management: A practical approach for educators.* Upper Saddle River, NJ: Merrill/Prentice Hall.

Werner, E. E. (2000). Protective factors and individual resilience. In J. P. Shonkoff & S. J. Meisels (Eds.), *Handbook of early childhood intervention* (pp. 115–132). New York: Cambridge University Press.

Wolraich, M. L. (2006). Attention-deficit/hyperactivity disorder: Can it be recognized and treated in children younger than 5 years? *Infants and Young Children, 19*(2), 86–93.

Chapter 7

Apgar, V. & James, L. S. (1962). Further observations on the Newborn Scoring System. *American Journal of Diseases of Children, 104,* 419–428.

Ayres, A. J. (1979). *Sensory integration and the child.* Los Angeles: Western Psychological Services.

Ayres, A. J. (1994). *Sensory integration and learning disorders.* Los Angeles: Western Psychological Services.

Ayres, A. J. (2005). *Sensory integration and the child: 25th anniversary edition.* Los Angeles: Western Psychological Services.

Batshaw, M. L. (2002). *Children with disabilities.* Baltimore: Brookes.

Best, S. J., Heller, K. W., & Bigge, J. L. (2004). *Teaching individuals with physical and multiple disabilities.* Upper Saddle River, NJ: Merrill/Prentice Hall.

Blasco, P. M. (2001). *Early intervention services for infants, toddlers and their families.* Boston: Allyn & Bacon.

Bobath, K. & Bobath, B. (1984). The neuro-developmental treatment. In D. Scurtton (Ed.), *Management of the motor disorders of children with cerebral palsy.* Philadelphia: J. Lippincott.

Brazelton, T. B. (1996). *Neonatal Behavioral Assessment Scale.* London: Cambridge University Press.

Bricker, D. (2002). *Assessment, evaluation, and programming system for infants and children.* Baltimore: Brookes.

Copeland, M. E. & Kimmel, J. R. (1989). *Evaluation and management of infants and young children with developmental disabilities.* Baltimore: Brookes.

Dunn, W. (2001). The sensations of everyday life: Empirical, theoretical, and pragmatic considerations. *American Journal of Occupational Therapy, 55,* 608–620.

Erikson, E. (1993). *Childhood and society.* New York: Norton.

Finnie, N. (1997). *Handling the young child with cerebral palsy at home.* New York: Dutton.

Greenspan, S. I. (2001). Working with children who have motor difficulties. *Scholastic Early Childhood Today, 15*(4), 20–21.

Hanson, M. J. & Harris, S. R. (1986). *Teaching the young child with motor delays.* Austin, TX: PRO-ED.

Heller, K. W., Forney, P. A., Alberto, P. A., Schwartzman, M. N., & Goeckel, T. M. (2000). *Meeting physical and health needs of children with disabilities.* Belmont, CA: Wadsworth/Thomson Learning.

Hooper, S. & Umansky, W. (2003). *Young children with special needs.* Upper Saddle River, NJ: Merrill/Prentice Hall.

Howard, V. F., Williams, B. F., & Lepper, C. (2005). *Very young children with special needs.* Upper Saddle River, NJ: Merrill Prentice Hall.

Howe, M. B., Brittain, L. A., & McCathren, R. B. (2004). Meeting the sensory needs of young children in classrooms. *Young Exceptional Children, 8*(1), 11–19.

Humpal, M. E. & Wolf, J. (2003). Music in the inclusive environment. *Young Children, 58*(2), 103–107.

Klein, M. D., Cook, R. E., & Richardson-Gibbs, A. M. (2001). *Strategies for including children with special needs in early childhood settings.* Albany, NY: Delmar.

Lacy, A. (1981). *Dear Mom and Dad.* San Diego, CA: Project Hope, Superintendent of Schools, Department of Education, San Diego County.

Linder, T. (1996). *Transdisciplinary play-based assessment: A functional approach to working with young children.* Baltimore: Brookes.

Linder, T. (2000). Transdisciplinary play-based assessment. In K. Gitlin-Weiner, A. Sandgrund, & C. Schaefer (Eds.),

Play diagnosis and assessment (pp. 139-166). New York: Wiley.

Morris, S. E. & Klein, M. D. (1998). *Pre-feeding skills: A comprehensive resource for feeding development.* San Antonio, TX: Psychological Corporation.

Noonan, M. J. & McCormick, L. (2006). *Young children with disabilities in natural environments.* Baltimore: Brookes.

Nugent, J. K., Keefer, C. H., O'Brien, S. A., Johnson, L., & Blanchard, Y. (2007). *Understanding newborn behavior and relationships: The newborn behavior observation (nbo) system handbook.* Baltimore: Brookes.

Palmer, H. (2001). The music, movement and learning connection. *Young Children, 56*(5), 13-17.

Piaget, J. (1952). *The origins of intelligence in children* (M. Cook, trans.). New York: International University Press.

Rogers-Warren, A. K. (1982). Behavioral ecology in classrooms for young handicapped children. *Topics in Early Childhood Special Education, 2*(1), 21-32.

Snell, M. E. & Brown, F. (Eds.) (2000). *Instruction of students with severe disabilities.* Upper River, NJ: Merrill/Prentice Hall.

Stern, F. M. & Gorga, D. (1998). Neurodevelopmental treatment (NDT): Therapeutic intervention and efficacy. *Infants and Young Children, 1, 22-32.*

Chapter 8

Ackley, R. S., & Decker, T. N. (2006). Audiological advancement and the acquisition of spoken language in deaf children. In P. Spencer & M. Marschark (Eds.), *Advances in the spoken language development of deaf and hard-of-hearing children* (pp. 64-84). New York: Oxford University Press.

Adler, S. (1979). *Poverty children and their language: Implications for teaching and treating.* New York: Grune & Stratton.

Alpert, C. L. & Kaiser, A. P. (1992). Training parents as milieu language teachers. *Journal of Early Intervention, 16*(1), 31-52.

American Psychiatric Association. (2000). *Diagnostic and statistical manual of mental disorders* (Text revision). Washington, DC: Author.

American Speech-Language-Hearing Association. (1991). Report: Augmentative and alternative communication. *American Speech-Language-Hearing Association, 33*(Suppl. 5), 9-12.

Bates, E. & McWhinney, B. (1988). What is functionalism? *Papers and Reports on Child Language Development, 27,* 137-152.

Beukelman, D. R. & Mirenda, P. (1998). *Augmentative and alternative communication: Management of severe communication disorders in children and adults.* Baltimore: Brookes.

Bountress, N. G. (1980). The Ann Arbor decision: Implications for the speech-language pathologist. *American Speech-Language-Hearing Association, 22,* 543-545.

Bruner, J. (1983). *Child's talk.* New York: Norton.

Bunce, B. (2003). Children with culturally diverse backgrounds. In L. McCormick, D. Loeb, & R. L. Schiefelbusch (Eds.), *Supporting children with communication difficulties in inclusive settings.* (2nd ed., pp. 367-408). Boston: Allyn & Bacon.

Campbell, A. & Namy, L. (2003). The role of social referential context and verbal and nonverbal symbol learning. *Child Development, 74,* 549-563.

Coates, D. L. & Lewis, M. (1984). Early mother infant interaction and cognitive status as predictors of school performance and cognitive behavior in six year olds. *Child Development 55,* 1219-1230.

Cross, T. (1984). Habilitating the language-impaired child: Ideas from studies of parent-child interaction. *Topics in Language Disorders, 4,* 1-14.

Fazzi, D. (2002). Developing cognition, concepts and language. In R. Pogrund & D. Fazzi (Eds.), *Early focus: Working with young children who are blind or visually impaired and their families* (2nd ed., pp. 107-153). New York: AFB Press.

Fraiberg, S. (1977). *Insights from the blind.* New York: Basic Books.

Frost, L. & Bondy, A. (1994). *The Picture Exchange Communication System training manual.* Cherry Hill, NJ: PECS, Inc.

Girolametto, L., Verbery, M. & Tannock, R. (1994). Improving joint engagement in parent-child interaction: An intervention study. *Journal of Early Intervention, 18,* 155-167.

Guitar, C. (1998). *Stuttering: An integrated approach to its nature and treatment* (2nd ed.) Baltimore: Williams and Wilkins.

Hage, C. & Leybaert, J. (2006). The effect of cued speech on the development of spoken language. In P. Spencer & M. Marschark (Eds.), *Advances in the spoken language development of deaf and hard-of-hearing children* (pp. 193-211). New York: Oxford University Press.

Halle, J.W., Alpert, C., & Anderson, S. (1984). Natural environment language assessment and intervention with severely impaired pre-schoolers. *Topics in Early Childhood Special Education, 4,* 36–56.

Halliday, M. A. K. (1975). Learning how to mean. In E. Lenneberg & E. Lenneberg (Eds.), *Foundations of language development* (Vol. 1, pp. 17–32). New York: Academic Press.

Hendrick, J. (1980). *The whole child: New trends in early education.* St. Louis, MO: Mosby.

Hulit, L. (2004). *Straight talk on stuttering* (2nd ed.). Springfield, IL: Thomas.

Hulit, L. M. & Howard, M. R. (2006). *Born to talk: An introduction to speech and language development* (4th ed.). Boston: Pearson/Allyn & Bacon.

Hunt, N. & Marshall, K. (1994). Children who are deaf and hard-of-hearing. In N. Hunt & K. Marshall (Eds.), *Exceptional children and youth* (pp. 336–385). Boston: Houghton Mifflin.

Kelly, J. E., & Barnard, K. E. (2000). Assessment of parent-child interaction: Implications for early intervention. In J. P. Shonkoff & S. J. Meisels (Eds.), *Handbook of early childhood intervention* (2nd ed., pp. 258–289). New York: Cambridge University Press.

Klein, M. D. & Briggs, M. H. (1987). Facilitating mother–infant communicative interaction in mothers of high-risk infants. *Journal of Childhood Communication Disorders, 10*(2), 95–106.

Klein, M. D. & Chen, D. (2001). *Working with children from culturally diverse backgrounds.* Albany, NY: Delmar.

Klein, M. D., Chen, D., & Haney, M. (2000). *Promoting learning through active interactions.* Baltimore: Brookes.

Koegel, R. L. & Koegel, R. K. (2006). *Pivotal response treatments for autism.* Baltimore: Brookes.

Krashen, S. E. & Terrell, T. (1983). *The natural approach: Language acquisition in the classroom.* Oxford: Pergamon.

Lahey, M. (1988). *Language disorders and language development.* Upper Saddle River, NJ: Merrill/Prentice Hall.

Landry, S. H., Smith, K. E., & Miller-Loncar, D. (1997). Predicting cognitive, language and social growth curves from early maternal behaviors in children at varying degrees of biological risk. *Developmental Psychology, 33,* 1040–1053.

Landry, S. H., Smith, K. E., Swank, P. R., & Miller-Loncar, C. L. (2000). Early maternal and child influences on children's later cognitive and social functioning. *Child Development, 71,* 358–375.

Leonard, L. B. (1998). *Children with specific language impairment.* Cambridge, MA: MIT Press.

Light, J. C. & Drager, K. D. 2002. Improving the design of augmentative and alternative technologies for young children. *Assistive Technology, 14*(1), 17–32.

Ling, D. (Ed.). (1984). *Early intervention for hearing impaired children: Oral options.* San Diego, CA: College-Hill Press.

Loeb, D. F. (2003). Diagnostic and descriptive assessment. In L. McCormick, D. F. Loeb, & R. L. Schiefelbusch (Eds.), *Supporting children with communication difficulties in inclusive settings* (2nd ed., pp. 189–234). Boston: Allyn & Bacon.

Mahoney, G. & Perales, F. (2003). Using relationship-focused intervention to enhance the social-emotional functioning of young children with autism spectrum disorder. *Topics in Early Childhood Special Education, 23*(2), 77–89.

Manolson, A. (1985). *It takes two to talk.* Toronto: Hanen Early Language Resource Center.

MacDonald, J. D. (1989). *Becoming partners with children: From play to conversation.* San Antonio, TX: Special Press.

McCormick, L., Loeb, D. F., & Schiefelbusch, R. L. (2003b). *Supporting children with communication difficulties in inclusive settings* (2nd ed.). Boston: Allyn & Bacon.

McEachin, J., Smith, T., & Lovaas, O. I. (1993). Long-term outcomes for children with autism who received early intensive behavioral treatment. *American Journal on Mental Retardation, 98,* 359–372.

McGee, G. G., Morrier, M. J., & Daly, T. (1999). An incidental teaching approach to early intervention for toddlers with autism. *Journal of the Association for the Severely Handicapped, 24,* 133–146.

Meadows, D., Elias, G., & Bain, J. (2000). Mothers' ability to identify infants' communicative acts. *Journal of Child Language, 27,* 393–406.

Montgomery, J. (1992). Perspectives from the field: Language, speech, and hearing services in schools. *Language, Speech, and Hearing Services in Schools, 23,* 363–364.

Mundy, P. & Crowson, M. (1997). Joint attention and early social communication: Implications for research on

intervention with autism. *Journal of Autism and Developmental Disorders, 27*(6), 653–676.

Nelson, K. (1986). *Event knowledge: Structure and function in development.* Hillsdale, NJ: Lawrence Erlbaum Associates.

Nicholas, J. G. & Geers, A. (2006). The process and early outcomes of cochlear implantation by three years of age. In P. Spencer & M. Marschark (Eds.), *Advances in the spoken language development of deaf and hard-of-hearing children* (pp. 271–297). New York: Oxford University Press.

Ogletree, B. & Oren, T. (1998). Structured yet functional: An alternative conceptualization of treatment for communication impairment in autism. *Focus on Autism, 13*(4), 228–233.

Owens, R. (2004). *Language disorders: A functional approach to assessment and intervention* (4th ed.). Boston: Allyn & Bacon.

Owens, R. E., Jr. (2000). *Language development* (3rd ed.). Upper Saddle River, NJ: Merrill/Prentice Hall.

Peck, C. A. (1985). Increasing opportunities for social control by children with autism and severe handicaps: Effects on learner behavior and perceived classroom climate. *Journal of the Association for Persons with Severe Handicaps, 10,* 183–193.

Pogrund, R. & Fazzi, D. (Eds.). (2002). *Early focus: Working with young children who are blind or visually impaired and their families* (2nd ed.). New York: AFB Press.

Prizant, B. M., Wetherby, A. M., & Rydell, P. J. (2000). Communication intervention issues for young children with autism spectrum disorders. In A. M. Wetherby & B. M. Prizant (Eds.), *Autism spectrum disorders* (pp. 193–224). Baltimore: Brookes.

Prutting, C. & Kirchner, D. (1987). A clinical appraisal of the pragmatic aspects of language. *Journal of Speech and Hearing Disorders, 52,* 105–119.

Raver, S. A. (1987). Practical procedures for increasing spontaneous language in language delayed pre-schoolers. *Journal of the Division for Early Childhood, 11,* 226–232.

Richard-Amato, P. A. (1988). *Making it happen: Interaction in the second language classroom.* White Plains, NY: Longman.

Roberts, J. & Burchinal, M. R. (2001). Otitis media and mediating effects on early literacy development. In S. Neuman & D. K. Dickinson (Eds.), *Handbook of early literacy research* (pp. 232–244). New York: Guilford Press.

Rogers-Warren, A. K., & Warren, S. (1984). The social basis of language and communication in severely handicapped preschoolers. *Topics in Early Childhood Special Education, 4,* 57–72.

Rogow, S. M. (2000). Communication and language: Issues and concerns. In B. Silverstone, M. A. Lang, B. P. Rosenthal, & E. Faye (Eds.), *The lighthouse handbook on vision impairment and vision reha-bilitation: Vol. 1. Vision impairment* (pp. 395–408). New York: Oxford University Press.

Rossetti, L. M. (2001). *Communication intervention: Birth to three* (2nd ed.). Albany, NY: Singular Press.

Sachs, J. (2001). Communication development in infancy. In J. B. Gleason (Ed.), *The development of language* (5th ed., pp. 40–69). Boston: Allyn & Bacon.

Stokoe, W. C. (2001). *Language in hand.* Washington, DC: Gallaudet University Press.

Tabors, P. O. (1997). *One child two languages: A guide for preschool educators of children learning English as a second language.* Baltimore: Brookes.

Tait, M. & Luttman, M. (1994). Comparison of early com-municative behavior in young children with cochlear implants and hearing aids. *Ear and Hearing, 15*(5), 352–361.

Tallal, P., Miller, S., Bedi, G., Byma, G., Wang, X., Nagarajan, S., et al. (1996). Language comprehension in language-learning impaired children improved with acousti-cally modified speech. *Science, 271,* 81–84.

Tannock, R., Girolametto, L., & Siegel, L. (1992). Language intervention with children who have developmental delays: Effects of an interactive approach. *American Journal on Mental Retardation, 97,* 145–160.

Vygotsky, L. (1978). Mind in society: The development of higher order psychological processes. In M. Cole, J. Scribner, J. John-Steiner, & E. Souberman (Eds.), *Culture and thought: A psychological introduc-tion.* Cambridge, MA: Harvard University Press.

Warren, S. & Kaiser, A. (1986). Incidental language teach-ing: A critical review. *Journal of Speech and Hearing Disorders, 51,* 291–298.

Weitzman, E. & Greenberg, J. (2002). *Learning language and loving it: A guide to promoting children's social, language, and literacy development in early childhood settings* (2nd ed.). Toronto: Hanen Centre.

Wetherby, A. M. & Prizant, B. M. (Eds.). (2000). *Autism spectrum disorders.* Baltimore: Brookes.

Yoshinaga-Itano, C. (2006). Early identification, commu-nication modality, and the development of spoken

language skills. In P. Spencer & M. Marschark (Eds.), *Advances in the spoken language development of deaf and hard-of-hearing children* (pp. 298-327). New York: Oxford University Press.

Chapter 9

Adams, M. (1990). *Learning to read: Thinking and learning about print.* Cambridge, MA: MIT Press.

Adams, M., Foorman, B., Lundberg, I., & Beeler, T. (1998). *Phonemic awareness in young children.* Baltimore: Brookes.

Atkinson, P. C. & Shiffrin, P. M. (1968). Human memory: A proposed system and its control processes. In K. W. Spence & J. T. Spence (Eds.), *The psychology of learning and motivation: Advances in research and theory* (Vol. 2). New York: Academic Press.

Bell-Gredler, M. E. (1986). *Learning and instruction: Theory into practice.* Upper Saddle River, NJ: Merrill/Prentice Hall.

Bidell, R. R. & Fischer, W. W. (1989). Commentary. *Human Development, 32*, 363-368.

Boehm, A. E. (2001). *Boehm Test of Basic Concepts—3 Preschool.* New York: Psychological Corporation.

Bunce, B. H. (2003). Children with culturally diverse backgrounds. In L. McCormick, D. R. Loeb, & R. L. Schiefelbusch (Eds.), *Supporting children with communication difficulties in inclusive settings* (2nd ed., pp. 367-408). Boston: Allyn & Bacon.

Case, R. (1985). *Intellectual development: A systematic reinterpretation.* New York: Academic Press.

Catts, H. W. & Kamhi, A. G. (Eds.). (2005). *Language and reading disabilities* (2nd ed.). Boston: Pearson.

Cook, R. E. & Slife, B. D. (1985). Developing problem solving skills. *Academic Therapy, 21,* 5-13.

Dickinson, D. K. & Tabors, P. O. (Eds.). (2001). *Beginning language with literacy: Young children learning at home and school.* Baltimore: Brookes.

Gallagher, J. M. & Reid, D. K. (1981). *The learning theory of Piaget and Inhelder.* Monterey, CA: Brooks/Cole.

Gardner, H. (2006). *Multiple intelligences: New horizons.* Jackson, TN: Perseus Books.

Gee, J. P. (2001). A sociocultural perpective on early literacy development. In D. Neuman & D. Dickinson (Eds.), *Handbook of early literacy research* (pp. 30-42). New York: Guilford Press.

Gelman, R. & Brenneman, K. (2004). Science learning pathways for young children. *Early Childhood Research Quarterly, 19*(1), 150-158.

Goodman, K. & Goodman, Y. (1986). *What is whole about whole language.* Portsmouth, NH: Heinemann.

Hart, B. & Risley, T. R. (1999). *The social world of children learning to talk.* Baltimore: Brookes.

Heath, S. B. (1983). *Ways with words: Language, life and work in communities and classrooms.* Cambridge: Cambridge University Press.

Heath, S. B. (1986). Taking a cross-cultural look at narratives. *Topics in Language Disorders, 7*(1), 84-96.

Hemmeter, J. L., McCollum, J., & Hsieh, W. (2005). Practical strategies for supporting emergent literacy in the preschool classroom. In E. Horn & H. Jones (Eds.), *Supporting early literacy development in young children* (pp. 59-74) (Young Exceptional Children Monograph Series No. 7). Missoula, MT: Division for Early Childhood.

Hohmann, M. & Weikart, D. P. (2002). *Educating young children: Active learning practices for preschool and child care.* Ypsilanti, MI: High/Scope Press.

Katims, D. S. (1991). Emergent literacy in early childhood special education: Curriculum and instruction. *Topics in Early Childhood Special Education, 11*(1), 69-84.

McCathren, R. B. & Allor, J. H. (2005). Using storybooks with preschool children: Enhancing language and emergent literacy. In E. Horn & H. Jones (Eds.), *Supporting early literacy development in young children* (pp. 75-86) (Young Exceptional Children Monograph Series No. 7). Missoula, MT: Division for Early Childhood.

Moats, L. C. (2000). *Speech to print.* Baltimore: Brookes.

Morrison, G. S. (1991). *Early childhood education today* (5th ed.). Upper Saddle River, NJ: Merrill/Prentice Hall.

National Research Council. (2005). *Mathematical and scientific development in early childhood: A workshop summary.* Washington, DC: National Academy Press.

Neuman, S. B., Copple, C., & Bredekamp, S. (2000). *Learning to read and write: Developmentally appropriate practices for young children.* Washington, DC: National Association for the Education of Young Children.

Neuman, S. B. & Dickinson, D. K. (Eds.). (2001). *Handbook of early literacy research.* New York: Guilford Press.

Palakian, R. (2004). Early literacy and very young children. *Zero to Three, 25*(1), 37-44.

Piaget, J. (1954). *The construction of reality in the child.* New York: Basic Books.

Piaget, J. (1977). *The development of thought: Equilibration of cognitive structure*. New York: Viking Press.

Piaget, J. & Inhelder, B. (1969). *The psychology of the child*. New York: Basic Books.

Snow, C. E., Barnes, W. S., Chandler, J., Goodman, I. F., & Hemphill, L. (1991). *Unfulfilled expectations: Home and school influences on literacy*. Cambridge, MA: Harvard University Press.

Snow, C. E., Burns, M. S., & Griffin, P. (Eds.). (1998). *Preventing reading difficulties in young children*. Washington, DC: National Academy Press.

Strickland, D. S. & Shanahan, T. (2004). What the research says about reading: Laying the groundwork for literacy. *Educational Leadership, 61*(6), 74-77.

Tager-Flusberg, H. (2000). Understanding the language and communicative impairments in autism. In L. M. Glidden (Ed.), *Autism* (pp. 185-205). New York: Academic Press.

van Kleeck, A. (1990). Emergent literacy: Learning about print before learning to read. *Topics in Language Disorders, 10*(2), 25-45.

Vygotsky, L. S. (1986). *Thought and language*. Cambridge, MA: MIT Press.

Watson, L. R., Layton, T. L., Pierce, P. L., & Abraham, M. A. (1994). Enhancing emerging literacy in a language preschool. *Language, Speech and Hearing Services in Schools, 25*(3), 136-145.

Westby, C. (1985, August). *Cultural differences in caregiver child interaction*. Paper presented at the annual meeting of the American Speech-Language-Hearing Association, Albuquerque, NM.

Whitehurst, G. J. & Lonigan, C. J. (2001). Emergent literacy: Development from prereaders to readers. In S. Neuman & D. Dickinson (Eds.), *Handbook of early literacy research* (pp. 11-29). New York: Guilford Press.

Chapter 10

The content of this chapter is partly based on the works of M. D. Klein, A. M. Richardson-Gibbs, S. Kilpatrick, and K. Harris, in the implementation of Project Support, U.S. Office of Special Education Programs Grant H086U60026, 1997-2002.

Appl, D. (2006). First-year early childhood special education teachers and their assistants: "Teaching along with her." *Teaching Exceptional Children, 38*(6), 34-40.

Bridges, W. (1991). *Managing transitions: Making the most of change*. Reading, MA: Addison-Wesley.

Brown, D., Pryzwansky, W., & Schulte, A. (2006). *Psychological consultation: Introduction to theory and practice*. Boston: Allyn & Bacon.

Carroll, D. (2001). Considering paraeducator training, roles, and responsibilities. *Teaching Exceptional Children, 34*(2), 60-64.

Causton-Theoharis, J. & Malmgren, K. (2005). Building bridges: Strategies to help paraprofessionals promote peer interaction. *Teaching Exceptional Children, 37*(6), 18-24.

Dettmer, P., Thurston, L. P., & Dyck, N. (2002). *Consultation, collaboration and teamwork for students with special needs* (4th ed.). Boston: Allyn & Bacon.

Dinnebeil, L. A., McInerney, W., Roth, J., & Ramaswamy, V. (2001). Itinerant early childhood special education services. *Journal of Early Intervention, 24*(1), 35-44.

Ellis, D. G. & Fisher, B. A. (1994). *Small group decision making: Communication and the group process* (4th ed.). New York: McGraw-Hill.

French, N. K. (2003). Paraeduators in special education programs. *Focus on Exceptional Children*.

Friend, M. & Cook, L. (2003). *Interactions: Collaboration skills for school professionals* (4th ed.). Boston: Allyn & Bacon.

Frith, G. H. & Mims, A. (1985). Burnout among special education paraprofessionals. *Teaching Exceptional Children, 17*, 225-227.

Frost, L. & Bondy, A. (1994). *The Picture Exchange Communication System*. Cherry Hill, NJ: PECS, Inc.

Gately, S. E. & Gately, F. J. (2001). Understanding co-teaching components. *Teaching Exceptional Children, 33*(4), 4-7.

Giangreco, M. F. & Doyle, M. B. (2002). Students with disabilities and paraprofessional supports: Benefits, balance, and band-aids. *Focus on Exceptional Children, 34*(7), 1-12.

Giangreco, M. F., Edelman, S. W., Broer, S. M., & Doyle, M. B. (2001). Paraprofessional support for students with disabilities: Literature from the past decade. *Exceptional Children, 68*, 45-63.

Giangreco, M. F., Yuan, S., McKenzie, B., Cameron, P., & Fialka, J. (2005). "Be careful what you wish for . . .": Five reasons to be concerned about the assignment of individual paraprofessionals. *Teaching Exceptional Children, 37*(5), 28-34.

Grisham-Brown, J., Pretti-Frontczak, K., Hemmeter, M. L., & Ridgley, R. (2002). Teaching IEP goals and objectives in the context of classroom routines and activities. *Young Exceptional Children, 6*(1), 18–27.

Guralnick, M. J. (2000). An agenda for change in early childhood inclusion. *Journal of Early Intervention, 23*(4), 213–222.

Hanson, M. J., Horn, E., Sandall, S., Beckman, P., Morgan, M., Marquart, J., et al. (2001). After preschool inclusion: Children's educational pathways over the early school years. *Exceptional Children, 68*(1), 65–83.

Harris, K. & Klein, M. D. (2002). Itinerant consultation in ECSE: Issues and changes. *Journal of Educational and Psychological Consultation, 13*(3), 237–247.

Heron, T. E. & Harris, K. C. (2001). *The educational consultant: Helping professionals, parents and mainstreamed students* (4th ed.). Austin, TX: PRO-ED.

Homans, G. C. (1992). *The human group.* New York: Transaction.

Horn, E., Lieber, J., Li, S. M., Sandall, S., & Schwartz, I. (2000). Supporting young children's IEP goals in inclusive settings through embedded learning opportunities. *Topics in Early Childhood Special Education, 20,* 208–223.

Horn, E., Lieber, J., Sandall, S., & Schwartz, I. (2001). Embedded learning opportunities as an instructional strategy for supporting children's learning in inclusive programs. In M. Ostrosky & S. Sandall (Eds.), *Teaching strategies: What to do to support young children's development* (YEC Monograph No. 3, pp. 59–70). Longmont, CO: Sopris West.

Hoskins, B. (1996). *Developing inclusive schools: A guide.* Port Chester, NY: National Professional Resources.

Idol, L., Nevin, A., & Paolucci-Whitcomb, P. (2000). *Collaborative consultation* (3rd ed.). Austin, TX: PRO-ED.

Klein, M. D., Cook, R., & Richardson-Gibbs, A. M. (2001). *Strategies for including young children with special needs in early childhood settings.* New York: Delmar.

Klein, M. D., Richardson-Gibbs, A. M., Kilpatrick, S., & Harris, K. (2001). *A practical guide for early childhood inclusion support specialists.* Los Angeles: Project Support, California State University Los Angeles, Division of Special Education.

Kurpius, D. (1978). Consultation theory and process: An integrated model. *Personnel and Guidance Journal, 56,* 335–338.

Margolies, H. & McCabe, P. P. (1988). Overcoming resistance through a new remedial program. *The Clearing House, 62*(3), 131–134.

Mueller, P. (1997). *The Vermont paraeducator survey.* Retrieved January 15, 2006, from http://www.2nea.org/esp/resource/csppubl.htm

Odom, S. L. (2000). Preschool inclusion: What we know and where we go from here. *Topics in Early Childhood Special Education, 20*(1), 20–27.

Pretti-Frontczak, K., Barr, D., Macy, M., & Carter, A. (2003). Research and resources related to activity-based intervention, embedded learning opportunities, and routines-based instruction. *Topics in Early Childhood Special Education, 23*(1), 24–39.

Warger, C. (2003). *Supporting paraeducators: A summary of current practices* (ERIC Digest #E642). Arlington, VA: ERIC Clearinghouse on Disabilities and Gifted Education. http://ericec.org/digests/ e642.html

Wesley, P. (2002). Early intervention consultants in the classroom. *Young Children, 57*(4), 30–34.

Wesley, P., Buysse, V., & Keyes, L. (2000). Comfort zone revisited: Child characteristics and professional comfort with consultation. *Journal of Early Intervention, 23*(2), 106–115.

Wesley, P., Buysse, V., & Skinner, D. (2001). Early interventionists' perspectives on professional comfort as consultants. *Journal of Early Intervention, 24*(2), 112–128.

appendix A

Chart of Typical Development

	Gross Motor Skills	Fine Motor Skills	Language Comprehension	Expressive Communication
0 to 3 months	Holds head up in prone position. Lifts head when held at shoulder. Kicks reciprocally. Rolls from side to supine position.	Moves arms symmetrically. Follows with eyes to midline. Brings hands to midline in supine position. Activates arms on sight of toy.	Responds to voice. Watches speaker's eyes and mouth. Searches with eyes for sound.	Cries when hungry or uncomfortable. Makes comfort sounds.
3 to 6 months	Holds head in line with body when pulled to sitting. Bears weight on hands in prone position. Sits with light support. Holds head steady in supported sitting position. Rolls from supine position to side.	Follows with eyes without moving head. Keeps hands open most of time. Uses palmar grasp. Reaches and grasps objects.	Quiets to mother's voice. Distinguishes between friendly and angry voices. Responds to own name.	Coos variety of vowel sounds. Laughs. Takes turns. Responds to speech by vocalizing. Expresses displeasure and excitement.
6 to 9 months	Exhibits body-righting reaction. Extends arms protectively.	Transfers object. Manipulates toy actively with wrist movement.	Looks at pictures briefly. Looks for family members or pets when named.	Babbles to people. Produces variety of consonants in babbling.

Sources. Adapted from the following:

The Carolina Curriculum for Handicapped Infants and Infants at Risk, by N. Johnson-Martin, K. G. Jens, and S. M. Attermeier, 1986, Baltimore: Brookes.

The Carolina Curriculum for Preschoolers with Special Needs, by N. Johnson-Martin, S. M. Attermeier, and B. Hacker, 1990, Baltimore: Brookes.

Help for Special Preschoolers Assessment Checklist, 1987, Palo Alto, CA: VORT Corporation.

HELP Hawaii Early Learning Profile Activity Guide, by S. Furuno, K. A. O'Reiley, C. M. Hosaka, T. T. Inatsuka, T. L. Allman, and B. Zeisloft, 1985, Palo Alto, CA: VORT Corporation.

Mainstreaming Preschoolers, by CRC Education and Human Development, Inc. for the Administration for Children, Youth and Families, 1978, Washington, DC: U.S. Government Printing Office (1979620-182/5708).

Transdisciplinary Play-Based Assessment: A Functional Approach to Working with Young Children, by T. W. Linder, 1990, Baltimore: Brookes.

Cognitive Skills	Self-Help Skills	Social Skills
Inspects surroundings. Shows anticipation. Inspects own hands.	Opens mouth in response to food stimulus. Coordinates sucking, swallowing, and breathing.	Regards face. Enjoys physical contact; molds, relaxes body when held. Makes eye contact. Expresses distress.
Begins rattle play. Repeats/continues familiar activity. Uses hands and mouth for sensory exploration of objects. Plays with own hands, fingers, toes.	Brings hand to mouth holding toy or object. Swallows strained or pureed foods. Inhibits rooting reflex.	Smiles socially. Discriminates strangers. Demands attention. Vocalizes pleasure or displeasure. Enjoys social play, e.g., "This Little Piggy." Lifts arms to mother.
Works to obtain desired out-of-reach object. Finds object observed being hidden.	Uses tongue to move food in mouth (4 to 8 months).	Recognizes mother (4 to 8 months). Displays stranger anxiety.

	Gross Motor Skills	Fine Motor Skills	Language Comprehension	Expressive Communication
6 to 9 months *(continued)*	Sits independently, but may use hands. Stands holding on. Pulls to stand. Crawls backward. Gets into sitting position without assistance.	Reaches and grasps with extended elbow.	Responds to simple requests with gesture.	Babbles with adult inflection. Babbles reduplicated syllables, "mama," "baba," etc. Vocalizes loudly to get attention.
9 to 12 months	Creeps on hands and knees. Moves from sitting to prone position. Stands momentarily. Walks holding on to furniture (cruises).	Takes objects out of container. Uses both hands freely. Tries to imitate scribble. Puts object into container. Releases object voluntarily. Pokes with index finger. Uses neat pincer grasp.	Understands "no no." Listens selectively to familiar words. Enjoys looking at books.	Babbles single consonant–vowel syllables, e.g., "ba." Responds to certain words (e.g., "wave bye bye") with appropriate gesture. Uses behaviors and vocalization to express needs.
12 to 18 months	Stands from supine position. Walks without support. Throws ball. Creeps up stairs. Pulls toy while walking. Carries large toy while walking. Moves to music.	Uses two hands in midline, one holding, one manipulating. Scribbles spontaneously. Places pegs in pegboard. Builds two- to three-cube tower.	Responds to simple verbal requests; identifies one body part. Understands many nouns. Brings objects from another room on request.	Combines gestures and vocalizations to express a variety of communicative functions. Says "Dada" or "Mama" purposefully. Uses single words. Uses exclamations, e.g., "Oh, oh!" Says "no" meaningfully. Uses 10 to 15 words (by 18 months).

Cognitive Skills	Self-Help Skills	Social Skills
Touches adult's hand or toy to restart an activity. Plays 2 to 3 minutes with single toy. Follows trajectory of fast-moving object. Shows interest in sounds of object.	Holds own bottle. Mouths and gums solid foods. Bites voluntarily; inhibits bite reflex. Feeds self a cracker.	Smiles at mirror image. Shows anxiety to separation from mother.
Overcomes obstacle to obtain object. Retrieves object using other material. Imitates gestures. Unwraps a toy. Enjoys looking at books.	Finger feeds variety of foods. Holds spoon. Cooperates with dressing by extending arm or leg. Chews by munching.	Enjoys turn-taking game. Resists supine position. Shows like and dislike for certain people, objects, or situations. Shows toys to others; does not release. Tests parents' reactions at feeding and bedtime by new and mischievous behavior.
Understands adult's pointing. Hands toy back to adult. Matches objects. Places round and square pieces in form board. Nests two or three cans. Identifies self in mirror.	May refuse food; appetite decreases. Brings spoon to mouth. Drinks from cup with some spilling. Indicates discomfort over soiled pants. Removes socks.	Displays independent behavior; may be difficult to discipline. May display tantrum behavior. Demonstrates sense of humor. Is easily distractible; has difficulty sitting still.

	Gross Motor Skills	Fine Motor Skills	Language Comprehension	Expressive Communication
18 to 24 months	Moves on "ride-on" toys without pedals. Walks upstairs holding railing, both feet on step. Picks up toy from floor without falling. Runs.	Imitates circular scribble. Imitates horizontal stroke. Holds crayon with fist.	Identifies three to six body parts. Matches sounds to animals. Understands personal pronouns, some action verbs, and some adjectives. Enjoys nursery rhymes.	Uses intelligible words about 65% of the time. May use jargon (syllable strings that sound like speech). Tells experience using jargon and words. Uses two-word sentences. Names two or three pictures. Attempts to sing songs with words. Imitates three- to four-word phrase.
24 to 36 months	Runs forward well. Jumps in place, two feet together. Stands on one foot, with aid. Walks on tiptoe. Kicks ball forward.	Strings four large beads. Turns pages singly. Snips with scissors. Holds crayon with thumb and fingers, not fist. Uses one hand consistently in most activities. Paints with some wrist action; makes dots, lines, circular strokes. Rolls, pounds, squeezes, and pulls clay.	Points to pictures of common objects when they are named. Can identify objects when told their use. Understands question forms *what* and *where*. Understands negatives *no*, *not*, *can't*, and *don't*. Enjoys listening to simple storybooks and requests them again.	Joins vocabulary words together in two-word phrases. Gives first and last name. Asks *what* and *where* questions. Makes negative statements (e.g., "Can't open it"). Shows frustration at not being understood. Sustains conversation for two or three turns.

Cognitive Skills		Self-Help Skills	Social Skills
Finds object not observed being hidden. Activates mechanical toy. Matches objects to pictures. Sorts objects. Explores cabinets and drawers. Remembers where objects belong. Recognizes self in photo.		Scoops food, feeds self with spoon. Chews with rotary jaw movements. Plays with food. Removes shoe when laces undone. Zips/unzips large zipper. Shows awareness of need to eliminate.	Expresses affection. Expresses wide range of emotions including jealousy, fear, anger, sympathy, embarrassment, anxiety, and joy. Attempts to control others; resists control; peer interaction is somewhat aggressive. Engages in parallel play. Enjoys solitary play occasionally.
Selects and looks at picture books, names pictured objects, and identifies several objects within one picture. Matches and uses associated objects meaningfully (e.g., given cup, saucer, and bead, puts cup and saucer together). Stacks rings on peg in order of size. Uses self and objects in pretend play.	Can talk briefly about what he or she is doing. Imitates adult actions (e.g., housekeeping play). Has limited attention span; learning is through exploration and adult direction (as in reading of picture stories). Is beginning to understand functional concepts of familiar objects (e.g., that a spoon is used for eating) and part/whole concepts (e.g., parts of the body).	Gets drink from fountain or faucet unassisted. Opens door by turning handle. Takes off coat. Puts on coat with assistance. Washes and dries hands with assistance.	Watches other children; joins briefly in their play. Defends own possessions. Begins to play house. Participates in simple group activity (e.g., sings, claps, dances). Knows gender identity.

	Gross Motor Skills	Fine Motor Skills	Language Comprehension	Expressive Communication
36 to 48 months	Runs around obstacles. Walks on a line. Balances on one foot for 5 to 10 seconds. Hops on one foot. Pushes, pulls, steers wheeled toys. Rides (i.e., steers and pedals) tricycle. Uses slide without assistance. Jumps over 15-centimeter (6 inch)-high object, landing on both feet together. Throws ball over head. Catches ball bounced to him or her.	Builds tower of nine small blocks. Drives nails and pegs. Copies circle. Imitates cross. Manipulates clay materials (e.g., rolls balls, snakes, cookies).	Begins to understand sentences involving time concepts (e.g., "We are going to the zoo tomorrow"). Understands size comparatives such as *big* and *bigger*. Understands relationships expressed by *if . . . then* or *because* sentences. Carries out a series of two to four related directions. Understands when told, "Let's pretend."	Talks in sentences of three or more words, which take the form agent-action-object ("I see the ball") or agent-action-location ("Daddy sit on chair"). Tells about past experiences. Uses *-s* on nouns to indicate plurals. Uses *-ed* on verbs to include past tense. Refers to self using pronouns *I* or *me*. Repeats at least one nursery rhyme and can sing a song. Speech is understandable to strangers, but there are still some sound errors.
48 to 60 months	Walks backward toe-heel. Jumps forward 10 times without falling. Walks up and down stairs alone, alternating feet. Turns somersault.	Cuts on line continuously. Copies cross. Copies square. Prints a few capital letters.	Follows three unrelated commands in proper order. Understands comparatives such as *pretty, prettier,* and *prettiest.* Listens to long stories, but often misinterprets the facts. Incorporates verbal directions into play activities. *(Continued)*	Asks *when, how,* and *why* questions. Uses modals such as *can, will, shall, should,* and *might.* Joins sentences together (e.g., "I went to the store and I bought some ice cream"). Talks about causality by using *because* and *so.* Tells the content of a story but may confuse facts.

Cognitive Skills		Self-Help Skills	Social Skills
Recognizes and matches six colors. Intentionally stacks blocks or rings in order of size. Draws somewhat recognizable picture that is meaningful to child, if not to adult; names and briefly explains picture. Asks questions for information: *why* and *how* questions requiring simple answers. Knows own age. Knows own last name.	Has short attention span; learns through observing and imitating adults, and by adult instruction and explanation; is easily distracted. Has increased understanding of concepts of the functions and grouping of objects (e.g., can put doll house furniture in correct rooms); part/whole (e.g., can identify pictures of hand and foot as parts of body). Begins to be aware of past and present (e.g., "Yesterday we went to the park. Today we go to the library.").	Pours well from small pitcher. Spreads soft butter with knife. Buttons and unbuttons large buttons. Washes hands unassisted. Blows nose when reminded. Uses toilet independently.	Joins in play with other children; begins to interact. Shares toys; takes turns with assistance. Begins dramatic play, acting out whole scenes (e.g., traveling, playing house, pretending to be animals). Comforts peers in distress.
Points to and names four to six colors. Matches pictures of familiar objects (e.g., shoe, sock, foot, apple, orange, banana). Draws a person with two to six recognizable parts, such as head, arms, legs; can name or match drawn parts to own body.

(Continued) | Knows own street and town. Has more extended attention span; learns through observing and listening to adults as well as through exploration; is easily distracted. Has increased understanding of concepts of function, time, part/whole relationships.

(Continued) | Cuts easy foods with a knife (e.g., hamburger patty, tomato slice). Laces shoes. | Plays and interacts with other children. Plays dress-up. Shows interest in exploring gender differences. |

	Gross Motor Skills	Fine Motor Skills	Language Comprehension	Expressive Communication
48 to 60 months *(continued)*			Understands sequencing of events when told them (e.g., "First we have to go to the store, then we can make the cake, and tomorrow we will eat it").	
60 to 72 months	Runs lightly on toes. Walks on balance beam. Can cover 2 meters (6½ feet) hopping. Skips on alternate feet. Jumps rope. Skates.	Cuts out simple shapes. Copies triangle. Traces diamond. Copies first name. Prints numerals 1 to 5. Colors within lines. Has adult grasp of pencil. Has handedness well established (i.e., child is left- or right-handed). Pastes and glues appropriately. Uses classroom tools appropriately.	Demonstrates preacademic skills.	There are few obvious differences between child's grammar and adult's grammar. Still needs to learn such things as subject–verb agreement and some irregular past tense verbs. Can take appropriate turns in a conversation. Gives and receives information. Communicates well with family, friends, or strangers. Retells story from picture book with accuracy.

Cognitive Skills		Self-Help Skills	Social Skills
Draws, names, and describes recognizable picture. Rote counts to 5, imitating adults. Describes what will happen next. Dramatic play is closer to reality, with attention paid to detail, time, and space.	Function or use of objects may be stated in addition to names of objects. Time concepts are expanding. The child can talk about yesterday or last week (a long time ago), about today, and about what will happen tomorrow.		
Names some letters and numerals. Rote counts to 10. Sorts objects by single characteristics (e.g., by color, shape, or size—if the difference is obvious). Is beginning to use accurately time concepts of *tomorrow* and *yesterday*.	Begins to relate clock time to daily schedule. Attention span increases noticeably; learns through adult instruction; when interested, can ignore distractions. Concepts of function increase as well as understanding of why things happen; time concepts are expanding into an understanding of the future in terms of major events (e.g., "Christmas will come after two weekends").	Dresses self completely. Ties bow. Brushes teeth unassisted. Crosses street safely.	Chooses own friend(s). Plays simple table games. Plays competitive games. Engages in cooperative play with other children involving group decisions, role assignments, fair play.

appendix **B**

Find Your Child's Speech and Hearing Age

Instructions: Read each question through your child's age group and check yes or no. Add the total and score:

 All yes = Good! Your child is developing hearing, speech, and language normally.

 1–3 no = Caution! Your child may have delayed hearing, speech, and language development.

 More than 3 no = Action! Take your child for professional help.

Check One		Hearing and Understanding	Child's Age	Talking	Check One	
Yes	No	**Hearing and Understanding**	**Child's Age**	**Talking**	Yes	No
☐	☐	Does your child hear and understand most speech in the home?	*5 years*	Does your child say all sounds correctly except perhaps *s* and *th?*	☐	☐
☐	☐	Does your child hear and answer when first called?		Does your child use the same sentence structure as the family?	☐	☐
☐	☐	Does your child hear quiet speech?		Does your child's voice sound clear, like other children's?	☐	☐
☐	☐	Does everyone who knows your child think he or she hears well (teacher, babysitter, grandparent, etc.)?				
☐	☐	Does your child understand conversation easily?	*2½–4 years*	Does your child say most sounds, except perhaps *r, s, th,* and *l?*	☐	☐
☐	☐	Does your child hear you when you call from another room?		Does your child sometimes repeat words in a sentence?	☐	☐
☐	☐	Does your child hear television or radio at the same loudness level as other members of the family?		Does your child use 200–300 words?	☐	☐
☐	☐	Does your child understand differences in meaning ("go—stop"; "the car pushed the truck—the truck pushed the car")?		Does your child use two- to three-word sentences?	☐	☐
☐	☐	Can your child point to pictures in a book upon hearing them named?		Does your child ask lots of "why" and "what" questions?	☐	☐
☐	☐	Does your child notice sounds (dog barking, telephone ringing, television sound, knocking at door, and so on)?		Does your child like to name things?	☐	☐

Source. Adapted from public information materials of the American Speech-Language-Hearing Association. Used with permission.

Check One		Hearing and Understanding	Child's Age	Talking	Check One	
Yes	No				Yes	No
☐	☐	Can your child follow two requests ("Get the ball and put it on the table")?	$1\frac{1}{2}$-2 years	Does your child have 10-15 words (by age 2)?	☐	☐
				Does your child sometimes repeat requests?	☐	☐
				Does your child ask one- to two-word questions ("Where kitty? Go bye-bye? More?")?	☐	☐
				Does your child put two words together ("more cookie")?	☐	☐
☐	☐	Has your child begun to respond to requests ("Come here";"Do you want more?")?	9 months-1 year	Does your child say words (8-10 words at age 1/2; 2-3 words at age 1)? Words may not be clear.	☐	☐
☐	☐	Does your child turn or look up when you call?		Does your child enjoy imitating sounds?	☐	☐
☐	☐	Does your child search or look around when hearing new sounds?		Does your child use jargon (babbling that sounds like real speech)?	☐	☐
☐	☐	Does your child listen to people talking?		Does your child use voice to get attention?	☐	☐
☐	☐	Does your child respond to "no"and her or his name?	6 months	Does your child's babbling sound like the parent's speech, only not clear?	☐	☐
☐	☐	Does your child notice and look around for the source of new sounds?		Does your child make lots of different sounds?	☐	☐
☐	☐	Does your child turn her or his head toward the side where the sound is coming from?				
☐	☐	Does your child try to turn toward the speaker?	3 months	Does your child babble?	☐	☐
☐	☐	Does your child smile when spoken to?		Does your child cry differently for different needs?	☐	☐
☐	☐	Does your child stop playing and appear to listen to sounds or speech?		Does your child repeat the same sounds a lot?	☐	☐
☐	☐	Does your child seem to recognize Mother's voice?				
☐	☐	Does your child listen to speech?	Birth	Does your child coo or gurgle?	☐	☐
☐	☐	Does your child startle or cry at noises?				
☐	☐	Does your child awaken at loud sounds?				

Reflexes, Reactions, and Implications

Normal Age Range	Reflex	How to Elicit	Motor Response	Implications
Birth to 3 to 5 months	Biting	Rub index finger on child's upper lateral gum area. Both sides. (Do not attempt on child with teeth.)	Child will rhythmically open and close mouth.	If retained, it will inhibit lateral jaw movement necessary for chewing.
Birth to 3 to 4 months	Rooting	Stroke with finger from corner of child's mouth to across cheek to earlobe.	Turns head to stimulated side.	If retained, the reflex will interfere with development of natural feeding patterns.
	Grasping	Place object (pencil, rattle, index finger) on palm just below child's fourth and fifth fingers.	Grasps examiner's finger, rattle, pencil, etc.	If not present at birth, indicates abnormality in motor area. If retained, prevents normal grasp and release.
	Stepping	Hold child upright in standing position with weight on feet and lean baby's body slightly forward.	Child will take a few high steps (as if walking).	If not present at birth, indicates neurological problem. If retained, will interfere with gross motor skills.
Birth to 4 to 6 months	Asymmetrical tonic neck reflex (ATNR)	Child on back with head in midline, arms and legs relaxed.	Child will partially or totally straighten the arm and leg on side of body toward which the head is turned. The opposite arm and leg are partially or totally bent (fencer's position).	Hand use activities in midline, sitting, balance, and control of extremities will be impaired when the head is turned.

Age	Reflex/Reaction	Testing Procedure	Response	Significance
Birth to 6 months	Moro	With child on back with head in midline, arms by side, examiner places hand on the back of child's neck and raises head off surface. Release support, letting the head drop back. *Catch child's head before it reaches the surface.*	Child's arms straighten out sideways and then move to midline.	If not present at birth, there are indications of neurological immaturity or abnormality. If retained, reflex interferes with general motor control.
Birth to 6 months	Neck righting (log rolling)	Child on back with head in midline, arms straight down by sides. Put your hands on each side of head and turn it to the side.	The body rotates as a unit in the same direction as head is turned.	If retained, reflex will interfere with sequential rolling.
6 months to 18 months	Segmental rolling (body righting on body)	Stimulate as for neck righting.	First head turns, then shoulders, then pelvis.	Becomes voluntary and provides trunk rotation for normal rolling patterns (i.e., leading from hip).
6 months to 24 months	Landau reaction	Hold the child horizontally in space with support under the trunk between the shoulders and pelvis. (Use two hands to support.)	Child fully straightens head, trunk, and hips ("swan dive" position).	If not present, development of extensor pattern necessary for standing and walking will be delayed or possibly prevented.
6 months and beyond	Protective extensor reaction (parachute)	1. Child is held in air, stomach toward ground with support under stomach. Rapidly lower child, head first toward testing table or floor.	Child moves arms forward and catches weight on open hands. Note if child does not use both arms for protection.	If not present, child cannot maintain sitting balance.
		2. Child is sitting independently. Gently push forward or backward or sideways.	Child extends arms and catches weight for support.	

Sources. Adapted from the following:
Normal and Abnormal Development: The Influence of Premature Reflexes on Motor Redevelopment, by M. R. Fiorentino, 1972, Springfield, IL: Thomas.
Psychological Assessment of Handicapped Infants and Young Children, by G. Ulrey and S. J. Rogers, 1982, New York: Thieme-Stratton.

Referral Signals Checklist

AUDITORY SIGNALS			
Observable Signs, Symptoms, or Complaints	**Sometimes**	**Yes**	**No**
Has fluid running from ears.	[ ]	[ ]	[ ]
Has frequent earaches.	[ ]	[ ]	[ ]
Has frequent colds or sore throats.	[ ]	[ ]	[ ]
Has recurring tonsillitis.	[ ]	[ ]	[ ]
Breathes through mouth.	[ ]	[ ]	[ ]
Complains of noises in head.	[ ]	[ ]	[ ]
Voice is too loud or too soft.	[ ]	[ ]	[ ]
Has delayed or abnormal speech, excessive articulation errors.	[ ]	[ ]	[ ]
Seems to "hear what he or she wants to hear."	[ ]	[ ]	[ ]
Seems to be daydreaming.	[ ]	[ ]	[ ]
Often looks puzzled, frowns, or strains when addressed.	[ ]	[ ]	[ ]
Appears uninterested in things others find interesting.	[ ]	[ ]	[ ]
Observable Behaviors			
Turns or cocks head to hear speaker.	[ ]	[ ]	[ ]
Scans when called rather than turning to source.	[ ]	[ ]	[ ]
Does not pay attention.	[ ]	[ ]	[ ]

Note. One or two symptoms do not a problem make. Tables of typical development found in Appendix A should be checked carefully because preschoolers naturally exhibit some degree of many of these behaviors. Patterns should be noted and observation continued when there is a question. Language signals can be found in Chapter 8.

Sources: Adapted from the following:

Educating Young Handicapped Children, by by S. G. Garwood et al., eds., 1979, Germantown, MD: Aspen Systems Corp.

The Exceptional Student in the Regular Classroom, by B. R. Gearheart and M. W. Weishahn, 1984, Columbus, OH: Charles E. Merrill.

	Sometimes	Yes	No
Is especially inattentive in large groups.	[ ]	[ ]	[ ]
Exhibits extreme shyness in speaking.	[ ]	[ ]	[ ]
Has difficulty in following oral directions (and records).	[ ]	[ ]	[ ]
Acts out; appears stubborn, shy, or withdrawn.	[ ]	[ ]	[ ]
Exhibits marked discrepancy between abilities in verbal and performance test items.	[ ]	[ ]	[ ]
Watches classmates to see what they are doing before beginning to participate.	[ ]	[ ]	[ ]
Often does not finish work.	[ ]	[ ]	[ ]
Hears teacher only when he or she sees teacher.	[ ]	[ ]	[ ]
Hears some days but not others.	[ ]	[ ]	[ ]
Gives answers totally unrelated to question asked.	[ ]	[ ]	[ ]
Frequently requests repetition or says "Huh?"	[ ]	[ ]	[ ]

VISUAL SIGNALS

Observable Signs, Symptoms, or Complaints

	Sometimes	Yes	No
Red eyelids.	[ ]	[ ]	[ ]
Pupils turned in, out, up, or down (perhaps independent of each other).	[ ]	[ ]	[ ]
Watery eyes or discharges.	[ ]	[ ]	[ ]
Crusts on lids or among the lashes.	[ ]	[ ]	[ ]
Recurring styes or swollen lids.	[ ]	[ ]	[ ]
Pupils of uneven size.	[ ]	[ ]	[ ]
Excessive movement of pupils.	[ ]	[ ]	[ ]
Drooping eyelids.	[ ]	[ ]	[ ]
Excessive rubbing of eyes (seems to brush away blurs).	[ ]	[ ]	[ ]
Shutting or covering one eye.	[ ]	[ ]	[ ]
Tracking or focusing difficulties.	[ ]	[ ]	[ ]
Headaches or nausea after close work.	[ ]	[ ]	[ ]
Tensing up during visual tasks.	[ ]	[ ]	[ ]
Squinting, blinking, frowning, and distorting face while doing close work.	[ ]	[ ]	[ ]

Observable Behaviors

	Sometimes	Yes	No
Tilts head (possibly to use one eye) or thrusts forward.	[ ]	[ ]	[ ]
Tries to avoid or complains about light.	[ ]	[ ]	[ ]
Complains of pain or ache in eyes.	[ ]	[ ]	[ ]
Holds objects close to face.	[ ]	[ ]	[ ]
Complains of itchy, scratchy, or stinging eyes.	[ ]	[ ]	[ ]
Avoids or is irritable when doing close work.	[ ]	[ ]	[ ]
Moves head rather than eyes to look at object.	[ ]	[ ]	[ ]
Tires easily after visual tasks.	[ ]	[ ]	[ ]
Frequently confuses similarly shaped letters, numbers, or designs.	[ ]	[ ]	[ ]
Is unusually clumsy or awkward; trips over small objects.	[ ]	[ ]	[ ]
Has poor eye-hand coordination.	[ ]	[ ]	[ ]
Cannot follow a moving target held 25 to 30 centimeters (10 to 12 inches) in front of him or her.	[ ]	[ ]	[ ]

HEALTH OR PHYSICAL SIGNALS

Observable Signs, Symptoms, or Complaints	Sometimes	Yes	No
Flushes easily or has slightly bluish color to cheeks, lips, or fingertips.	[ ]	[ ]	[ ]
Has excessive low-grade fevers or colds.	[ ]	[ ]	[ ]
Has frequently dry coughs or complains of chest pains after physical exertion.	[ ]	[ ]	[ ]
Is unusually breathless after exercise.	[ ]	[ ]	[ ]
Is extremely slow or sluggish.	[ ]	[ ]	[ ]
Is abnormal in size.	[ ]	[ ]	[ ]
Is excessively hungry or thirsty.	[ ]	[ ]	[ ]
Complains of pains in arms, legs, or joints.	[ ]	[ ]	[ ]
Has poor motor control or coordination.	[ ]	[ ]	[ ]
Walks awkwardly or with a limp.	[ ]	[ ]	[ ]
Shows signs of pain during exercise.	[ ]	[ ]	[ ]
Moves in a jerky or shaky manner.	[ ]	[ ]	[ ]
Walks on tiptoe; feet turn in.	[ ]	[ ]	[ ]
Has hives or rashes.	[ ]	[ ]	[ ]
Loses weight without dieting.	[ ]	[ ]	[ ]
Appears to be easily fatigued.	[ ]	[ ]	[ ]
Has excessive or frequent bruises, welts, or swelling.	[ ]	[ ]	[ ]

Observable Behaviors

	Sometimes	Yes	No
Moves extremely slowly or in a sluggish manner.	[ ]	[ ]	[ ]
Is excessively hungry or thirsty.	[ ]	[ ]	[ ]
Complains of pains in arms, legs, or joints.	[ ]	[ ]	[ ]
Is excessively restless or overactive.	[ ]	[ ]	[ ]
Is extremely inactive; avoids physical exercise.	[ ]	[ ]	[ ]
Faints easily.	[ ]	[ ]	[ ]
Is extremely inattentive.	[ ]	[ ]	[ ]
Is unable to chew and swallow well.	[ ]	[ ]	[ ]
Exhibits difficulty with motor tasks, including balance.	[ ]	[ ]	[ ]
Complains of pain or discomfort in the genital area.	[ ]	[ ]	[ ]

LEARNING SIGNALS

Observable Signs, Symptoms, or Complaints

	Sometimes	Yes	No
Cries easily; is easily frustrated.	[ ]	[ ]	[ ]
Is clumsy, awkward; has visual motor difficulties (for example, unusual difficulty with coloring, puzzles, or cutting).	[ ]	[ ]	[ ]
Exhibits visual or auditory perceptual difficulties.	[ ]	[ ]	[ ]
Appears easily disturbed by loud noises.	[ ]	[ ]	[ ]
Often seems confused or unsure of self.	[ ]	[ ]	[ ]

Observable Behaviors

	Sometimes	Yes	No
Works very slowly or rushes through everything.	[ ]	[ ]	[ ]
Has difficulty working independently.	[ ]	[ ]	[ ]
Is highly distractible, impulsive.	[ ]	[ ]	[ ]

	Sometimes	Yes	No
Has extremely short attention span.	[ ]	[ ]	[ ]
Is unable to follow directions.	[ ]	[ ]	[ ]
Is excessively active or excessively inactive.	[ ]	[ ]	[ ]
Perseverates (repeats activity over and over).	[ ]	[ ]	[ ]
Seems to catch on quickly in some areas but not in others.	[ ]	[ ]	[ ]
Is extremely inconsistent in performance.	[ ]	[ ]	[ ]
Does not transfer what is learned in one area to another.	[ ]	[ ]	[ ]
Actively resists change.	[ ]	[ ]	[ ]
Constantly disrupts class.	[ ]	[ ]	[ ]
Does not remember classroom routine; has other memory problems.	[ ]	[ ]	[ ]
Has difficulty making choices.	[ ]	[ ]	[ ]
Lacks inventiveness; has interests below age level.	[ ]	[ ]	[ ]
Learns so slowly that he or she cannot participate well with others.	[ ]	[ ]	[ ]

Competencies for Trainees in Early Childhood Special Education

	Nonexistent	Poor	Satisfactory	Good	Excellent
I. *Appropriately and competently assesses strengths and needs.*					
A. Selects appropriate formal instruments.	1	2	3	4	5
B. Selects appropriate informal strategies.	1	2	3	4	5
C. Monitors child's progress frequently and systematically.	1	2	3	4	5
D. Evaluates family involvement and satisfaction.	1	2	3	4	5
II. *Plans effective intervention programs.*					
A. Works collaboratively with parents in selecting goals and objectives and strategies.	1	2	3	4	5
B. Goals are related to assessment results.	1	2	3	4	5
C. Goals and objectives are clear and relevant to high-priority child and family needs.	1	2	3	4	5
D. Plan is communicated to parents clearly both verbally and in writing.	1	2	3	4	5
III. *Demonstrates understanding of how children learn and ability to utilize generic teaching strategies, including the following:*					
A. Role of social interaction.	1	2	3	4	5
B. Motivation (e.g., identifies high-preference objects, people, and events).	1	2	3	4	5
C. Arrangement of physical environment.	1	2	3	4	5
D. Use of play as both context and method.	1	2	3	4	5
E. Behavioral analysis (including task analysis and identification of antecedents and consequences).	1	2	3	4	5
F. Behavioral analysis (including use of positive reinforcement, use of cues and prompts, shaping, fading, chaining, and stimulus generalization).	1	2	3	4	5

	Nonexistent	Poor	Satisfactory	Good	Excellent
G. Repetition and routines.	1	2	3	4	5
H. Appropriate caregiver–child interaction.	1	2	3	4	5
I. Critical role of family in child's development.	1	2	3	4	5
IV. *Manages classroom environment to optimize learning.*					
A. Effectively arranges physical environment.	1	2	3	4	5
B. Creates appropriate classroom schedule.	1	2	3	4	5
C. Utilizes daily routines for training.	1	2	3	4	5
D. Creates effective play routines.	1	2	3	4	5
E. Provides opportunity for rest and quiet time.	1	2	3	4	5
F. Creates comfortable atmosphere for parent involvement.	1	2	3	4	5
G. Takes responsibility for children's safety.	1	2	3	4	5
H. Effectively manages, coordinates, and involves paraprofessionals, volunteers, and consultants.	1	2	3	4	5
I. Selects highly motivating activities.	1	2	3	4	5
J. Utilizes individual as well as small and total group formats appropriately.	1	2	3	4	5
K. Integrates all developmental domains (i.e., language, cognition, motor, social-emotional, and self-help) into each activity.	1	2	3	4	5
V. *Facilitates the development of communication skills.*					
A. Recognizes and correctly interprets communicative cues.	1	2	3	4	5
B. Understands the stages and characteristics of language and speech development.	1	2	3	4	5
C. Establishes turn taking.	1	2	3	4	5
D. Is responsive to child's communicative intents; follows child's lead.	1	2	3	4	5
E. Uses repetition and recasts.	1	2	3	4	5
F. Uses appropriate pacing and speech rate; waits for child's response.	1	2	3	4	5
G. Appropriately labels objects and key events.	1	2	3	4	5
H. Expands child's utterance.	1	2	3	4	5
I. Knows how to "up the ante" (i.e., prompt for better turn).	1	2	3	4	5
J. Utilizes play routines.	1	2	3	4	5
K. Selects relevant and functional communication goals.	1	2	3	4	5
L. Develops augmentative communication systems and skills as needed.	1	2	3	4	5
M. Provides opportunity for choices.	1	2	3	4	5
N. Facilitates literate, autonomous uses of language (e.g., narrative, explanation, story telling).	1	2	3	4	5
VI. *Facilitates the development of cognitive skills.*					
A. Understands the stages and characteristics of typical cognitive development.	1	2	3	4	5
B. Creates opportunities for all children to experience "effectance" (i.e., to develop intentional behavior), and assists child to understand cause and effect.	1	2	3	4	5

	Nonexistent	Poor	Satisfactory	Good	Excellent
C. Effectively encourages exploration and trial and error behavior through modeling, scaffolding, and use of cues and prompts.	1	2	3	4	5
D. Teaches object permanence.	1	2	3	4	5
E. Utilizes activities and materials that encourage mental representation and memory.	1	2	3	4	5
F. Develops symbolic behavior such as pretend play and recognition of graphic symbols.	1	2	3	4	5
G. Creates opportunities for problem solving and assists children in discovering solutions.	1	2	3	4	5
VII. *Facilitates emotional and social growth.*					
A. Understands stages of social and emotional development.	1	2	3	4	5
B. Engages in positive reciprocal interactions with child.	1	2	3	4	5
C. Models and labels a wide range of emotions.	1	2	3	4	5
D. Interprets and validates child's emotional reactions and states.	1	2	3	4	5
E. Uses symbolic play to enhance social and emotional development (at appropriate developmental stage).	1	2	3	4	5
F. Builds self-esteem through emotional nurturing, encouraging trust, and mastery and independence.	1	2	3	4	5
G. Sets appropriate limits and consistent, yet flexible, behavioral guidelines (i.e., "rules").	1	2	3	4	5
H. To the extent possible, assists in providing a stable caregiving environment for child.	1	2	3	4	5
I. Effectively fosters peer–peer interaction, with both peers with disabilities and nondisabled peers.	1	2	3	4	5
J. Encourages altruistic behavior and "manners" in developmentally and culturally appropriate ways.	1	2	3	4	5
VIII. *Facilitates development of motor skills.*					
A. Understands stages and characteristics of typical motor development.	1	2	3	4	5
B. (In consultation with appropriate therapists if necessary), *positions* child appropriately for each activity in order to encourage optimal fine and gross movement and to maximize participation and independence.	1	2	3	4	5
C. Changes child's position frequently.	1	2	3	4	5
D. Effectively builds child's motor competence and self-confidence by gradually moving toward independent ambulations.	1	2	3	4	5
E. Utilizes appropriate assistive devices.	1	2	3	4	5
F. Utilizes effective teaching strategies to encourage functional fine motor skills and eye-hand coordination.	1	2	3	4	5

	Nonexistent	Poor	Satisfactory	Good	Excellent
G. Utilizes outdoor activities for development of large muscle skills such as running, climbing, and throwing.	1	2	3	4	5

IX. *Facilitates learning of self-help skills.*

	Nonexistent	Poor	Satisfactory	Good	Excellent
A. Creates positive mealtime environment.					
B. Assists child in development of chewing and swallowing a variety of foods and textures; finger feeding; use of utensils (adapted as necessary).	1	2	3	4	5
C. Establishes appropriate toileting schedule.	1	2	3	4	5
D. In cooperation with parent, develops consistent and appropriate toilet training procedures.	1	2	3	4	5
E. Provides frequent opportunities in natural contexts to learn dressing skills.	1	2	3	4	5
F. Adapts clothing as necessary to support independence.	1	2	3	4	5
G. When necessary, applies task analysis and behavioral techniques in teaching self-help skills.	1	2	3	4	5

X. *Facilitates academic readiness.*

	Nonexistent	Poor	Satisfactory	Good	Excellent
A. Uses developmentally appropriate techniques and materials and everyday contexts to teach cognitive operations such as classification, conservation, and seriation.	1	2	3	4	5
B. Demonstrates functional use of print (i.e., teacher models use of writing and reading in ways that are meaningful to children and displays print throughout classroom).	1	2	3	4	5
C. Creates opportunity for children to experience function and relevance of literacy behavior (e.g., treasure hunt clues, playing mail carrier, etc.).	1	2	3	4	5
D. Teaches important preacademic concepts such as opposites ("same" and "different," "big" and "little"); comparative terms ("taller," "tallest"); spatial terms ("in front of," "beside," "behind"); and quantity ("many," "few," "more") in *natural* contexts.	1	2	3	4	5
E. Teaches number and quantity concepts in meaningful ways (i.e., teaches "twoness" and "threeness," not simply rote counting).	1	2	3	4	5
F. Teaches auditory recognition, discrimination, and rhyming of sounds and sound combinations.	1	2	3	4	5

XI. *Encourages "normalization."*

	Nonexistent	Poor	Satisfactory	Good	Excellent
A. Creates opportunity for involvement with peers without disabilities.	1	2	3	4	5

	Nonexistent	Poor	Satisfactory	Good	Excellent
B. Creates opportunity for child and family to participate in and utilize community resources.	1	2	3	4	5
C. Develops child's ability to engage in age-appropriate and culturally appropriate activities through instruction and environmental adaptation.	1	2	3	4	5
XII. *Demonstrates collaborative and interpersonal skills.*					
A. Facilitates team approaches and works collaboratively with other disciplines.	1	2	3	4	5
B. Facilitates the development of children with low-incidence disabilities and medical risk conditions in consultation and close collaboration with disability specialists.	1	2	3	4	5
C. Understands roles of each discipline in providing early intervention services.	1	2	3	4	5
D. Effectively manages staff and develops competence and self-esteem of each staff member.	1	2	3	4	5
E. Develops positive work relations with both professional and nonprofessional staff.	1	2	3	4	5
F. Establishes appropriate partnerships with parents.	1	2	3	4	5
G. Communicates with parents in clear and culturally sensitive ways.	1	2	3	4	5
H. Demonstrates flexibility and approaches difficult situations with problem-solving strategies.	1	2	3	4	5

Building Collaborative Relationships and Conflict Resolution: Effective Communication Strategies

I. Barriers to effective communication. The effective consultant must be aware of her own communication behaviors, both verbal and nonverbal. After carefully examining her own communication style via videotape, self-reflection, or feedback from a colleague, she must seek to eliminate interfering behaviors from her professional repertoire. Several factors that can lead to less effective communication or even breakdowns in communication include the following:

1. **Advice—too much or too quickly.** Giving advice can foster dependence; in some cases, though well intended, the advice may simply be *bad* advice. Avoid giving advice too quickly, or too strongly.

2. **False reassurances, minimizing feelings.** Don't say things like, "Oh, I'm sure she'll be fine. It's just a new experience for her." Don't dismiss the problem, or minimize others' feelings (e.g., "You're just overreacting. You're being overprotective.").

3. **Misdirected questions.** Try to maintain some direction in the interaction. Don't ask questions that are unrelated to the topic.

4. **Wandering attention.** Pay attention! If you realize your attention has wandered, seek clarification through paraphrase or questions (e.g., "I'm sorry; what was that last point?").

5. **Interruptions.** An effective communicative interaction cannot occur if there are interruptions (e.g., cell phones ringing, colleagues stopping by, etc.). Try to minimize interruptions as much as possible.

6. **Distractions and fidgeting.** You may not even be aware of your own nonverbal behaviors that interfere with good communication. For example, doodling, tapping your pen, shuffling papers, avoiding eye contact, jiggling your leg, and so on give the impression that you are not listening, even if you are. Try to eliminate them from your professional interactions.

7. **Quick fixes.** Trying to find a solution too quickly can be dangerous. Make sure you've heard all the concerns as well as the person's thoughts about possible solutions.

II. *Effective nonverbal communication.* The old saying "It's not what you say, but what you do" holds a great deal of truth when it comes to effective communication skills. Nonverbal communication can often have a greater effect (both positive and negative) than verbal communication. The impact and meanings of nonverbal communication are culturally determined. The positive or negative impact of a particular behavior or expression will be influenced by the conventions and rules of social interaction in any given group. The successful consultant will have a good understanding of other people's cues and will develop a keen awareness of the impact of her own nonverbal behavior. Amazingly, body language can either inflame or diffuse conflict; thus, it is important to learn to avoid sending certain negative messages with nonverbal behaviors and to use other nonverbal behaviors to help deescalate potential conflicts. Equally important is learning to read the body language of others to better understand their perspectives and feelings. Of course, it is also possible to use body language to reduce tension and resistance. There are several nonverbal elements of this positive interaction: facing the speaker with arms open and relaxed, mirroring the speaker's affect and movements, and providing nonverbal backchanneling by smiling and nodding are examples of nonverbal communication that tend to reduce conflict.

1. **Appropriate eye contact.** Perhaps one of the most variable nonverbal communicative behaviors is eye contact. In mainstream U.S. culture, direct eye contact indicates interest and attention, and lack of eye contact or shifting eye contact may be interpreted as a lack of sincerity or honesty. In other cultures, however, direct eye contact may be experienced as intimidating; children particularly may be taught to look downward and avoid direct eye contact with adults.

2. **Facial expression.** It is important that you monitor your facial expression for inappropriate smiling, or irritated expression. Generally your face should express welcome and genuine concern. In mainstream U.S. culture an expressive, smiling face is usually positive. Generally you should avoid "mismatched" expression of affect. That is, if your listener is trying to be positive and is smiling, your own furrowed brow or stern expression can create a significant communication barrier. (It should also be noted, though, that members of some cultures may avoid expressing their own or reflecting others' emotions through facial expression, or they may smile when they are distressed.)

3. **Backchanneling.** In U.S. culture "backchanneling" is an important behavior on the part of the listener because it indicates attention and interest in what the speaker is saying. These include such nonverbal behaviors as head nodding and animated changes in facial expression and spoken responses such as "Oh my," "No kidding," "I see," and so on. Although backchanneling may not be common in all cultures, it usually has the effect of validating what the speaker is saying. Conversely, an absence of backchanneling may be interpreted as disagreement or inattention.

4. **Body language.** What you do with your body while engaging in conversations can be a powerful communicator. Folded arms, turning away from the speaker, looking at one's watch, shuffling papers, and so forth are all examples that may add to the tension of a difficult situation. Consider the following:

OPEN/VULNERABLE VERSUS CLOSED/PROTECTED POSITIONS. Sitting with arms folded and legs crossed may convey an image of being closed minded and self-defensive. On the other hand, a more open position may convey willingness to listen and receptivity.

MIRRORING MOVEMENT. One way of making another person feel validated and encouraging communication is to physically mirror (in subtle ways, of course) the other person's movements. For example, if your communication partner leans forward in the seat, you can move slightly forward. Or if she leans elbows on the table, you can do the same. On the other hand, if the person moves back (possibly expressing, "I need to regroup" or "I'm not feeling safe at this moment"), a responsive listener can reciprocate by also leaning back a bit, thus giving the nonverbal message that you respect whatever the person is feeling.

PERSONAL SPACE. One's culture determines what is considered a "comfortable distance" when communicating with a person you do not know intimately. Being too close may be considered intimidating and uncomfortable; being too far away may be interpreted as aloofness or wariness.

PHYSICAL BARRIERS. Where you position your body in relationship to a desk or table also affects communication. Hiding behind a large desk will inhibit the free flow of conversation. Sitting across from someone in a chair with no table or "buffer" may also be uncomfortable. Often the best physical arrangement is at a small round table or at the corner of a square table.

5. **Use of silence.** Most of us have very low tolerance for long pauses in a conversation. We rush to fill in the silence after about 2 seconds. Again, this tends to be culturally determined. It is very important, however, to learn to *wait* for someone to respond and to resist the temptation to answer for the other person or to move the conversation along. Creating a slower pace in an accepting environment may give others the opportunity to reflect and express difficult or complex thoughts and feelings.

6. **Listening.** One of the best communication strategies is listening! Your body language will convey that you are listening to understand.

7. **Awareness of one's own nonverbal communication.** Make sure your body language encourages rather than discourages open communication.

8. **Careful observation of others' nonverbal communication.** Paying attention to the cues of others can often provide important clues regarding their concerns and perspectives, even when they are reluctant to voice them.

III. *Effective verbal conversational strategies.* Verbal conversational strategies can also have negative or positive effects on group processes and the establishment of relationships. For example, simply talking too much or interrupting can significantly interfere with collaborative efforts. Also, rather than focusing on defending one's own positions while the other person is speaking, it is important to sincerely focus on understanding the meaning of what each person says. Specific verbal conversational strategies include the following:

1. **Avoid dominating the conversation.** Talking too much makes it difficult for less assertive members of the team to "weigh in" on the topic. Also, you can't listen if you're talking! Listening is crucial to effective consultation.

2. **Build rapport.** In the long run, true collaboration is difficult to establish if there is a lack of trust. Building rapport can be a beginning step in the development of trust. Simple strategies for building rapport include use of humor, use of nonthreatening, neutral conversation prior to dealing with more difficult issues (e.g., "The traffic was unbelievable. I was afraid I might be late"), and offering amenities such as shaking hands, offering coffee, and so on.

3. **Determine the other person's perspective.** You cannot solve problems effectively if you cannot take other people's views. Ask yourself, "How does he view the situation?" If you don't know, find out. For example, "How do you think the

program is working for Joshua?" "Do you have any ideas about why Maria gets so upset at circle time?"

4. **Use reflective listening.** State what you think the person is expressing (e.g., "So you're saying Jane's tantruming is really upsetting for the other children?" or "What I think I hear you saying is . . ."). This will prompt the speaker to either acknowledge that your understanding is correct or to restate the position more clearly.

5. **Use "I" messages.** "I'm feeling like this is very unrealistic" demonstrates the use of an "I" message in which the speaker owns her own feeling or preference. Using "I" messages (e.g., "I'm really upset about this") rather than judging others' ideas ("Your strategy just doesn't make any sense") or attributing some higher authority to your own view ("Everybody knows this is the most effective strategy") can help diffuse a conflict situation.

6. **Request more information.** Say, for example, "Tell me a little more about what happens just before lunch."

7. **Request clarification.** Say to the person, "I'm not sure I'm following you."

8. **Ask what the person wants.** Ask, "Tell me what you'd like to have happen." "What can I do to help?"

9. **Pause and wait.** Be patient, don't create a rushed atmosphere and don't interrupt. Avoid lengthy explanations or rationales. Provide enough time for others to respond.

This section has summarized a variety of specific conversational strategies that may make collaborations more effective. Ultimately these communication strategies, together with specific conflict resolution strategies, can have very positive benefits for children. (It is important to note, however, that these specific strategies will not be effective in the absence of a genuine concern for the best interests of the child and family and a genuine respect for the contributions of all the individuals involved in the inclusive setting.)

Strategies for Helping Children with Specific Disabilities Participate in Inclusive Settings

Note. The following are some specific strategies and adaptations that often prove helpful. For more detailed disability-specific information, refer to Klein, Richardson-Gibbs, Kilpatrick, and Harris (2001) referenced in chapter 10.

The following suggestions have been field tested and are based on discussions with inclusion specialists and professionals in the fields of special education and low-incidence disabilities. The information is organized according to different play or work areas and group settings typically found in child development centers and preschools. Suggestions are listed by disability (cognitive delays, physical disabilities, deafness or hard of hearing, visual disabilities, and so on).

Tips for Helping the Child with Cognitive Delays

Art Area

- Be aware of small objects that may be choking hazards to the child with developmental delays who still puts things in his mouth.
- Choose activities that emphasize process.

- Choose activities that the child can participate in at varying developmental levels (e.g., collage making, scribbling, painting, using clay or playdough).

Manipulatives Area

- Be aware of small objects that may be choking hazards to the child with developmental delays who still puts things in his mouth.
- Provide containers for the child to put smaller items in and take out rather than assembling to create an end product.
- Use see-through containers with lids that need adult help to open. The child needs to ask for help, resulting in less dumping and more control within manipulatives area.

Block Area

- See suggestions for the manipulatives area.

Pretend Play Area (e.g., dress-up, transportation)

- Provide opportunities for the child to use representations of real objects (e.g., dolls, bottles, cars) to engage in imitative play.

- Use play scripts to help the child understand "what comes next" and learn key words associated with play.

- Use simple dress-up items (hat, scarf, bag, purse, shoes) and have a mirror available.

Gross Motor Area or Activities and Outside Play

- Allow the child to use whole body when interacting with objects from other areas (e.g., push the baby in the cart, transport blocks in a small wagon).

- Weight the carts or wagons for sensory feedback.

- Allow the child to stand, if preferred, when doing tabletop activities so he can move but still focus on activities.

- Use classroom equipment to create obstacle courses: on, in, up, over, under, through, and so on.

- Give the child opportunities to engage in sliding, swinging, and bouncing on equipment but be aware of possible health concerns: *a child with Down syndrome may have serious problems with his spine and should never be encouraged to do somersaults.*

Large-Group Activities

- Try to have shorter group activities rather than longer activities in which the child may begin to lose interest.

- Allow the child to bring a transitional object to the circle that represents a favorite activity and helps ease the transition into a large-group activity.

- Provide photos or symbols in a "What's next" format so the child can see what will happen after circle time.

- Suggest appropriate ways for the child to ask to leave a large group if it becomes too overwhelming (e.g., using words, such as *out,* signaling with a picture or symbol; going to a specific adult).

- Use music! Even a silent child will often vocalize during music or singing.

- Use switches and loop tapes to give the child a "voice" during activities.

- Use preferential seating for the child to make the most use of his sight, hearing, body, and so on.

- Try to conduct a large-group activity in an area of the room with the *least* amount of distractions (e.g., avoid areas with open shelves with toys easily seen, walls with things to poke at or rip or pull, large objects like rocking chairs to climb on or under, and so on).

Books

- Choose books that have repetitive phrases or refrains.

- Choose books that relate to child's everyday experience.

- Choose books with clear pictures and high contrast between foreground and background.

- Choose books with uncluttered pictures (i.e., many things happening in same picture, "busy" backgrounds, and so on).

Tips for Helping the Child with Physical Disabilities

Art Area

- Use Velcro handles on brushes, markers, and so forth and make a Velcro hand holder for the child.

- Build up handles of brushes, markers, crayons, and so on with masking or duct tape so the child has large enough handle to grasp.

- Melt leftover crayon pieces and pour into small-sized paper cups; before wax solidifies, add length of ribbon or yarn across diameter with several centimeters (inches) excess on either side; when wax is set, remove from cup; use ribbon to tie around the child's hand as he grasps the chunky crayon. Ribbon helps keep

the crayon in the hand even if grasp is not consistent.

- Use Dy-Cem mats, suction cups, mounting tape, and so on to help keep materials in place as the child works on projects.

- Try to use art materials to help facilitate grasp rather than pieces of cutout paper which are difficult to pick up off flat surfaces (i.e., cut pieces of pipe cleaners rather than flat pieces of construction paper to make a picture of silkworms).

Manipulatives Area

- Use large Rubbermaid-type containers (sweater sized) and cut out part of one side so the child can slide arms in to play with manipulatives or other textures and won't "lose" material.

- Cut out empty bleach bottle to make scoop; use the Velcro idea above if needed; the child can scoop up smaller objects that he may not be able to pick up with fingers.

- Encourage the child to cross midline and use both hands, even if very difficult.

Block Area

- See suggestions for the manipulatives area.

Pretend Play Area (e.g., dress-up, transportation)

- Provide dress-up clothes with Velcro instead of buttons and zippers.

- Use simple dress-up items (hat, scarf, bag, purse, shoes) and have a mirror available.

- Position the child on the floor to encourage self-dressing from a stable position.

Gross Motor Area or Activities and Outside Play

- Weight the carts or wagons for sensory feedback.

- Adapt tricycles by using Velcro or straps to help keep the child's feet on the pedals.

- Give the child opportunities to engage in sliding, swinging, and bouncing on equipment but be aware of possible health concerns: a child with shunts may not be able to tolerate being upside down because the shunt may not work in that position.

- Partially deflate beach-type balls to allow easier grasp for catching and tossing.

- Consider purchasing adapted bikes that may be propelled by using arms instead of legs.

Large-Group Activities

- Use preferential seating for the child to make the most use of his sight, hearing, body, and so on to help maintain the child's attention and access to sensory cues.

- Be sure that the child is seated at same level as peers—not in a wheelchair or stander if everyone else is on floor.

- Use objects with magnets such as calendars so the child can slide the objects around rather than try to pick them up or knock them off the work surface.

- Add prosthetic devices to musical instruments or other group-time objects to allow the child to hold on to them more easily.

Environment

- Arrange the environment so there is space for the child to independently manipulate the walker or wheelchair to different areas of the room.

Tips for Helping the Child Who Is Deaf or Hard of Hearing

Circle Time/Story Time

- Determine family's preference regarding communication modality: signing, speech, or both.

- Seat the child close to the speaker in the best position to see and hear.

- Be aware of acoustic resonance and ambient noise in room. Try to reduce wherever possible (e.g., use carpets, sound absorbent materials, and decorations; do not seat the child near a noisy air conditioner or open window with traffic noise; and so on).
- Make sure the child's hearing aid is working properly.
- Use music with a strong bass beat.

Outside Play

- Use touch and visual cues to obtain the child's attention if he doesn't respond to your verbal cues.
- To increase the child's hearing in a noisy environment, move closer rather than yelling. (The child's hearing aid transmits clearest sounds from near distance.)

Art and Crafts Activity

- Support verbal instructions with demonstrations and pictures.

Tips for Helping the Child with Visual Impairment

Art Area

- Emphasize textures to increase interest and awareness.
- Emphasize contrasts (i.e., dark paper with light-colored paint, chalk, and so on or light paper with dark materials).
- Use additional lighting at work areas.
- Confine the child's work to the tray or an area that has edges so the child can organize and find needed materials.
- Reduce the amount of clutter in and around the child's work area.
- Have the child place his hand on top of the teacher's hand to introduce new materials: the teacher holds the new material, object, art media; the teacher lets the child feel the new material with his fingertips; and as the child becomes comfortable, the teacher gently rolls the child's hand around so the child feels more of the material that the teacher is holding.

Manipulatives Area

- Use large Rubbermaid-type containers (sweater sized) and cut out part of one side so the child can slide arms in to play with manipulatives or other textures and won't "lose" material.
- Reduce clutter so the child can easily find what he needs to build.
- Place objects in the child's work area with spaces between them so the child can find separate objects (if objects are clustered together, a child with low vision may think it's on a solid object and not several pieces).
- See suggestions under the art area above for ideas about lighting, space, and so on.

Block Area

- See suggestions for the manipulatives area.

Pretend Play Area (e.g., dress-up, transportation)

- Use play scripts to help the child understand "what comes next" and learn key words associated with play.
- Help the child learn where objects are: dolls, dress-up clothes; pretend food, cups, plates, and so forth.

Gross Motor Area or Activities and Outside Play

- Weight the carts or wagons for sensory feedback.
- Be aware of how glare from a sunny day may slow down a child with vision impairment. Contrast between darker inside rooms and

outside can be exaggerated for a child with vision impairment.

- Encourage the child to move around the yard—discourage the child from playing only on the swing or in the sandbox (the safest places on playground!).

- A child with vision impairment may have great fear of the outdoors—the environment is larger and changing all the time. Provide extra time and support to dispel the "fear factor."

Large-Group Activities

- Use preferential seating for the child to make the most use of his sight, hearing, body, and so on.

- Purchase and use a braille lap calendar during calendar time for an older child.

Environment

- For a blind child, label all parts of the environment in braille (that the child can reach).

- Use texture cues (e.g., a piece of sandpaper, cloth, rubber) to identify the child's chair, cubby, and so on.

- Use color to maximize visual contrast between different areas of the room.

Books

- Choose books that relate to the child's everyday experiences.

- Choose books with clear pictures and high contrast between foreground and background.

- Choose books with uncluttered pictures (i.e., many things happening in same picture, "busy" backgrounds, and so on).

- Use braille imprint and tactile books.

- Give a child with low vision his own book (same one) to follow along in while the teacher reads to the class.

Common Sequence of Training Steps Used in Milieu Approaches

Step 1. Conduct High Preference Inventory.

Identify the objects, persons, and events that interest and motivate the infant or young child.

Step 2. Create the need or opportunity to communicate.

Using procedures like time delay or violation of routines, manipulate environmental variables to encourage attempts to communicate. Keep in mind that identifying the objects, persons, and events that interest and motivate the infant or young child is a critical prerequisite to this step.

Step 3. Pause and wait. Give the child an opportunity to initiate communication.

For children with severe disabilities, this may take 10 to 20 seconds (as opposed to individuals without disabilities, who can organize and produce a behavior in 1 or 2 seconds). There are two ways in which the pause-and-wait strategy can be used. Early in teaching it is often helpful to look expectantly at the child. Many teachers will find it very difficult to look at a child without saying anything for 10 to 20 seconds. However, in some

cases the use of this time delay can produce previously unseen communicative behaviors. When the child has acquired the behavior (e.g., directed eye gaze, pointing at an object, pointing at a picture, and so on), instead of looking expectantly at the child during the wait period, the teacher can move or turn away as though busy doing something else. This procedure can be used to encourage the use of an attention-getting behavior such as vocalizing or activating an augmentative and alternative communication (AAC) switch. Initially, this procedure will require two teachers: one teacher to implement the delay while another observes the child's unsuccessful attempts and provides prompts and cues.

Step 4. Provide a natural cue.

Initially in teaching a communicative behavior, cues and prompts can be provided when the child is unable to respond or responds inappropriately during the pause period. It is important, however, that cues and prompts *not* be provided every time, lest the child learn to simply wait through a series of prompts to eventually obtain the desired communicative consequence. Occasionally, the

opportunity to communicate should simply be terminated until a later time during the day. This is particularly appropriate for optional situations such as choosing a toy or a dessert. When a child does not respond during the pause period, employ a *natural* cue. A natural verbal cue is one that is likely to occur in the natural environment, for example, someone asking, "What do you want?" or "Can I help you?" or "Tell me what you want to do now." If the child still does not respond, prompts may be used.

Step 5. Use prompts and assistance.

A wide variety of prompts may be used to assist the child in communicative behavior. Many of these are borrowed from behavioral teaching strategies. Perhaps the most commonly used prompting strategy is the use of ***modeling***. Modeling can be an effective prompt for children who have a generalized imitation strategy and who will attempt to imitate the teacher's model. Unfortunately, many children with severe disabilities do not have a generalized ability to imitate a model. For these children, physical prompting and shaping may be necessary.

Physical prompting involves physically guiding the child through the behavior. For example, if you are teaching a child to reach or point toward a desired object, a physical prompt moves the child's hand and arm through the motion of pointing. Using traditional behavioral methods, gradually fade this physical prompt until the child can produce the behavior on his own.

To use physical prompting effectively, the "topography" of the behavior must be accessible. Unfortunately, vocalization—one very important communicative modality—does not lend itself to physical prompting. Control of vocalization is completely internal. A teacher cannot force or assist a child in vocalizing other than by use of an imitative prompt. Thus, it is important to realize that when physical prompts must be used, communicative behaviors other than vocal behaviors must be selected.

Step 6. Comply with the communicative request.

Within this sequence of steps, provide the desired object or activity at any point at which the child produces an acceptable approximation to the targeted communicative behavior. That is, the child should get the toy, be moved to a favorite location, have the record player turned on, or whatever is desired.

In addition, the teacher should always accompany his or her compliance with the appropriate verbal input. The input strategies described earlier are very important here, particularly the use of repetition and recast sentences. As the teacher provides the desired item, he or she should say, "Oh, you want the *doll*, huh! Here's your *doll*. What a cute *doll*." If the child then appears to be paying attention to the doll, the teacher can semantically expand these utterances by adding a bit more information. For example, "Oh, the *doll* has a new *dress*. Look."

Inclusion Support Itinerant Procedures

The following section provides specific suggestions for establishing an itinerant inclusion support program. Forms referenced in the text are found at the end of this appendix.

I. Getting Started

A. Gather information from referral sources (include individualized family service plan [IFSP] and individualized education plan [IEP] progress notes and assessment data).

B. Meet with the family:
   1. Discuss family's concerns, priorities, and resources.
   2. Remember, parents know their child better than anyone and will have accurate perceptions of both the challenges and potential benefits in the inclusive setting.

C. Determine who the contact person is at the site (e.g., administrator, teacher) and make an initial phone call.

D. Contact any other support providers (e.g., therapists, behavior specialist, disability specialist, and so on).

E. Explain the kinds of services you can provide to all parties involved; determine their expectations and needs. *(Note: For many communities, inclusion support may be a relatively new and unfamiliar service. Families may not understand your role, and early childhood educators (ECE) may believe you will be critically evaluating them in some way. It is extremely important to clarify these issues before beginning your visits to the site.)*

F. Using the "Inclusion Planning Checklist" in conjunction with the "Possible Modifications for Effective Inclusion" (see the forms at the end of this appendix) may be helpful in working out specific details of how you will provide service, including:
   1. Frequency of visits and written reports
   2. Strategies and times for providing feedback
   3. Opportunities for suggestions and questions from parents and ECE staff

II. The First Visit

A. It is important that the initial contacts above be made before you observe the child at the site.

B. Set up a time for the initial visit:
   1. Be sure to touch base with the site administrator.

2. Ask him or her to show you to the classroom and introduce you to the staff.

C. If the initial contact described above was not with the classroom teacher, you will need to briefly explain your role.

D. If possible, provide written material describing the possible services and activities you can offer. *(Keep in mind that you may be the first person the teacher has had contact with who has expertise and knowledge related to the nature of the child's disability.)*

NOTE. Be prepared to answer questions and be willing (if necessary) to obtain additional information to share with the staff.

E. During the first one or two visits it may be best to just observe the child, take careful notes, and (without being intrusive) chat with the teacher. This is a critical time for building trust. The inclusion consultant must be aware of two important issues at this point:

1. ECE staff are extremely busy and often shorthanded.
2. They are unsure of your role. (Common misperceptions of your role can range from believing you are there to directly teach the child or do therapy to suspicions that you are there to evaluate their setting and their teaching skills.)

F. Document each visit. Copy a form similar to the "Inclusion Observation/Support" form at the end of the appendix on NCR paper so that you, the ECE teacher, and the parent have a record of your visit and your suggestions.

1. The form can include:
   a. Date and time of visit.
   b. Your observation of the child's progress (be as positive as possible, giving credit to ECE staff for supporting the child's adjustment, using adaptations, and so on).
   c. Specific suggestions to address problems identified by staff or parents.
   d. A statement of what you will do (e.g., make communication board, help with behavior analysis, make referral, discuss something with parents, etc.).
   e. Date and time of your next visit.
   f. Your name and phone number.

2. A copy of the form should be provided to the parents.

NOTE. Observations documented using the "Inclusion Observation/Support" form should emphasize the itinerant consultant's observation of the *child* and related supports, not the teacher.

G. During initial visits try to learn other children's names. Developing relationships with several children in the class can be a helpful strategy for encouraging peer interactions.

NOTE. It is important that the children in the class become comfortable with you. Also, try not to highlight the fact that you are there to help a particular child—although children will eventually figure this out.

III. Ongoing Visits

A. Individualize your inclusion support activities.

1. Determine the child's needs.
2. Determine what is most comfortable for the ECE staff. Remember, it may take time to feel comfortable in the setting. You will react differently to different sites because of personality factors, program philosophy, location, physical characteristics of the site, and so on.
3. Select strategies that best fit the needs of both the child and the staff:
   Observing and giving written or verbal feedback/recommendations
   Providing direct instruction with the child
   Modeling intervention procedures for the staff
   Coaching the staff

Coaching peers

Making adaptations of equipment and materials

Obtaining resources

   4. Use the "Individual Support Schedule" form at the end of the appendix to plan how the child's goals can be met within each daily activity.

B. Adjust the frequency of visits as needed in consultation with parents, staff, and the funding agency.

C. Learn to balance the needs and expectation of the family and the ECE staff.

   1. One of the most difficult challenges for many inclusion consultants is the feeling of being "caught in the middle" of differing perspectives and priorities of key stakeholders.

   2. The inclusion consultant must prioritize family preferences yet must work within the existing parameters and realities of the inclusive setting.

   3. Often it will be necessary for the inclusion support specialist to set aside individual biases about what is best for the child or the desire to change the practices or the philosophy of the community setting.

D. When conflicts arise that are not easily solved, learn to use conflict resolution strategies.

E. At least quarterly, write a detailed report documenting the child's progress and current needs and agreed-upon next steps and short-term goals. The "A Quick Look at the IEP" form at the end of the appendix may be useful in simplifying the IEP for use in the inclusive setting to be sure that all IEP goals are being met. Revisiting the "Inclusion Planning Checklist" and the "Inclusion Action Plan" can also assist the team in assessing planning specific revisions to ensure steady progress toward achievement of IEP goals and objectives.

F. At transition ages or as the need or desire arises for the family to consider a new placement, assist the family in this often difficult decision-making process.

G. Provide ongoing team coordination support. More often than not, the inclusion support specialist must take the lead in coordinating the activities and communication of other team members (e.g., parents, disability specialists, therapists). This is a logical role for two reasons: (a) coordination is a very time-consuming activity, making it difficult for ECE staff to take on this responsibility, and (b) the inclusion support provider often has the most regular contact with the child and family.

SOURCE Adapted from *Centro de Niños y Padres Inclusion Consulting Handbook,* by V. Bridges and A. M. Richardson-Gibbs, 1998, unpublished document, Los Angeles: California State University.

Possible Modifications
for Effective Inclusion

Personnel

_____ No extra support necessary

_____ Part-time extra support (specific parts of day)

_____ Full-time extra support (1:1 aide)

Physical Assistance

_____ No physical help necessary

_____ Physical help as needed

_____ Partial physical help

_____ Full physical help

Curriculum

_____ Adapt for lower cognitive level

_____ Adapt for vision impairments

_____ Adapt for hearing impairments

_____ Adapt for physical disabilities

Pacing and Amount of Time per Activities

_____ Same pace and time as all other children

_____ Less time than other children (e.g., less attention)

_____ More time than other children (e.g., goes slower)

_____ Slower pacing necessary for understanding (e.g., more wait time for comprehension and/or action)

Hierarchy of Prompts

_____ Full physical help to complete activities

_____ Partial physical help to complete activities

_____ Direct verbal reminders to complete activities (e.g., "Sit down")

_____ Indirect verbal reminders to complete activities (e.g., "What do you need to do?")

_____ Gestures to complete activities (e.g., pointing)

Environment

_____ Seating adaptations (e.g., chairs too high, child does better sitting next to specific peers, and so on)

_____ Reduce or minimize distractions or stimulation

_____ Define limits (e.g., physical and/or behavioral)

Behavior

_____ Define limits (e.g., physical and/or behavioral)

_____ Use positive reinforcement

_____ Determine behavior plans through use of ABC (antecedent, behavior, consequences)

Inclusion Planning Checklist

Child _____ Inclusion Site _____

I. Planning for inclusion *(Have you compiled, received, or had access to the following information?)*
_____ IEP/IFSP
_____ Relevant reports about child
_____ Types of available supports or resources

II. Planning for teaming *(Have you developed an ongoing communication plan?)*
_____ Who is part of the "team"?
_____ When will we meet?
_____ How often will we meet?
_____ Do all people have to be present for all meetings?
_____ How will agendas be developed and by whom?

III. Designing modifications *(How do we determine when, what, and how much?)*
_____ For each part of the daily schedule (large- and small-group periods, free play, meals, and so on), answer the question, "What should the child gain from this part of the routine?"
_____ Review modification options and levels. (What needs to be changed or added to help child learn during each part of routine?)

IV. Implementation *(How can we follow through with modification plans?)*
_____ Who will make/develop the modification or alternative material/activity?
_____ What implementation steps are involved?
_____ Determine material and personnel needs for modification.
_____ Determine allocation of supports (i.e., need for 1:1 aide).
_____ How will modification be used/explained to child and peers?
_____ How will we determine modification is working?

V. Evaluation *(How well did modification(s) work?)*
_____ Was (were) the modification(s) and implementation successful for child?
_____ Will you keep it, reuse it, change it, or throw it out?

Source. From *A Practical Guide for Early Childhood Inclusion Support Specialists,* by M. D. Klein, A. M. Richardson-Gibbs, S. Kilpatrick, and K. Harris, 2001, Los Angeles: Project Support, California State University, Los Angeles, Division of Special Education.

A Quick Look at the IEP

Child _____   Date _____   Teacher(s) _____

Goal #1 _____
Objective(s)
a.
b.
c.
d.
e.
f.

Goal #2 _____
Objective(s)
a.
b.
c.
d.
e.
f.

Goal #3 _____
Objective(s)
a.
b.
c.
d.
e.
f.

Goal #4 _____
Objective(s)
a.
b.
c.
d.
e.
f.

Goal #5 _____
Objective(s)
a.
b.
c.
d.
e.
f.

Goal #6 _____
Objective(s)
a.
b.
c.
d.
e.
f.

Inclusion Action Plan

Child:

Goal/Vision:

Current Situation:

Setting/Population:

Activities	Expected Outcomes	Person Responsible	Timeline	Evaluation

IEP Objectives Within Daily Classroom Routine

Name _____   Date _____

IEP Objectives	Daily Schedule							

Individual Support Schedule

Child: **Date:**

Teacher(s):   **Center:**

Inclusion Consultant:

Schedule	Specific Supports/Adaptations (what staff will do for child that will help child be part of activities)
Arrival	
Morning Activities (Free Play)	
Cleanup	
Toilet/ Handwash	
Snack	
Circle Time	
Small Group (Work Time)	
Outside Play	

Source. From *A Practical Guide for Early Childhood Inclusion Support Specialists,* by M. D. Klein, A. M. Richardson-Gibbs, S. Kilpatrick, and K. Harris, 2001, Los Angeles: Project Support, California State University, Los Angeles, Division of Special Education.

Inclusion Observation/Support

Date _____ Child _____ Center _____

Teacher(s) _____ Inclusion Consultant _____

Schedule	Observations (what consultant observes)	Supports/Adaptations (suggestions for teachers that may help child be part of activities)

Note. This form should be copied on NCR paper so copies may be left for parents and staff after each visit.

Websites Related to Young Children with Special Needs and Their Families

Assistive Technology

Assistive Technology Education Network (ATEN)
http://www.webable.com

The Boulevard
http://www.blvd.com

Closing the Gap
http://www.closingthegap.com

Comforty Media Concepts
http://www.comforty.com

Augmentative and Alternative Communication

American Speech-Language-Hearing Association
http://www.asha.org

Disability Specific Centers and Organizations

American Foundation for the Blind (AFB)
http://www.afb.org

American Speech-language-Hearing Association (ASHA)
http://www.asha.org

Autism Society of America
http://www.autism-society.org

Center for the Study of Autism
http://www.autism.com

Council for Children with Behavioral Disorders
http://www.ccbd.net

Down Syndrome: Health Issues
http://www.ds-health.com

Epilepsy Foundation
http://www.epilepsyfoundation.org

National Association for Down Syndrome
http://www.nads.org

National Association of the Deaf
http://www.nad.org

National Down Syndrome Society
http://www.ndss.org

National Organization for Rare Diseases (NORD)
http://www.rarediseases.org

The Arc of the United States (facts about mental retardation)
http://www.thearc.org

United Cerebral Palsy Association
http://www.ucp.org

Early Childhood

Early Head Start National Resource Center
http://www.ehsnrc.org

Head Start Bureau
http://www.acf.dhhs.gov/programs/hsb

Hilton/Early Head Start Training Program
http://www.specialquest.org

National Head Start Association
http://www.nhsa.org

Education

Early Childhood Outcomes Center (ECO)
http://www.fpg.unc.edu/~eco

ERIC (Education Resources Information Center)
http://www.eric.ed.gov

Native Child
http://www.dhhs.gov

Puckett Institute
http://www.puckett.org

U.S. Department of Education
http://ed.gov/offices/OSERS/OSEP

Families

Beach Center on Families and Disability
http://www.beachcenter.org

Center for Child and Family Studies
http://www.wested.org/ccfs

Family Education Network (Exceptional Parent)
http://www.familyeducation.com/home

Fathers Network
http://www.fathersnetwork.org

Foundation Center Library
http://www.foundationcenter.org

Individuals with Disabilities Education Act
http://www.ideapractices.org

National Center for Fathering
http://www.fathers.com

National Parent Information Network
http://npin.org

Pacer Center
http://www.pacer.org

Parents Helping Parents
http://www.php.com

Policy Action Network
http://www.movingideas.org

Positive Parenting
http://www.positiveparenting.com

Health

Indian Health Service
http://www.his.gov

KidsHealth
http://www.kidshealth.org

National Library of Medicine
http://www.nlm.nih.gov

The Department of Health and Human Services
http://www.dhhs.gov

Literacy

Foundation for Family Literacy
http://www.barbarabushfoundation.com

Houston READ Commission
http://www.houread.org

National Center for Family Literacy
http://www.famlit.org

Nutrition

Food and Nutrition Information Center
http://www.nal.usda.gov/fnic

U.S. Food and Drug Administration
http://www.fda.gov

Organizations Relevant to Early Childhood Special Education

Association for Childhood Educational International
http://www.acei.org

Center for Effective Collaboration and Practice
http://www.cecp.air.org

Council for Exceptional Children (CEC)
http://www.cec.sped.org

Division for Early Childhood (DEC) of the Council for Exceptional Children
http://www.dec-sped.org

National Association of Early Childhood Teacher Educators (NAECTE)
http://www.naecte.org

National Association for the Education of Young Children (NAEYC)
http://www.naeyc.org

National Information Center for Children and Youth with Disabilities (NICHCY)
http://www.nichcy.org

Society of Research in Child Development
http://www.srcd.org

Zero to Three: National Center for Infants, Toddlers and Families
http://www.zerotothree.org

Safety

Consumer Product Safety Commission
http://www.cpsc.org

Safe Kids Worldwide
http://www.safekids.org

Periodicals Relevant to Early Childhood Special Education

American Journal of Speech-Language Pathology:
A Journal of Clinical Practice
American Speech-Language-Hearing Association
10801 Rockville Pike
Rockville, MD 20852-3279
http://www.asha.org

Child Development
Society for Research in Child Development
University of Michigan
3131 South State Street, Suite 302
Ann Arbor, MI 48108-1623
http://www.srcd.org

Child Welfare Journal
Child Welfare League of America, Inc.
440 First Street NW, Third Floor
Washington, DC 20001-2085
http://www.cwla.org

Childhood Education
Association for Childhood Education International
17904 Georgia Avenue, Suite 215
Olney, MD 20832
http://www.acei.org

Exceptional Children
Council for Exceptional Children
1110 North Glebe Road, Suite 300
Arlington, VA 22201-5704
http://www.cec.sped.org

The Exceptional Parent
Psy-Ed Corporation
EP Global Communications

5151 Main Street
Johnstown, PA 07675
http://www.exceptionalparent.com

Focus on Autism and Other Developmental
Disabilities
PRO-ED
8700 Shoal Creek Boulevard
Austin, TX 78757-6897
http://www.proedinc.com

Infant Mental Health Journal
John Wiley & Sons, Inc.
111 River Street, Suite 2000
Hoboken, NJ: 07030
http://www.wiley.com

Infants and Young Children
Lippincott Williams & Wilkins, Inc.
P. O. Box 1620
Hagerstown, MD 21741
http://lww.com

Journal of Early Childhood Teacher Education
National Association of Early Childhood Teacher
Educators
Taylor & Francis Group
325 Chestnut Street
Philadelphia, PA 19106
http://www.naecte.org

Journal of Early Intervention
Division for Early Childhood
The Council for Exceptional Children
1110 North Glebe Road, Suite 300

Arlington, VA 22201-5704
http://www.dec-sped.org

Journal of Speech, Language, and Hearing Research
American Speech-Language-Hearing Association
10801 Rockville Pike
Rockville, MD 20852-6897
http://www.asha.org

Language, Speech, and Hearing Services in Schools
American Speech-Language-Hearing Association
10801 Rockville Pike
Rockville, MD 20852-3279
http://www.asha.org

Monographs of the Society for Research in Child Development
Blackwell Publishing
350 Main Street
Malden, MA 02148
http://www.customerservices@blackwell publishing.com

Teaching Exceptional Children
The Council for Exceptional Children
1110 North Glebe Road, Suite 300
Arlington, VA 22201-5704
http://www.cec.sped.org

Topics in Early Childhood Special Education
PRO-ED
8700 Shoal Creek Boulevard
Austin, TX 78757-6897
http://www.proedinc.com

Topic in Language Disorders
Lippincott Williams & Wilkins, Inc.
P. O. Box 1620
Hagerstown, MD 21740-2116
http://www.lww.com

The Volta Review
The Alexander Graham Bell Association for the Deaf, Inc.
3417 Volta Place NW
Washington, DC 20007
http://www.agbell.org

Young Children
National Association for the Education of Young Children
1313 L Street NW, Suite 500
Washington, DC 20005
http://www.naeyc.org

Young Exceptional Children
Division for Early Childhood
1380 Lawrence Street, Suite 650
Denver, CO 80204-2076
http://www.dec-sped.org

Zero to Three
National Center for Clinical Infant Programs
2000 M Street NW, Suite 200
Washington, DC 20036-3307
http://www.zerotothree.org

Glossary

active listening Listening intently for feelings as well as content, being impartial, and reflecting back what is understood of the feelings and the content.

abduction Movement of a limb outward (away) from the body.

acquired Referring to a feature, state, or disease that happened after birth (acquired conditions are not inherited but rather are a response to the environment).

acquired immune deficiency syndrome (AIDS) A communicable disease that reduces the body's ability to fight some types of infection.

acuity Degree to which one is able to hear sounds and see visual images.

adapt To change or modify while retaining the basic model.

adaptive behavior The ability to adjust to new situations and to apply familiar or new skills to those situations.

adaptive equipment Any device that is modified to enhance the independence of the user.

adduction Movement of a line inward (toward) the body.

advocate One who acts on behalf of another.

affective Pertaining to emotion, feeling, or attitude.

affective conflict Emotional clashes between individuals.

affective domain The state of feeling and expression of feelings.

anecdotal record A factual account of a child's behavior.

anomaly Abnormality.

anoxia The lack of oxygen.

apnea A pause in breathing that lasts 20 seconds or longer.

apnea monitor A monitor that sounds an alarm when an infant has a period of apnea.

apraxia A loss of the ability to perform voluntary, purposeful movements due to damage to the brain (e.g., inability to perform movements of a command such as "Clap your hands").

arena assessment The process of one professional conducting assessment while other team members, including the family, observe and contribute.

arthritis Inflammation of a joint or joints.

articulation The manner in which speech sounds are produced.

assessment Either a test or an observation that determines a child's strengths or weaknesses in a particular area of development.

association The process of relating one concept to another.

asthma A complicated pulmonary symptom characterized by obstruction, labored breathing, and wheezing.

asymmetrical Unequal; lack of similarity in form between two sides of the body.

ataxia Characterized by disturbance of balance and awkward movements caused by damage to brain or spinal cord.

ataxic Unbalanced and jerky.

athetoid movement patterns Moving uncontrollably and continuously.

atrophy Wasting away or diminution in size.

atypical Not typical. Different from the norm or average.

audiologist A trained professional who measures hearing acuity, diagnoses hearing impairments, and assists in planning for remediation, including hearing aids and educational adaptations.

auditory discrimination The ability to distinguish one sound from another.

auditory memory The ability to retain and recall what has been heard.

augmentative communication (AAC) Any method of communicating without speech, such as using signs, gestures, picture boards, and electronic or nonelectronic devices.

backward chaining Teaching the steps of a skill backward, beginning with the last step.

behavior modification Systematic, consistent efforts to change an individual's behavior. Carefully planned consequences for specific behaviors are designed to help a learner develop new and more appropriate responses to situations and experiences.

behavioral objective (also referred to as performance objective) Identifies exactly what the teacher will do, provide, or restrict, describes the learner's observable behavior, and defines how well the learner must perform.

best practices Strategies recommended by members of a profession usually derived from evidence-based practices.

bilateral Both sides.

biological risk Insult to bodily systems that makes typical development problematic.

body awareness (image) Awareness of one's own body and its position in time and space.

bolster or therapy roll A cylindrical piece of equipment (often made of foam) on which infant is placed to help develop muscle strength, balance, and protective reactions.

bonding The establishment of a bond of affection between child and caring adults.

case management Responsible for coordinating services for a family and ensuring that individual family service plans are written and carried out. Currently referred to as service coordination.

categorical placement Placement of children according to classification of their suspected disabilities. Classrooms that are categorical usually group children according to disability labels, for example, classes for children who have learning disabilities or emotional disturbance.

catheter Small, flexible tube inserted into a body channel to distend or maintain an opening to an internal cavity.

cerebral palsy Disorder of posture, muscle tone, and movement resulting from brain damage.

child-find The process of finding and identifying children with special needs.

choreoathetosis Type of cerebral palsy in which there are uncontrolled muscle movements in all four limbs of the body and sometimes in the face.

chromosomal abnormality A genetic disorder caused by too few or too many chromosomes or by chromosomes with extra or missing pieces. Down syndrome is caused by a chromosomal abnormality (an extra chromosome 21).

chronological age (CA) A child's actual age in years and months.

classification Distinguishing characteristics of things, then sorting, matching, or otherwise grouping them.

cognition Analytical, logical acts of mental behavior that result in the act of knowing.

collaboration Two or more co-equal partners voluntarily working side by side with mutual respect and cooperation to reach a common goal through shared decision making.

concepts Mental images or ideas.

confidentiality Records and other information about children must not be shown to anyone other than those who have been approved to have the information. Parental consent in writing must be obtained before information can be released to other individuals or facilities.

conflict resolution A systematic process for managing disagreements and conflicts that seeks a "win-win" outcome.

congenital Presumed to be present at birth.

consultation In early childhood education, a triadic process in which a professional assists another individual to address a problem concerning a third party.

contracture Permanently tight muscles and joints.

coordination Harmonious functioning of muscles or groups of muscles in movement.

corrected age (of infants) Calculated by subtracting the number of weeks of prematurity from the chronological age.

correlation The relationship between factors.

coteaching A form of teaming in which a general educator and a special educator jointly design and implement educational activities for children in a single classroom.

Council for Exceptional Children (CEC) A national professional organization for anyone working for and with children who are gifted and children with disabilities.

criterion A norm or standard for a behavior or item.

criterion-referenced tests Tests or observations that compare a child's performance on a particular task to a standard established for that specific task. Such tests identify what a child can and cannot do.

cross-categorical program A program designed to serve children who have differing disabling conditions.

curriculum All the specific features of a master teaching plan that have been chosen by a particular teacher for his or her classroom. Curricula may vary widely from school to school, but each curriculum reflects the skills, tasks, and behaviors that a school has decided are important for children to acquire.

custodial care Usually refers to the constant supervision and care of bodily needs provided in institutional settings.

cystic fibrosis A chronic disorder often causing respiratory and digestive problems.

decibel Unit used to measure hearing intensity or loudness.

decoding The act of deciphering or obtaining meaning from what is seen or heard.

developmental age The age at which a child is functioning (demonstrating specific abilities) based on assessment of the child's skills and comparison of those skills to the age at which they are considered typical.

developmental curriculum checklist A checklist of behavior often prepared by choosing items from standardized tests or scales. Duplicate items are deleted and those remaining are arranged in a developmental sequence. The checklist is then used as a guide in designing curriculum and in providing a record of individual children's progress through the curriculum.

developmental delay Classification for children with or without established diagnosis who perform significantly behind developmental norms.

developmental quotient (DQ) A score similar to an IQ that describes an infant's developmental level.

developmentally appropriate practices (DAP) Strategies and activities that are appropriate for the child's age and developmental level.

developmentally disabled (delayed) Persons who have an identifiable delay in mental or physical development compared with established norms are referred to in this way rather than as "impaired" or "retarded."

diabetes mellitus A metabolic disorder related to insufficient insulin.

diagnosis A diagnosis is an effort to confirm the presence or absence of a delay or disability by observing the child and considering the results of tests.

diplegia Condition of cerebral palsy with major involvement of the legs and minor involvement of the arms.

directionality The ability to know right from left, up from down, forward from backward, and other directional orientation.

discrimination The ability to differentiate among similar stimuli.

distal Further from the point of origin. For example, the fingers are distal to the shoulder, whereas the elbow is proximal to the shoulder.

divergent thinking Thinking that is unusual, different, and searching.

dyskinesia Difficulty in performing voluntary movement, usually due to damage to basal ganglia of the brain. Examples are *chorea* and *athetosis*.

dystonia 1. Abnormal muscle tone, either increased or decreased. 2. A genetic disorder in which child experiences severe muscle spasms and exhibits abnormal movements and postures, especially when walking.

dystrophy Weakness and degeneration of muscle.

early intervention Services for children (and families) from birth to school age.

echolalia A habit of repeating (without meaning), or "echoing," what is said by others.

eclecticism Method or practice of selecting what seems best from various theories, systems, or programs.

ecological validity Occurs when assessment includes observations in natural settings that reveal what demands are made on children and what skills are

demonstrated during daily routines with familiar caregivers.

ecologically relevant Skills that are functional; skills that assist the child with coping with daily, environmental demands.

efficacy Positive effects or impact of a program, strategy, or procedure.

emerging skills As children learn, they may use a new skill some but not all of the time. A skill observed at least some of the time is said to be emerging.

empathy An active process in which one tries to learn all he or she can about another person in order to vicariously experience their feelings, thoughts, and experiences.

empowerment (empowered) Being in a state of having control over one's life; being able to take action to get what is wanted and needed.

en route behaviors Tasks to be mastered or behaviors to be demonstrated as the child moves from one level of functioning (entry behavior) to a designated goal or objective (terminal behavior).

encoding The act of expressing oneself in words or gestures.

entry behavior The level of functioning or behavior already acquired before beginning a series of tasks.

environment Everything the child encounters. The rooms, furniture, toys, the opportunity to experience new and different places, and the behaviors of those around the child constitute the environment.

environmental risk conditions The presence of factors in the family or community that lead to experiences that may result in developmental delay.

epilepsy A brain disorder frequently resulting in seizure activity that may be very mild or severe enough to cause loss of consciousness.

equivalent practice To prevent boredom in repetition, the teacher provides equivalent practice by offering a variety of materials and activities that are designed to develop the same skill. The task must also be at the same level of difficulty and provide the same kind of practice to be equivalent.

established risk condition The presence of a diagnosed physical or medical condition that is likely to lead to developmental delay.

etiology The study of the causes of diseases or disabilities.

evaluation 1. The process of making value judgments based on behavioral information about the effectiveness of a program in meeting the needs of children enrolled. 2. Under Part H, the term *evaluation* refers to the assessment procedures used to determine a child's eligibility for services.

eversion Turning out.

evidence-based practice Practice based on integration of the best available research evidence with family and professional wisdom and values.

expansion Adults expand a child's utterance by stating the child's idea in a longer phrase or sentence.

expressive language What is said or written to communicate an idea or a question.

extension Straightening of trunk and limbs of body.

extensor pattern A pattern of muscle movement that causes a straightening out of a limb.

family-centered approach to assessment A practice of involving family members as primary decision makers on the assessment team.

family-focused early intervention Concentrating intervention equally on the child's family and on the child.

family functions One of the elements of family systems theory that refers to interrelated activities (outputs) necessary for the family to function effectively (i.e., affection, economics, daily care, socialization).

family subsystems The relational or interactive subsystems according to family systems theory including the marital (adult partners), parental (parents–children), sibling (child–child), and extended family (nuclear family–relatives).

family systems perspective The family is viewed as an interactive unit; what affects one member affects all.

feedback The receipt of knowledge of results (the effect) of one's own behavior.

figure-ground discrimination The ability to attend to one aspect of a visual or auditory field while relegating other aspects of the environment to the background.

fine motor skills Activities with the fingers and hands.

First Chance programs Preschool programs for children with disabilities funded by the Bureau of Education for the Handicapped.

flexion Bending of elbows, hips, knees, and so on.

floppy Loose or weak posture and movements.

forward chaining A method of teaching a skill in which it is broken down into steps, beginning with the least difficult step.

fragile X syndrome An X-linked disorder that often but not always causes mild to severe mental retardation. Some children with fragile X have average intelligence, with or without a learning disability.

free appropriate public education (FAPE) Designed by Public Law 94–142 to mean special education and related services provided at public expense. Such services are to be described in the individualized education program, appropriate to the child's individual needs, and meet requirements of the state agency.

functional skills Skills that will be immediately useful to the child and that will be used relatively frequently in the child's typical environment.

genetic Having to do with the principles of heredity.

gestational age The age of a fetus or infant stated in weeks from first day of the mother's last menstrual period before conception until the body reaches term (40 weeks).

goals The general statement on the individualized education program that states what teaching is expected to accomplish; for example, "To improve Johnny's fine motor skills."

grammar The linguistic rules of language.

gross motor skills Activities such as running, climbing, throwing, and jumping that use large muscles.

hand-over-hand guidance Physically guiding a child through movements involved in a fine motor task (e.g., helping the child grasp a spoon and bring it to his or her mouth).

hemiplegia Condition of cerebral palsy with major involvement of one side of the body.

hereditary Referring to a trait (such as eye color) or defect or disease (such as cystic fibrosis). Not all hereditary disorders are apparent at birth and not all birth defects are hereditary.

high-preference items A child's most preferred activities, objects, and people.

high-preference inventory Identification of a child's high-preference items determined through care giver interviews and careful observation of a child's likes and dislikes; information can be used to identify ways of motivating, engaging, and reinforcing a child.

high-risk signals Those signs that when observed in very young children have been known to be predictive of more than normal likelihood of future disabilities or developmental delays.

hydrocephalus Congenital condition in which the accumulation of the fluid in the brain causes enlargement of the skull.

hyperactivity Exceedingly active behavior not typical of most children.

hyperresponsive Unregulated reactive behavior. Children who are hyperresponsive may actually avoid stimuli as if they have a lower tolerance for it.

hypertonicity Condition in which muscles are stretched and constantly excited.

hypoactivity Opposite of hyperactivity; lethargy.

hyporesponsive Lack of appropriate reactive behavior. Children who are hyporesponsive may be slow to respond to stimuli and actually seek more of it.

hypotonicity Condition in which muscles are limp and do not exhibit resistance to stretching.

identification The process of finding and screening individuals to determine whether they might benefit from specialized services.

inclusion Another term used for integration of children with and without disabilities.

inclusive settings Sites, classrooms, and programs where inclusion takes place.

individualize Match a teaching task to the capacity of the particular individual being taught.

individualized education plan (IEP) A collaborative process that culminates in a written program plan that includes the child's present level of functioning; specific areas that need special services; annual goals; short-term objectives; services to be provided; and the method of evaluation to be implemented. An individualized education program is required for every child receiving services while P.L. 101–476 is in effect.

individualized family service plan (IFSP) A collaborative process that culminates in a written service plan that includes the child's present level of functioning; a statement of the family's concerns, priorities, and resources; measurable results or outcomes expected to be achieved for the child and family; the criteria, procedures, and time lines to determine progress; specific services to be provided; natural environments;

dates of service initiation; and name of the service coordinator.

innate Inherent within an individual.

inner language The language in which thinking occurs. The process of internalizing and organizing experiences that can be expressed by symbols.

instructional objectives These define specific accomplishments to be achieved. See "behavioral objective."

integration Education of children with disabilities together with their classmates without disabilities to the maximum extent appropriate.

interdisciplinary team approach Professionals from different disciplines work together to assess and provides intervention based on mutual decision making.

interindividual differences Differences between individuals.

intraindividual differences Differences in performance within one child on different factors or on the same factor at different times.

inversion Turning in.

involuntary movements Unintended movements.

itinerant consultant An individual who travels from place to place, providing services via consultation model.

kinesthesia The muscle sense by which the child is aware of his or her body position and his or her movements in relation to the environment.

labeling Giving a categorical term (label) to a disabling condition and to those who exhibit such a condition, for example, "emotionally disturbed" or "mentally retarded."

laterality Awareness of sidedness; left and right of the body.

least restrictive environment (LRE) A concept inherent in P.L. 94-142 that requires children with disabilities to be educated with peers without disabilities in regular educational settings to the maximum extent appropriate.

litigation The act or process of contesting by law through lawsuits.

locomotor Pertaining to movement from one location to another.

low tone/low muscle tone Hypotonia.

mainstreaming The practice of placing children with special needs in regular classrooms whenever appropriate.

medically fragile Referring to an infant or child whose health status either is unstable or renders him or her at risk for developmental delay (often due to poor health or limitations on the infant's ability to participate in typical activities).

mental age Level of mental functioning. A child with a mental age (MA) of 4-0 is thought to be mentally functioning like a 4-year-old.

metacognition Having knowledge of one's thought processes and how to regulate strategies for thought or learning.

microcephaly An abnormally small head size, resulting in poor brain growth and mental retardation.

mixed-type cerebral palsy A form of cerebral palsy in which both spasticity and choreoathetoid movements are present.

modality The pathways through which an individual receives information and thereby learns. Some individuals are thought to learn more quickly through one modality than another; for example, some process auditory information more efficiently than visual information and would thus be classified as auditory learners.

modeling Providing a demonstration of an expected behavior.

motor planning The ability to organize sensory information in order to plan and carry out the appropriate sequence of movements required to complete a task.

multidisciplinary team approach Individuals from different disciplines carry out evaluations, and intervention may be offered with little opportunity for professional interaction or integrated planning.

multiple sclerosis A progressive central nervous system disease affecting motor control.

multisensory learning A technique to facilitate learning that employs a combination of sense modalities at the same time.

muscular dystrophy A central nervous system disease that affects skeletal and respiratory functions.

natural environments A philosophy that emphasizes services in settings most natural and comfortable for children and their families.

neonatal intensive care unit (NICU) The hospital unit staffed with specially trained medical practitioners who care for critically ill newborns, both premature babies and sick full-term babies.

neurological examination An examination of sensory or motor response to determine whether there are impairments of the nervous system.

noncategorical Grouping children together without labeling or categorizing according to suspected disabilities.

nonlocomotor Lack of movement from one place to another.

nonverbal ability Having skill to perform a task that does not involve using words.

norm-referenced tests These are tests that report a particular child's performance in relation to other children of the same chronological age. Such tests are highly standardized and usually do not include individuals with disabling conditions in the normative sample against which behavior is being compared.

norms A sample of a large number of people's behavior against which a particular behavior can be compared.

observable behavior Behavior that can be seen, heard, or felt.

observational learning Learning by watching those around us.

occupational therapy Treatment given to improve movement for daily living.

ocular pursuit Following an object with the eye.

olfactory Pertaining to the sense of smell.

ophthalmologist A physician trained in the diagnosis and treatment of diseases of the eyes.

optometrist A vision specialist trained to measure refraction and prescribe glasses but not licensed to treat eye diseases.

oral stimulation Referring to the natural mouthing of toys that emerges in the infant between 3 and 6 months of age or to the specific activities (such as massaging the gums or lips) designed to help the child with *oral tactile defensiveness* tolerate having things placed in his or her mouth.

orthosis Any assistive device used to support, align, prevent, or correct bone, joint, or muscle deformities.

orthotic A custom-made orthopedic appliance (such as a brace, splint, or cast) used to promote proper body alignment, to stabilize joints, or to passively stretch muscle or other soft tissue.

otitis media Inflammation of the middle ear; a common infection.

otolaryngologist A medical doctor who specializes in the diagnosis and treatment of disorders of the ear, nose, and throat.

otologist A physician trained to treat problems of the ear.

parallel talk Parents of young children often talk about what their children are doing as it is happening. Their "talk" occurs parallel to what the child is doing. This practice appears to help young children learn language.

paraplegia Paralysis of both legs.

paraprofessional A trained assistant to a professional teacher, often referred to as a teacher aide or paraeducator.

parity Equality of value or standing.

patterning Guiding the child's arms or legs through a series of passive movements in order to stimulate normal movement patterns.

pediatrician A physician whose specialty is working with and treating infants and young children.

percentile rank The percentage of persons in a normal distribution who score below a particular point.

perception The process of interpreting what is received by the five senses.

perceptual-motor The interaction of various channels of perception with motor activity; for example, the act of kicking is a perceptual-motor interaction between sight and gross motor responses.

performance objectives See "behavioral objective."

perinatal Around the time of birth.

perseveration Continuous repetition of the same action characterized by the inability to shift readily from one activity to another.

physical therapist A therapist who assesses gross motor skills and treats disorders of movement and posture.

physiotherapy Treatment of disorders of movement.

pincer grasp Coordination of index finger and thumb.

positioning Placing a child in certain postures in order to promote symmetrical body alignment, normalize muscle tone, and promote functional skills.

positive behavior support Behavioral technique that focuses on *prevention* of problem behaviors and providing support for more positive behaviors by identifying the *function* of the problem behavior and teaching the child a *replacement* behavior that is more acceptable. The technique also identifies the antecedents of problem behaviors as clues to possible "triggers" or causes of the behavior and attempts to modify or eliminate those causes.

post-ictal sleep The sleep that occurs naturally after seizures.

pragmatics The use of language in social contexts, including how language is used for communication.

premature infant A baby born before 37 weeks' gestation.

prenatally exposed to drugs (PED) Referring to an infant who was exposed to drugs as a fetus due to maternal substance abuse.

primitive reflex A reflex response to a stimulus such as touch or movement that is normal in infants. The word *primitive* refers to the fact that these are involuntary survival responses with which infants are born.

prognosis A forecast of the probable course of disease or illness.

prompting Using cues and partial cues to build desired behavior. Verbal prompting often involves saying a single sound or word to help a child remember what to say or do. Physical prompting that involves physical assistance or touch can be helpful to initiate a motor or self-help skill. Prompts should be reduced gradually (faded) until they can be eliminated.

pronation Turning of the palm downward or backward.

prone Lying on the stomach.

prosthesis Artificial device used to replace a missing body part.

psycholinguistics The field of study that combines psychology and linguistics to create an understanding of the total language process.

punishment A consequence that decreases the future likelihood of the behavior that it follows.

quadriplegia Condition of cerebral palsy with major involvement of arms and legs.

range of motion The total distance through which a joint can be moved in natural directions.

rapport A harmonious relationship. When working with a child, establishing rapport involves developing a climate or atmosphere in which the child feels comfortable enough to perform as well as possible.

receptive language The ability to understand the intent and meaning of someone's effort to communicate.

reciprocal movement Alternating movements of arms and legs, such as movement involved in walking or in creeping on hands and knees.

reflexes Postures and movements completely out of the child's control.

reinforcer An event or consequence (reward) that increases the likelihood of a behavior that it follows being repeated. May be concrete or social.

reliability Extent to which a test measures a given performance consistently. The degree to which it is dependable, stable, and relatively free from errors of measurement.

remission Period during which the symptoms of a condition disappear for an unpredictable period.

residual hearing Auditory acuity of an individual after an impairment without amplification.

respite care Skilled child-care service that can be provided in place of the parent of a child who is seriously ill or disabled.

retarded Traditionally this term was used to describe any individual who was slow to learn or difficult to teach. The term is not precise and is less often used today. Laws specify that one must correlate test scores, adaptive behavior, and other factors before this term can be used appropriately.

retinopathy of prematurity (ROP) An eye disorder that can develop in premature infants. There is an increased incidence in infants who are given high levels of oxygen for long periods.

reversal A transposition of letters.

reverse chaining Top down; begin teaching with the last step of a task and work backward. Particularly useful with self-help skills.

reverse mainstreaming Children without disabilities are integrated into classes composed primarily of children with identifiable special needs.

righting Ability to put in or restore the head and body to a proper position when in an abnormal or uncomfortable position.

rigidity A type of cerebral palsy characterized by widespread continuous muscle tension. Muscles of the body become very stiff.

role release The systematic training of other professionals in one's own discipline-specific skills.

schemata Patterns.

scissor pattern Body movement in which one leg crosses over the other.

screening The process of sorting out form a total group children who may have problems. It is often a part of total program called child-find or child-check. The intent is to test all children with specially designed screening instruments to determine those who need further diagnostic testing and to determine if a problem really does exist.

self-fulfilling prophecy The tendency for individuals to behave in accordance with views they perceive others to have of them.

self-regulation The ability to regulate one's emotional state and to organize an appropriate behavioral response to a stimulus. In infants, self-regulation refers to the ability to attain an optimal level of arousal.

sensorimotor The combination of input of sense organs and output of motor activity.

sensory integration The ability of the central nervous system to receive, process, and learn from sensation (such as touch, movement, sight, sound, smell, and the pull of gravity) in order to develop skills.

sensory overload The condition that occurs when one or more senses have been overstimulated beyond the child's level of tolerance. It may occur as a result of too much noise, light, or movement.

seriation Ordering according to relative differences.

service coordination Professional assistance designed to help families procure, coordinate, and manage the diverse services needed by a child and family. (See "case management.")

sexually transmitted disease (STD) A contagious disease transmitted through sexual contact. STDs can also be transmitted in other ways, such as through blood contact (as with drug users who share needles).

shaping A technique of behavior modification in which behaviors that are successive approximations of the target behavior are reinforced until target behavior is acquired.

sickle cell anemia A hereditary condition in which misshapen blood cells clump together in the blood vessels causing varied symptoms: painful joints, chronic ulcers of the ankles, episodes of abdominal pain, and neurological disturbances.

small for gestational age (SGA) A newborn whose weight is low (below the 10th percentile) for his or her gestational age.

soft sign Any of several neurological indicators that collectively suggest the presence of damage to the central nervous system. They include disturbance of balance, visual motor difficulties, a lack of motor coordination, and so on.

sorting Discrimination and separation according to differences.

spasm Sudden tightening of the muscles.

spasticity Muscular incoordination resulting from sudden, involuntary contractions of the muscles; a type of cerebral palsy.

spatial relationships The ability to perceive the position of two or more objects in relation to oneself and in relation to each other.

spina bifida A disorder of the spinal column that may affect motor coordination and body functions.

standardization The procedure of having standard directions and scoring so that normative data about others who have taken the test can be used.

standardized tests Tests that are administered in a specifically described standard way, scored in a particular way, and then compared with the performance of a standard group.

standards based practices Strategies and activities based on professionally determined expectations for the learning and development of young children.

stanine A single digit derived score based on the normal curve. It ranges in value from 1 to 9 with a mean of 5.

status epilepticus Refers to a situation in which a person has two major seizures, one right after the other; signals that an ambulance should be called immediately.

stimuli Information that can be received by the senses.

stoma Opening in the abdominal wall, created through surgery, to allow the urine from the kidneys to drain into a collecting bag.

strabismus A condition in which the eyes do not work together, in that one eye deviated (wanders) from its position relative to the other eye. It may go inward (cross-eye) or outward (walleye).

stuttering A speech impairment evidenced by hesitations, repetitions, or spasm of breathing.

substantive conflict Arises from intellectual differences and is content based (i.e., differences in philosophy, priorities, and so on).

successive approximation The process of gradually increasing expectations for a child to display behaviors that are more like the desired target behavior; used in shaping behaviors not previously a part of the child's behavior pattern.

sudden infant death syndrome (SIDS) The unexpected and sudden death of an infant who has appeared to be healthy. SIDS occurs during sleep and is the most common cause of death in infants 1 month to 1 year. Cause is still unknown.

supine Lying on back.

symmetrical Similarity in form between two sides of the body.

syndactyly A congenital anomaly in which there is partial or complete webbing or fusion of fingers or toes.

systematic fading The gradual removal of any support that assists a child's learning.

systemic Refers to a disease that can exist throughout the body (e.g., arthritis).

tactile Refers to the sense of touch.

tactile defensiveness An abnormal sensitivity to touch, indicated by infant's avoidance or rejection of touching and handling.

target behavior The terminal objective or final desired behavior that is the goal of shaping when using behavioral (performance) objectives. This same term, when used in relation to behavior modification, refers to the negative behavior to be changed.

task analysis Breaking down a difficult talk into small steps that lead to doing the difficult task. En route behaviors are behavioral objectives that state the individual subskills leading toward the terminal objective or the difficult task.

terminal objective The behavioral objective that a particular teacher has chosen as the highest level of skill he or she intends to strive toward to help a child or children achieve.

tone Firmness of muscles.

tongue thrust The strong involuntary (reflexive) protrusion of the tongue. It may be seen in some forms of cerebral palsy.

tonic neck reflex Uncontrollable movement in which turning of the head causes one arm to straighten and stiffen and the other to bend.

total communication A philosophy involved in teaching individuals with hearing impairments that includes using aural, manual, and oral methods to ensure effective communication.

tracking Following an object with one's eyes.

transdisciplinary team approach The use of a team approach to services in which team members work across disciplinary boundaries to plan and provide integrated services. This approach includes sharing of roles through support and consultation from other team members.

transition The purposeful, organized process of helping children who are at risk or have developmental disabilities move from one program to the next, such as from an infant development program to an inclusive preschool program.

trauma The condition, physical or mental, that results from shock or a violently produced wound or injury.

tremor Involuntary vibration in large muscles.

utterance Something that is said or produced orally. It is not necessary that an utterance be spoken correctly to be counted in the child's mean length of utterance (MLU).

validity The extent to which an instrument measures what it is supposed to measure or what the test giver needs it to measure.

verbal expression The ability to express one's ideas verbally.

vestibular stimulation An activity that stimulates the vestibular apparatus (the structures contained in the inner ear that provide the sense of balance) and helps the child develop awareness of body position in space as well as balance reactions.

visual association The process of relating concepts that have been presented visually.

visual discrimination The ability to differentiate between and among various shapes, sizes, colors, numbers, and letters.

visualization Imagery; the ability to retrieve a mental image or to produce a mental image.

voluntary muscles The muscles in the body over which there is conscious control of contraction.

women, infants, and children program (WIC) A federally funded program that provides pregnant women, new mothers, infants, and young children with food vouchers, nutrition counseling, and referrals to health care.

"W" sitting position Sitting on the buttocks between the heels of the feet (the knees are bent, forming a *W*).

zero project The principle that no child should be refused a free appropriate education if other children the same age are being served.

Source. Many definitions came from *The Early Intervention Dictionary*, by J. G. Coleman, 1999, Rockville, MD: Woodbine House.

Name Index

Subject Index

480   Subject Index

Teacher Preparation

P9-DFR-145

TEACHER PREP

**MERRILL
PRENTICE HALL**

See a demo at
www.prenhall.com/teacherprep/demo

Your Class. Their Careers. Our Future. Will your students be prepared?

We invite you to explore our new, innovative and engaging website and all that it has to offer you, your course, and tomorrow's educators! Preview this site today at www.prenhall.com/teacherprep/demo. Just click on "go" on the login page to begin your exploration.

Organized around the major courses pre-service teachers take, the Teacher Preparation site provides media, student/teacher artifacts, strategies, research articles, and other resources to equip your students with the quality tools needed to excel in their courses and prepare them for their first classroom.

This ultimate online education resource will provide you and your students access to:

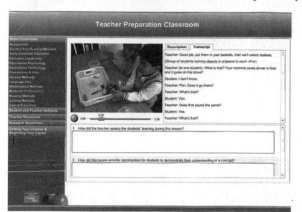

Online Video Library. More than 250 video clips—each tied to a course topic and framed by learning goals and Praxis-type questions—capture real teachers and students working in real classrooms.

Student and Teacher Artifacts. More than 200 student and teacher classroom artifacts—each tied to a course topic and framed by learning goals and application questions—provide a wealth of materials and experiences to help your students observe children's developmental learning.

Lesson Plan Builder. Step-by-step guidelines and lesson plan examples support students as they learn to build high-quality lesson plans.

Articles and Readings. Over 500 articles from ASCD's renowned journal *Educational Leadership* are available. The site also includes Research Navigator, a searchable database of additional educational journals.

Strategies and Lessons. Over 500 research-supported instructional strategies appropriate for a wide range of grade levels and content areas.

Licensure and Career Tools. Resources devoted to helping your students pass their licensure exam; learn standards, law, and public policies; plan a teaching portfolio; and succeed in their first year of teaching.

How to ORDER *Teacher Prep* for you and your students:

For students to receive a *Teacher Prep* Access Code with this text, instructors **must** provide a special value pack ISBN number on their textbook order form. To receive this special ISBN, please email **Merrill.marketing@pearsoned.com** and provide the following information:
*   Name and Affiliation
*   Author/Title/Edition of Merrill text
Upon ordering *Teacher Prep* for their students, instructors will be given a lifetime *Teacher Prep* Access Code.